T0228869

Managing Gigabytes

Compressing
and Indexing
Documents and Images

The Morgan Kaufmann Series in Multimedia Information and Systems

Series Editor, Edward Fox

Managing Gigabytes: Compressing and Indexing Documents and Images,
Second Edition
Ian H. Witten, Alistair Moffat, and Timothy C. Bell

Digital Compression for Multimedia: Principles and Standards
Jerry D. Gibson, Toby Berger, Tom Lookabaugh, Dave Lindbergh, and Richard L.
Baker

Practical Digital Libraries: Books, Bytes, and Bucks
Michael Lesk

Readings in Information Retrieval
Edited by Karen Sparck Jones and Peter Willett

Introduction to Data Compression
Khalid Sayood

Forthcoming

Multimedia Servers: Design, Environments, and Applications
Dinkar Sitaram and Asit Dan

Introduction to Data Compression, Second Edition
Khalid Sayood

Managing Gigabytes

Compressing and Indexing Documents and Images

SECOND EDITION

Ian H. Witten
University of Waikato

Alistair Moffat
University of Melbourne

Timothy C. Bell
University of Canterbury

MORGAN KAUFMANN PUBLISHERS

An Imprint of Elsevier

SAN FRANCISCO   SAN DIEGO   NEW YORK   BOSTON
LONDON   SYDNEY   TOKYO

Senior Editor	Jennifer Mann
Director of Production and Manufacturing	Yonie Overton
Production Editor	Elisabeth Beller
Cover Design	Ross Carron
Cover Photo	Ian Beesley/Photonica
Text Design	Side by Side Studios/Mark Ong
Copyeditor	Ken DellaPenta
Proofreader	Jennifer McClain
Composition	Babel Press/Ed Sznyter

Designations used by companies to distinguish their products are often claimed as trademarks or registered trademarks. In all instances where Morgan Kaufmann Publishers is aware of a claim, the product names appear in initial capital or all capital letters. Readers, however, should contact the appropriate companies for more complete information regarding trademarks and registration.

ACADEMIC PRESS
An Imprint of Elsevier

525 B Street, Suite 1900, San Diego, CA 92101-4495, USA
http://www.academicpress.com

Academic Press
Harcourt Place, 32 Jamestown Road, London NW1 7BY United Kingdom
http://www.hbuk.co.uk/ap/

Morgan Kaufmann Publishers
340 Pine Street, Sixth Floor, San Francisco, CA 94104-3205, USA
http://www.mkp.com

ⓒ 1999 by Academic Press
All rights reserved

Printed and bound by CPI Group (UK) Ltd, Croydon, CR0 4YY
Transferred to Digital Print 2011

No part of this publication may be reproduced, stored in a retrieval system, or transmitted in any form or by any means—electronic, mechanical, photocopying, recording, or otherwise—without the prior written permission of the publisher.

Permissions may be sought directly from Elsevier's Science and Technology Rights Department in Oxford, UK. Phone: (44) 1865 843830, Fax: (44) 1865 853333, e-mail: permissions@elsevier.co.uk. You may also complete your request on-line via the Elsevier homepage: http://www.elsevier.com by selecting "Customer Support" and then "Obtaining Permissions".

Library of Congress Cataloging-in-Publication Data.
Witten, I. H. (Ian H.)
      Managing gigabytes : compressing and indexing documents and images
      / Ian H. Witten, Alistair Moffat, Timothy C. Bell. – 2nd ed.
          p.   cm.
      Includes bibliographical references and index.
      ISBN-13: 978-1-55860-570-1   ISBN-10: 1-55860-570-3
      1. Image processing–Digital techniques. 2. Data compression
(Telecommunication) 3. Text processing (Computer science)
4. Document imaging systems. I. Moffat, Alistair. II. Bell,
Timothy C. III. Title.
Ta1637.W58 1999
651.5'0285574–dc21
                                                                                    99-26345
                                                                                    CIP

This book is printed on acid-free paper.

Contents

List of Tables

List of Figures

Preface

The computer revolution has produced a society that feeds on information. Yet much of the information is in its raw form: data. There is no shortage of this raw material. It is created in vast quantities by financial transactions, legal proceedings, and government activities; reproduced in an overwhelming flood of reports, magazines, and newspapers; and dumped wholesale into filing cabinets, libraries, and computers. The challenge is to manage the stuff efficiently and effectively, so that pertinent items can be located and information extracted without undue expense or inconvenience.

The traditional method of storing documents on paper is expensive in terms of both storage space and, more importantly, the time it takes to locate and retrieve information when it is required. It is becoming ever more attractive to store and access documents electronically. The text in a stack of books hundreds of feet high can be held on just one computer disk, which makes electronic media astonishingly efficient in terms of physical space. In addition, the information can be accessed using keywords drawn from the text itself. Compared with manual document-indexing schemes, this approach provides both flexibility (all words are keywords) and reliability (because indexing is accomplished without any human interpretation or intervention). Moreover, organizations nowadays have to cope with diverse sources of electronic information such as machine-readable text, fax and other scanned documents, and digitized graphics. All these can be stored and accessed efficiently using electronic media rather than paper.

This book discusses how to manage large numbers of documents—gigabytes of data. A *gigabyte* is approximately one thousand million bytes, enough to store the text of a thousand books, about the size of an office wall packed floor to ceiling. The term has gained currency only recently, as the capacity of mass storage devices has grown. Just two decades ago, requirements measured in megabytes (one million bytes) seemed extravagant, even fanciful. Now personal computers come with gigabytes of storage, and it is commonplace for even small organizations to store many gigabytes of data. Since the first edition of this book, the explosion of the World Wide Web has made terabytes (one trillion bytes) of data available to the public, making even more people aware of the problems involved in handling this quantity of data.

There are two challenges when managing such huge volumes of data, both of which are addressed in this book. The first is storing the data efficiently. This is done by *compressing* it.[1] The second is providing fast access through keyword searches. For this, a tailor-made electronic *index* must be constructed. Traditional methods of compression and searching need to be adapted to meet these challenges. These are the two topics examined in this book. The end result of applying the techniques described here is a computer system that can store millions of documents and retrieve the documents that contain any given combination of keywords in a matter of seconds, or even in a fraction of a second.

Here is an example to illustrate the power of the methods described in this book. With them, you can create a database from a few gigabytes of text and use it to answer a query like "retrieve all documents that include paragraphs containing the two words 'managing' and 'gigabytes' " in just a few seconds on an office workstation. In truth, given an appropriate index to the text, this is not such a remarkable feat. What is impressive, though, is that the database that needs to be created, which includes the index and the complete text (both compressed, of course), is less than half the size of the original text alone. In addition, the time it takes to build this database on a workstation of moderate size is just a few hours. And, perhaps most amazing of all, the time required to answer the query is *less* than if the database had not been compressed!

Many of the techniques described in this book have been invented and tested recently and are only now being put into practice. Ways to index the text for rapid search and retrieval are thoroughly examined; this material forms the core of the book. Topics covered include text compression and modeling, methods for the compression of images, techniques for compressing textual images such as scanned or fax documents, and page layout recognition to separate pictures and diagrams from text.

Full-text indexes are inevitably very large and therefore potentially expensive. However, this book shows how a complete index to every word—and, if desired, every number—in the text can be provided with minimal storage overhead and extremely rapid access.

The objective of this book is to introduce a new generation of techniques for managing large collections of documents and images. After reading it, you will understand what these techniques are and appreciate their strengths and applicability.

---

1 We use *data* in the singular throughout this book. To us, data seems like a large—often formidably large—entity in itself, rather than a collection of "datums."

Accompanying software

A comprehensive system, mg (standing for "managing gigabytes"), has been created to illustrate the ideas in the book. Complete source code for mg is freely available on the Internet (start at *www.cs.mu.oz.au/mg/*). Written in ANSI C and running under Unix, it is an operational example of the techniques that we develop and explain. It compresses, stores, and accesses a collection of text, scanned documents, and images in a fully integrated fashion. Any Boolean combination of keywords can be used to retrieve all documents meeting the specification. Informal ranked queries, where the user merely specifies a list of words and relevant documents are retrieved in order, are also supported. Consider the query mentioned earlier, to retrieve all documents that include paragraphs containing the two words *managing* and *gigabytes*. With a database of 750,000 documents, amounting to 2 gigabytes (Gbytes) of text, it took mg just 1 second to access and decode the index entries for these two words—159,458 and 961 appearances, respectively—and well under a minute to fetch and decompress the 7 megabytes (Mbytes) containing the 554 documents that match the query.

Audience

This book should be of interest to general readers who want to learn about this subject, to information professionals who need to become acquainted with the new technology for information management, and to those who wish to gain a detailed technical understanding of what is involved. It is written for an eclectic audience of information systems practitioners, programmers, consultants, librarians, information distributors, professors, students, developers, specification writers, patent examiners, and curious lay people who need an accessible description of this new technology. Distributors of CD-ROM databases, such as books, encyclopedias, and even computer software, will benefit directly from the techniques described. We have avoided requiring any specific theoretical or mathematical knowledge, except in some sections that are marked by a light gray bar in the margin. These contain material for the more technical or theoretically inclined reader, and they may be skipped without loss of continuity. We have also highlighted "rules of thumb" in the body of the text.

There are several ways in which this book can be used as the basis of courses at the senior undergraduate, graduate, and professional levels. Each chapter deals with a different component of a full-text retrieval system, including compression methods for the text, index, and pictures; consequently, many of the chapters are suitable for short courses in their own right. For example, Chapter 2 is a comprehensive survey of text compression methods and has been used for a short course on compression. Whole books could be written on this subject—indeed, they have been[2]—but this

---

2 One such book is *Text Compression*, by two of the authors of this book in collaboration with John G. Cleary (Bell, Cleary, and Witten 1990).

chapter provides a self-contained, practical guide to the methods that are most commonly used in practice, giving the right amount of information to learn how each one works. Likewise, Chapter 6 is a self-contained account of current techniques and international standards for the compression of images. Chapter 4 covers the basic notions of information retrieval using Boolean and ranked queries and gives a detailed discussion of the issues involved in their implementation.

This book has been organized so that two groups of chapters provide deep and extensive coverage of particular subareas. Chapters 1, 3, 4, and 5 have been used as the basis of a graduate course on information retrieval, while Chapters 6, 7, and 8 form a stand-alone module on the analysis and compression of document images. A more comprehensive senior undergraduate or graduate course on information systems and data compression would cover the entire book, or the text can be used to supplement general undergraduate courses on information systems or practical data structures.

Finally, if you are more concerned with the concepts involved than the technical details, you will get the general message of the book by reading the first and last chapters. Chapter 1 introduces the problems tackled and illustrates them with real-world examples. It looks at how concordances have been constructed in the past and how they are being replaced by full-text retrieval systems. It also introduces the key ideas of the book: compressing and indexing large collections of text and images. Chapter 10 looks to future developments and applications for this new technology. One such development is the integration of audio and multimedia information into indexed retrieval systems. This is surprisingly straightforward; any kind of information that needs to be retrieved on the basis of a specified set of keywords can be incorporated into an indexed compression system, and any compression scheme for such information can be incorporated as well. It seems certain that such systems will see rapidly increasing use in the future to store large collections of disparate kinds of information.

Where more detail is required, readers can turn to the initial parts of other chapters. In all cases the more technical material does not begin until well into the chapter, and the first part provides a general overview of what is involved. Many of the chapters contain some sections that are "optional" (marked by a light gray bar in the margin) and need not be studied unless the material is felt to be particularly relevant to your interests.

Updated and revised content

The first edition of this book was published in 1994, and now, in March 1999, we are just polishing this second edition. What a lot has happened in the world of information during the intervening five years—the rise of the World Wide Web, the idea of digital libraries, the internationalization of information, Java and the "network computer," virtual reality in your living room (and, on the downside, pornography, virtual sex, gambling). Today, the largest information system that humanity has ever known is pushed "in your face" daily—whoever you are—by TV, magazines, and advertisements everywhere. Today, information workers experience the power—and the frustration—of full-text searching of vast masses of data—gigabytes—on a routine basis, every working day. All this in just five years. One of the more esoteric topics this book covers (or so we thought), textual image compression, is being turned into an international standard and will soon be used in your fax machine. Some of the changes that were foreseen in 1993 have not happened (yet): for example, this second edition is not called *Managing Terabytes* as we rashly hinted it might be. So much for technology forecasting.

On the one hand, the world of information has become assimilated into everyday life to an extent that would have stretched our credulity in 1993. On the other, the topics covered in this book are not dated: indeed, they are ever more relevant to today's scene. The need to compress and index documents and images is even stronger. The basic ideas of compression, information science, full-text retrieval, and image representation are just the same. The idea of *compressed* full-text indexing is just as good and almost as unusual. So far as we know, no commercial search engines yet use all of the techniques we espouse: they do it the hard way—the hardware way—with enormous disk and main memory installations. (And they don't store the text, only the index. The new catch phrase for technology failure—"404 Not Found: The requested URL was not found on this server"—makes "Bus error: core dumped" seem quaint, almost friendly.) This book is just as timely and important now as when it was first published.

While the basic core of material in this second edition is the same as in the previous edition, we have made the most of our opportunity to update it to reflect the changes that have taken place over five years. Of course, there have been errors to fix, errors that we had accumulated in our publicly available errata file. In fact, surprisingly few were found, and we are hopeful that there are even fewer in this second edition. (The errata for the second edition may be found via the home page at *www. cs.mu.oz.au/mg/*.) We have thoroughly edited the chapters and brought them up-to-date where appropriate, inserting many new references into the "Further reading" sections. The most enjoyable part has been adding new material—here are the major additions.

Chapter 2 has been updated to include recent developments in text compression, including the block-sorting method (Burrows-Wheeler transform), approximate arithmetic coding, and fast Huffman coding algorithms. More details of some of the methods have been added, the performance comparison has been updated to include recent compression programs, and comparative results have been obtained using the more recent Canterbury corpus instead of the Calgary corpus as before.

Chapter 3 discusses indexing techniques, and a new section has been added on context-based index compression, including a description of the recently developed technique of "interpolative coding." The material on signature files and their performance relative to inverted files has been extensively revised.

Four sections have been added to Chapter 4. The first describes the use of blocked inverted indexes, which provide fast Boolean querying. The second covers frequency-sorted inverted indexes, which improve performance for ranked queries. The third describes some of the operational issues associated with the World Wide Web search engines that we now—millions of us—take for granted. The fourth new section discusses distributed querying. The sections describing ranked querying and the *TREC* project have been extensively revised to incorporate the substantial developments that have taken place over the last five years.

Chapter 6 includes significant new material on lossless image compression, including de facto image compression standards that are in widespread use for pictures in Web pages (GIF and PNG), a high-performance lossless image compression algorithm called CALIC, and the JPEG-Lossless or JPEG-LS scheme that has been proposed as a new international standard for lossless compression.

Chapter 7 includes a new section on JBIG2, an upcoming international standard for the compression of document images. Although the details will not be finalized until approaching the year 2000—well after this edition is published—the form that the standard will take is reasonably clear, and it will incorporate many of the techniques described in this chapter.

The discussion in Chapter 9 has been revised and the various experimental results updated to reflect developments in compression technology and computer hardware that have taken place over the last five years. In particular, a detailed section (including new figures) has been added that describes length-limited Huffman coding.

Chapter 10 contains new information on the Internet and World Wide Web, a major new section on digital libraries, and new material on Web search engines and agent-based information retrieval.

An important new appendix (Appendix B) has been added describing a large-scale application of some of the key ideas presented in this book, the New Zealand Digital Library. This is a repository of public information, freely available on the World Wide Web, that uses mg as its kernel. It is intended to demonstrate the utility and flexibility of the mg software for information retrieval. This appendix explains the facilities that are offered and the mechanisms that are necessary to provide them.

Finally, from our experience in teaching this material in a variety of classroom settings, we have put together an "Instructor's Supplement" that includes review and test questions for use when teaching from the book. It is a separate booklet, available to teachers on request from Tim C. Bell, Department of Computer Science, University of Canterbury, Christchurch, New Zealand.

Older but wiser, we are refraining from making any forecasts of what will have changed when we begin work on the third edition of *Managing Gigabytes*, probably around the year 2003.

Acknowledgments

Writing the acknowledgments is always the nicest part! A lot of people helped us, and it is lovely to have this opportunity to thank them. We have been fortunate to receive a great deal of encouragement and assistance in this book from many of our highly esteemed colleagues in the data compression and information retrieval areas, principally Abe Bookstein, Nigel Horspool, Tomi Klein, Glen Langdon, Timo

Raita, and Jim Storer. We have learned a great deal from all these people, and part of what we have learned is reflected in this book. Worthy of special mention are John Cleary, Radford Neal, Ron Sacks-Davis, and Justin Zobel, with whom we have worked extensively over the years. The results we present here are theirs just as much as they are ours. Rob Akscyn and Bob Kruse gave valuable help and advice at critical points of this project, and Rod Harries and Todd Bender have provided helpful information and advice on concordances. Several other people have also contributed either directly or indirectly at some stage over the last five years: Gill Bryant, Sally Jo Cunningham, Tony Dale, Daryl D'Souza, Mike Fleischmann, Peter Gutmann, Jan Pedersen, Bill Pennebaker, Art Pollard, Marcelo Weinberger, and Ross Wilkinson. David Abrahamson was heavily involved in the early stages of the book: he helped us decide what should—and should not—be included. He also provided the motivation for our work on textual image compression and contributed some material to Chapter 7. We also thank the reviewers who were there at the beginning to convince our publisher that we were worth supporting and who were there again at the end when the manuscript was nearly complete. Douglas Campbell provided particularly detailed and helpful comments for the second edition. Valuable input in the review process was also provided by Ron Murray, Rob Akscyn, Robert Gray, David Hawking, Paul Kantor, Yann LeCun, Michael Lesk, Darryl Lovato, Karen Sparck Jones, Jan Pedersen, and Peter Willett.

Jennifer Mann and Karyn Johnson of Morgan Kaufmann have worked hard to shape the second edition, and Elisabeth Beller, our production editor, has made the process go very smoothly for us. Joan Mitchell of IBM has provided valuable practical assistance in helping us to define, refine, and produce this book.

Many of our students have been extremely helpful. Mary-Ellen Harrison and Mark James at the University of Calgary, Canada, and Hugh Emberson at the University of Canterbury, New Zealand, were instrumental in the development of our ideas on textual image compression. Stuart Inglis and Abdul Saheed at the University of Waikato, New Zealand, have done sterling work on document layout recognition and template matching using model-based compression. Craig Nevill-Manning at Waikato and Calgary was involved in some of our early research on index compression and has been a great source of all sorts of practical help. Peter Thompson at the University of Melbourne, Australia, contributed to the material presented in Chapter 5. We are grateful to students who field-tested various sections of the book, including Tim A. H. Bell (a student at the University of Melbourne, and not to be confused with the Tim C. Bell who is an author of this book), Gwenda Bensemann, Mike Ciavarella, Craig Farrow, Andrew Kelly, Alex McCooke, Chris Stephens, John Tham, Bert Thompson, Lang Stuiver, Andrew Turpin, and Glenn Wightwick, who relished their role as guinea pigs and provided valuable comments.

In producing the second edition, we are most grateful to Peter Fenwick of the University of Auckland for his assistance with the new material on the Burrows-Wheeler transform. Nasir Memon kindly supplied some information for Chapter 6, and much of the section on JPEG-LS is derived from a paper that he wrote. Paul Howard reviewed our description of the embryonic new standard for textual image compression, JBIG2. Harold Thimbleby made valuable comments on Appendix B.

Yvonne Simmons helped with the indexing. Andrew Turpin provided an improved implementation of the *huffword* program, together with some of the length-limited coding results listed in Chapter 9. Owen de Kretser and Lang Stuiver reran many of the results listed in Chapters 3 and 4. Tim A. H. Bell assisted with a perceptive proofreading service for almost all of the revised book, and Tetra Lindarto, Elizabeth Ng, and Bronwyn Webster also helped in the proofreading effort. Nelson Beebe has been a source of useful information and encouragement since the first edition was published.

The first mg system was developed with the support of the Australian Research Council and the Collaborative Information Technology Research Institute and with assistance from Lachlan Andrew, Gary Eddy, and Neil Sharman. Since then many people have contributed: Owen de Kretser, Tim Shimmin, and William Weber, to name just those directly involved. There are many others who have developed modifications for specific purposes, and space precludes us naming them all. The minimal perfect hashing routines were written by Bohdan Majewski at the University of Queensland, and his permission to incorporate these procedures is gratefully acknowledged. A lot of other people also went well beyond the call of duty in helping us with technical aspects of the book. All the images in Chapter 6 were produced by Neil Sharman, as were some of the figures in Chapter 2 and Appendix A. Many of the illustrations in Chapters 7 and 8 were produced by Kerry Guise and Stuart Inglis.

Figure 1.1 is reproduced by permission of T. & T. Clark Ltd. Figure 1.2 is reproduced by permission of Cornell University Press. Figure 1.3 is reproduced by permission of Garland Publishing. Figure 1.5 was drawn by Gail Williams. Figure 1.6 is reproduced by permission of Faber and Faber Limited and Crown Publishers Inc. The text of Figure 3.4 is reproduced with the permission of Ziff Communications Inc. The "peppers" picture used for Figures 6.1, 6.18, and 6.20 is from the University of Southern California Image Processing Institute (USC-IPI) image database. The magazine page shown in Figure 6.11 and also used in Figures 8.1, 8.2, and 8.5 is from *Canadian Artificial Intelligence Magazine*. Figure 7.1 is reproduced with the permission of the Board of Trinity College, Dublin. The page shown in Figure 8.16 is reproduced with permission from *Communications of the ACM* (copyright 1987, Association for Computing Machinery Inc.). Figures 8.25 and 8.26 are reprinted from *IEEE Computer* by permission of the Institute of Electrical and Electronics Engineers, Inc.

Parts of this research have been funded by the Australian Research Council and the Natural Sciences and Engineering Research Council of Canada. Furthermore, the departments of computer science at Calgary, Canterbury, Melbourne, and Waikato have all been very supportive of our work.

Last, but definitely not least, we are grateful to our families, who were quite aware of the implications of having an author in the house but let us go ahead and write the book anyway. Thank you Judith, Pam, and Thau Mee for your support. You have helped us in innumerable ways, and this is your book too. We are grateful to our children, Andrew, Anna, Anne, Kate (who arrived shortly after the first edition), Michael, and Nikki, who are growing up immersed in the information age, for keeping us in touch with reality and continually reminding us that managing gigabytes is not all *that* important.

Overview

I n 1911, Professor Lane Cooper published a concordance of William Words-worth's poetry so that scholars could readily locate words in which they were interested. The 1,136-page tome lists all 211,000 nontrivial words in the poet's works, from *Aäliza* to *Zutphen's,* yet remarkably, it took less than 7 months to construct. The task was completed so quickly because it was undertaken by a highly organized team of 67 people—3 of whom had died by the time the concordance was published—using 3-by-5-inch cards, scissors, glue, and stamps.

The task of constructing concordances has traditionally been very onerous and time-consuming. As an example, a concordance for the Greek version of the New Testament was compiled by William Moulton and Alfred Geden and first published in 1897. The work has undergone several revisions since then, and responsibility for the task has been passed down through three generations of the Moulton family. Figure 1.1 shows part of the concordance entry for the word ἐραυνάω, a Greek verb for *search.* The task is not entirely mechanical, since several inflections of the verb are recorded under the one heading.

The Greek New Testament concordance was just one of many comprehensive indexes to various books—such as the Bible, the works of Shakespeare, and the writings of classical philosophers—produced by hand in the 19th and early 20th centuries. The prefaces of these works tell of many years of painstaking toil, presumably driven by a belief in the worthiness of the text being indexed. The term *concordance* originally applied just to biblical indexes. Its root, *concord,* means unity, and the term apparently arose out of the school of thought that the unity of the Bible should be reflected in consistency between the Old and New Testaments, which could be demonstrated by a concordance.

The 1960s and 1970s saw another ebullition of concordance making, this time fueled by the ease with which indexes could be constructed with the aid of a computer. All that was required was enough motivation to type a work into a machine-readable format and access to a sufficiently powerful computer system and suitable software.

ἘΡΑΥΝΆΩ 2037.5

Jo 5 39 ἐραυνᾶτε τ. γραφάς
7 52 ἐραύνησον κ. ἴδε
Ro 8 27 ὁ δὲ ἐραυνῶν τ. καρδίας οἶδεν
1 Co 2 10 τὸ γὰρ πνεῦμα πάντα ἐραυνᾷ
1 Pe 1 11 ἐραυνῶντες εἰς τίνα ἢ ποῖον καιρὸν ἐδή-
λου τὸ ἐν αὐτοῖς πνεῦμα Χριστοῦ
Re 2 23 ἐγώ εἰμι ὁ ἐραυνῶν νεφροὺς κ. καρδίας

Figure 1.1 A concordance entry for the verb *to search* from the Greek New Testament (Moulton and Geden 1977). Reprinted by permission from T & T Clark, Ltd.

In this way concordances came into being for all sorts of literature, from Charlotte Brontë to Dylan Thomas, from the Tao-Tsang to Charles Darwin. There are even concordances of musical compositions and of mathematical sequences and values. A 1965 index of Byron's works was not computer-generated but concedes that the computer will be the concordance maker of the future, predicting that the author's work "may be considered the last of the hand-made concordances." Its construction was begun in 1940, well before computers were available for this tedious task, and we can sense the compiler's frustration that in 1965 it may have been better to discard the 285,000 cards compiled over 25 years and have a computer construct the information in a matter of days. Nevertheless, the compiler rightly points out that there are advantages to manually constructed concordances, including the opportunity to spot errors in the original text. It was also noted that the pleasure of working with Byron's poetry would have been lost on a machine (Young 1965).

As computers capable of constructing concordances become more and more accessible, the task of compiling such an index becomes less and less significant. What was once the work of a lifetime—or longer—is now a relatively modest project. In 1875, Mary Cowden Clarke proudly wrote in the preface to her concordance of Shakespeare that "to furnish a faithful guide to this rich mine of intellectual treasure . . . has been the ambition of a life; and it is hoped that the sixteen years' assiduous labour . . . may be found to have accomplished that ambition" (Clarke 1875). It may have been hard for Mrs. Clarke to imagine that a century later, just one person, Todd K. Bender, professor of English at the University of Wisconsin, would produce nine concordances in the time it took her to construct one.[1] Mrs. Horace Howard Furness, the author of a concordance of Shakespeare's poetry that was also published in 1875 and whose husband and son both wrote books about Shakespeare's

1 Bender is the sole author of 9 concordances, but has coauthored 22 more.

```
SHEEPFOLD
        THE SHEEPFOLD OF MICHAEL SURVIVES   •  •  •  •  •  •   228 YOUTH OF NATURE     21

SHEET
        OER THE BLANCHD SHEET HER RAVEN HAIR  •  •  •  •  •  •   146 TRISTRAM 2       107
        AND REACH THAT GLIMMERING SHEET OF GLASS  •  •  •  •   310 OBERMANN         119

SHEETS
        THERE WHERE DOWN CLOUDY CLIFFS THROUGH SHEETS OF FOAM   262 SCHOLAR-GIPSY     248
        IN SHEETS OF SCATHING FIRE   •  •  •  •  •  •  •   319 OBERMANN MORE     202
        FAR OER THE GLISTENING SHEETS OF WINDY CORN    •  •   473 CROMWELL          36

SHELF
        AND FROM SOME SWARDED SHELF HIGH UP THERE CAME   •  •    25 DREAM            11

SHELL
        THE WIND IS DOWN BUT SHELL NOT COME TO-NIGHT   •  •   139 TRISTRAM 1        300
        SHELL LIGHT HER SILVER LAMP WHICH FISHERMEN    •  •   151 TRISTRAM 3         79
        AND TAKE HER BROIDERY-FRAME AND THERE SHELL SIT  •  •   152 TRISTRAM 3         82
        WHOSE STRIPED SHELL FOUNDED   •  •  •  •  •  •  •   392 MEROPE          1628
```

Figure 1.2 Entries from a concordance of Matthew Arnold (Parrish 1959). Reprinted from *A Concordance to the Poems of Matthew Arnold.* Copyright © 1959 by Cornell University. All rights reserved.

work, describes herself as a "harmless drudge" (Furness 1875). Clearly, concordance making is an ideal task for mechanization.

The computer may make a good "harmless drudge," but in its early years it was also a very expensive one. The preface to one of Bender's concordances relates how most of his computer budget for 1970 was spent on just one computer run to generate the work (Bender and Higdon 1988). Furthermore, early machine-compiled concordances were often produced as line printer output, in uppercase letters, with punctuation omitted. Figure 1.2 shows some entries from a 1959 concordance of Matthew Arnold. Note that *she'll* is indistinguishable from *shell*.

As computers became cheaper and more powerful, it became more and more economical to produce concordances, and the quality of the output improved. Figure 1.3 shows an entry from a 1988 concordance of *The Spoils of Poynton* by Henry James. The work was generated and printed on a personal computer, yet the quality of the output is comparable to that of handmade concordances—possibly even better.

With the advent of personal computers that were sufficiently powerful to perform the concordancing task, individual scholars could generate their own concordances. The only hurdle to being a prolific author of concordances was getting the text into a machine-readable form. The preface to a concordance of Darwin's *Origin of the Species* suggests at least one economical option for text entry: the original text was apparently entered as a labor of love by undergraduate students (Barrett, Weinshank, and Gottleber 1981). More recently it has become possible to accomplish this task effectively by use of optical character recognition or by obtaining the document in electronic form from a publisher who uses computer typesetting. Even having a book entered by a typist is relatively inexpensive. The ease with which a concordance can now be generated is often acknowledged in how it is cataloged: the author being indexed (such as Shakespeare or Darwin) is listed as one of the authors of the concordance, and the person creating the concordance may well be given the designation of "editor" or "programmer" rather than "author."

```
Scruple 4
proved what he had to offer her? That was a scruple 24,9
keener now and her scruple more absent; the pro- 138,15
Mona, but now that scruple was swept away. If he 158,9
times yes — her choice should know no scruple: the 260,30
Scruples 3
up to satiety. Preoccupations and scruples fell away 22,3
was simply that all Mrs. Gereth's scruples were on 37,23
scruples?" Her resentment rose to a high insolence 219,28
Sea 2
person she loved jump into the sea. Mrs. Gereth 213,23
long sea. Something, in a dire degree at this last 262,23
Seal 2
to Ricks, under her hand and seal; but no sense of 146,5
in her own room, late at night, she broke the seal 258,17
Sealed 2
at any rate their fate was sealed: Owen, as soon as 35,11
show me his release as quite signed and sealed. Oh 215,22
Seams 1
with black seams and an umbrella as fine as a lance; 150,21
Search 2
Her companion again seemed to search her. "I 156,8
```

Figure 1.3 Entries from a concordance of *The Spoils of Poynton* by Henry James (Bender and Higdon 1988). Reprinted by permission of Garland Publishing.

The natural outcome of the increasing computing power now available to scholars is for concordances to be constructed on demand for any text whatever, and this is exactly what is happening. Instead of purchasing a concordance, you can visit a Web site that provides access to a text or collection of texts. For example, the "British National Corpus" (*info.ox.ac.uk/bnc/*) allows visitors to search over 4,000 texts, containing a total of 100 million words. The user can search the text for terms of interest as and when required. This makes complex operations possible, such as seeking combinations of words that appear together or having the output sorted in order of expected usefulness.

Computer searching of a large text database using an automatically constructed concordance is called *full-text retrieval,* since the full text is available for searching, rather than some much more restricted list of keywords as used to be the case in earlier computer-based text retrieval systems. All sorts of people use full-text retrieval to locate information. A historian may use it to find references to a certain event in archives; a personnel manager might use it to search a collection of résumés to find a person with the right skills; a secretary could use it to track down some old correspondence; a newspaper or magazine reporter could use it to scan back issues for background material for a new story; a legal assistant might use it to determine which previous cases are relevant to a new one; an engineer might use it to locate information in the manuals for a large project; and a cook might use it to find a recipe that uses particular ingredients or techniques. Over the past few years, it has become common to employ full-text retrieval for searching for information on the World Wide Web, using one of the popular commercial search engines. Full-text retrieval is very attractive: all that is needed is an electronic version of the documents that might be consulted and a computer system with sufficient storage to accommodate them.

Searching a full text is not quite so simple as having a computer go through the text from start to finish looking for keywords. Despite their reputation for speed and blind obedience, an exhaustive search is still a lengthy business for a computer. For example, even a fast system takes several minutes to read an entire CD-ROM, and on the enormous volumes of text managed by the World Wide Web search engines, an exhaustive search would take longer than any user would be prepared to wait.

Imagine trying to find a book in a library that has no catalog and where the librarians had always placed the books on the shelves in the order in which they were acquired, simply moving to a new shelf when the old ones became full. Although the required information is there, for all intents and purposes it is inaccessible, and unless you are prepared to spend days, and perhaps months, walking the bookshelves looking for what you are after, you would probably give up. This is analogous to the computer trying to find information by reading through the text from start to finish.

Of course, this is exactly why we expect the books in a library to be cataloged. The catalog allows people to search for information about a particular topic, which can then be located using a map of the library. If such a catalog is available, it matters little where the books are actually stored on the shelves—they might be ordered by a code for their subject or by author name, but even if they were simply numbered in order of accession to the library, a particular book could be located quickly. The ordering might save some walking if several related books are being sought, but it is the catalog that makes the query viable. Likewise with computer-based searches—a machine-readable index to the text being searched greatly speeds up access.

The price usually paid for such fast access is that a significant amount of extra space is required to store the index. Although a card catalog does not take up much space in a library (and a computerized catalog occupies even less), it does not provide nearly as comprehensive an index as we hope for in a full-text retrieval system. The card catalog would be a lot bigger if it indicated the location of each occurrence of every possible word in every book in the library! One of the main ideas in this book is that it is possible to provide very fast searching and yet *reduce* the amount of space needed to store documents on a computer.

All sorts of possibilities are opened up by being able to store vast collections of documents in relatively little space, yet with fast searching for retrieval. We can imagine scanning onto a computer every document that we read—including letters, books, papers, messages, and advertisements—so that at some later stage a particular fact could be recalled using a full-text retrieval system. This would provide a powerful supplement to our memory. The precursors of the sort of portable technology required to make this possible are already available in the form of notebook computers and personal digital assistants, so a comprehensive system may not be too far in the future. In fact, such a system was envisaged as long ago as 1945 in a seminal article by Vannevar Bush, the highest-ranking scientific administrator in the U.S. war effort (Bush 1945):

> The human mind ... operates by association. With one item in its grasp, it snaps instantly to the next that is suggested by the association of thoughts, in accordance with some intricate web of trails carried by the cells of the brain. It has other characteristics, of course; trails that are not frequently followed are prone to fade, items are not fully permanent, memory is transitory. Yet the speed of action, the intricacy of trails, the detail of mental pictures, is awe-inspiring beyond all else in nature.... Consider a future device for individual use, which is a sort of mechanized private file and library. It needs a name, and, to coin one at random, "memex" will do. A memex is a device in which an individual stores all his books, records, and communications, and which is mechanized so that it may be consulted with exceeding speed and flexibility.... When numerous items have been thus joined together to form a trail, they can be reviewed in turn, rapidly or slowly, by deflecting a lever like that used for turning the pages of a book.... It is exactly as though the physical items had been gathered together from widely separated sources and bound together to form a new book. It is more than this, for any item can be joined into numerous trails.

The "memex" is widely viewed as the precursor of hypertext. However, hypertext systems do not really address the question of how to consult such a huge collection of documents with "exceeding speed and flexibility." For this we need mechanisms for full-text retrieval that are efficient and whose performance does not deteriorate even when dealing with immense document databases.

1.1 Document databases

A library is just one form of document database—a large collection of books, magazines, and newspapers, of which, at any given time, a particular user is interested in only a tiny fraction. As a very rough estimate, we might suppose that one printed page contains about 400 words, or, including formatting and punctuation, about 2,500 characters; then a 400-page book contains about one million characters. For example, the present book contains over 200,000 words, nearly 1,400,000 characters—excluding pictures. Continuing the calculation, if we assume that a 400-page book is 2 centimeters thick, then a library stores information at the rate of 50 million characters per linear meter. A book stack has two sides and might be five shelves high and 5 meters long, so it stores perhaps two and a half billion characters, or, in computer terms, 2.5 gigabytes. Even a small library has 10 or more stacks; a large one might have hundreds. In total, then, we might expect even a relatively small document collection to contain several billion characters.

Document databases are so large, and so common, that it is well worthwhile to consider how they might be stored as efficiently as possible—that is what this book is about. It is possible to reduce significantly the amount of space required to store text on computers using compression techniques. These methods change the representation of a document so that it can be stored in less space, yet recovered quickly in its original form.

It is important to store documents efficiently in terms of storage space, but it is equally important that they can be located and retrieved efficiently—hence our interest in concordances. A major theme of the book is the combination of compression techniques with indexing techniques, which together address the two main problems in document retrieval: the space required to store large quantities of text, and the time needed to search it. Much has been written about solutions to each of the problems in isolation, but there are obstacles to combining compression and indexing that have, in the past, prevented their being used together. However, elegant ways to circumvent the obstacles have been devised, and it is these that are presented in this book. The most remarkable result is that it is possible, given a particular text, to produce a compressed and indexed version that is usually less than half the size of the original and yet can be searched extremely rapidly for any given combination of terms. We measure a computer system's speed in terms of the number of accesses made to disk, because this access time—which is measured in fractions of a second—dominates the total time that is involved in a search. Searches require just a few disk accesses, and so the technique is clearly very satisfactory for all but the most impatient interactive user.

A document database system should be able to store more than just text. Images—usually in the form of diagrams or photographs—are an important part of many documents. The above rough estimate of the amount of storage needed for a document database conveniently ignores the cost of storing images. It is much more difficult to estimate the amount of space required for pictures than it is for text, but it is likely to be considerable. For example, the 175-odd pictures in the present book (they occur mainly in Chapters 6, 7, and 8, although figures like the ones in this chapter are also stored as pictures) total almost 40 Mbytes on the computer, which is about 40 times the size of the text in the book. However, to be fair, they are—for technical convenience—stored in an unnecessarily redundant representation, and perhaps these numbers should be reduced by a factor of around five to give a more realistic feeling for the magnitude of the space occupied by the pictures. Even so, they occupy several times as much space as the text.

Sometimes a document that is predominantly text must be stored as an image because it may be necessary to reproduce it later in its original form for legal or historical reasons. Storing it as plain text generally loses a host of information, from spacing and typeface details to illegible or nontextual marks. For example, a document database might include credit card slips, and an accurate facsimile of the slip might be needed for legal purposes, though a textual version could be more useful for the purpose of routine consultation. Moreover, any document database system must provide a way to cope with the vast amount of text that is already on paper, and by far the simplest way of doing this is to scan existing documents into the system, using an optical scanning device, and treat them as a succession of images.

For these reasons, it is important to consider how images can be compressed and indexed alongside the text. A particularly important kind of image in document databases is one made up primarily of text, and we call this a *textual image*. Examples include fax documents and archives that have been digitally scanned for long-term storage. Special techniques are available to store textual images effectively; these are discussed in later chapters.

In this book we take a fairly liberal view of what is meant by a "document database." We have already expanded the term to include images. Document databases are now beginning to include other material, such as sound and video recordings. Although we do not specifically look at techniques for incorporating these kinds of data, what is involved is really just an extension of the ideas used for incorporating still images into a document database, coupled with appropriate, tailor-made compression methods.

The book focuses on full-text retrieval techniques, as opposed to conventional databases in which there are only a small number of preselected keys (such as "account number" or the mysterious codes like "J6NHYQ" used by airlines to identify reservation records) that can be used to access the stored data. In a full-text system, *every* part of each record is indexed, so *any* part may be used as the basis for a query. Imagine trying to extract, from an airline database, a list of all the people on your street who have departures on the same day as yours, so that you can try to hitch a ride to the airport. Airline databases are not likely to be indexed in a way that supports this kind of query, yet this is exactly the type of query of which a full-text system is capable. An example of this sort of query is "find all the documents about meetings between United States presidents and New Zealand and Australian prime ministers in which defense treaties are discussed."

Although full-text retrieval systems are a kind of very large database, the latter term is generally used to refer specifically to very large *conventional* databases, which form a major area of study in themselves. Full-text retrieval and database systems are also part of the larger field known as *information retrieval*, which can be defined loosely as the study of methods and structures used to represent and access information. Again, we do not intend to deal in full with this larger field but have drawn in the appropriate material.

Many of the ideas in this book have been incorporated into a public domain full-text retrieval system called mg, a suite of programs that can index, compress, and search large quantities of documents, including both text and images. The mg system uses some of the better techniques now available and is intended to give practitioners an idea of the kind of performance that can be achieved. Information about obtaining and using the mg system is provided in Appendix A.

In the remainder of this chapter we introduce some of the main issues that the book deals with—namely, compression, indexes, images and textual images, and the mg system. Each of these is examined in more detail in the chapters that follow. Inspired by the biblical origins of indexing, the problems addressed in this book are lightheartedly expressed in the allegory of Figure 1.4: this is the order in which we develop our theme.

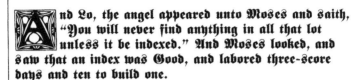

In the beginning there was the text, and the text was words, and yea, verily, I say unto you, there was too much of it and it had to be compressed.

And Lo, the angel appeared unto Moses and saith, "You will never find anything in all that lot unless it be indexed." And Moses looked, and saw that an index was Good, and labored three-score days and ten to build one.

Then the Devil appeared in the guise of a computer salesperson and tempted the people by shewing them how beautiful a graven 24-bit full color image could be, and how little disk space would be needed to store just a few of these images, and how easy they were to scan. And the people succumbed to temptation.

As the cursor follows the mouse, so too did seven years of disk drought follow the seven days of plentiful file space, and Moses was in a foul mood and in severe need of more tablets.

But the Lord spoke, and saith that the images must also be compressed, and shewed Moses a nifty method for compression and for separation of the text from the nontext.

Figure 1.4 The story behind the book.

1.2 Compression

Figure 1.5 shows an example of a compression system that represents a technique commonly used on computers. In the figure, missing text can be obtained by following an arrow back to where the text has occurred before.[2] For example, the first empty box should contain a letter *e*. The first empty box on the second line refers to the phrase *Pease porridge* on the first line. Because all the arrows point backward, the original text can be reconstructed by working in natural reading order. On a computer, the arrows are represented by two numbers that indicate where the text has occurred before and how many characters should be copied. These "pointers" usu-

---

2 This method has been "invented" by many people over the years. The variation shown here was conceived at age five by the son of one of the authors. The family of methods based on this idea is discussed in Section 2.6.

Figure 1.5   A compressed representation (Bell, Witten, and Fellows 1998).

ally take less space to store than the text they represent, so compression is achieved. Notice that single characters are sometimes represented by a pointer and sometimes by the actual character, depending on how far back the reference is. This is very close to how some compression systems work, as will be discussed in Chapter 2.

The motivation for compressing text is that it requires less storage space or, if it is being transmitted over a communication link, it takes less time and costs less money to send. The original text can still be reconstructed exactly from the compressed version. The chief price paid is that some computing time is required to encode and decode the text. Another significant factor for full-text retrieval is that random access to the text is difficult. With uncompressed text, accessing the part that begins a specified number of characters from the beginning can generally be done very rapidly using appropriate calls to the operating system. However, when a file is compressed, it is usually necessary to decode the entire text from the beginning until the desired part is reached.

One way to provide faster random access to a very large text is to break the text up into *blocks* and compress each one independently. In that way, only the block containing the desired text needs to be decoded, not all preceding ones. However, the more blocks there are, the less each one is compressed. For example, for the method shown in Figure 1.5, there is little opportunity to replace characters near the start of a block with pointers, and so compression is poorer than it would have been if more previous text were available to be referenced.

The whole question of text compression is taken up in Chapter 2, which is a comprehensive survey of compression techniques that provides a practical guide to the methods most commonly used in practice. An extensive comparison of the performance of the most popular schemes is included, in terms of both compression efficiency and speed on current computers.

1.3 Indexes

Although the use of text compression can save much space, it does not help with the question of how the information should be organized so that queries can be resolved and relevant portions of the data located and extracted. Indexes are crucial for efficient access to all sorts of information. They appear at the ends of books, in the year-end issues of journals, as catalogs for libraries, and as telephone directories and building directories. Special indexes have been constructed for locating non-textual information too: books are available that enable you to look up a musical theme, such as "G G G E♭," and discover that it is the opening of Beethoven's Fifth Symphony; to look up a sequence of integers such as 1, 2, 1, 2, 2, 3, 1, 2, 2, 3, 2, 3, 3, 4, . . . , and determine that it is the number of ones in the binary expansion of $n+1$; or to look up the real number 0.93371663 . . . to find that it is approximately equal to $2 \log_{10} \frac{1}{2}(e + \pi)$.

Indexes can range in detail from a few key terms at the end of a book to a complete concordance of every word in a text showing each context in which it was used. Not only do indexes make it easy to locate particular terms, but they show terms together that might not have been previously associated.

For example, Figure 1.6a shows part of an index of musical themes. To locate a theme, we must transpose it to C major and look up the letter names of the opening notes. The part of the index shown in Figure 1.6a includes a Beethoven piano

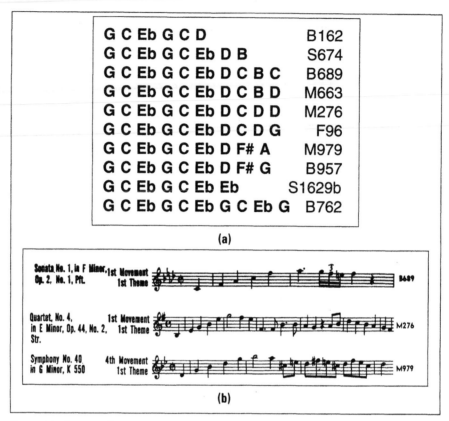

Figure 1.6 Excerpts from a concordance of musical themes (Barlow and Morgenstern 1949): (a) the index of themes transposed to C major; (b) some of the themes beginning with the "Mannheim motif."

sonata (labeled B689 and shown in Figure 1.6b), which begins with a minor arpeggio. Nearby entries in the index show other works that begin with the same theme,[3] including a Mendelssohn string quartet (M276) and a Mozart symphony (M979). The same effect occurs in textual indexes, such as those shown in Figures 1.2 and 1.3, and could be used to find places where material may have been reused, reinvented, or even plagiarized.

Alphabetically ordered indexes can be searched very quickly using a binary search. Each probe into the index halves the number of potential locations for the target of the search. For example, some 300,000 word appearances are indexed in Cruden's concordance of the Bible, from *Aaron* to *Zuzims*, printed on 774 pages. The correct page for an entry can be located by looking at no more than 10 pages, and even fewer if the searcher can interpolate the position of an entry from the position of its

---

3   This theme is sometimes called the "Mannheim motif."

search
enquire and made *s.*   *Deut* 13:14
that *s.* may be made in.   *Ezra* 4:15
                                    5:17
s. hath been made, and it. 4:19; 6:1
prepare thyself to the *s.*   *Job* 8:8
hast thou walked in the *s.?*   38:16*
accomplish a diligent *s.*   *Ps* 64:6
my spirit made diligent *s.*   77:6
not found it by secret *s.*   *Jer* 2:34

search, *verb*
he shall not *s.* whether.   *Lev* 27:33
to *s.* out a resting place. *Num* 10:33
that they may *s.* the land.   13:2
which we have gone to *s.* it.   32
passed through to *s.* it, is.   14:7
of the men that went to *s.*   38
men, and they shall *s.*   *Deut* 1:22
before to *s.* you out a place.   33
men to *s.* the country.   *Josh* 2:2, 3
the Danites sent men to *s.* *Judg* 18:2
land, I will *s.* him out. *1 Sam* 23:23
servants unto thee to *s.* the city ?
        2 Sam 10:3; *1 Chr* 19:3
servants, and they shall *s.* *1 Ki* 20:6
s. that none of the servants.
                            2 Ki 10:23
is it good that he should *s.?* *Job* 13:9
shall not God *s.* this out ? *Ps* 44:21

Figure 1.7 Entries for the word *search* in Cruden's concordance of the Bible (Cruden et al. 1941). Reprinted by permission of Lutterworth Press.

initial letter in the alphabet. A term can usually be located in a few seconds, which is not bad considering that only very elementary technology is being employed. Once an entry is located, the searcher has a list of references that can be followed up. Figure 1.7 shows some of Cruden's concordance entries for the word *search*.

On modern full-text systems, the searching is done by a computer rather than by a person, but essentially the same techniques are used. The difference is that things happen a little faster. Usually it is possible to keep a list of terms in the computer's main memory, and this can be searched in a matter of microseconds. The computer's equivalent of the concordance entry is usually too large to store in main memory, so an access to secondary storage (usually disk) is required to obtain the list of references. Then each of the references must be retrieved from the disk. Depending on the type of disk, how local it is to the computer, and the extent of mechanical movement that is required in devices such as jukebox arrays, this might take anything from a few milliseconds to a few seconds.

When indexing a large text it rapidly becomes clear that just a few common words—such as *of, the,* and *and*—account for a very large number of the entries in the index. People have argued that these words should be omitted since they take up so much space and are not likely to be needed, and for this reason they are often called *stop words*, a term that is used frequently throughout this book. However, several index compilers and users have observed that it is usually better to leave stop words in. As long ago as 1875, Mrs. Furness observed that these seemingly unimportant words may be of more interest than their commonness might suggest, citing a German scholar who had published a study of Shakespeare's use of the verb *to do*. As Mrs. Furness said, "No discretionary powers should be granted to a 'harmless drudge' compiling a Concordance" (Furness 1875). Strong's concordance of the Bible contains the word *exhaustive* in its title because he too held the view that the indexer could not predict what the researcher would want to find. He claims that his concordance is the first comprehensive index of the Bible and notes that "in this respect no Concordance can ever be made more perfect."[4]

Although a few dozen stop words may account for around 30 percent of the references that an index contains, it is possible to represent them in a way that uses relatively little space. The compression techniques described in Chapter 3 are so efficient for stop words that these words increase the size of the index file by as little as 4 percent—a small price to pay to relieve the harmless drudge of the responsibility of having to predict the interests of future users.

A comprehensive index that is designed to give instant access to all documents that satisfy a particular query is a very large data structure, particularly if the index is fine-grained—that is, if locations are recorded to within a small unit, such as a phrase or sentence, rather than a large one, such as a chapter or document. Its very size compromises not only compression performance but also retrieval time, since the computer must read and interpret appropriate parts of it to access the desired information. Fortunately, there are interesting data structures and algorithms that can be applied to solve these problems, and these are described in Chapter 3.

Techniques for answering queries are covered in Chapter 4. A common approach is the *Boolean query,* by which documents are located using keywords that are combined using the logical operations AND, OR, and NOT. An alternative approach is the *ranked query,* in which a list of keywords is provided and the system returns a set of documents in order of decreasing relevance. Chapter 4 examines the details of both these types of queries and looks at how they can be implemented efficiently—particularly in an environment where the index structure is compressed.

Chapters 3 and 4 carefully avoid the question of how the index was created. In fact, constructing an index for a very large text can be rather tricky. It is not difficult conceptually, for all that is needed is to extract the index terms, group together their occurrences, and sort the list alphabetically. But the business becomes rather challenging when dealing with databases containing gigabytes of text, millions of different index terms, and hundreds of millions of index entries. Simple implementations can place incredible demands on computer resources—as much as several gigabytes of primary memory might be required, or if disk memory is used instead, perhaps a human lifetime in terms of disk access time (which is well beyond a disk

---

4 It is rumored that Strong lost his sanity as a result of the struggle for perfection in such an extended and tedious project.

lifetime). As you might expect, there are techniques that can be used to construct indexes efficiently, and they are discussed in Chapter 5. Achieving a suitable trade-off between the three principal variables—primary memory, disk space, and time—is surprisingly intricate.

Archimedes is reputed to have claimed that given a sufficiently long lever and a place to stand, he could move the earth. In the same way, an index provides a powerful lever for locating an item in a text. Suppose that an index were created that referenced every word in every book in the Library of Congress. The books in this library number around 20 million and contain perhaps 5 trillion words. Using a binary search, you could locate any word by looking up just 42 entries in the index.[5] Of course, it is exceedingly unlikely that such an index will be obtained—just as it was exceedingly unlikely that Archimedes would find a suitable lever to move even the Library, let alone the world. Nevertheless, it illustrates how powerful an index can be.

1.4 Document images

Many different technologies and standards are used for storing and interchanging documents, but the most universal format is still the printed page. No special interface is required to read it—it can be stored using technology as simple as a shoebox or a magnet on a refrigerator door—and there are many ways to transmit it, including mail, courier, and fax. It can be read anywhere, anytime, without any special equipment. It is easy to duplicate, edit, and mark up. It is not expensive, and the setup cost is minimal. Consequently, documents are printed, photocopied, and faxed in great quantities, and we are still a long way from the much-vaunted "paperless office."

It is therefore inevitable that a large proportion of the documents we would like to store in a full-text retrieval system can be obtained only from paper. These documents must be scanned into a computer, where they will be represented as a digital image of the page, made up of picture elements (or *pixels*) as shown in Figure 1.8. This sort of image is often referred to as a *document image*. It must be processed by an optical character recognition system before the text can be searched or edited. We refer to document images that are predominantly text (rather than pictures or diagrams) as *textual images*. We distinguish this type of image because special processing methods can be applied to it, not just for optical character recognition but for compression and page analysis.

In many circumstances it is necessary for an archive to store images. The images may be correspondence received by mail or fax, or they might be old records that had previously been stored on paper. Some organizations—such as the military— must store records for decades because they are required to for legal reasons or

---

5 Is it just a coincidence that this number is said to be the answer to "life, the universe, and everything"?

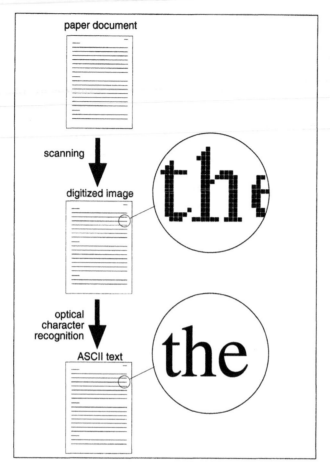

Figure 1.8 Scanning text into a computer.

perhaps for pension purposes. Other organizations—such as department stores—maintain records for months or years. For example, an image of a check or credit card slip may be needed to settle a dispute, and the *way* in which the document is written may be as significant as *what* is written—perhaps the signature is wrong, or the handwriting indicates haste or carelessness. Images of a text may also be important for historical reasons. Scholars retrieving a document may be interested in the original typeface, layout, alterations, or notes in the margin.

Pictures present a very different kind of compression problem from text. When compressing text it is essential that the decoded document be absolutely identical to the one that was encoded, but for images this may be less important. Digital images are usually the result of converting a continuous range of shades or colors into a finite number of values. This means that a digital image is already an approximation of the original, and it does not necessarily make sense to store very fine details because they may not have existed even in the source document. Substantial gains in compression can generally be made if inexact reproduction is tolerated, and often the difference is so small that the human eye cannot detect it or has great difficulty in doing so. Such methods are called *lossy* since they lose some of the original document's detail. In contrast, methods for text compression are generally *lossless*—what is decompressed is supposed to be exactly the same as what was compressed. Although index compression is lossless on the whole, it is not necessarily so. For example, it is acceptable for an index entry to point to a few passages that do *not* contain the index term, along with all those passages that do, if other advantages (like increased compression) are gained thereby. Inappropriate passages can easily be weeded out by an automatic scan through the retrieved material.

There is a wide variety in the kinds of images that information systems must accommodate. Depending on their content and purpose, different images tolerate different amounts of loss. Some are black and white, while in others each pixel can take a shade of gray, and still others are reproduced in color. A further variation relates to how the image is to be uncompressed and displayed: sometimes, particularly when browsing, it is nice to see an approximation of the final image as quickly as possible and have it gradually build up to the full level of detail—that way, the user can interrupt and move to another image before the current one is complete. Because images can take considerable time to decompress, this can provide a very real advantage. Due to all these possibilities, there are many different methods for dealing with images.

Chapter 6 describes both lossy and lossless methods of compression that are suitable for images. Some of these are well-established international standards, like the current fax machine standard for black-and-white images. Some are emerging standards. Some are not standards but are nevertheless included because of their simplicity and performance or because they play an important role in the textual image compression discussed in Chapter 7. Lossy techniques are also appropriate for compressing data from other analog sources, such as voice and moving images, although these methods are not discussed in detail in this book. Many of the image compression methods we describe are lossless because for many purposes—such as medical, legal, and archival—it may not be acceptable in practice to tolerate even the slightest chance of a discrepancy from the original. But some are not, and even some of the lossless ones use lossy techniques and then construct and store a "difference" image to re-create the original exactly.

Many of the images stored in an archival database are textual images. This special case provides new opportunities—and new challenges—for compressing and indexing. One obvious strategy is to perform optical character recognition (OCR) on the text, and represent the document as character codes in some standard alphabet such as ASCII. However, OCR is not a completely reliable technology, and terrible mistakes could be perpetrated, and perpetuated, by archiving documents in this form. It is far more reliable to combine a lossy technique, in which the compression factor is high but what is reconstructed is an approximation to the original digitized document, with a lossless one, which enables the original document to be reproduced exactly from its compressed form. This is achieved by separating the text and noise in the document and compressing the two components separately using a method appropriate to each. Because the components occupy very different amounts of storage space, it can be advantageous to have both versions available—the lossy one for quick previewing and scanning and the lossless one where exact reproduction is required for printing or close examination.

Special techniques for compressing and indexing textual images are introduced in Chapter 7. These work by looking for frequently occurring "shapes" in the image, which are likely to correspond to characters. These shapes, or *marks*, are then given special codes so that their shapes need not be delineated every time they occur. The list of mark identifiers is tantamount to an encoding of the characters in the text and is susceptible to the same compression methods that are used for ordinary text. This technique involves matching against a library of character templates formed by processing the textual image, so Chapter 7 also includes an extensive discussion of template-matching techniques. Indexing can be performed by attempting to recognize the characters using optical character recognition.

Textual image compression is more effective if parts of the image that contain line art or halftone graphics are identified and treated differently from the text itself. Chapter 8 shows how to separate the textual part of a document image from line drawings and halftones, so that each component can be compressed effectively. The first step is to check the orientation of the image and correct it for skew. The next is to segment the document into visually distinct regions, such as blocks of text (columns, paragraphs, or perhaps individual lines), headers and footers, and illustrations. The final step is to classify the regions into text, line drawings, and photographs. This is important because the different components are best compressed and stored in different ways.

1.5   The mg system

This book shows that it is possible to construct a full-text retrieval system that gives instant access to a collection of documents, yet requires far less storage space than the original documents. It hardly seems fair to describe such an attractive prospect without actually demonstrating it. For this reason we have implemented a public domain full-text retrieval system called mg (for *managing gigabytes*), which uses some of the better techniques described in this book. The mg system has two main parts: a program that turns a collection of documents into a compressed and indexed full-text database and a program that services interactive queries for words that appear in the documents.

Mg is not intended as a production system—for example, it has only a rudimentary command-line interface—but it does give the user a good idea of what can be achieved. It demonstrates the kind of compression possible with different sorts of documents, as well as the speed of indexing, compression, and retrieval. It has already had considerable use—for archiving documents such as electronic mail and letters, as a testbed for research involving large-scale information retrieval, and as a foundation for digital libraries.

Chapter 9 looks in some detail at the design and construction of the mg system. The choice of compression and indexing methods is justified with reference to earlier chapters, and the overall structure of the system is explained. This description will help the technically inclined to see how the components introduced in previous chapters can be incorporated into a useful system and also provides the information needed by programmers to modify the system or use parts of the code for another purpose. The chapter includes performance figures for compression, response times, and retrieval effectiveness using a set of large document databases.

A user manual for mg is provided in Appendix A. This is a brief guide and tutorial, aimed at the nontechnical person who wishes to use the system as it stands. The function of the various commands is described, and sample sessions are examined to show how these commands interact and the alternatives they present. A step-by-step guide to the construction of a retrieval system using the software is given, including the initialization of directories and various environment options. The system, written in the C programming language, is designed to be used on a Unix system. It should be relatively easy to port to different environments by modifying the input and output sections. The system requirements will depend on the volume of data to be manipulated; obviously, multigigabyte databases will require commensurate disk and memory capacity. The mg software is available by ftp on the Internet. Information on obtaining and installing it can be found in Appendix A.

Appendix B describes a particular digital library system, the New Zealand Digital Library, which is a large-scale application of some of the key ideas described in this book. Using mg as its kernel, it also serves to demonstrate the utility and flexibility of this software for information retrieval. The facilities that are provided are described, and the mechanisms that are necessary to provide them are explained.

Further reading

Where they are directly relevant, citations are provided in the text of each chapter to indicate the source of included material. All citations are detailed in the References. The "Further reading" section at the end of each chapter—of which this is the first—then draws together those citations into a concise summary describing the papers, books, and other resources relevant to the material covered in that chapter. Any Internet addresses that are given can also be found at *www.cs.mu.oz.au/mg/*.

Historical concordances. The concordance of Wordsworth was published by Lane Cooper (1911). The Greek concordance that has been edited by three generations of the Moulton family was originally published in 1897 (Moulton and Geden 1897) and was revised more recently in 1977 (Moulton and Geden 1977); Figure 1.1 is from the latter. Two early Shakespeare concordances were produced manually by Mrs. Mary Cowden Clarke (1875) and Mrs. Horace Howard Furness (1875). The earliest Bible concordance seems to be one constructed in the 13th century by Frère Hewe of S. Victor (apparently also known as Hugo de St. Caro, or Cardinal Hugo). More recent versions include Cruden's "complete" concordance (some of which is shown in Figure 1.7), first published in 1737 (Cruden et al. 1941), Young's "analytical" concordance, first published in 1879 (Young 1939), and Strong's 1894 "exhaustive" concordance (Strong 1894).

Modern concordances. In the past few decades a large number of concordances have been produced for a variety of books; one of the more prolific compilers is Todd K. Bender, professor of English at the University of Wisconsin. The remark about using a year's computing budget for one run is from one of his later works (Bender and Higdon 1988). Some of the more unusual indexes mentioned include an index of musical themes (Barlow and Morgenstern 1949), a book that lists over 5,000 integer sequences (Sloane and Plouffe 1995), and a dictionary of over 100,000 real numbers (Borwein and Borwein 1990).

Applications of full-text indexing. The applications of computerized full-text retrieval are legion: digital libraries and Web search engines provide full-text retrieval for general searches, and organizations now build up their own full-text databases using off-the-shelf document capture systems that scan, recognize, store, and retrieve text. More specialized areas include résumé scanning (Newstrack 1993b), litigation support (Deets 1989), and searching published journals online (Newstrack 1993a).

Other topics mentioned in this chapter. The pictorial representation of Ziv-Lempel coding in Figure 1.5 is from a book about computer science for children (Bell, Witten, and Fellows 1998), which is available through the Internet. Further reading on text and image compression can be found at the end of Chapters 2 and 6, respectively, and Chapter 4 lists sources of additional information connected with information retrieval. Common abbreviations that are not used in this book but might be encountered in the literature are FTR for *full-text retrieval,* VLDB for *very large database*, and IR for *information retrieval.*

The question as to the meaning of "life, the universe, and everything" is raised in *The Hitchhiker's Guide to the Galaxy* by Douglas Adams (1979).

Text Compression

00001
00010
00011
00100
00101
two

A paradox of modern computer technology is that despite an almost incomprehensible increase in storage and transmission capacities, more and more effort has been put into using compression to increase the amount of data that can be handled. No matter how much storage space or transmission bandwidth is available, someone always finds something to fill it with. It seems that Parkinson's law applies to space as well as time.

The problem of representing information efficiently is nothing new. People have always been interested in means for storing and communicating information, and methods for compressing text to improve this process predate computers. For example, the Braille code for the blind can include "contractions," which represent common words with two or three characters, and Morse code also "compresses" data by using shorter representations for common characters.

Text compression on a computer involves changing the representation of a file so that it takes less space to store or less time to transmit, yet the original file can be reconstructed exactly from the compressed representation. *Text* compression techniques are distinguished from the more general *data* compression methods because the original file can always be reconstructed exactly. For some types of data other than text, such as sound or images, small changes, or *noise*, in the reconstructed data can be tolerated because it is a digital approximation to an analog waveform anyway. However, with text it must be possible to reproduce the original file exactly.

Many compression methods have been invented and reinvented over the years. These range from numerous ad hoc techniques to more principled methods that can give very good compression. One of the earliest and best-known methods of text compression for computer storage and telecommunications is Huffman coding.[1]

---

1 David Huffman, then a student at M.I.T., devised his celebrated coding method in response to a challenge from his professor, and as a result managed to avoid having to take the final exam for the course!

This uses the same principle as Morse code: common symbols—conventionally, characters—are coded in just a few bits, while rare ones have longer codewords. First published in the early 1950s, Huffman coding was regarded as one of the best methods of compression for several decades, until two breakthroughs in the late 1970s—Ziv-Lempel compression and arithmetic coding—made higher compression rates possible. Both these ideas achieve their power through the use of *adaptive compression*—a kind of dynamic coding where the input is compressed relative to a model that is constructed from the text that has just been coded. By basing the model on what has been seen so far, adaptive compression methods combine two key virtues: they are able to encode in a single pass through the input file, and they are able to compress a wide variety of inputs effectively rather than being fine-tuned for one particular type of data such as English text.

Ziv-Lempel methods are adaptive compression techniques that give good compression yet are generally very fast and do not require large amounts of memory. The idea behind them was developed by two Israeli researchers, Jacob Ziv and Abraham Lempel, in the late 1970s. *Arithmetic coding* is really an enabling technology that makes a whole class of adaptive compression schemes feasible, rather than a compression method in its own right. Early implementations of character-level Huffman coding were typically able to compress English text to about five bits per character. Ziv-Lempel methods reduced this to fewer than four bits per character—about half the original size. Methods based on arithmetic coding further improved the compression to just over two bits per character. The price paid is slower compression and decompression, and more memory required in the machines that do the processing.

Some of the best compression methods available are variants of a technique called *prediction by partial matching* (PPM), which was developed in the early 1980s. PPM relies on arithmetic coding to obtain good compression performance. Since then, there has been little advance in the amount of compression that can be achieved, other than some fine-tuning of the basic methods, and the development of a new method called *block sorting* that gives similar performance to PPM. On the other hand, many techniques have been discovered that improve the speed or memory requirements of compression methods. Most of these achieve a significant reduction in computing requirements in exchange for a slight loss of compression.

Present compression techniques give compression of about two bits per character for general English text, depending on what you mean by "general English text." Evidence suggests that compression better than one bit per character is not likely to be achieved, and in order to approach this bound, compression methods will have to draw both on the semantic content of the text and external world knowledge. This is discussed further in Section 2.8.

Improvements are still being made in processor and memory utilization during compression, although both of these resources are becoming cheaper and more plentiful. Generally speaking, the amount of compression achieved by the PPM method increases as more memory becomes available. It is not competitive with Ziv-Lempel methods until 100 Kbytes or more are available, and it does not approach its best performance until 500 Kbytes to 1 Mbyte is allocated. Because of this requirement, when PPM was first proposed in the early 1980s it was a laboratory curiosity, requiring a large minicomputer to test it. Now, most PCs have sufficient computing power to execute it quite effectively. Furthermore, processor speed is currently improving at a faster rate than disk speeds and capacities. Since compression decreases the demand on storage devices at the expense of processing, it is becoming more economical to store data in a compressed form than uncompressed.

Most text compression methods can be placed in one of two classes: *symbolwise* methods and *dictionary* methods. Symbolwise methods work by estimating the probabilities of symbols (often characters), coding one symbol at a time, using shorter codewords for the most likely symbols in the same way that Morse code does. Dictionary methods achieve compression by replacing words and other fragments of text with an index to an entry in a "dictionary." The Braille code is a dictionary method since special codes are used to represent whole words.

Symbolwise methods are usually based on either Huffman coding or arithmetic coding, and they differ mainly in how they estimate probabilities for symbols. The more accurately these estimates are made, the greater the compression that can be achieved. To obtain good compression, the probability estimate is usually based on the context in which a symbol occurs. The business of estimating probabilities is called *modeling*, and good modeling is crucial to obtaining good compression. Converting the probabilities into a bitstream for transmission is called *coding*. Coding is well understood and can be performed very effectively using either Huffman coding or arithmetic coding. Modeling is more of an art, and there does not appear to be any single "best" method.

Dictionary methods generally use quite simple representations to code references to entries in the dictionary. They obtain compression by representing several symbols as one output codeword. This contrasts with symbolwise methods, which rely on generating good probability estimates for a symbol, since the length of the output codeword is what determines compression performance; for this reason, symbolwise methods are sometimes referred to as *statistical* methods, since they rely on estimating accurate statistics. The most significant dictionary methods are based on Ziv-Lempel coding, which uses the idea of replacing strings of characters with a reference to a previous occurrence of the string. This approach is adaptive, and it is effective because most characters can be coded as part of a string that has occurred earlier in the text. Compression is achieved if the reference, or *pointer*, is stored in fewer bits than the string it replaces. There are many variations on Ziv-Lempel coding, with different pointer representations and different rules governing which strings can be referenced.

The key distinction between symbolwise and dictionary methods is that symbolwise methods generally base the coding of a symbol on the context in which it occurs, whereas dictionary methods group symbols together, creating a kind of implicit context. Hybrid schemes are possible, in which a group of symbols is coded together and the coding is based on the context in which the group occurs. This does not necessarily provide better compression than symbolwise methods, but it can improve the speed of compression.

The following sections describe in more detail the main compression techniques introduced above. We look at the modeling and coding components separately. First the general idea of modeling is introduced, and then a particularly powerful class of models, adaptive models, is discussed. Before looking at how models are used in practice, we describe the two principal methods of coding used to represent symbols based on the probability distributions generated by models. Each of these descriptions begins with an overview of what the method is and how it works, and each is followed by a much more detailed description of how the coding can be implemented efficiently. These details are included because, although they lead to extremely effective implementations, they are not obvious and are hard to come by in the literature; they should be skipped on a first reading. The two main classes of models, symbolwise and dictionary, are then examined. There is a section that deals with the problem of providing random access to compressed text, which is important for full-text retrieval systems. Finally, the practical performance of various text compression methods is discussed.

2.1 Models

Compression methods obtain high compression by forming good models of the data that is to be coded. The function of a model is to *predict* symbols, which amounts to providing a probability distribution for the next symbol that is to be coded. For example, during the encoding of a text, the "prediction" for the next symbol might include a probability of 2 percent for the letter *u*, based on its relative frequency in a sample of text. The set of all possible symbols is called the *alphabet*, and the probability distribution provides an estimated probability for each symbol in the alphabet.

The model provides this probability distribution to the encoder, which uses it to encode the symbol that actually occurs. The decoder uses an identical model together with the output of the encoder to find out what the encoded symbol was. Figure 2.1 illustrates the whole process.

The number of bits in which a symbol, s, should be coded is called the *information content* of the symbol. The information content, $I(s)$, is directly related to the symbol's predicted probability, $\Pr[s]$, by the function $I(s) = -\log \Pr[s]$ bits.[2] For example, to transmit a symbol representing the fact that the outcome of a fair coin toss was "heads," the best an encoder can do is to use $-\log(1/2) = 1$ bit. The average amount of information per symbol over the whole alphabet is known as the *entropy* of the probability distribution, denoted by H. It is given by

$$H = \sum_{s} \Pr[s] \cdot I(s) = \sum_{s} -\Pr[s] \cdot \log \Pr[s].$$

---

2 All logarithms in this book are to base two unless indicated otherwise.

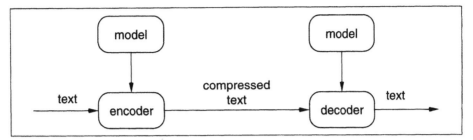

Figure 2.1 Using a model to compress text.

Provided that the symbols appear independently and with the assumed probabilities, H is a *lower* bound on compression, measured in bits per symbol, that can be achieved by *any* coding method. This is the celebrated source coding theorem of Claude Shannon, a Bell Labs scientist who single-handedly developed the field of information theory, and provides a bound that we can strive to attain but can never beat (Shannon 1948).

Huffman coding often achieves compression performance close to the entropy, but can, in some cases, be very inefficient. One such situation is when very good predictions are being made, in which case probabilities close to one are generated. This is exactly when entropy is minimized and "compressibility" is maximized and is what we hope to achieve when designing data compression systems; hence it is unfortunate that Huffman coding is inefficient in this situation. By way of contrast, the more recent method of arithmetic coding comes arbitrarily close to the entropy even when probabilities are close to one and the entropy of the probability distribution is close to zero. These two methods are discussed in Sections 2.3 and 2.4. What is important for the model is to provide a probability distribution that makes the probability of the symbol that actually occurs as high as possible. The above relationship means that a low probability results in a high entropy and vice versa. In the extreme case when $\Pr[s] = 1$, only one symbol s is possible, and $I(s) = 0$ indicates that zero bits are needed to transmit it. This follows intuitively: if a symbol is certain to occur, then it conveys no information and need not be transmitted. To paraphrase a well-worn truism, $I(\text{death}) = 0$ and $I(\text{taxes}) = 0$.

Conversely, I becomes arbitrarily large as $\Pr[s]$ approaches zero, and a symbol with zero probability cannot be coded. In practice, all symbols must be given a nonzero probability because a zero-probability symbol could not be coded if, by unlucky chance, it did occur. Moreover, it is not possible for the encoder to peek at the next symbol and artificially boost its probability just for this step; the encoder and decoder must use the *same* probability distribution, and the decoder clearly cannot look ahead at symbols that have not yet been decoded. Hence the model must take into account all the information available to the decoder and then gamble on what the next symbol will be. The best compression is obtained when the model is backing the symbols that actually occur.

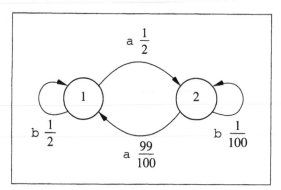

Figure 2.2 A simple finite-state model.

At the beginning of this section the probability of a u was estimated as 2 percent. This corresponds to an information content of 5.6 bits; that is, if it does happen to be the next symbol, u should be transmitted in 5.6 bits. Nothing has been said yet about *how* the probabilities should be estimated. It turns out that predictions can usually be improved by taking account of the previous symbol. If a q has just been encountered, the probability of u may jump to 95 percent, based on how often q is followed by u in a sample of text. This gives a much lower information content for u of 0.074 bits. Of course, other symbols must have lower probabilities and therefore longer codewords to compensate, and if the prediction is incorrect (as in *Iraq* or *Qantas*), the price paid is extra bits in the output. But averaged over many appearances of the context q, the number of bits required to decode each appearance of u can be expected to decrease.

Models that take a few immediately preceding symbols into account to make a prediction are called *finite-context* models of order m, where m is the number of previous symbols used to make the prediction. Such models are effective in a variety of compression applications, and the best text compression methods known are based on this approach.

Other approaches to modeling are possible, and although potentially more powerful, they have not proved as popular as finite-context models. One approach is to use a *finite-state* model, in which each state of a finite-state machine stores a different probability distribution for the next symbol. Figure 2.2 shows such a model. This particular model is for strings in which the symbol a is expected to occur in pairs. Encoding starts in state 1, where a and b are predicted with equal probability, $1/2$. Using the formula above, we find that each should be coded in one bit (not surprisingly). If a b is received, the encoder stays in state 1 and uses the same probability distribution for the next symbol. However, if an a is received, it moves to state 2, where the probability of a b is now only $1/100$ and requires 6.6 bits to be encoded, as opposed to 0.014 bits to encode an a. This model captures behavior that cannot be represented accurately by a finite-context model because a state model is able to keep track of whether an odd or even number of as have occurred consecutively.

It is important that the decoder works with an identical probability distribution in order to decode symbols correctly. This is achieved by ensuring that it has an identical model to the encoder's and that it starts in the same state as the encoder. The encoder transmits the symbol and then follows a transition; the decoder recovers the symbol and can then follow the same transition, so it is now in the same state as the encoder and will use the same probability distribution for the next symbol. Error-free transmission is assumed, for if any errors were to occur, the encoder and decoder would lose synchronization, with potentially catastrophic results.

If the text being compressed is in a formal language such as C or Java, a grammar can be used to model the language. The text is represented by sending the sequence of *productions*, or rules, that would generate the text from the grammar. By estimating the probability of a particular production occurring, more frequently used productions can be coded in fewer bits, thus achieving good compression. It is hard to obtain a formal grammar for texts written in natural languages, so to date, grammar models have been applied only to artificial languages such as programming languages.

2.2   Adaptive models

There are many ways to estimate the probabilities in a model. We could conceivably guess suitable probabilities when setting up a compression system and use the same distribution for all input texts. However, it is easier, and more accurate, to estimate the probabilities from a sample of the kind of text that is being encoded.

The method that always uses the same model regardless of what text is being coded is called *static* modeling. Clearly, this runs the risk of receiving an input that is quite different from the one for which the model was set up—for example, a model for the English language will probably not perform well with a file of numbers and vice versa. One example of such a mismatch occurs when numeric data is transmitted using Morse code. Because the digits are all relatively rare in normal text, they are assigned long codewords, and so transmission times increase if documents such as financial statements are sent. Another example is shown in Figure 2.3, which is the opening sentence of a rather contorted book—*Gadsby* by E. V. Wright, published in 1939. You may care to try to work out what is unusual about the text before reading on. In fact, the reason that the text reads strangely is that it does not contain a single occurrence of what is usually the most common letter in normal English text—*e*. A static model designed for normal English text would perform poorly in this case.

One solution is to generate a model specifically for each file that is to be compressed. An initial pass is made through the file to estimate symbol probabilities, and these are transmitted to the decoder before transmitting the encoded symbols. This approach is called *semi-static* modeling. (Semi-static modeling has also been referred to as semi-adaptive modeling, but we prefer the term "semi-static" because the implementation of these models has more in common with static models than adaptive ones.) Semi-static modeling has the advantage that the model is invariably

```
If Youth, throughout all history, had had a champion to stand
up for it; to show a doubting world that a child can think;
and, possibly, do it practically; you wouldn't constantly run
across folks today who claim that ''a child don't know anything.''
```

Figure 2.3 The first sentence of an unusual book.

```
"I never heerd a skilful old married feller of twenty
years' standing pipe ''my wife'' in a more used note
than 'a did," said Jacob Smallbury.  "It migh
```

Figure 2.4 Sample text.

better suited to the input than a static one, but the penalty paid is having to transmit the model first, as well as the preliminary pass over the data to accumulate symbol probabilities. In some situations, such as interactive data communications, it may be impractical to make two passes over the data, and for complex models the cost of pretransmitting the model might be a considerable overhead.

Adaptive modeling is an elegant solution to these problems. An adaptive model begins with a bland probability distribution and gradually alters it as more symbols are encountered. As an example, consider an adaptive model that uses the previously encoded part of a string as a sample to estimate probabilities. We will use a model that operates character by character, with no context used to predict the next symbol—in other words, each character of the input is treated as an independent symbol. Technically, this is called a *zero-order* (equivalently, *order-0*) model: in full, an adaptive, zero-order, character-level model. Now consider the text of Figure 2.4, excerpted from Thomas Hardy's book *Far from the Madding Crowd*. It is from the final scene in the book, in which a group is jesting with a newlywed couple. The archaic language in this excerpt is another reminder of the desirability of using adaptive codes.

The zero-order probability that the next character after the excerpt is t is estimated to be $49,983/768,078 = 6.5$ percent, since in the previous text, $49,983$ of the $768,078$ characters were ts. Using the same system, an e has probability 9.4 percent, and an x has probability 0.11 percent. The model provides this estimated probability distribution to an encoder such as an arithmetic coder (see Section 2.4). In fact, the next character is a t, which an arithmetic coder represents in about $-\log 0.065 = 3.94$ bits. The decoder is able to generate the same model since it has just decoded all the characters up to (but not including) the t. It makes the same probability estimates as the encoder and so is able to decode the t correctly when it is received. In practice, the encoder and decoder do not extract the statistics from the prior text each time they are needed, but instead keep a running tally of the character counts.

Some details of the adaptive system need to be considered. First, the system must avoid the situation in which a character is predicted with a probability of zero. In the example above, the character Z has never occurred in the text up to this point and would be predicted with zero probability. Such events cannot be coded, yet they might occur; this is referred to as the *zero-frequency problem* (Witten and Bell 1991). The text *It mighZ* is very unlikely, but it can occur. If nowhere else, it has just occurred in this book.

There are several ways to solve the zero-frequency problem. One is to allow one extra count, which is divided evenly among any symbols that have not been observed in the input. In the Hardy example, the total count would be increased by one to 768,079. A total of 82 different characters have been seen so far, so 46 of the 128 ASCII characters have not occurred by this point. Each of these gets 1/46 of the spare proportion of 1/768,079. Thus, a Z character is given a probability of $1/(46 \times 768,079) = 1/35,331,634$, corresponding to 25.07 bits in the output.

Another possibility is to artificially inflate the count of every character in the alphabet by one, thereby ensuring that none has a zero frequency. This is equivalent to starting the model assuming that we have already processed a stretch of text in which each possible character appeared exactly once. In the above example, allowing for the ASCII alphabet of 128 characters, 128 would be added to the total number of characters seen so far, giving Z a relative frequency of $1/768,206 = 0.00013$ percent, corresponding to 19.6 bits in the output.

Several other solutions to the zero-frequency problem are possible, although in general none offers a particularly significant compression performance advantage over the others. The problem is most acute near the beginning of a text where there are few, if any, samples on which to base estimates; so at face value the choice of method is more critical for small texts than for large ones. The method is also important for models that use very many different contexts because many of the contexts will be used only a few times.

The example above used a zero-order model, in which each character's probability was estimated without regard to context. For a higher-order model, such as a first-order model, the probability is estimated by how often that character has occurred in the current context. For example, the excerpt used above to illustrate a zero-order model was coding the letter t in the context of the phrase *It migh*, but in reality made no use at all of the characters comprising that phrase. On the other hand, a first-order model would use the final h as a context with which to *condition* the probability estimates. The letter h has occurred 37,525 times in the prior text, and 1,133 of these times it was followed by a t. Ignoring for a moment the zero-frequency problem, the probability of a t occurring after an h can be estimated to be $1,133/37,525 = 3.02$ percent, which would have it coded in 5.05 bits. This is actually worse than the zero-order estimate because the letter t is rare in this context—an h is much more likely to be followed by an e, and so here is an example where use of more information caused inferior compression. On the other hand, a second-order model does substantially better. It uses the relative frequency that the context gh is followed by a t, which is 1,129 times out of 1,754, or 64.4 percent, and results in the t being coded in just 0.636 bits.

So far we have suggested how the probabilities in a model can be adapted, but it is also possible—and effective—to adapt a model's *structure*. In a finite-context model, the structure determines which contexts are used; in a finite-state model, the structure is the set of states and transitions available. Adaptation usually involves adding more detail to an area of the model that is heavily used. For example, if the first-order context *h* is being used frequently, it might be worthwhile to add more specific contexts, such as the second-order contexts *th* and *sh*. So long as the encoder and decoder use the same rules for adding contexts, and the decision to add contexts is based on the previously encoded text only, they will remain synchronized.

Adaptive modeling is a powerful tool for compression and is the basis of many successful methods. It is robust, reliable, and flexible. The principal disadvantage is that it is not suitable for random access to files—a text can be decoded only from the beginning, since the model used for coding a particular part of the text is determined from all the preceding text. Hence, adaptive modeling is ideal for general-purpose compression utilities but is not necessarily appropriate for full-text retrieval. This point will be taken up again in Section 2.7.

2.3 Huffman coding

Coding is the task of determining the output representation of a symbol, based on a probability distribution supplied by a model. The general idea is that a coder should output short codewords for likely symbols and long codewords for rare ones. There are theoretical limits on how short the average length of a codeword can be for a given probability distribution, and much effort has been put into finding coders that achieve this limit. Another important consideration is the speed of the coder—a reasonable amount of computation is required to generate near-optimal codes. If speed is important, we might use a coder that sacrifices compression performance to reduce the amount of effort required. For example, if there are 256 possible symbols to be coded, we might use a coder that represents the 15 most probable symbols in 4 bits and the remainder in 12 bits. The extreme of this sort of approximation is just to code all symbols in 8 bits. It gives no compression but is very fast. In fact, many dictionary-based methods use a simple coder like this, with the implicit assumption that the symbols (which in this kind of model are actually groups of characters) are equally likely.

In contrast to dictionary methods, symbolwise schemes depend heavily on a good coder to achieve compression, and most research on coders has been performed with symbolwise methods in mind. This section and the next describe the two main methods of coding: *Huffman coding* and *arithmetic coding*. Huffman coding tends to be faster than arithmetic coding, but arithmetic coding is capable of yielding compression that is close to optimal given the probability distribution supplied by the model. For each of these two types of coder, we first look at the principle by which they achieve compression and then give details of how they are implemented in practice. We begin with Huffman coding (Huffman 1952).

Table 2.1 Codewords and probabilities for a seven-symbol alphabet.

Symbol	Codeword	Probability
a	0000	0.05
b	0001	0.05
c	001	0.1
d	01	0.2
e	10	0.3
f	110	0.2
g	111	0.1

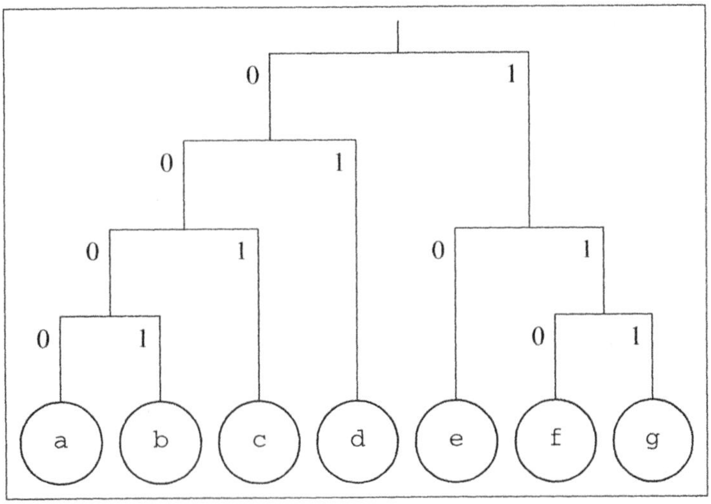

Figure 2.5 A Huffman code tree.

Table 2.1 shows codewords for the seven-symbol alphabet *a*, *b*, *c*, *d*, *e*, *f*, and *g*. A phrase is coded by replacing each of its symbols with the codeword given by the table. For example, the phrase *eefggfed* is coded as 10101101111111101001. Decoding is performed from left to right. The input to the decoder begins with 10 . . . , and the only codeword that begins with this is the one for *e*, which is therefore taken as the first symbol. Decoding then proceeds with the remainder of the string, 1011011 . . . .

Figure 2.5 shows a tree that can be used for decoding. The tree is traversed by starting at the root and following the branch corresponding to the next bit in the coded text. The path from the root to each symbol (at a leaf) corresponds to the codewords in Table 2.1. This type of code is called a *prefix* code—or more accurately, a *prefix-free* code—because no codeword is the prefix of another symbol's codeword.

If that were not the case, the decoding tree would have symbols at internal nodes, which leads to ambiguity in decoding.

The code in Table 2.1 was produced by the technique of Huffman coding, which generates codewords for a set of symbols, given some probability distribution for the symbols. The codewords generated yield the best compression possible for a prefix-free code for the given probability distribution.

Huffman's algorithm works by constructing the decoding tree from the bottom up. For the example symbol set, with the probabilities shown in Table 2.1, it starts by creating for each symbol a leaf node containing the symbol and its probability (Figure 2.6a). Then the two nodes with the smallest probabilities become siblings under a parent node, which is given a probability equal to the sum of its two children's probabilities (Figure 2.6b).

The combining operation is repeated, choosing the two nodes with the smallest probabilities and ignoring nodes that are already children. For example, at the next step the new node formed by combining a and b is joined with the node for c to make a new node with probability $p = 0.2$. The process continues until there is only one node without a parent, which becomes the root of the decoding tree (Figure 2.6c). The two branches from every nonleaf node are then labeled 0 and 1 (the order is not important) to form the tree.

Figure 2.7 shows the general algorithm for constructing a Huffman code. The algorithm is expressed in terms of a set T that recursively contains other sets, with each subset corresponding to a node in the tree. When the algorithm terminates, T contains one set, which itself contains two sets—the descriptions of the two subtrees of the root. A more detailed description of how Huffman coding is implemented appears later in this section.

Huffman coding is generally fast for both encoding and decoding, provided that the probability distribution is static. There are also algorithms for adaptive Huffman coding, where localized adjustments are made to the tree to maintain the correct structure as the probabilities change (Gallager 1978; Cormack and Horspool 1984; Knuth 1985; Vitter 1989). However, the better adaptive symbolwise models usually use many different probability distributions at the same time, with the appropriate distribution being chosen depending on the context of the symbol being coded. Huffman coding requires that multiple trees be maintained in this situation, which can become demanding on memory. The alternative is for each tree to be regenerated whenever it is required, but this is slow. Hence, for adaptive compression, arithmetic coding (described in the next section) is usually preferable, as its speed is comparable to that of adaptive Huffman coding, yet it requires less memory and is able to achieve better compression—particularly when high-probability events are being coded.

Nevertheless, Huffman coding turns out to be very useful for some applications. For example, when coupled with a word-based (rather than character-based) model, it gives good compression, and its speed and ease of random access make it more attractive than arithmetic coding. Furthermore, there is a slightly different representation of a Huffman code that decodes very efficiently despite the extremely large models that might arise with a word-based model. This representation is called the

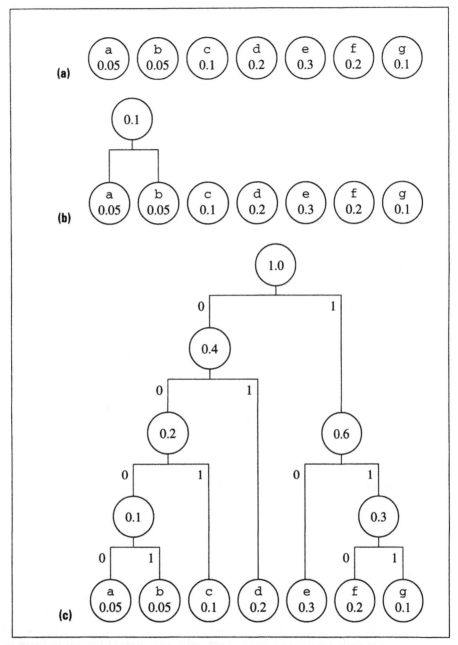

Figure 2.6 Constructing the Huffman tree: (a) leaf nodes; (b) combining nodes; (c) the finished Huffman tree.

To calculate a Huffman code,

1. Set $T \leftarrow$ a set of n singleton sets, each containing one of the n symbols and its probability.

2. Repeat $n - 1$ times

    (a) Set m_1 and $m_2 \leftarrow$ the two subsets of least probability in T.

    (b) Replace m_1 and m_2 with a set $\{m_1, m_2\}$ whose probability is the sum of that of m_1 and m_2.

3. T now contains only one item, which corresponds to the root of a Huffman tree; the length of the codeword for each symbol is given by the number of times it was joined with another set.

Figure 2.7 Assigning a Huffman code.

canonical Huffman code (Hirschberg and Lelewer 1990). It uses the same codeword *lengths* as a Huffman code, but imposes a particular choice on the codeword *bits*.

Table 2.2 shows part of a canonical Huffman code for the Hardy book, where the alphabet has been chosen to be the words that appear in the book. The frequency of each word has been counted, and, as in the conventional Huffman method, the codewords have been chosen to minimize the size of the compressed file for this model. In the terminology introduced on page 28, this is a static zero-order word-level model. The codewords are shown in decreasing order of length, and therefore in increasing order of word frequency—except that within each block of codes of the same length, words are ordered alphabetically rather than by frequency. The list begins with the thousands of words (and numbers) that appear only once. Words that occur only once in a text are called *hapax legomena*, a term that we will meet again on several occasions. Many of the words, such as *yopur* and *youmg*, occur only once because they are typographical errors. The numbers 100, 101, . . . come from page numbers that are recorded in the file. (They start at 100 rather than a smaller number because words of the same codeword length are sorted in lexical— not numerical—order, so that 90, 91, . . . appear later in the sequence.)

The table shows the codewords sorted from longest to shortest. An important feature of a canonical code like this is that when the codewords are sorted in lexical order—that is, when they are in the sequence they would be in if they were entries in a dictionary—they are also in order from the longest to the shortest codeword. On the other hand the code of Table 2.1 does not exhibit this property: although the codewords are ordered lexicographically, this does not result in them being sorted by length.

The key to using canonical codes efficiently is to notice that a word's encoding can be determined quickly from the length of its codeword, how far through the list it is, and the codeword for the first word of that length. For example, the word *said* is the 10th seven-bit codeword. Given this information and that the first seven-bit

Table 2.2 A canonical Huffman code.

Symbol	Codeword	
	Length	Bits
100	17	00000000000000000
101	17	00000000000000001
102	17	00000000000000010
103	17	00000000000000011
. . .	. . .	. . .
yopur	17	00001101010100100
youmg	17	00001101010100101
youthful	17	00001101010100110
zeed	17	00001101010100111
zephyr	17	00001101010101000
zigzag	17	00001101010101001
11th	16	0000110101010101
120	16	0000110101010110
. . .	. . .	. . .
were	8	10100110
which	8	10100111
as	7	1010100
at	7	1010101
for	7	1010110
had	7	1010111
he	7	1011000
her	7	1011001
his	7	1011010
it	7	1011011
s	7	1011100
said	7	1011101
she	7	1011110
that	7	1011111
with	7	1100000
you	7	1100001
I	6	110001
in	6	110010
was	6	110011
a	5	11010
and	5	11011
of	5	11100
to	5	11101
the	4	1111

codeword is 1010100, we can obtain the codeword for *said* by incrementing 1010100 nine times, or, more efficiently, adding nine to its binary representation.

Canonical codes come into their own for decoding because it is not necessary to store a decode tree. All that is required is a list of the symbols ordered according to the lexical order of the codewords, plus an array storing the first codeword of each distinct length. For example, with the code in Table 2.2, if the upcoming bits to be decoded are 1100000101 . . . , then the decoder will quickly determine that the next codeword must come after the first seven-bit word, *as* (1010100), and before the first six-bit word, *I* (110001). Therefore, the next seven bits are read (1100000), and the difference of this binary value from the first seven-bit value is calculated. In this example, the difference is 12, which means that the word is 12 positions after the word *as* in the list, so it must be *with*.

Compared with using a decoding tree, canonical coding is very direct. An explicit decode tree of the kind illustrated in Figure 2.5 requires a lot of space and is accessed randomly. With the canonical representation, only the first codeword of each length is accessed, plus one access to a lookup table to determine what the word is. Storing the first codeword of each length takes negligible space—the example in Table 2.2 has just 14 different lengths, ranging from 4 to 17. The list of symbols in lexical order of their codewords replaces the randomly accessed Huffman tree and is consulted only once for each symbol decoded.

Canonical Huffman codes

We now take a more detailed look at the implementation of a Huffman encoder and decoder pair. These details are quite intricate and can be skipped on the first reading, which is why this section is marked "optional" with a gray bar in the margin.

A canonical code is carefully structured to allow extremely fast decoding, with a memory requirement of only a few bytes per alphabet symbol. The code is called "canonical" (standardized) because much of the nondeterminism of normal Huffman codes is avoided. For example, in normal construction of the Huffman tree, some convention such as using a 0 bit to indicate a left branch and a 1 bit to indicate a right is assumed, and different choices lead to different, but equally valid, codeword assignments.

It is easiest to show this effect with an example. Consider the information shown in Table 2.3. The second column shows the observed symbol frequencies for the symbols in column 1. Three possible prefix-free codes for these symbols are shown in the columns headed *Code 1*, *Code 2*, and *Code 3*. Of course, in word-based codes there would be thousands of symbols instead of the six shown here, with frequencies ranging from 1 for *hapax legomena* to many thousands for common words (like *the*)—just as in Table 2.2.

The derivation of the first two codes in Table 2.3 is exactly as described in Figure 2.6. At each step, the two smallest items are extracted and coalesced, with one of the items having all its codewords prefixed by a 0 bit and the symbols represented by the other item being prefixed by a 1 bit. To obtain Code 1, for example, the sideways tree in Figure 2.8 was used, in which the convention is adopted that the upper

Table 2.3 Possible Huffman codes.

Symbol	Count	Code 1	Code 2	Code 3
a	10	000	111	000
b	11	001	110	001
c	12	100	011	010
d	13	101	010	011
e	22	01	10	10
f	23	11	00	11

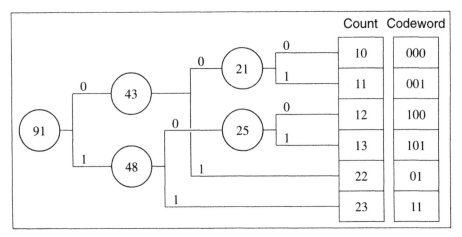

Figure 2.8 Constructing a Huffman code; "upper" edge is assigned a 0 bit.

branches are consistently assigned the 0 bit and the lower branches the 1 bit.

There is no particular requirement for this labeling convention, and Code 2 of Table 2.3 is formed by adopting the opposite rule, that upper edges are assigned 1 bits. In fact, this choice can be made at each of the internal nodes of the tree. A Huffman tree for an alphabet of n symbols has $n - 1$ internal nodes—for example, the tree of Figure 2.8 has five—and so there are 2^{n-1} equivalent, equally optimal, Huffman codes. Table 2.3 lists Code 1 and Code 2; to be exhaustive, it should really list Codes 1 through 32.

Code 3 in Table 2.3 is a little different. It is not just another relabeling of the edges in the Huffman tree. Although it is certainly an optimal prefix-free code for the symbols listed—it must be, because all of the codewords are the same length as they are in Codes 1 and 2—there is in fact no edge relabeling that will derive it. Strictly speaking, Code 3 is not a Huffman code at all because Huffman's algorithm is incapable of generating it, since it will always produce a tree with the shape of the one in Figure 2.8. Rather than be pedantic, let us sidestep the issue of exactly what Huffman intended and define a Huffman code to be "any prefix-free assignment of codewords where the length of each code is equal to the depth of that symbol in a Huffman tree." That is, Huffman's algorithm should be used to calculate the *length* of each codeword, and then some bit pattern of this length can be assigned as the code.

Consider again Code 3 in Table 2.3. All the three-bit codewords form a neat sequence and the two-bit codewords likewise. Interpreted as integers, the three-bit codes are 0, 1, 2, and 3, and the two-bit codes are 2 and 3. More important, the first two bits of the three-bit codewords are all 00 or 01, that is, integer 0 or 1. This pattern makes decoding very easy. First, two bits from the input stream are read and interpreted as an integer. If their value is 2 or 3, a codeword has been identified, and the corresponding symbol can be output. If their value is 0 or 1, a third bit is appended, and the three bits are again interpreted as an integer and used to index a table to identify the correct symbol.

On such a small example this may not seem much of an improvement over the storage of a detailed code tree with left and right pointers and so on. However, an explicit decode tree raises two problems. First, it can consume a great deal of space. A Huffman tree for n symbols requires n leaf nodes and $n - 1$ internal nodes. Each leaf stores a pointer to a symbol and the information that it is in fact a leaf, and each internal node must store two pointers. In total, this structure requires around $4n$ words, and for an alphabet of one million symbols, 16 Mbytes of memory might be consumed—not even including the strings that are the actual symbols.

The second problem is that traversing a tree from root to leaf involves a lot of pointer chasing through memory, and the nodes accessed show little locality of reference. Each bit of compressed data that is decoded will require a new page of memory to be referenced, causing either page faults or—at best—numerous cache misses.

On the other hand, use of the canonical code means that decoding can be accomplished in a little over n words of memory, and with one random access per symbol rather than one random access per bit. This means that decompression is faster and requires substantially less memory than if an explicit code tree were used.

Let us now describe the use of a canonical code in detail. First, Huffman's algorithm is used to calculate, for each symbol i in the alphabet, the desired length l_i of the corresponding codeword. Exactly how this computation should be performed is described in the following subsection, "Computing Huffman code lengths." Next, the number of codewords of each possible length from 1 to *maxlength* is counted by passing over the set l_i and counting the frequency of each value. This allows the set of possible codes to be partitioned into groups, where each code within the group has the same length and the codewords form consecutive integers. For example, suppose there are to be four codewords of five bits, one of three bits, and three of two bits. At the completion of the partitioning step the five-bit codes will be 00000 through to 00011, the three-bit code will be 001, and the two-bit codes will be 01, 10, and 11. Finally, once the starting codeword for each length has been decided, it is straightforward to process the symbols one by one, simply assigning the next

To assign a canonical Huffman code to a set of symbols, supposing that symbol i is to be assigned a code of l_i bits, that no codeword is longer than *maxlength*, and that there are n distinct symbols,

1. For $l \leftarrow 1$ to *maxlength* do
      Set $numl[l] \leftarrow 0$.
   For $i \leftarrow 1$ to n do
      Set $numl[l_i] \leftarrow numl[l_i] + 1$.
   Number of codes of length l is stored in $numl[l]$.

2. Set $firstcode[maxlength] \leftarrow 0$.
   For $l \leftarrow maxlength - 1$ downto 1 do
      Set $firstcode[l] \leftarrow (firstcode[l + 1] + numl[l + 1])/2$.
   Integer for first code of length l is stored in $firstcode[l]$.

3. For $l \leftarrow 1$ to *maxlength* do
      Set $nextcode[l] \leftarrow firstcode[l]$.

4. For $i \leftarrow 1$ to n do
   (a) Set $codeword[i] \leftarrow nextcode[l_i]$.
   (b) Set $symbol[l_i, nextcode[l_i] - firstcode[l_i]] \leftarrow i$.
   (c) Set $nextcode[l_i] \leftarrow nextcode[l_i] + 1$.
   The rightmost l_i bits of the integer $codeword[i]$ are the code for symbol i.

Figure 2.9   Assigning a canonical Huffman code.

codeword of that length. This process is described in detail by the algorithm of Figure 2.9, in which *nextcode[l]* is an integer storing the next codeword of length l that should be assigned. The array *symbol* is used during the decoding process, described below.

An example of the application of this algorithm is shown for a small collection of symbols in Table 2.4. The last two rows show the values calculated for the arrays *numl*, the number of codewords of each possible length, and *firstcode*, the integer value corresponding to the first codeword of each length. These values are used to assign the integer codes shown in the third column. The fourth column shows the corresponding bit patterns when the rightmost l_i bits of *codeword[i]* are taken. These are the prefix-free codes that are generated.

The right-hand part of Table 2.4 shows the integer values that result when the first l bits of each codeword are extracted and considered as an integer, for $1 \leq l \leq 5 = maxlength$. Note that all the two-bit prefixes for codewords longer than two bits are less than *firstcode[2]*, all the three-bit prefixes for codewords longer than three bits are less than *firstcode[3]*, and all the four-bit prefixes for codewords longer than four bits are less than *firstcode[4]*. Indeed, all the five-bit prefixes for codewords

Table 2.4 Construction of a canonical Huffman code.

Symbol i	Code length l_i	codeword[i]	Bit pattern	l-bit prefix 1	2	3	4	5
1	2	1	01	0	1			
2	5	0	00000	0	0	0	0	0
3	5	1	00001	0	0	0	0	1
4	3	1	001	0	0	1		
5	2	2	10	1	2			
6	5	2	00010	0	0	0	1	2
7	5	3	00011	0	0	0	1	3
8	2	3	11	1	3			
			numl[l]	0	3	1	0	4
			firstcode[l]	2	1	1	2	0

To decode a symbol represented in a canonical Huffman code,

1. Set $v \leftarrow nextinputbit()$.

   Set $l \leftarrow 1$.

2. While $v < firstcode[l]$ do

   (a) Set $v \leftarrow 2 * v + nextinputbit()$.

   (b) Set $l \leftarrow l + 1$.

   Integer v is now a legitimate code of l bits.

3. Return $symbol[l, v - firstcode[l]]$.

   This is the index of the decoded symbol.

Figure 2.10 Decoding using a canonical Huffman code.

longer than five bits are less than *firstcode*[5] too. (There are none of these in the example because no codewords are longer than five bits.)

This observation is the heart of the decoding process, and it is the reason why canonical codes are of such interest. Figure 2.10 shows how the decoding algorithm makes use of these relationships. The function *nextinputbit*() returns an integer 0 or 1, depending on the next input bit from the compressed stream that is being decoded. The array *symbol* is the mapping established by the code construction process of Figure 2.9. The space required by this array is discussed below.

For example, suppose the codewords of Table 2.4 are being used and that the bit-stream 00110 ... is to be decoded. Variable v in Figure 2.10 is initialized to 0, which as an integer is less than *firstcode*[1] = 2, so a second bit is appended to give v the value 00. This in turn is less than *firstcode*[2], and a third bit is added. This gives v the value 001 or integer 1, and now the test guarding the *while* loop (step 2) fails, since *firstcode*[3] = 1. Now a code has been parsed, and *symbol*[3, 0] is output—the correct symbol number 4. At the next decoding step v is initialized to 1, and the process repeats to form the code 10, which is identified as being *symbol*[2, 1], or symbol 5.

How much memory space is required during decoding? Surprisingly, the only large structure is the array *symbol*. The three other arrays—only one of which is required for decoding—require one word of memory for each possible code length, $1 \ldots maxlength$. For most implementations, a convenient value is $maxlength = 32$, so that integers can be used to store the codewords. (The restrictions imposed by this decision are discussed in Section 9.1, as is a mechanism for guaranteeing that no codeword exceeds such a limit.) Thus, only $3 \times 32 = 96$ words are required by the three small arrays together, irrespective of the size of the alphabet. Figures 2.9 and 2.10 use the array *symbol* as though it were two-dimensional. However, it can be implemented as a single one-dimensional array, in which the lth component is exactly $numl[l]$ words long. The amount of space required for this array is $\sum_{l=1}^{maxlength} numl[l] = n$, which is the number of symbols. Thus, the mapping stored in *symbol* can be achieved in n words. In total, about $n + 100$ words of storage are required during decoding in addition to the space required to describe the n symbols. Note that it is not even necessary to store the length of symbol i since it is implicit in the sequential arrangement of codewords.

The implementation described in Figure 2.10 is also fast. One array lookup, one addition, and one integer comparison occur for each input bit, and the array lookup is to consecutive elements in a small array of just 32 words. If the processor is using memory caching, there will be no cache misses during the execution of this loop, and the logic is almost identical to that required to decode binary numbers of arbitrary length. Indeed, if the minimum codeword length is greater than one, there is no need to commence the linear search (step 2 of Figure 2.10) at one—it can instead be started at the minimum codeword length, with variable v assigned that number of input bits in a single operation. In this way binary decoding can be seen to be just a special case of canonical decoding.

Once a length and offset pair have been decoded, the array *symbol* is consulted, and a symbol number located. This might cause a cache miss. However, it takes place at most once per output symbol, and since the array *symbol* is organized with the frequent symbols (those with short codes) close together, it will on average occur even less often than that. Furthermore, in a word-level model each "symbol" represents several characters, so the time per character of output is relatively small.

Computing Huffman code lengths

An important area that has not been addressed so far in our discussion is determining the lengths for a Huffman code, which is required for canonical Huffman coding. In this section we will look at what this problem involves and then describe the heap data structure, which is a useful data structure for Huffman coding. Next, we will describe a memory-efficient three-phase algorithm that uses a heap to determine the code lengths. Finally, two improvements are examined that can improve the speed of the algorithm and take advantage of the distribution of symbol frequencies found in practice.

The efficiency of computing Huffman code lengths affects only the cost of encoding, so it is not usually crucial, but elegant and efficient solutions are available and can make a big difference if the alphabet is large. The tree algorithm described earlier could be used to determine the lengths, and it has, over the years, proved to be an area rich in programming assignments for computer science students. However, for canonical coding there is no need to calculate the actual codewords, but just the code lengths. Also, in a word-based model, the alphabet is likely to contain thousands or even millions of symbols, and memory space for an explicit tree data structure might be a problem.

For these two reasons it is interesting to consider other techniques for calculating the code lengths of an optimal prefix-free coding. The algorithm presented in this section assumes that a file of n integers is supplied, where the ith integer is the number of times symbol i has appeared in the text. That is, if c_i is the ith value in the file, a code is to be built in which the probability of symbol i is $c_i/(\sum_{i=1}^{n} c_i)$. The output of the calculation is a second file, also of length n, in which the ith integer is the length in bits l_i of the code to be assigned to symbol i.

Since all the frequencies must be read into memory before any calculation can be performed, and it seems similarly impossible to write any of the lengths until all have been generated, a minimum requirement of $2n$ nodes with three four-byte fields (that is, $24n$ bytes) appears inevitable to store an explicit tree. On an alphabet of one million symbols, this corresponds to 24 Mbytes of memory. The process described in this section is substantially more economical and requires just $2n$ four-byte words (that is, $8n$ bytes), or 8 Mbytes for a model of one million symbols. The process is also efficient in terms of time.

The efficiency of the process comes from using a heap data structure, which can repeatedly find the smallest frequency very quickly with practically no memory overhead for storing the data structure. A *heap* is an implicit binary tree, with values stored at all leaves and internal nodes, and an ordering rule that requires values to be nonincreasing along each path from a leaf to the root. Figure 2.11a shows, in tree form, an example heap of 10 items. The immediate consequence of the ordering is that the smallest value is stored at the root of the tree. Although visualized as a binary tree, a heap is actually stored in an array, as shown in Figure 2.11b. The mapping of a heap to storage in memory is particularly elegant: the root is stored in location 1 of an array; the left child of the node stored in location i is stored in location $2i$; and the right child of location i is stored in location $2i + 1$. These rules mean that the parent of the node in position i occupies location $\lfloor i/2 \rfloor$.

A heap is very good for repeatedly finding and removing the smallest item. The trick at each stage is to remove the smallest item, replace it with another, and reinstate the heap order, all without spending too much effort. Suppose in the example that the smallest item, 2, is removed from location 1, and the last item in the

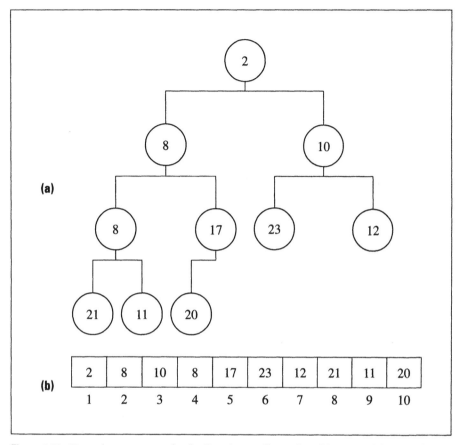

Figure 2.11 Heap data structure for finding the smallest value: (a) tree with heap ordering property; (b) implicit storage of tree in array.

array—item 20 in location 10—replaces it, as shown in Figure 2.12a for the heap of Figure 2.11a. To rebuild the ordering at the top level of the tree, item 8—the smaller of the two children of the root—must be swapped with 20. This localizes the order violation to the left subtree, and the process is repeated until heap order is restored. Figure 2.12b shows the reestablished heap after that item has been sifted back down the tree. The worst that can happen is that the item just promoted from the bottom leaf level returns all the way back to the bottom.

Using a heap, the smallest of n items can be found with one of these sifting operations. Since the depth of the tree is $\lceil \log n \rceil$, and just two comparisons are required at each level as an item is sifted down the tree, the total cost of finding the next smallest item is no more than $2\lceil \log n \rceil$ comparisons. Alterations to the weight associated with any item are handled in exactly the same way, and an item weight can be reassigned at a cost of at most $2\lceil \log n \rceil$ comparisons.

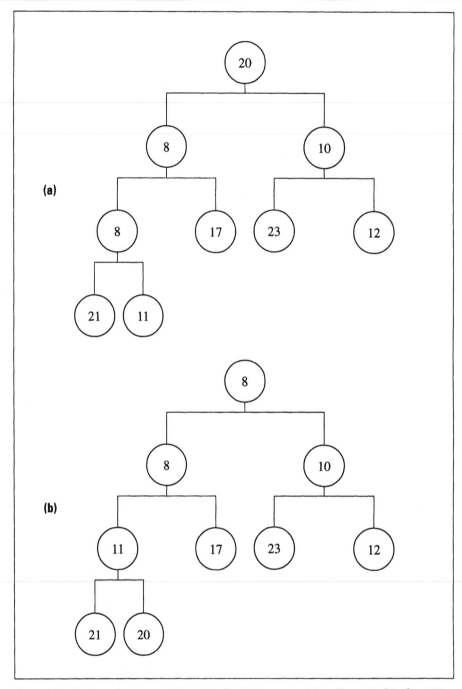

Figure 2.12 Finding the next smallest: (a) after 20 is swapped into the root; (b) after 20 is sifted down the tree.

Not included so far is the cost of constructing the initial heap from an unsorted list of n items. The algorithm for doing so makes use of the same sift operation, applying it to the root of every subtree in the heap from right to left and bottom to top. This stage requires approximately $2n$ comparisons.

The heap is used to calculate Huffman code lengths in the algorithm described in Figure 2.13. It uses an array of $2n$ entries to calculate the lengths for an alphabet of n symbols. Figure 2.14 illustrates how the array is used. Initially (Figure 2.14a), the frequencies of the symbols occupy the last n entries in the array. The first half of the array stores a heap that is used to efficiently locate the symbol with the lowest frequency for the node-combining step of Huffman's algorithm. As entries are removed from the heap, the space vacated is reused to store pointers that correspond to branches in the Huffman tree (Figure 2.14b). The frequency counts are also overwritten to store these pointers. At the end of processing, the heap contains only one item, and the rest of the array stores the shape of a Huffman tree. This is the arrangement shown in Figure 2.14c.

The details of the three main stages are as follows. In the first, the file of frequencies is read into locations $n + 1 \ldots 2n$ of an array A of $2n$ words. Each of the first n words in locations $1 \ldots n$ of A is set to point at the corresponding frequency in location $n + 1 \ldots 2n$. Next, the bottom half of A is turned into a heap using the method described above. The values used to drive the ordering in the heap are the frequencies pointed at by the items compared, not the items themselves. That is, the heap construction process must ensure that $A[A[i]] \leq A[A[2i]]$ and $A[A[i]] \leq A[A[2i + 1]]$ for all i in $1 \leq i \leq n/2$. Once the heap is constructed, $A[1]$ is the index in the range $n + 1 \leq A[1] \leq 2n$ of the smallest frequency in the second half of the array.

Now the second phase begins. As described earlier, the symbols, or aggregates of symbols, are considered in pairs, in each case taking the two smallest remaining items. In Figure 2.13, each of the items yet to be considered is represented in $A[1 .. h]$ by a pointer to its value, with the smallest always at the root of the heap. Thus, to find the two smallest, the root is taken from the heap, the leaf at $A[h]$ is moved into the root to fill the gap, h is decreased by one to indicate that position $A[h]$ is no longer included in the heap, and the heap is sifted. This brings the second smallest to the root of the heap. It is combined with the previously noted smallest, the weight of the combination is recorded at the empty location $A[h + 1]$, and $A[1]$ is set to point at this new aggregate value. To record the combination that took place, the two individual frequency counts for the two smallest items, $m1$ and $m2$—neither of which is required anymore—are changed into tree pointers that indicate the logical parent of these two nodes. This is the statement $A[m1] \leftarrow A[m2] \leftarrow h + 1$. Finally, the heap is sifted again to reestablish the invariant that the root of the heap indicates the smallest frequency count.

Figure 2.15 shows an example of this process at several stages. In Figure 2.15a, the last item in the heap is $A[h]$, and $A[m1]$ and $A[m2]$ are the two smallest entries in the heap, with values 4 and 5, respectively. Figure 2.15b shows the heap after the smallest item has been removed and the heap has been sifted. Now $m2$ is at the root of the heap, h has been decremented, and location $h + 1$ is empty. Next, the two

To calculate codeword lengths for a Huffman code,

1. /* Phase One */
   Create an array A of $2n$ words.

2. For $i \leftarrow 1$ to n do
   > Read c_i, the ith integer in the input file,
   > Set $A[n+i] \leftarrow c_i$ and $A[i] \leftarrow n+i$.

   $A[n+i]$ is now the frequency of symbol i.
   $A[i]$ points at $A[n+i]$.

3. Set $h \leftarrow n$.
   Build a min-heap out of $A[1 \ldots h]$.
   $A[1]$ stores $m1$ such that $A[m1] = \min\{A[n+1 \ldots 2n]\}$.

4. /* Phase Two */
   While $h > 1$ do

   (a) Set $m1 \leftarrow A[1]$, $A[1] \leftarrow A[h]$, and $h \leftarrow h - 1$.
       $A[m1]$ is the current smallest.

   (b) Sift the heap $A[1 \ldots h]$ down from $A[1]$,
       Set $m2 \leftarrow A[1]$.
       $A[m2]$ is the second smallest.

   (c) Set $A[h+1] \leftarrow A[m1] + A[m2]$, $A[1] \leftarrow h+1$, and
       $A[m1] \leftarrow A[m2] \leftarrow h+1$.
       $A[h+1]$ now represents $(m1 + m2)$.

   (d) Sift the heap $A[1 \ldots h]$ down from $A[1]$.

   For $3 \leq i \leq 2n$, the value of $A[i]$ represents the parent of i in the Huffman tree, the leaves are in $A[n+1 \ldots 2n]$.

5. /* Phase Three */
   For $n+1 \leq i \leq 2n$ do

   (a) Set $d \leftarrow 0$ and $r \leftarrow i$.

   (b) While $r > 2$ do
       > Set $d \leftarrow d + 1$ and $r \leftarrow A[r]$.

   (c) Set $A[i] \leftarrow d$.

6. For $i \leftarrow 1$ to n do
   > Write $A[n+i]$ as l_i, the length of the code for symbol i.

Figure 2.13 Calculating Huffman code lengths.

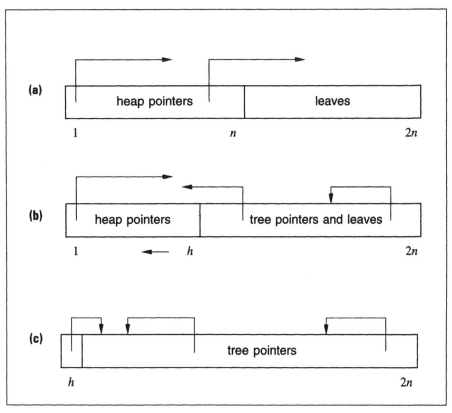

Figure 2.14 Use of an array to generate Huffman code lengths: (a) two sections, heap on left, frequencies on right; (b) heap shrinking, and pointers replacing frequencies; (c) one item remaining in heap.

smallest items are combined. Their total frequency is 9, which is stored at location $h + 1$. To get this new aggregate into the heap, $A[1]$ is made to point at location $h + 1$, and, to note the composition of the aggregate, both $A[m1]$ and $A[m2]$ also point at $h + 1$—the arrangement shown in Figure 2.15c. Finally, the heap is sifted, and the next smallest item moves up to position $A[1]$. In Figure 2.15d, this is the last item, with frequency 7. It will be the first element in the next combination and may, perhaps, be merged with the aggregate just formed.

At the completion of each such step, two items have been combined into one. As a result, the heap contains one less item, and one item has been added to the superstructure of internal tree nodes that records what combinations took place. After $n - 1$ iterations, a single aggregate remains in the heap. The frequency of this item is stored in $A[2]$, and $A[1]$ must contain 2 since there is just one item in the heap. All the other $2n - 2$ values in A contain parent pointers. To find the depth in the tree of any particular leaf, we can now simply start at that leaf and count how

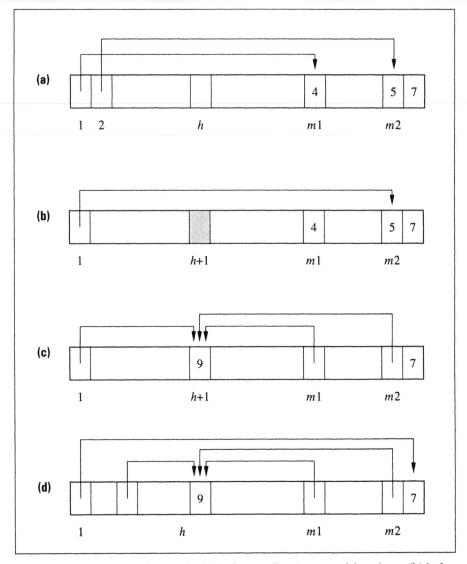

Figure 2.15 Building a Huffman code: (a) before smallest is removed from heap; (b) before second smallest is removed from heap; (c) after smallest and second smallest have been removed and combined; (d) after heap has been sifted.

many parent pointers must be followed to get to location 2, the root of the entire code tree.

This is the third phase of the algorithm. Starting from each leaf in turn—recall that the symbols of the alphabet are indicated by positions $n + 1 \ldots 2n$—the parent pointers are followed and the depth of that particular leaf stored in place of the

5′. /* Revised Phase Three */
    Set $A[2] \leftarrow 0$.
    For $i \leftarrow 3$ to $2n$ do
        Set $A[i] \leftarrow A[A[i]] + 1$.

Figure 2.16 Improved counting of leaf depths.

parent pointer. For example, in Figure 2.15, the paths from both $m1$ and $m2$ will pass through $h + 1$, and one bit is counted toward their code lengths for that part of their path. Thereafter, both traversals follow the same path to the root.

When this process is finished, the array $A[n + 1 \ldots 2n]$ stores the desired Huffman code lengths. These can be written to disk or used to construct a code. If it were more convenient, the values could be written as they are calculated in phase three.

Now consider the running time of the algorithm in Figure 2.13. The first phase is linear and takes n steps. Even when $n = 1,000,000$, this represents just a few seconds of computation. In the second phase, a heap of at most n items is sifted about $2n$ times. Each sift operation takes $\lceil \log h \rceil \leq \lceil \log n \rceil$ iterations, and each iteration takes a constant number of steps. In total, the second phase will take $kn \log n$ steps, where k is a small constant. Typical workstations execute about one million steps per second, and so with $n = 1,000,000$ the time taken by the second phase is at most a few tens of seconds.

Analysis of the third phase is a little more problematic. It would appear that one loop iteration is required for each bit of code length for each symbol, so we should calculate how many bits there could be. In the fastest case, the distribution of symbol frequencies will be uniform, and all codes will be approximately $\log n$ bits long. The total counting time will thus be $n \log n$ steps. Another way to analyze this is simply to assume in the implementation that no code will be longer than, say, 32 bits—this automatically provides an upper bound on the number of loop iterations.

In the worst case, however, it is possible for a pathological distribution of frequencies to drive the code for the ith symbol to i bits. This in turn means that the cost of computing the code lengths is proportional to $\sum_{i=1}^{n} i \approx n^2/2$, and this dominates the time required during phases one and two. (In fact, if the ith symbol received a code i bits long in any nontrivial application, there would probably be serious repercussions elsewhere in the system.) To avoid this blow-out in computation time during the third phase of the algorithm, a further refinement is necessary. Figure 2.16, which replaces step 5 of Figure 2.13, describes such an alternative. The modified phase three is based on the observation that all the pointers in the array produced by phase two point from right to left, so a labeling process from left to right will label each parent node before either of its children is encountered. Hence, if the root in $A[2]$ is labeled with a depth of 0, each following item can, in turn, be labeled with depth 1 greater than the depth of its parent—$A[A[i]] + 1$ in Figure 2.16. The resulting algorithm takes some effort to understand but is very simple

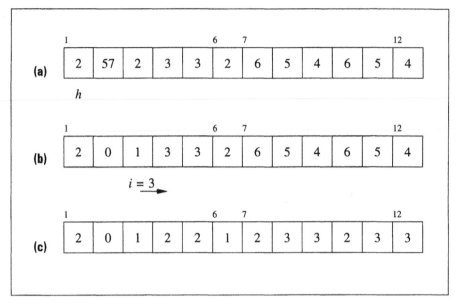

Figure 2.17 Traversing the tree: (a) before traversal; (b) after processing $i = 3$; (c) after the traversal is complete.

to code and executes extremely quickly. It takes time proportional to the number of symbols in the alphabet and even for an alphabet of one million symbols requires just a few seconds.

Figure 2.17 shows an example of the processing carried out by the revised depth-counting mechanism. Figure 2.17a shows one possible state of the array A immediately prior to step 5. The total count of all symbols is recorded in $A[2]$ and is 57. The combination $h = 1$ and $A[1] = 2$ indicates that this is the only item still in the heap. The other 10 locations indicate parent nodes for the six symbols represented in the leaves in locations $7 \ldots 12$. Figure 2.17b shows the situation when $i = 3$ has been completed, and Figure 2.17c shows the arrangement when the loop of Figure 2.16 has terminated. In Figure 2.17c, $A[i + 6]$ for $1 \le i \le 6$ records the number of bits to be allocated to the Huffman code of symbol i.

There is a further way that the code calculation process can be improved. For some alphabets, particularly very large ones such as the one shown in Table 2.2, it is common—indeed, all but inevitable—for many symbols to have the same frequency. In particular, *hapax legomena* typically account for as many as 50 percent of the distinct words, and in this case half of the frequency counts will be 1. If 50 percent of the symbols have a count of 1, then half the Huffman aggregation operations will involve joining two symbols with a count of 1. The repetition of counts can be exploited using an algorithm that represents the list of symbol frequencies using run-length coding, where a sequence of identical counts are represented by just two numbers, one giving the count and the other giving the number of repetitions (Moffat and Turpin 1998). The combining rule—which requires aggregating the smallest two frequencies—becomes rather more complex, but a substantial reduction in time and space is possible, provided only that the list of input symbol frequencies is already in sorted order. Run-length coding can also be applied to the output (such as the lengths shown in Table 2.2), which also inevitably contains long runs of identical code lengths. Analysis of the run-length method for calculating Huffman codes shows that the time taken is proportional to $r + r \log(n/r)$ for an alphabet of n symbols in which there are r distinct symbol frequencies (Moffat and Turpin 1998). Furthermore, the space required is proportional to the running time. For typical large-alphabet values $n = 1,000,000$ and $r = 10,000$, these bounds represent a considerable saving in resources, and the mechanism is very useful in situations when the $n \log n$ cost of sorting the symbol frequencies can be either avoided or amortized over more than one calculation.

Summary

Now, at last, we have seen how to generate and use Huffman codes efficiently for alphabets containing thousands of symbols. This is an essential prerequisite for virtually all large-scale information retrieval systems that use compression. Although Huffman codes are standard fodder for undergraduate courses in computer science, the methods described in the usual textbooks do not scale up effectively. Considerable savings can be made in both the time and the main memory required for decoding by using canonical Huffman codes instead of the standard decoding tree, and decoding is one of the principal ongoing operations in compressed information retrieval systems. Although encoding is done far less often—just once every time the database is reconstructed—it is still necessary to accomplish it within reasonable resource constraints, and again substantial savings in both time and space can be reaped by using the nonstandard, and by no means obvious, techniques that we have described.

2.4   Arithmetic coding

Arithmetic coding is a technique that has made it possible to obtain excellent compression using sophisticated models. Its principal strength is that it can code arbitrarily close to the entropy. It has been shown that it is not possible to code better than the entropy on average (Shannon 1948), so in this sense arithmetic coding is optimal.

To compare arithmetic coding with Huffman coding, suppose symbols from a binary alphabet are to be coded, where the symbols have probabilities of 0.99 and 0.01. The information content of a symbol s with probability $\Pr[s]$ is $-\log \Pr[s]$ bits, so the symbol with probability 99 percent can be represented using arithmetic coding in just under 0.015 bits. In contrast, a Huffman coder must use at least one bit per symbol. The only way to prevent this situation with Huffman coding is to "block" several symbols together at a time. A block is treated as the symbol to be coded, so that the per-symbol inefficiency is now spread over the whole block.

Blocking is difficult to implement because there must be a block for every possible combination of symbols, so the number of blocks increases exponentially with their length; this effect is exacerbated if consecutive symbols come from different alphabets, as is the case in the high-performance schemes that are described in the next few sections.

The compression advantage of arithmetic coding is most apparent in situations like the previous example, in which one symbol has a particularly high probability. More generally, it has been shown that the inefficiency of Huffman coding is bounded above by

$$\Pr[s_1] + \log \frac{2 \log e}{e} \approx \Pr[s_1] + 0.086$$

bits per symbol, where s_1 is the most likely symbol (Gallager 1978). For the extreme example described above, the inefficiency is thus 1.076 bits per symbol at most (a bound that can trivially be reduced to one bit per symbol), which is many times higher than the entropy of the distribution. On the other hand, for English text compressed using a zero-order character-level model, the entropy is about five bits per character, and the most common character is usually the space character, with a probability of about 0.18. With such a model the inefficiency is less than $0.266/5 \approx 5.3$ percent. In many compression applications $\Pr[s_1]$ is even smaller, and the inefficiency becomes almost negligible. Moreover, this is an *upper* bound, and in practice the inefficiency is often significantly less than the bound might indicate. On the other hand, when images are being compressed, it is common to deal with two-symbol alphabets and highly skewed probabilities, and in these cases arithmetic coding is essential unless the symbol alphabet is altered using a technique like blocking.

Another advantage of arithmetic coding over Huffman coding is that arithmetic coding calculates the representation on the fly, so less primary memory is required for operation and adaptation is more readily accommodated. Canonical Huffman codes are also fast, but they are suitable only if static or semi-static modeling is being used. Arithmetic coding is particularly suitable as the coder for high-performance adaptive models, where very high probabilities (confident predictions) are occurring, where many different probability distributions are stored in the model, and where each symbol is coded as the culmination of a sequence of lower-level decisions.

One disadvantage of arithmetic coding is that it is slower than Huffman coding, especially in static or semi-static applications. Also, the nature of the output means that it is not easy to start decoding in the middle of a compressed stream. This contrasts with Huffman coding, in which it is possible to index "starting points" in a compressed text if the model is static. In full-text retrieval, both speed and random access are important, so arithmetic coding is not likely to be appropriate. Furthermore, for the types of models used to compress full-text systems, Huffman coding gives compression that is practically as good as arithmetic coding. Thus, in large collections of text and images, Huffman coding is likely to be used for the text and arithmetic coding for the images.

How arithmetic coding works

Arithmetic coding can be somewhat difficult to grasp. Though it is interesting, understanding it is not essential. Source code is readily available for efficient arithmetic coders (see *www.cs.mu.oz.au/mg/*), which can be plugged into a compression system to perform the coding part. Only the interface to the coder needs to be understood in order to use it.

The output of an arithmetic coder, like that of any other coder, is a stream of bits. However, it is easier to describe arithmetic coding if we prefix the stream of bits with 0. and think of the output as a fractional binary number between 0 and 1. In the following example, the output stream is 1010001111, but it will be treated as the binary fraction 0.1010001111. In fact, for the sake of readability, the number will be shown as a decimal value (0.64) rather than as binary, and some possible efficiencies will be overlooked initially.

As an example we will compress the string *bccb* from the ternary alphabet {*a, b, c*}. We will use an adaptive zero-order model and deal with the zero-frequency problem by initializing all character counts to one.

When the first *b* is to be coded, all three symbols have an estimated probability of $1/3$. An arithmetic coder stores two numbers, *low* and *high*, which represent a subinterval of the range 0 to 1. Initially, *low* = 0 and *high* = 1. The range between *low* and *high* is divided according to the probability distribution about to be coded. Figure 2.18a shows the initial interval, from 0 to 1, with a third of it allocated to each symbol. The arithmetic coding step simply involves narrowing the interval to the one corresponding to the character to be coded. Thus, because the first symbol is a *b*, the new values are *low* = 0.3333 and *high* = 0.6667 (working to four decimal places). Before coding the second character, *c*, the probability distribution adapts because of the *b* that has already been seen, so $\Pr[a] = 1/4, \Pr[b] = 2/4$, and $\Pr[c] = 1/4$. The new interval is now divided up in these proportions, as shown in Figure 2.18b, and coding of the *c* involves changing the interval so that it is from *low* = 0.5834 to *high* = 0.6667. Coding continues as shown in Figure 2.18c, and at the end the interval extends from *low* = 0.6390 to *high* = 0.6501.

At this point, the encoder transmits the code by sending any value in the range from *low* to *high*. In the example, the value 0.64 would be suitable. The decoder simulates what the encoder must have been doing. It begins with *low* = 0 and *high* = 1 and divides the interval as shown in Figure 2.18a. The transmitted number, 0.64, falls in the part of the range corresponding to the symbol *b*, so *b* must have been the first input symbol. The decoder then calculates that the range should be changed to *low* = 0.3333 and *high* = 0.6667, and, because the first symbol is now known to be *b*, the new probability allocation where $\Pr[b] = 2/4$ (shown in Figure 2.18b) can be calculated. Decoding proceeds along these lines until the entire string has been reconstructed.

A general algorithm for calculating the range during encoding is shown in Figure 2.19, and Figure 2.20 shows how a symbol is decoded and the range is updated afterward. Since arithmetic coding deals with ranges of probabilities, it is usual for a model to supply *cumulative probabilities* to the encoder and decoder; this makes

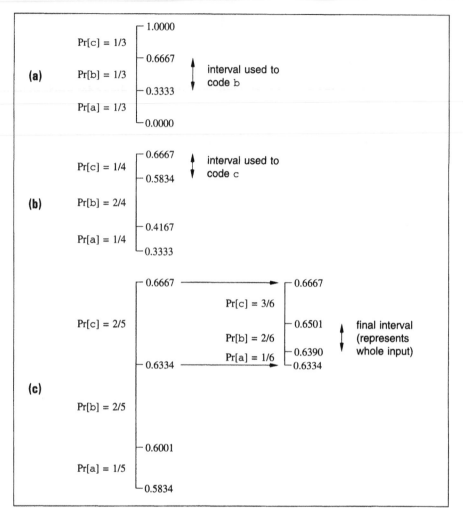

Figure 2.18 Arithmetic coding example for the string *bccb*: (a) first symbol; (b) second symbol; (c) third and fourth symbols.

the first steps of each algorithm easy to implement. For static and semi-static coding, the cumulative probabilities can be stored in an array. The encoder accesses the array by symbol number, and the decoder accesses it by binary search or through the use of a lookup table. Adaptive coding requires a more sophisticated structure so that cumulative probabilities can be adjusted on the fly. More commonly, frequency counts are kept for each symbol, and these are normalized to probabilities as an integral part of the arithmetic coding process.

Informally, compression is achieved because high-probability events do not decrease the interval from *low* to *high* very much, while low-probability events result in a much smaller next interval. A small final interval requires many digits (bits)

To code symbol s, where it is assumed that symbols are numbered from 1 to n, and that symbol i has probability $\Pr[i]$,

1. Set *low_bound* $\leftarrow \sum_{i=1}^{s-1} \Pr[i]$.
2. Set *high_bound* $\leftarrow \sum_{i=1}^{s} \Pr[i]$.
3. Set *range* $\leftarrow$ *high* $-$ *low*.
4. Set *high* $\leftarrow$ *low* + *range* $\times$ *high_bound*.
5. Set *low* $\leftarrow$ *low* + *range* $\times$ *low_bound*.

Figure 2.19   The arithmetic encoding step.

To decode a symbol, assuming that the symbols are numbered from 1 to n, that symbol i has probability $\Pr[i]$, and that *value* is the arithmetic code to be processed,

1. Find s such that

$$\sum_{i=1}^{s-1} \Pr[i] \leq (value - low)/(high - low) < \sum_{i=1}^{s} \Pr[i].$$

2. Perform the range-narrowing steps described in Figure 2.19, exactly as if symbol s is being *en*coded.
3. Return symbol s.

Figure 2.20   The arithmetic decoding step.

to specify a number that is guaranteed to be within the interval—for example, at least six decimal digits are needed to specify a number that is between 0.378232 and 0.378238. In contrast, a large interval requires few digits—for example, any number beginning with 0.4 is between 0.378232 and 0.578238, so the decoder only needs to know that the number begins with 0.4. The number of digits necessary is proportional to the negative logarithm of the size of the interval, just as the number of digits needed to represent numbers on the other side of the decimal point is proportional to the positive logarithm of the number. The size of the final interval is the product of the probabilities of the symbols coded, and so the logarithm of this quantity is the same as the sum of the logs of the individual probabilities. Therefore, a symbol s of probability $\Pr[s]$ contributes $-\log \Pr[s]$ bits to the output, which is equal to the symbol's information content and results in a code that is identical to the bound given by the entropy formula. This is why arithmetic coding produces a near-optimal number of output bits and is, in effect, capable of coding high-probability symbols in just a fraction of a bit. In practice, arithmetic coding is not exactly optimal because of the use of limited precision arithmetic and because a whole number of bits (or even bytes) must eventually be transmitted, but it is extremely close.

As we have described arithmetic coding so far, nothing appears in the output until all the encoding has been completed. In practice, it is possible to output bits *during* encoding, which avoids having to work with higher and higher precision numbers. The trick is to observe that when *low* and *high* are close in value, they have a common prefix. For example, after the third character has been coded (Figure 2.18c), the range is *low* = 0.6334 and *high* = 0.6667. Both are prefixed with 0.6, so no matter what happens to the range from there on, the first symbol transmitted must be a 6 (or would be, if the encoder were working in decimal). Thus, an output symbol can be transmitted at this point and then removed from *low* and *high* without any effect on the remaining calculations. In the example, the first decimal digit (which is 6) can be removed from *low* and *high*, changing them to 0.334 and 0.667, respectively. Working with these new values, the top of the *a* interval is now calculated to be 0.390 instead of 0.6390. The same output is being constructed, but the need for increasing precision has been avoided, and the output is generated incrementally, rather than having to wait until the end of coding.

As mentioned earlier, the final output value is really transmitted as a binary fractional number, and the 0. on the front is unnecessary because the decoder knows that it will appear. The values *low* and *high* are stored in binary; in fact, with suitable scaling they can be stored as integers rather than as real numbers. Working with finite precision causes compression to be a little worse than the entropy bound, but 16- or 32-bit precision usually degrades compression by an insignificant amount. Witten, Neal, and Cleary (1987), in a seminal paper, describe a general-purpose arithmetic coder based upon the use of integer arithmetic, and they also give analysis to bound the inefficiency arising from calculation errors. So although the example used unlimited-precision floating-point decimal numbers, in practice arithmetic coding can be implemented using fixed-precision integers, and the output is a stream of bits. Each symbol coded requires just a few arithmetic operations in the arithmetic coder. In the following section, we look more carefully at exactly how many operations are necessary.

Implementing arithmetic coding

This section describes a practical implementation of arithmetic coding. As well as examining how the interface between the model and coder works in practice, we will look at the special cases where the alphabet is very small (perhaps just two symbols) or very large (thousands or millions of symbols).

The interface between an arithmetic coder and a model is a little unusual because of the way that arithmetic coding works. To divide up the range, the coder needs to know which part of it corresponds to the symbol to be coded. We now describe three routines that are found in the mg source code: *arithmetic_encode*, *arithmetic_decode_target*, and *arithmetic_decode*.

The interface to the encoder is through the single routine *arithmetic_encode*. Instead of using probabilities, the coder is passed integers related to the counts of symbols. The procedure *arithmetic_encode* has three parameters: *low_count*, *high_count*, and *total*. The *total* parameter is the sum of all the counts for all possible symbols. In the example in Figure 2.18, for the coding of the fourth symbol, the total would be 6. The *low_count* parameter is the sum of the counts of all symbols prior (in the alphabet ordering) to the one to be encoded, so that the cumulative probability *low_bound* in Figure 2.19 is then easily calculated as *low_count/total*. In the example, the fourth character coded was *b*, and *a* is the only one that comes before it in the alphabet, so *low_count* = 1 (the count for *a*). The *high_count* parameter is the top of the range corresponding to *b* — that is, *low_count* plus the count of *b*. The example would have *high_count* = 3. Thus the *b* would be coded by calling *arithmetic_encode*(1, 3, 6). If the fourth character had been *a* or *c*, then it would have been coded by calling *arithmetic_encode*(0, 1, 6) or *arithmetic_encode*(3, 6, 6), respectively.

Two routines are required to interface to the arithmetic decoder. The first, function *arithmetic_decode_target*, has *total* as a parameter, obtained from the decoder model. It returns a number corresponding to the encoded symbol, in the range from 0 to *total* − 1. The range is closed below and open at the top, so the values "in the range" of 1 to 3 (for the example symbol *b*) are 1 and 2. If either of these targets is received, then a *b* is decoded. Similarly, *a* has a range of 1, so it has only one target value, which is 0; a target of 3, 4, or 5 indicates that a *c* is to be decoded. The decoder must use the model to determine to which symbol the target value belongs, and then the full range must be adjusted by a call to *arithmetic_decode*. The parameters for *arithmetic_decode* should be identical to the ones that were given to *arithmetic_encode*; in the example, the call would be *arithmetic_decode*(1, 3, 6). Use of the identical parameters enables the decoder to narrow the range correctly.

There are two important issues surrounding implementation of arithmetic coding. One is how the cumulative counts can be maintained efficiently, since it would usually be too slow to perform a summation every time one is needed. We return to this in the following subsection, "Maintaining cumulative counts."

The other issue, which we address immediately, is exactly how the arithmetic should be performed to make the coder work as fast as possible.

The key operations performed during arithmetic coding are the operations to adjust the range as sketched in Figure 2.19. In practice, the cumulative probabilities are represented using integers (*low_count*, *high_count*, and *total*), so, for example, *low_bound* is actually *low_count/total*. This means that step 5 of Figure 2.19 is now

$$low \leftarrow low + range \times low\_count/total.$$

To perform this calculation accurately, double-precision integer arithmetic is needed for the intermediate results of the multiplication/division component. It turns out that by choosing the ordering of the calculations carefully, and allowing a little loss of precision, it is possible to simultaneously avoid the use of high-precision arithmetic and reduce the number of operations required. The exact details of the trade-off will depend on the architecture of the machine; if high-precision integer

To *arithmetic_encode*(*low_count*, *high_count*, *total*) using low-precision arithmetic and assuming that the state variables *low* and *range* are to be modified to reflect the new range,

1. Set $r \leftarrow range$ div *total*.

2. Set $low \leftarrow low + r \times low\_count$.

3. If *high_count* < *total* then
   Set $range \leftarrow r \times (high\_count - low\_count)$
   else
   Set $range \leftarrow range - r \times low\_count$.

4. Renormalize *low* and *range*.

To *arithmetic_decode_target*(*total*), returning an integer in the range [0, *total*), where D buffers the compressed bits being decoded and corresponds to *value* − *low* in Figure 2.20,

1. Set $r \leftarrow range$ div *total*.

2. Return min{*total* − 1, D div r}.

To *arithmetic_decode*(*low_count*, *high_count*, *total*) using low-precision arithmetic, assuming that r has been set by *arithmetic_decode_target* and that the state variables D and *range* are to be modified to reflect the new range,

1. Set $D \leftarrow D - r \times low\_count$.

2. If *high_count* < *total* then
   Set $range \leftarrow r \times (high\_count - low\_count)$
   else
   Set $range \leftarrow range - r \times low\_count$.

3. Renormalize *range* and load new bits into D to match the renormalization.

Figure 2.21 An efficient arithmetic coding implementation.

multiplications are fast, then it may not be so beneficial. The cost of using approximations will be a small loss in compression performance, but for the method shown below, this generally amounts to a fraction of a percent in practice and is a worthwhile optimization.

An effective algorithm that achieves this is shown in Figure 2.21. A significant difference from the version described in Figures 2.19 and 2.20 is that instead of representing the current range using its boundaries *low* and *high*, it is represented using the lower boundary *low* and *range*, the size of the current interval. The speed efficiency is gained by using the temporary variable r, which can be stored to relatively low precision. In fact, because r is typically a small integer, it can be more efficient to perform the multiplicative operations in which it is involved using shifting and adding, which results in a further speed gain on some architectures.

Notice that a special case is made when *high_count* is at the top of the range. This serves two purposes. First, the separate calculation ensures that the new high point is the same as before; if it were rounded down because of the truncation when r is calculated, some compression inefficiency would be introduced unnecessarily. Second, the calculation $r \times$ *low_count* has already been performed in the second step and need not be repeated here, saving one multiplication. This can happen relatively often if the most probable symbol is allocated the top part of the range.

The renormalization step involves transmitting bits from the left-hand side of *low*, and shifting *range* left, until excessive leading 0 bits at the start of *range* have been eliminated.

The decoder mirrors the state of the encoder, except that instead of storing *low*, it stores the difference D between *low* and the value in the input. This saves some operations in the decoder by simplifying the renormalization step—only D needs to be renormalized instead of both *low* and the incoming value.

This approximate method is from Moffat, Neal, and Witten (1998), who evaluate a number of improvements to arithmetic coding. Source code for their methods is available by ftp from *ftp://munnari.oz.au/pub/arith_coder/*; the original 1987 implementation of Witten, Neal, and Cleary is available at *ftp://ftp.cpsc.ucalgary.ca/ pub/projects/ar.cod/cacm-87.shar*. Other enhancements improve the speed by using shift/add operations instead of multiplications and divisions (Rissanen and Mohiuddin 1989; Chevion, Karnin, and Walach 1991; Feygin, Gulak, and Chow 1994; Stuiver and Moffat 1998) or looking up approximate arithmetic calculations in a precomputed table (Howard and Vitter 1993a). Approximating the calculations leads to higher compression throughput but is at the cost of degraded compression effectiveness because less care is taken with the accuracy of the arithmetic.

One special case where approximate arithmetic coding has been used very effectively is for binary input alphabets. In this case there is only one point between *high* and *low* to be calculated, and the order of the two symbols in the range can easily be swapped so that the most probable one is at the top. The split point is therefore guaranteed to be below halfway. If it is approximated with a power of two, the multiplication can be replaced with a single shift operation, and because the split point is less than 0.5 (and often a lot less than this), the loss of compression efficiency can be bounded and is usually very small. This kind of approximation is exploited by the IBM Q-coder, which is used for various applications including the JBIG and JPEG image compression standards described in Chapter 6.

Maintaining cumulative counts

For nonbinary alphabets, the speed of arithmetic coding is strongly affected by how quickly the cumulative counts can be calculated, so it is important to use a data

i	1	2	3	4	5	6	7	8	9	
$F[i]$	c_1	$c_1 + c_2$	c_3	$c_1 + \ldots + c_4$	c_5	$c_5 + c_6$	c_7	$c_1 + \ldots + c_8$	c_9	$\cdots$

Figure 2.22 Array storing implicit tree for cumulative count calculation.

structure that makes it easy to calculate the cumulative count for a symbol and easy to search the cumulative counts for a target. If the probability distribution is very skew, so that only a small subset of the possible symbols are being regularly used (or if the alphabet contains in total only a few symbols), then a move-to-front list is suitable. This uses a linear search, but the list being searched is reorganized by moving an element to the head of the list when it is accessed. If only a few symbols are being coded, they will quickly end up near the front of the list, and most accesses will only require a short search. This is the case for a simple zero-order character-level model, where for typical English text only about 10 elements in a move-to-front list are probed on average for each symbol coded.

If the alphabet is used sparsely (which occurs in high-order contexts for coders such as the PPM method, described in Section 2.5), even a simple linked list may be suitable since only a few counts will be kept for the few symbols that are observed in each context. For binary alphabets—one of the main applications of arithmetic coding—the problem of calculating cumulative counts is trivial.

For larger alphabets, such as the set of words in a document, the probability distribution will be less skew and a better structure is needed. A particularly elegant structure for this situation has been developed that uses an implicit tree, where each node contains the cumulative sum of a specific range of counts (Fenwick 1994). The tree can be traversed from the root to a symbol's node in such a way that the selection of ranges encountered on the path will exactly cover the entire range up to the symbol for which a cumulative count is required. For an alphabet of n symbols, the maximum depth of the tree is $\log_2 n$, so the cumulative count can be determined in logarithmic time. The tree is implicit and is actually stored without pointers in an array. The fast Huffman implementation described earlier also uses an implicit tree (a heap) but with different rules for the structure. Like the heap, the implicit tree used for cumulative counts is very efficient; only n integers are stored to represent n counts, so there are no storage overheads.

Figure 2.22 shows the beginning of the array F that is used to store the implicit tree. Each entry $F[i]$ in the array contains the sum of the counts for a contiguous group of symbols including c_i, the frequency of symbol i; from these the required cumulative sums can be readily calculated.

To calculate the cumulative count for symbol i, we start at entry $F[i]$ and work backward toward $F[1]$, adding a selected subset of the array entries. For example, for $i = 11$ the entries summed are $F[11]$, $F[10]$, and $F[8]$. The set of entries to visit is easily determined from the binary representation of i; the next entry to visit is found by setting the rightmost one in the binary representation to a zero. In the previous example, the index 11 is represented as 1011 in binary. Setting the

> "I never heerd a skilful old married feller of twenty
> years' standing pipe ``my wife'' in a more used note
> than 'a did," said Jacob Smallbury. "It might have been
> a little more true to nater if't had been spoke a little
> chillie

Figure 2.23 Sample text.

rightmost bit to zero gives 1010 and then 1000, which in decimal are 10 and 8, respectively.

To increment the count for symbol i, the appropriate entries beyond the one for i must be incremented. For example, if symbol 3 is to have its count incremented, then the array entries at $F[3]$, $F[4]$, and $F[8]$ must be incremented. This sequence is also easily determined from the binary representation of the numbers.

This implicit tree technique calculates cumulative sums in logarithmic time. Another mechanism exists that uses a tree in which the shape depends on the counts, and as a result the time taken is linear in number of input and output bits that would be used if the counts are used for an arithmetic coder (Moffat 1990b). Although asymptotically optimal, in practical applications this structure is no faster than the Fenwick tree described above, and it uses more memory.

2.5 Symbolwise models

Now we look at symbolwise models that can be combined with the coders described in the two previous sections. Compression methods that work in a symbolwise manner and make use of adaptively generated statistics give excellent compression—in fact, they include the best-known methods—and so are well worth studying. Four main approaches will be discussed in detail: PPM, which makes predictions based on previous characters; block sorting, which transforms the text to bring similar contexts together; DMC, which uses a finite-state machine for the model; and word-based methods, which use words rather than letters as the atomic symbols for compression. Each of these methods generates predictions for the input symbols. The predictions take the form of probability distributions that are provided to a coder—usually either an arithmetic or Huffman coder.

Prediction by partial matching

Prediction by partial matching (PPM) uses finite-context models of characters (Cleary and Witten 1984b). Rather than being restricted to one context length, it uses different sizes, depending on what contexts have been observed in the previously coded text—hence the term "partial matching" in the name.

Suppose Hardy's book is being coded by PPM and the encoder is up to the passage shown in Figure 2.23. The characters *chillie* have just been encoded, and the character r is about to be coded. PPM starts with a reasonably large context, typically three or four characters. For illustration, suppose a context of five characters (*illie*) is used to try to make a prediction. This string has never occurred before in the prior text, so the encoder switches to a context of four characters (*llie*). The decoder is able to do likewise, since it has seen the same prior text as the encoder and also recognizes that the context has not occurred before. This smaller four-character context *has* occurred previously. However, it has only appeared once, and it was followed by the character *s*. This is a zero-frequency situation—the character *r* is to be coded, but it has a count of zero. Rather than code it explicitly using one of the zero-frequency methods described above, PPM sends a special "escape" symbol—available in every context—that tells the decoder that the symbol cannot be coded in the current context and that the next smaller context should be tried. Assigning a probability to the escape symbol is really just another form of the zero-frequency problem. One effective method is to allocate a count of one to the escape symbol. This is sometimes referred to as *escape method A,* and the version of PPM that uses it is referred to as *PPMA.* In the example, the escape symbol has a probability of 1/2 (and the character *s* has the remaining 1/2). The escape symbol is transmitted, and both encoder and decoder shift down to a context of three symbols. One bit has been transmitted so far and one arithmetic coding step completed.

The three-symbol context *lie* has occurred 201 times in the prior text, and 19 of those were followed by an *r.* Allowing one count for the escape symbol, the *r* can now be coded with a probability of 19/202, which requires 3.4 bits. In total, the *r* requires two encoding steps and is represented in 4.4 bits.

If the *r* character had not occurred in the order-3 context, another escape would have been used to get to the order-2, and then, if necessary, order-1 or order-0 contexts. If a symbol has never occurred in the prior text, even the order-0 model cannot be used, and a further escape symbol is transmitted to revert to a simple model in which all characters are coded with equal probability. In this case, six arithmetic encoding steps would be required. This may seem extreme, but actually it is very rare—during the early parts of the text, while the model is still learning, it is unlikely that fifth-order contexts will be repeated, and once the model is up to speed it is unlikely that any of the low-order contexts will be required. As a result, compression using the PPM method is only a little slower than using a straightforward zero-order character-based model that uses exactly one arithmetic coding step per symbol.

The probability estimates used above can be improved a little using a technique called *exclusions.* In the example, although the three-symbol context *lie* had occurred 201 times, 22 of these occurrences were followed by the letter *s*, yet an *s* will not be coded in that context since it was available to be coded in the four-symbol context. Therefore *s* can be excluded from the count. This means that only 179 occurrences of the context will be used as a sample, and an *r* will have an estimated probability of 19/180 instead of 19/202. Performing exclusion takes a little extra time but gives a reasonable payback in terms of extra compression (and an improvement is guaranteed since all nonexcluded characters have their probabilities increased). There are several other variations that offer different trade-offs between speed and compression (Lelewer and Hirschberg 1991; Howard and Vitter

1993a; Willems, Shtarkov, and Tjalkens 1995, 1996; Åberg, Shtarkov, and Smeets 1997; Bunton 1997b).

PPM is very effective. Figure 2.24 shows the number of bits used to code an excerpt extracted from the end of the Hardy book, assuming that the prior part of the book has already been processed to establish the contexts and frequency counts. The number of bits for each character includes any escape characters necessary to get the decoder to the correct context; for the example in this figure, the coder attempts to code each character first in a third-order context. Notice that many characters are very predictable. For example, the letter *d* in the word *old* in the first line is coded in just 0.19 bits; a *d* is very common in this context. The space character after the *d* is coded in 0.86 bits; it is not quite so predictable because the letter *e* is also considered likely since the prior text contains words like *older* and *beholder*. The unpredictable characters stand out. For example, longer representations are generated for the last three characters of the word *heerd* in the first line, and the closing parenthesis in the penultimate line takes 11.06 bits because, although that context occurs very frequently in the text, this is only the second time that *now* is followed by a parenthesis. Despite these exceptions, the majority of the symbols are predicted with high probabilities and so are coded in two to three bits each. Because PPM generates so many high probabilities, it is best to code its output with an arithmetic coder.

The amount of compression achieved by PPM is affected by the method used to estimate escape probabilities. One of the better methods, referred to as *method C*, estimates the probability of an escape to be $r/(n + r)$, where n is the total number of symbols seen previously in the current context and r is the number of them that were *distinct* (Moffat 1990a). A character with a count of c_i in the context would have a probability of $c_i/(n + r)$. Using method C, the probability of an escape character increases as the relative frequency of novel characters increases, but also decreases as the total number of times the context has occurred increases. Using PPMC (PPM with escape method C) combined with arithmetic coding, Hardy's book can be coded in an average of 2.5 bits per character; that is, it is compressed to 31 percent of its original size.

A number of improvements to the PPM method can shave a little more off the size of compressed files. For example, the PPMD method (which is consistently slightly better than PPMC) only gives half the weight to novel events, so the probability of an escape character is $r/(2n)$, and the probability of a symbol that has been observed c_i times in the current context is $(2c_i - 1)/(2n)$ (Howard 1993). Another way of calculating escape probabilities is method X, proposed by Witten and Bell (1991). In method X, the number of *hapax legomena* (symbols of frequency one) is used as an estimate of the number of symbols of frequency zero. That is, if t_1 is the number of symbols i for which $c_i = 1$, then the escape probability is calculated as $t_1/(n + t_1)$, and the probability of symbols with $c_i \geq 1$ as $c_i/(n + t_1)$. To avoid the problems that arise when $t_1 = 0$, and no symbols have appeared only once, further approximations can be used: $(t_1 + 1)/(n + t_1 + 1)$ and $c_i/(n + t_1 + 1)$, respectively.

As well as refinements to the escape calculation strategy, researchers have explored using arbitrarily large contexts instead of a fixed size for the starting point

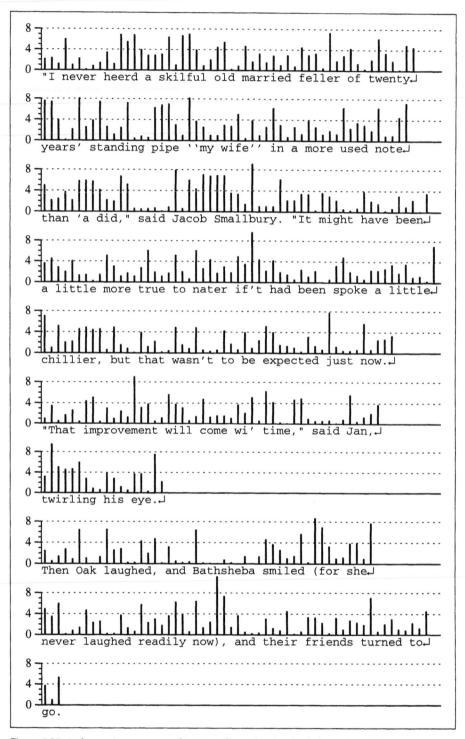

Figure 2.24 Information content of PPM coding of individual characters (bits per character).

(Cleary, Teahan, and Witten 1995). This general technique is referred to as PPM*, and one implementation, PPMZ, can compress *Far from the Madding Crowd* to about 2.2 bits per character. This places PPM-based methods among the best known for achieving good compression.

Some generalized PPM systems have been developed for experimenting with different forms of the basic algorithm. One is known as the Swiss Army Knife Data Compression (SAKDC) method (Williams 1991a). As its name suggests, SAKDC is actually many variations rolled into one, with some 25 parameters to control how the model is used. The parameters include the maximum context, how memory is managed, how probabilities are estimated, and how new contexts are added to the model. It includes several other techniques as special cases. Like its namesake, the large number of parameters makes it unsuitable for regular use, but it has been valuable in exploring the bounds of how much compression can be achieved with PPM-style models.

In her 1997 doctoral dissertation, Suzanne Bunton described a similar heavily parameterized program. Indeed, her "executable taxonomy" also includes the DMC model (described on page 69) as a variant, as well as many other possibilities.

Block-sorting compression

Block-sorting compression is an intriguing approach that was first published in 1994 (Burrows and Wheeler 1994). It is unusual because it works by transforming the text into a form that is more amenable to compression. The transformed text is compressed and transmitted to the decompressor, which reverses the compression and then applies the inverse transform. This is analogous to the discrete cosine transform, used for compressing images, or the Fourier transform, which converts signals from the time domain to the frequency domain. One disadvantage of block sorting is that the input must be broken up into blocks that are processed one at a time, rather than the process being continuously adaptive as characters arrive.

The transformation used for block-sorting compression is sometimes called the Burrows-Wheeler transform, after its inventors. It permutes the characters in a text so that those occurring in similar contexts end up near each other. The permuted text is the same size as the original, but it is easily compressed using simple techniques because only a limited selection of characters tends to occur in similar contexts. The decompressor must rearrange it back to its original order. It is remarkable that this reverse permutation can be done with little computational effort (in fact, it is remarkable that it can be done at all!).

The transformation is performed by sorting each character in the text, using its context as the sort key. Figure 2.25 shows some of the sorted characters for the Hardy book, preceded by their contexts. Notice that the contexts are compared for sorting by working from right to left. The comparisons go back as far as necessary to order any two contexts; if the beginning of the file is reached in a comparison, then it wraps around to the end of the file, although, as Figure 2.25 shows, most of the time only a few characters are needed to distinguish contexts. The transformed text is simply the characters in the order of their sorted contexts, so the permuted text

```
nly thrown into greater relie    f
n. Nevertheless, he⏎was relie    v
eba, feeling a nameless relie    f
rise, experienced great relie    f
thsheba was momentarily relie    v
P 398>⏎foreheads, quite⏎relie    v
t such times is a great⏎relie    f
e droning of⏎blue-bottle flie    s
and the reasonable probabilie    s
tions, pinks, picotees, lilie    s
  her head and feet,⏎the lilie    s
eads, all⏎about their familie    s
e as common among the⏎familie    s
d been spoke a little⏎chillie    r
no absurd sides to the follie    s
lways be your⏎friend,' replie    d
s I've got no chance,' replie    d
⏎'O no -- not at all,' replie    d
  'tis my only doctor,' replie    d
```

Figure 2.25 Sorted contexts for the Burrows-Wheeler transform.

for the Hardy book will contain the sequence *fvffvvfsssssssrsdddd* from the right-hand column of Figure 2.25.

The two main issues that arise at this point is how the permuted text should be coded and how the original text can be reconstructed from the permuted one. We will deal with the coding first.

Notice that characters occur in clusters in the permuted text. For example, in the context *relie* in Figure 2.25, only the letters f and v occur. This pattern is conveniently coded using a *move-to-front* coder, which maintains a list of characters, moving them to the front of the list each time they are coded. Characters near the front of the list are assigned shorter codes. In the example, f and v will be in the first two characters of the list for a while, and then will be displaced by s and, later, d.

But how can the original source text be reconstructed from a permutation like *fvffvvfsssssssrsdddd*? The permuted text gives us the last column of characters from Figure 2.25. One important observation is that the second to last column (containing only the symbol e in Figure 2.25) can be constructed by sorting the permuted text, so the decoder has access to both of these columns.

The shorter text *mississippi* will be used as an example to describe the reverse transformation. Figure 2.26 shows the encoding of this text. In Figure 2.26a, each character is shown with its context, where wraparound is used to get a full con-

	(a)			(b)			(c)		(d)	
1	ississippi	m	1	sissippimi	s	1	s	1	i	s
2	ssissippim	i	2	ississippi	m	2	m*	2	i	m
3	sissippimi	s	3	sippimissi	s	3	s	3	i	s
4	issippimis	s	4	pimississi	p	4	p	4	i	p
5	ssippimiss	i	5	ssissippim	i	5	i	5	m	i
6	sippimissi	s	6	imississip	p	6	p	6	p	p
7	ippimissis	s	7	mississipp	i	7	i	7	p	i
8	ppimississ	i	8	issippimis	s	8	s	8	s	s
9	pimississi	p	9	ippimissis	s	9	s	9	s	s
10	imississip	p	10	ssippimiss	i	10	i	10	s	i
11	mississipp	i	11	ppimississ	i	11	i	11	s	i

Figure 2.26 Burrows-Wheeler transform of the string *mississippi*: (a) rotations of the string; (b) sorted by contexts; (c) permuted string (transmitted), with * indicating the starting character; (d) sorted string (last character of context) and permuted string.

text. In Figure 2.26b, the contexts have been sorted into order, and the permuted string is transmitted (Figure 2.26c). The number of the context corresponding to the first character, which is 2 in this case, must also be transmitted; this is indicated by an asterisk in Figure 2.26c. The last character of the contexts is reconstructed in Figure 2.26d by sorting the permuted string.

Reversing the transformation relies on the key observation that the order in which the corresponding characters appear in the two columns are the same. For example, the letter *s* appears four times in each column. Looking at Figure 2.26b, in each column, the first appearance corresponds to the first *s* in *mississippi* (lines 1 and 8), the second appearance corresponds to the third *s* in the word (lines 3 and 9), the third appearance corresponds to the second (lines 8 and 10), and the fourth to the fourth (lines 9 and 11). This relationship can be used as follows to reconstruct the original string.

Using the information in Figure 2.26d, the decoder starts with the indicated first row (line 2), which gives the first character, *m*. Looking down the left-hand column, the context ending with *m* only occurs once (line 5), so this gives the next character, *i*. The context *i* has occurred four times. However, the one that was just decoded is the first *i* in the second column, so we should use the first *i* in the first column as the next context (line 1), giving the next character, *s*. This is the first *s* in the permuted string, so the next context is the first *s* (line 8), which is followed by another *s*. This latest *s* is the third one, so the next context is the third *s* (line 10), which is followed by *i*. The rest of the text is decoded by going through contexts 3, 9, 11, 4, 6, 7, and 2, at which point the whole text has been decoded.

To encode using the Burrows-Wheeler transform, and produce a permuted version
of the input that is amenable to symbol-ranking coding,

1. Sort the N input characters using the preceding characters as the sort key,
   creating a permuted array $P[1 \ldots N]$.

2. Output the position in P that contains the first character from the
   compressed file.

3. Output the permuted array P.

To decode using the Burrows-Wheeler transform,

4. Set $p \leftarrow$ the position of the first input character (from the encoder).

5. Set $P[1 \ldots N] \leftarrow$ the permuted symbols (from the encoder).

6. Set $K[s] \leftarrow$ the number of times symbol s occurs in P.

7. Set the array $M[s]$ to be the position of the first occurrence of s in the array
   that would be obtained by sorting P:

   (a) Set $M[\text{first symbol in lexical order}] \leftarrow 1$.

   (b) For each symbol s (in lexical order)
       Set $M[s] \leftarrow M[s-1] + K[s-1]$.

8. For each input symbol position i from 1 to N

   (a) Set $s \leftarrow P[i]$.

   (b) Set $L[i] \leftarrow M[s]$.

   (c) Set $M[s] \leftarrow M[s] + 1$,

   Array L now stores the links with which to traverse the permuted string.

9. Traverse the link array to reconstruct the original string:

   (a) Set $i \leftarrow p$ (initial position).

   (b) Repeat N times (until $i = p$ a second time)
       Output $P[i]$,
       Set $i \leftarrow L[i]$.

Figure 2.27 Encoding and decoding using the Burrows-Wheeler transform.

In practice the block sorting can be implemented quite efficiently. For example,
there is no need to create all the substrings as shown in Figure 2.26a since they can be
represented by an array of pointers to the input text. The inverse transform can be
performed efficiently by making a single pass through the strings in Figure 2.26d,
storing links to the next context, which avoids searching through the contexts for
each character.

Algorithms for encoding and decoding using the Burrows-Wheeler transform are
shown in Figure 2.27. Encoding simply involves permuting the input symbols using

each symbol's prior context as a sort key. The entire prior context is not usually needed for sorting; most of the time only a few previous characters will be required to determine the lexical order of the context. The sorted characters are coded using a coder that exploits the locality of reference in the permuted string.

The decoder recovers the permuted string into the array P. Although the example above showed a sorted version of P used to determine the permuted order (the first column of Figure 2.26d), it is not necessary for this sorted array to be constructed explicitly. Instead, two arrays (K and M) store it implicitly. Each different symbol in the sorted array will occur in one contiguous group. The array K stores how long each group is for each symbol, and from this M is constructed, which stores the position of the start of each group. These are easily constructed from P.

The decoding is facilitated by a link array, L, which stores the order in which characters should be taken from P. The link array is constructed from one pass through P using M to keep track of which occurrence of a symbol is being used. Finally, P is traversed using the order given by L, to produce the original uncompressed file.

The method used to code the permuted string is crucial to the compression performance of the system. The permuted string has quite different characteristics than normal text, and a specialized coding method is called for. A context-based coder is not appropriate because almost all of the contextual information has been removed by the permutation. As mentioned earlier, one suitable method is to use a move-to-front coder, which assigns a higher probability to characters that have occurred recently in the input. For text files, the position numbers in the move-to-front list usually follow an inverse square frequency distribution, which the coder must exploit. A variety of codes have been proposed for this, including zero-order arithmetic or Huffman coding or even fixed codes that approximate a typical distribution.

Figure 2.25 indicates that the sorted contexts correspond quite closely to the PPM method. For example, the context *chillie* appears adjacent to the context *follie*, which was the longest matching PPM context (order-4) and predicts an *s* after *llie*. This came up in coding the same character in the example of PPM coding (page 62). In fact, block sorting is very closely related to the PPM* method, which is a variant of PPM that allows arbitrary-length contexts. Not surprisingly, in practice the compression performance of block sorting is similar to that of PPM-based methods.

Dynamic Markov compression

Dynamic Markov compression (DMC) is a modeling technique based on a finite-state model (Cormack and Horspool 1987). Such a model is often called a Markov model after the Russian mathematician A. A. Markov (1856–1922). DMC is capable of achieving compression comparable to that of PPM, making it one of the better compression methods currently known. It is also quite easy to implement a working version of DMC, although it tends to be slow unless some effort is put into making it efficient.

DMC is adaptive. Both the probabilities and the structure of the finite-state machine change as coding proceeds. Figure 2.28 shows a model created by DMC. The

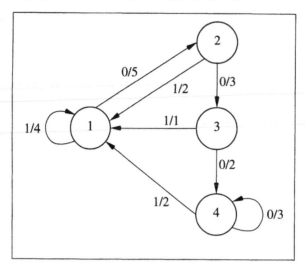

Figure 2.28 A model generated by the DMC method.

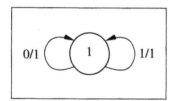

Figure 2.29 A simple initial model for DMC.

input alphabet comprises single bits, rather than bytes. Each transition out of a state records how often it has been traversed, and these counts are used to estimate the probabilities of the transitions. For example, the transition out of state 1 labeled 0/5 indicates that a 0 bit in state 1 has occurred five times. The decoder constructs an identical model using the symbols decoded and keeps track of which state the encoder is in. In practice, the values on the transitions are not necessarily integers because counts are divided up when states are cloned, as explained later.

The zero-frequency problem is avoided by initializing unused transitions to a count of one. Probabilities are estimated using the relative frequencies of the two transitions out of the current state. For example, if an encoder using the model in Figure 2.28 is in state 2 and the next input bit is a 0, then that input is coded with a probability of $3/(2 + 3) = 0.6$, corresponding to 0.737 bits. The count on the 0 transition is then incremented to 4, and the transition is followed so that state 3 is now the current state. The next input bit is coded from this new state.

The adaptation of the *structure* of a DMC model is achieved by a heuristic called *cloning*. In its simplest form, DMC starts with the elementary model shown in Figure 2.29. When a transition appears to be heavily used, the state that it leads to is

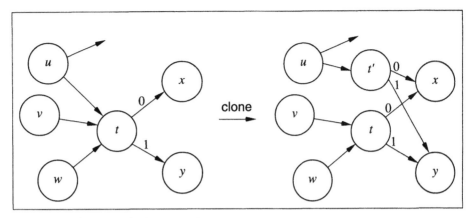

Figure 2.30 The DMC cloning operation.

cloned into two states. Figure 2.30 shows the cloning of state t. The heavy use of the transition into it from state u has triggered the cloning, and so a new state, t', is created. The transition from state u now goes to t', while transitions from other states (v and w) to t remain the same. The transitions out of state t' are set to be the same as those out of state t. The counts on the transitions out of t' are in the same ratio as the counts out of t, and the counts for the transitions out of t and t' are adjusted so that their sum is equal to the sum of counts on transitions coming in. This is a logical equivalent of Kirchoff's law for electrical circuits, which states that the algebraic sum of the currents flowing into any node must be zero. The extended structure means that a new state is now available to record independent probabilities for symbols occurring after a transition from state u to state t. Previously, these probabilities were confused with those of states v and w.

The encoding algorithm for DMC is shown in Figure 2.31. The structure of the finite-state machine is stored using the array T. Entry $T[t][e]$ in the array stores the state reached on transition e out of state t. The array $C[t][e]$ stores the number of times the input has traversed transition e out of state t, with one added to avoid the zero-frequency problem. Initially there is just one state, number 1, with both transitions going to state 1 (although more sophisticated initial models could be used). Linking in a new cloned state requires just three assignments to the entries in T, plus some work to redistribute the counts. The pseudocode shown here contains most of the details for implementing a DMC model—just a little over a dozen lines of code are required, with a simple data structure. The decoder is similar.

Being a finite-*state* model rather than a finite-*context* model, DMC is potentially more powerful than, for example, PPM. However, it has been shown that the choice of initial models and the nature of the cloning heuristic mean that only finite *contexts* are generated (Bell and Moffat 1989). This is borne out in the compression performance of DMC, which is similar to that of PPM.

The use of bits rather than bytes simplifies the implementation of DMC, although it has the disadvantage that every bit in the input must be coded individ-

To encode using the DMC method,

1. Set $s \leftarrow 1$. /* the current number of states */
2. Set $t \leftarrow 1$. /* the current state */
3. Set $T[1][0] \leftarrow 1$ and $T[1][1] \leftarrow 1$. /* initial model */
4. Set $C[1][0] \leftarrow 1$ and $C[1][1] \leftarrow 1$. /* set counts to 1 to avoid zero-frequency problem */
5. For each input bit e do
   (a) Set $u \leftarrow t$.
   (b) Set $t \leftarrow T[u][e]$. /* follow the transition */
   (c) Code e with probability $C[u][e]/(C[u][0] + C[u][1])$.
   (d) Set $C[u][e] \leftarrow C[u][e] + 1$.
   (e) If cloning thresholds are exceeded then
       Set $s \leftarrow s + 1$ /* the new state (t') */,
       Set $T[u][e] \leftarrow s$,
       Set $T[s][0] \leftarrow T[t][0]$,
       Set $T[s][1] \leftarrow T[t][1]$, and
       Move some of the counts from $C[t]$ to $C[s]$.

Figure 2.31 Encoding using DMC.

ually, and this can be slow. Bitwise DMC is probably one of the easiest models to implement—only a few lines of code are needed to perform the counting and cloning—yet DMC is one of the best compression methods in terms of compression performance. Its speed can be improved by adapting it to work with bytes rather than bits, but this requires more sophisticated data structures to avoid excessive memory usage. In this case, the implementation effort becomes comparable to that of other high-performance methods, such as PPM, and the difference between the two methods—both in implementation effort and compression efficiency—becomes small.

Word-based compression

Word-based compression methods parse a document into "words" (typically, contiguous alphanumeric characters) and "nonwords" (typically, punctuation and white-space characters) between the words. The words and nonwords become the symbols to be compressed. There are various ways to compress them. Generally, the most effective approach is to form a zero-order model for words and another for nonwords. It is assumed that the text consists of strictly alternating words and nonwords (the parsing method needs to ensure this), and so the two models are used alternately. If the models are adaptive, a means of transmitting previously unseen words and nonwords is required. Usually, some escape symbol is transmitted, and then the novel word is spelled out character by character. The explicit characters can be compressed using a simple model, typically a zero-order model of the characters.

Although this approach seems to be specific to textual documents, it does not perform too badly on other types of data. This is because if few "words" are found, then the model effectively reverts to the simple zero-order model of characters, and for nontextual data such as images, this sort of model is reasonably appropriate. A well-tuned word-based compressor can achieve compression performance close to that of PPM, and it has the potential to be substantially faster because it codes several characters at a time.

There are many different ways to break English text into words and the intervening nonwords.[3] One scheme is to treat any string of contiguous alphabetic characters as a word and anything else as a nonword. More sophisticated schemes could take into account punctuation that is part of a word, such as apostrophes and hyphens, and even accommodate some likely sequences, such as a capital letter following a period. This kind of improvement does not have much effect on compression but may make the resulting list of words more useful for indexing purposes in a full-text retrieval system.

One aspect of parsing that deserves attention is the processing of numbers. If digits are treated in the same way as letters, a sequence of digits will be parsed as a word. This can cause problems if a document contains many numbers—such as tables of financial figures. The same situation occurs, and can easily be overlooked, when a large document contains page numbers—with 100,000 pages, the page numbers will generate 100,000 "words," each of which occurs only once. Such a host of unique words can have a serious impact on operation: in an adaptive system, each one must be spelled out explicitly, and in a static system, each will be stored in the compression model. In both cases this is grossly inefficient because the frequency distribution of these numbers is quite different from the frequency distribution of normal words for which the system is designed. One solution is to limit the length of numbers to just a few digits. Longer numbers are broken up into shorter ones, with a null punctuation marker in between. This moderates the vocabulary generated by the numbers and can result in considerable savings in decode-time memory requirements.

Word-based schemes can generate a large number of symbols since there is a different symbol for each word and word variant that appears in the text being coded. This means that special attention must be given to efficient data structures for storing the model. In a static or semi-static situation, a canonical Huffman code is

---

3 Note, however, that not all languages are so cooperative. Most Asian languages are written and stored without any equivalent of the white-space characters that are taken for granted in English, and they are very difficult to segment into words. For compression purposes, this is not a serious handicap, as other methods can be used. But for information retrieval purposes (see Chapter 4), where discrete words are employed as the terms used to search for documents relevant to a query, segmentation is an important problem indeed.

ideal. It provides efficient decoding, and because even the most common words occur with a relatively low frequency, coding inefficiency is small. Details of exactly such a scheme are given in Section 9.1.

This section has described a relatively small selection of symbolwise models for compression. Many other models have been proposed. They are generally based on the principles discussed above and differ chiefly in how they compromise between speed, memory requirements, and compression performance. The "Further reading" section at the end of this chapter cites books and surveys that discuss some of these methods in more detail.

2.6 Dictionary models

Dictionary-based compression methods use the principle of replacing substrings in a text with a codeword that identifies that substring in a *dictionary*, or *codebook*. The dictionary contains a list of substrings and a codeword for each substring. This type of substitution is used naturally in everyday life, for example, in the substitution of the number 12 for the word *December*, or representing "the chord of B minor with the seventh added" as *Bm7*. Unlike symbolwise methods, dictionary methods often use fixed codewords rather than explicit probability distributions because reasonable compression can be obtained even if little attention is paid to the coding component.

The simplest dictionary compression methods use small codebooks. For example, in *digram coding*, selected pairs of letters are replaced with codewords. A codebook for the ASCII character set might contain the 128 ASCII characters, as well as 128 common letter pairs. The output codewords are eight bits each, and the presence of the full ASCII character set in the codebook ensures that any input can be represented. At best, every pair of characters is replaced with a codeword, reducing the input from seven bits per character to four bits per character. At worst, each seven-bit character will be expanded to eight bits. Furthermore, a straightforward extension caters to files that might contain some non-ASCII bytes—one codeword is reserved as an escape, to indicate that the next byte should be interpreted as a single eight-bit character rather than as a codeword for a pair of ASCII characters. Of course, a file consisting of mainly binary data will be expanded significantly by this approach; this is the inevitable price that must be paid for use of a static model.

Another natural extension of this system is to put even larger entries in the codebook—perhaps common words, like *and* and *the*, or common components of words, such as *pre* and *tion*. Strings like these that appear in the dictionary are sometimes called *phrases*. A phrase may sometimes be as short as one or two characters, or it may include several words. Unfortunately, having a dictionary with a predetermined set of phrases does not give very good compression because the entries must usually be quite short if input independence is to be achieved. In fact, the more suitable the dictionary is for one sort of text, the less suitable it is for others. For example, if this book were to be compressed, then we would do well if the codebook contained phrases like *compress, dictionary,* and even *arithmetic coding,* but such a codebook would be unsuitable for a text on, say, business management.

One way to avoid the problem of the dictionary being unsuitable for the text at hand is to use a semi-static dictionary scheme, constructing a new codebook for each text that is to be compressed. However, the overhead of transmitting or storing the dictionary is significant, and deciding which phrases should be put in the codebook to maximize compression is a surprisingly difficult problem.

The elegant solution to this problem is to use an adaptive dictionary scheme. Practically all adaptive dictionary compression methods are based on one of just two related methods developed by Jacob Ziv and Abraham Lempel in the 1970s (Ziv and Lempel 1977, 1978). We label the methods LZ77 and LZ78, respectively, after the years in which they were published; some authors refer to the two methods as LZ1 and LZ2, respectively. They are only rarely referred to as being "ZL" methods, even though this is the ordering of the authorship of the seminal papers in which they are described. These methods are the basis for many schemes that are widely used in utilities for compressing and archiving, although they have undergone much fine-tuning since their invention.

Both methods use a simple principle to achieve adaptivity: a substring of text is replaced with a pointer to where it has occurred previously. Thus, the codebook is essentially all the text prior to the current position, and the codewords are represented by pointers. The prior text makes a very good dictionary since it is usually in the same style and language as upcoming text; furthermore, the dictionary is transmitted implicitly at no cost because the decoder has access to all previously encoded text. The many variants of Ziv-Lempel coding differ primarily in how pointers are represented and in the limitations they impose on what the pointers are able to refer to.

The LZ77 family of adaptive dictionary coders

One of the key features of LZ77 (Ziv and Lempel 1977) and its successors is that it is relatively easy to implement, and decoding can be performed extremely quickly using only a small amount of memory. For these reasons it is particularly suitable when the resources required for decoding must be minimized, such as when data is distributed or broadcast from a central source to a number of small computers.

Like many compression methods, LZ77 is most easily explained in terms of its decoding. Figure 2.32 shows some output from an LZ77 encoder, supposing for the purposes of the example that the input alphabet consists of just *as* and *bs.* The output consists of a series of triples. The first component of a triple indicates how far back to look in the previous (decoded) text to find the next phrase, the second component records how long the phrase is, and the third gives the next character from the input. The first two items constitute a pointer back into the text. Strictly, the third is necessary only when the character to be coded does not occur anywhere in the previous input; it is included in every triple for the sake of simplicity.

In Figure 2.32, the characters *abaabab* have already been decoded, and the next characters to be decoded are represented by the triple $\langle 5, 3, b \rangle$. Thus the decoder

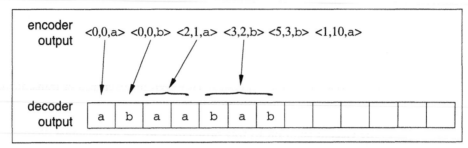

Figure 2.32 Example of LZ77 compression.

goes back five characters in the decoded text (to the third one from the start) and copies three characters, yielding the phrase *aab*. The third item in the triple, *b*, is then added to the output. The next triple, $\langle 1, 10, a \rangle$, is a recursive reference. To decode it, the decoder starts copying from one character back (the *b*) and copies the next 10 characters. Despite the recursive reference, each of the characters will be available before it is needed, yielding 10 consecutive *b*s. In this way, a kind of run-length coding is achieved.

LZ77 places limitations on how far back a pointer can refer and the maximum size of the string referred to. For English text there is little advantage in allowing the reach of pointers to exceed a window of a few thousand characters. For example, if the window is limited to 8,192 characters, then the amount of text it holds is equivalent to several book pages, and the first component of the triple can be represented in 13 bits. Extending the reach of the pointer beyond this makes more text available for referencing, but the gain is generally offset by the extra cost of storing the pointer. The second component of the triple, the length of the phrase, is also limited, typically to about 16 characters. Again, matches longer than this are rare and do not justify allocating extra space to the number representing the length of the phrase.

Algorithms for LZ77 encoding and decoding are shown in Figure 2.33. The search for a match may return a length of zero, in which case the position of the match is not relevant. Notice that the decoder is simply a small loop that copies from an array. In practice the array can be a circular buffer of W characters, and characters are written to the output as they are decoded.

The LZ77 method has gradually been refined into systems that have fast implementations and give good compression. There are some straightforward ways to improve the method described above. It is common to use different representations for the pointers. For the first component (the offset), it can be effective to use shorter codewords for recent matches and longer codewords for matches further back in the window, because recent matches are more common than distant ones. The second component of a pointer (the match length) can be represented more efficiently with variable-length codes that use fewer bits to represent smaller numbers. Also, in many schemes the third element of the triple, the character, is included only when necessary. For example, a one-bit flag can be used to indicate whether the next

---

To encode the text $S[1 \ldots N]$ using the LZ77 method, with a sliding window of W characters,

1. Set $p \leftarrow 1$. /* the next character of S to be coded */
2. While there is text remaining to be coded do
   (a) Search for the longest match for $S[p \ldots]$ in $S[p - W \ldots p - 1]$. Suppose that the match occurs at position m, with length l.
   (b) Output the triple $\langle p - m, l, S[p + l] \rangle$.
   (c) Set $p \leftarrow p + l + 1$.

To decode the text $S[1 \ldots N]$ using the LZ77 method, with a sliding window of W characters,

1. Set $p \leftarrow 1$. /* the next character of S to be decoded */
2. For each triple $\langle f, l, c \rangle$ in the input do
   (a) Set $S[p \ldots p + l - 1] \leftarrow S[p - f \ldots p - f + l - 1]$.
   (b) Set $S[p + l] \leftarrow c$.
   (c) Set $p \leftarrow p + l + 1$.

Figure 2.33 Encoding and decoding using LZ77.

```
"I never heerd a skilful old married
feller of twenty↵years' standing
pipe ''my wife'' in a more used not
e↵than 'a did," said Jacob Smallbury. "
It might have been↵a little more true
to nater if't had been spoke a little↵
chillier, but that wasn't to be
 expected just now.↵"That improvement
will come wi' time," said Jan,↵
twirling his eye.↵Then Oak laughed
, and Bathsheba smiled (for she↵never
laughed readily now), and their friends
 turned to↵go.↵
```

Figure 2.34 Coding of Hardy's book using an LZ77-type method.

item in the output is a pointer (offset and match length) or a character. Figure 2.34 shows how part of the Hardy book is coded using an LZ77-based method. Boxes are drawn around characters that can be coded as pointers. The rest of the characters could not be coded economically as part of a pointer and were transmitted as "raw" characters. It is interesting to compare this coding with the one shown in Figure 2.24 on page 64, which shows the PPM algorithm: both methods tend to have difficulty with the same parts of the text.

Encoding for LZ77 involves searching the window of prior text for the longest match with the upcoming phrase. A naive linear search is very time-consuming and can be accelerated by indexing the prior text with a suitable data structure, such as a trie,[4] hash table, or binary search tree. A simple but effective method of searching is to use an index of pairs of characters in the window. Each entry in the index is the head of a linked list that points to each occurrence of the given pair of characters in the window. This can greatly decrease the number of matches that need to be evaluated. The index could be a two-dimensional array, a hash table, or a structure that stores just the more popular character pairs. Speed can be guaranteed at the expense of slight compression loss by limiting how much of the linked list is searched. The characters in the window can be stored in a circular buffer, so very little data movement is required to maintain the window.

Decoding for LZ77-type methods is very fast because each character decoded requires just one array lookup; moreover, the array is small compared to the cache size of current computers, so the lookup is likely to be very fast. The decoding program is very simple, so it can be included with the data at very little cost—in fact, the compressed data is stored as part of the decoder program, so the user sees just one file. This makes the data self-expanding, in that the original compression software is not needed to read it. For example, a compressed file could be downloaded from a network and expanded without needing any extra software. It is common to distribute files using this technique. When executed, this "program" generates the original file or files, greatly simplifying the distribution and installation of software and data.

The *gzip* variant of LZ77

One of the higher-performance compression methods based on LZ77 is *gzip*, distributed by the Gnu Free Software Foundation in Cambridge, Massachusetts (Gailly 1993). It contains many worthwhile refinements and so is described in a little more detail here.

Gzip uses a hash table to locate previous occurrences of strings. The next three characters to be coded are hashed, and the resulting value is used to look up a table entry. This is the head of a linked list that contains places where the three characters have occurred in the window. At the expense of a small loss in compression, the length of the linked list is restricted to prevent search time from growing too much. The size of the limit on the list length can be chosen at encoding time, so that the speed/compression trade-off is made by the user. Having a limit is particularly important if the input contains long runs of the same character because this results in a very long list of references. Long lists are time-consuming to maintain and are un-

---

4 A trie is a multiway tree with a path for each string inserted in it, which allows rapid location of strings and substrings, and is discussed in more detail on page 80.

necessary because the first few items in the list will usually be more than sufficient to find a good match. Compression can be improved slightly by storing recent occurrences at the beginning of the linked list, in order to favor recent matches. Matches are represented in the encoded file by a pointer consisting of an offset and a length. If no suitable previous occurrence can be found, a raw character is transmitted. The offset of a pointer is represented using a Huffman code so that more frequent offsets (usually recent ones) are coded in fewer bits. The match length is represented by another Huffman code, and the same code is also used for raw characters. It may seem contradictory to combine the match lengths and raw characters into one code, but in fact this gives better compression because if they were separated, an extra bit would need to be transmitted to indicate whether the next input is a match length or a character; the combined code, however, can use less than one bit on average. The match length is sent before the offset of a pointer so that the decoder can tell whether a pointer or a raw character is being transmitted.

As described so far, the matching algorithm for *gzip* is "greedy"—it codes the upcoming characters as a pointer if at all possible. Sometimes, long-term compression is actually better if a raw character is transmitted, even though a pointer could be used. This occurs when the use of a raw character gives a better match for the characters immediately following the one about to be coded. If the user specifies that compression is more important than speed, *gzip* checks for this situation and transmits a raw character if that yields better compression in the long run.

The Huffman codes for *gzip* are generated semi-statically. Blocks of up to 64 Kbytes from the input file are processed at a time. The appropriate canonical Huffman codes are generated for the pointers and raw characters, and a code table is placed at the beginning of the compressed form of the block. This means that *gzip* is not really a single-pass method. However, the blocks are small enough to be held in memory. As a result, the input file need be read only once, and the program behaves as if it operates in one pass.

Because of the fast searching algorithm and compact output representation based upon Huffman codes, *gzip* outperforms most other Ziv-Lempel methods in terms of both speed and compression effectiveness. One implementation that is faster is the LZRW1 method, which achieves extremely fast encoding and decoding by limiting the search of previous text to just one candidate phrase (Williams 1991b). As with *gzip*, a hash table is used to locate previous occurrences of triples of characters. However, the table has just one entry for each hashed value, so a collision results in the previous phrase at that hash location being lost. Further time is saved by updating the hash table only with triples that begin a coded phrase; that is, it is updated only once per phrase coded, rather than once per byte in the input. Simple byte-aligned binary codes are used for all output components. This ruthless housekeeping results in considerable speed, at the price of compression performance. Performance measurements for these methods are given in Section 2.8.

The LZ78 family of adaptive dictionary coders

In contrast to the LZ77 method, in which pointers can refer to any substring in the window of prior text, the LZ78 method (Ziv and Lempel 1978) places restrictions

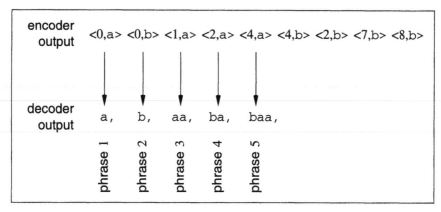

Figure 2.35 A string compressed by LZ78.

on which substrings can be referenced. However, it does not have a window to limit how far back substrings can be referenced. By restricting the set of strings that can be referenced, LZ78 avoids the inefficiency of having more than one coded representation for the same string, which occurs frequently in LZ77 methods since the window will often contain many repeated substrings.

Figure 2.35 shows a string being decoded by LZ78. The text prior to the current coding position has been parsed into substrings, and only these parsed phrases can be referenced. They are numbered in sequence, so phrase number 1 is *a*, number 2 is *b*, number 3 is *aa*, and so on. The characters about to be encoded are represented by the number of the longest parsed substring that the characters match, followed by an explicit character. The next part of the encoder output to be decoded is the pair $\langle 4, b \rangle$, which represents phrase 4 (*ba*) followed by a *b*. The characters just decoded (*bab*) are added to the dictionary as a new phrase, number 6. The remaining pairs represent a run of consecutive *b*s. The code $\langle 2, b \rangle$ represents *bb*, and in the remainder of the example the phrases used to code the run gradually increase in length, one character at a time.

Phrase 0 is the empty string, so if there is no match with a previous phrase then the next character, say, *c*, can always be coded as $\langle 0, c \rangle$.

The parsing strategy can be implemented efficiently by storing the phrases in a trie data structure (sometimes also known as a digital search tree). Figure 2.36 shows the trie for the parsed phrases of Figure 2.35. The characters of each phrase specify a path from the root of the trie to the node that contains the number of the phrase. The characters that are about to be encoded are used to traverse the trie until the path is blocked, either because there is no onward path for the indicated character or because a leaf is reached. The node at which the block occurs gives the phrase number to output. The next character from the input is then used to add a new node below this one, and this is how new phrases are added to the codebook. In the example, when the phrase *bab* was being encoded, the first two characters (*ba*) were used to traverse the trie to node 4, and then the extra branch from this node was

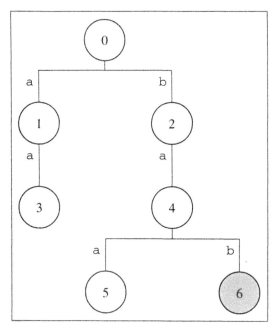

Figure 2.36 Trie data structure for LZ78 coding.

added to create node 6 (shown shaded in Figure 2.36). Thus, the longest previous phrase (phrase 4) is found, and the structure is updated with the new phrase at the same time. In practice, the multiway branches of a trie are tricky to implement efficiently because most nodes have relatively few children if the input alphabet is large, requiring an efficient representation for the sparse array of pointers. It can be faster and simpler to use a hash table in which the current node number and the next input character are hashed to determine where the next node can be found.

The data structure for an LZ78 compressor continues to grow throughout coding, and eventually growth must be stopped to avoid using too much memory. Several strategies can be used when memory is full. The trie can be removed and reinitialized; it can be used as it is, without further updates; or it can be partially rebuilt using the last few hundred bytes of coded text, thereby avoiding much of the learning penalty of starting again from scratch.

Although encoding for LZ78 can be faster than for LZ77, decoding is slower because the decoder must also store the parsed phrases. Nevertheless, the scheme is attractive, and one of its variants, LZW, forms the basis of several widely used compression systems.

The LZW variant of LZ78

LZW (Welch 1984) is one of the more popular variants of Ziv-Lempel coding, partly because the paper describing it is more accessible than Ziv and Lempel's 1978 one in

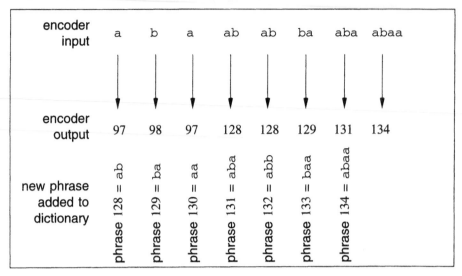

Figure 2.37   Example of LZW coding.

which the original idea was proposed. It has been used as the basis of several popular programs, including the Unix *compress* program and some personal computer archiving systems.

The main difference between LZW and LZ78 is that LZW encodes only the phrase numbers and does not have explicit characters in the output. This is made possible by initializing the list of phrases to include all characters in the input alphabet. A new phrase is constructed from a coded one by appending the first character of the *next* phrase to it. Figure 2.37 shows a string that has been partially coded. The phrases are numbered from 128 because 0 to 127 are used to represent the 128 characters of the ASCII alphabet. Each phrase is coded as a single number that identifies a previously parsed phrase. For example, the eighth and ninth characters, *ba*, are represented by transmitting the number 129 to identify a phrase that was constructed earlier. The new phrase to be added after the *ba* is received is constructed by adding the next character, *a* (not yet coded), to the phrase, creating the new phrase *baa*, which is number 133. Next, the phrase *aba* is coded as the number 131. It is only at this point that the decoder can construct phrase 133 because it needs to use the first character of phrase 134 (*abaa*).

This lag in construction of phrases is not a problem unless a new phrase is used by the encoder immediately after it is constructed. The last phrase in Figure 2.37 shows how this situation can arise for the decoder. The first seven phrases have been decoded, and the phrase *abaa* (number 134) has just been added to the encoder's dictionary. The decoder does not yet know what the last character of the phrase is, so it cannot be added to the decoder's dictionary. The next input codeword, 134, now requires the use of the new phrase. Fortunately, the decoder knows the beginning of the new phrase—it is *aba*—and the last (currently unknown) character

To encode the text $S[1 \ldots N]$ using the LZW method,

1. Set $p \leftarrow 1$. /* the next character of S to be coded */

2. For each character $d \in 0 \ldots q - 1$ in the alphabet do /* initial dictionary */
   Set $D[d] \leftarrow$ character d.

3. Set $d \leftarrow q - 1$. /* d points to the last entry in the dictionary */

4. While there is text remaining to be coded do

   (a) Search for the longest match for $S[p \ldots]$ in D.
       Suppose that the match occurs at entry c, with length l.

   (b) Output the code c.

   (c) Set $d \leftarrow d + 1$. /* add an entry to the dictionary */

   (d) Set $p \leftarrow p + l$.

   (e) Set $D[d] \leftarrow D[c] ++ S[p]$. /* concatenation */

To decode using the LZW method,

1. Set $p \leftarrow 1$. /* the next character of S to be decoded */

2. For each character $d \in 0 \ldots q - 1$ in the alphabet do
   Set $D[d] \leftarrow$ character d.

3. Set $d \leftarrow q - 1$. /* d points to the last entry in the dictionary */

4. For each code c in the input do

   (a) If $d \neq (q - 1)$ then /* first time is an exception */
       Set last character of $D[d] \leftarrow$ first character of $D[c]$.

   (b) Output $D[c]$.

   (c) Set $d \leftarrow d + 1$. /* add an entry to the dictionary */

   (d) Set $D[d] \leftarrow D[c] ++ ?$. /* last character is currently unknown */

Figure 2.38   Encoding and decoding using LZW.

of the phrase is the first character of the next phrase (number 135). Since phrase 135 will be constructed by appending one character to phrase 134, phrase 135 must begin with the same character as phrase 134, an *a*. Thus, phrase 134 must be *abaa*, and decoding can proceed. In fact, whenever a phrase is referenced as soon as the encoder has constructed it, the last character of the phrase must be the same as its first, so the decoder can construct the phrase too. Despite the slight inelegance of having to deal with this exception, LZW gives good compression and is relatively easy to implement efficiently.

The LZW algorithms for encoding and decoding are shown in Figure 2.38. The dictionary D is initialized to contain the q symbols in the alphabet (typically $q = 256$ for bytewise coding). The text is coded by looking for the longest match in

```
"I never heerd a skilful old married
 feller of twenty↵years' standing
 pipe ''my wife'' in a more used note
↵than 'a did," said Jacob Smallbury. "I
t might have been↵a little more true
to nater if't had been spoke a little↵c
hillier, but that wasn't to be
expected just now.↵"That improvement w
ill come wi' time," said Jan,↵twirli
ng his eye.↵Then Oak laughed, and
 Bathsheba smiled (for she↵never laughe
d readily now), and their friends
 turned to↵go.↵
```

Figure 2.39 Phrases parsed by Unix *compress* coding the Hardy book.

the dictionary, and a new entry is created at each step by concatenating the next input symbol with the code just used (concatenation of strings is represented by "++"). The decoder begins with the same initial dictionary and adds an entry each time an input code is processed. However, the last character of the last entry in the dictionary (entry *d*) is unknown until the next code is read from the input, and it is represented by a question mark in Figure 2.38.

There are several variants to LZW, which are the result of fine-tuning. The Unix utility *compress* is one of the more widely used variants. Here, the number of bits used to indicate phrases is gradually increased instead of using more bits than necessary when there are few phrases in the dictionary. *Compress* also places a maximum on the number of phrases that are constructed, which in turn limits the amount of memory required for coding. When the dictionary is full, adaptation ceases. Compression performance is monitored, and if it deteriorates significantly, the dictionary is cleared and rebuilt from scratch. Figure 2.39 shows how the Hardy book is parsed into phrases by *compress*. A box is drawn around each phrase that is transmitted. This segment is from the end of the book, and each phrase is represented in 15 bits. The dictionary contains many common phrases at this stage, such as *never* and *ave been.* Only rarely is a single character coded as a 15-bit reference, and whole words are often represented by a single pointer.

Many other variations on Ziv-Lempel coding have been proposed. They can be classified according to how they parse strings from the input, how they represent pointers in the output, and how they prevent the dictionary from using too much memory. Hybrids of LZ77 and LZ78 have also been described; these build up a limited list of previous strings that can be referenced but also allow the length of the string to be specified so that partial matches can be used.

2.7   Synchronization

Good compression methods, including most of the schemes described above, perform best when compressing large files. This tends to preclude random access because the decompression algorithms are sequential by nature. Full-text retrieval systems require random access, and special measures need to be taken to facilitate this.

There are two reasons that the better compression methods require files to be decoded from the beginning: they use variable-length codes, and their models are adaptive. With variable-length codes, it is not possible to begin decoding at an arbitrary position in the file since we cannot be sure of starting on the boundary between two codewords. The situation is even worse for arithmetic coding because there isn't a boundary between codewords. This section describes how this can be overcome by creating synchronization points.

Adaptive modeling exacerbates the situation because, even if a codeword boundary is known, the model required for decoding can be constructed only using all of the preceding text. To achieve synchronization with adaptive modeling, large files must be broken up into small sections of, say, a few kilobytes. It is not likely that good compression can be obtained by compressing each of the small sections independently. Instead, the compression model needs to be "primed" before the section is compressed. A good choice for the priming text is a sample of the text being compressed. The same sample can be used for all the sections, provided that their styles are similar. Alternatively, the sections could be grouped according to the kind of text that they store and a separate priming text used for each group. If speed is important, the system could store a primed model, rather than reconstruct it each time it is needed. However, the size of a model is generally much greater than the size of the text from which it is built.

For full-text retrieval it is usually preferable to use a static model rather than an adaptive one. Static models are more appropriate given the static nature of a large textual database, and the need for random access decoding is of paramount importance.

In this section we will look at two methods for achieving random access in compressed files. The first is *synchronization points*, where the coding is reset to a known state at certain points, and the second is *self-synchronizing codes*, which allow decoding to start at a random point because it will automatically come into synchronization after a while.

Creating synchronization points

In a full-text retrieval system, the main text usually consists of a number of *documents*, which represent the smallest unit to which random access is required. In an uncompressed text, a document can be identified simply by specifying how many bytes it is from the start of the file. However, when a Huffman code or other variable-length code is used, a document will not necessarily begin on a byte boundary. One solution is to give the bit offset of the document from the start of the file, requiring an additional three bits in each entry of the index.

An alternative to storing bit offsets is to insist that documents begin on byte boundaries, which means that the last byte of each document may contain some wasted bits. On average, 3.5 bits are wasted per document (a minimum of zero and a maximum of seven). Furthermore, with bit offsets, a Huffman decoder knows when it has reached the end of a document because the exact position of the start of the next document is known; but with byte offsets, the end of the document must be identified explicitly to prevent the decoder from trying to make sense of any waste bits in the last byte.

There are various ways to let a Huffman decoder know when to stop decoding. One way is to specify the length of each document at its beginning. Alternatively, a special "end of document" symbol could be encoded at the end of the text. Both of these methods use several bits—in fact, both typically require about $\log n$ bits for a document that is n characters long. A more efficient method, which wastes only one bit per document on average, is to store a code into the waste bits to say how many of them there are. The first waste bit is set to 0, and the remainder are set to 1. If there are no waste bits, then an extra byte must be added to create some waste bits so that the code can be stored. The decoder can now identify the waste bits by working backward from the last bit of the last byte of the compressed document, discarding all the 1s and the first 0 encountered. The next bit (still working from right to left) is the last meaningful bit of the document. The only cost of this code is the extra byte that must be added if there were no waste bits in the first place. This will happen once in eight documents on average and costs an extra eight bits, so the average cost is one bit per document. The same technique can be used for even coarser resolutions of addressing, with the same average cost of one bit per document. Hence, if compressed documents are quad-byte (word) aligned, then the average total synchronization cost is 16.5 bits per document.

Determining the trade-off between using bit and byte addressing (or even coarser resolutions) also depends on how many pointers are stored for each document—it may be that the document is referenced from more than one place. Furthermore, the document is very likely to be stored on disk, while the offsets may be stored in primary memory. One bit of memory is likely to be worth many bits of secondary storage, and in this case there can be no question that the offset representation should be minimized at the expense of extra space for the compressed documents.

An even more pressing reason for having coarse offsets is to fit them into a machine word. It is likely that 32 bits is a convenient limit to impose on the offset representation, at least until 64-bit computers become commonplace. With bit resolution addressing, this can address texts that are compressed to 2^{32} bits or less, which is about 512 Mbytes, or at most about 2 Gbytes of uncompressed data. It would not be unusual for this bound to be exceeded in a full-text retrieval system. A byte resolution address could deal with up to 16 Gbytes of uncompressed text. For larger texts, it may well be better to consider even coarser resolutions, rather than use a larger offset representation. Minimizing the length of offset representations is likely to be much more important than trying to save a few bits in the compressed document, unless the documents are very small (such as sentences or lines of text)—and even then only if disk space is at a premium.

The discussion above applies to integral-length codes, such as Huffman codes. Synchronization of arithmetic codes incurs an even larger overhead than Huffman codes. An arithmetic encoder must be stopped and have its output flushed before each boundary because the coder usually has some output pending that is needed by the decoder to complete the decompression of the data. There is a small overhead in stopping the encoder—the output is typically about one bit longer than the entropy of the model. A more significant overhead is caused by the need to mark the end of a file. Because several input characters may be represented as one output bit, reaching the last bit of a compressed document does not identify exactly when to stop decoding. The length of the uncompressed document must be stored explicitly or an "end of document" symbol stored. Both of these cost about $\log n$ bits. These overhead bits are often sufficient to make an arithmetic coder give *worse* compression than a Huffman coder in full-text retrieval applications, an effect that is most pronounced when documents are short (Bookstein and Klein 1993). The number of bits needed to identify the end of the file could be reduced by storing only the number of symbols that should be decoded from the last bit of the compressed file, which is likely to be a very small number, but the saving is unlikely to justify the level of complexity introduced.

Self-synchronizing codes

A possible alternative to creating synchronization points in a text is to use a self-synchronizing code. With a self-synchronizing code, if decoding begins in the middle of a compressed file, the decoder soon latches on to the correct synchronization cycle and thereafter remains in step. Self-synchronizing codes are not particularly useful for full-text retrieval because it is not always possible to guarantee how quickly they will synchronize. They deserve mention, however, since we are talking about random access to compressed text. The original motivation for self-synchronizing codes was to enable a message to be decoded even if an early part of it is corrupted or if the beginning is missing, but they are also suitable if the system is to begin reading from a random point in the text.

Table 2.5 shows a variable-length code for the English alphabet. The code has been designed to be self-synchronizing. Figure 2.40a shows how the word *andrew* is represented using the code. Figure 2.40b shows what would be decoded if the decoder started two bits too late. The decoder synchronizes after the *d* is transmitted, and the remainder of the message is decoded correctly.

It turns out that it is remarkably difficult to construct a variable-length code that is *not* self-synchronizing, although it is a matter of chance how quickly synchronization occurs if decoding begins at a randomly chosen point (Gilbert and Moore 1959). Figure 2.41 shows the result of a single bit being corrupted in a compressed file. Figure 2.41a shows the correct decoding of the text, while Figure 2.41b shows the effect of nine different single bits being corrupted in a file that has been compressed using a zero-order model and a Huffman code. Notice that the decoder usually resynchronizes within one or two characters. The worst case of the nine lines shown resulted in eight of the decoded characters being corrupted. Figure 2.41c

Table 2.5 A self-synchronizing code.

Symbol	Codeword	Symbol	Codeword
a	0011	n	0100
b	100010	o	0001
c	10010	p	00100
d	11011	q	1000000000
e	011	r	1010
f	00001	s	1011
g	100001	t	111
h	1100	u	10011
i	0101	v	100011
j	10000001	w	000001
k	1000001	x	100000001
l	11010	y	000000
m	00101	z	1000000001

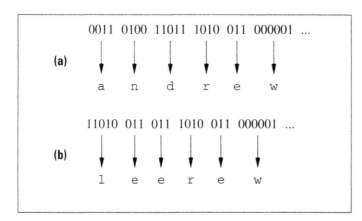

Figure 2.40 Decoding a self-synchronizing code: (a) without errors; (b) with errors.

shows the result of a single bit error when the same model is combined with arithmetic coding. Once the decoder goes off the track, it becomes hopelessly lost and never resynchronizes.

It has been shown that if a code is able to self-synchronize at all, there must be some sequence (or sequences) of input characters that always guarantee synchronization; that is, regardless of how the code got out of synchronization, it will resynchronize as soon as this special sequence occurs (Gilbert and Moore 1959). For example, for the code in Table 2.5, synchronization is guaranteed whenever the

(a)	chillier, but that wasn't to be expected just now.
(b)	chillier, bic that wasn't to be expected just now.
	chillier, bP that wasn't to be expected just now.
	chillier, bft that wasn't to be expected just now.
	chillier, b,t that wasn't to be expected just now.
	chillier, bmt that wasn't to be expected just now.
	chillier, budse, eonasn't to be expected just now.
	chillier, bueea aieonasn't to be expected just now.
	chillier, buh that wasn't to be expected just now.
	chillier, butan, eonasn't to be expected just now.
(c)	chillier, but thaswhrs eree " maem hcL t otaedgsrkeh

Figure 2.41 Effect of one corrupted bit in compressed files: (a) original text; (b) Huffman code with one bit flipped; (c) arithmetic coding with one bit flipped.

character d or k is coded. If an error occurs, there is a very high probability that one of these synchronizing characters will occur shortly afterward, and the effect of the error will be minimal. It is, however, possible to generate infinite sequences that never synchronize. For example, the reader might care to experiment with the sequence *hahahahaha . . .* —if the very first bit is dropped, the output is decoded as *gtftf . . . .* Of course, it is most unlikely that such sequences will occur in practice; nevertheless, the possibility remains.

We can force a code to be self-synchronizing by periodically inserting a special sequence that is not part of any other codeword, but this results in a loss of compression. In fact, any error-free compressed output that contains synchronization information must have room for more compression, since this information is available implicitly by decoding the text from its beginning.

Fixed-length codes cannot be self-synchronizing because once the decoder begins out of phase there is no way for it to get into step. However, the starting points of codewords can be calculated in this situation because they occur at multiples of the codeword length. Some static dictionary compression methods are particularly convenient for random access because they use fixed-length codes. For example, the digram coding method described in Section 2.6 uses eight-bit codewords, so decoding can begin at any byte. The price paid for such simple synchronization is that the method does not give particularly effective compression, and this makes it of limited interest. However, in conjunction with a standard pattern-matching program, digram coding does permit searching directly in compressed text—the pattern is simply compressed using the same algorithm and then the compressed pattern matched against the compressed text, saving both decoding time and file transfer time (Manber 1997). This is an appropriate mechanism for retrieving information from small data files, but linear search cannot be contemplated for large

Table 2.6 Representative compression methods.		
Method	Reference	Description
pack	Section 2.3	Zero-order, character-based, semi-static Huffman coder
char	Section 2.4	Zero-order, character-based, adaptive arithmetic coder
ppm	Section 2.5	Variable-order, character-based, adaptive arithmetic coder
bzip2	Section 2.5	Block-sorting compression, Huffman coder
dmc	Section 2.5	Variable-order, bit-based, adaptive arithmetic coder
huffword	Section 2.5	Zero-order, word-based, semi-static Huffman coder
gzip-f	Section 2.6	LZ77 paradigm, semi-static Huffman coder, *fast* option
gzip-b	Section 2.6	LZ77 paradigm, semi-static Huffman coder, *best compression* option
lzrw1	Section 2.6	LZ77 paradigm, binary coder, tuned for speed
compress	Section 2.6	LZ78/LZW paradigm, the Unix *compress* utility

collections, and, as we shall see in Chapter 3, there are much more elegant ways to attain the same result, using less disk space and less processor time.

Adaptive compression precludes self-synchronization because the encoder and decoder models become different as soon as any symbols are decoded incorrectly, and it is all but impossible for them to ever regain synchronization.

2.8   Performance comparisons

Choosing an appropriate compression method from the bewildering array of techniques available can be difficult. One method might be faster than others, while another gives better compression and yet another requires very little memory. The balance between computing resources needed to compress and decompress might be a significant consideration, or the main requirement may be the ability to access text randomly. In this section we summarize the main performance characteristics of the key players in the text compression stakes.

It is difficult to give definitive results because methods are gradually being improved, and the performance can depend on the type of data that is being compressed. Some recent results on compression performance can be accessed via the Web page *corpus.canterbury.ac.nz*. In this section, in order to quantify the performance of various compression methods, we give results for programs that implement a representative selection of the techniques described in this chapter.

Table 2.6 lists the programs compared. The *pack* program is a two-pass Huffman coder. The first pass counts the frequency of characters and uses them to generate a canonical Huffman code. The code—or rather, the codeword lengths—are placed at the beginning of the compressed file. The *char* program is a zero-order character-based adaptive coder using arithmetic encoding, with a modeling method similar to that of *pack*. Because the model is constructed adaptively, it can encode in a single pass. It is not intended to be useful in practice: much better models would normally be used with arithmetic coding. However, it does give an indication of the speed of arithmetic coding relative to Huffman coding. The *ppm* program uses a context model of five characters to predict characters, truncating this to smaller contexts where necessary.[5] An arithmetic coder is used to code characters with respect to the model. The *bzip2* program uses block-sorting compression with a Huffman coder (this is version 2; version 1 used arithmetic coding). Unlike the other methods, *dmc* codes a bit at a time instead of a character at a time. The bits are predicted by a finite-state model and coded using an arithmetic coder. The *huffword* program breaks the text up into words and nonwords, then uses canonical Huffman coding to represent these. It makes use of an auxiliary file to store the compression vocabulary, and this file must be counted as part of the space required by the compressed file. For a small compressed file, this overhead can be relatively large, but for files of several megabytes or more the cost is small. As we shall see later, this method is particularly suitable for integration with full-text retrieval systems.

Several Ziv-Lempel methods are also represented. As was described above, the *gzip* program is one of the better LZ77 implementations around. The output, which mainly comprises pointers to previous text, is coded using Huffman coding. In the experiments reported here, it was used in two modes: *gzip-f* gives *fast* compression by limiting how much searching it does for matches, while *gzip-b* gives *best* compression by searching extensively for previous occurrences of phrases. The *lzrw1* method is another LZ77-based coder. It achieves only moderate compression but does so extremely quickly by having very limited searches and a simple encoding of the output. The *compress* program is an LZ78-style coder that has been used widely on a variety of machines for some time.

Most of these programs are well tuned and are the culmination of a good deal of effort on the part of their authors. In some cases this effort has been invested most heavily in favor of speed, and in others the effort has been spent to obtain high compression rates. Any parameters needed for these methods have been chosen to reflect how each one is used in practice. Generally, the parameters are chosen to give good compression without being unduly slow or using too much memory.

Compression performance

The relative performance of various methods depends on the type of data that is being compressed. For example, a method that is good for bilevel images may not do so well on English text and vice versa. Fortunately, if we restrict ourselves

---

5 Results for *ppm* are better than in the first edition of this book because there we used a context of only three characters. The present five-character context is more in keeping with today's memory sizes. The escape calculation is also refined: these results use method D.

Table 2.7   The Canterbury corpus of text used to evaluate compression methods.

File	Bytes	Content
text	152,089	The text of Lewis Carroll's *Alice's Adventures in Wonderland*
fax	513,216	A fax bitmap image (CCITT test document 5)
Csrc	11,150	C source code
Excl	1,029,744	Excel spreadsheet
SPRC	38,240	Executable object code for Sun SPARC architecture
tech	426,754	Technical writing (workshop proceedings)
poem	481,861	*Paradise Lost* by John Milton
HTML	24,603	Hypertext Markup Language source
lisp	3,721	A Lisp program
man	4,227	A Unix manual page in the *roff* format
play	125,179	Shakespeare's play, *As You Like It*

to a particular style, such as English text, the relative performance of methods is quite consistent. In this section, the Canterbury corpus is used as a benchmark. This corpus is a collection of 11 texts that were chosen to test compression systems; it is a more modern form of the Calgary corpus, which has been widely used to evaluate compression methods since it was established in 1989. The Canterbury corpus—as was the Calgary corpus—is freely available to researchers (see the Web page *corpus.canterbury.ac.nz*), and results from many compression methods are available for both. Table 2.7 describes the files it contains: there are a variety of them, including English text, program source code, a bilevel fax image, HTML source, and a spreadsheet.

Figure 2.42 shows the compression performance of the methods in Table 2.6 for selected files from the Canterbury corpus. Here, compression is shown in bits per character, which is the average number of bits used to represent each character, or byte, of the input. We use this measure here because this figure can be related directly to the details given in this chapter—in Figure 2.24, for example. Various other measures of compression are in wide use. Another that we will use later is the percentage remaining, which is useful in many situations because it indicates more directly the amount of disk space required to store the compressed text.

The zero-order character coders (*pack* and *char*) give the worst compression on average, and *gzip*, *dmc*, *bzip2*, and *ppm* the best. All of the better systems are the subject of ongoing refinement, and the results given here are only coarse indications of relative performance. The *huffword* program does well on the files that naturally break up into words (English text and source code) but not so well on the other files, and on all of the files the cost of storing the list of words is a nontrivial component

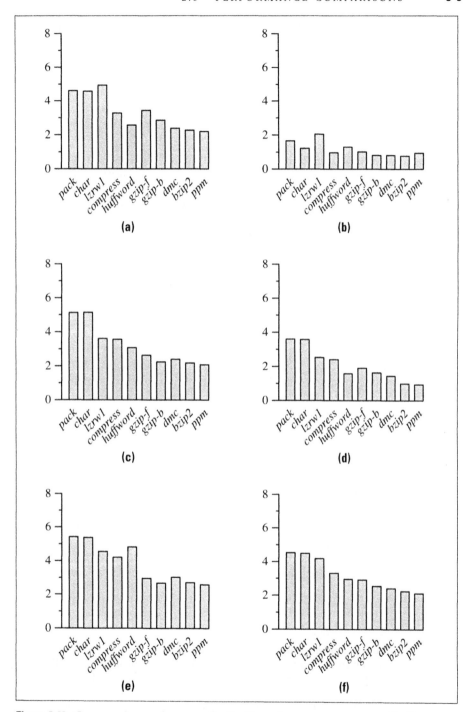

Figure 2.42 Compression performance for the Canterbury corpus, measured in bits per character: (a) English text; (b) fax image; (c) C program source code; (d) spreadsheet; (e) SPARC object code; (f) overall average.

of the compressed size. *Huffword* gives its best performance on files much larger than those used here, a point that is returned to in Chapter 9. The other Ziv-Lempel methods (*compress* and *lzrw1*) perform somewhere between the two extremes, and the tuning that has gone into *gzip* is apparent. All the methods perform well on the image file. This is because the long runs of zero entries in the file are picked up quickly by all the models. In the symbolwise models, zeros are soon given a high probability, while the dictionary models rapidly accumulate phrases to represent the long runs.

Will new methods be developed that give significantly better compression performance than the ones described here? Two indicators can be used to predict what might happen to compression performance in the future. One is an experiment in which human subjects are asked to make predictions of what characters will appear next in a text (Shannon 1951). A more refined form of the experiment involves having people place bets on the characters (Cover and King 1978). For example, you could show the phrase *There is no reverse on a motorcyc* to human subjects and ask them to gamble on what the next character would be. These bets can be used to make a probability estimate to code the next character. The experiment is repeated with many characters and on many subjects. Assuming that people have a better model of English text than any computer is likely to have, the compression performance that can be achieved with these human estimates gives a lower bound.[6] Researchers who have performed this type of experiment agree that the inherent entropy of English text seems to be about one bit per character. At present, the better compression methods can compress a version of the Bible to around 1.7 bits per character, while Hardy's book that was used in examples in this chapter can be compressed to about 2.2 bits per character. It is impossible to say which of the two contains the more typical English text (perhaps neither!), but either way there is apparently some room for improvement before machines can predict text as well as people can.

Another way to gain an idea of what might be achieved in the future is to extrapolate from past events. Figure 2.43 shows the amount of compression achieved by some of the more historically significant methods, plotted against the year in which they were published. Because it contains historic results that would in some cases be next to impossible to recompute, this illustration is based on the Calgary corpus, established in 1989, instead of the more recent Canterbury corpus of Table 2.7. Two points are plotted for PPM, the later one incorporating some improvements and

---

6   Of course, implementing a system that uses humans to make the estimates poses some practical problems. For a start, both encoder and decoder must use exactly the same probabilities, and if the authors of this book are typical, the two people involved would be completely unable to agree. Nor would the process be especially fast. And finally, even if a single person was responsible for making the probability estimates in both the encoder and, some time later, the decoder, it seems all but impossible that they could use *exactly* the same world knowledge when performing the two tasks.

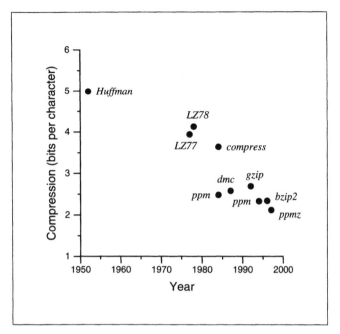

Figure 2.43 Compression effectiveness versus year of discovery of methods.

also being based on a five-character context rather than the earlier three-character one.

The graph shows that little progress has been made in the past decade. It appears that it is becoming increasingly difficult to achieve better compression and that researchers may be close to an inherent limit around the two bits per character mark. Some sort of breakthrough is needed for compression performance to increase significantly in the future. Such a breakthrough is likely to use grammatical or semantic information to increase the accuracy of predictions.

Compression speed

Measuring the speed of compression methods is difficult because it depends on how well the method has been implemented, the architecture of the machine that it runs on, and how good the compiler is. It can also be influenced by the type of file being compressed. We can get an idea of the speed of a method from the type of computation that must go on during encoding—for example, the sort of searching that is required—and the kind of operations that are needed to generate bits in the output.

As a rule of thumb:

The better the compression, the slower the program runs or the more memory it uses.

Table 2.8 Throughput (relative to the encoding speed of *compress*) for encoding and decoding, and average compression on the Canterbury corpus (bits per character and percent remaining).

Method	Relative speed		Compression	
	Encoding	Decoding	bpc	%
dmc	24.3	24.5	2.40	30.0
ppm	5.3	5.9	2.11	26.4
char	2.9	4.0	4.49	56.1
bzip2	5.5	2.0	2.23	27.9
pack	0.6	0.9	4.53	56.6
huffword	2.2	0.9	2.95	36.9
compress	1.0	0.6	3.31	41.4
lzrw1	0.7	0.4	4.18	52.3
gzip-f	1.1	0.4	2.91	36.4
gzip-b	7.0	0.3	2.53	31.6
null	0.2	0.2	8.00	100.0

To give a more concrete measure of speed, Table 2.8 shows the relative time taken by various compression programs to compress and decompress a 4 Mbyte text (the experiments were run on a 170 MHz Sun SPARCstation 5). The times are expressed relative to the compression time of version 4.0 of the *compress* program, a widely available compression utility. For example, a method with a relative time of 2 would take twice as long to compress a text as the *compress* program. Decompression times are normalized against the same value, so each program's compression time can be compared directly with its decompression time. The table is in order of increasing decoding speed. By coincidence, a normalized value of 1.0 represents about 1 second to encode 1 Mbyte of text on the SPARCstation 5. The speed measurements need to be taken with a grain of salt since one program might be more suited than others to the particular compiler or machine architecture being used.

The null method is well known to Unix users as the command *cat*, and it simply copies the input to the output. It is included to give an indication of the maximum speed that might be expected, although a compression program could potentially be faster than the null method because it has less output.

From the table it can be seen that the LZ77 methods (*gzip* and *lzrw1*) are the fastest for decoding, then the LZ78 technique, then the Huffman coders, while the slowest are those that use arithmetic coding. The amount of compression averaged over the 11 files of the Canterbury corpus is also shown in Table 2.8—these are the values plotted in Figure 2.42f. The *bzip2* program decodes particularly quickly considering the level of compression it achieves.

For the Ziv-Lempel methods, decoding is generally considerably faster than encoding. Decoding for the LZ77 methods is very fast indeed. Notice that the decoding speeds for *gzip-f* and *gzip-b* are nearly the same since it is only the encoder that does extra work. In fact, *gzip-b* decodes a little faster than *gzip-f* because it has less input to process. Methods for which encoding is slow but decoding is very fast are sometimes called *distribution* algorithms since they are useful in situations where a file is being distributed and is compressed once but decompressed many times. Notice that compared with *gzip-f*, *compress* gives worse compression, decodes slower, and encodes at nearly the same speed, so *compress* is effectively obsolete. However, since it may be necessary to decompress old files, *gzip* includes procedures to decompress *compress*-coded files, *pack*-coded files, and a third obsolete Unix compression tool called *compact*, which used a zero-order character-based model coupled with an adaptive Huffman coder and was noted for its slow performance.

For the two-pass methods—*huffword* and *pack*—the encoding time includes the cost of the preprocessing pass during which the model parameters are accumulated. This accounts for about half of the total encoding time for *huffword* but less than one-quarter of the time for *pack*. Even with two passes over the text during encoding, the static Huffman-based *pack* is about five times faster than the model-equivalent *char* program. The difference in speed is caused more by the complexity of arithmetic coding compared with canonical Huffman coding than by the fact that it is adaptive. For example, a static arithmetic coder would be about twice as fast as the adaptive coder that was tested. On the other hand, a dynamic Huffman coder would be slower than the adaptive arithmetic coder, and its slow speed is why the program *compact* never became popular. The general rule is the following:

Huffman coding is far better for static applications, and arithmetic coding is preferable in situations when the coding must be both adaptive and online.

When delayed one-pass coding is acceptable—when the input text may be buffered in memory until enough has been accumulated that a semi-static code can be economically used—Huffman coding again becomes the mechanism of choice. Note also that many of the LZ methods use binary or other ad hoc coding methods, neatly avoiding the resource implications of both Huffman and arithmetic coding.

Another interesting observation is that the zero-order *char* and third-order *ppm* are adjacent when ranked on speed. In fact, *ppm* uses an older (and slower) arithmetic coding implementation than the one described on page 56, and if instead it used the same routines as *char*, it would operate at an almost identical speed. Both perform roughly one arithmetic encoding step per character, and to do so they must spend some effort searching a list to locate each character. Hence, they have similar CPU requirements. Achieving high compression need not be at the cost of increased computing requirements. The bit-based *dmc* method is slower still, primarily because it does roughly eight times as many arithmetic encoding steps, although its model is simpler to maintain.

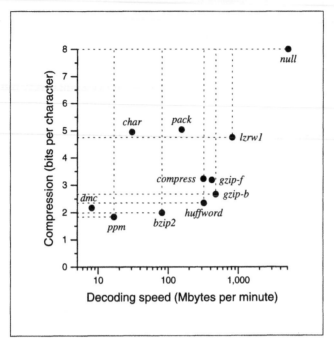

Figure 2.44 Compression effectiveness versus decompression speed (266 MHz Pentium II, 2 Gbytes of English text).

The evaluation presented above has concentrated on using the compression systems for general-purpose applications, with moderate-sized files. When considering the suitability of methods for very large full-text retrieval systems, the most important criteria are the decoding speed and the amount by which the file size is reduced. Figure 2.44 summarizes the performance observed on a file of about 2 Gbytes containing articles from a variety of newspaper and other published sources (this *TREC* collection will be described further in Chapter 3). The graph plots decompression rate versus compression effectiveness for all the methods discussed. Speeds are given in megabytes per minute to give a concrete idea of the throughput rates users can expect. All these experiments were run on a 266 MHz Pentium II under Debian GNU/Linux. Better compression and faster decoding are both desirable, and since points inside the envelope marked by the dotted lines (for example, *char* and *pack*) can be beaten both in terms of decoding speed and compression efficiency, they are not of practical interest. On the other hand, the points that establish the envelope (for example, *gzip-b* and *lzrw1*) are worthy of note since for each there is no single method that can beat it in terms of both speed and compression.

From the graph it is clear that compression systems based upon arithmetic coding incur a significant penalty in speed compared with those based on Huffman coding or Ziv-Lempel modeling. Also, the requirement of semi-static models to make two passes through the data does not necessarily mean that they will be slower, and the two-pass *pack* program is still faster than the adaptive but arithmetically coded *char*. Use of long symbols is also helpful. Much of the reason that *huffword*, *gzip*, and so on are fast for decoding is that each step decodes several characters at once, and this is an important principle to be borne in mind when designing a compression system.

Other performance considerations

When choosing the appropriate compression method to apply in a given situation, influential factors are the amount of memory available and any special features of the problem—such as the need for random access—that render certain methods particularly suitable.

All adaptive compression methods require a significant amount of memory during encoding and decoding in order to store tables specific to the text being encoded. In the case of Ziv-Lempel methods, the tables contain previously occurring strings, usually in some sort of indexed structure that allows rapid access. Symbolwise methods, such as *ppm* and *dmc*, store tables of contexts and the probability distributions of characters appearing within those contexts. In general, methods that give better compression use more detailed tables and require more memory to store them. The exact amount depends on what sort of data structure is used and may even depend on the type of data being encoded. In general, the Ziv-Lempel methods use a few tens of kilobytes of memory, while high-performance symbolwise methods such as *dmc*, *bzip2*, and *ppm* work best with hundreds of kilobytes, or even megabytes.

Further reading

Text compression. Several books about text compression are available. Bell, Cleary, and Witten (1990) and Salomon (1998) discuss many of the methods described in this chapter in more detail, and Nelson and Gailly (1995) provide source code for a variety of compression mechanisms.

Williams (1991a) gives a very detailed survey, as well as the results of extensive experiments with symbolwise methods. Storer (1988) covers many compression techniques, with a focus on dictionary-based methods. Recent research in data compression can be found in the proceedings of the annual IEEE *Data Compression Conference* (for example, Storer and Cohn 1997, 1998). There are also papers surveying text compression (Lelewer and Hirschberg 1987; Bell, Witten, and Cleary 1989) and a collection of papers covering several key areas (Storer 1992). A recent issue (Volume 2, 1997) of the *Computer Journal* was devoted to the subject of lossless compression. Jayant (1997) surveys a wide range of compression techniques and applications. A Web page that points to many data compression sites can be found at *www.internz.com/compression-pointers.html*.

Information theory. The foundations of information theory were laid by Shannon (1948) and Shannon and Weaver (1949) well before data compression itself became practical. The idea of separating the model and coder in compression systems was presented by Rissanen and Langdon (1981). A comparison of adaptive and nonadaptive compression has been made by Cleary and Witten (1984a).

The zero-frequency problem is discussed by Witten and Bell (1991), and a further estimation method is described by Howard and Vitter (1993a, 1994).

Huffman coding. Huffman coding was originally presented in 1952 (Huffman 1952). Several adaptive versions have been proposed (Gallager 1978; Cormack and Horspool 1984; Knuth 1985; Vitter 1989), and bounds on the inefficiency of Huffman coding have been derived by Gallager and others (Gallager 1978; Capocelli, Giancarlo, and Taneja 1986; Capocelli and De Santis 1991). Turpin and Moffat (1997) present a pseudoadaptive coder that combines in a one-pass online coder the adaptivity of a fully dynamic coder and the speed of a semi-static canonical coder. The same authors have also considered the details of using semi-static coding over blocks (Turpin and Moffat 1998). Andrew Turpin's 1998 Ph.D. thesis describes a range of prefix-coding techniques (Turpin 1998).

Lelewer and Hirschberg (1987) provide a summary of early work on prefix codes and have also examined the implementation of canonical coding (Hirschberg and Lelewer 1990). Choueka, Klein, and Perl (1985) and Siemiński (1988) have also examined the implementation of Huffman coding. Moffat and Turpin (1997) show how the canonical coding mechanism described in Section 2.3 can be further improved.

The Huffman code calculation mechanism described in Figure 2.13 is the unpublished work of Alistair Moffat. Katajainen and Moffat (1998) give an efficient mechanism for calculating Huffman codeword lengths when the set of symbol frequencies is presorted. Moffat and Turpin (1998) describe and analyze the use of run lengths to efficiently calculate Huffman codes for large alphabets. Most texts on data structures mention heaps (see, for example, Cormen, Leiserson, and Rivest 1990).

Arithmetic coding. One of the earliest discussions of arithmetic coding is by Rissanen and Langdon (1979). The approach to arithmetic coding described in this chapter is from Witten, Neal, and Cleary (1987). Other studies of arithmetic coding have been published (Rubin 1979; Howard and Vitter 1992a, 1994; Gräf 1997; Schindler 1998). The tree structure for cumulative counts was devised by Peter Fenwick at the University of Auckland in New Zealand (Fenwick 1994). A linear-time structure for maintaining cumulative frequency counts is described by Moffat (1990b). Structures for storing cumulative counts are discussed by Moffat, Neal, and Witten (1998). A comparison of several different coding methods, including Huffman and arithmetic coding, has been made by Moffat et al. (1994).

The PPM method. The PPM model was first described by Cleary and Witten (1984b) and refined by Moffat (1990a), Lelewer and Hirschberg (1991), and Howard and Vitter (1993a). The PPM* method was first discussed by Cleary, Teahan, and Witten (1995). The Swiss Army Knife Data Compression system, covering many variants of PPM, was developed by Williams (1991a). Bunton (1997a, 1997c) has examined context-based compression in painstaking detail, and her 1997 Ph.D. thesis is a definitive work in the area. Recent ideas relating to improving PPM escape probabilities are discussed by Willems, Shtarkov, and Tjalkens (1995, 1996) and Åberg, Shtarkov, and Smeets (1997).

Block-sorting compression. Block-sorting compression is also known as the Burrows-Wheeler transform after its developers: the original description can be found in Burrows and Wheeler (1994). The description in this text has the contexts reversed from conventional descriptions, where a character is normally considered in terms of the context that it *precedes* rather than *follows*. Our reversal was done to make it more comparable with the PPM method, based on a paper about PPM* (Cleary, Teahan, and Witten 1995). A detailed study of block sorting is given by Fenwick (1996a, 1996b), who devised the *mississippi* example used in Figure 2.26. Implementation details and source code for a Burrows-Wheeler transform system are given by Nelson (1996).

The DMC method. The DMC method is described by Cormack and Horspool (1987), and its performance has been investigated by Bell and Moffat (1989) and Bunton (1995). The CRAM method is related to DMC (Ramabadran and Cohn 1989).

Word-based compression. Experiments with word-based compression are described by Moffat (1989), and other authors have also considered similar mechanisms (Bentley et al. 1986; Horspool and Cormack 1992). An implementation of an adaptive word-based compressor is included with the arithmetic coding routines mentioned above (Moffat, Neal, and Witten 1998). Moffat, Zobel, and Sharman (1997) consider the effect of using a partial first pass to establish a semi-static word-based compression model. One interesting development in modeling has been the use of the syntax of the Pascal programming language to aid compression (Cameron 1988; Katajainen, Penttonen, and Teuhola 1986).

Ziv-Lempel methods. There are many variations of LZ methods in the literature. The original methods are LZ77 (Ziv and Lempel 1977) and LZ78 (Ziv and Lempel 1978). Figure 2.34 shows the LZB method, described by Bell (1986b). This chapter also discusses the LZW method described in Welch (1984). A hybrid of the LZ77 and LZ78 methods is described by Fiala and Greene (1989). A variation of LZ coding called ACB (Associative Coder of Buyanovsky) that gives very good compression by using contexts has been described by Buyanovsky (1994). Nongreedy parsing for LZ coding is discussed by Horspool (1995). Data structures for accelerating the searching for LZ coding have also been examined (Bell 1986a; Williams 1991a; Bell and Kulp 1993).

The relationship between symbolwise and dictionary methods is discussed by Langdon (1983) and Witten and Bell (1991).

Synchronization. The self-synchronizing code in Table 2.5 is from Fergusson and Rabinowitz (1984). Gilbert and Moore (1959) show that variable-length codes are very likely to be self-synchronizing. Figure 2.41 is based on an example given by Bookstein and Klein (1993). Manber (1997) examines some of the issues raised when compression and string searching are coupled.

Evaluating compression performance. Extensive compression performance results and more information about the Canterbury corpus can be found on the World

Wide Web at *corpus.canterbury.ac.nz*. This site has recent evaluations and information about most of the programs discussed in this chapter. The Calgary corpus is also available via that site. Both corpora are discussed by Arnold and Bell (1997).

The programs evaluated in Section 2.8 are from a variety of sources: *pack* was written by Syzmanski at Princeton University; *char* is part of the package described by Moffat, Neal, and Witten (1998), with implementation carried out by John Carpinelli, Wayne Salamonsen, and Lang Stuiver; the *ppm* program was written by Alistair Moffat (1990a) based on the seminal description of Cleary and Witten (1984b); *bzip2* is version 2 of the *bzip2* program by Julian Seward based upon work by David Wheeler and Peter Fenwick; the *dmc* program is by Gordon Cormack at the University of Waterloo based on work jointly authored with Nigel Horspool (1987); *huffword* was written by Alistair Moffat, Gary Eddy, Justin Zobel, and Andrew Turpin (Zobel and Moffat 1995; Moffat and Turpin 1997) at the University of Melbourne; *gzip* by Mark Adler, Richard Wales, and Jean-loup Gailly of the Info-ZIP group (Gailly 1993); *lzrw1* by Ross Williams (1991b); and *compress* by S. Thomas and Joe Orost as an implementation of Welch's ideas (1984). The *ppmz* program is the work of Charles Bloom.

Entropy of natural languages. Shannon's experiments to measure the entropy of English (1951) have been developed further by Cover and King (1978). Bell, Cleary, and Witten (1990) give a summary of estimates of the entropy of several natural languages. The book without any *es* is *Gadsby* by E. V. Wright (1939). The recent doctoral thesis of Teahan (1998) provides a comprehensive overview and includes results for a range of word- and language-based compression models.

Indexing

Compressing the information to be stored in a full-text database is only part of the solution to the information explosion. The techniques described in Chapter 2 may save a great deal of disk space, making it possible to store far more than might otherwise be handled, but compression does nothing to address the issue of how the information should be organized so that queries can be resolved efficiently and relevant portions of the data extracted quickly. For that, an index is necessary.

Most people are familiar with the use of an index in a book—there is one at the end of this book, for example, and if you look up the word *index* in it, it should refer you to this page. Using an index, it is possible to find information without resorting to a page-by-page search, and, provided that the index itself can be understood, it is possible to locate relevant pages in a book even if the book is written in another language. Indeed, if you wanted to obtain information from a book written in a foreign language, having an index would save an enormous amount of effort, since a translator could then be employed to "decode" just the pages actually required rather than the entire book. Although this scenario may sound far-fetched, it is in fact exactly the situation we are advocating in this book since the compressed documents that are stored in an information retrieval system might as well be stored in a foreign language, and some translation cost must certainly be paid to access them.

A book without an index can give rise to great frustration. Most people, at some time or another, have looked through a book for something they are sure is there but they simply cannot find. Tracking down the telephone number of a government department in a telephone directory is one such task that immediately springs to mind—you are never quite sure whether to look for "Taxation Department," or "Department of Taxation," or "Federal Office of Revenue," and so on. (In New Zealand, the correct answer is "Inland Revenue Department"; in Australia, it is the

"Australian Taxation Office"; in Canada, it is "Revenue Canada" or "Revenu Canada"; and in the United States, it is universally known as the "IRS.")

This difficulty of searching is the result of an inadequate index or no index at all. Of course, with a normal book (including this one) it is possible to skim-read every page, with a reasonable chance of being able to zero in, by various contextual clues, to the desired section. But with computers we are talking about gigabytes of data, millions of pages rather than hundreds, and with little structure and no contextual clues such as headings. Casual browsing of this much data by human means would be very costly, and even exhaustive searching by mechanical means is expensive. If no index is available, efforts to extract information are doomed to failure. For this reason, it is crucial to the success of an automated retrieval system that the stored information be accurately and comprehensively indexed; otherwise we might as well not have bothered accumulating the documents in the first place.

In this chapter we discuss a variety of indexing methods and show how the resulting indexes can themselves be compressed. For the most part it is supposed that a *document collection* or *document database* can be treated as a set of separate *documents*, each described by a set of *representative terms*, or simply *terms*, and that the index must be capable of identifying all documents that contain combinations of specified terms or are in some other way judged to be relevant to the set of query terms. A document will thus be the unit of text that is returned in response to queries.

For example, if the database consists of a collection of electronic office memoranda, and each memo is taken to be one document, then the representative terms might be the recipient's name, the sender's name, the date, and the subject line of the memo. It would then be possible to issue queries such as *find memos from Jane to John on the subject of taxation*. If a more detailed index is required, the entire text of the message might be regarded as its own set of representative terms, so that any words contained in the message could be used as query terms. If the documents are images, the terms to be indexed might be a few words describing each image, and a query might, for instance, ask that all images containing an *elephant* be retrieved. Note that in this latter case it is supposed that someone has examined the collection of images and decided in advance (by creating representative terms) which ones show elephants. The task of taking an arbitrary image and deciding mechanically what objects are portrayed is a major research area in its own right and is certainly not the subject of this book. Nevertheless, for certain restricted types of image, such as faxes and other scanned text, it is sometimes possible to infer a set of representative terms using OCR.

There will also be situations in which it is sensible to choose a document in the database to be one paragraph, or even just one sentence, of a source document. This would allow paragraphs that meet some requirement to be extracted, independent of the text in which they are embedded. In the previous example of office memos, it would be of dubious merit, but certainly possible, to define each field as one document—one document storing the sender, another the recipient, another the subject, and a fourth the actual message text. Similarly, it would be possible, but probably confusing, to store as a document a group of 10 memos on disparate topics. As in this example, it is normally easy to decide, for a given collection, what the documents should be.

The database designer is also free to choose the *granularity* of the index—the resolution to which term locations are recorded within each document. Having decided for the office information system that a document will be a single memo, the system implementer may still require that the index be capable of ascertaining a more exact location within the document of each term, so documents in which the words *tax* and *avoidance* appear in the same sentence can be located using only the index, without recourse to extensive checking of every document in which they appear anywhere.

In the limit, if the granularity of the index is taken to be one word, then the index will record the exact location of every word in the collection, and so (with some considerable effort) the original text can be recovered from the index. In this case it is unlikely that the index can be stored in less space than the least amount that is possible for the main text using a normal text compression algorithm. If it could, the index compression method could be used as a better text compression algorithm, and, given the discussion in Chapter 2, that seems unlikely.

When the granularity of the index is coarser—to the sentence or document level—the input text can no longer be reproduced from the index, and a more economical representation becomes possible. Most of this chapter is devoted to *index compression*, the problem of representing the index efficiently. Each entry in a document-level index is a pointer to a particular document, and for a collection of a million documents, such a pointer would take 20 bits uncompressed. However, it is possible to reduce this to about 6 bits for typical document collections, a very worthwhile saving indeed.

The database designer is also free to decide how the representative terms for textual documents should be created. One simple possibility is to take each of the words that appears in the document and declare it verbatim to be a term. This tends to both enlarge the vocabulary of the collection—the number of distinct terms that appear—and increase the number of document identifiers that must be stored in the index. Having an overlarge vocabulary not only affects the storage space requirements of the system but can also make it harder to use since there are more potential query terms that must be considered when formulating requests of the system. For these reasons it is more usual for each word to be transformed in some way before being included in the index.

The first of these transformations is known as *case folding*—the conversion of all uppercase letters to their lowercase equivalents (or vice versa). For example, if all uppercase letters are folded to lowercase, *ACT*, *Act*, and *act* are all indexed as *act* and are regarded as equivalent at query time, irrespective of which original version appeared in the source document. This transformation is carried out so that those querying the database need not guess the exact case that has been used and can pose case-invariant queries. Certainly, we would not wish to distinguish between the two sentences *Data compression . . .* and *Compression of data . . .* when querying on *data* AND *compression*—both sentences (or rather, the documents containing them) should be retrieved. Of course, as with most generalizations, there are counterexamples. In Australia, "ACT" stands for Australian Capital Territory, which is the seat of the federal government. This is quite different from the verb *to act* and only tenuously related to the noun *Act* (of parliament). And, given the authorship of this book, unification of *Bell* and *bell* might also introduce problems.

A second, less obvious, transformation is for words to be reduced to their morphological roots—that is, for all suffixes and other modifiers to be removed. For example, *compression*, *compressed*, and *compressor* all have the word *compress* as their common root. This process is known as *stemming* and is carried out so that queries retrieve relevant documents even if the exact form of the word is different. If the representative terms are created using stemming, and all query terms are also stemmed, the query *data* AND *compression* would retrieve documents containing phrases such as *compressed data is* and also documents containing the likes of *to compress the data*. It is difficult to deny the usefulness of this transformation, but the user needs to remember that it is taking place, as it can easily cause the retrieval of seemingly extraneous material.

A final transformation that is sometimes applied is the omission of *stop words*—words that are deemed to be sufficiently common or of such small information content that their use in a query would be unlikely to eliminate any documents since they are likely to be present in almost every document. Hence, nothing will be lost if they are simply excluded from the index. At the top of any stop word list for English is usually *the*, closely followed by *a*, *it*, and so on. Other terms might also be stopped in particular applications—in an online computer manual, appearances of the terms *options* and *usage* might not be indexed, and a financial archive might choose to stop words such as *dollar* and *stock* and perhaps even *Dow* and *Jones*. One automatic method that is sometimes used to derive a set of stop words is to determine, for each term, the extent to which it can be described by a random process, accepting as stop words those that appear in the collection as if they were randomly distributed.

All these transformations, and the effect they have upon index size, are considered in this chapter. A further possible transformation that we do not consider is that of *thesaural substitution*, where synonyms—*fast* and *rapid*, for example—are identified and indexed under a single representative term.

3.1   Sample document collections

To allow practical comparison of various algorithms and techniques, experiments have been performed on some real-life document collections. This section describes the four collections that have been used in preparing this book.[1] Some statistics for

---

1 Three of the four collections were modified slightly (to correct errors in the data) between 1993, when the results of the first edition of this book were prepared, and 1998, when the second edition was prepared. The stemming program used in 1998 is also different from that used in 1993. This is why most of the collection statistics listed in Table 3.1 are different from

Table 3.1 Statistics of document collections.

		Collection			
		Bible	*GNUbib*	*Comact*	*TREC*
Documents	N	31,101	64,343	261,829	741,856
Number of terms	F	884,994	2,570,906	22,805,920	333,338,738
Distinct terms	n	8,965	46,488	36,660	535,346
Index pointers	f	701,412	2,226,300	12,976,418	134,994,414
Total size (Mbytes)		4.33	14.05	131.86	2070.29

```
Genesis 1 1
In the beginning God created the heaven and the earth.

Genesis 1 2
And the earth was without form, and void; and darkness was
upon the face of the deep.  And the Spirit of God moved upon
the face of the waters.
```

Figure 3.1 Sample text from the *Bible* collection.

them are listed in Table 3.1. In Table 3.1, and throughout the remainder of this book, N is used to denote the number of documents in some collection; n is the number of distinct terms—that is, stemmed words—that appear; F is the total number of terms in the collection; and f indicates the number of *pointers* that appear in a document-level index. That is, f is the number of distinct "document, word" pairs to be stored—the size of the index.

Collection *Bible* is the King James version of the Bible, with each verse taken to be a document, including the book name, chapter number, and verse number. The first two documents in this collection, shown in Figure 3.1, are the well-known verses from Genesis.

The second collection, *GNUbib*, is a set of about 65,000 citations to papers that have appeared in the computing literature. These documents are again very short; for example, all of document number 8,425 is shown in Figure 3.2.

Collection *Comact* stores the Commonwealth Acts of Australia, from the 1901 constitution under which Australia became a federation through legislation passed in 1989. Each document in this collection corresponds to one physical page of an original printed version and contains 50 to 100 words. Two typical pages are

---

those listed in the corresponding table in the first edition. The various compression results in the remainder of this chapter are correct for the modified collections.

```
%A Ian H. Witten
%A Radford M. Neal
%A John G. Cleary
%T Arithmetic coding for data compression
%J Communications of the ACM
%K cacm
%V 30
%N 6
%D June 1987
%P 520--540
```

Figure 3.2 Sample text from *GNUbib*.

```
Page 92011
EVIDENCE AMENDMENT ACT 1978 No. 14 of 1978---SECT. 3.
``derived'' means derived, by the use of a computer or
otherwise, by calculation, comparison, selection, sorting or
consolidation or by accounting, statistical or logical
procedures;
``document'' includes---
(a) a book, plan, paper, parchment, film or other material
on which there is writing or printing, or on which there are
marks, symbols or perforations having a meaning for persons
qualified to interpret them;

Page 92012
EVIDENCE AMENDMENT ACT 1978 No. 14 of 1978---SECT. 3.
(b) a disc, tape, paper, film or other device from which
sounds or images are capable of being reproduced; and
(c) any other record of information;
``proceeding'' means a proceeding before the High Court or
any court (other than a court of a Territory) created by the
Parliament;
``qualified person,'' in relation to a statement made in the
course of, or for the purposes of, a business, means a
person who---
```

Figure 3.3 Sample text from *Comact*.

shown in Figure 3.3. As in all these examples, some liberties have been taken with formatting—line breaks have been altered and some white space has been removed.

The final collection that has been used is the first two disks of *TREC*, an acronym for Text REtrieval Conference. This is a very large document collection distributed to research groups worldwide for comparative information retrieval experiments. The documents in the first two disks of *TREC* are taken from five sources: the Associated Press newswire; the U.S. Department of Energy; the U.S. Federal Register; the *Wall Street Journal*; and a selection of computer magazines and journals published by Ziff-Davis. In these five subcollections there is a total of more than 2 Gbytes of text and nearly 750,000 documents. These documents are much longer than those of the other three collections, averaging about 450 words. One document in the Federal Register subcollection is more than 2.5 Mbytes long. All the documents contain embedded standard generalized markup language (SGML) commands; one document (selected because it matched the query *managing* AND *gigabytes*) is shown in part in Figure 3.4. In dealing with *TREC*, all the SGML tags were stripped out before any indexing took place, and the values reported in Table 3.1 exclude the SGML markup.

It is also worth stating the definition of *word* that was used to obtain the statistics in Table 3.1. A practical rule of thumb for identifying words for indexing is

---

A word is a maximal sequence of alphanumeric characters, but limited to at most 256 characters in total and at most four numeric characters.

The latter restriction is to avoid sequences of page numbers becoming long runs of distinct words. Without this restriction, the size of the vocabulary might be unnecessarily inflated. For example, *Comact* contains 261,829 pages, beginning with page 1. Using this definition, a string such as *92011* is parsed as two distinct words, *9201* and *1*. Similarly, queries on *92011* are expanded to become *9201* AND *1*, introducing some small but acceptable likelihood of *false matches*—documents that satisfy the query according to the index but in fact are not answers—on queries involving large numbers. For example, a document containing the text *totalling 9201, of which 1* would be retrieved as a false match. (A more robust but more expensive strategy is to expand a query on *92011* into *9201* AND *2011*, supposing that a similar rule had been used during the creation of the index.) Years, such as *1901*, at four digits, were preserved as words. Of course, this whole strategy would have to be revised for a document such as the dictionary of real numbers mentioned in Chapter 1 (page 11) (Borwein and Borwein 1990).

All the words thus parsed are then stemmed to produce index terms, as described in Section 3.7.

3.2 Inverted file indexing

An index is a mechanism for locating a given term in a text. There are many ways to achieve this. In applications involving text, the single most suitable structure is an *inverted file*, sometimes known as a *postings file* and in normal English usage as a *concordance*. Other mechanisms—notably *signature files* and *bitmaps*—can also be used and may be appropriate in certain restricted applications. The emphasis in this section is on inverted file indexing; signature file and bitmap indexing are discussed

```
<DOC>
<DOCNO> ZF07-781-012 </DOCNO>
<DOCID> 07 781 012.  </DOCID>
<JOURNAL> Government Computer News Oct 16 1989 v8 n21 p39(2)
* Full Text COPYRIGHT Ziff-Davis Pub.  Co.  1989.
</JOURNAL>
<TITLE> Compressing data spurs growth of imaging.  </TITLE>
<AUTHOR> Hosinski, Joan M. </AUTHOR>
<DESCRIPTORS> Topic:  Data Compression, Data Communications,
Optical Disks, Imaging Technology.  Feature:  illustration
chart.  Caption:  Path taken by image file.  (chart)
</DESCRIPTORS>
<TEXT>
Compressing Data Spurs Growth of imaging

Data compression has spurred the growth of imaging
applications, many of which require users to send large
amounts of data between two locations, an Electronic Trend
Publications report said.
    Data compression is an ''essential enabling technology''
and the ''importance of the compression step is comparable
to the importance of the optical disk as a cost-effective
storage medium,'' the Saratoga, Calif., company said in the
report, Data Compression Impact on Document and Image
Processing Storage and Retrieval.
    Document images need to be viewed at a resolution of 100
to 300 dots per inch, and files quickly grow to the gigabyte
or terabyte range, the report said.  Data typically
compresses at a 10-to-1 ratio, but can go up to a 60--to-1
ratio.
    ''Use of document imaging has been slow to unfold,'' but
it is gaining acceptability beyond desktop publishing, where
document imaging already has been used, researchers said.
However, document imaging can be complex and can be
misapplied, they said.  Also, vendors have changed standards
or used only subsets of the standards in their products.
    The Defense Department's Computer-Aided Logistics Support
(CALS) program and use of image compression format standards
will help the government avoid problems with interchanging
data between systems, researchers said.

[Three paragraphs omitted]

</TEXT>
</DOC>
```

Figure 3.4 Sample text from *TREC*.

Table 3.2   Example text; each line is one document.

Document	Text
1	Pease porridge hot, pease porridge cold,
2	Pease porridge in the pot,
3	Nine days old.
4	Some like it hot, some like it cold,
5	Some like it in the pot,
6	Nine days old.

in Section 3.5, and then Section 3.6 examines the factors that influence the choice of indexing method. However, as an initial rule of thumb:

In most applications inverted files offer better performance than signature files and bitmaps, in terms of both size of index and speed of query handling.

Let us now define exactly what we mean by an inverted file index. An inverted file contains, for each term in the lexicon, an *inverted list* that stores a list of pointers to all occurrences of that term in the main text, where each pointer is, in effect, the number of a document in which that term appears. The inverted list is also sometimes known as a *postings list* and the pointers as *postings*. This is perhaps the most natural indexing method, corresponding closely to the index of a book and to the traditional use of concordances as an adjunct to the study of classical tracts such as the Bible and the Koran.

An inverted file index also requires a *lexicon*—a list of all terms that appear in the database. (The word "vocabulary" is also used to denote this list. We prefer "lexicon" when talking about the data structure that holds the list and "vocabulary" when referring to linguistic aspects of the text.) The lexicon supports a mapping from terms to their corresponding inverted lists and in its simplest form is a list of strings and disk addresses.

As an example of an inverted file index, consider the traditional children's nursery rhyme in Table 3.2, with each line taken to be a document for indexing purposes. The inverted file generated for this text is shown in Table 3.3, where the terms have been case-folded but with no stemming applied and no words stopped. Because of the unusual nature of the example, each word appears in exactly two of the lines. This would not normally be the case, and in general, the inverted lists for a collection are of widely differing lengths.

A query involving a single term is answered by scanning its inverted list and retrieving every document that it cites. For conjunctive Boolean queries of the form *term* AND *term* AND . . . AND *term*, the intersection of the terms' inverted lists is formed. For disjunction, where the operator is OR, the union is taken; for negation

Table 3.3 Inverted file for text of Table 3.2.

Number	Term	Documents
1	cold	$\langle 2; 1, 4 \rangle$
2	days	$\langle 2; 3, 6 \rangle$
3	hot	$\langle 2; 1, 4 \rangle$
4	in	$\langle 2; 2, 5 \rangle$
5	it	$\langle 2; 4, 5 \rangle$
6	like	$\langle 2; 4, 5 \rangle$
7	nine	$\langle 2; 3, 6 \rangle$
8	old	$\langle 2; 3, 6 \rangle$
9	pease	$\langle 2; 1, 2 \rangle$
10	porridge	$\langle 2; 1, 2 \rangle$
11	pot	$\langle 2; 2, 5 \rangle$
12	some	$\langle 2; 4, 5 \rangle$
13	the	$\langle 2; 2, 5 \rangle$

using NOT, the complement is taken. The inverted lists are usually stored in order of increasing document number, so that these various merging operations can be performed in a time that is linear in the size of the lists. As an example, to locate lines containing *some* AND *hot* in the text of Table 3.2, the lists for the two words—$\langle 4, 5 \rangle$ and $\langle 1, 4 \rangle$, respectively—are merged (or, strictly speaking, intersected), yielding the lines that they have in common, in this case the list $\langle 4 \rangle$. This line is then fetched, using whatever mechanism is being used to store the main text, and finally displayed.

The *granularity* of an index is the accuracy to which it identifies the location of a term. A coarse-grained index might identify only a block of text, where each block stores several documents; an index of moderate grain will store locations in terms of document numbers; while a fine-grained one will return a sentence or word number, perhaps even a byte number. Coarse indexes require less storage, but during retrieval, more of the plain text must be scanned to find terms. Also, with a coarse index, multiterm queries are more likely to give rise to *false matches*, where each of the desired terms appears somewhere in the block, but not all within the same document. At the other extreme, word-level indexing enables queries involving adjacency and proximity—for example, *text compression* as a phrase rather than as two individual words *text* AND *compression*—to be answered quickly because the desired relationship can be checked before the text is retrieved. However, adding precise locational information expands the index by at least a factor of two or three compared with a document-level index since not only are there more pointers in the index (as explained below), but each one requires more bits of storage because it indicates a more precise location. Unless a significant fraction of the queries are expected to be proximity-based, the usual granularity is to individual documents. Proximity-

Table 3.4 Word-level inverted file for text of Table 3.2.

Number	Term	(Document; Words)
1	cold	$\langle 2; (1;6), (4;8) \rangle$
2	days	$\langle 2; (3;2), (6;2) \rangle$
3	hot	$\langle 2; (1;3), (4;4) \rangle$
4	in	$\langle 2; (2;3), (5;4) \rangle$
5	it	$\langle 2; (4;3,7), (5;3) \rangle$
6	like	$\langle 2; (4;2,6), (5;2) \rangle$
7	nine	$\langle 2; (3;1), (6;1) \rangle$
8	old	$\langle 2; (3;3), (6;3) \rangle$
9	pease	$\langle 2; (1;1,4), (2;1) \rangle$
10	porridge	$\langle 2; (1;2,5), (2;2) \rangle$
11	pot	$\langle 2; (2;5), (5;6) \rangle$
12	some	$\langle 2; (4;1,5), (5;1) \rangle$
13	the	$\langle 2; (2;4), (5;5) \rangle$

and phrase-based queries can then be handled by the slightly slower method of a postretrieval scan.

Table 3.4 shows the text of Table 3.2 indexed by word number within document number, where the notation $(x; y_1, y_2, \dots)$ indicates that the given word appears in document x as word number $y_1, y_2, \dots$. To find lines containing *hot* and *cold* less than two words apart, the two lists are again merged, but this time pairs of entries (one from each list) are only accepted when the same document number appears and the word number components differ by less than two. In this example there are no such entries, so nothing is read from the main text. The coarser inverted file of Table 3.3 gives two false matches, which require certain lines of the text to be checked and discarded.

Notice that the index has grown bigger. There are two reasons for this. First, there is more information to be stored for each pointer—a word number as well as a document number—and, given the discussion in Chapter 2, it is not surprising that more precise locational information requires a longer description. Second, several words appear more than once in a line. In the index of Table 3.3, duplicate appearances are represented with a single pointer, but in the word-level index of Table 3.4, both appearances require an entry. A word-level index must, of necessity, store one value for each word in the text (the value F in Table 3.1), while a document-level index benefits from multiple appearances of the same word within the document and stores fewer pointers (listed as f in Table 3.1).

More generally, an inverted file stores a hierarchical set of addresses—in an extreme case, a word number within a sentence number within a paragraph number within a chapter number within a volume number within a document number.

Each term location could be considered to be a vector (d, v, c, p, s, w) in coordinate form. However, within each coordinate the list of addresses can always be stored in the form illustrated in Table 3.4, and all the representations described in this chapter generalize readily to the multidimensional situation.

For this reason, throughout the following discussion it will be assumed that the index is a simple document-level one. In fact, given that a document can be defined to be a very small unit, such as a sentence or verse (as it is for the *Bible* database), in some ways word-level indexing is just an extreme case in which each word is defined as a document.

Uncompressed inverted files can consume considerable space and might occupy 50 to 100 percent of the space of the text itself. For example, in typical English prose the average word contains about five characters, and each word is normally followed by one or two bytes of white space or punctuation characters. Stored as 32-bit document numbers, and supposing that there is no duplication of words within documents, there might thus be four bytes of inverted list pointer information for every six bytes of text. If a two-byte "word number within a document" field is added to each pointer, the index consumes six bytes for roughly each six bytes of text.

For a text of N documents and an index containing f pointers, the total space required with a naive representation is $f \cdot \lceil \log N \rceil$ bits, provided that pointers are stored in a minimal number of bits.[2] Using 20-bit pointers to store the *TREC* document numbers gives a 324 Mbyte inverted file. This is already a form of compression compared to the more convenient 32-bit numbers usually used when programming, but even so, the index occupies a sizable fraction of the space taken to store the text. For the same collection, a word-level inverted file using 29-bit pointers requires approximately 1,200 Mbytes.

The use of a stop list (or rather, the omission of a set of stop words from the index) yields significant savings in an uncompressed inverted file since common terms usually account for a sizable fraction of total word occurrences. However, as will be demonstrated in the next section, there are more elegant ways to obtain the same space savings and still retain all terms as index words. Our favored approach is that all terms should be indexed—even if, to make query processing faster, they are simply ignored when present in queries.

3.3 Inverted file compression

The size of an inverted file can be reduced considerably by compressing it. This section describes models and coding methods to achieve this.

The key to compression is the observation that each inverted list can, without any loss of generality, be stored as an ascending sequence of integers. For example, sup-

---

2 The notation $\lceil x \rceil$ indicates the smallest integer greater than or equal to x; hence, $\lceil 3.3 \rceil = 4$. Similarly, $\lfloor x \rfloor$ denotes the greatest integer less than or equal to x; $\lfloor 3.3 \rfloor = 3$.

pose that some term appears in eight documents of a collection—those numbered 3, 5, 20, 21, 23, 76, 77, 78. This term is described in the inverted file by a list:

$$\langle 8; 3, 5, 20, 21, 23, 76, 77, 78 \rangle,$$

the address of which is contained in the lexicon. More generally, the list for a term t stores the number of documents f_t in which the term appears and then a list of f_t document numbers:

$$\langle f_t; d_1, d_2, \ldots, d_{f_t} \rangle,$$

where $d_k < d_{k+1}$. Because the list of document numbers within each inverted list is in ascending order, and all processing is sequential from the beginning of the list, the list can be stored as an initial position followed by a list of d-gaps, the differences $d_{k+1} - d_k$. That is, the list for the term above could just as easily be stored as

$$\langle 8; 3, 2, 15, 1, 2, 53, 1, 1 \rangle.$$

No information has been lost, since the original document numbers can always be obtained by calculating cumulative sums of the d-gaps.

The two forms are equivalent, but it is not obvious that any saving has been achieved. The largest d-gap in the second representation is still potentially the same as the largest document number in the first, and so if there are N documents in the collection and a flat binary encoding is used to represent the gap sizes, both methods require $\lceil \log N \rceil$ bits per stored pointer. Nevertheless, considering each inverted list as a list of d-gaps, the sum of which is bounded by N, allows improved representation, and it is possible to code inverted lists using on average substantially fewer than $\lceil \log N \rceil$ bits per pointer.

Many specific models have been proposed for describing the probability distribution of d-gap sizes. The ones we will look at are listed in Table 3.5, along with references to papers where they are described. They are grouped into two broad classes: *global* methods, in which every inverted list is compressed using the same common model, and *local* methods, where the compression model for each term's list is adjusted according to some stored parameter, usually the frequency of the term. Local models tend to outperform global ones in terms of compression and are no less efficient in terms of the processing time required during decoding, though they tend to be somewhat more complex to implement. Global models themselves divide into *parameterized* and *nonparameterized*, the latter being fixed codes and the former involving some parameter that can be tailored to the actual distribution of gap sizes. Local methods are always parameterized—otherwise there would be no point in using them.

Global models are generally outperformed by local ones, and the following rule holds:

For the majority of practical purposes, the most suitable index compression technique is the local Bernoulli method, implemented using a technique called Golomb coding.

Table 3.5 Some methods for compressing inverted files.

Method	Reference
Global methods	
Nonparameterized	
Unary	
Binary	
γ	Elias (1975); Bentley and Yao (1976)
δ	Elias (1975); Bentley and Yao (1976)
Parameterized	
Bernoulli	Golomb (1966); Gallager and Van Voorhis (1975)
Observed frequency	
Local methods	
Bernoulli	Witten, Bell, and Nevill (1992); Bookstein, Klein, and Raita (1992)
Skewed Bernoulli	Teuhola (1978); Moffat and Zobel (1992)
Hyperbolic	Schuegraf (1976)
Observed frequency	
Batched frequency	Moffat and Zobel (1992)
Interpolative	Moffat and Stuiver (1996)

In the subsections that follow, we work our way through these coding methods. If you are in a hurry, you can skip to the sections on global Bernoulli models (page 119) and local Bernoulli models (page 121), but the material on the other schemes provides a fascinating account of the development of different coding methods. These apply not just to index compression: they can be used for different purposes and in other applications.

Nonparameterized models

The simplest global codes are fixed representations of the positive integers. For example, as has already been considered, if there are N documents in the collection, a flat binary encoding might be used, requiring $\lceil \log N \rceil$ bits for each pointer.

Shannon's relationship between ideal code length l_x and symbol probability $\Pr[x]$, namely, $l_x = -\log \Pr[x]$, allows the probability distribution implied by any particular encoding method to be determined. The implicit probability model associated with a flat binary encoding is that each d-gap size in each inverted list will be uniformly random in $1 \ldots N$, which is not a very accurate reflection of reality.

Thinking of a code in terms of the implied probability distribution is a good way to assess intuitively whether it is likely to do well, and when considered in this light, it seems unlikely that all gap sizes are equally probable. For example, common

Table 3.6 Example codes for integers.

Gap x	Coding Method				
	Unary	γ	δ	Golomb	
				$b = 3$	$b = 6$
1	0	0	0	0 0	0 00
2	10	100	1000	010	001
3	110	101	1001	011	0100
4	1110	11000	10100	100	0101
5	11110	11001	10101	1010	0110
6	111110	11010	10110	1011	0111
7	1111110	11011	10111	1100	1000
8	11111110	1110000	11000000	11010	1001
9	111111110	1110001	11000001	11011	10100
10	1111111110	1110010	11000010	11100	10101

words are likely to have small gaps between appearances—otherwise, they could not end up occurring frequently. Similarly, infrequent words are likely to have gaps that are very large, although if documents are stored in chronological or some other logical sequence, it may well be that appearances of rare terms tend to cluster and be nonuniform throughout the collection. Thus, variable-length representations should be considered in which small values are considered more likely, and coded more economically, than large ones.

One such code is the unary code. In this code an integer $x \geq 1$ is coded as $x - 1$ one bits followed by a zero bit, so that the code for integer 3 is 110. The second column of Table 3.6 shows some unary codes. Although unary coding is certainly biased in favor of short gaps, the bias is usually far too extreme. An inverted list coded in unary will require d_{f_t} bits, since the code for a gap of x requires x bits, and in each inverted list the sum of the gap sizes is the document number d_{f_t} of the last appearance of the corresponding word. In total, an inverted file coded in unary might thus consume as many as $N \cdot n$ bits, and this quantity will generally be extremely large.

Looking at probabilities, it is apparent that the unary code is equivalent to assigning a probability of $\Pr[x] = 2^{-x}$ to gaps of length x, and this is far too small. However, unary coding does have its uses, and Chapters 4 and 5 describe some situations in which it is the method of choice.

There are many codes whose implied probability distributions lie somewhere between the uniform distribution assumed by a binary code and the binary exponential decay implied by the unary code. One is the γ code, which represents the number x as a unary code for $1 + \lfloor \log x \rfloor$ followed by a code of $\lfloor \log x \rfloor$ bits that represents the value of $x - 2^{\lfloor \log x \rfloor}$ in binary. The unary part specifies how many bits are required to code x, and then the binary part actually codes x in that many bits. For example, consider $x = 9$. Then $\lfloor \log x \rfloor = 3$, and so $4 = 1 + 3$ is coded in unary (code 1110) followed by $1 = 9 - 8$ as a three-bit binary number (code 001), which combine to give a codeword of $1110\,001$.

Other examples of γ codes are shown in the third column of Table 3.6. Although they are of differing lengths, the codewords can be unambiguously decoded. All the decoder has to do is first extract a unary code c_u, and then treat the next $c_u - 1$ bits as a binary code to get a second value c_b. The value x to be returned is then easily calculated as $2^{c_u-1} + c_b$. For the code $1110\,001$, $c_u = 4$, and $c_b = 1$ is the value of the next three bits, and so the value $x = 9 = 2^3 + 1$ is returned. Although it can be outperformed by some of the methods described below, the γ code is nevertheless much better for coding inverted file gaps than either a binary encoding or a unary encoding, and it is just as easy to encode and decode. It represents a gap x in $l_x \approx 1 + 2 \log x$ bits, so the implied probability of a gap of x is

$$\Pr[x] = 2^{-l_x} \approx 2^{-(1+2\log x)} = \frac{1}{2x^2}.$$

This gives an inverse square relationship between gap size and probability.

A more general way of looking at the γ code is to break it into two components: a unary code representing a value $k + 1$ relative to some vector $V = \langle v_i \rangle$ such that

$$\sum_{i=1}^{k} v_i < x \leq \sum_{i=1}^{k+1} v_i,$$

followed by a binary code of $\lceil \log v_k \rceil$ bits representing the residual value

$$r = x - \sum_{i=1}^{k} v_i - 1.$$

In this framework, the γ code uses the vector

$$V_\gamma = \langle 1, 2, 4, 8, 16, \ldots \rangle,$$

and $x = 9$ is coded with $k = 3$ and $r = 1$. Similarly, the unary code is relative (somewhat recursively) to the vector

$$V_U = \langle 1, 1, 1, 1, 1, \ldots \rangle.$$

Later in this section we will refer back to this general view of coding with respect to vectors.

A further development is the δ code, in which the prefix indicating the number of binary suffix bits is represented by the γ code rather than the unary code. Taking the same example of $x = 9$, the unary prefix of 1110 coding 4 is replaced by 11000, the γ code for 4. That is, the δ code for $x = 9$ is $11000\,001$.

In general, the δ code for an arbitrary integer x requires

$$l_x = 1 + 2 \lfloor \log(1 + \lfloor \log x \rfloor) \rfloor + \lfloor \log x \rfloor = 1 + 2 \lfloor \log \log 2x \rfloor + \lfloor \log x \rfloor$$

bits. Inverting this, the distribution implied is approximated by

$$\Pr[x] \approx 2^{-(1+2\log\log x + \log x)} = \frac{1}{2x(\log x)^2}.$$

Table 3.6 gives examples of δ codes for various values x. Although for the small values of x shown the δ codes are longer than γ codes, in the limit, as x becomes large, the situation is reversed. For a value of x such as 1,000,000, the δ code is superior, requiring 28 bits compared with the 39 bits of γ.

Global Bernoulli model

One obvious way to parameterize the model and perhaps obtain better compression is to make use of the actual density of pointers in the inverted file. Suppose that the total number of pointers to be stored (the quantity f in Table 3.1) is known. Dividing this by the number of index terms, and then by the number of documents, gives a probability of $f/(N \cdot n)$ that any randomly selected document contains any randomly chosen term. The pointer occurrences can then be modeled as a Bernoulli process with this probability, by assuming that the f pointers of the inverted file are randomly selected from the $n \cdot N$ possible word-document pairs in the collection. For example, using the information contained in Table 3.1, the probability that any randomly selected word of *Bible* appears in any randomly chosen verse is calculated as $701,412/(31,101 \times 8,965) = 0.0025$, assuming that words are scattered completely uniformly across verses.

Making this assumption, the chance of a gap of size x is the probability of having $x - 1$ nonoccurrences of that particular word, each of probability $(1 - p)$, followed by one occurrence of probability p, which is $\Pr[x] = (1 - p)^{x-1}p$. This is called the *geometric* distribution and is equivalent to modeling each possible term-document pair as appearing independently with probability p. If arithmetic coding is to be used, the required cumulative probabilities can be calculated by summing this distribution:

$$low\_bound = \sum_{i=1}^{x-1}(1-p)^{i-1}p = 1 - (1-p)^{x-1}$$

$$high\_bound = \sum_{i=1}^{x}(1-p)^{i-1}p = 1 - (1-p)^{x}$$

When decoding, the cumulative probability formula $1 - (1 - p)^x$ must be inverted to determine x and inverted exactly in order for the decoder to proceed correctly. The inverse function $x = 1 + \lfloor(\log(1 - v))/(\log(1 - p))\rfloor$, where v is the current fractional value of the arithmetic coding target, yields the decoded value x.

The probabilities generated by the geometric distribution can also be represented by a surprisingly effective Huffman-style code, and this turns out to be a more useful alternative to arithmetic coding. The following method was first described in 1966 by Solomon Golomb of the University of Southern California and is referred to as the *Golomb code* (Golomb 1966). For some parameter b, any number $x > 0$ is coded

Table 3.7 Probability ranges for Golomb coding.

b	Probability of "1"
1	$0.3820 \leq p \leq 1.0000$
2	$0.2452 \leq p \leq 0.3819$
3	$0.1809 \leq p \leq 0.2451$
4	$0.1434 \leq p \leq 0.1808$
5	$0.1188 \leq p \leq 0.1433$
6	$0.1014 \leq p \leq 0.1187$
7	$0.0885 \leq p \leq 0.1013$
8	$0.0785 \leq p \leq 0.0884$
9	$0.0705 \leq p \leq 0.0784$
10	$0.0640 \leq p \leq 0.0704$

in two parts: first, $q + 1$ in unary, where the quotient $q = \lfloor (x - 1)/b \rfloor$; then the remainder $r = x - qb - 1$ coded in binary, requiring either $\lfloor \log b \rfloor$ or $\lceil \log b \rceil$ bits. For example, with $b = 3$ there are three possible remainders r, and these are coded as 0, 10, and 11, respectively, for $r = 0$, $r = 1$, and $r = 2$. Similarly, for $b = 6$, there are six possible remainders r, with values 0 through 5, and these are assigned codes of 00, 01, 100, 101, 110, and 111. Then, if the value $x = 9$ is to be coded relative to $b = 3$, calculation yields $q = 2$ and $r = 2$ because $9 - 1 = 2 \times 3 + 2$; so the encoding is 110 followed by 11. Relative to $b = 6$, the values calculated are $q = 1$ and $r = 2$, resulting in a code of 10 followed by 100. Other code values for small x and both $b = 3$ and $b = 6$ are given in Table 3.6.

Gallager and Van Voorhis (1975) showed that if b is chosen to satisfy

$$(1 - p)^b + (1 - p)^{b+1} \leq 1 < (1 - p)^{b-1} + (1 - p)^b \qquad (3.1)$$

this coding method generates an optimal prefix-free code for the geometric distribution corresponding to Bernoulli trials with the probability of success given by p. In a sense, Golomb's construction is a one-step method for calculating the Huffman code for this particular infinite set of probabilities, which would clearly not be possible using the conventional Huffman algorithm described in Chapter 2. Solving Equation 3.1 for b gives

$$b^A = \left\lceil \frac{\log(2 - p)}{-\log(1 - p)} \right\rceil \qquad (3.2)$$

where the superscript A indicates that the *average* number of bits required to code the inverted file is being minimized. (In Chapter 5 it will also be useful to calculate a value for b to minimize the *worst* that can happen on any particular inverted list, and there a corresponding formula to calculate b^W is given.) The range of (approximate) probabilities for which some small values of b are appropriate is shown in Table 3.7.

Assuming that $p = f/(N \cdot n) \ll 1$, a useful simplification is

$$b^A \approx \frac{\log_e 2}{p} \approx 0.69 \cdot \frac{N \cdot n}{f}.$$

For example, on *Bible*, the best value is $b = 276$, calculated using the values $N = 31{,}101$, $n = 8{,}965$, and $f = 701{,}412$ taken from Table 3.1. For the *TREC* collection, the parameter that should be used is $b = 2{,}039$.

The Golomb code is closely related to the unary code and, like the unary code, assigns exponentially decreasing probabilities. However, in the Golomb code the base of the exponential decay is a function of b and is normally very close to one. Indeed, it is these exponentially decreasing probabilities that render the Golomb code suitable for use when the underlying distribution is geometric. In terms of the vector representation introduced above, the Golomb code is an encoding relative to the vector

$$V_G = \langle b, b, b, b, \ldots \rangle.$$

Golomb coding gives results within a few percent of the compression obtained by a Bernoulli model with arithmetic coding if $p \ll 1$ and $b \gg 1$, which is the normal case in inverted file compression. Only when many terms appear with very high probabilities does the optimality of arithmetic coding lead to a significant improvement, and for most applications involving a Bernoulli model, the fact that the Golomb approach yields much faster decoding makes it the method of choice. It is also worth noting that if p exceeds 0.5, the Golomb code is more efficient if the inverted file is complemented before compression—that is, if the numbers of the documents that do not contain the term are stored rather than the numbers of the documents that do. The reason is that in this case some of the outputs need to be coded in less than one bit, which is not possible with Golomb codes. However, arithmetic coding handles these extreme situations without modification.

Global observed frequency model

Another global technique for modeling interword gaps is to build an exact distribution based upon the observed frequencies of the numbers that appear as gap sizes in the inverted lists, and then use this distribution to drive either an arithmetic or a Huffman coder. In theory, this should give better compression than predetermined fixed codes. However, in practice, an observed frequency model is only slightly better than γ and δ, which is evidence that the probability models assumed by γ and δ are appropriate. More to the point, an exact global model of this type can be outperformed by simple local codes that are parameterized by individual term frequencies rather than the distribution of gap sizes in the entire inverted file. This is because pointers are not scattered randomly in the inverted file, and knowing the frequency of each term allows much better conditional estimates of gap probabilities.

Local Bernoulli model

At this point, we leave the global models of Table 3.5 and turn to the local models.

If f_t, the frequency of term t, is known, a Bernoulli model on each individual inverted list can be used. Again, the Golomb code is less demanding computationally than arithmetic coding and gives similar compression. If, for example, the inverted list of page 115 was drawn from a collection of exactly $N = 78$ documents, Equation 3.2 stipulates that $b_t^A = 6$.

Using this method, frequent words are coded with small values of b, while less frequent ones are coded with larger values. In *TREC*, a *hapax legomena*—a word that appears only once—is coded with $b \approx 500{,}000$, in either 19, 20, or 21 bits. On the other hand, a word that appears in 10 percent of the documents is coded with $b = 7$, and in this case a gap of one is represented in just 3 bits. This compares favorably with the minimum of 11 bits—1 for a minimal unary part plus 10 for a minimal binary part—required using the globally optimal value of $b = 2{,}036$.

Very common words are coded with $b = 1$. When $b = 1$, the code degenerates to a set of unary codes for the gap sizes, with no binary components. This is tantamount to storing the inverted list as a *bitvector*, that is, as a binary vector with one bit for each document, the bit being set if the term appears in that document. Thus, the compressed inverted file representation using the Huffman-coded Bernoulli model can never be worse than an index comprising one bitvector per term. This latter structure is referred to as a *bitmap* and is discussed further in Section 3.5.

To exploit this local model, it is necessary to store the parameter f_t with each inverted list, so that the correct value of b can be used during decoding. The overhead cost of doing this is small—indeed, the example on page 115 already shows it as part of the inverted list. Each compressed inverted list is easily prefixed with a γ code for f_t—the γ code is a good choice because most of the frequencies can be expected to be small. Indeed, in *TREC*, about half of the frequencies f_t are one, and storing f_t is a relatively small overhead.

Skewed Bernoulli model

As discussed earlier, the Golomb code can be described in the same general framework as the γ code. The vector for the Golomb code is

$$V_G = \langle b, b, b, \dots \rangle$$

and because of the uniform bucket size used, a great deal of the skewness of the γ distribution is lost. For this reason, the local Golomb code performs only marginally better than global γ or δ codes.

In reality, it is unreasonable to expect that each particular term is scattered randomly throughout the documents comprising a collection. Rather, it is probable that there are long periods of inactivity, interspersed by clumps, or *clusters*, of documents containing a certain word—clusters that are grouped together in the collection perhaps because they originate from the same source or perhaps because they discuss some topical material and the documents in the collection were inserted in chronological order. Words such as *Chernobyl*, *Vincennes*, and *Waco* in news archives serve to illustrate this point. Moreover, clustering is not restricted

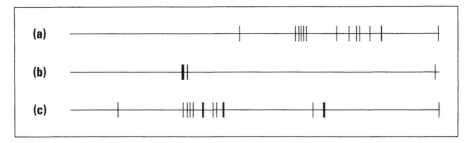

Figure 3.5   Word positions in *Bible*: (a) *bridegroom*; (b) *Jezebel*; (c) *twelfth*.

to proper names. Figure 3.5 shows diagrammatically the locations in *Bible* of three different words, each of which appears in exactly 20 verses; only *Jezebel* is a proper name. Even the word appearances for commonplace words such as *twelfth* are not uniformly scattered in their inverted lists, and it is desirable to allow for clustering in the inverted file compression model.

One way of distorting the geometric probability distribution to allow for clustering is to boost the implicit probabilities of small *d*-gaps, without overpenalizing the large gaps. To do this, a cross between the γ and Golomb codes can be used, employing a coding vector that has small initial buckets that grow larger (rather than maintaining all the buckets at the same size) and allows the first bucket to contain *b* values (rather than just one). One possible vector is

$$V_T = \langle b, 2b, 4b, \ldots, 2^i b, \ldots \rangle,$$

in which a value of *b* that gives good results is the median gap size in each inverted list. This means that half of the gaps will fall into the first bucket of the code, with a single unary prefix bit. For any given value of f_t, skew distributions have a smaller median than random distributions, so the binary suffix component for half or more of the list pointers are also likely to be shorter than with the V_G code. At worst, on an inverted list that really is random, the median will be close to the mean, and this V_T code will perform only slightly worse than the Golomb code.

To use the V_T code, a value from which *b* can be calculated must be stored in each inverted list, as f_t is no longer sufficient. Since *b* is large for rare terms, a γ-coded representation of the ratio N/b should be added, from which *b* can be calculated at runtime.

Local hyperbolic model

Another possibility for a local model is to use a hyperbolic distribution, where the probability $\Pr[x]$ of a gap of *x* is

$$\Pr[x] = \mu/x, \text{ for } x = 1, 2, \ldots, m.$$

To ensure that the distribution is normalized and the probabilities sum to not more than one, μ should be chosen as

$$\mu = \frac{1}{\log_e(m + 1) + 0.5772},$$

where the value $0.57721566\ldots$ is usually referred to as Euler's constant. While m could be taken to be the largest gap that occurs for a particular term, it is more robust to determine m by matching the expected value of this distribution with the average gap size defined by the term's frequency count. The expected value is

$$\sum_{x=1}^{m} x \cdot \Pr[x] = m\mu.$$

For a word that occurs f_t times in a text of N documents, the average gap is N/f_t. Thus, m can be obtained from

$$\frac{m}{\log_e(m + 1) + 0.5772} = \frac{N}{f_t}.$$

This equation can be solved by an iterative computation.

In practice, the gap will occasionally exceed m. To enable this to be encoded, any gap of m or greater is treated as a gap of m, followed by a flat encoding of the extra length. This rarely occurs and has a negligible effect on the code length.

This method typically gives better performance than the Bernoulli model but is more complex to implement and requires the use of arithmetic coding, so it does not offer the same decoding performance. No simple Huffman code is known for this model.

Local observed frequency model

The ultimate in local modeling is based on observed frequencies. Here, one of the interesting dilemmas in data compression is encountered—when to stop modeling and when to start coding. For example, consider the list of gaps in the inverted list for the word *bridegroom* (this inverted list was shown graphically in Figure 3.5a):

$$\langle 20; 14174, 4680, 6, 294, 192, 199, 242, 2541, 1067,$$
$$615, 4, 1, 4, 261, 1, 861, 1, 962, 45, 4867 \rangle.$$

In this inverted list there are 17 distinct gap values. If a model on an observed frequency basis is to be built, the prelude to the inverted list must somehow indicate what the 17 gap values are and the length of the Huffman or arithmetic code that should be assigned to each. Each gap value is in the range $1 \ldots N$, and even if they are coded using the Golomb code, about 12 bits per gap will be required, plus some bits to represent the corresponding code length. In total, the model description must consume at least 200 bits. Then, and only then, can the actual gaps be coded—at a further cost of 4 bits each. That is, the cost of recording the model is two and a half times greater than the cost of coding the data, and the total cost—more than 14 bits per pointer—is greater than the 12.05 bits per pointer required by the simple δ code. Clearly, this is taking modeling too far.

To resolve this dilemma, the cost of model storage must somehow be amortized over several terms. One way to do this is by *batching* various inverted lists. For example, all words with $f_t = 20$—including *bridegroom*, *Jezebel*, and *twelfth*—could share a single model. Using this approach, one model would be needed for each different f_t value that occurs, and, what is worse, each such model will be dense, in that most possible gap sizes will appear. This combination again means that model storage may require too much space. The batching process must be even broader.

Another possibility is to batch not by f_t but by $\lfloor \log f_t \rfloor$. This means that the number of batches is tightly constrained, and so, even if each of the models is dense and records information about a wide range of gaps, the total space required to store the models is moderate. For example, on a collection of one million documents, just 20 models are required. There is no reason for the base of the logarithmic selector to be binary, and other bases can also be considered, such as a batching based on the well-known Fibonacci sequence—using individual models for frequencies $f_t = 1, 2$, and 3, then a fourth model for all words with $3 < f_t \le 5$, a fifth model to cover all words with $5 < f_t \le 8$, and so on. Here, the base of the logarithm is approximately 1.62, and the number of models required will be about 40 percent greater than if a binary logarithm were used. In the limit, if the base of the logarithm becomes one, the situation reverts to that of the previous paragraph, with one model for each distinct f_t value.

In practice, the binary logarithmic batching method works well (Moffat and Zobel 1992). Although each gap is coded from one of just a handful of different models, there is enough discrimination remaining that frequent words are coded according to an appropriate distribution of gap sizes, and infrequent words are similarly coded according to their own probability distribution. In this method—*batched frequency*—each inverted list must be prefixed with a *model selector*, either f_t or, more economically, the value of $\lfloor \log f_t \rfloor$. If f_t is not already being stored, then the latter quantity can be coded very economically using the γ code. Either Huffman or arithmetic coding can be used with this model, since the probabilities are derived from a table of frequencies. Huffman coding is faster and only slightly less economical than arithmetic coding, and it is the preferred choice.

Context-sensitive compression

Despite being motivated as a mechanism to cope with clustering of word appearances, the V_T code described on page 123 is still a static code and is the equivalent of a zero-order model for the d-gaps. Use of a higher-order model also allows the compression to be sensitive to clustering since a sequence of small d-gaps is strong evidence that the next d-gap will also be small. One mechanism that has been suggested is that the parameter b used for each d-gap should be the average of some number of previously decoded d-gaps. While attractive in theory, the extra compression gain is usually small, and, because there are more cases to be handled, implementation is more complex. Care must also be taken to ensure that it is possible to recover quickly from incorrect estimates. Any savings will be immediately lost if, for example, a parameter $b = 1$ is calculated at some point, and a subsequent long gap coded in unary. For this reason, codes based upon the V_T-style vector should be used rather than a V_G-style vector.

A rather elegant way in which the compression of each inverted list can be made sensitive to clustering has been developed (Moffat and Stuiver 1996). This *interpolative code* is best illustrated with an example. Consider the inverted list

$$\langle 7; 3, 8, 9, 11, 12, 13, 17 \rangle$$

in a collection of $N = 20$ documents. The various index compression mechanisms described above would convert this to a list of d-gaps $\langle 7; 3, 5, 1, 2, 1, 1, 4 \rangle$ and code it in a left-to-right manner, possibly recognizing the cluster between the second and sixth pointers.

Suppose instead that the value of the second pointer is somehow known before the first must be coded. In the example, if it is known that the second pointer is to document 8, then the first pointer is restricted to some document number in the range 1 to 7 inclusive. A simple assignment of binary codewords then suffices to represent this first document pointer in three bits.

Suppose now that the fourth as well as the second document number is known. The fourth document pointer is to document 11, so the third pointer is constrained to the range 9 to 10. Again, a simple code—in this case just one bit long—can be used to represent the third pointer. The brevity of this codeword is a direct consequence of the fact that there is a cluster and that both the upper and lower bounding pointers are also in the cluster. As an even more extreme example, if both the fourth and the sixth pointers are known (to documents 11 and 13, respectively), then the fifth document pointer can be represented using a codeword zero bits long—it must be to document 12.

This representation is based upon the supposition that the second, fourth, and sixth pointers are known. To represent them, a list $\langle 3; 8, 11, 13 \rangle$ must have been previously coded. The same technique can be used for this list too. If the second pointer (to document 11) is known, then the first pointer (to document 8) takes at most four bits. Indeed, since there must be a pointer to the left and a pointer to the right of this document, the range can be further narrowed to $2 \ldots 9$ inclusive, and a three-bit code can be used. By a similar argument, the third pointer must lie between $13 = 12 + 1$ and $19 = 20 - 1$ inclusive, and $3 = \lceil \log 7 \rceil$ bits suffice.

The only remaining problem is to code the pointer to document 11. A five-bit code in the range $1 \ldots 20$ inclusive is certainly adequate, and if the knowledge that there are three document pointers to the left and three to the right of this middle pointer is exploited, the range can be further narrowed to $4 \ldots 17$ inclusive, and four bits are sufficient.

The recursive process of calculating ranges and codes is captured in Figure 3.6. Function *binary_code*(x, lo, hi) is assumed to encode a number $lo \leq x \leq hi$ in some appropriate manner. The simplest mechanism for doing this (as assumed above) requires $\lceil \log(hi - lo + 1) \rceil$ bits. The operation ++ in step 4 denotes concatenation of codewords.

To *interpolative_code*(L, f, lo, hi), where $L[0 \ldots (f - 1)]$ is a sorted list of f
document numbers, all in the range $lo \ldots hi$,

1. If $f = 0$ then return the empty string.

2. If $f = 1$ then return *binary_code*$(L[0], lo, hi)$.

3. Otherwise,

    (a) Set $h \leftarrow f$ div 2 and $m \leftarrow L[h]$.

    (b) Set $f_1 \leftarrow h$ and $f_2 \leftarrow f - h - 1$.

    (c) Set $L_1 \leftarrow L[0 \ldots h - 1]$ and $L_2 \leftarrow L[(h + 1) \ldots (f - 1)]$.

4. Return *binary_code*$(m, lo + f_1, hi - f_2)$ ++
    interpolative_code$(L_1, f_1, lo, m - 1)$ ++
    interpolative_code$(L_2, f_2, m + 1, hi)$.

Figure 3.6 Interpolative coding.

For the example list, the full sequence of (x, lo, hi) triples processed by function *binary_code* is

$$(11, 4, 17), \ (8, 2, 9), \ (3, 1, 7), \ (9, 9, 10), \ (13, 13, 19), \ (12, 12, 12), \ (17, 14, 20).$$

With a simple implementation of *binary_code*, the lengths of the corresponding codes are 4, 3, 3, 1, 3, 0, and 3 bits, respectively, for a total of 17 bits. By way of comparison, a Golomb code for the same list with $b = 2$ requires 18 bits.

The compression can be further improved by using a minimal binary code. For example, when the triple $(13, 13, 19)$ is being processed, there are only seven numbers in the range, so one of the codewords can be one bit shorter; if there are six possible values, two of the codewords can be one bit shorter. In general, the middle codewords in each range should be the shorter ones since it is more likely that the middle value in a list of pointers will be near the middle of the range than near the ends. But at the last step of the process, when there is only one pointer left in each interval, the allocation should be reversed. Then the one-bit-shorter codewords should be assigned at the ends of the range since the fundamental assumption of the whole method is that the document pointers are clustered.

It is possible to show that at its worst the interpolative code is only slightly inefficient compared with a Golomb code, and, because contiguous sets of values can be coded in less than one bit each, at its best it can be dramatically better. Moreover, in practice the interpolative code usually results in very good compression (Moffat and Stuiver 1996). Indeed, the only real drawback of the method is its complexity of implementation—encoding and each decoding make use of a stack of pending values, and the encoding and decoding loops become rather more detailed than for the simpler Golomb and γ codes.

3.4 Performance of index compression methods

Table 3.8 shows the compression obtained on the four test collections by the various methods described above. Output sizes are expressed as bits per pointer. The total size of the index can be calculated by multiplying by the appropriate f value from Table 3.1. For example, use of the interpolative code yields a *TREC* index of 83.4 Mbytes, or just 4 percent of the text that it indexes. This is quite a remarkable achievement when it is remembered that a document number for *every* word and number in this 2 Gbyte collection is stored in the index. As a reference point, the second row of values shows the space that would be required, per pointer, by an ordinary binary encoding of the gap sizes.

The results of Table 3.8 include any necessary overheads, such as the γ-coded f_t values for the local Bernoulli model and the complete set of models and model selectors for the batched frequency model. The figures for unary-coded compression are less than what the average would be for a pure bitmap because in the unary-coded file γ is used to represent the local value f_t for each inverted list, followed by f_t unary codes rather than a complete bitvector. For example, a word with $f_t = 1$ that appears in the first document (number one) would be counted as taking two bits in the unary-coded implementation—one bit for the γ code for f_t and one bit for the unary code for 1.

Though it is the best of the global models, the global observed frequency model is outperformed by remarkably simple local models. The frequency of a term is a much better predictor of the distribution of its gap sizes than is the overall gap size distribution for all terms. Furthermore, given that the local Bernoulli or skewed Bernoulli models need just one parameter to be stored in memory during decoding, compared with the hundreds and possibly thousands of parameters required by the various observed frequency models, there is no contest—the local models are significantly better. Even the global γ and δ codes come surprisingly close to the compression attained by the global observed frequency model. These latter two codes also have the major advantage of requiring no parameters. This is useful when storing dynamic collections, which will be discussed in Chapter 5.

Of the results listed, only the hyperbolic model assumes the use of arithmetic coding. All of the other mechanisms rely upon prefix codes, so slight compression gains might result if the underlying probability distributions were used to drive an arithmetic coder instead. It is, however, unlikely that any gains would be sufficiently large to warrant the extra decoding time.

The interpolative code gives the best results on all four of the test files, followed by the batched frequency model and the skewed Bernoulli model, with the parameter b chosen as the median gap size in each inverted list. Furthermore, all of these codes require relatively modest computational resources during index compression and decompress as quickly during index access as do simple binary codes. The local Bernoulli model, coded using the Golomb code, is also a good choice, obtaining slightly less compression than the interpolative code but with a correspondingly simpler implementation. Compared to both of these mechanisms, the batched frequency model has the extra disadvantage that during inverted file decompression,

Table 3.8 Compression of inverted files in bits per pointer.

Method	Bits per pointer			
	Bible	*GNUbib*	*Comact*	*TREC*
Global methods				
Unary	262	909	487	1918
Binary	15.00	16.00	18.00	20.00
Bernoulli	9.86	11.06	10.90	12.30
γ	6.51	5.68	4.48	6.63
δ	6.23	5.08	4.35	6.38
Observed frequency	5.90	4.82	4.20	5.97
Local methods				
Bernoulli	6.09	6.16	5.40	5.84
Hyperbolic	5.75	5.16	4.65	5.89
Skewed Bernoulli	5.65	4.70	4.20	5.44
Batched frequency	5.58	4.64	4.02	5.41
Interpolative	5.24	3.98	3.87	5.18

either the appropriate model must be read off disk and stored in memory while the inverted list is being decoded, at the cost of an extra disk access, or the complete set of models must be held resident in memory. The latter choice can involve significant memory resources.

3.5 Signature files and bitmaps

Signature files and bitmaps are two further approaches to indexing. In certain combinations of circumstances both can offer faster query processing than inverted files but in those same situations are likely to require a great deal more storage space, which often outweighs that advantage. Signature files have been particularly popular in the past because they are, in a sense, implicitly compressed and so can consume less storage space than uncompressed inverted files.[3] The previous two sections have shown how much has been learned about inverted index representations in the last 10 years, and signature files no longer enjoy the relative advantage that they used to.

---

3 For example, the 1992 text *Information Retrieval: Data Structures and Algorithms* by Frakes and Baeza-Yates includes a chapter on signature files but no material on the compression of indexes.

Table 3.9   Hash values for text of Table 3.2.

Term	Hash string
cold	1000 0000 0010 0100
days	0010 0100 0000 1000
hot	0000 1010 0000 0000
in	0000 1001 0010 0000
it	0000 1000 1000 0010
like	0100 0010 0000 0001
nine	0010 1000 0000 0100
old	1000 1000 0100 0000
pease	0000 0101 0000 0001
porridge	0100 0100 0010 0000
pot	0000 0010 0110 0000
some	0100 0100 0000 0001
the	1010 1000 0000 0000

In this section we examine these two alternative index representations and compare them to the compressed inverted files described above in terms of both storage cost and processing requirements. We examine them in considerable detail, not because we recommend their use, but in order to allay any concerns that signature files may prove to offer a superior solution. In fact:

Compressed inverted indexes are almost always superior to signature files and bitmaps in practical situations, in terms of both the space required for the index and the time needed to respond to typical queries.

Signature files

A signature file is a probabilistic method for indexing text. Each document has an associated *signature*, or *descriptor*, a string of bits that captures in some sense the content of the document. To create the descriptor for a document, each term in the document is used to generate several hash values, and the bits of the document signature corresponding to those hash values are set to one.

For example, consider again the text of Table 3.2 on page 111, and suppose that the words have the 16-bit signatures shown in Table 3.9. These descriptors are constructed by taking three hash functions generating values in the range 1 . . . 16 and setting the corresponding bits in the signature. That is, each word is hashed three times using different functions, and the bits so indicated are the "one" bits in the signature of that word. Collisions may result in fewer than three bits being set in some of the term signatures, but no account need be taken of this. For example, in

Table 3.10 Signature file for text of Table 3.2.

Document	Text	Descriptor
1	Pease porridge hot, pease porridge cold,	1100 1111 0010 0101
2	Pease porridge in the pot,	1110 1111 0110 0001
3	Nine days old.	1010 1100 0100 1100
4	Some like it hot, some like it cold,	1100 1110 1010 0111
5	Some like it in the pot,	1110 1111 1110 0011
6	Nine days old.	1010 1100 0100 1100

Table 3.9 the term *hot* has only two bits set. Describing these bit strings as signatures is a very apt use of the word—as with human signatures, they bear little resemblance to the words (names) they represent but are the result of a repeatable operation (the act of signing), and it is relatively unlikely, but not impossible, that the signatures of two words (people) are identical.

Now consider the resultant descriptors when the signatures for the words in each document (in this case, each line) are superimposed—that is, ORed together to make document signatures. For example, the last line of Table 3.2 contains the three words *nine*, *days*, and *old*, so the signature for this line is the disjunction of 0010 1000 0000 0100 (the signature for *nine*), 0010 0100 0000 1000 (the signature for *days*), and 1000 1000 0100 0000 (representing *old*); that is, 1010 1100 0100 1100. The complete set of document signatures is shown in Table 3.10.

To test whether a query term occurs in a given document, the values of the hash functions for the term are calculated. If all corresponding bits in the descriptor of some document are set, the term probably occurs in that document. Or, more to the point, it cannot yet be said that the term does not appear in the document, as some other combination of words might by coincidence have set all of the bits examined for the query term. To resolve this uncertainty, the document must be fetched and scanned to check that the term really does occur. The probability of such a *false match* can be kept arbitrarily low by setting several bits for each term and making the signatures sufficiently long, but false-match checking is always required with signature file indexes and can add substantially to query processing costs since each document checked must be completely decoded, parsed into words, and the words all restemmed.

For example, a query using the index of Table 3.10 to find lines containing the word *cold* searches in the file of signatures for descriptors in which bits 1, 11, and 14 are set since if a document contains *cold*, these bits must be set. The only lines that satisfy this requirement are lines 1 and 4, and both are determined by the false-match check to be correct answers to the query. Suppose instead that the search is for *old*. In this case, lines with 1 bits in positions 1, 5, and 10 must be examined, and four lines—2, 3, 5, and 6—are indicated as possible answers, only two of which actually contain the word. For any given conjunctive query, the index only eliminates documents: it never definitively selects them.

Signature files become more effective as queries become more specific because queries involving the conjunction of several terms can check more bits in the signature file. Only one bit needs to be 0 to cause the match to fail, and this leads to a low probability for false matches when the number of bits specified in the query is large. Conversely, using a signature file to process single-term queries necessitates either slow processing, while many false matches are eliminated, or a large signature file, so that each term can set many bits.[4]

If queries include negated terms, the logic becomes more complex, and there is a quite surprising reversal of roles. For example, consider the query NOT *hot* (which is not the same as the query *cold*). The descriptor for *hot* has bits 5 and 7 set, so documents in which one of the indicated bit positions is not set can be accepted as answers without further checking because if the term is present, the bit would be set. In the example, documents 3 and 6 are definitely answers and cannot be false matches. On the other hand, even if a document descriptor does have both of these bits set, it might still be an answer and so cannot be rejected without further checking—as before, the bits in question might have been set by other terms that appear in that document. In the example, lines 2 and 5 both have bits 5 and 7 set, but since neither contains *hot*, both are answers. To process this query and determine that lines 2, 3, 5, and 6 are the correct answers, lines 1, 2, 4, and 5 must all be fetched and checked—that is, one way or another every document in the collection is handled.

In either type of query, the document collection is partitioned into two categories. If the term is not negated, then the categories are *No*, meaning that a document is definitely not an answer, and *Maybe*, meaning that the document may be an answer. False-match checking is then necessary on the set of *Maybe* documents. When the term is negated, the two categories are *Maybe* and *Yes*, and again false-match checking is required on the *Maybe* set. More complex queries, such as (*some* OR NOT *hot*) AND *pease*, must be evaluated in a three-valued logic, where for each document each subexpression is either *Yes*, *No*, or *Maybe* and the combining rules for the Boolean operations are as described in Figure 3.7. For example, *Maybe* AND *Yes* results in *Maybe*; *Maybe* OR *Yes* results in *Yes*. Once all the operators in the query expression have been evaluated and a single value obtained for each document, all the *Yes* documents can be accepted as answers without further processing, all the *No* documents can be rejected without being inspected, and all the *Maybe* documents must be fetched and evaluated directly against the terms of the query. Fast query processing is possible only when the final *Maybe* set is small.

Table 3.11 shows the evaluation of the query (*some* OR NOT *hot*) AND *pease* for the sample collection, where *s* stands for *some*, *h* for *hot*, and *p* for *pease*. Each column

---

4 Although single-term queries may seem hopelessly inadequate in a huge collection such as the World Wide Web, they are nevertheless very widely used. Average queries to Web search engines contain only two or three terms.

AND	N	M	Y		OR	N	M	Y		NOT	
N	N	N	N		N	N	M	Y		N	Y
M	N	M	M		M	M	M	Y		M	M
Y	N	M	Y		Y	Y	Y	Y		Y	N

Figure 3.7 Boolean operations in a three-valued logic.

Table 3.11 Evaluation of (*some* OR NOT *hot*) AND *pease*.

Document	s	h	p	NOT h	s OR NOT h	(s OR NOT h) AND p
1	M	M	M	M	M	M
2	M	M	M	M	M	M
3	N	N	N	Y	Y	N
4	M	M	N	M	M	N
5	M	M	M	M	M	M
6	N	N	N	Y	Y	N

represents the *Yes*, *Maybe*, or *No* value for that subexpression. When the expression has been fully evaluated, no documents are category *Yes*; three are still *Maybe*; and three are definitely *No*. A false-match check of the three *Maybe* documents shows that only document 2 is an answer to this query. In general, most queries are simple conjunctions with only AND operations specified, and, as was discussed above, in the absence of any NOT operations, these partition the documents into two sets, *No* and *Maybe*. Hence, the only way a conjunctive query can return any *Yes* answers is if every term in the query is negated, a reasonably unlikely proposition.

Bitsliced signature files

Access to signature files can be accelerated by transposing the matrix of bits, a technique that is called *bitslicing*. Table 3.12 shows the idea. The bits associated with a particular hash value are now grouped together so that they can be obtained with one disk access. In the example, the word *cold* is hashed to obtain the values 1, 11, and 14, as above. The corresponding bitslices in the stored index are then fetched with three disk accesses, and the bitstrings 111111, 110110, and 101101 are read. The conjunction of these bitslices yields 100100, indicating that documents 1 and 4 should be checked by the false-match processing phase since they might contain the word *cold*.

The advantage of storing the signature file in bitsliced form is that instead of needing to read the entire signature file to process each query, only a small fraction of it is required, resulting in considerable savings in disk transfer time. In the limit,

Table 3.12 Bitsliced signature file for index of Table 3.10.

Pos.	Slice	Pos.	Slice	Pos.	Slice	Pos.	Slice
1	111111	5	111111	9	000110	13	001001
2	110110	6	111111	10	011011	14	101101
3	011011	7	110110	11	110110	15	000110
4	000000	8	110010	12	000000	16	110110

the bitsliced signature file is somewhat akin to a randomized inverted file, where, instead of one bitvector for each term, there is one slice for each pseudoterm, and each actual term is randomly assigned to multiple pseudoterms. This idea will be developed in more detail below.

The size of a signature file is determined by three parameters. Once the characteristics of the documents and likely queries are known, values can be chosen for these parameters to obtain a desired level of performance. We first describe the parameters and give typical values for them—anticipating the discussion that follows on how to choose their values to meet given design criteria.

The first parameter is the number b of bitslices to be accessed for each query. If this is too large, query processing will be slow because many bitslices must be retrieved even when there are only a few answers. A fine balance must be maintained between the time spent retrieving potential answers from the disk and the time spent retrieving bitslices, and a large value of b can push the balance too far, requiring more work to be spent on bitslice processing than is saved on false-match checking. Typical values for b are in the range of 6 to 12.

If the signature file is being designed for simple conjunctive queries, the second parameter to be chosen is q, the minimum number of terms expected to be present in each query. A conservative choice is $q = 1$, and in this case each term must be hashed b times to guarantee that b bitslices can be accessed. Larger values of q mean that the size of the signature file can be reduced because each term needs to set fewer bits. However, this also increases the risk that queries will be specified with fewer than q terms. Such queries run very slowly because of the many false matches that result when fewer than b bitslices are available.

The final parameter controlling the size of the signature file is z, the desired bound on the expected number of false matches per query. Small values of z mean that query processing is fast since few false-match records are retrieved, but to obtain this discrimination the index must be large. On the other hand, large values of z reduce the size of the index at the expense of query processing time. Typically, z is assumed to be one. That is, provided that at least q query terms are specified and a query of b bitslices can be built up, the expected number of false-match records is one or less.

Given values for these three parameters, it is possible to calculate the necessary signature width W so that a query of q terms has an expected number of false matches of z or fewer. Details of this calculation are given in the next section, "Analysis of signature files." Taking *TREC* as an example, and specifying $b = 8$, $q = 1$, and $z = 1$, the required value of W is 7,130 or more; that is, the descriptor for each document in *TREC* must be at least 7,130 bits wide to get the desired performance. Thus, in total, the signature file will occupy 631 Mbytes.

Using this signature file, a single-term query with just one answer will require at least 10 disk accesses on average—8 to retrieve bitslices, 1 to access the true match, and 1 to retrieve a second record that is later discovered to be a false match. In contrast, an inverted file index answers the query with 2 accesses if the lexicon is held in main memory and 3 if it is on disk. Moreover, the inverted file approach involves minimal computational effort—the decoding of one pointer—whereas the signature file search requires seven AND operations, each involving a 91 Kbyte bitslice. Clearly, this type of query strongly favors inverted files over signature files.

Conversely, the bitsliced signature file is most strongly favored by a query of b or more terms that are very common individually but together serve to identify just one answer. The inverted file approach must perform at least one disk access for every term, retrieve and decode all of the inverted lists, and perform a merging operation. On the other hand, the signature file involves approximately the same work as before because when processing a query of b or more terms there is no need to access more than one bitslice for each term—b slices are, by design, already enough to reduce the false-match rate to less than one. There is no decoding, and the ANDing of the bitslices is fast. In this case, the signature file index can also resolve such a query with one disk access per term. Indeed, if at any stage the number of remaining candidates falls below the number of remaining terms, it may be more efficient to proceed directly to the false-match-checking stage and search for the remaining terms directly in the documents themselves than it is to continue processing bitslices since false-match checking has to be carried out regardless. For these queries, the number of disk accesses for inverted files and signature files are comparable, but the signature file index requires less computational effort. It is, however, unlikely that such queries would be common.

Table 3.13 shows the sizes of the signature files required for the example document collections. The calculation is based upon the "speed before space" assumptions that $z = 1$ and $q = 1$. As b, the number of bitslices accessed per query, increases from $b = 6$, the size of the index decreases. To allow comparison with Table 3.8 (page 129), the sizes are given in terms of bits per pointer, even though there is no explicit storage of pointers in a signature file index. The method used to calculate the values given in Table 3.13 is described in the following section, "Analysis of signature files."

There are two points to note in the table. First, even for quite large values of b, the signature file is relatively big—well over 20 bits for each pointer nominally represented. This is comparable to the space that was calculated for an uncompressed inverted file and is much greater than the space required by a compressed inverted file. Second, increasing b beyond a certain limit makes the signature file larger as well as queries slower—too many bits are being set, and the signature has to become wider to keep the ratio of 1 bits at an acceptable level.

Table 3.13 Signature file sizes assuming $z = 1$ and $q = 1$.

b	Bits per pointer			
	Bible	GNUbib	Comact	TREC
6	30.6	34.9	44.9	54.0
8	25.0	27.7	33.9	39.2
10	22.8	24.9	29.5	33.4
12	21.9	23.7	27.5	30.6
16	21.6	23.1	26.1	28.5
20	22.1	23.4	26.1	28.1

Table 3.14 Signature file sizes assuming $z = 4$ and $q = 2$.

b	Bits per pointer			
	Bible	GNUbib	Comact	TREC
6	11.8	13.5	17.5	21.1
8	10.1	11.3	13.9	16.1
10	9.6	10.5	12.5	14.2
12	9.4	10.2	11.9	13.3
16	9.5	10.1	11.6	12.7
20	9.8	10.5	11.7	12.7

In a less demanding situation, where slower response can be tolerated to achieve reduced space, the results are closer to those obtained with a compressed inverted file. Table 3.14 shows the result of the same calculations but with $q = 2$ and $z = 4$—that is, assuming that at least two terms are supplied for every query and that an average of four false matches per query is tolerable.

The signature files have decreased in size. However, they are still more than twice as large as the compressed inverted files summarized in Table 3.8. Furthermore, this liberal approach now makes some queries extremely slow. Consider what happens when a query with one term is issued rather than the two that were assumed when the index was designed. Only half the required number of bitslices can be accessed, and so the probability that false-match documents are eliminated is low. On *TREC*, the expected number of false matches climbs from four when two terms are specified to nearly two thousand when only one term is given. An inescapable conclusion is that signature file parameters must be chosen extremely conservatively if performance is to be good across a variety of query types.

Throughout the calculations summarized in Tables 3.13 and 3.14, a variety of uniform random distributions have been assumed, and any deviation increases the number of false matches. Of these assumptions, by far the most crucial is that all of the documents are the same length. In a document database this is most unlikely, and merely using the average document length—which is what has been done to generate Tables 3.13 and 3.14—is foolhardy. As is discussed below and in Section 3.6, just one long document in a collection can enormously disrupt the performance of a signature file index.

The real message to be understood from these caveats is that text is not at all random, so when designing signature files, model-based figures such as those given in the two tables should be viewed with enormous suspicion until the performance of actual data on actual queries can be measured. Moreover, extreme care should be taken when designing hash functions themselves, to be sure that they yield uniformly random values—it is surprisingly easy for the performance characteristics of a signature file to be badly distorted by an uninformed choice of hash function.

These results also show that the design of signature files involves many trade-offs. For example, very wide, sparse signatures mean that false-match rates can be forced low after just a few bitslices have been accessed. On the other hand, shorter, denser signature files are compact but require more disk accesses—either more bitslices must be processed to obtain the same false-match rate or more documents from the database must be accessed because of a higher false-match rate. Because of these trade-offs, the space required by a signature file is, to some extent, variable. When indexing text, most implementations set the signature width to allow about 30 to 40 bits per index term, which is about 15 to 30 bits per word when multiple appearances of the word within the same document are taken into account. Within this range, the storage required for a signature file is roughly comparable to an equivalent uncompressed inverted file, at about 30 to 70 percent of the original text.

As well as requiring more space than compressed inverted files, signature files have other disadvantages when used to index text. As was noted earlier, they are inefficient if the documents vary in size because the same number of signature bits are allocated to each record, and long documents, with more unique "term, document" pairs and hence more bits set, become much more likely to be picked up as false matches than are short ones. Unfortunately, variability in record length is the normal situation in full-text retrieval. One solution is to block the text into fixed-size units, but this makes it more difficult to answer even simple Boolean queries. Another possibility is to use large sparse signatures and compress each bitslice. However, the ultimate in sparsity is a bitmap—with one bit per document per term—and since a deterministic bitmap has fewer 1 bits than a signature file of the same size, it is both more compressible and less costly to decompress.

Many refinements have been described for the signature file method. These are primarily applicable to very large conventional databases in which record lengths are relatively short and of low variability. For example, a two-level system has been suggested in which a master signature file serves to locate relevant blocks and secondary files locate records within those blocks (Sacks-Davis, Kent, and Ramamohanarao

1987; Kent, Sacks-Davis, and Ramamohanarao 1990). To give better discrimination, the block descriptor is much longer than the record descriptor, and an element of cross-indexing is provided by using a different logical blocking for each of several secondary signature files. Nevertheless, the storage requirement is still 20 to 30 bits per term, compared with a typical pointer size of just 6 to 8 bits for each term represented in a compressed inverted file. And, as always with signature file indexes, time must be spent on false-match checking.

Analysis of signature files

To calculate the size of a signature file, some decisions must be made about the desired performance. Values must be chosen for b, the maximum number of bitslices to be processed while answering any query, and z, the expected number of false matches that is to be tolerated. Typical values for b are in the range of 6 to 12: if b is too small, the width of the signature is pushed too high to maintain the required false-match rate; if b is made larger, the time to evaluate queries grows; and if b is too large, the required signature width again increases. Similarly for z: the signature file can be designed so that, on average, there is just one false match per query, which makes the signature wide, or, trading response time for index size, z might be chosen to permit 10 or more false matches for a large collection. Let p be the probability that a randomly chosen bit in a signature is on, assuming that each term in each document selects its signature bits at random. If the signature is wide, for example, then p will be small because the signature will be sparse. Hence, to minimize the signature width for a given value of b, the maximal value of p should be calculated so that b randomly chosen bits, each of which has a probability p of being set, will select on average z records from the database. Because the hash functions are assumed to be random, these three quantities are related by

$$z = p^b \cdot N \tag{3.3}$$

since the probability that *all* of the b bits selected by some query are on is p^b and there are N records in the collection. Hence, the value of p that minimizes the signature width while complying with the requirement that the expected number of false-match records be z or less is

$$p = \left(\frac{z}{N}\right)^{1/b}. \tag{3.4}$$

Now suppose that q terms are to be supplied in each query. If interterm collisions are ignored (which is reasonable provided b is small compared to the signature width), then b/q bits must be set in the signature by each indexed term if a query is to be capable of supporting b bitslices. Hence B, the total number of hashings in the signature of an average document, is given by

$$B = \frac{f}{N} \cdot \frac{b}{q}. \tag{3.5}$$

Here f is the number of unique "term, document" pairs in the collection, as shown in Table 3.1. Hidden in this calculation is the crucial assumption that all the documents contain roughly the same number of distinct terms.

It is now possible to calculate W, the required signature width, since W must be sufficiently large that B random selections out of W, with replacement, must give a probability of p or less that a randomly selected bit is 1. These quantities are related by

$$p = 1 - \left(\frac{W - 1}{W}\right)^B$$

since for a bit to remain off, it must avoid selection a total of B times, and the probability of not being selected once is $(W - 1)/W$. All other bits will be hit at least once and so turned on. Hence

$$W = \frac{1}{1 - (1 - p)^{1/B}}. \tag{3.6}$$

Finally, given W, the size of the signature file can be calculated as $N \cdot W$ bits.

For example, if a signature file is to be constructed for *TREC*, single-term queries are to be processed with a maximum of eight bitslices being read, and one false match can be tolerated on average, then $q = 1$, $b = 8$, and $z = 1$ for a collection in which $N = 741,856$. Using Equation 3.4, p is calculated as $p = 0.185$. That is, at most about one bit in six in the signature file should be on if a random selection of eight bitslices is to yield a probability of less than $1/741,856$ for a false match. Similarly, dividing f by N gives about 182 unique "term, document" pairs for the average document, and, with $q = 1$, Equation 3.5 results in $B = 1,456$—the number of independent hashings to be used to create the signature of an average document. Finally, the signature width needed to allow 1,456 random selections of bits, while still retaining a probability of at most 0.185 that a bit is on, is calculated from Equation 3.6. This gives $W = 7,134$, and a signature whose width is 7,134 bits must be allocated—631 Mbytes in total. This corresponds, on average, to 39.2 bits per unique term appearance and is the value listed for *TREC* with $b = 8$ in Table 3.13.

If these strong requirements are relaxed to allow $q = 2$ and $z = 4$—that is, every query will have two terms specified and four false matches can be tolerated—then each term need set only four of the eight required bits, and Equations 3.4, 3.5, and 3.6 give $p = 0.220$, $B = 728$, and $W = 2,937$, respectively. In this case, the signature file will require 259 Mbytes, or 16.1 bits per nominal pointer, as shown in Table 3.14.

To calculate the false-match rate when only one term is specified, Equation 3.3 can be used, in which it is assumed that p has been fixed. With $b = 4$ bits specified, and $p = 0.220$, the expected number of false-match queries for the example *TREC* index discussed in the previous paragraph exceeds 1,700.

Table 3.15 Bitmap index for text of Table 3.2.

Number	Term	Bitvector
1	cold	100100
2	days	001001
3	hot	100100
4	in	010010
5	it	000110
6	like	000110
7	nine	001001
8	old	001001
9	pease	110000
10	porridge	110000
11	pot	010010
12	some	000110
13	the	010010

Bitmaps

In the limit, when each term in a bitsliced signature file index sets one bit in a signature that is as wide as the number of distinct terms in the collection, and the hash function is one-to-one, the index becomes a bitmap. This structure is also a special case of inverted files—it corresponds to a unary code of gaps between term occurrences. Let us now consider the bitmap in its own right.

A bitmap is a very simple indexing structure. For every term in the lexicon, a bitvector is stored, each bit corresponding to a document. A bit is set to 1 if the term appears anywhere in that document and 0 otherwise. Table 3.15 shows a bitmap index for the text in Table 3.2. In this example, the word *pot* appears in lines 2 and 5, so bits 2 and 5 are set in the corresponding bitvector 010010.

Bitmaps are particularly efficient for answering Boolean queries. To resolve this kind of query, the bitvectors for the terms are simply combined using the appropriate Boolean operations, which are often available in fast hardware because of their usefulness in supporting bitmapped graphics displays. In the example, lines containing the words *pot* and *some* are located by evaluating the conjunction of the two bitvectors—010010 and 000110—to yield 000010, or, in other words, line 5.

Bitmaps are fast and easy to use but enormously extravagant of storage, a facet of their behavior that is not demonstrated by the small examples considered here. For a text of N documents and n distinct words, a bitmap occupies Nn bits. To see how large this can be, consider the *TREC* database: a bitmap requires in excess of 40 Gbytes, 20 times more than the text it indexes.

The size of the bitmap can be reduced by removing stop words, but the saving is marginal since there are usually just a few hundred of these. Indeed, uncompressed bitmaps are most efficient for representing common words, since a relatively high proportion of the bits are set. Bitmaps have sometimes been used in this way as an adjunct to an uncompressed inverted index or signature file. On the other hand, there is no reason to explicitly add them as an auxiliary structure to a compressed inverted index since terms that are sufficiently common will automatically be represented with a compression parameter that causes them to be stored as a bitmap.

Compression of signature files and bitmaps

Signature files have traditionally been considered a space-efficient way to store indexing information. Furthermore, their size is adjustable. A signature file that is too large can be made smaller at the expense of an increased number of false matches, and if there is storage to spare, the index can be enlarged, yielding faster retrieval. This variability is a useful option with static databases on fixed-volume secondary storage devices like CD-ROM or digital videodisk.

The information content of a signature file is maximized when exactly half the bits are 1s. In this case, it is impossible to compress the file, since the pattern of bits is supposed to be random, and the best compression obtainable is one bit per symbol. However, it is normal in bitsliced signature file implementations for the number of 1 bits to be substantially less than the number of 0 bits, so that a given level of false-match behavior can be reached after relatively few of the bitslices have been retrieved. Signature files, including those implied by the values of Tables 3.13 and 3.14, are usually designed so that about 10 to 20 percent of the bits are set. In this case, each of the bitslices could be compressed using the Golomb code described above. However, accessing the database through the compressed bitslices would be very costly. For example, a typical query accesses 8 to 12 bitslices, and several hundred kilobytes of bitslices must be processed. If these slices must be decompressed as well as conjoined, then, even with a fast compression code, the time required will be prohibitive.

In some ways, a signature file is already in compressed form since it was created probabilistically based upon the original text. Furthermore, the compression is lossy because the original data cannot be reconstructed from the signature file. Lossy compression is common when dealing with images and analog signals, where small changes (noise) are acceptable on decompression. Much better compression factors can be obtained for images and analog signals if lossy methods are employed instead of lossless ones. This suggests that a signature file has the potential to give better compression than the methods discussed for inverted files. The difficulty is the degree of noise that can be tolerated. Noise appears in the form of a bit that is a 1 when it should be set to 0 for one of the terms indexed and so results in false matches. Errors in the other direction—bits that should be 1 but are set to 0—are still unacceptable. As a consequence, better compression causes more noise and therefore slower retrieval. This is another manifestation of the trade-off between storage space and computing time.

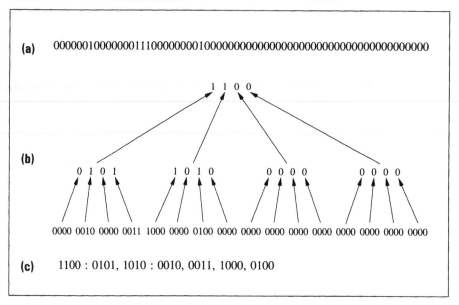

Figure 3.8 Hierarchical bitvector compression: (a) original bitvector; (b) hierarchical structure; (c) flattened tree as a string of bits.

Bitmaps can be compressed, of course. They are very sparse (at these sizes, they must be) and so are amenable to compression. But there is no distinction between a compressed bitmap and a compressed inverted file, and the performance advantages of a bitmap have been lost. For this reason, there is little place for the bitmap in large-scale information retrieval, and they are seldom used in their raw form.

Despite this similarity between bitmaps and inverted lists, it can sometimes be helpful to think in terms of bitmaps. Suppose that the cost of sequentially decoding the d-gaps in a compressed inverted list is too high (we will see why this is important in Chapter 4), and some kind of random access facility is required. Figure 3.8 illustrates one way this can be achieved simultaneously with bitvector compression. Groups of bits (in the example, groups of four bits) are combined disjunctively in a hierarchical manner to make a treelike description of the original bitvector. A 0 in any position indicates that all its descendants are also 0, obviating the need to store those lower levels, in a manner somewhat akin to the pyramid coding techniques for images that are described in Chapter 6. Finally, leaf nodes that contain 1 bits are replaced by short bitvectors showing the locations of the 1 bits in that node. In this manner the bitmap is compressed.

In the example, Figure 3.8a shows a bitvector of 64 bits, of which five are set. Figure 3.8b shows the tree that results if this bitvector is combined in groups of four bits. The bitstring in Figure 3.8c shows what would actually be stored. The first four bits represent the root node of the tree and indicate that the next two groups of four bits contain details of the first and second children and that the third and fourth children are all 0. The next pair of four-bit strings are the two middle nodes of the tree. The final sequence of four four-bit quantities at the end of the bitstring are the blocks of the original bitvector that actually contain the 1 bits. In other words, the colons—which need not be stored explicitly—separate the levels of the tree, and the bitvector at one level dictates which groups of bits are present at the next level below. In total, the original 64 bits are represented in 28 bits. Note that for the example it has been assumed that the expansion ratio from one level to the next is four, but larger values are more normal in practice. Eight-way and sixteen-way branching allow particularly fast implementation, since all of the codes can be processed as 8-bit bytes or 16-bit words.

Because a fixed branching ratio is used throughout the bitmap, the compression is not as good as the Bernoulli/Golomb combination for inverted files. On the other hand, on average only a relatively small fraction of each compressed list needs to be checked to determine if a term appears in a particular document. In the example, if document 22 is to be checked, only two of the tree nodes—eight bits—must be inspected. Faster still, the absence of this term from any of documents 32 through 64 can be known after just the root node has been inspected. That is, regarding the inverted list as a bitvector has resulted in an alternative index representation with desirable properties. Interpolative coding can be regarded as a dynamic form of the tree method, where branches are formed so that the number of 1s is balanced on each side of a node. Every leaf has exactly one bit set, which means that only the position of the bit needs to be coded. Chapter 4 describes other hierarchical strategies that allow compressed inverted files to be processed quickly for conjunctive queries.

3.6 Comparison of indexing methods

The three indexing methods discussed in this chapter are really variations of the same basic idea. For example, an inverted list is one particular sparse matrix method for storing a single row of a bitmap, and a bitsliced signature file can be thought of as a bitmap that has been squeezed into fewer rows, with multiple words represented probabilistically in each. Similarly, a bitmap is equivalent to an inverted file in which word positions are represented by coding in unary the gaps between successive words. A bitmap is also equivalent to the degenerate form of a signature file, in which a single hash function is applied and the signature is extremely wide.

Despite these similarities, there are differences that affect the choice of strategy in practice. Signature files and inverted files consume an order of magnitude less secondary storage than bitmaps, and this difference alone is probably enough to rule out bitmaps in all practical situations.

Signature files can cause unnecessary accesses to the main text because of false matches, but these can be reduced to an insignificant proportion if the signature is large enough and an appropriate number of bits are set for each term. However, this means that some minimum number of bitslices—typically 6 to 12—must always be retrieved, so there is a fine balance between bitslice access and false-match access. In contrast, if inverted lists are accessed in order of increasing length, and the collection's lexicon is held in main memory, then an inverted file scheme requires no more disk accesses in total than a bitsliced signature file scheme except in a few pathological situations. Moreover, signature file manipulations become complex if disjunction and negation are allowed as operators, and, as will be explained in Chapter 4, signature files cannot be used to support ranked, or informal, queries.

And, as was noted above, signature files can be especially disastrous when the record lengths are highly variable. Consider again the *TREC* signature file that was described on page 134 of Section 3.5. Each signature was 7,134 bits wide. There is, however, one document in *TREC* that is nearly 3 Mbytes long and contains more than 400,000 words. Even supposing that just one in a hundred of these words is unique, there are 4,000 terms to be indexed, and (using typical values for b, q, and z) there will be about 32,000 bits selected in the document's signature. Only a handful of signature bits will remain 0, and this document will be retrieved as a false match for almost every query on the system. Worse, the entire document must be processed—decompressed, parsed into words, and stemmed—before it can be determined whether or not it matches the query. Much of the time it will not match, and this enormous effort has been wasted. Unless some preventive action is taken, this document alone will contribute many tens of seconds to the processing time of most queries.

For typical choices of parameters, signature file indexes are also two to three times larger than compressed inverted file indexes:

The two drawbacks of signature file performance—slow speed and greater index size required—form a comprehensive argument in favor of compressed inverted files for applications involving text databases.

The big advantage of signature files is that there is no need to maintain an in-memory lexicon during query processing. On a collection with a very rich vocabulary, an inverted file index might require a lexicon that is a substantial fraction of the total index size, and if fast access is desired, this lexicon needs to be held in memory. The cost of using an inverted file, but with the lexicon on disk, is one extra disk access per query term; if typical queries are on tens or hundreds of terms, the inverted file might require more disk accesses than the signature file since it is never necessary to retrieve more than one bitslice per term on multiterm signature file queries in order to reduce the false-match rate to tolerable levels. Thus, when the lexicon is too large for main memory, the signature file might require only half the disk accesses of an inverted file.

In some circumstances, signature files require less processor time during the resolution of conjunctive queries than do compressed inverted files, particularly if dedicated hardware is available to perform bitslice AND operations. But these circumstances are unlikely to arise in practice. For example, for a Boolean query constructed from the 33 most frequent terms in *TREC*, a compressed inverted file mechanism must decode and merge nearly 15 million document numbers, and this will take tens of seconds of processing time. On the same query, the signature file index would simply retrieve and AND together at most 33 bitslices, each of about 91 Kbytes. This is much faster, a few seconds at most.

In summary, signature files may be appropriate in applications where record lengths are constrained and the vocabulary is very large or where many queries involve common terms. However, compared to compressed inverted files, signature files do not reduce index space as has often been claimed, nor do they offer faster resolution for typical conjunctive queries. Moreover, they cope poorly with non-conjunctive queries, offer no special advantage for dynamic collections (examined in Chapter 4), and require the same or more resources during database creation (discussed in Chapter 5).

Hybrid combinations of inverted files, bitmaps, and signature files have been proposed, where the indexing method for each term is based on the term's frequency. For example, frequent words could be represented by bitmaps and infrequent ones by an inverted file. Alternatively, a bitmap can be used as a preliminary filter to reduce the number of accesses to the inverted file. Another proposal is to store a complete inverted file and fill any remaining disk space with bitvectors since, on a read-only disk, the space would otherwise be wasted. Although such hybrid schemes appear to offer the best of both worlds, retrieval becomes more complex to implement. More to the point, a suitable compression scheme obviates all of these considerations since common terms are stored very compactly and never less densely than in a bitmap. Compressed inverted files are without a doubt the most useful method of indexing a large collection of variable-length text documents.

3.7 Case folding, stemming, and stop words

We have described many trade-offs that are available when designing an index; now it is time to reconsider the exact nature of what should be indexed. The most straightforward approach is to treat each alphabetic or alphanumeric string that appears in the text as an index term. Numbers should not be ignored: queries include them surprisingly often, and a retrieval scheme is seriously handicapped if they cannot be specified. For example, the *GNUbib* document shown in Figure 3.2 on page 108 should certainly be locatable by *arithmetic* AND *coding* AND *1987* AND *cacm*.

There are two problems with this simplistic approach. First, searches will fail if there is a mismatch between the case of the query term and that of the index term. Second, users will want to search in a way that ignores suffixes. Here we examine these two problems and their effect upon index size. A further facility appreciated by users is the option of specifying wildcard characters in their query terms—for example, searching for **compress** to find documents that talk about *decompression* and *decompressers*. Mechanisms for providing this facility are considered in detail in Chapter 4.

```
the other proces is stem which allow a littl leewa when
match qu term to indic term so that for exampl compres and
compres are both accept as equival to compres stem involut
strip one or mor suffic off a word to reduc it to root form
convers it to a neutr term that is dev of tens and plur the
easiest way to appreci the proces is to look at som exampl
text
```

Figure 3.9 Stemmed text.

Case folding

The first problem, that of case mismatches causing queries to fail, is easily solved by *case folding*—the action of replacing all uppercase characters in a string with their lowercase equivalents. For example, *the*, *The*, *THE*, and five other combinations would all be folded to the representative term *the* and indexed accordingly. Similarly, any occurrence of these three letters in the query would be converted to the query term *the* before any attempt was made to resolve the term against the search lexicon and access the inverted file. There will be situations when the user wishes to disable this feature and perform an exact-match search, perhaps looking for documents containing *General* AND *Motors* (the automotive manufacturer) and not wanting to be flooded with answers about *general repairs to all kinds of motors*. This kind of exception can always be handled by a postretrieval scan, in which an exact pattern matcher is used and case differences are respected; the need to check for these false matches means that these queries are slower. In some situations, as in the system described in Appendix B, it may be worthwhile providing an index structure that allows both case-folded and case-sensitive queries.

Stemming

The other process is *stemming*, which allows a little leeway when matching query terms to index terms so that, for example, *compressed* and *compression* are both accepted as equivalent to *compress*. Stemming involves stripping one or more suffixes off a word to reduce it to root form, converting it to a neutral term that is devoid of tense and plurality. The easiest way to appreciate the process is to look at some example text. Figure 3.9 shows the first few lines of this paragraph, after being processed by a stemmer. To create index terms, all punctuation has been removed, and, as discussed above, the alphabetic characters have been case-folded.

At first glance, the result of stemming is little short of rubbish—it looks as though the algorithm is seriously flawed. Note, however, that first, the final representation of the root word does not really matter providing it is unique for a class of source terms, and second, the transformation is repeatable. The transformation does not, of course, need to be invertible, since stemming is used only to create index terms and the text itself is always stored exactly; nor does the root word need to be any meaningful English word. Indeed, *compress*, *compression*, and *compressed* might as well all be converted to *ppzxg* by the stemmer, providing no other words are. Humans are rarely, if ever, required to read stemmed text.

Stemming is not necessarily appropriate for all parts of a collection. If this book were being sought in a library catalog, and the very precise query *Witten* AND *Moffat* AND *Bell* AND *Managing* AND *Gigabytes* were entered, the stemmer used to generate Figure 3.9 would map the search into one for *wit* AND *moffat* AND *bel* AND *man* AND *gigabys*, leading perhaps to some ambiguity. (And a search for work by *Cleary* AND *Witten* turns into a quest for *clear wit*.) In the author field of a bibliographic database, it may well be more appropriate to disable stemming; the restriction of stemming to certain parts of the documents is another option available to the database designer. In the library system in Appendix B, for example, users can specify for each individual word in their query whether or not it should be stemmed.

Actual implementation of a stemming process requires a detailed knowledge of English and a great deal of patience. The first few cases—the suffixes *-s*, *-ed*, *-ing*, *-ly*, and so on—are easy. But then exceptions to these simple rules are found and further rules added to prevent them from being stripped; then exceptions to the exceptions are identified, and so on. The stemmer used to produce Figure 3.9 contains more than 500 rules and exceptions, coded as a finite-state machine.

Effect on index size

The principal purpose of stemming and case folding is to simplify the construction of queries. However, with them comes a bonus—a substantial reduction in the size of the inverted file. This occurs for two reasons. First, there are fewer inverted lists to be stored, and those that are stored become denser, making their storage cost, on a per-pointer basis, cheaper. Second, the average frequency of terms within documents tends to increase, meaning that there are fewer pointers in total.

For example, after case-folding and stemming the raw index for the *TREC* collection, the number of pointers is reduced by about 16 percent, the number of distinct terms by about 40 percent, and the total space used by a Golomb-coded index is reduced by about 30 percent. However, the saving arising from the use of a stemmed index must be offset to some extent by the cost of storing the stemmed lexicon. An unstemmed, unfolded lexicon can be shared between the text compression components of the system and the indexing subsystem, but a stemmed lexicon cannot. On *TREC*, the lexicon requires about 5 Mbytes, so the balance is still in favor of stemming, with a net saving of about 35 Mbytes.

In a signature file, the effect of stemming and case folding is to reduce the number of distinct terms appearing in each record, thereby reducing the width of the signature that is needed for a given false-match rate, so similar savings accrue. In a bitmap index, savings arise simply because fewer terms are indexed, and similar reductions result.

Stop words

Another mechanism that is sometimes used with the aim of reducing the size of the index is to *stop* certain frequently occurring terms and simply not index them at all.

$$\boxed{f_t > 283{,}591; \quad b = 1}$$

```
the of and to a in for is with on by that s are at from as
be an th it was has new which hav 1 said or wil its not but
```

$$\boxed{f_t > 182{,}627; \quad b = 2}$$

```
2 year been wer als other m compan one mor two about than
bas us produc st 3 up he tim their all t inclus no who can 5
pres system would u had 10 after p offic when
```

$$\boxed{f_t > 134{,}223; \quad b = 3}$$

```
som part ap first i int may strees 4 top j report fin out
million act dat last ther unit mak nr over we if o inc oper
such man gener onl wal tak becaus markes 6 most plan under
nat associ result thre 8 high 000 journ any his corp r work
bus month presid direct co between giv servic 7 89
```

Figure 3.10 The most frequent 135 index terms in *TREC*.

The set of stop words is referred to as the *stop list*. In a conventional uncompressed inverted file index, a stop list can yield a substantial saving in space. For example, in *TREC* there are 33 terms that appear in more than 38.2 percent of the documents (the lower threshold percentage for the use of a Golomb code with $b = 1$ from Table 3.7 on page 120), a very small fraction of the total vocabulary; but these 33 terms account for almost 30 percent of all term appearances and 11 percent of the pointers stored in the inverted file. A further 39 terms appear in 24.5 percent to 38.2 percent of the documents, accounting for another 6.3 percent of pointers, and the next 63 terms, with probabilities down to 18.1 percent, contribute 7.3 percent of pointers. In combination, these three groups of terms—just 135 in total—generate 25 percent of the pointers in the inverted file. Figure 3.10 lists, in decreasing f_t order, these 135 words. (Recall that although there is SGML markup in every document, it is stripped out before any indexing takes place.) You might wish to try to guess the word (or words) corresponding to each stemmed version.

In an uncompressed index, a quarter of the inverted file space would be saved by eliminating these frequent terms. Provided we are reasonably confident that a plausible query will not be posed entirely out of stop words, there seems little reason to retain them. However, frequency alone is not necessarily a reliable indicator of words that it is safe to exclude. For example, consider the phrase *The head and president of an American computer system company based in Washington said she expected to make a million systems by the end of the year*. It turns out that every word in this sentence occurs in 10 percent or more of the *TREC* documents, so any attempt to find further information, using this phrase as a query, would fail if the stop list were based solely upon frequency. The only recourse would be a linear search of the entire text, which is very time-consuming.

Furthermore, in applying a stop list, the index creator is anticipating that future users will not be interested in these terms. In reality, it is not so easy to predict what will be of interest to researchers. For example, in Section 1.3 we mentioned a study of Shakespeare's use of the verb *to do*. A traditional concordance that did not list stop words would be of little assistance in such a study. In a more recent context, the researchers who created an online version of the *Trésor de la Langue Française*, a comprehensive collection of French literature, have noted that their decision to omit certain stop words caused problems for someone who was looking for occurrences of the phrase *un de ces* ("one of these"). All three of these words were stopped, so the only way to locate the phrase was to search the entire text (Klein, Bookstein, and Deerwester 1989).

A further problem with stop words is that some of the most common words—notably, *may*, *can*, and *will*—are verbs that are homonyms for rarer nouns, so, for example, stopping the word *may* also removes references to the month of May.

When the inverted file is stored compressed, the value of removing stop words is even less clear. Applying a stop list still reduces the size of the index, but the words that are stopped are exactly those that require the fewest bits per pointer to store, and the overall saving on the inverted file is far smaller than might be expected. For example, on *TREC*, the inverted lists for the 33 most frequent words are stored (using the Golomb code) with $b = 1$, so the corresponding inverted lists are at most 741,856 bits long—about 91 Kbytes. The saving generated by stopping all 33 words is less than 3 Mbytes. Similarly, the other two groups of words listed in Figure 3.10 are coded with $b = 2$ and $b = 3$ and consume 3.0 Mbytes and 4.2 Mbytes, respectively. Since the total *TREC* inverted file, when compressed, occupies around 93 Mbytes, the saving is of doubtful benefit, particularly considering the inconvenience of processing queries that might contain any of these words.

Stop words have little effect on the size of signature files and bitmaps. A few bitslices or bitvectors might be saved, but compared to the size of the original index, the benefit is negligible because very few words are actually removed from the lexicon.

The idea of including stop words in an index is not new, but previously a different representation has been used. In Strong's exhaustive concordance of the Bible (discussed in Chapter 1), 47 common words are printed separately at the end of the main concordance. Unlike the main entries, the contexts of these words are not quoted since, as Strong points out, this would be tantamount to quoting practically the whole Bible in each of the words' entries. The words are represented more efficiently by giving references to where they occur, and the stop words use only 119 pages, compared with 1,212 pages for the remaining words. Eliminating the stop words altogether would have reduced the size of Strong's concordance by less than 10 percent, yet would greatly increase the effort to find, for example, the frequencies or co-occurrences of words such as *him* and *her*.

By using a suitable representation, the issue of whether stop words should be used becomes much less serious, whether we are concerned about the length of a printed book or the size of an online index for a retrieval system. Using an appropriate compressed representation means that the amount of space allocated to stop words is commensurate with their status and relieves the indexer—the "harmless drudge"—of the task of predicting the needs of future users.

Further reading

Much of the material presented in this chapter is drawn from the survey of Bell et al. (1993).

Coding methods. The γ and δ codes were described by Elias (1975) and subsequently by Bentley and Yao (1976). The use of a local Bernoulli model for index compression has been considered by Witten, Bell, and Nevill (1992) and Bookstein, Klein, and Raita (1992). The Golomb code was first described in the mid-1960s (Golomb 1966) and further analyzed by Gallager and Van Voorhis (1975); it has other applications too (McIlroy 1982). The skewed Bernoulli model was described by Teuhola (1978), and further experiments were carried out by Moffat and Zobel (1992). Other index compression methods are described by Abraham Bookstein and S. T. (Tomi) Klein and their coworkers (Fraenkel and Klein 1985; Bookstein and Klein 1991a, 1991b; Bookstein, Klein, and Raita 1992). The hyperbolic model was introduced by Schuegraf (1976). Moffat and Zobel (1992) examine the batched frequency method for assigning codes. Context-sensitive index compression has been considered by Bookstein, Klein, and Raita (1994). The interpolative code was described by Moffat and Stuiver (1996), and Figure 3.6 is derived from that paper.

Example collections. The four example collections used in this chapter have rather different origins. *Bible* is a public domain version of the King James Bible, broken into verses with a simple "book, chapter, verse" prefix included in each. *GNUbib* is a large database of computing citations collected by Zoltan Somogyi, Isaac Balbin, and others at the University of Melbourne in the late 1980s. Not only did they collect the data, entering much of it manually themselves, they also wrote a suite of programs to manipulate it and support a variety of access needs (Somogyi 1990). *Comact* is a result of the celebration in 1988 of 200 years of European settlement in Australia. As one bicentennial project, it was decided to make all legislation available in machine-readable form. This was achieved by scanning the 261,829 pages of text covering the constitution of 1901 and all subsequent legislation through 1989. Finally, the *TREC* collection is the result of support from several federal research organizations in the United States. The foreword by Donna Harman (1992a) in the proceedings of the first *TREC* conference provides an overview of this project and describes the scale of the investigation that is being undertaken, with more than 20 groups involved worldwide within the first two years. A special issue of the journal *Information Processing and Management* describing the work undertaken by some of the groups involved in *TREC* was issued in 1995 (Harman 1995). Now in its sixth year, the *TREC* resource includes more than 5 Gbytes of text, 300 query topics, and several hundred thousand relevance judgments; there are approximately 50 research groups committed to the project (in 1998). There is further mention of the *TREC* project in Chapter 4.

Implementations of inverted file retrieval systems. Descriptions of the implementation of inverted file retrieval systems have been given by numerous authors (McDonell 1977; Buckley and Lewit 1985; Lucarella 1988; Harman and Candela 1990; Somogyi 1990; Fox, Harman, et al. 1992). Moffat and Zobel (1994) describe some of the problems caused by the magnitude of the *TREC* collection and discuss the performance of a retrieval system based on inverted files.

Signature files. The trade-off between storage space and the probability of false matches in signature files is examined by Faloutsos and Christodoulakis (1984) (see also Faloutsos 1985). Various structures based upon signature files, including a two-level scheme, are described by Sacks-Davis, Kent, and Ramamohanarao (1987) and Kent, Sacks-Davis, and Ramamohanarao (1990). Faloutsos (1992) surveys signature file techniques. Another type of signature file index is described by Lesk (1988), and the spelling checker of McIlroy (1982) also involves an element of probabilistic indexing. McKenzie, Harries, and Bell (1990) have examined hash functions for strings and described some of the common pitfalls that can lead to bad behavior. Further work in this area has been carried out by Ramakrishna and Zobel (1997).

Bitmaps. Choueka et al. (1986) describe the hierarchical bitmap representation.

Stemming and stop words. Lovins (1968) and Porter (1980) are two of many authors who have examined the problem of stemming. Frakes surveys this area in a chapter in the book he coedited (Frakes and Baeza-Yates 1992). Lennon et al. (1981) have also examined the problem. The stemmer reported in Section 3.7 is based on the paper by Lovins (1968). The sentence composed entirely of frequent *TREC* words is taken from Buckley, Salton, and Allan (1992). The *un des ces* anecdote comes from a paper discussing the implementation of a retrieval system for the *Trésor de la Langue Française* (Klein, Bookstein, and Deerwester 1989).

Comparison of indexing methods. Zobel, Moffat, and Ramamohanarao (1998) compare compressed inverted files and bitsliced signature files in both theory and practice and give detailed experiments for various types of queries. In a separate paper, the same authors discuss the various criteria that should be used to assess indexing methods (Zobel, Moffat, and Ramamohanarao 1996).

Querying

Now that we have seen what an index contains and how to store it efficiently, we move on to consider how best to use an index to locate information in the text it describes. Two types of queries will be examined in this chapter. The first is a conventional *Boolean* query; this form was tacitly assumed during the discussion in Chapter 3. The second is a *ranked* query; we will discuss what this means shortly.

A Boolean query comprises a list of *terms*—words to be sought in the text—that are combined using the connectives AND, OR, and NOT. The *answers*, or *responses*, to the query are those documents that satisfy the stipulated condition. For example, an appropriate query to search for material relevant to this book is

> *text* AND *compression* AND *retrieval.*

All three words (or variants considered equivalent by a stemming algorithm) must occur somewhere in every answer. They need not be adjacent nor appear in any particular order. Documents containing phrases like *the compression and retrieval of large amounts of text is an interesting problem* will be returned as answers. Also returned would be a document containing *this text describes the fractional distillation scavenging technique for retrieving argon from compressed air*—perhaps not quite what is sought, but nonetheless a correct answer to the query.

A problem with all retrieval systems is that answers are invariably returned that are not relevant, and these must be filtered out manually. A difficult choice must be made between casting a broad query to be sure of retrieving all relevant material, even if it is diluted with many irrelevant answers, and posing a narrow one, which ensures that most documents retrieved are of interest but risks eliminating others sight unseen because the query is too restrictive. A broad search that identifies virtually all the relevant documents is said to have *high recall*, while one in which virtually all the retrieved documents are relevant has *high precision*. An enduring theme in information retrieval is the tension between these two virtues. We must choose in any particular application whether to prefer high precision or high recall and cast the query appropriately—just as a fisherman might choose to use a hand net to select a single prized catch or to trawl the ocean floor to make sure that nothing escapes, but in the process catching a great deal of junk as well.

Another problem with Boolean retrieval systems is that small variations in a query can generate very different results. The query *data* AND *compression* AND *retrieval* is likely to produce quite a different answer set to *text* AND *compression* AND *retrieval*, yet the person issuing these requests probably sees them as very similar. To be sure of catching all the required documents, users become adept at adding extra terms and learn to pose queries like

(*text* OR *data* OR *image*) AND
(*compression* OR *compaction* OR *decompression*) AND
(*archiving* OR *retrieval* OR *storage* OR *indexing*)

where the parentheses indicate operation order. This, perhaps, is one reason why librarians guard access to the large international databases. Formulating queries is an art, and librarians have the necessary insight and linguistic skills to guide a query toward an acceptable set of answers.

Despite these problems, Boolean retrieval systems were the primary mechanism used to access online information for more than three decades, in both commercial and scientific applications. They have satisfied countless users. Nevertheless, they are not the only way a database can be queried. Typical fishers of information might find it even better simply to list words that are of interest and have the retrieval mechanism supply the documents that seem most relevant, rather than seeking exact Boolean answers. For example, to locate material for this book, the query

text, data, image, compression, compaction, archiving, storage, retrieval, indexing, gigabyte, megabyte, document, database, searching, information

is, to a person at least, probably a clearer description of the topic than the Boolean query above.

Identifying documents relevant to a list of terms is not just a matter of converting the terms to a Boolean query. It would be fruitless to connect these particular terms with AND operations since vanishingly few documents are likely to match. (We cannot, of course, say that no documents will match. This page certainly does.) It would be just as pointless to use OR connectives since far too many documents will match and very few are likely to be useful answers.

One solution is to use a ranked query. This involves a heuristic that is applied to gauge the *similarity* of each document to the query. Based on this numeric indicator, the r most closely matching documents are returned as answers—r being perhaps 10 or 100. If the heuristic is good, or r is small, or (better still) both, there will be a predominance of relevant answers—high precision. If the heuristic is good and r is large, most of the documents in the collection that are relevant will fall within the top r—high recall. In practice, low precision invariably accompanies high recall since many irrelevant documents will almost certainly come to light before the last of the relevant ones appears in the ranking. Conversely, when the precision is high, recall will probably be low, since precision will be high only near the beginning of the ranked list of documents, at which point only a few of the total set of relevant ones will have been encountered.

Great effort has been invested over the years in a quest for similarity measures and other ranking strategies that succeed in keeping both recall and precision reasonably high. Simple techniques just count the number of query terms that appear somewhere in the document: this is often called *coordinate matching*. A document that contains five of the query terms will be ranked higher than one containing only three, and documents that match just one query term will be ranked lower still. An obvious drawback is that long documents are favored over short ones since by virtue of size alone they are more likely to contain a wider selection of the query terms. Furthermore, common terms appearing in the query tend to discriminate unfairly against documents that do not happen to contain them, even ones that match on highly specific ones. For example, a query concerning *the electronic office* might rank a document containing *the office garbage can* ahead of one that discusses *an electronic workplace*. A word such as *the* in the query should probably not be given the same importance as *electronic*.

More sophisticated ranking techniques take into account the length of the documents and assign a numeric *weight* to each term. One such technique—the *cosine* measure—is examined in this chapter as an example of a *vector space* (also sometimes called *statistical*) method. Many other schemes have been proposed for ranking documents, some of which are also surveyed here.

Throughout this book our primary concern is with implementation issues and resource implications. Nevertheless, results are provided to show how useful the various ranking methods are. For example, on a set of 50 queries applied to the *TREC* collection, the cosine measure achieves an average precision exceeding 40 percent on the top 100 answers to each query. In other words, when a ranked query is posed to *TREC*—which contains nearly three-quarters of a million documents—40 of the top 100 documents returned for each query will be relevant. Such performance is difficult to achieve with a Boolean query, and, as will be illustrated below, the queries formulated from the *TREC* topics were anything but carefully phrased. Set against this improved retrieval is the extra expense of ranked queries. More complex index information is required than for Boolean queries, and processing costs are greater.

Before any of these issues can be tackled, a mechanism must be provided that locates the query terms in the collection's lexicon and identifies the addresses of the corresponding inverted lists. Although this is a simple task for small collections, it is not easy to do efficiently for large ones. The first section of this chapter deals with the problem of searching the lexicon to identify query terms.

There is also the possibility that query terms might include wildcard characters. For example, *lab*r* might be used to cover both *labor* (the American spelling) and *labour* (the British spelling); economy of typing might prompt the use of *superc*fra*exp*do*s* when looking for information about the movie *Mary Poppins*. The former query would also match *labrador*, an expansion that probably does

Table 4.1 Storage requirements for a million-term lexicon using various data structures.

Method	Storage
Fixed-length strings	28 Mbytes
Terminated strings	20 Mbytes
Four-entry blocking	18 Mbytes
Front coding	15.5 Mbytes
Minimal perfect hashing	13 Mbytes

not yield the desired effect, and so even at this level of query, there is a question of relevance. Methods for handling partially specified terms are considered in Section 4.2.

4.1 Accessing the lexicon

The lexicon for an inverted file index stores both the terms that can be used to search the collection and the auxiliary information needed to allow queries to be processed. The minimal information that must be stored for each term t in the lexicon is the address in the inverted file of I_t, the corresponding list of document numbers. To allow inverted lists to be retrieved in order of increasing term frequency, it is usual to store f_t, the number of documents containing the term, as well. The reason for this is discussed in Section 4.3. Other values, such as compression parameters, are normally stored as part of the inverted list since they are required only after the list has been retrieved.

In this section we develop ways to store lexicons. A poor choice of data structure can waste many megabytes of storage space during query processing, and since the intention is that query processing will be carried out on a relatively low-powered machine, this memory might be needed for other purposes. Table 4.1 summarizes the storage required by the data structures we develop, for a collection with one million terms. The first three techniques are very simple; the fourth is more involved, and the fifth, minimal perfect hashing, is distinctly subtle. In the end we will conclude that for querying purposes, the main memory requirement can be eliminated almost entirely simply by placing the lexicon on disk. However, there are situations, such as the index construction process described in Chapter 5, when this solution is inadequate, and minimal perfect hashing becomes the method of choice.

Access structures

A simple structure for the lexicon is to store an array of records, each comprising a string along with two integer fields. If the lexicon is sorted, a word can be located by a binary search of the strings, as was suggested in some of the calculations in

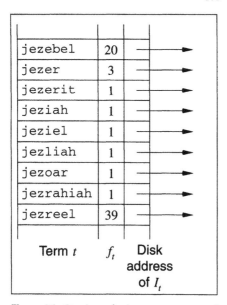

Term t	f_t	Disk address of I_t
jezebel	20	→
jezer	3	→
jezerit	1	→
jeziah	1	→
jeziel	1	→
jezliah	1	→
jezoar	1	→
jezrahiah	1	→
jezreel	39	→

Figure 4.1   Storing a lexicon as an array of records.

Chapter 1, and access is very fast. This structure is shown in Figure 4.1; the words used are part of the lexicon for the *Bible* collection.

Storing the strings in this way will consume a great deal of space. The lexicon for a large collection might contain one million terms. This is not extreme: in the 2 Gbyte *TREC* collection, for example, there are $n = 535,246$ distinct terms even after stemming (many of them are spelling mistakes, but that is unavoidable), and so one million terms could correspond to a collection of perhaps 5 Gbytes. Stored as 20-byte strings (and optimistically assuming that none is longer than 20 bytes), with a 4-byte inverted file address and a 4-byte f_t value, the lexicon requires more than 28 Mbytes.

The space for the strings is reduced if they are all concatenated into one long contiguous string and an array of 4-byte character pointers is used for access. Then each term consumes its exact number of characters, plus four for the pointer. This is likely to result in a net saving since the average length of terms in a large lexicon is typically about eight characters in English. Note that the average length of terms in a lexicon is considerably longer than the average length in the corresponding text, which is usually about four to five characters. For example, the average length in the 538,000-term *TREC* lexicon is 7.36 letters, whereas the average length in the 334,000,000-term *TREC* corpus is 3.86 letters. This difference in average length is because most of the very common terms are short; they are repeated many times in the text, but each appears only once in the lexicon.

The string and pointer structure is sketched in Figure 4.2. When every string is indexed, it is not necessary for a string length field or terminator character to be stored since the next pointer in the array indicates the end of the string. For the

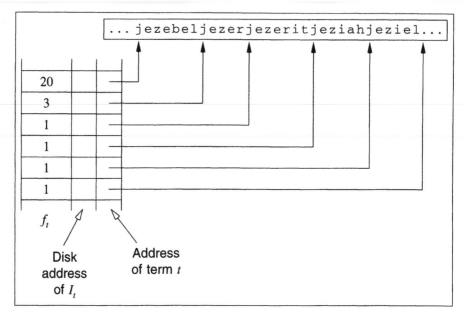

Figure 4.2 Storing a lexicon as an array of string pointers.

same hypothetical vocabulary of one million words, the memory space is reduced by 8 Mbytes to 20 Mbytes.

The memory required can be further reduced by eliminating many of the string pointers. Although it is clear that n inverted file addresses and f_t values must be stored, it is not necessary to use n pointers to index the array of words. Suppose that one word in four is indexed, and each stored word is prefixed by a 1-byte length field. The length field allows the start of the next string to be identified and the block of strings traversed. In each group of four words, a total of 12 bytes of pointers is saved, at the cost of including 4 bytes of length information. This structure is illustrated in Figure 4.3. For the one-million-word lexicon, the space required drops by another 2 Mbytes, and a total of 18 Mbytes suffices. For larger blocks, the savings continue to accrue but are less dramatic. For example, blocks of eight words rather than four save a further 0.5 Mbyte; blocks of 16 words, another 0.25 Mbyte; and so on.

Blocking makes the searching process somewhat more complex. To look up a term, the array of string pointers is first binary-searched to locate the correct block of words. This block is then scanned in a linear fashion to find the term, and its ordinal term number is inferred from the combination of block number and position within block. Once the ordinal term number has been calculated, the f_t array and the vector of inverted file addresses can be accessed in the usual way.

Best of all, using blocks of four words has only a very small effect on the cost of searching. This is because a linear search on the last three words within the block, should it be necessary, requires, on average, two string comparisons. This is only

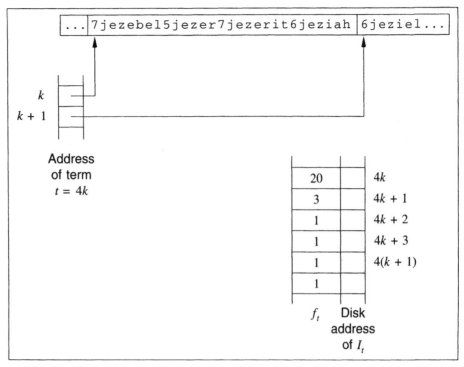

Figure 4.3 Storing a lexicon with one word in four indexed.

slightly more than the average of 1.7 comparisons spent if all strings are indexed and the binary search continued through to completion.

Front coding

Front coding is a further worthwhile improvement. It utilizes the fact that consecutive words in a sorted list are likely to share a common prefix. Two integers are stored with each word: one to indicate how many prefix characters are the same as the previous word and the other to record how many suffix characters remain when the prefix is removed. The two integers are followed by the stipulated number of suffix characters. Table 4.2 shows part of the lexicon of the *Bible* text. The first column gives the words in full, each one prefixed by its length in bytes. Allowing 1 byte for each length field, the storage required by this set of strings is 96 bytes.

The second column of Table 4.2 shows the front-coded version of Figure 4.1. The amount of saving depends on the lexicon, but typically an average of three to five prefix characters will match, at the cost of 1 extra byte to store the second integer. For the set of words shown, which were extracted from a relatively small lexicon, the average net saving is 2.5 bytes per word. The larger the lexicon, the more matching prefix characters there are, simply because more strings are forced into the same range of possible characters. To see this, recall that uppercase characters are folded

Table 4.2 Front coding (the word before *jezebel* was *jezaniah*).

Word	Complete front coding	Partial "3-in-4" front coding
7, jezebel	3, 4, ebel	, 7, jezebel
5, jezer	4, 1, r	4, 1, r
7, jezerit	5, 2, it	5, 2, it
6, jeziah	3, 3, iah	3, , iah
6, jeziel	4, 2, el	, 6, jeziel
7, jezliah	3, 4, liah	3, 4, liah
6, jezoar	3, 3, oar	3, 3, oar
9, jezrahiah	3, 6, rahiah	3, , rahiah
7, jezreel	4, 3, eel	, 7, jezreel
11, jezreelites	7, 4, ites	7, 4, ites
6, jibsam	1, 5, ibsam	1, 5, ibsam
7, jidlaph	2, 5, dlaph	2, , dlaph

to lowercase, leaving 10 digits and 26 letters, and imagine each alphanumeric string to be a radix-36 fractional number between zero and one. Character *0* is interpreted as digit 0, *1* as digit 1, and so on; characters *a* to *z* are interpreted as digits 10 through 35, respectively.

Further, assume a radix-36 point immediately to the left of the first digit. That is, instead of the ordinary radix-10 representation of numbers in which 10 digits are used, suppose that a number system with 36 digits is used. For example, the string *01* is represented by the decimal number $0.00077 = 0 \times 36^{-1} + 1 \times 36^{-2}$; the string *a* corresponds to the decimal number $0.27777 = 10 \times 36^{-1}$; the word *bed* corresponds to $0.31664 = 11 \times 36^{-1} + 14 \times 36^{-2} + 13 \times 36^{-3}$; and *zzzzz* ... is, for all practical purposes, equivalent to 1.0. If a lexicon has n strings, the average gap between strings interpreted in this way must be less than $1/n$, and if one string in the sorted lexicon corresponds to the value x, the next one will, on average, correspond to the value $x + 1/n$. For any random value x in $[0, 1)$, the expected number of matching radix-k digits between x and $x+1/n$ is $\log_k n - 1$ for all but small values of k. Thus, for the text *Bible*, the average prefix match length must be at least $\log_{36} 9,020 - 1 = 1.5$, and for the hypothetical lexicon of $n = 1,000,000$ strings, it is at least $\log_{36} 1,000,000 - 1 = 2.9$.

Of course, the strings are not random. In any dictionary, some prefixes are used extensively, while others never appear. This means that the actual saving reaped from front coding considerably exceeds the amount just calculated. In *Bible*, the average prefix length is 3.6 characters, and the average string length is 6.1. This amounts to a net saving of 2.6 bytes out of each 7.1 bytes of string storage. On the

TREC lexicon, the corresponding values are 4.8 and 7.3, amounting to a net saving of 3.8 bytes per 8.3 bytes. As a general rule of thumb:

Front coding yields a net saving of about 40 percent of the space required for string storage in a typical lexicon for the English language.

The problem with the "Complete front coding" column of Table 4.2 is that binary search is no longer possible. Even if a string pointer leads directly to the entry *3, 4, ebel*, it is impossible to know what the word is. The third column shows a good strategy to use in practice. Here, every fourth word—the one indexed by the block pointer—is stored without front coding, so that binary search can proceed. Just one integer field—the length—need accompany these indexed words, as Table 4.2 shows. However, they might be stored with a prefix length of zero, introducing a small amount of redundancy for the sake of consistency. Similarly, the second suffix-length integer is omitted from the last string of each block since it can be inferred from the next string pointer.

On a large lexicon, a 3-in-4 front-coding strategy can be expected to save about 4 bytes on each of three words, at the cost of 2 extra bytes of prefix-length information—a net gain of 10 bytes per four-word block. This reduces the storage required for the hypothetical lexicon by a further 2.5 Mbytes, bringing the total to 15.5 Mbytes.

Each entry in the three arrays can be squeezed into less space. For example, $\lceil \log N \rceil$ bits is sufficient for each f_t value, where N is the number of documents in the collection; similarly, the inverted file pointer and string pointer can be stored as minimal binary codes in their respective ranges. The calculations above assumed four bytes for each f_t value and inverted file pointer, but coded in this way they will occupy perhaps 28 bits each, saving a further 1 Mbyte. The prefix- and suffix-length fields in the list of strings can be extracted and stored in their own parallel arrays, the former occupying perhaps three or four bits and the latter five or six bits. Placing a limit of 8 or 16 on the maximum prefix match length is not restrictive. If more characters match, a prefix length of too few characters can nevertheless be coded: this just means that a few extra bytes must be stored, an insignificant penalty compared to the saving of four or five bits for every word in the lexicon.

These efforts to reduce the size of the lexicon data structure are prompted by a desire to store the index entry address and f_t value in main memory. It seems that the only remaining mechanism to reduce the storage space would be to dispense with the strings entirely. Incredible as it may sound, this is exactly what we do next.

Minimal perfect hashing

A *hash function h* is a mechanism for mapping a set L of n keys x_j into a set of integer values $h(x_j)$ in the range $0 \le h(x_j) \le m-1$, with duplicates allowed. This is a standard method for implementing a lookup table and provides fast average-case behavior. When the data consists of n integer keys, for example, a common hash function is to take $h(x) = x \bmod m$ for some value $m > n/\alpha$, where α is the *loading*, the ratio of records to available addresses, and m is usually chosen to be a prime number. Thus, if asked to provide a hash function for 1,000 integer keys, a programmer might suggest something like $h(x) = x \bmod 1,399$ to give a load factor of $\alpha = 0.7$ in a table declared to have 1,399 locations.

The smaller the value of α, the less likely it is that two of the keys *collide* at the same hash value. Nevertheless, collisions are almost impossible to avoid. This fact is somewhat surprising when first encountered and is demonstrated by the well-known *birthday paradox*, which asks, "Given that there are 365 days in the year, how many people must be collected together before the probability that two people share a birthday exceeds 0.5?" In other words, given 365 hash slots, how many keys can be randomly assigned before the probability of collision exceeds 0.5? The initial reaction is usually to say that lots of people are needed. In fact, the answer is just 23, and the chance that a hash function of realistic size is collision-free is insignificant.[1] For example, with 1,000 keys and 1,399 randomly selected slots, the probability of there being no collisions at all is 2.35×10^{-217}. (The derivation of this probability can be found in the next subsection: it is given by Equation 4.1 with $m = 1,399$ and $n = 1,000$.) The inevitability of collisions has led to a large body of literature on how best to handle them. Here, however, we seek instead those one-in-a-million hash functions that do manage to avoid all collisions.

If the hash function has the additional property that, for x_i and x_j in L, $h(x_i) = h(x_j)$ if and only if $i = j$, it is a *perfect* hash function. In this case, no collisions arise when hashing the set of keys L.

If a hash function h is both perfect and maps into the range $m = n$, each of the n keys hashes to a unique integer between 1 and n and the table loading is $\alpha = 1.0$. Then h is a *minimal perfect hash function*, or MPHF. An MPHF provides guaranteed one-probe access to a set of keys, and the table contains no unused slots.

Finally, if a hash function has the property that if $x_i < x_j$ then $h(x_i) < h(x_j)$, it is *order preserving*. Given an order-preserving minimal perfect hash function (abbreviated OPMPHF and pronounced "oomph!"), keys are located in constant time without any space overhead and can be processed in sorted order should that be necessary. An OPMPHF simply returns the sequence number of a key directly.

Of course, an MPHF or OPMPHF h for one set L will not be perfect for another set of keys, and so it is nothing more than a precalculated lookup function for a single set. Nevertheless, there are occasions when the precalculation is warranted, and the space saving can be great.

---

1   It is always interesting to try this experiment with groups of people. Having tried this experiment many times with students while teaching them about hash tables, there is one important tip that we would like to pass on: the participants should be asked to write down their birthday (or any other date) *before* the collation process is commenced, so that the temptation for mysterious negative feedback is eliminated. In our experience, unless this is done, it can sometimes take 366 students before the first collision. Perhaps there is a psychology paradox here too.

Table 4.3 Tables for a minimal perfect hash function: (a) terms and hash functions; (b) function g.

(a)	Term t	$h_1(t)$	$h_2(t)$	$h(t)$		(b)	x	$g(x)$
	jezebel	5	9	0			0	0
	jezer	5	7	1			1	4
	jezerit	10	12	2			2	0
	jeziah	6	10	3			3	7
	jeziel	13	7	4			4	6
	jezliah	13	11	5			5	0
	jezoar	4	2	6			6	1
	jezrahiah	0	3	7			7	1
	jezreel	6	3	8			8	3
	jezreelites	8	4	9			9	0
	jibsam	9	14	10			10	2
	jidlaph	3	1	11			11	2
							12	0
							13	3
							14	10

As an example, Table 4.3 gives an OPMPHF for the same set of 12 keys that was used earlier. The methodology leading to this hash function is described in the next section. The construction presumes the existence of two normal hash functions $h_1(t)$ and $h_2(t)$ that map strings into integers in the range $0 \ldots m - 1$ for some value $m \geq n$, with duplicates permitted. One way to define these is to take the numeric value for each character of a string radix 36, as before, and compute a weighted sum for some set of weights w_j,

$$h_j(t) = \left(\sum_{i=1}^{|t|} t[i] \times w_j[i] \right) \bmod m,$$

where $t[i]$ is the radix-36 value of the ith character of term t and $|t|$ is the length in characters of term t. Then two different sets of weights $w_1[i]$ and $w_2[i]$ for $1 \leq i \leq |t|$ yield two different functions $h_1(t)$ and $h_2(t)$. As well as these two functions, a rather special array g is needed that maps numbers $0 \ldots m - 1$ into the range $0 \ldots n - 1$; this is shown in Table 4.3b.

To evaluate the OPMPHF $h(t)$ for some string t, calculate

$$h(t) = g(h_1(t)) +_n g(h_2(t)),$$

where $+_n$ means addition modulo n—that is, add the two numbers together, and take the remainder on division of the sum by n. (For example, $4 +_9 7 = 2$.) In other words, evaluate the two nonperfect hash functions, convert the resulting values using the mapping g, and then add them modulo n. The result of this calculation for the example lexicon is shown in the fourth column of Table 4.3a. As if by magic, the final hash values are exactly the ordinal positions within the list of strings.

To make this work, the array g must meet some very special constraints. A detailed description of how it can be obtained appears shortly. Let us simply accept that for any given set of strings it is possible to construct functions h_1, h_2, and g so that $h(t) = g(h_1(t)) +_n g(h_2(t))$ is the ordinal number of string t.

Suppose that an OPMPHF h is calculated for the set of index terms in a given lexicon. There is no need to store the strings or the string pointers—all that is required is for f_t and the inverted file address for term t to be stored in the $h(t)$th positions of their respective arrays.

There is a catch, which is the space required for the description of the hash function h. It has been shown that at least $1.44n$ bits of storage are required by *any* MPHF (Fox, Heath, et al. 1992), and more typically, easily calculable MPHFs for large values of n require from 4 to 20 bits per key. The specification of OPMPHFs is even more lengthy and requires at least $n \log n$ bits of storage (Fox et al. 1991). In the OPMPHF described, the two functions h_1 and h_2 are determined by small tables of weights w_1 and w_2, so they require negligible space. On the other hand, array g is m items long and occupies $m \log n$ bits even when stored as compactly as possible. The method detailed in the next section operates with $m \approx 1.25n$, and this is why, in the example of Table 4.3, the $n = 12$ strings were handled using $m = 15$ entries in the array g. This means that array g occupies at least 25 bits per string, or, in practical terms with each entry stored as a four-byte integer, $1.25 \times 4 \times 1{,}000{,}000 = 5$ Mbytes for the hypothetical lexicon of $n = 1{,}000{,}000$ words. Another 8 Mbytes is still required for the disk pointers and term frequencies. In total, if an OPMPHF of the type described here is used, this lexicon can be reduced to 13 Mbytes, compared with 15.5 Mbytes for a 3-in-4 front-coded representation.

Design of a minimal perfect hash function

To set the scene for the development of an algorithm for finding minimal perfect hash functions, let us first calculate the probability for the birthday paradox. Suppose that n items are to be hashed into m slots. The first item can be placed anywhere without risk of collision. The second item will avoid collision with probability $(m-1)/m$ since one slot is now occupied; the third, with probability $(m-2)/m$; and so on. The probability of inserting n consecutive items without collision is the product of these probabilities:

$$\prod_{i=1}^{n} \frac{m - i + 1}{m} = \frac{m!}{(m-n)!\, m^n}. \tag{4.1}$$

When $m = 365$ and $n = 22$, the probability is 0.524, and when $n = 23$, the probability decreases to 0.493, so if there are 23 people in a room, it is more likely than not that at least two of them will have the same birthday.

Now let us turn to the construction of the array g that is the secret of the MPHF shown in the example in Table 4.3. Recall that

$$h(t) = g(h_1(t)) +_n g(h_2(t))$$

and that

$$h_1(t) = \left(\sum_{i=1}^{|t|} t[i] \times w_1[i] \right) \bmod m,$$

$$h_2(t) = \left(\sum_{i=1}^{|t|} t[i] \times w_2[i] \right) \bmod m,$$

where $t[i]$ is the ith character of the string being hashed. The first step in developing an OPMPHF is to choose mappings randomly for the functions h_1 and h_2. There are several ways to do this, the easiest of which is to generate random integers into the two arrays w_1 and w_2 used in their definition. Once this is done, the search for a function g can be commenced.

One way to visualize the situation is as an m-vertex graph, with vertices labeled $0 \ldots m - 1$ and edges defined by $(h_1(t), h_2(t))$ for each of the terms t. Each term in the lexicon corresponds to one edge of the graph, and the values of the two hash functions define to which vertices that edge is incident. Finally, suppose that each edge is labeled with a value $h(t)$, where $h(t)$ is the desired value of the hash function for term t. The graph corresponding to the functions h_1 and h_2 in Table 4.3a is shown in Figure 4.4. It has $m = 15$ vertices and $n = 12$ edges. Graph algorithms are normally described with n as the number of vertices and m the number of edges, but consistency has required the opposite convention for this discussion.

What is needed now is a mapping g from vertices to integers $0 \ldots n - 1$ such that, for each edge $(h_1(t), h_2(t))$, the mapping yields $g(h_1(t)) +_n g(h_2(t)) = h(t)$, the label on the edge.

For a general graph, finding such a labeling, if it exists, is difficult. But suppose that the graph is known to be *acyclic*; that is, it has no closed cycles of edges. For example, the graph of Figure 4.4 is acyclic, but if there were an edge from vertex 2 to vertex 8, then a cycle 2–4–8–2 would be formed, and it would no longer meet this requirement.

The desired function g for an acyclic graph is easily derived. Any unprocessed vertex v is chosen and assigned $g(v) = 0$. The edges out of that vertex are then traced, and the destinations of those edges are labeled with the h value of the edge used. In the next step, a second generation of vertices is labeled, this time with the *difference* between the tag on the edge used and the label of the vertex that is the source of the edge. If there are unlabeled vertices, another root is chosen and the process repeats. Work continues until all vertices are labeled, at which point the mapping g is complete.

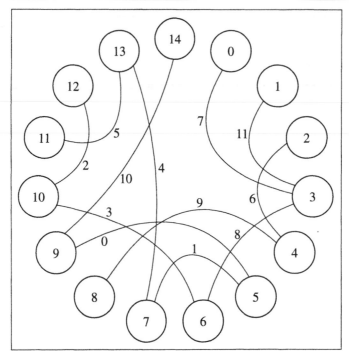

Figure 4.4 Graph corresponding to hash function of Table 4.3.

For example, suppose that vertex 0 in Figure 4.4 is chosen as the root of one of these connected components, and the assignment $g[0] = 0$ is made. Then $g[3]$ can be set to 7, which in turn means that $g[6]$ can be set to 1 and $g[1]$ can be set to 4. But if $g[6] = 1$, then $g[10]$ must be 2, and if $g[10] = 2$, then $g[12]$ must be 0. This is the end of the component rooted at vertex 0, and the next unlabeled vertex—in this case vertex 2—is selected as the root of a new component, giving $g[2] = 0$, $g[4] = 6$, and $g[8] = 3$. Finally, vertex 5 is taken as a root, and the remaining vertices are assigned values for g during the processing of that component.

If the graph were not acyclic, this labeling process might trace around a cycle and insist on relabeling some already-processed vertex with a different label than the one that has already been assigned to it. On an acyclic graph this cannot happen, and labeling is always possible. Because of this, the test for acyclicity can be built into the labeling process. Figure 4.5 describes this process for an arbitrary undirected graph $G = (V, E)$. It is assumed that *adjacent(v)* is a list of vertices that share an edge with vertex v and that $h((v, u))$ is the label associated with the edge joining v and u.

This mechanism requires a linear number of steps to either fully assign the mapping g or to report that the graph is not acyclic, and the function *LabelFrom* will be called at most $2m$ times. Figure 4.6 describes an iterative process that generates and

To label an acyclic graph,

1. For $v \in V$,

   Set $g[v] \leftarrow$ *unknown*.

2. For $v \in V$,

   If $g[v] =$ *unknown* then

       LabelFrom$(v, 0)$.

where the function *LabelFrom*(v, c) is defined by

1. If $g[v] \neq$ *unknown* then

   If $g[v] \neq c$ then

       return with failure—the graph is not acyclic,

   else

       return—this vertex has already been visited.

2. Set $g[v] \leftarrow c$.

3. For $u \in$ *adjacent*(v),

   LabelFrom$(u, h((v, u)) - g[v])$.

Figure 4.5 Checking for acyclicity and assigning a mapping.

To generate a perfect hash function,

1. Choose a value for m.

2. Randomly choose weights $w_1[i]$ and $w_2[i]$ for $1 \leq i \leq \max_{t \in L} |t|$, where L is the set of strings to be hashed and $|t|$ is the length of string t.

3. Generate the graph $G = (V, E)$, where

   $V = \{1, \ldots m\}$ and

   $E = \{(h_1(t), h_2(t)) \,|\, t \in L\}$.

4. Use the algorithm of Figure 4.5 to attempt to calculate the mapping g.

5. If the labeling algorithm returns with failure, go back to step 2.

6. Return the arrays w_1, w_2, and g.

Figure 4.6 Generating a perfect hash function.

tests hash functions. The essence of this algorithm is simple: new functions h_1 and h_2 are generated until an acyclic graph results.

The single remaining question is crucial to the usefulness of this technique: how likely is it that the graph G produced at steps 2 and 3 is acyclic? The answer to this question depends upon the value of m that is chosen in the first step. Clearly, the larger the value of m, the sparser the graph G and the more likely it is to be acyclic.

Analysis based upon the theory of random graphs shows that for $m \leq 2n$, the probability of generating an acyclic graph tends toward zero as n grows—the edges are too dense, and it becomes inevitable that a cycle is formed somewhere in the graph (Czech, Havas, and Majewski 1992). On the other hand, when $m > 2n$, the probability of a random graph of m vertices and n edges being acyclic is approximately

$$\sqrt{\frac{m - 2n}{m}}.$$

Hence the expected number of graphs generated until the first acyclic graph is found is

$$\sqrt{\frac{m}{m - 2n}}.$$

For example, if $m = 3n$, then on average $\sqrt{3} \approx 1.7$ graphs will be tested before one suitable for use in the hash function is generated. In total, the time taken to generate the hash function is proportional to the number of items in the set L, provided that $m > 2n$.

The drawback of using $m = 3n$ is the space required by the array g. If this array takes three four-byte integers per term, then it is no cheaper than storing the terms themselves. On the other hand, reducing m/n below 2 means that many graphs must be generated before an acyclic one is found. This is tolerable only if the set of keys is small and the time taken to generate the mapping is of no concern.

There is, however, another way to reduce the ratio m/n. The example given in Table 4.3 and Figure 4.4 assumes the use of a 2-graph, where each edge connects two vertices. Suppose a third random hash function h_3 is introduced, and a 3-graph is formed on m vertices, where each edge is a triple of the form $(h_1(t), h_2(t), h_3(t))$, and the hash function is given by

$$h(t) = g(h_1(t)) +_n g(h_2(t)) +_n g(h_3(t)).$$

The requirement for the existence of a mapping function g becomes somewhat more complex, but the logic is the same: a graph can be used if there is some sequence of edge deletions such that each edge deleted has at least one vertex of degree one, and the sequence removes all the edges. Another way to state this requirement is to ask that no subgraph contain only vertices of degree two or greater.

Experiment and analysis have shown that with 3-graphs, the critical ratio of m to n is about 1.23 (Havas et al. 1993; Majewski et al. 1996). That is, if $m > 1.23n$, then a graph with the desired property will be constructed on average after a constant number of trials. All the other steps continue to take time proportional to the size of the graph and in practice are extremely fast. For example, it takes less than 1 minute of processor time to build a minimal perfect hash function for the more than 500,000 terms in the *TREC* lexicon.

Finally, we should admit to a small inconsistency. To avoid confusion, the example used in Table 4.3 and Figure 4.4 shows $n = 12$ and $m = 15$ in the ratio 1.25 but

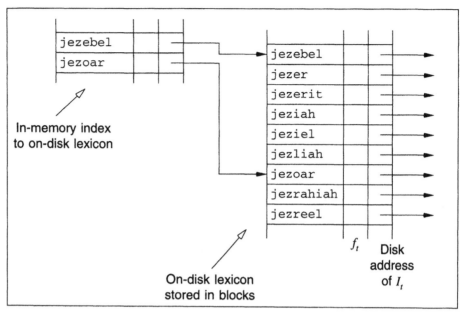

Figure 4.7 Disk-based lexicon storage.

employs two hash functions rather than three. This worked because the example was carefully chosen.

Disk-based lexicon storage

There is a much simpler way to reduce the amount of primary memory required by the lexicon: put it on disk, with just enough information retained in primary memory to identify the disk block corresponding to each term t. Using 4 Kbyte disk blocks, the 20 Mbyte example lexicon of strings, inverted file pointers, and f_t values together occupy about 5,000 disk blocks. Provided that the 5,000 first-in-block terms are held in memory in a searchable array, as little as 100 Kbytes are sufficient to store this memory-resident index table. Figure 4.7 shows how the example strings from *Bible* might be stored.

To locate the information corresponding to a given term, the in-memory index is searched to determine a block number; that block is read into a buffer, and the search is continued within the block. More generally, a B-tree or other dynamic index structure can be used, with leaf pages on disk and a single root page in memory.

This approach is attractive because it is simple and requires a minimal amount of primary memory. However, a disk-based lexicon is many times slower to access than a memory-based one. One disk access per lookup is required—perhaps 10 milliseconds even on a fast machine, compared with the few microseconds required by an in-memory binary search. This extra time is tolerable when just a few terms are being looked up, and this is certainly the case when queries are being processed. Typical queries involve no more than 50 terms, so lexicon lookup takes less than a second. Moreover, it is dominated by other tasks such as decoding the inverted lists and accessing and decompressing responses. It is generally quite acceptable to store the lexicon on disk, particularly when retrieval is performed on a small workstation or personal computer.

However, there are also situations in which enormous numbers of terms must be located—in some cases, every term in the text. One such situation occurs during index construction, the subject of Chapter 5. At a rate of 10 milliseconds per lookup, it would take several months to process a 5 Gbyte text. In this case it is essential to keep the lexicon in memory, and index construction is feasible only on a machine large enough to support this.

4.2   Partially specified query terms

So far we have assumed that a term t is given, and it is necessary to find its lexicon entry. Suppose, however, that terms may contain a wildcard character, *, that serves to match any sequence of letters. If the wildcard is played at the end of the query term—for example, *lab**—a binary search on the prefix will still locate all matching terms. However, if the wildcard is not at the end, or if there is more than one, different techniques are needed to locate the corresponding words in the lexicon. All these require access to the words themselves, so partial specification of query terms is incompatible with minimal perfect hashing. Pattern matching in general is a problem rich in algorithms; for an overview see Cormen, Leiserson, and Rivest (1990); Gonnet and Baeza-Yates (1991); and Baeza-Yates (1992).

Brute-force string matching

Assuming that the entire lexicon is held in main memory, it is possible to scan all terms and compare them with the pattern using a fast pattern-matching algorithm. On the hypothetical lexicon, one million individual tests might be required. No extra space is needed—the words can still be front-coded, and the string pointers can still be one in four. Furthermore, this is the worst case. If the lexicon is ordered, any initial characters that are specified can be used to narrow down the region in which the exhaustive search must be applied.

Indexing using *n*-grams

Faster pattern matching can be achieved if additional memory is available. One method is to decompose query terms into their constituent n-grams, for some small value of n. For example, the word *labor* comprises the digrams *la*, *ab*, *bo*, and *or*. It is convenient to mark the start and end of the word by including two extra digrams: *$l* and *r$*, where $ is a special end-of-string character. To find terms in the lexicon that match *lab*r*, answers to the query

$l AND *la* AND *ab* AND *r$*

Table 4.4 Use of an *n*-gram inverted index into lexicon strings, with *n* = 2: (a) stemmed lexicon; (b) index into the lexicon. (For simplicity, the lists in the inverted index for some digrams have been omitted.)

(a) Number	Term		(b) Digram	Term numbers
1	abhor		$a	1
2	bear		$b	2
3	laaber		$l	3, 4, 5, 6, 7
4	labor		$s	8
5	laborator		aa	3
6	labour		ab	1, 3, 4, 5, 6, 7, 8
7	lavacaber		bo	4, 5, 6
8	slab		la	3, 4, 5, 6, 7, 8
			or	1, 4, 5
			ou	6
			ra	5
			ry	5
			r$	1, 2, 3, 4, 5, 6, 7
			sl	8

are sought. These answers must still be checked by the pattern matcher, since false matches might turn up, such as *laaber* and *lavacaber*,[2] which include all the specified digrams but not in the right order. This mechanism is a filter that reduces the number of strings to be checked with the pattern matcher, rather than the final index. The word *labrador*, which will also be returned by this particular search, is not a false match, but it may not be a desired solution either. Wildcards certainly ease query construction, but there are definite risks associated with their use.

Table 4.4 shows a digram index for a very small lexicon. The inverted lists for the *n*-grams would, of course, normally be stored compressed using the methods described in Section 3.3.

One noteworthy point about *n*-gram indexing is that, since false-match checking with an exact pattern matcher must still be performed, an almost continuous trade-off of time for space is possible by a kind of blocking. Table 4.4 tacitly assumes that the granularity of the index is to individual words. But, as with a document index, a coarser index is smaller. Moreover, for a document-level index, false matches

---

2 Both of these words are in the stemmed *TREC* vocabulary. *Laaber* is a town in Bavaria, mentioned in an Associated Press news report; *Lavacaberry* appears in a federal regulation about blackberries and other berry fruit.

cannot be tolerated since they cause disk accesses, but here false-match resolution is relatively cheap. To test a single extra term with the exact pattern matcher is a small penalty compared to the cost of decoding and merging inverted lists since we are already assuming that the lexicon is present in main memory. Blocking involves recording $\lfloor$ term number$/b \rfloor$ in the index, for some appropriate value of b, instead of the term number itself, and can in some cases actually make the search faster. This occurs when the time saved by decoding the shorter inverted lists outweighs the extra cost of false-match checking.

In the *TREC* lexicon, a compressed inverted index of trigrams, each pointing to a group of eight words in the in-memory lexicon, requires a 50 percent space overhead in addition to the space occupied by the words in the lexicon. However, the index cuts the search time for a set of partially specified query terms from more than 6 seconds each for a brute-force search to less than 0.05 second, a 100-fold speedup. Moreover, since partially specified query terms generally contain just a handful of n-grams, the n-gram index lists might even be relegated to disk, adding a seek time of perhaps 10 milliseconds per n-gram. Zobel, Moffat, and Sacks-Davis (1993a) describe the inverted file lexicon indexing approach to partially specified query terms and give results for the *TREC* collection.

Rotated lexicons

A further order-of-magnitude improvement can be achieved by using even more memory (Bratley and Choueka 1982). Suppose an indexing pointer is maintained for each character of the lexicon, rather than for each word. For example, the word *labor* would have six pointers—one to each letter plus one to the string-terminating character. Suppose also that the array of character pointers is sorted, and, to determine the sort order, the characters of the word are considered to be *rotated* from the one indexed by the pointer. Thus, the strings addressed by the pointers are considered to be *labor$*, *abor$l*, *bor$la*, *or$lab*, *r$labo*, and *$labor*. If this is done, any pattern that contains a single wildcard can be located by a binary search. For example, the pattern *lab*r* is rotated until the wildcard is at the end, obtaining *r$lab**; then the sorted list of pointers is searched for strings having *r$lab* as a prefix. All strings that match this in the augmented lexicon also match the original query.

Part of the rotated lexicon for the words listed in Table 4.5a is shown in Table 4.5b. For example, the pointer $(4, 5)$ for *r$labo* indicates word number 4 and character number 5 within the word. In practice, of course, these two components would be combined into a single-byte address. The first column of Table 4.5b is for illustration only and would not actually be stored; it shows the string indexed by the pointer and the sort order that results. Many of the entries have been omitted from the example. A search for the rotated pattern *r$lab** yields the range from *r$labo* through to *r$labou*, and these three words, when re-rotated, are the answers. (The string *laborator* is the stemmed representation of *laboratories*.)

The important case in which there are wildcards at beginning and end of the word can also be handled in this way: **lab** is rotated to generate *lab**, and the search proceeds as before. Other incompletely specified terms with multiple wildcards cannot

Table 4.5 Use of a rotated lexicon to handle wildcard queries: (a) stemmed lexicon; (b) some of the rotated terms and their corresponding pointers.

(a)	Number	Term		(b)	Rotated form	Address
	1	abhor			$abhor	(1, 0)
	2	bear			$bear	(2, 0)
	3	laaber			$laaber	(3, 0)
	4	labor			$labor	(4, 0)
	5	laborator			$laborator	(5, 0)
	6	labour			$labour	(6, 0)
	7	lavacaber			$lavacaber	(7, 0)
	8	slab			$slab	(8, 0)
					aaber$l	(3, 2)
					abhor$	(1, 1)
					aber$la	(3, 3)
					abor$l	(4, 2)
					aborator$l	(5, 2)
					abour$l	(6, 2)
					aber$lavac	(7, 6)
					ab$sl	(8, 3)
					r$abho	(1, 5)
					r$bea	(2, 4)
					r$laabe	(3, 6)
					r$labo	(4, 5)
					r$laborato	(5, 9)
					r$labou	(6, 6)
					r$lavacabe	(7, 9)
					slab$	(8, 1)

be handled directly and are processed as follows. First, a set of candidates is established. This can be based either upon the longest (rotated) sequence of characters specified in the query or on the smallest set of candidates that remains after each specified component is considered in turn. Then, as before, a pattern matcher is used as a second checking stage.

Experiments show that using this *rotated* (or *permuted*) *lexicon*, the same set of *TREC* test terms is expanded in 0.006 second per term, 10 times faster than the indexing approach described in the previous section, but at a memory overhead of 250 percent, five times as much (Zobel, Moffat, and Sacks-Davis 1993a).

4.3 Boolean query processing

The simplest type of query is the Boolean query, in which terms are combined with the connectives AND, OR, and NOT. It is relatively straightforward to process such a query using an inverted file index. The lexicon is searched for each term; each inverted list is retrieved and decoded; and the lists are merged, taking the intersection, union, or complement, as appropriate. Finally, the documents so indexed are retrieved and displayed to the user as the list of answers. For a typical query of 5 to 10 terms, a second or so is spent reading and decoding inverted lists; then—depending on the number of answers—accessing, decoding, and writing the documents takes anything from tenths of a second to hundreds of seconds.

Conjunctive queries

Let us examine this process in detail. In the next few pages we suppose that the query is a *conjunction*, consisting of terms connected with AND operations such as

text AND *compression* AND *retrieval.*

Although this is not the only form of Boolean query, it is sufficiently common to warrant special discussion.

Suppose a conjunctive query of r terms is being processed. First, each term is stemmed and then located in the lexicon. As discussed in Section 4.1, the lexicon might be resident in memory, if space is available, or on disk. In the latter case, one disk access per term is required. The next step is to sort the terms by increasing frequency; all subsequent processing is carried out in this order. This is one reason why we stipulated earlier that the lexicon should hold, for each term t, its frequency of appearance f_t. If this information were held with the inverted list instead, it would not be possible to process terms in increasing frequency order without fetching and buffering all the inverted lists. Processing the least frequent term first is not essential, but it makes retrieval significantly more efficient.

Next, the inverted list for the least frequent term is read into memory. This list establishes a set of *candidates*, documents that have not yet been eliminated and might be answers to the query. All remaining inverted lists are processed against this set of candidates, in increasing order of term frequency. This strategy is described in Figure 4.8, where C is the set of candidate document numbers and I_t the inverted list for term t.

In a conjunctive query, a candidate cannot be an answer unless it appears in all inverted lists; if it is omitted from any list, it can be discarded at once. This means that the size of the set of candidates is nonincreasing. To process a term, each document in the set is checked and removed if it does not appear in the term's inverted list. From this perspective, the dominant operation when processing conjunctive queries is not so much merging as "looking up" since the set of candidates is never larger than the inverted lists and shrinks as more terms are processed and the inverted lists grow longer.

To evaluate a conjunctive Boolean query,

1. For each query term t,

    (a) Stem t.

    (b) Search the lexicon.

    (c) Record f_t and the address of I_t, the inverted file entry for t.

2. Identify the query term t with the smallest f_t.

3. Read the corresponding inverted file entry I_t.
   Set $C \leftarrow I_t$. C is the list of *candidates*.

4. For each remaining term t,

    (a) Read the inverted file entry, I_t.

    (b) For each $d \in C$,

    if $d \notin I_t$ then

    set $C \leftarrow C - \{d\}$.

    (c) If $|C| = 0$,

    return, there are no answers.

5. For each $d \in C$,

    (a) Look up the address of document d.

    (b) Retrieve document d and present it to the user.

Figure 4.8   Evaluating conjunctive Boolean queries.

When all inverted lists have been processed, the remaining candidates, if there are any, are the desired answers.

Term processing order

There are two reasons to select the least frequent term to initialize the set of candidates. The first is to minimize the amount of temporary memory space required during query processing. Since the size of the set is nonincreasing, it is largest when it is initialized, so the memory required is minimized by selecting the shortest inverted list first. Processing the remaining terms in increasing frequency order does not affect the peak memory space required. It is still a good idea, though, because it may quickly reduce the number of candidates, perhaps even to zero. Obviously, if the candidate set becomes empty, no further terms need be considered at all. A query that returns no answers is not particularly informative; nevertheless, a surprising fraction of actual queries have just this result. Such queries are, of course, typically followed by broader queries formed by removing one or more query terms.

The second reason to process terms in order of frequency is that it is faster because each inverted list involves a sequence of lookup operations rather than a merge operation. Merging takes time proportional to the sum of the sizes of the two sets. If there are $|C|$ candidates and f_t pointers in the inverted list, then a linear merge takes $|C| + f_t$ steps. This is unnecessarily expensive if $|C|$ is much smaller than f_t. For example, suppose that $|C| = 60$ and $f_t = 60,000$—not unreasonable figures with a large collection like *TREC*. Then merging will take 60,060 steps, or 1,000 steps per candidate.

Since the list of document numbers in any inverted list is sorted, instead of a linear merge the inverted list can be binary-searched for each of the candidates. This is not possible if the list is stored compressed, but we will continue the calculation just to see what might be achieved. Each binary search will take $\log 60,000 \approx 16$ computation steps, and the entire inverted list can be processed with just 1,000 steps.

Each inverted list must be read from disk, so the elapsed time to process term t remains proportional to f_t. Still, much less processor time is needed—if a binary search can be used. But a binary search is possible only when the document numbers are in sorted order within list I_t, and if they can be accessed randomly. Unfortunately, the use of compression destroys random access capabilities since it is impossible to index into the middle of a compressed inverted list and decode a document number. Thus, if the inverted file is compressed, not only must a linear merge be used irrespective of the length of the inverted list, but each inverted list must be fully decompressed in order to perform the merge. The cost is still linear, but the constant of proportionality is large. At face value, then, the use of compression saves a great deal of space in the inverted file but imposes a substantial time penalty during conjunctive query processing.

Random access and fast lookup

What is needed is some provision for random access into the inverted list to support faster searching. This is the problem of synchronization and was discussed in Section 2.7. Suppose that the compressed inverted list for some term t is partially indexed itself, and that every b_tth pointer is duplicated into an index array. For example, if $b_t = 4$, every fourth pointer in the inverted file is indexed, and both the bit address within the inverted file of that pointer and the document number it corresponds to are stored in some auxiliary structure. If a document number x is to be looked up, it is first sought in the auxiliary index. The result tells which block of the inverted file that document number appears in, if it does appear, and also gives the bit address in the inverted file at which decoding should commence to access it. This is much the same structure as was described in Section 4.1 for disk-based storage of the lexicon, except that here both components are read from disk when required, and the purpose of indexing is to save decompression time rather than memory space.

Several issues must be resolved. The first is the storage mechanism used for the index. The second is a suitable value for b_t, the blocking constant for term t. The third concerns the trade-off of time for space—how much time is saved and at what cost in space.

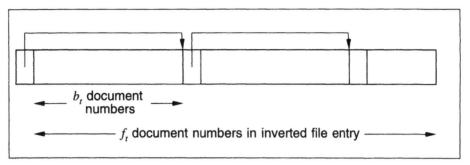

Figure 4.9 Interleaving index information in an inverted file entry.

The first issue has already been treated in Section 3.3. Both lists of numbers in the auxiliary structure are sorted. The document numbers appear in order because they are sorted in the inverted list that is being indexed, and so do the bit addresses. This means that the index can be stored as a sequence of pairs of differences, with the first difference indicating a document number and the second a difference in bit address. This in turn means that to look up a document number, the index must be fully decoded, even if the inverted list is not. However, this cost is amortized over all the searches performed on this list and does not dominate the cost of searching within the block.

There is no need for the auxiliary structure to be stored separately from the inverted list. It is most easily stored as a sequence of *skips* interleaved with the blocks they create in the inverted list. Figure 4.9 shows an example of an inverted list with skips inserted. Interleaved storage means that one disk access is sufficient to fetch both components, and it allows each inverted list to be constructed easily.

The second question—how to choose b_t—requires a little more thought. Suppose that there are $|C| = k$ candidates, and an inverted list of f_t pointers is indexed every b_t pointers. Suppose also that decoding a "document number, bit address" pair in the auxiliary index costs twice as many steps as decoding a document number in the inverted list; that all of the index is decoded to process the inverted list; and that half of each of k blocks in the inverted list must be decoded to determine the presence or absence of the k candidates. This final assumption is based upon the expectation that, on average, the desired document numbers are located at the midpoint of their blocks. Then the cost in steps of processing one inverted list is

$$\frac{2f_t}{b_t} + \frac{kb_t}{2},$$

which is minimized when

$$b_t = 2\sqrt{f_t/k}$$

and has minimal value

$$2\sqrt{kf_t}.$$

Now we can calculate the answer to the third question: how much time might be saved. If $f_t = 60,000$ and $k = 60$, as assumed for the earlier calculations, then $b_t = 63$ is the appropriate value, and the total number of decoding steps performed is 3,800.

Before concluding that this technique can speed compressed inverted file operations by a factor of 15, four caveats are necessary. First, one step in a merging algorithm might be quite different from one decoding step in a compression algorithm. Second, these calculations take no account of the cost of actually reading the inverted list, and since this cost is by and large the same whether the list is skipped or not, it tends to favor the nonskipped method. Third, the values for k and f_t that have been used in these calculations may be quite inappropriate. Finally, the space overhead caused by the auxiliary information will tend to increase the reading time for each inverted file slightly.

Experiments with a skipped inverted file indicate that, because of these effects, the speedup calculation is optimistic (Moffat and Zobel 1996). Nevertheless, there is still a substantial saving. When processed with a skipped index constructed assuming that $k = 100$, conjunctive Boolean queries of 5 to 10 terms on the *TREC* collection run approximately five times faster in terms of both processing time and total elapsed time (which includes the cost of disk accesses). The index grows by just over 5 percent. Further details of these experiments appear in Section 9.6.

Blocked inverted files

The skipped inverted file uses blocks each containing a fixed number of pointers, and so the blocks themselves are of differing lengths. Another way in which the index can be modified to provide faster checking of individual candidates is to break the inverted lists into blocks that all have the same number of bits (Moffat, Zobel, and Klein 1995). The advantage is that the blocks themselves can be accessed by pointer arithmetic since if b is the number of bits used for each block of some inverted list, then the kth block of the list starts at bit location $1 + (k - 1)b$. Each block must contain as a prefix the document number corresponding to the first pointer stored in the block, but the second "address of the next block" offset required in the skipped organization can be omitted. Counterbalancing this gain, a few bits will be wasted at the end of each block since an integral number of pointers per fixed-length block means that on average the equivalent of half a pointer per block will be lost. Each compressed $(d, f_{d,t})$ posting in an inverted list occupies about eight bits, so four bits per block will be unused.

If these were the only trade-offs, then there would be little reason to prefer this blocking approach since blocked indexes are harder to build and harder to actually decode—care must be taken to avoid interpreting the vacant bits at the end of the block, and having to continually test for this condition slows down decoding. However, by allowing even more space inefficiency, considerably faster processing can be achieved for conjunctive Boolean queries. Suppose that the first document number in each block—the *critical value* for the block—is stored completely uncompressed. Then to search for a candidate in the compressed inverted list a binary search on *blocks* can be carried out, inspecting only the critical values, since none of them rely for decoding upon any other values. Then, when the search has been refined to just one block, the normal processing mode is resumed, using a Golomb or other code within the block, with each document number dependent sequentially upon the previous one in the block.

This clearly offers much faster access to candidates than the skipping method since there is no decoding of the critical values required, and only logarithmically many of them have to be examined, compared to the square root relationship that was derived for the skipped index. As an estimate of the additional space wastage, suppose that a collection of $N = 1,000,000$ documents is to be stored. Then the critical pointer in each block is stored in 20 bits rather than about 6, a further per-block overhead of 14 bits. A typical block size using this mechanism might be 128 bits (around 15–20 pointers per block), so the use of an uncompressed critical pointer adds about 10 percent to the size of the inverted file.

And it is possible to do better. Recall the interpolative code that was introduced in Section 3.3 on page 126. A similar technique can be used to code the critical document numbers in a blocked index. The middle block of the list—which is the one that will be required first by the binary search for a candidate—has its critical value stored uncompressed. The binary search then moves either left or right, to the one-quarter or three-quarter blocks, and both of these can have their critical values coded relative to the middle block critical value since the binary search has already traversed that block. The same logic then applies at the next level, and so on. The net effect is that all of the critical document numbers are coded using the interpolative code, and binary search at the block level is still possible. For the hypothetical $N = 1,000,000$ record database, the cost of the binary search facility is considerably reduced from the 14 bits per block that was estimated above, and the critical values cost essentially the same as they do in the skipping approach, in which they are Golomb-coded in a sequential manner.

As the final component of the blocked organization, it now makes sense for the middle block of the file to be stored first since it is always the one from which all decoding must commence. Similarly, the remaining blocks are stored in the sequence that results from a preorder traversal of the binary search tree, in the same way in which the interpolative codes were stored in Section 3.3.

On the downside, simple sequential decoding of the inverted list is no longer possible since the critical value in the first block cannot be decoded until the critical value in the second block is known, and so on. If pointers are required in sequential order, perhaps because this term is being used to establish the list of candidates, a stack must be employed. The decoding cost is still linear in the length of the list, but the constant factor is higher. Nor is it at all obvious how each inverted list should be constructed since the contents of each block cannot be finalized until the previous block is built, and the previous block cannot be built until the next block is finalized. In practice, an iterative approach based upon estimated lengths of critical codes provides an excellent approximation.

Nonconjunctive queries

So far we have considered only conjunctive queries. Another common form is a con-junction of disjunctions, where several alternatives are specified for each component of what is basically a conjunctive query:

(*text* OR *data* OR *image*) AND
(*compression* OR *compaction*) AND
(*retrieval* OR *indexing* OR *archiving*).

In this case, the terms comprising each conjunct can be processed simultaneously, candidates remaining in the set if they appear in any member of the OR group. The set of candidates should be initialized to the union of the members of the smallest conjunct. As a pessimistic approximation, the size of each conjunct can be estimated by summing the f_t values for its constituent terms, ignoring the possibility of over-lap in the OR component. This strategy should allow time savings similar to those described above to be achieved.

Even more general queries, such as

(*information* AND (*retrieval* OR *indexing*)) OR
((*text* OR *data*) AND (*compression* OR *compaction*)),

can be transformed into a conjunction of disjunctions by the query processing sys-tem, although this may cause terms to be duplicated. The above example could be recast as

(*information* OR *text* OR *data*) AND
(*retrieval* OR *indexing* OR *text* OR *data*) AND
(*information* OR *compression* OR *compaction*) AND
(*retrieval* OR *indexing* OR *compression* OR *compaction*).

When a Boolean query expression becomes as complex as this, it is time to consider changing tack entirely and using another information retrieval paradigm—*informal* or *ranked* queries.

4.4   Ranking and information retrieval

Boolean queries are not the only method of searching for information. If some exact subset of the document being sought is known, then they are certainly ap-propriate, which is why they have been so successful in areas such as commercial databases and bibliographic retrieval systems. Often, however, the information re-quirement is less precisely known. For this reason, it is sometimes useful to be able to specify a list of terms that give a good indication of which documents are *rele-vant*, though they will not necessarily all be present in the documents sought. The system should rank the entire collection with respect to the query, so that the top 100, say, ranked documents can be examined for relevance and those that constitute the answer set extracted. In this section we study how to assign a *similarity measure* to each document that indicates how closely it matches a query.

Table 4.6   A small document collection: six documents over 10 terms.

d	Document D_d
1	Pease porridge hot, pease porridge cold,
2	Pease porridge in the pot,
3	Nine days old.
4	In the pot cold, in the pot hot,
5	Pease porridge, pease porridge,
6	Eat the lot.

Coordinate matching

One way to provide more flexibility than a simple binary yes-or-no answer is to count the number of query terms that appear in each document. The more terms that appear, the more likely it is that the document is relevant. This approach is called *coordinate matching*. The query becomes a hybrid, intermediate between a conjunctive AND query and a disjunctive OR query: a document that contains any of the terms is viewed as a potential answer, but preference is given to documents that contain all or most of them. All necessary information is in the inverted file, and it is relatively straightforward to implement this strategy.

Consider, for example, the six documents shown in Table 4.6—a revision of the doggerel already used as an example in Chapter 3. For the query *eat*, it is clear that document 6 is the best (and only) answer. But what about the query *hot porridge*? In a conjunctive Boolean sense, document 1 is the only answer. But three other documents might also be relevant, and coordinate matching yields a ranking $D_1 > D_2 = D_4 = D_5 > D_3 = D_6 = 0$. Documents containing only one of the terms are available as answers, should the user wish to inspect them.

Inner product similarity

This process can be formalized as an inner product of a query vector with a set of document vectors. Table 4.7a shows the same collection, with a set of binary document vectors represented by n components, n being the number of distinct terms in the collection. For convenience the terms are abbreviated to three letters, and to keep the example manageable it is assumed that the terms *in* and *the* are stopped. The two example queries can also be represented as n-dimensional vectors and are shown in Table 4.7b.

Using this formulation, the similarity measure of query Q with document D_d is expressed as

$$M(Q, D_d) = Q \cdot D_d$$

Table 4.7 Vectors for inner product calculation: (a) document vectors; (b) query vectors.

(a)	d	Document vectors $\langle w_{d,t} \rangle$									
		col	day	eat	hot	lot	nin	old	pea	por	pot
	1	1	0	0	1	0	0	0	1	1	0
	2	0	0	0	0	0	0	0	1	1	1
	3	0	1	0	0	0	1	1	0	0	0
	4	1	0	0	1	0	0	0	0	0	1
	5	0	0	0	0	0	0	0	1	1	0
	6	0	0	1	0	1	0	0	0	0	0
(b)	eat	0	0	1	0	0	0	0	0	0	0
	hot porridge	0	0	0	1	0	0	0	0	1	0

where the operation · is inner product multiplication. The *inner product* of two n-vectors $X = \langle x_i \rangle$ and $Y = \langle y_i \rangle$ is defined to be

$$X \cdot Y = \sum_{i=1}^{n} x_i y_i.$$

For example,

$M(hot\ porridge, D_1) = (0, 0, 0, 1, 0, 0, 0, 0, 1, 0) \cdot (1, 0, 0, 1, 0, 0, 0, 1, 1, 0) = 2.$

Despite the additional power introduced by the notion of ranking, this simple coordinate-matching approach has three drawbacks. First, it takes no account of term frequency. In Table 4.6, *porridge* appears twice in document 1 and only once in document 2, yet on the query *porridge* the two documents are ranked equally. Second—and this may seem the same point, but it is not—the formula takes no account of term scarcity. Since *eat* appears in only one document, it is, at face value at least, a more important term than *porridge*, which appears in three of the documents. Third, long documents with many terms will automatically be favored by the ranking process because they are likely to contain more of any given list of query terms merely by virtue of the diversity of text present in a long document.

The first problem can be tackled by replacing the binary "present" or "not present" judgment with an integer indicating how many times the term appears in the document. This occurrence count is called the *within-document frequency* of the term and is denoted $f_{d,t}$. When the inner product is calculated, the $f_{d,t}$ values are then taken into account. For example, the similarity calculation for the sample query would become

$M(hot\ porridge, D_1) = (0, 0, 0, 1, 0, 0, 0, 0, 1, 0) \cdot (1, 0, 0, 1, 0, 0, 0, 2, 2, 0) = 3$

since document D_1 contains *hot* once and *porridge* twice. More generally, term t in document d can be assigned a *document-term weight*, denoted $w_{d,t}$, and another weight $w_{q,t}$ in the query vector. The similarity measure is the inner product of these two—the sum of the products of the weights of the query terms and the corresponding document terms:

$$M(Q, D_d) = Q \cdot D_d = \sum_{t=1}^{n} w_{q,t} \cdot w_{d,t}.$$

It is normal to assign $w_{q,t} = 0$ if t does not appear in Q, so the measure can be stated as

$$M(Q, D_d) = \sum_{t \in Q} w_{q,t} \cdot w_{d,t}.$$

This suggests an evaluation mechanism based on inverted files. However, before discussing implementation options, let us explore the other two problems mentioned above.

The second problem is that no emphasis is given to scarce terms. Indeed, a document with enough appearances of a common term will always be ranked first if the query contains that term, irrespective of other words. The solution is for the term weights to be reduced for terms that appear in many documents, so that a single appearance of *the* counts far less than a single appearance of, say, *Jezebel*. This can be done by weighting terms according to their *inverse document frequency*, often abbreviated to IDF. This suggestion is consistent with the observations of George Zipf, who published a remarkable book about naturally occurring distributions called *Human Behavior and the Principle of Least Effort* (Zipf 1949). Zipf observed that the frequency of an item tends to be inversely proportional to its rank. That is, if rank can be regarded as a measure of importance, then the weight w_t of a term t might be calculated as

$$w_t = \frac{1}{f_t},$$

where, as before, f_t is the number of documents that contain term t.

The term weight can then be used in three different ways. First, and most obvious, it can be multiplied by a *relative term frequency* value, denoted $r_{d,t}$, to generate the document-term weight $w_{d,t}$, where $r_{d,t}$ itself can be calculated in several different ways and is discussed further below. Second, the term weight can be combined multiplicatively with $r_{q,t}$ to yield a query-term weight $w_{q,t}$. Third, it can be used in calculating both $w_{d,t}$ and $w_{q,t}$, that is, applied twice. Nor is the formulation above the only possibility for w_t, the IDF component. Others that have appeared in the literature include

$$w_t = \log_e \left(1 + \frac{N}{f_t} \right),$$

$$w_t = \log_e \left(1 + \frac{f^m}{f_t} \right),$$

and

$$w_t = \log_e \frac{N - f_t}{f_t},$$

where N is the number of documents in the collection and f^m is the largest $f_{d,t}$ value in the collection. The first of these three is now regarded as being the "usual" mechanism, with the logarithm included to prevent a term for which $f_t = 1$ from being regarded as twice as important as a term for which $f_t = 2$.

Similarly, the relative term frequency component $r_{d,t}$ can be calculated in several different ways as a function of $f_{d,t}$, the within-document frequency:

$$r_{d,t} = 1,$$
$$r_{d,t} = f_{d,t},$$
$$r_{d,t} = 1 + \log_e f_{d,t},$$
$$r_{d,t} = \left(K + (1 - K) \frac{f_{d,t}}{\max_i f_{d,i}} \right),$$

and so on. The third formula uses a logarithm to give diminishing returns as term frequencies increase. No explicit upper bound is enforced, but a term must be very frequent indeed to have a term frequency contribution of greater than four. In the fourth formula, the first appearance of a term in a document contributes much more than the second and subsequent occurrences, with the constant $0 \le K \le 1$ controlling the balance between initial and later appearances. This is quite plausible, in that the first appearance of a term should contribute more of the available similarity than, say, the fifth. The factor $\max_i f_{d,i}$ is the maximum frequency of any term in document d and is introduced to keep the term frequency multiplier from becoming greater than one.

The document vectors are then calculated as either

$$w_{d,t} = r_{d,t}$$

or

$$w_{d,t} = r_{d,t} \cdot w_t \qquad \text{(TF} \times \text{IDF)}.$$

The latter method for assigning document-term weights is called the TF×IDF rule: term frequency times inverse document frequency. Note that neither the TF nor the IDF components should be interpreted literally as being the functions that their names suggest. A similarity heuristic is called "TF×IDF" whenever it uses the term frequency $f_{d,t}$ in a monotonically increasing way, and the term's document frequency f_t in a monotonically decreasing way.

The query-term weights $w_{q,t}$ are calculated similarly. The within-query frequency $f_{q,t}$ may or may not be taken into account, and the term weight w_t may or may not be taken into account.

There is no particular magic in any of several hundred similarity formulas allowed by these various expressions, and no single combination of them outperforms any of the others over a range of different queries—Zobel and Moffat (1998) have evaluated a large number of them against the *TREC* data. Furthermore, the above lists are certainly not exhaustive—there are plenty of other formulations for both w_t and $r_{d,t}$ that have been proposed. What is worthy of note is that all of the suggestions comply with two straightforward monotonicity constraints:

A term that appears in many documents should not be regarded as being more important than a term that appears in a few, and a document with many occurrences of a term should not be regarded as being less important than a document that has just a few.

Beyond that, which is used in any particular situation tends to be a subjective choice rather than an objective one.

It is, however, helpful to assume a particular formulation in the development of the next section, and for the sake of concreteness, it will be supposed that the document and query vectors are described by

$$w_t = \log_e(1 + N/f_t)$$
$$r_{d,t} = 1 + \log_e f_{d,t} \qquad r_{q,t} = 1 \qquad (4.2)$$
$$w_{d,t} = r_{d,t} \qquad w_{q,t} = r_{q,t} \cdot w_t$$

Whatever the weighting rule, all inner product methods are vulnerable to the third effect described above: long documents are favored over short ones since they contain more terms and so the value of the inner product increases.

For this reason, it is also common to introduce a *normalization* factor to discount the contribution of long documents. Hence another variation of the inner product rule is to measure similarity by

$$M(Q, D_d) = \frac{\sum_{t \in Q} w_{q,t} \cdot w_{d,t}}{|D_d|}$$

where $|D_d| = \sum_i f_{d,i}$ is the *length* of document D_d, obtained by counting the number of indexed terms. Another proposal is to use the square root of this length.

Fortunately, there is a simple way to understand these various rules using vector space models.

Vector space models

Whatever term weights w_t and relative term and document frequencies $r_{d,t}$ and $r_{q,t}$ are assigned, and whatever document-term weights $w_{d,t}$ and query-term weights

$w_{q,t}$ arise from these assignments, the result is the same—each document is represented by a vector in n-dimensional space, and the query is also represented as an n-dimensional vector.

One obvious similarity measure for a pair of vectors is the familiar Euclidean distance:

$$M(Q, D_d) = \sqrt{\sum_{t=1}^{n} |w_{q,t} - w_{d,t}|^2}$$

This is actually a *dissimilarity* measure since a large numeric value indicates that the vectors are very different; to turn it into a similarity measure, the reciprocal is taken. This measure suffers from the opposite fault to the inner product—because the query is usually much shorter than the documents, it discriminates *against* long documents.

What is really of interest is the *direction* indicated by the two vectors, or, more precisely, the *difference* in direction, irrespective of length. Moreover, difference in direction is a well-understood concept in geometry—it is the angle between the two vectors.

Simple vector algebra yields an elegant method for determining similarity. If X and Y are two n-dimensional vectors $\langle x_i \rangle$ and $\langle y_i \rangle$, the angle θ between them satisfies

$$X \cdot Y = |X||Y| \cos\theta$$

where $X \cdot Y$ is the vector inner product defined above and

$$|X| = \sqrt{\sum_{i=1}^{n} x_i^2}$$

is the Euclidean length of X. The angle θ can be calculated from

$$\cos\theta = \frac{X \cdot Y}{|X||Y|} = \frac{\sum_{i=1}^{n} x_i y_i}{\sqrt{\sum_{i=1}^{n} x_i^2}\sqrt{\sum_{i=1}^{n} y_i^2}}$$

This has two implications. First, it justifies the normalization that was described at the end of the previous section. The normalization factor is the Euclidean length of the document—that is, the length in n-space of the set of document-term weights describing the document. Second, this formula provides a clear visualization of what the ranking rule accomplishes. Imagine the set of documents being points in the positive region of n-dimensional space, with short documents close to the origin and long ones farther away from it. A query can be imagined as a ray emanating from the origin, piercing this space in some desired direction. Within this framework, the task of the ranking method is to select those documents lying closest to this ray in an angular sense. Since $\cos\theta = 1$ when $\theta = 0$ and $\cos\theta = 0$ when the vectors are orthogonal, the similarity measure can be taken as the cosine of the angle between the document and query vector—the larger this cosine, the greater the similarity.

These considerations lead to the *cosine rule* for ranking:

$$cosine(Q, D_d) = \frac{Q \cdot D_d}{|Q||D_d|}$$

$$= \frac{1}{W_q W_d} \sum_{t=1}^{n} w_{q,t} \cdot w_{d,t}$$

where

$$W_d = \sqrt{\sum_{t=1}^{n} w_{d,t}^2}$$

is the Euclidean length—the *weight*—of document d and

$$W_q = \sqrt{\sum_{t=1}^{n} w_{q,t}^2}$$

is the weight of the query.

This rule can be used with any of the term-weighting methods described above. Suppose, for example, that the variant described in Equation 4.2 is used. The similarity calculation is then described by

$$cosine(Q, D_d) = \frac{1}{W_d W_q} \sum_{t \in Q \cap D_d} (1 + \log_e f_{d,t}) \cdot \log_e \left(1 + \frac{N}{f_t}\right). \qquad (4.3)$$

Indeed, there is no need to factor in W_q since it is constant for any given query, and while it affects the numeric similarity scores, the document ordering is unaffected.

Table 4.8 applies the cosine measure to the collection of $N = 6$ documents and $n = 10$ terms given in Table 4.6. Table 4.8a shows the corresponding document vectors, where the entry for row d and column t is $w_{d,t}$, the weight of term t in d. Also recorded are f_t, the number of documents containing t, and w_t, calculated using the inverse document frequency rule $w_t = \log_e(1 + N/f_t)$.

Table 4.8b shows four queries Q and the resulting values of $cosine(Q, D_d)$. For the single-term query *eat*, the ranking is simple since it appears in only one document. Not so straightforward is the second query, *porridge*—document 5 beats document 1 because it is shorter. The final query—*eat nine day old porridge*—is best matched by line 3, despite the fact that it does not contain the word *eat*, illustrating the power (and perhaps also a drawback) of ranked queries. Someone looking for this doggerel in a retrieval system would almost certainly find it with the last query.

Table 4.8 Application of the cosine measure: (a) term frequencies $f_{d,t}$ and document weights; (b) cosine similarities for queries.

(a) d	Document vectors $\langle w_{d,t} \rangle$										W_d
	col	*day*	*eat*	*hot*	*lot*	*nin*	*old*	*pea*	*por*	*pot*	
1	1.0	0.0	0.0	1.0	0.0	0.0	0.0	1.7	1.7	0.0	2.78
2	0.0	0.0	0.0	0.0	0.0	0.0	0.0	1.0	1.0	1.0	1.73
3	0.0	1.0	0.0	0.0	0.0	1.0	1.0	0.0	0.0	0.0	1.73
4	1.0	0.0	0.0	1.0	0.0	0.0	0.0	0.0	0.0	1.7	2.21
5	0.0	0.0	0.0	0.0	0.0	0.0	0.0	1.7	1.7	0.0	2.39
6	0.0	0.0	1.0	0.0	1.0	0.0	0.0	0.0	0.0	0.0	1.41
f_t	2	1	1	2	1	1	1	3	3	2	
w_t	1.39	1.95	1.95	1.39	1.95	1.95	1.95	1.10	1.10	1.39	

(b) d	Query			
	eat	*porridge*	*hot porridge*	*eat nine day old porridge*
	$W_q = 1.95$	$W_q = 1.10$	$W_q = 1.77$	$W_q = 3.55$
1	0.00	0.61	0.66	0.19
2	0.00	0.58	0.36	0.18
3	0.00	0.00	0.00	0.63
4	0.00	0.00	0.36	0.00
5	0.00	0.71	0.44	0.22
6	0.71	0.00	0.00	0.39
Top	6	5	1	3

4.5 Evaluating retrieval effectiveness

There are many variations on these ranking rules, some of which were described above. In order to compare them, we need some way to quantify their performance. A ranking rule's performance should be based on the total ranking it imposes on the collection with respect to a query. A number of methods have been suggested for this. None are entirely satisfactory, but this is a natural consequence of attempting to represent multidimensional behavior with a single representative value. First we define two important measures of effectiveness: recall and precision.

Recall and precision

The most common way to describe retrieval performance is to calculate how many of the relevant documents have been retrieved and how early in the ranking they were listed. This leads to the following definitions.

The *precision* P_r of a ranking method for some cutoff point r is the fraction of the top r ranked documents that are relevant to the query:

$$P_r = \frac{\text{number retrieved that are relevant}}{\text{total number retrieved}}.$$

For example, if 50 documents are retrieved in answer to some query and 35 of them are relevant, then the precision at 50 is $P_{50} = 70$ percent. With the precision metric, we measure the accuracy of the search—how close we were to the target.

In contrast, the *recall* R_r of a method at some value r is the proportion of the total number of relevant documents that were retrieved in the top r:

$$R_r = \frac{\text{number relevant that are retrieved}}{\text{total number relevant}}.$$

If, on the same query as before, there are 70 relevant documents, then the recall at 50 is $R_{50} = 50$ percent, since 35/70 of the relevant documents were selected within the top 50. Recall measures the extent to which the retrieval is exhaustive and quantifies the coverage of the answer set.

Table 4.9a shows an example of this calculation applied to a ranking in response to some query. The first column shows the rank ordering of documents, and the second indicates whether the document is relevant to the query. For Table 4.9, it is assumed that there are 10 relevant documents in the entire collection and that 25 documents have been retrieved and displayed. Of course, at the time the algorithm is asked to supply the ranking, the relevance is not known; otherwise, the algorithm could simply discard the irrelevant documents and never show them. Relevance is a decision made after the event by one or more human assessors. Nor should it be assumed that relevance is absolute. One assessor may well judge a document to be relevant, while another says it is not. The designers of large information retrieval experiments must consider all of these problems, and establishing a plausible experimental regime is nontrivial.

The third column shows the *recall level*—the fraction of relevant documents that have been returned. By definition, recall is nondecreasing as the rank list is processed. The final column in Table 4.9a shows the precision at that point—the fraction of documents retrieved that are relevant. Since the first document is relevant, the precision at that point is 100 percent.

Table 4.9b shows how the ranking of Table 4.9a is reported as standardized recall-precision values. The first column shows 11 standard recall points, from 0 percent through 100 percent. For each of these points, the second column shows the corresponding precision value, measured at the number of documents required to achieve that level of recall. The third column shows the *interpolated* precision. This is the maximum precision at this and all higher recall levels. In the case of 0 percent recall, the precision is actually extrapolated rather than interpolated, and it is set to the maximum precision achieved at any point in the ranking.

Finally, these 11 precision values are often combined into a single overall value for retrieval *effectiveness*. There are two standard ways to do this. The first is to average the precision at recall values of 20 percent, 50 percent, and 80 percent, giving a

Table 4.9 Example showing calculation of recall and precision: (a) rank order; (b) calculating effectiveness.

(a)	r		R_r	P_r	(b)	Recall	Precision	Interpolated precision
	1	R	10%	100%				
	2	—	10%	50%		0%	—	100%
	3	—	10%	33%		10%	100%	100%
	4	R	20%	50%		20%	50%	60%
	5	R	30%	60%		30%	60%	60%
	6	—	30%	50%		40%	57%	57%
	7	R	40%	57%		50%	42%	50%
	8	—	40%	50%		60%	46%	50%
	9	—	40%	44%		70%	50%	50%
	10	—	40%	40%		80%	50%	50%
	11	—	40%	36%		90%	47%	47%
	12	R	50%	42%		100%	45%	45%
	13	R	60%	46%		3-point average		53%
	14	R	70%	50%		11-point average		61%
	15	—	70%	47%				
	16	R	80%	50%				
	17	—	80%	47%				
	18	—	80%	44%				
	19	R	90%	47%				
	20	—	90%	45%				
	21	—	90%	43%				
	22	R	100%	45%				
	23	—	100%	43%				
	24	—	100%	42%				
	25	—	100%	40%				

3-point effectiveness, which in this example is 53 percent. The second is to use an 11-point average, where the 0 percent level is also included, giving an 11-point effectiveness in the example of about 61 percent.

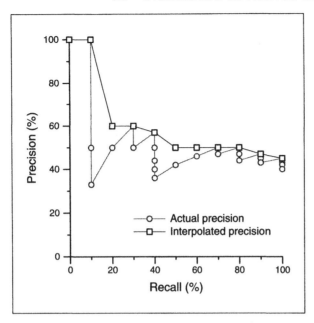

Figure 4.10 Recall-precision curve for ranking of Table 4.9.

Recall-precision curves

Since recall is a nondecreasing function of rank, precision can be regarded as a function of recall rather than of rank. Indeed, this is effectively what is shown in Table 4.9b. The relationship is formalized in a diagram known as a *recall-precision curve*, which plots precision as a function of recall. Because precision is usually high at low recall levels and low at high recall levels, the curve generally decreases. The recall-precision curve for the example in Table 4.9 is shown in Figure 4.10, where the two lines show actual precision and interpolated precision. If the interpolated precision values are used, the curve is nonincreasing.

If a perfect ranking algorithm could be developed, all relevant documents would be ranked ahead of all irrelevant documents. In this case, precision would be 100 percent at all recall levels, and the recall-precision curve would be a horizontal line at 100 percent. This provides one way to compare two ranking algorithms: plot their recall-precision curves, and if one curve lies completely above the other, then that algorithm is better. Unfortunately, this simple situation is rarely the case, and the curves usually intersect, perhaps several times.

This method of evaluating a similarity measure also presupposes that some standard set of documents and queries is available and that a complete set of *relevance judgments*—decisions as to which documents in the collection are answers to each query—is available. This is an onerous requirement, particularly if the experiment is performed on real-world examples and large databases.

```
<top>
<head> Tipster Topic Description
<num> Number:   094
<dom> Domain:   Science and Technology
<title> Topic:   Computer-aided Crime
<desc> Description:   Document must identify a crime
perpetrated with the aid of a computer.
<narr> Narrative:   To be relevant, a document must describe
an illegal activity which was carried out with the aid of a
computer, either used as a planning tool, such as in target
research; or used in the conduct of the crime, such as by
illegally gaining access to someone else's computer files.
A document is NOT relevant if it merely mentions the illegal
spread of a computer virus or worm.   However, a document
WOULD be relevant if the computer virus/worm were used in
conjunction with another crime, such as extortion.
<con> Concept(s):
1.   crime, fraud
2.   illegal access, corporate spying, extortion
<fac> Factor(s):
<def> Definition(s):
</top>
```

Figure 4.11   Sample *TREC* query.

The *TREC* project

The worldwide *TREC* (Text Retrieval Conference) project has, as one of its aims, the evaluation of methods for querying databases of realistic size and scope. An overview of the first two years of the project appears in a special issue of *Information Processing and Management* (Harman 1995). The research groups involved receive three resources: several (currently five) gigabytes of textual data, a set of sample queries (currently 300), and a set of relevance judgments that allow retrieval effectiveness to be measured and compared (currently several hundred thousand). The 741,856 documents comprising the first 2 Gbytes of *TREC* were described in Section 3.1, and a small sample of the text was shown in Figure 3.4 on page 110. Figure 4.11 shows one of the *TREC* query topics.

Prior to the establishment of *TREC*, there were no large test data sets, and information retrieval research was dominated by measured performance on some small databases for which sample queries and relevance judgments were available. Fortunately, several U.S. federal agencies cooperated in the early 1990s to rectify this situation and invested significant resources into the collection of text and queries, and the evaluation of relevance judgments.

Even when underwritten by the U.S. government, it was clear that assessing a set of $150 \times 741,856 = 111$ million relevance judgments, these being the requirement of the first two years of *TREC*, was an impossible task. Instead, a subset of the judgments were made for each query, and all other documents were assumed to be irrelevant. To establish a pool of possibly relevant documents for each query, the top r documents found by each of the participating research groups for that query were inspected manually, with r typically being taken to be 100. In the first two years of the project this process generated 224,311 judgments—an average of about 1,500 per query. Of these, 45,746 were that the document is relevant, an average of 300 per query. Even when restricted to this subset, producing the judgments has been a tremendous effort by those involved.

Since then, an annual round of experimentation has taken place, each year adding either new subcollections, or running on a different subset of the collection, or both, and each year adding around 50 fresh queries. This allows groups to tune system performance on a steadily growing pool of test data and at the same time respond to the challenge of fresh queries without any knowledge of performance until the official results are announced. The form of the topics has slowly evolved, and they have tended to become shorter. The number of participants has also increased (to about 50 in 1998). A variety of specialist streams have now been established. One, initiated in 1997, is the very large collection (VLC) track. Participants in this stream are provided with 20 Gbytes of data and have the computational performance of their retrieval system monitored as well as its retrieval effectiveness. With this volume of data, retrieval effectiveness is evaluated by comparing the precision achieved after a fixed number of documents have been examined since the cost of performing even pooled relevance judgments is too high.

In the first round of *TREC* experiments, using queries 51 to 100, and assuming both that all nonjudged documents are irrelevant and (pessimistically) that all relevant documents outside the top 200 retrieved are ranked lower in the ordering than all other documents, a straightforward implementation of the cosine measure (using $w_t = \log(n/f_t)$, $w_{d,t} = f_{d,t} \cdot w_t$ and $w_{q,t} = w_t$, the calculation used by the RMIT/Melbourne group) gives an average 11-point effectiveness of 17.4 percent—surprisingly good, considering the volumes of text involved and the fact that many of the precision figures going into the average are zero. Perhaps an easier statistic to digest is that, on these 50 queries, the cosine measure produces a precision-at-10 average of 56 percent, and a precision-at-100 average of 41 percent. In pulling 100 documents out of 740,000, the cosine rule gives a two-in-five chance that any document retrieved within the top 100 is relevant.

There is still plenty of room for improvement. Figure 4.12 shows the actual list of terms—after stopping and case folding—created from the query topic shown in Figure 4.11. Because the queries were created from the topics automatically, several problems have crept in. Perhaps the most glaring of these is that the word *not* has been stopped out of the query, so the query asks about *illegal, spread, virus, computer, worm*. Instead of these words appearing in a negative sense to discourage the selection of material, they actively support some irrelevant answers. Had the queries been created manually, the exception clause would, at the least, have been simply removed. Another problem was caused by the use of the word *document*; it was not stopped out of the queries, so many of the incorrect responses were articles about *software engineering and documentation standards*. In the collection, *document* is an

```
document identify crime perpetrated aid computer relevant document
describe illegal activity carried aid computer planning tool target
research conduct crime illegally gaining access computer files
document relevant merely mentions illegal spread computer virus worm
document relevant computer virus worm conjunction crime extortion
crime fraud illegal access corporate spying extortion
```

Figure 4.12 Sample *TREC* query as executed during experiments.

information-carrying word, but in the queries it is not and should be added to the query stop list.

The best results reported at the first *TREC* Conference in 1992, measured as the average of fifty 11-point averages, were higher than 20 percent, using the same assessment methodology. Needless to say, the research groups that achieved these results created their queries in a somewhat more elegant manner than the mechanism described here.

A second round of experimentation was held in 1993 using query topics 101 to 150, each of which contained an average of 53.6 terms. Figure 4.13 shows the recall-precision curve obtained by the cosine method described in Equation 4.3 (and a similar query creation process) on these queries. In this round, the top $r = 100$ documents from each group were again judged by the relevance assessors, but retrieval effectiveness figures are calculated using the top $r = 1,000$ retrieved documents rather than the top $r = 200$.

The curve shows quite clearly the trade-off between recall and precision. A search with high recall also accesses a large number of irrelevant documents, and a large number of the answers must be discarded. On the other hand, when precision is high, only a small fraction of the relevant documents are returned.

World Wide Web searching

One application in which the techniques described in this chapter have had enormous impact is World Wide Web searching. Few of us have not at some time, probably within the last week or month, clicked on the "Search" button of our browser or visited a favorite search engine, be it Infoseek, AltaVista, Excite, or one of the myriad other such facilities.

The service provided by these search engines is a result of two distinct activities. The first, of course, is information gathering. Programs known as "spiders" trawl the publicly readable sections of the Web, following links as they are encountered in an endless quest for new or updated Web pages. Visits to pages can also be explicitly requested, and so greatly do the majority of us value the transitory fame achieved when our page appears at the top of a query answer list that most information harvesting facilities have no shortage of work ahead of them. Indeed, it may be many months between visits to established sites, and one frequent complaint made

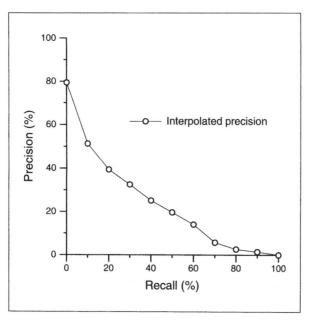

Figure 4.13 Recall-precision curve for cosine method on *TREC* topics 101–150 with top
$r = 1{,}000$ documents retrieved.

of Web search engines is that their indexes are not up-to-date. Various techniques
are used by the spiders to limit the amount of information they fetch: taking only
the first few hundred bytes of each page (so as to be sure of indexing the title and
primary heading fields); limiting the depth in each Web hierarchy from which pages
are retrieved; and, in extreme cases, blacklisting entire sites. Of course, as soon as
techniques like these become even suspected, the authors of the affected pages re-
act and change their formatting or layout or hostname in an attempt to spoof the
spider. Such behavior—deliberately seeking to bias the search results in favor of a
particular page—is known as index "spamming." Search engine companies create
antispam filters at almost exactly the same rate as users find ways to finesse them.

Once the data has been harvested, the engines construct lexicons and indexes,
very much as described in this book.[3] It is then that the more public face of Web
searching takes over. Users enter queries and expect answers that match them.
The default for most engines is that the input is interpreted as a ranked query, but
most engines also offer Boolean operators to specify that a term must or must not
be present in the documents returned. The majority of engines also offer phrase
searching, which can be extremely useful in restricting the search. One of the

---

3 Of course, for reasons of competitive advantage, the companies that run search engines do
not release technical details of their implementations.

authors was searching recently for information about the eight queens problem (a well-known chess puzzle), and the obvious query *eight queens* drew a wide range of answers, including one about "eight cut-out drag queens and their fabulous, over-the-top ensembles," and another about "Henry the Eighth and his queens." On the other hand, the quoted query phrase *"eight queens"* eliminated these spurious results.

Most queries posed to Web search engines are very short, just two or three terms. Indeed, the most common query is the empty query—exactly zero terms long. Whether this is an artifact of dropped network packets or a sad reflection of our technical competence is unclear. And if the anecdotal evidence that flows from search companies is correct, a depressingly large fraction of nonempty queries—as much as one-fifth—involve terms like *adult* and *xxx*. Analysis of logs reveals that around 1,000 common queries account for well over 10% of all search engine usage, and some engines do not actually consult their index to resolve such queries, returning precomputed answers instead.

Another way in which search engines increase their query throughput is through the use of enormous tracts of memory in order to avoid disk accesses. For example, the AltaVista engine maintains its entire index in memory so that processing of queries can be accomplished without any recourse to disk-based indexes.

Because the source of the original information is completely anarchic, unexpected behavior can sometimes occur. In a keynote address at the 1998 Information Retrieval Conference, Steve Kirsch, the principal of the search company Infoseek, described how not to search for the "Barney" home page. (Barney is a large green and purple dinosaur that sings and dances for four-year-olds and their parents.) Kirsch reported that most search engines, when asked the obvious query

Barney dinosaur,

return some sites that are clearly hits but also some vehemently anti-Barney sites—including some that you might not want your children to see. (Barney, though loved by four-year-olds, inspires derision in much of the rest of the community, especially those with the power to author Web pages.) A better search is

Barney dinosaur −kill −maim −destroy,

in which the "−" Boolean operator restricts answers to pages not containing the corresponding term. There is a clear lesson here, and as users of such services we should think carefully about what information we are seeking and what information we are not.

Another interesting side of Web searching is the placement of advertisements. Most search companies provide free searching, and the cost of their operation is essentially borne by advertisers who pay a few cents at a time for marketing that appears in the answer page. Moreover, in many instances the advertisers only pay the placement fee if the user actually follows the link through the ad and accesses the information it relates to—known as a "click through." Hence, to maximize revenue, a search engine company should target the advertisement to the particular user asking the query, and, of course, the information upon which that targeting should be based is right at hand in the query. Hence, if you search for information on Barney on an Australian search engine site, you may well be offered details of a "Bananas in Pyjamas" (Australia's answer to Barney) video in the banner advertisement; if your query is *xxx*, you might be offered adult videos. That is, your query is executed twice: once against the index of Web pages and once against an index describing possible advertisements.

The final aspect of Web searching that is worth noting is that in terms of assessing effectiveness, precision reigns supreme. A user that obtains a relevant answer in the first page of document pointers is satisfied, irrespective of the recall level that answer represents. Similarly, a user who has to wade through to the third page of answers in order to find a relevant document is unimpressed, even if that one answer is the only relevant document in the entire indexed Web.

Other effectiveness measures

Methods other than recall-precision averages have been suggested for generating a single number to quantify the usefulness of ranking algorithms. One possibility is to measure the precision when the number of retrieved documents, r, is just sufficient to include all the relevant documents. In effect, a single point is sampled from the recall-precision curve, and that point is chosen as the minimum point at which recall *could* be 100 percent. For example, the ranking of Table 4.9 has 10 relevant documents, and the value of P_{10} is 40 percent. This is known as the R-value.

None of the measures discussed so far takes into account the size of the collection. The ranking of Table 4.9 would be far more impressive if it were from a collection of one million documents rather than just 25. Indeed, if the collection only has 25 documents and there are 10 answers, it is hard to see how the 11-point effectiveness could be less than 40 percent. We will briefly discuss three measures of retrieval effectiveness that attempt to account for the size of the collection.

The first is the receiver operating characteristics (ROC) curve. Rather than plotting precision as a function of recall, the probability of *detection* is plotted as a function of the probability of a *false alarm* (also known as *fallout*). The detection probability is just the recall, as previously defined. The probability of false alarm is the ratio of nonrelevant items that are retrieved to the number of nonrelevant items in the collection. A good retrieval mechanism will offer low false alarm probabilities at reasonable detection probabilities.

The second effectiveness measure—which, as noted above, is particularly applicable to users of Web search engines—is to assess system performance solely by taking the precision at a fixed value such as 10 or 20. Supporters of this metric argue that user satisfaction is the criterion that should be assessed, and an interactive user tends to view only a few screens of document titles before terminating their search, either successfully if a relevant document was discovered or unsuccessfully if not.

The third measure, which also attempts to assess this notion of user effort, is simply to use the rank position of the first relevant document, possibly combining scores for different experiments using a geometric mean rather than an arithmetic mean, to avoid one poor run distorting otherwise good results. For example, a system that on average returns the first relevant document as the second in the rank list would be assessed as being better than one that scores the first relevant document in the fifth position on average.

4.6 Implementation of the cosine measure

We now examine the implementation of the cosine measure. Clearly, more information is required than for Boolean query processing, and there are important decisions to be made about how this information should be structured to make the ranking process efficient in terms of the time and memory required. In the sections that follow, several components of an implementation are studied in detail.

The first problem addressed is that ranking requires more information than Boolean queries, and there is the need for within-document frequencies $f_{d,t}$ to be added to the index. Methods for representing these are discussed in the first subsection below.

We then turn to how the cosine formula is evaluated. Although the rule is succinctly summarized by Equation 4.3, it turns out that efficient evaluation of the rule on a large collection is potentially expensive, in terms of CPU time, disk bandwidth, and memory requirements. Various mechanisms have been proposed for reducing these requirements, including efficient representation of the document weights W_d, limiting the number of documents that can be *candidates* in the ranking, and the use of skipped or frequency-sorted inverted files to speed query processing. These aspects are examined in detail below. Finally, we examine algorithms for solving a deceptively simple problem: given a set of N numbers, how to identify the r largest of them when $r \ll N$.

In combination, the techniques developed here allow ranked queries to be evaluated on large collections using not much more memory space and CPU time than is required by Boolean query evaluation.

Within-document frequencies

Suppose that some query Q is to be used to rank a collection of documents. If the term frequencies f_t are stored in the lexicon, then for most of the term weight assignment rules described above, the document-term weight $w_{d,t}$ can be calculated provided that $f_{d,t}$ is known, since N, the only other value required, is global. For this reason, $f_{d,t}$ can be stored in the inverted list along with the document number d.

Consider again the example document collection shown in Table 4.6 on page 181. In the inverted file structures described in Chapter 3, the inverted list for the term *porridge* would have the form

$$\langle 3; 1, 2, 5 \rangle,$$

indicating that the term appears in $f_{\text{porridge}} = 3$ documents, namely, documents 1, 2, and 5.

Now, this inverted list must be augmented by including with each document pointer the number of times the term appears, which we refer to as the *within-document frequencies* and denote by $f_{d,t}$:

$$\langle 3; (1, 2), (2, 1), (5, 2) \rangle.$$

This indicates that *porridge* appears two times in document 1, once in document 2, and twice in document 5. More generally, each inverted list is *augmented*:

$$\langle f_t; (d_{t,1}, f_{d_{t,1},t}), (d_{t,2}, f_{d_{t,2},t}), \ldots, (d_{t,f_t}, f_{d_{t,f_t},t}) \rangle,$$

where $i = d_{t,k}$ is the number of the kth document that contains term t; w_t is the term weight, described above; and $f_{d_{t,k},t} = f_{i,t}$ is the within-document frequency of term t in this document. Note that although f_t is logically a field in the inverted list, it is more likely to be stored in the lexicon together with t (the term), I_t (the inverted file address), and, if it is explicitly stored and not derived, w_t (the term weight).

Each inverted list must store the $f_{d,t}$ values. In fact, the unary code is an effective method for compressing the within-document frequencies. In Section 3.3 it was found to be inappropriate for representing the gaps in the inverted list; however, it turns out to be almost ideal for representing the within-document frequency values $f_{d,t}$. If a word appears once in a document, it requires a one-bit code; if it appears twice, a two-bit code; and so on. In fact the inverted list for term t grows by a number of bits exactly equal to the total number of appearances, in the entire collection, of that term, and this provides an easily calculated upper bound on the amount by which the compressed inverted file must grow. Let F_t be the total number of appearances of term t, where duplicate occurrences within the same document are counted separately. That is,

$$F_t = \sum_{d=1}^{N} f_{d,t}.$$

Then

$$\sum_{t=1}^{n} F_t = F$$

where F is the total number of words in the collection, as defined in Section 3.1 and Table 3.1 (page 107).

Since a unary code for x requires x bits, the inverted list for term t grows by exactly F_t bits, and the total inverted file grows by exactly F bits. From Table 3.1, it is clear that the ratio F/f indicates that, on average, most $f_{d,t}$ values are relatively small and must frequently be 1 or 2. This is borne out by the compression results attained using the unary code for the $f_{d,t}$ values.

The cost, measured in bits per term, is shown for the four sample collections of Chapter 3 as the first line of Table 4.10. The γ and δ codes described in Section 3.3 are other obvious candidates for coding these values. Compared with unary, γ is

Table 4.10 Adding frequency information, bits per pointer.

Method	Bits per pointer			
	Bible	GNUbib	Comact	TREC
Unary	1.27	1.16	1.74	2.49
γ	1.38	1.23	1.88	2.13
δ	1.53	1.32	2.15	2.41
Observed frequency	1.27	1.15	1.72	2.02
Interpolative	0.76	0.45	1.41	1.77

longer for only two values ($x = 2$ and $x = 4$) and then by only one bit (Table 3.6 on page 117). Surprisingly, the distribution of $f_{d,t}$ values is sufficiently skewed that unary outperforms the γ code for three of the four test databases, and γ outperforms δ for all four. The observed frequency row corresponds to a global Huffman code based on the actual frequencies of each number coded, so it represents the best that any of these codes might achieve (although, as will be considered below, a different organization within each inverted list allows this limit to be beaten). The interpolative code of page 126 can also be used for the $f_{d,t}$ values, by forming a list of cumulative sums and treating them as a list of "document numbers." It achieves excellent compression and on *Bible* and *GNUbib*, in which the documents are short and most of the $f_{d,t}$ values are one, averages at less than one bit per stored number. For the three small collections, the closeness of the results for the observed frequency code to those for the unary code indicates that the $\Pr[x] = 2^{-x}$ probability distribution implied by the unary code is an excellent approximation to the actual distribution. Only on the relatively long documents in the *TREC* collection, where within-document frequencies sometimes exceed 4 or 5, is the unary code less economical.

Adding the costs per pointer of Table 3.8 (page 129) and Table 4.10 reveals a rather remarkable fact:

It is possible to index every term in a large text using less than one byte per pointer, even when the index file contains term frequencies.

For the *TREC* collection, for example, an interpolative coded augmented inverted file—indexing every word and every number—can be stored in 112 Mbytes, just 5.4 percent of the data that it indexes.

Of the simple codes, the fact that the unary code admits a tight upper bound on the number of bits required to represent the frequency information for all terms t renders it very useful during the index construction process, as described in Chapter 5 ("In-place multiway merging" section, page 239). On the other hand, γ has a significant advantage: it can never be much worse than unary, but it can be much better. Integer x requires a unary code of x bits, whereas the corresponding γ code consumes about $1 + 2\log x$ bits (for large x). The latter quantity can be considerably smaller on collections in which there are many terms with very high within-document frequencies. And when the documents are very short, the worst that can result is that the γ codes are one bit longer than the unary alternative, a situation that is most unlikely—it would require that all within-document frequencies be either 2 or 4. Hence, γ is the method of choice if a simple code is to be used, and the interpolative method is the appropriate choice if reducing the size of the index is the dominant concern.

Calculating the cosine value

We are now ready to evaluate the cosine measure using the TF$\times$IDF weighting rule. The simplest strategy is to read each document of the collection, calculate a cosine value for it, and maintain a sorted list of the top r cosine values found so far, together with the text of the corresponding documents. But this is prohibitively expensive: to read a gigabyte of text and parse it into terms takes several hours of computation. Fortunately, a more economical alternative is provided by the information stored in the augmented inverted file.

Consider again the formulation for the cosine measure given by Equation 4.3 on page 187:

$$cosine(Q, D_d) = \frac{1}{W_d W_q} \sum_{t \in Q \cap D_d} (1 + \log_e f_{d,t}) \cdot \log_e \left(1 + \frac{N}{f_t}\right).$$

If the summation is evaluated by processing in turn each inverted list, the ranking can be evaluated without recourse to the text of the document collection. Furthermore, the presence of $f_{d,t}$ in the inverted lists means that W_d, the weight of document d, is the only remaining value to be specified. Let us assume for now that the W_d values have been precomputed—which is feasible because they are independent of the query and, for this particular formulation, dependent only upon the $f_{d,t}$ values for the terms that appear—into an array in memory, indexed by d. The cost of this array is considered in the next subsection.

To perform the processing term by term, one more temporary structure is required—a set of *accumulators* indexed by document number d, in which the value $cosine(Q, D_d)$ can be accrued in a random access manner. In its simplest form, this is an array in which each element is initially zero, but, as discussed below, other data structures can be used.

Figure 4.14 shows the algorithm used to calculate $cosine(Q, D_d)$ for each document d and to extract and display the top r ranked documents. In this calculation, each inverted list is processed in full. Each document number that appears in an inverted list causes a cosine contribution to be added to the corresponding accumulator, so each document that contains any of the query terms ends up with a nonzero accumulator. Once all the cosine contributions have been accrued, they are normalized by the corresponding document weights into values that are proportional to the

To retrieve r documents using the cosine measure,

1. Set $A \leftarrow \{\ \}$. A is the set of accumulators.

2. For each query term $t \in Q$,

   (a) Stem t.

   (b) Search the lexicon.

   (c) Record f_t and the address of I_t, the inverted file entry for t.

   (d) Set $w_t \leftarrow 1 + \log_e(N/f_t)$.

   (e) Read the inverted file entry, I_t.

   (f) For each $(d, f_{d,t})$ pair in I_t,

       i. If $A_d \notin A$ then
          Set $A_d \leftarrow 0$,
          Set $A \leftarrow A + \{A_d\}$.

       ii. Set $A_d \leftarrow A_d + \log_e(1 + f_{d,t}) * w_t$.

3. For each $A_d \in A$,
       Set $A_d \leftarrow A_d/W_d$.
       A_d is now proportional to the value $cosine(Q, D_d)$.

4. For $1 \le i \le r$,

   (a) Select d such that $A_d = \max\{A\}$.

   (b) Look up the address of document d.

   (c) Retrieve document d and present it to the user.

   (d) Set $A \leftarrow A - \{A_d\}$.

Figure 4.14 Evaluation of the cosine measure to retrieve r documents.

cosine measure. The final step is to select the r largest from among all these values and retrieve and display the documents they represent.

This algorithm raises three points. First, W_q is ignored since it is a constant for any particular query and so does not affect the ranking. Second, large amounts of memory are used. The document weights W_d typically occupy four bytes per document, and if the accumulators are implemented as an array, they too cost four bytes each. On a collection such as *TREC*, these two alone will consume several megabytes of memory, and a number of techniques for reducing the space required are discussed in the next two sections. Third, only $r \ll N$ documents are presented. This means that at step 4 there is no need to completely sort the set A. Algorithms for efficiently extracting the top r items from a large set are discussed in the "Sorting" subsection (page 210).

Memory for document weights

Once all the inverted lists have been processed, the document weights W_d must be factored in. The algorithm in Figure 4.14 does this by processing the entire array of accumulators A_d, dividing each by the corresponding weight W_d drawn from a memory-resident array W. This has the advantage of being both simple and fast. It is, however, expensive in memory. For example, a W array for the 740,000 documents of the *TREC* collection requires nearly 3 Mbytes, an appreciable amount of space.

One way to reclaim this space is to store the array W on disk. It is accessed only sequentially, never randomly, so disk storage is certainly a reasonable way to trade time for space. To normalize the accumulators into cosine values, the entire weights file must then be read. Assuming a transfer rate of 1 Mbyte per second, this adds about 3 seconds to the time taken to process a query on *TREC*, accounting for approximately 20 to 30 percent of the query processing time. (Detailed times for query processing are given in Section 9.6.)

Another method that has been suggested for eliminating the memory required by document weights is to store $f_{d,t}/W_d$ instead of $f_{d,t}$ in the inverted list, so that the value accumulated in A_d is automatically scaled by W_d. When the inverted file is stored compressed, however, this is extravagantly expensive. Having taken reasonable care to store the $f_{d,t}$ values in under 2 bits each, the cost of storing $f_{d,t}/W_d$, where W_d may have 16 or 32 bits of precision, is a substantial imposition, tantamount to storing each document weight once for every word in the document. This approach is suitable only when it has already been decided for other reasons that 16- or 32-bit integers will be used to store the $f_{d,t}$ values. It is quite inappropriate if compression is being used to minimize the space required by the inverted file.

As a compromise between the all-in-memory and all-on-disk extremes, if some limited amount of main memory is available, it is possible to store *approximate weights* in memory and use these to guide access into an on-disk file storing the exact document weights (Moffat, Zobel, and Sacks-Davis 1994). In this method, as little as six to eight bits of main memory per document is enough that the number of accesses to the full weights file can be restricted to only slightly more than r, the number of documents to be presented. To achieve this, a code must be devised for representing weights in a small number of bits.

Suppose that b bits are to be used for coding an approximation of some value x. Suppose also that upper and lower bounds on x are known—namely, that

$$L \le x \le U$$

for some constants L and U. One way to code x onto an integer c in the range $0 \le c < 2^b$ is to assume uniform-sized buckets over the range and to represent x by the corresponding bucket number:

$$c = \left\lfloor \frac{x - L}{U - L + \epsilon} 2^b \right\rfloor$$

Table 4.11　Geometric approximate code for $L = 10.0$, $U = 18.0$, and $b = 2$.

Code c	Code value	Corresponding range for x	$\hat{x} = g(c + 0.5)$
00	0	[10.00, 11.60)	10.77
01	1	[11.60, 13.46)	12.49
10	2	[13.46, 15.61)	14.49
11	3	[15.61, 18.01)	16.81

for some suitably small value ϵ. However, when the weights are eventually used in the cosine method, they are applied in a multiplicative sense rather than an additive sense, so this method has a disproportionately large relative error for small values of x.

It is better to keep the relative error constant by using a set of buckets that grow in width as a geometric sequence. A base B is calculated as

$$B = \left(\frac{U + \epsilon}{L}\right)^{2^{-b}}$$

and the code c for x is then given by

$$f(x) = \lfloor \log_B(x/L) \rfloor = \left\lfloor \frac{\log(x/L)}{\log B} \right\rfloor.$$

The range of values x corresponding to a code c is

$$g(c) \leq x < g(c + 1)$$

where

$$g(c) = L \cdot B^c.$$

As an example, suppose that values in the range $10 \leq x \leq 18$ are to be approximated by $b = 2$ bit codes. Taking $\epsilon = 0.1$, calculate

$$B = \left(\frac{18.1}{10.0}\right)^{2^{-2}} = (1.81)^{0.25} = 1.160.$$

The value 15.3 would then be coded as

$$c = f(15.3) = \left\lfloor \log_{1.16} \frac{15.3}{10.0} \right\rfloor = \left\lfloor \frac{\log 1.53}{\log 1.16} \right\rfloor = \lfloor 2.865 \rfloor = 2$$

so the two-bit pattern 10 would be used.

When the approximate weights are being used, the code 10, or $c = 2$, is expanded to give the range $13.456 \leq x < 15.610$. Table 4.11 shows the complete set of codes for this example.

The final column of Table 4.11 shows the approximation $\hat{x}$ that would, in a general situation, be used upon decoding, where $\hat{x} = g(c + 0.5)$ and the 0.5 is added to minimize the average error arising from the truncation in the encoding formula. In the particular application being considered here, there is no need to add the 0.5 because all that is important is the resultant relativities, not the exact values.

A simple way to take the approximate weights into account when ranking is to use $\hat{W}_d$ to normalize the accumulator values, where $\hat{W}_d = g(c_d)$ and $c_d = f(W_d)$ is the b-bit code used to represent W_d. When B is close to one, the approximate value is very close to the actual one, and positions within the rank ordering may alter a little, but the only documents that can move in or out of the top r are those with cosine values in a narrow band around the cutoff value for the query. Given that ranking is approximate in any case, it seems reasonable to put another heuristic step into the chain and accept this slight reordering.

Another possibility is for the approximate weights to be used as a guide to determine those full weights that must be fetched from disk to calculate an exact ranking. Suppose that the coded weight of document d is c_d. Then $g(c_d)$ is a lower bound on the actual weight W_d. Given the accumulator value A_d, a lower bound on W_d allows an *upper* bound on the cosine value to be calculated. This bound can be used to eliminate the bulk of the documents from further consideration on most queries, and only those that remain in contention need to have their weights checked. The algorithm for deciding which weights are needed is shown in Figure 4.15. It uses A_d as the accumulator value for document d, c_d for the coded approximation to W_d, and $g(c)$ as the inverse function for this approximation. The set H holds the r answers to be returned. It is initialized to the top r approximate cosine values using the lower bound on W_d and is resolved by the end of the algorithm into the final top r exact cosine values. The mechanism to be used at step 2 to identify these top r approximate values during this first phase is described in the "Sorting" subsection (page 210).

The second phase reconsiders every cosine value, asking if any of the documents currently outside the top r might conceivably belong in that set. This is done by comparing the smallest of the top r final cosine values in H with the upper bound A_d previously calculated for document d. If $A_d > \min\{H\}$, then the exact weight must be read and a more detailed check performed. If the exact cosine of document d (which is less than the approximate value) is still greater than the smallest value in H, then it supplants that item, and its document address is noted. This process ensures that only a small number of exact weights are required over and above the r that are resolved between the two phases.

For example, on *TREC*, with an array of eight-bit approximate weights, the top 25 ranked documents could be identified by retrieving just 30 exact weights, averaged over 50 of the standard queries. Random access to these weights takes well under a second. Given that the document addresses are also likely to be stored on disk and that 25 of these accesses would have been required anyway to fetch addresses for the answers, the overhead of using approximate weights is just 5 disk accesses. The query has already performed more than 50 disk accesses by the time the answers are displayed, and 5 extra ones can buy the release of 2 Mbytes of main memory.

To determine the top r documents using approximate weights,

1. For $1 \leq d \leq N$,

 Set $A_d \leftarrow A_d/g(c_d)$.

 A_d is approximate *cosine* value; $A_d \geq cosine(Q, D_d)$.

2. Set $H \leftarrow$ top r values of A_d.

3. For $d \in H$,

 (a) Read W_d from disk.

 (b) Record address of document d.

 (c) Set $A_d \leftarrow A_d * g(c_d)/W_d$.

 Documents in H have exact *cosine* values.

4. For $1 \leq d \leq N$,

 (a) If $A_d \notin H$ and $A_d > \min\{H\}$ then

 i. Read W_d from disk.

 ii. Set $A_d \leftarrow A_d * g(c_d)/W_d$.

 iii. If $A_d > \min\{H\}$ then

 Set $H \leftarrow H - \{\min\{H\}\} + \{A_d\}$,

 Record address of document d.

 H now contains the top r exact *cosine* values.

Figure 4.15 Using approximate weights to eliminate documents.

Memory for accumulators

The accumulators place another demand on main memory during query processing. There are two obvious ways to store this information.

The first is to use a simple array of N items, indexed by the document number d. In this case, N words of storage—$4N$ bytes on a 32-bit machine—are required for every query, and the accumulators take the same space as the document weights.

The second, which is appropriate if there are expected to be far fewer accumulators than documents, is a dynamic search structure such as a tree or a hash table. A constant amount of memory space will be required for each candidate: four bytes for a document number; four bytes for the actual accumulator; and perhaps six bytes overhead for a chained hash table search structure. Hashing is probably the best method to use because insertion and lookup are fast. However, when the query is such that many documents have nonzero accumulators, a dynamic structure might require a great deal of space.

Various heuristics have been proposed to restrict the number of nonzero accumulators (Buckley and Lewit 1985; Lucarella 1988; Harman and Candela 1990;

Wong and Lee 1993; Moffat and Zobel 1996; Anh and Moffat 1998). They all rely on the inverted lists being accessed in increasing f_t (that is, decreasing w_t) order, so f_t must be stored in the lexicon, just as for Boolean queries. These heuristics may mean that the ranking will no longer be exactly that specified by the cosine rule. Of course, the cosine rule is itself a heuristic, and additional approximations will not necessarily degrade retrieval effectiveness.

The simplest rule is to place an a priori bound on the number of nonzero accumulators permitted and stop adding new ones when the bound is reached. In effect, terms of high weight are permitted to select accumulators, but terms of low weight are denied this opportunity. There are then two ways in which the remaining terms can be handled. The easiest approach is to *quit*, ignoring the cosine contribution of all unprocessed terms even if they are for documents that have already been granted accumulators. The alternative is to *continue* processing inverted lists. Documents that do not yet have an accumulator are ignored, but documents for which accumulators have already been created continue to have their cosine contributions accrued. When processing ends, the full cosine values have been built up for a subset of the documents, but some documents have been denied a position in the ranking.

The advantage of the *quit* rule is that query processing is very fast since the inverted lists that remain unprocessed are exactly those that are longest. This strategy does, however, result in markedly poorer retrieval effectiveness; even the last few inverted lists contribute positively to the final ranking. On the other hand, the *continue* strategy gives retrieval performance comparable to the exact cosine method. Experiments with the *TREC* collection and the standard set of queries have shown that as few as 5,000 accumulators are sufficient to extract the top 1,000 documents; when the number of accumulators is 30,000, retrieval effectiveness is actually *greater* than for the exact cosine method. Details of these experiments are given in Chapter 9 ("Ranked queries" subsection, page 425).

Fast query processing

The *continue* strategy also allows faster query processing than the exact cosine rule. At face value, every inverted list must be processed, and it is not clear that any time can be saved. But processing every inverted list is not the same as processing *all* of every inverted list. Section 4.3 (page 178) describes a skipping strategy that allows Boolean queries to be processed quickly, making use of the fact that a small set of candidates is being resolved against a longer inverted list. During the first part of *continue* processing, before the accumulator limit is reached, every document number must be examined, and the logic is that of an OR query. But in the second phase, when no new accumulators are created, the processing is more like an AND query since only existing accumulators must be checked. Thus, skipping can also be used in ranking, provided that the number of accumulators is restricted. The saving is less dramatic than for Boolean queries since the number of accumulators is much larger than the number of candidates left after the first few terms of a Boolean query have been processed. Experiments with the *TREC* collection have shown that the time taken to resolve a ranked query of 40–50 terms can be halved by skipping, without degradation of retrieval effectiveness. This time saving is an added benefit: the primary motivation for limiting the number of accumulators is to save memory during query processing.

There are two more elegant heuristics for limiting the number of accumulators, though they cannot guarantee to operate within some prior bound on available memory. The first is a *pruning* strategy that processes inverted lists in decreasing w_t order, allowing new accumulators to be created only so long as $w_t > \max_{t \in Q}\{w_t\}/3$. The remaining terms are processed in the same AND mode described above, and similar time savings accrue. The only terms allowed to establish accumulators are those that are at least one-third as important as the query term of highest weight. The second heuristic is to process an inverted list only if the term weight w_t of that term plus all other remaining terms is sufficiently large that the document currently ranked $r + 1$ could be pushed into the top r if it contains all these terms. In this case, the correct r documents are guaranteed to be returned, but not necessarily in the same order as they would be by the exact cosine measure.

Frequency-sorted indexes

Another way in which the inverted index structure can be modified, this time specifically to ease ranked query evaluation, is to *frequency-sort* each of the inverted lists (Persin 1994; Persin, Zobel, and Sacks-Davis 1996). Consider the list for some word that appears, say, twice in each of documents 1, 2, and 5 in a collection; once in document 4; and five times in document 3. Stored in document number order, and with each pair representing a document number d and the within-document frequency $f_{d,t}$, the inverted list would be

$$\langle 5; (1,2), (2,2), (3,5), (4,1), (5,2) \rangle.$$

Suppose instead that the list is sorted first by decreasing $f_{d,t}$ value and then by document number:

$$\langle 5; (3,5), (1,2), (2,2), (5,2), (4,1) \rangle.$$

This means that the documents for which the $f_{d,t}$ values are the greatest can be found quickly. Before we exploit this observation, we first consider how frequency-sorted lists might be represented.

The pointers in each list are no longer in ascending document number order, so taking d-gaps over the whole list is not possible. The list can, however, be broken into chunks within which all the $f_{d,t}$ values are the same and d-gaps can be used. In the example list, the first chunk contains just one pointer, the second chunk contains three, and the final chunk contains one. If each chunk is prefixed by the common $f_{d,t}$ value that is shared by the pointers within the chunk, together with a counter to say how many pointers there are in each chunk, the list can be represented as

$$\langle 5; (5, 1 : 3), (2, 3 : 1, 2, 5), (1, 1 : 4) \rangle,$$

where a tuple $(f, k : d_1, d_2, \dots, d_k)$ records that in the original inverted list for this term there are k documents in which the term has frequency f, namely, $d_1, d_2,$

and so on through to d_k. Within each tuple, the document numbers can now be represented using d-gaps. But because there are fewer pointers in each chunk than there were in the original list, and each chunk still spans the same potential range of document numbers (1 to N) as the full list, each pointer will require more bits than previously. For example, if a document d is the only document that contains the term f times, then approximately $\log N$ bits will be required for the d-gap code. The extra counter k must also be paid for. However, set against these extra costs is the saving that accrues through not repeating the duplicate $f_{d,t}$ values. For the majority of lists, there are very many pointers for which $f_{d,t}$ is one or two—after all, this was the basis upon which the unary and γ codes performed so well in Table 4.10 on page 200—which means both that the removal of duplicate $f_{d,t}$ values results in a nontrivial saving and that the loss caused by each document pointer being in a sparser range is small. Moreover, the $f_{d,t}$ values can be coded as negative differences from the first one, which is the largest such value in the list, and the values k can be economically coded using the γ code. Experiments with databases such as TREC have shown that frequency-sorted indexes are rarely larger than comparable document-sorted indexes and are usually a few percent smaller (Persin 1994; Persin, Zobel, and Sacks-Davis 1996).

Now that the inverted lists have been reorganized, how should they be employed? Consider a ranked query. For each term, a weight w_t is calculated in advance and used to order the terms, so that the rarer terms are processed first. This is especially important if a bound has been placed upon the number of nonzero accumulators, the rationale being that the bigger the numeric value of the contribution of some term to a document's accumulator, the more necessary it is that the contribution be properly recorded. But in fact the contribution made to the score of any document by a term is not solely a function of w_t. Equation 4.3 clearly shows that $f_{d,t}$ is also important—a term that has a small w_t value may still be crucial to the query if some document contains it many times. So instead of processing the inverted lists in decreasing w_t order, suppose that they are all processed in parallel using a frequency-sorted index, one chunk at a time. That is, the first chunk of inverted list for each query term is read, and then the products $(1 + \log_e f_{d,t}) \cdot w_t$ are calculated for those chunks. The largest value of this expression determines the greatest accumulator contribution and should be processed first, even if it is not the largest w_t value. All of the documents indicated by this chunk will get the same accumulator contribution. Then the second chunk from that list is read to replace the first in the tournament and the comparison performed again to determine which of the current chunks should be processed next.

This strategy has four advantages and one drawback. First, it is more accurate. Each chunk of each term is processed at exactly the right time, so as to ensure that the amounts being added to the accumulators are strictly nonincreasing. If an accumulator bound is being enforced, processing can again either *quit* or *continue* when the limit is reached, and now we can be even more confident than before that the contributions that are being discounted are small.

Second, it can involve less processing. Suppose that a relatively modest number of accumulators is enforced. It is quite likely that *none* of the $f_{d,t} = 1$ pointers from *any* of the inverted lists are processed. As always, these pointers form the bulk of most inverted lists. Thus a frequency-sorted index allows faster processing of ranked queries.

Third, disk transfer time will also be saved since there is no longer any requirement to read all of every list. Instead, lists can be read in, say, 4 Kbyte blocks and chunks decoded off the front of the lists in an on-demand manner. It is quite unlikely that long lists—which are those for frequent terms and hence have low w_t values—will be read in entirety. It is instead quite possible that only one block will be read from the long lists, a considerable saving in disk transfer costs.

Fourth, experiments have shown that this processing strategy gives retrieval effectiveness as good as, and in many cases slightly better than, the use of *quit* and *continue* strategies with a document-sorted index (Persin 1994; Persin, Zobel, and Sacks-Davis 1996).

The drawback of using a frequency-sorted index is, of course, more complex processing for Boolean queries. It is most appropriate in systems that will only be required to support ranked queries, and the extra processing cost for Boolean queries may be a sufficient disadvantage so as to discourage its use if both ranked and Boolean queries are to be handled in the same system.

Sorting

The final component of the ranking process outlined at the beginning of Section 4.6 (page 198) is sorting. Conventional sorting algorithms require at least $N \log N$ comparisons to sort N records, and for $N \approx 1,000,000$ this corresponds to 20 million operations, or several seconds on typical computers (see, for example, Cormen, Leiserson, and Rivest 1990 and Sedgewick 1990).

A variety of mechanisms have been suggested to reduce the sorting time. One is to sort only the accumulators that are nonzero. In many cases, the set A might contain accumulators for only a small proportion of the documents, particularly if their numbers are artificially restricted to save space, as was suggested above. Even with a relatively large fraction of nonzero accumulators—say, 10 percent—sorting time can be greatly reduced. Indeed, this saving has sometimes been used as an argument in favor of reducing the number of accumulators.

There is, however, a simpler approach. The key to this method is to note that r, the number of documents to be presented, is, in most cases, very small relative to N, and extracting the $r \ll N$ greatest values from a set is quite a different proposition from sorting the entire set. This problem is called *selection* and is well known in the field of algorithm design and analysis. The standard solution to the r-selection problem is to use the heap data structure that was introduced in Chapter 2 in connection with Huffman's algorithm. Now a *max-heap* is required, one in which the largest item is maintained at the root, but this is easy to arrange, and the operations are almost identical to those sketched in Figure 2.12 on page 44.

Suppose then that the top $r = 100$ documents are to be presented out of a collection of $N = 1,000,000$ documents. It takes about two million steps to build the initial heap, after which the 100 sifting operations are completed within a further 4,000

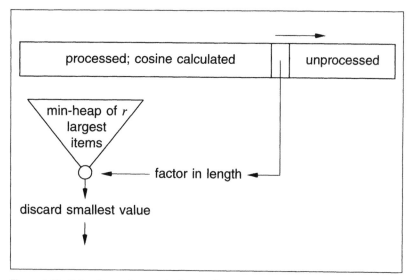

Figure 4.16   Selection using a min-heap of r items.

comparisons. The total effort is about 10 percent of the cost of a full sort. More-over, the techniques described above for controlling the number of accumulators continue to yield the same benefits in this heap-based arrangement.

There is, unfortunately, a drawback to using a heap in this way, and that is the space required to hold document addresses until they are needed. If a heap of N items is used in the manner suggested, then either the document addresses must be accessed from disk after the top r documents have been identified, at a cost of r further disk accesses, or a second array of N items must be maintained in memory to hold document addresses if they are to be accessed at the same time as the W_d values. The first option increases the time taken by ranking; the second increases the memory required. What would be ideal is to store in memory just the addresses of the top r ranked documents and to read those addresses at the same time that the weights W_d are processed from a combined document weights plus document addresses file.

The solution to this problem is rather surprising, and it involves returning to the use of a *min-heap*. Suppose that a min-heap of r items, instead of a max-heap of N items, is maintained. In most cases, r is small, so the cost of storing r document addresses, one for each item in the heap, is minimal. The basic idea now is to process the N accumulator values, storing in the heap the r largest values seen so far. A min-heap allows easy identification of the smallest of these r values, and this item—the rth largest of the values processed until now—is exactly the one that is next to drop out of the top r if a larger value is found. This is illustrated in Figure 4.16.

The algorithm operates as follows. To get started, the first r accumulators are copied into the heap, and their document weights factored in. When the weights are read, their document addresses are stored. These r cosine values are then converted into a min-heap, taking about $2r$ steps. At the end of this initialization stage, the smallest of the r cosine values is at the root of the heap.

Each remaining accumulator is then processed. To process one accumulator, its weight is read and factored in to calculate a cosine value. If this cosine value is larger than the smallest value in the heap, then that smallest item can be taken out of the heap—it is now known to have rank at least $r + 1$—and replaced by the new cosine value. In this case, the document address corresponding to this cosine value should also be noted as being in the (current) top r.

On the other hand, if the new cosine value is smaller than the root of the heap, it is the new value that is discarded since its rank must be at least $r + 1$. In fact, the only items that ever make it into the heap are within the top r at the time they are considered.

When all the accumulators have been filtered through the heap in this way, the heap contains exactly the r largest cosine values. These are then sorted into decreasing order, and, using the addresses already recorded, the documents can be fetched and displayed to the user. This process is described by the algorithm shown in Figure 4.17, which replaces steps 3 and 4 in Figure 4.14.

How long does this process take? In the worst case—when the list of cosine values is already in increasing order, for example—every cosine value can be forced to enter the heap only to be displaced r steps later. In this case, a total of $2r + (N - r) + 2(N - r)\log r + r \log r \approx N + 2N \log r$ steps are required. For $N = 1,000,000$ and $r = 100$, this is 15 million, not much less than the cost of fully sorting the values and obtaining a complete ranking. However, this is a very pessimistic accounting. Much more likely is that once a reasonable fraction of the cosine values have been considered, very few values will be bumped out of the heap. For the most part, new cosine values will be smaller than the r current largest candidates and will be discarded immediately.

Assuming that the cosine values are independently drawn from a random distribution, the expected number of comparisons can be estimated as follows. The heap contains the r largest values that have been encountered so far. If $i > r$ values have been seen, and they are uniformly distributed, then the chance of the next value being in the top r, and hence making it into the heap, is r/i. Once the first r values have been processed, the expected number of values that make it into the heap from then on is

$$\sum_{i=r+1}^{N} \frac{r}{i} = r \sum_{i=1}^{N} \frac{1}{i} - r \sum_{i=1}^{r} \frac{1}{i} \approx r \log_e(N/r) = 0.69r \log(N/r)$$

because

$$\sum_{i=1}^{n} \frac{1}{i} \approx \log_e(n+1) + \gamma$$

where γ is Euler's constant. Each insertion costs $2 \log r$ comparisons, so the total cost, on average, is $2r + N + 1.4r \log r \log(N/r) + r \log r$ comparisons. For the

To select the top r cosine values,

1. Set $H \leftarrow \{\}$. H is the heap.
2. For $1 \leq d \leq r$,
   (a) Set $A_d \leftarrow A_d/W_d$.
   (b) Record address of document d.
   (c) Set $H \leftarrow H + \{A_d\}$.
3. Build H into a heap.
4. For $r + 1 \leq d \leq N$,
   (a) Set $A_d \leftarrow A_d/W_d$.
   (b) If $A_d > \min\{H\}$ then
       i. Set $H \leftarrow H - \min\{H\} + \{A_d\}$.
       ii. Sift H.
       iii. Record address of document d.

   H now contains the top r exact *cosine* values.
5. For $1 \leq i \leq r$,
   (a) Select d such that $A_d = \max\{H\}$.
   (b) Retrieve document d and present it to the user.
   (c) Set $H \leftarrow H - \{A_d\}$.

Figure 4.17   Selecting the top r cosine values.

$N = 1,000,000$ and $r = 100$ scenario discussed earlier, this corresponds to about 1,013,000 comparisons—even fewer than the cost of using an N-item max-heap.

There is one further detail that needs to be reexamined: the role of the approximate weights. The algorithm described in Figure 4.17 makes use of the exact document weights. However, the top r approximate values can be determined using approximate weights, and then the strategy of Figure 4.15 can be employed to resolve them into exact cosine similarities.

This final variant is the technique that is best suited to the problem of identifying the r largest accumulators. It requires only a small amount of memory space—perhaps 12 bytes for each of the r documents to be displayed—and is also the fastest for typical values of N and r. Moreover, it allows document addresses to be interleaved on disk with the document weights, and they can be processed sequentially, saving a potentially large number of expensive disk seeks. Finally, it allows the use of in-memory approximate weights to further reduce the number of disk operations.

4.7 Interactive retrieval

Ranking does not normally take place offline and unattended. Rather, as with search engines on the World Wide Web, documents or document summaries are displayed one by one in a window on a workstation, and, as each appears, the user undertakes (possibly implicitly) some action that accepts relevant documents and rejects the remainder. Periodically, or even after each such decision, the retrieval engine may reevaluate the ranking, promoting documents that are similar to those accepted and demoting ones that resemble documents that have been rejected. *Relevance feedback* is the process of modifying the query to improve the effectiveness of the remainder of the search, based upon partial relevance judgments. In this section we consider techniques for providing relevance feedback and examine the related area of *probabilistic ranking*, where partial information about relevance is used to guide the process of selecting other relevant documents. Both were introduced by Maron and Kuhns (1960).

Relevance feedback

Suppose a query Q_0 is posed to a retrieval system and some documents are returned. The user then examines some or all of them and makes a decision as to whether or not they are relevant. In a batch processing environment, this is the end of the process—the system has been allowed to indicate the documents that it has calculated as being relevant, and then, without really questioning this choice, the user works with some subset of these. But it need not end there. Suppose that the user picks some of the documents and indicates to the system, "I like these, find me more of the same," and picks others and clicks a button to say, "No, these are red herrings, I don't want to see any more like this." This is iterative retrieval, continuing until the user is satisfied with the set of answers. It requires the query to be adapted, emphasizing some terms, deemphasizing others, and perhaps introducing some completely new ones extracted out of the preferred documents. Effectively, a sequence $\langle Q_i \rangle$ of queries is executed, where Q_{i+1} is intended to be closer in some sense to the "optimal" query than Q_i.

Several methods for iterating the query have been suggested (Salton and Buckley 1990; Harman 1992b, 1992c). All make use of the vector representation that was described above, in which document D_d and query Q are both considered as n-vectors of weights, where n is the number of distinct query terms. The simplest is the *Dec Hi* strategy:

$$Q_{i+1} = Q_i - D_n + \sum_{d \in R} D_d,$$

where D_n is the highest-ranked document tagged as nonrelevant and R is the set of documents identified as relevant. Only one nonrelevant document is allowed to negate terms in the query, but all relevant documents are allowed to support the terms they contain. Operationally, three decisions must be made. First, it is conventional to restrict the vector subtraction operation so that no term receives a weight of less than zero—the irrelevant document is not allowed to give any terms negative weights. Second, the documents tend to have far more nonzero weights than the initial query Q_0, so this expression can potentially create a new query with hundreds or thousands of terms, which would be expensive to evaluate. Hence, it is usual to sort the terms in the relevant documents by decreasing weight and select just a subset of them to influence the augmented query Q_{i+1}. Third, each of the three components in this expression can be weighted so as to bias Q_{i+1} either to remain near to Q_i or to move closer to the relevant documents.

More general feedback expressions allow a greater number of nonrelevant documents to influence the new query and include a provision for the initial query to exert influence over all subsequent queries:

$$Q_{i+1} = \pi Q_0 + \omega Q_i + \alpha \sum_{d \in R} D_d + \beta \sum_{d \in I} D_d,$$

where π, ω, α, and β are weighting constants (with $\beta \leq 0$); R is some subset of the documents tagged relevant; and I is a subset of documents known to be irrelevant because of the user's response to previous iterations of the query.

Evaluation of relevance feedback techniques is complicated by the fact that, in the revised ranking, precision will be high because the system has already been told what some of the relevant and irrelevant documents are. To avoid this inflation, it is usual to assume that documents already judged by the user are simply not present in the collection during the second round of evaluation and that the revised query is run against a revised collection. But because the documents removed were ranked highly in the first round, they are likely to be relevant, and in the second round the absence of these documents inevitably means that precision decreases. Hence, an iterated query may well be reported as having poorer retrieval performance at each evaluation, despite the fact that the feedback is working successfully to bring in new relevant documents. The alternative is to leave the collection untouched when assessing retrieval effectiveness during the second and subsequent rounds of query execution. In this case, quite spectacular rises in retrieval effectiveness can be recorded, simply because the documents that were judged relevant in one round are pushed to the top of the ranking in the next by virtue of their contents being included in the revised query.

Experience shows that one round of feedback often brings substantially better retrieval, and a second round brings some small additional benefit (Harman 1992b, 1992c). There are, however, many variables to be chosen, including the number of documents that should be presented and the various weighting factors included in the formulas above, and there are no clear-cut guidelines as to which techniques, with what parameters, are the best for any given situation. As with the choice of similarity measure in the first place, different feedback rules appear to be effective for different types of collection and different types of query.

At a simpler level are more pragmatic feedback schemes in which the system calculates a list of terms that, according to the weighting formula, are important in the relevant documents and then presents them to the user in weight order. The user is then free to pick among these terms, expanding the original query to include

Table 4.12 Conditional probabilities.

	Number of documents		
	Relevant	Nonrelevant	Total
Term t present	R_t	$f_t - R_t$	f_t
Term t absent	$R - R_t$	$N - f_t - (R - R_t)$	$N - f_t$
Total	R	$N - R$	N

words that were perhaps overlooked at the time the initial query was formulated. In a sense, the feedback comes from the system as an implicit message that "you say now that this is relevant, but you were actually lucky because these are the terms that *I* think are important in this document, and if you want more documents like this one, you had better include these terms in your query."

All these alternatives assume that at least one relevant document is extracted during the processing of the initial query Q_0. However, even if no documents are found, there are still several techniques that can be applied to extend the query. The simplest is to report that while there were no answers to the original query, the user might benefit by trying again with an alternative description and different words. More helpful is to employ an online thesaurus, either displaying a list of synonyms for each query term and asking the user to select additional words to be added to the query or automatically extending the query without checking with the user.

Probabilistic models

Once some documents have been identified as being relevant to the query, a second retrieval paradigm becomes available (Bookstein and Swanson 1974, 1975). In the *probabilistic model*, the appearance of a particular term in a document is interpreted either as evidence that the document is relevant or that it is not relevant. To establish a weight for each term, conditional probabilities of "relevant to the query, given that the term appears" and "irrelevant to the query, given that the term appears" are estimated based upon some known relevance judgments. In a collection of N documents, R of which are relevant, suppose that R_t of the relevant documents contain term t and that term t appears in f_t documents. For the purposes of this discussion, N, f_t, and R are the values for some training set of documents for which relevance judgments have already been decided. For example, they might result from showing a user some of the top-ranked documents from a first-round query evaluated using some other retrieval mechanism such as the cosine method. This arrangement is shown in Table 4.12.

The conditional probabilities can be estimated from Table 4.12. For example,

$$\Pr[\text{relevant} \mid \text{term } t \text{ is present}] = R_t/f_t,$$

and

$$\Pr[\text{irrelevant} \mid \text{term } t \text{ is present}] = (f_t - R_t)/f_t.$$

Similarly,

$$\Pr[\text{term } t \text{ is present} \mid \text{relevant}] = R_t/R,$$

and

$$\Pr[\text{term } t \text{ is present} \mid \text{irrelevant}] = (f_t - R_t)/(N - R).$$

From these estimates, a weighting w_t for term t is derived using Bayes' theorem:

$$w_t = \frac{R_t/(R - R_t)}{(f_t - R_t)/(N - f_t - (R - R_t))},$$

where values greater than one indicate that the appearance of term t should be taken as support for the hypothesis that the document is relevant, and values less than one indicate that appearance of the term suggests that the document is not relevant. Suppose that $N = 20$ documents have been judged; $R = 13$ are relevant. Suppose also that term t appears in $R_t = 11$ of the relevant documents and in one of the nonrelevant ones; that is, $f_t = 12$. Then the weight w_t assigned to this term is

$$w_t = \frac{11/(13 - 11)}{(12 - 11)/(20 - 12 - (13 - 11))} = \frac{5.5}{0.17} = 33,$$

and the term is strongly indicative of relevance since it frequently appears in relevant documents and rarely in irrelevant ones. Suppose, however, that instead $R_t = 4$ and $f_t = 7$. Then $w_t = (4/9)/(3/4) = 0.59$, and the training set suggests that the appearance of term t in a document counts slightly against that document being relevant to the query. A value of $w_t = 1$ indicates that the term is neutral and appears randomly across the relevant and irrelevant documents.

Assuming—rashly, perhaps—that the occurrences of terms in documents are independent, then the weight for a document D_d is calculated by multiplying the weight of the terms:

$$weight(D_d) = \prod_{t \in D_d} w_t$$

Documents with high weights are selected as answers to the query. Since all that is required is the document ordering, not the exact numeric value of the weight, it is conventional to express this as a sum of logarithms:

$$\sum_{t \in D_d} \log w_t = \sum_{t \in D_d} \log \frac{R_t/(R - R_t)}{(f_t - R_t)/(N - f_t - (R - R_t))}.$$

In this formulation, a negative outcome indicates that the document is predicted to be nonrelevant. An overall weight of zero indicates that there is as much evidence against relevance as there is for it and that the document could just as well have been generated by some random process.

4.8 Distributed retrieval

The previous discussion has implicitly assumed that the retrieval system is running on a single processor at a single site. While this will often be the case, there are also important applications in which the documents of the database are spread over multiple sites, and no single host has access to the full collection. For example, a Web search engine might rely on a number of associated indexing sites that are located in different regions, or even different countries, so a query could be distributed to the sites and the results collated. Similarly, an organization with a head office in one location and branch offices in several other locations might be structured so that each office maintains the files for a geographic region associated with that office, with correspondence generated by one branch office for a local client being held at that office. But the head office might also wish to query these local databases, or another branch might seek to gather information from across the entire organization, looking for, say, a precedent for some particular type of legal action that one of their customers wishes to pursue.

In such an environment there is a clear need for *distributed querying*. This question has recently attracted a great deal of attention and is discussed by, for example, Macleod et al. (1987); Tomasic and Garcia-Molina (1993); Viles and French (1995); Voorhees, Gupta, and Johnson-Laird (1995); Cahoon and McKinley (1996); Yuwono and Lee (1997); and de Kretser et al. (1998). From the point of view of the user, the collection should appear to be monolithic, but at a physical level the collection being queried may be the union of many smaller collections, each of which can also be individually queried. Indeed, the most desirable situation is one in which the user, as a routine facility offered by the query engine, is able to specify as part of the sign-on process a list of hostname/database name pairs, and, provided they have access rights to those collections, have that combination established as their working environment. Any queries they execute would then be run against the supercollection, as if that collection had been tailor-made for them and existed on their local machine.

It should also be possible for users to run a query engine on a local machine that accesses data from a remote machine, in the same way that a user can run a Web browser on their local machine and with it fetch data from anywhere in the world.

How should the querying process be organized? For Boolean queries, the answer is straightforward—the query must be transmitted to each of the desired remote collections, the answers from those collections combined into a single list of answers, and then that list presented to the user. An answer to a Boolean query returned by any one of the subcollections is, by definition, an answer for the supercollection. The only decision remaining is then whether or not to return the full text of answer documents from the subcollections, or return only a document identifier (perhaps a title or a short extract) and wait until the user explicitly requests the full document.

The first of these two strategies has a smaller number of handshakes between the various processes but transmits more data, and so is appropriate when latency and bandwidth are both high. The second strategy—documents on demand once the answer set is known—transmits less data but requires more handshaking.

For ranked queries it is a different story. Now the user seeks the r best documents from the collection as a whole, so it is not appropriate to simply issue the query to each of the subcollections. A more careful approach is required. Consider the formulation of the cosine method described by Equations 4.2 and 4.3. To determine the similarity score for a document, values are required for w_t, $f_{d,t}$, and W_d. One of the particular benefits of the formulation given in those two equations is that of these three quantities, only w_t is collection dependent. In particular, each document length W_d is unaffected by any factors external to the document d for which it is calculated. By using the IDF component only in the calculation of $w_{q,t}$ and not $w_{d,t}$, it is possible to cater to distributed collections, and the processing proceeds as follows.

First, the central host (dubbed the *receptionist* in some of the literature) receives the query from the user and passes it to the remote systems (the *librarians*). The librarians might not be physically remote and might even be executing on the same machine. (Each librarian might be in simultaneous communication with several receptionists, with many different logical supercollections formed at any point in time.) Each of the librarians then consults its lexicon and determines a local value for f_t for each term in the query, returning to the receptionist an augmented query that includes local term weights.

Once all the librarians have responded, the receptionist has all the information needed to construct global w_t values for the supercollection, and it can send these back to the librarians, who execute the query using those supplied weights. Each prepares a ranking of their top r documents and sends that back to the receptionist, including the actual similarity score attained by each of the listed documents. These lists are then merged by the receptionist, which prepares a final ranking of r documents. The receptionist then asks each librarian to supply the appropriate documents to be included in the final list presented to the user.

In total, six messages are exchanged between the receptionist and each librarian. The first three are proportional to the length of the query and so are short and involve negligible bandwidth but possibly considerable latency. The next two messages are longer, and the final message—the text of the answer documents—might be very long. Each of the receptionists has also executed the query against its collection, even though ultimately it might not supply any of the answer documents. Consequently, it is not surprising that the research effort in this area is centered on heuristics that allow subcollections to be eliminated at an early stage or at least reduce the amount of work each librarian is asked to perform. Heuristics that reduce the number of messages, or their total volume, are also of interest.

The extent to which any savings are possible is, of course, dependent upon the trade-offs that are made. We will discuss four possibilities: a full central index, a coarse-granularity central index, a central vocabulary comprising the lexicons of the individual subcollections, and no central information at all about the contents of the subcollections.

First, if the receptionist can maintain a superindex, constructed as the union of the indexes kept by the librarians, then the first four messages are eliminated, and the only message passing that takes place is for the receptionist to poll the librarians to supply documents. In this arrangement the librarians are little more than filing clerks. Maintaining a central index removes much of the flexibility we were hoping for at the outset. Even worse, like the Web search engines that store only pointers to the documents indexed, users may be frustrated to find themselves referred to information that matches their query but is no longer available. Nevertheless, there may be applications in which this is appropriate—a user can quickly query any one of a defined set of aggregate collections but cannot create new supercollections on the fly.

The central index arrangement has the disadvantage of requiring a completely duplicate index, which is wasteful of space. The second approach is to maintain a central index, but at a coarser granularity than the indexes of the individual subcollections. The receptionist would use the central index to determine blocks of records at each librarian that might be of interest and then ask each librarian to provide a detailed evaluation of all of the records in the nominated blocks. This has the advantage of requiring a smaller central index but the disadvantage of devolving more work to the librarians. The total amount of work might be reduced, however, since with a skipped inverted index only that part of each inverted list that relates to the blocks in question need be processed. Subcollections from which no blocks are nominated by the superindex are again not required to contribute any work, but the likelihood of this is less than when the central index is comprehensive because the coarse index introduces false matches.

The third possibility is for the receptionist to maintain a copy of the lexicon of each of the subcollections, thereby allowing the first two messages to be eliminated. It has also been suggested by some authors that knowledge of the vocabulary of each subcollection can be used to focus the query on the particular subcollections in which relevant documents might be found (Gravano and Garcia-Molina 1995; Zobel 1997), but the evidence to date has not been conclusive. It is certainly the case with the *TREC* topics, for example, that most of the subcollections contain at least some relevant documents.

The fourth possibility is to maintain no central information and simply accept the similarity scores that arise from the use of local weights at each librarian. Retrieval effectiveness may suffer because all of the term weights used are local, but flexibility is maintained and the use of network resources minimized. There may be some situations when even this is not possible: for example, when the individual retrieval systems are heterogeneous and scores are not comparable. One example of this situation are the so-called *metaengines* on the World Wide Web. They issue the user query to several different primary search engines and combine the results that come back, deciding which links are duplicates and may be culled and which engine is returning the highest-quality data for this query.[4]

Other merging rules can be imagined, aside from these four. For example, merging could be based upon the relative similarity scores of each document compared to the score of the best document returned from that subcollection; the perceived credibility of each source, as a function of how well it has performed in the past; the total number of documents held in that subcollection; and so on.

Further reading

Information retrieval. Standard reference works covering the area of information retrieval are by Salton (1989); Salton and McGill (1983); van Rijsbergen (1979); Frakes and Baeza-Yates (1992); Korfhage (1997); and Lesk (1997).

The annual ACM-SIGIR International Conference on Research and Development in Information Retrieval, held most recently in Zürich in 1996 (Frei et al. 1996), Philadelphia in 1997 (Belkin, Narasimhalu, and Willett 1997), and Melbourne in 1998 (Croft et al. 1998), is the major forum for the presentation of results in the area of information retrieval. The *TREC* proceedings are also published on an annual basis and are available from NIST in Washington (*trec.nist.gov*). Detailed results for the application of the techniques described in this chapter to the *TREC* collection have been reported (Moffat and Zobel 1994; Zobel et al. 1995). An overview of the first two years of *TREC* appears in a special issue of *Information Processing and Management* (Harman 1995). Cormack, Palmer, and Clarke (1998) and Zobel (1998) consider the experimental methodology employed by *TREC*.

Perfect hashing. The minimal perfect hashing method described in this chapter is from Czech, Havas, and Majewski (1992), Havas et al. (1993), and Majewski et al. (1996). Other methods are described by Fox et al. (1991) and Fox, Heath, et al. (1992).

Pattern matching. Pattern matching in general is a problem rich in algorithms; for an overview see Cormen, Leiserson, and Rivest (1990); Gonnet and Baeza-Yates (1991); and Baeza-Yates (1992). Recent papers include those by Wu and Manber (1992); Baeza-Yates and Gonnet (1992); and Owolabi (1993). Zobel, Moffat, and Sacks-Davis (1993a) describe the inverted file lexicon indexing approach to partially

---

4 As an interesting side note, the metaengine must also decide which of the advertisements returned by the individual engines is passed through to the user. One such metaengine simply takes the advertisement attached to the first-returning search engine. Since advertising revenue based upon actual placement counts is the primary income source for companies that provide search engines, this policy has the counterproductive effect of tempting the engines that do actually go to the trouble of indexing Web pages to identify queries that originate at the metaengines and immediately return a standard nonsensical answer when they detect queries from them. This then gives their advertisement a good chance of being passed through to the original querier, and since the search results appear under someone else's banner, their responsibility for the result is blurred.

specified query terms and give results for the *TREC* collection. The use of n-grams has also been suggested in connection with signature files, with and without the primary terms; see, for example, Faloutsos (1992). The rotated lexicon approach is described by Bratley and Choueka (1982).

Query processing. Moffat and Zobel (1996) describe the insertion of skips into compressed inverted files, including experimental results showing a speedup on typical Boolean queries of three to five times. The material on blocked inverted files is derived from Moffat, Zobel, and Klein (1995). Anh and Moffat (1998) describe further refinements of the blocked approach, including a method for coding inverted files based upon modified Rice codes that allows extremely fast checking of candidate document numbers and so further accelerates retrieval.

Zobel and Moffat (1998) have evaluated a large number of similarity formulations against subsets of the *TREC* data in an attempt to determine which formulations work consistently well.

The use of approximate weights during the ranking process is described by Moffat, Zobel, and Sacks-Davis (1994). Several authors have described heuristics for reducing the number of nonzero accumulators or the number of terms processed during ranked query evaluation (Buckley and Lewit 1985; Lucarella 1988; Harman and Candela 1990; Wong and Lee 1993; Moffat and Zobel 1996; Anh and Moffat 1998). The material on frequency-sorted indexes and their use in ranked queries is derived from work undertaken by Michael Persin and others at RMIT (Persin 1994; Persin, Zobel, and Sacks-Davis 1996).

A general discussion of the time required by sorting and selection algorithms can be found in textbooks such as those of Cormen, Leiserson, and Rivest (1990) and Sedgewick (1990).

Web searching. Most of the technical information about Web search engines is confidential. The site at *www.searchenginewatch.com* provides a collation of information from disparate sources, including estimates of index size. Jansen, Spink, Bateman, and Saracevic (1998) provide an analysis of a query log for one of the major search engines.

Interactive retrieval. Relevance feedback was first advocated by Maron and Kuhns (1960), and detailed experiments are described by Rocchio (1971) and Ide (1971). More recently the area has been examined by Salton and Buckley (1990) and surveyed by Harman (1992c, 1992b). Maron and Kuhns (1960) also discussed probabilistic retrieval in a seminal paper. Other work has been presented by Bookstein and Swanson (1974, 1975), Robertson and Sparck Jones (1976), and Bookstein (1983). Other query paradigms include fuzzy Boolean or fuzzy set methods, in which the AND and OR operations are real-valued rather than binary-valued. For example, 0.5 AND 0.5 might be defined as 0.25, while 0.5 OR 0.5 would be defined as 0.75. Bookstein (1981) compares the effectiveness of two such schemes.

Distributed retrieval. The question of distributed retrieval is discussed by Macleod et al. (1987); Tomasic and Garcia-Molina (1993); Viles and French (1995); Voorhees, Gupta, and Johnson-Laird (1995); Cahoon and McKinley (1996); Yuwono and Lee (1997); and de Kretser et al. (1998). Gravano and Garcia-Molina (1995) and Zobel (1997) examine the extent to which collection vocabularies can be used to determine likely subcollections in a distributed environment.

Index Construction

Chapters 3 and 4 avoid the question of how the index is created: they simply suppose that it exists and can thus be compressed or queried. In reality, constructing the index is one of the most challenging tasks to be faced when a database is built. This chapter addresses the problem of creating the various index structures described in Chapters 3 and 4. The emphasis here, as in those two chapters, is on inverted file indexing since this is the most practical form of index for both Boolean and ranked queries.

The process of building an index is known as the *inversion* of the text. The *Concise Oxford Dictionary* defines "inversion" as "turning upside down, reversal of normal position, order, or relation," and this is exactly what must be done to create an index. "Inversion" is also used in a technical sense by meteorologists, musicians, electrical engineers, and mathematicians, to name but a few. In fact, to a mathematician the operation being performed here is more usually known as *transposition* (which is also a musical term); when a mathematician inverts a matrix, it is to calculate a multiplicative inverse. And, of course, the author of a technical book knows the required process only too well; it is the task of *indexing*. Indeed, the task of indexing was known and described well before the computer made it easy, and there are books on the subject that make interesting reading. In *Indexing Books: A Manual of Basic Principles*, Collison (1962, 16–17) instructs us:

> Whether handwriting or a typewriter is used, it is essential to have on hand a large number of slips or thin cards of the same size. . . . Indexing needs a lot of stationery, and it is best to order ten thousand slips at a time.

Given that we propose to deal with texts containing more than 1,000 individual books, it is clear that a very large number of "slips" indeed might be required.

To illustrate the magnitude of the inversion problem, we will first describe, through the use of an example, what is perhaps the most obvious method. Consider again the simple text that was used in Chapter 3, reproduced in Table 5.1.

Table 5.1 Example text; each line is one document.

Document	Text
1	Pease porridge hot, pease porridge cold,
2	Pease porridge in the pot,
3	Nine days old.
4	Some like it hot, some like it cold,
5	Some like it in the pot,
6	Nine days old.

Table 5.2 Frequency matrix for text of Table 5.1.

	Term												
	cold	days	hot	in	it	like	nine	old	pease	porridge	pot	some	the
1	1	—	1	—	—	—	—	—	2	2	—	—	—
2	—	—	—	1	—	—	—	—	1	1	1	—	1
3	—	1	—	—	—	—	1	1	—	—	—	—	—
4	1	—	1	—	2	2	—	—	—	—	—	2	—
5	—	—	—	1	1	1	—	—	—	—	1	1	1
6	—	1	—	—	—	—	1	1	—	—	—	—	—

Each line (document) of this text contains some index terms, and each index term appears in some of the lines. This relationship can be expressed with a *frequency matrix*, in which each column corresponds to one word, each row corresponds to one document, and the number stored at any row and column is the frequency, in that document, of the word indicated by that column. The frequency matrix for the text of Table 5.1 is shown in Table 5.2.

In effect, each document of the collection is summarized in one row of this frequency matrix. To create an index, the matrix must be transposed, forming a new version in which the rows are the term numbers. The inverted frequency matrix is shown in Table 5.3. From this it is easy to construct an inverted file of the form described in Chapter 3 or an augmented inverted file of the form described in Chapter 4.

One algorithm to create an inverted file is now clear: build in memory a transposed frequency matrix, reading the text in document order, one column of the matrix at a time; then write the matrix to disk row by row, in term order. Despite the attractive simplicity of this approach, in reality inversion is a much more difficult task. The problem is the size of the frequency matrix. Suppose that the text *Bible* is

Table 5.3 Transposed equivalent of frequency matrix of Table 5.2.

Number	Term	Document					
		1	2	3	4	5	6
1	cold	1	—	—	1	—	—
2	days	—	—	1	—	—	1
3	hot	1	—	—	1	—	—
4	in	—	1	—	—	1	—
5	it	—	—	—	2	1	—
6	like	—	—	—	2	1	—
7	nine	—	—	1	—	—	1
8	old	—	—	1	—	—	1
9	pease	2	1	—	—	—	—
10	porridge	2	1	—	—	—	—
11	pot	—	1	—	—	1	—
12	some	—	—	—	2	1	—
13	the	—	1	—	—	1	—

to be inverted. From Table 3.1, *Bible* contains 8,965 distinct terms and 31,101 documents. If a four-byte integer is allowed for each entry in the frequency matrix, the matrix will occupy $4 \times 8{,}965 \times 31{,}101$ bytes of main memory. This is a little over 1 Gbyte, barely manageable even on a large machine. For the bigger *TREC* collection, the size of the matrix becomes even more daunting: $4 \times 535{,}346 \times 741{,}856$ bytes, or 1.4 Tbytes (terabytes).

Supposing that one byte is sufficient to record each within-document frequency $f_{d,t}$ (for *TREC* it is not adequate) does not help either: the space requirements for the two collections are 250 Mbytes and 350 Gbytes, respectively, and the algorithm still is not viable. If only Boolean access is required, then a Boolean matrix is sufficient, and the frequencies can be dispensed with, reducing the sizes to 31 Mbytes and 46 Gbytes, respectively—still an unpleasantly large amount of memory. Of course, we could use a machine with a large virtual memory and let the operating system be responsible for paging the array into and out of memory as required. But the column-by-column access as the matrix is created means that there will probably be one page fault for each pointer in the eventual index, and about 700,000 page faults would be required to build the *Bible* index. At a rate of perhaps 50 page replacements per second, this corresponds to 14,000 seconds, about 4 hours. For *TREC*, use of virtual memory to build an explicit frequency matrix results in an inversion process that takes two nonstop calendar months, which is reminiscent in computer-based terms of the dedication needed for the manual indexing processes described in Chapter 1.

For these reasons, more economical methods for constructing and inverting a frequency matrix must be considered—the main theme of this chapter. The final method described has been used to create an augmented inverted index for the *TREC* collection (2 Gbytes of text) in under 2 hours on a personal computer, consuming just 30 Mbytes of main memory and less than 20 Mbytes of temporary disk space over and above the space required by the final inverted file. Needless to say, this final method bears little resemblance to the method sketched in these introductory paragraphs. The construction of signature files and bitmaps is discussed in this chapter too.

Chapters 3 and 4 also avoided mention of *dynamic* collections and concentrated exclusively on *static* ones. Such techniques are appropriate if an archive of material is to be distributed on some read-only medium such as CD-ROM. Then it is acceptable for a large amount of effort to go into preparing the files that will comprise the distribution, provided that access to the data is fast. However, in other situations the collection may be required to be dynamic, with new documents being added, existing ones being modified, and, sometimes, old ones being deleted. Keeping an index up-to-date requires file structures that can cope with these operations efficiently without consuming inordinate amounts of extra space. The final section of this chapter considers the problems posed by dynamic collections and explains how to compress and index large volumes of text when individual documents are subject to change and the collection itself is subject to extension.

Before we begin to look at the details of the various index construction methods, we introduce a benchmark on which their performance will be compared and preview the panoply of methods that will be presented.

Computational model

In order to assess the efficiency of index construction algorithms, it is useful to have as a reference point the cost of inverting some typical database. Table 5.4 describes a hypothetical collection of 5 Gbytes and five million documents. It also gives some nominal performance figures, which will be used to estimate the overall time required by each inversion method. Although not specifically derived from the execution speed of any particular machine, these provide a useful basis for comparing algorithms and capture the relative costs of the various operations involved. When the first edition of this book was written in 1993, the listed performance roughly corresponded to the $30,000 workstation used for our experiments with *TREC*-sized document collections; now, in 1999, they somewhat underestimate the performance of the $5,000 personal computer we use for the same experiments.

Preview of index construction methods

Table 5.5 gives an advance peek at the methods that we will develop for index construction, and their performance on the 5 Gbyte collection of five million documents in Table 5.4. For example, the standard linked-list inversion algorithm is summarized in the first entry: it is described in Section 5.1, and pseudocode appears in Figure 5.1. Although it could invert the sample document collection of Table 5.4

Table 5.4 Typical sizes and performance figures.

Parameter	Symbol	Assumed value
Total text size	B	5×10^9 bytes
Number of documents	N	5×10^6
Number of distinct words	n	1×10^6
Total number of words	F	800×10^6
Number of index pointers	f	400×10^6
Final size of compressed inverted file	I	400×10^6 bytes
Size of dynamic lexicon structure	L	30×10^6 bytes
Disk seek time	t_s	10×10^{-3} sec
Disk transfer time per byte	t_r	0.5×10^{-6} sec
Inverted file coding time per byte	t_d	5×10^{-6} sec
Time to compare and swap 10-byte records	t_c	10^{-6} sec
Time to parse, stem, and look up one term	t_p	20×10^{-6} sec
Amount of main memory available	M	40×10^6 bytes

Table 5.5 Predicted resource requirements to invert 5 Gbytes.

Method	Section	Figure	Memory (Mbytes)	Disk (Mbytes)	Time (hours)
Linked lists (memory)	5.1	5.1	4,000	0	6
Linked lists (disk)	5.1	5.1	30	4,000	1,100
Sort-based	5.2	5.3	40	8,000	20
Sort-based compressed	5.3	—	40	680	26
Sort-based multiway merge	5.3	—	40	540	11
Sort-based multiway in-place	5.3	5.8 and 5.9	40	150	11
In-memory compressed	5.4	5.12	420	1	12
Lexicon-based, no extra disk	5.4	—	40	0	79
Lexicon-based, extra disk	5.4	—	40	4,000	12
Text-based partition	5.4	—	40	35	15

in 6 hours, it would consume 4 Gbytes of main memory in doing so. No extra disk space is required beyond what is needed to store the inverted file. For algorithms in which a memory limit is enforced, it is assumed that 40 Mbytes of memory is available to be exploited. The final method is the one used for the 2-hour inversion

To produce an inverted index for a collection of documents,

1. /* Initialization */
   Create an empty dictionary structure S.

2. /* Phase one—collection of term appearances */
   For each document D_d in the collection, $1 \leq d \leq N$,

   (a) Read D_d, parsing it into index terms.

   (b) For each index term $t \in D_d$,

      i. Let $f_{d,t}$ be the frequency in D_d of term t.

      ii. Search S for t.

      iii. If t is not in S, insert it.

      iv. Append a node storing $\langle d, f_{d,t} \rangle$ to the list corresponding to term t.

3. /* Phase two—output of inverted file */
   For each term $1 \leq t \leq n$

   (a) Start a new inverted file entry.

   (b) For each $\langle d, f_{d,t} \rangle$ in the list corresponding to t,
       append $\langle d, f_{d,t} \rangle$ to this inverted file entry.

   (c) If required, compress the inverted file entry.

   (d) Append this inverted file entry to the inverted file.

Figure 5.1 Memory-based inversion algorithm.

of *TREC* mentioned above, except that the 2-hour inversion was done on a rather faster machine than that specified in Table 5.4.

All these algorithms will be explained in the sections that follow. Table 5.5 is just intended as a preview and summary.

5.1 Memory-based inversion

Implementing a cross-reference generator is a commonly assigned student project in "Data Structures and Algorithms" courses. In reality, a cross-reference is just another name for an inverted index, in which each term of some text (for example, identifiers in program source code) is listed in alphabetical order, together with a list of the line numbers in which it appears.

When set as a student exercise, the intended solution is usually that some kind of dynamic dictionary data structure such as a hash table or binary search tree be used to record the distinct terms in the collection, with a linked list of nodes storing line numbers associated with each dictionary entry. Once all documents have been processed, the dictionary structure is traversed, and the list of terms and corresponding

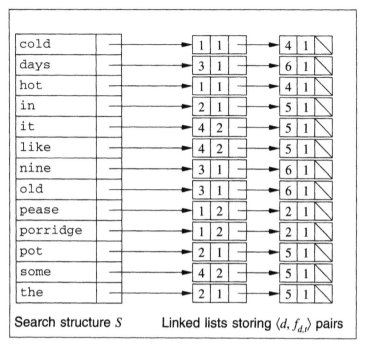

Figure 5.2 Data structure representing inverted file for text of Table 5.1.

line numbers is written. This process is detailed in Figure 5.1, and the state of the data structure at the completion of the first phase of processing on the sample text of Table 5.1 is shown in Figure 5.2. Here the terms are shown stored in sorted order in the dictionary, but this is not necessary. Any dynamic structure is suitable, but a hash table is generally the most economical choice in terms of both speed and space.

Now consider the cost of this inversion algorithm. At the assumed rate of 2 Mbytes per second, it takes about 40 minutes to read 5 Gbytes of text. Parsing and stemming to create index terms, and searching for these terms in the dictionary, takes much longer, more than 4 hours, at 20 microseconds per word. The second phase requires each list to be traversed so that the corresponding inverted list can be encoded and written. The encoding requires 2,000 seconds and the writing 200 seconds, a further 40 minutes.

More generally, the inversion time T required by this approach is

$$T = Bt_r + Ft_p + \qquad \text{(read and parse text)}$$
$$I(t_d + t_r) \qquad \text{(write compressed inverted file)}$$

seconds, where the symbols used are defined in Table 5.4. This simple linked-list inversion method corresponds to the first line in Table 5.5.

The above analysis predicts an inversion time of about 6 hours for the database of Table 5.4. This might sound like a long time, but when the enormous volume of data being processed is taken into account, it is very fast. For the *Bible* collection, for example, the same calculation gives an inversion time under 30 seconds.

There is, however, another resource to be considered: the memory space required by the algorithm. Each node in each list of document numbers typically requires at least 10 bytes: 4 for the document number d, 4 for the "next" pointer, and 2 or more for the frequency count $f_{d,t}$. For a small collection, this requirement is modest. But in the situation described in Table 5.4 there are 400 million such nodes, or 4 Gbytes of memory, and to require this much main memory is unrealistic, even given the advances in computing power noted above. Of course, as machine performance increases, so does the amount of memory supported, but it is also true that collection sizes are likely to grow at the same exponential rate and that memory will never overtake demand.

It is tempting to move the linked lists of document numbers from memory onto disk—or, equivalently, to run the program on a machine with a large virtual memory and a small physical memory—but this is not a viable alternative either. To see why, consider the steps of the algorithm again but assuming that the linked lists are stored on disk.

The sequence of disk accesses during the first phase is sequential, and generation of the threaded file containing the linked lists is largely unaffected. Each new node results in a record being appended to a file, so, in the example inversion, a file of 4 Gbytes is created in sequential fashion on disk, adding about 30 minutes to the 6 hours already allowed.

Now consider the cost of the second phase, when each list is traversed. The stored list nodes are interleaved in the same order on disk as they appeared in the text, and so each node access requires a random seek into the file on disk. At the assumed rate t_s of 10 milliseconds per seek, and with 10 bytes to be read per record, this corresponds to a phase two time of four million seconds, or 6 weeks. In terms of the parameters described in Table 5.4, the inversion time is now

$$
\begin{aligned}
T = Bt_r + Ft_p + 10ft_r + & \quad \text{(read and parse, write file)} \\
ft_s + 10ft_r + & \quad \text{(trace lists on disk)} \\
I(t_d + t_r) & \quad \text{(write compressed inverted file)}
\end{aligned}
$$

seconds, annoyingly slow for practical purposes. Indeed, the use of a similar disk-based random access inversion to invert an 806 Mbyte text—one-sixth the size considered in Table 5.4—has been reported to have required more than 13 days of processing, albeit on a minicomputer less powerful than the machine postulated here (Harman and Candela 1990). This disk-based linked-list inversion method corresponds to the second line in Table 5.5.

For the gigabyte collections that this book addresses, the linked-list approach is inadequate because it requires either too much memory or too much time. It is, however, an excellent project and the best method for small collections. For the *Bible*, an in-memory inversion takes half a minute and requires about 10 Mbytes of main memory, well within the reach of typical workstations.

5.2 Sort-based inversion

The main problem with the two methods discussed so far is that they require too much memory, and they use a data access sequence that is essentially random, preventing an efficient mapping from memory onto disk. Sequential access is the only efficient processing mode for large disk files since transfer rates are usually high and random seeks are time-consuming. Moreover, the use of disk seems inescapable for the volumes of data being considered, and so the inversion algorithm should perform sequential processing on whatever disk files are required. These considerations lead to a third inversion algorithm: a *sort-based* inversion, corresponding to the third line in Table 5.5.

The sort-based algorithm is outlined in Figure 5.3 and operates as follows. First, in step 2, the text is parsed into terms and a temporary file written. The temporary file stores one triple $\langle t, d, f_{d,t} \rangle$ for each combination of term number t and document d that appears in the text. The inverted file is then obtained by sorting these triples into ascending order of t. This collects all the entries for each term together, so the inverted list for that term can be created by scanning the sorted list sequentially.

Sorting, in step 3 of Figure 5.3, is accomplished by an external merge sort. During the sort the temporary file is read in blocks of k records, where k is the maximum number of records that can be accommodated in main memory. These records are all the same length, typically about 10 bytes long, comprising 4 bytes for the term number, 4 bytes for the document number, and 2 bytes to store the frequency of the term in that document. If available memory is limited to 1 Mbyte, for example, k would be 100,000. Each block so read is sorted into increasing order using the term number t as the primary key, with d used to break ties. An in-memory sorting technique such as Quicksort should be used for this step. The block is then written back to the temporary file as a sorted *run*.

The next phase, step 4 of Figure 5.3, is to merge a large number of sorted runs. This is achieved by cycling through the set of runs, merging the first and the second, then the third and the fourth, and so on, until each run has been merged once. Each such merging pass halves the number of runs in the temporary file and doubles their length. If there are R initial runs, after $\lceil \log R \rceil$ passes there will be a single run remaining, and the file is sorted. This is the standard method for performing an "external sort"—maximal runs are constructed using an internal sort and are then merged by a sequence of linear passes—and is the kind of sorting usually invoked when a large file is sorted using a standard system sort command. For clarity, this detail has been spelled out in Figure 5.3.

The final step in the inversion process, step 5 of Figure 5.3, is to read the sorted temporary file, generating a compressed inverted output file. Sorting the temporary file gives the required inverted file order: records are ordered by increasing t and, within equal values of t, by increasing d. Once the inverted file has been written, the space occupied by the temporary file can be released.

Figure 5.4 shows the dictionary and temporary file that would be created by a sort-based inversion of the sample text. In this example, it has been assumed that

To produce an inverted index for a collection of documents,

1. /* Initialization */
   Create an empty dictionary structure S.
   Create an empty temporary file on disk.

2. /* Process text and write temporary file */
   For each document D_d in the collection, $1 \leq d \leq N$,

   (a) Read D_d, parsing it into index terms.

   (b) For each index term $t \in D_d$,

      i. Let $f_{d,t}$ be the frequency in D_d of term t.

      ii. Search S for t.

      iii. If t is not in S, insert it.

      iv. Write a record $\langle t, d, f_{d,t} \rangle$ to the temporary file, where t is represented by its term number in S.

3. /* Internal sorting to make runs */
   Let k be the number of records that can be held in memory.

   (a) Read k records from the temporary file.

   (b) Sort into nondecreasing t order and, for equal values of t, nondecreasing d order.

   (c) Write the sorted run back to the temporary file.

   (d) Repeat until there are no more runs to be sorted.

4. /* Merging */
   Pairwise merge runs in the temporary file until it is one sorted run.

5. /* Output inverted file */
   For each term $1 \leq t \leq n$,

   (a) Start a new inverted file entry.

   (b) Read all triples $\langle t, d, f_{d,t} \rangle$ from the temporary file and form the inverted file entry for term t.

   (c) If required, compress the inverted file entry.

   (d) Append this inverted file entry to the inverted file.

Figure 5.3 Sort-based inversion algorithm.

term numbers are assigned in order of first appearance, rather than alphabetically as before. Thus, the lists in the resulting inverted file appear in an order different from that shown in Table 5.3 and Figure 5.2. The altered ordering has no effect on subsequent processing using the inverted file, but is convenient for a reason that will

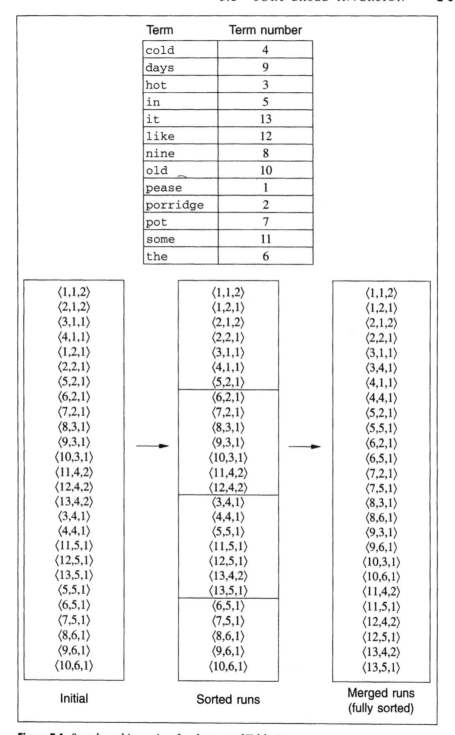

Figure 5.4 Sort-based inversion for the text of Table 5.1.

be explained in the next section (on page 237, under "Compressing the temporary files").

How much time does this method require to invert the hypothetical text collection? As with both of the earlier methods, the entire text must be read, parsed, and filtered through the dictionary S, taking about 5 hours. During this time, the temporary file is written, containing 400 million 10-byte records. Writing the temporary file adds another half hour. In terms of the computational model of Table 5.4, the time for this phase is

$$Bt_r + Ft_p + 10ft_r$$

seconds, where it is assumed that each temporary file record is 10 bytes long.

Next, the temporary file is sorted. If all of the 40 Mbytes of main memory are available (Table 5.4), then k can be taken to be 4 million. That is, there are about 100 blocks of 4 million records to be sorted using the in-memory sorting algorithm. Quicksort, widely considered to be the fastest internal sorting algorithm, takes about $1.2k \log k$ record comparisons and swaps to sort k items in a well-engineered implementation, so by the assumptions of Table 5.4, each execution of step 3 of Figure 5.4 takes about 110 seconds. In total, sorting all 100 blocks takes 3 hours. During this internal sorting, the entire temporary file is both read and written, so a further hour should be allowed to cover reading and writing time. Four hours after starting the sorting phase, the temporary file contains 100 sorted runs, each containing 4 million records. In terms of the model, the time for this phase is

$$20ft_r + R(1.2k \log k)t_c$$

seconds, where $k = M/10$ is the number of records that can be held in main memory and $R = \lceil f/k \rceil$ is the number of runs.

Finally, the external part of the sort (step 4) takes place: runs are merged in pairs. There are $\lceil \log 100 \rceil = 7$ merging passes required, and in each pass the entire temporary file is both read and written. This means that each pass takes about 1 hour, assuming that there is no concurrency between read and write operations. Processing time is also required during the merging—one comparison per triple—but this is an order of magnitude smaller than the time spent reading and writing the files.

In total, sorting the temporary file takes about 13 hours, depending on the exact arrangement of temporary files on the disks and the extent to which the merge routine provides for overlap of input, output, and merging operations. In general, the time for this phase is

$$\lceil \log R \rceil (20ft_r + ft_c)$$

seconds, where, as before, R is the number of runs.

Finally, the temporary file is again read, compressed, and written to disk, taking about 90 minutes. In general, this takes

$$10ft_r + I(t_d + t_r)$$

seconds.

The complete inversion takes about 20 hours and has made use of all of the 40 Mbytes of memory assumed to be available. Totaling the time required by the four phases, sorting time for this method according to the computational model is

$$T = Bt_r + Ft_p + 10ft_r +$$ (read and parse, write file)

$$20ft_r + R(1.2k \log k)t_c +$$ (sort runs)

$$\lceil \log R \rceil (20ft_r + ft_c) +$$ (merge runs)

$$10ft_r + I(t_d + t_r)$$ (write compressed inverted file)

The only remaining resource to be considered is disk space. Unfortunately, the sorting algorithm described requires *two* copies of the data at any given time. For example, consider the situation halfway through the last merge. There are two runs being merged, each approximately half the size of the original file. Moreover, at the halfway stage of the merge, both of these runs have been partially consumed. Because of this, it is impossible for the merged output to be written sequentially back to the same file since it might overwrite data yet to be processed. At the last instant, just before this merge finishes, the output file contains all of the records being sorted, and so do the two input files.

This means that two temporary files must be allowed for. For the example inversion, each of these contains 10×400 million bytes, so at the peak of the process a total of 8 Gbytes of disk space is required. This is 60 percent larger than the text being inverted and more than 20 times the size of the index that is eventually produced. Indeed, the text being inverted is probably stored compressed (of course), and so the temporary disk space required is more than twice the space required to store the raw collection. The enormous demand for disk space means that although this simple sort-based inversion is the best method for moderate-sized collections in the 10 to 100 Mbyte range, it is not suitable for truly large collections in the gigabyte range.

5.3   Exploiting index compression

There are two very different ways in which compression can be used to reduce the resources required by the inversion process, and both lead to inversion methods that are viable for very large collections. The first approach, described in this section, is straightforward—the temporary file required by the sort-based inversion is stored compressed, thereby alleviating the demand for excessive amounts of disk space. This approach was explored by Moffat and Bell (1995).[1] Three variants will be given, corresponding to the entries in Table 5.5 for compressed sort-based inversion, multiway merging, and in-place multiway merging. The use of an appropriate merging strategy allows the overhead disk space to be substantially reduced, and

---

1   As noted in the Preface, two Tim Bells work in this area. The one referenced here is Timothy A. H. Bell at the University of Melbourne.

the end result is a sort-based method that requires only about 35 percent more disk space than the final compressed inverted file. A second, completely different, way in which compression can be used is considered in Section 5.4.

Compressing the temporary files

The sort-based inversion technique is not practical because it requires too much disk space. But, as was demonstrated in Chapters 3 (Table 3.8) and 4 (Table 4.10), even with relatively simple compression methods such as the γ and δ codes, the inverted file requires only about one byte per $\langle d, f_{d,t} \rangle$ pair. For the hypothetical collection of Table 5.4, this is 400 Mbytes. Since the final inverted file can be compressed by a factor of six, similar compression might be obtained on the temporary file of $\langle t, d, f_{d,t} \rangle$ triples. It should then be possible to invert the hypothetical collection in 1.5 Gbytes of disk space rather than the 8 Gbytes calculated above. In fact, as Table 5.5 shows, things work out even better for compressed sort-based inversion.

Let us examine the details of such a scheme. There are three values that make up each record of the temporary file. Compression of the d and $f_{d,t}$ components has already been discussed in Chapters 3 and 4, and several methods are available (Tables 3.8 and 4.10). Of these, the nonparameterized codes have the advantage of avoiding two passes over the text. There is some compression leakage through the use of a slightly inefficient code, but the figures of Tables 3.8 and 4.10 indicate that this loss is small—of the order of 10 percent on the *TREC* collection if a "δ + unary" combination is used instead of the more efficient "local Golomb + γ" pair of codes. An economical representation of the t component is all that remains to be added, and this is achieved as follows.

Within each sorted run, the t values are nondecreasing—after all, t is the primary sort key used to order the records. Difference coding is a natural choice for representing t values. Each t-gap—the difference between t values of successive triples in the sorted file—is zero or more. Suppose that a t-gap of x is stored as the unary code for $x + 1$, requiring $x + 1$ bits. If a triple has the same t value as the previous triple, the t-gap is zero, and the code is 0; if a triple has a value of t one greater than its predecessor in the run, the t-gap is one, and the code is 10; if a triple has a t-gap of two, the code is 110; and so on. Of course, in the final inverted file, there is no need to store t-gaps—they are all zero, except for the first item in each inverted list, which is one, and the lexicon structure always indicates where each inverted list starts. The t components of the triples are required only in the temporary file, where any particular run may not contain all the terms.

The extra cost of storing t in this way is small provided that the initial runs are reasonably large. In an ordered list of k triples, the total number of bits to code the t-gaps is bounded above by $k + n$, where n is the number of distinct terms. This follows from the observation that the sum of all of the "t-gap plus one" values cannot exceed $k + n$. For the hypothetical text, each of the 100 initial sorted runs will require about 5 Mbytes: 4 Mbytes for the four million $\langle d, f_{d,t} \rangle$ pairs compressed using the final compression methods into one byte each; an allowance of about 0.4 Mbyte for the 10 percent compression leakage that results because the final compression methods are not in fact being used; and 0.6 Mbyte for the four million unary-coded t-gaps that are interleaved with these other values ($k + n$ bits, where k is four million $\langle d, f_{d,t} \rangle$ pairs and n is one million distinct terms). In total, about 500 Mbytes is required in each of the two files manipulated during the merging passes.

However, this calculation still is not quite complete. Because all runs are stored compressed, the unsorted temporary file—the left-hand column in Figure 5.4—cannot actually be stored on disk, because the t-gap representation accommodates only triples that have already been sorted. Consequently, internal sorting of runs must be interleaved with processing the text, blurring the distinction between steps 2 and 3 of the algorithm described in Figure 5.3. The first file written to disk must be the file of runs corresponding to the center column of Figure 5.4. This is necessary because there are no runs at all in the left-hand column and so no economical way to represent the t component of each triple.

A consequence of performing internal sorting of runs concurrently with parsing the text and creating the lexicon is that less buffer space is available to generate the sorted runs since a large amount of memory is occupied by the search dictionary S. The dictionary consumes three-quarters of the 40 Mbytes of available memory because about 30 bytes are required per unique term—a figure that will be justified below (page 244)—and Table 5.4 indicates that there are a million terms. So the initial runs can be only one-quarter as long, and there will be four times as many of them. Two extra merging passes during the second phase of the sort are required. Each of the 400 initial sorted runs requires about 1.325 Mbytes: 1 Mbyte for the four million $\langle d, f_{d,t} \rangle$ pairs, about 0.1 Mbyte compression leakage, and 0.25 Mbyte for the one million unary-coded t-gaps ($k + n$ bits, where k is one million $\langle d, f_{d,t} \rangle$ pairs and n is one million distinct terms). Thus, because of the increased length of the t-gap codes, the temporary files occupy 540 Mbytes each rather than 500 Mbytes.

The interleaved run generation forced by the use of compression makes it desirable for the term numbers t to be assigned in order of first appearance, as shown in the example of Figure 5.4. The first run must be written to disk before any more text is inspected, and there is no way that this can be achieved with a single pass if term numbers are to be assigned in lexicographic order for the entire collection.

The use of compression reduces the space requirements to a manageable level. As a "payment" for this saving, greatly increased processing time would normally be expected. However, in this application the extra computation is almost entirely offset by reduced disk transfer times, a very convenient trade-off. When the temporary file is not compressed, the seven merging passes are the dominant time cost and take about 1 hour each because of the cost of reading and writing the 4 Gbyte temporary file. With compression, just 540 Mbytes must be read and written, and disk transfer time drops from 1 hour to about 10 minutes per pass. To balance this, each pass must also decompress and then recompress 540 Mbytes, and, at the rate assumed in Table 5.4, this adds a further 90 minutes. Thus, instead of seven 60-minute, disk-intensive passes, there are nine 100-minute, processor-intensive passes and no separate internal sorting pass. Because of this, the overall increase in time caused by the use of compression is small. The predicted running time of this compressed sort-based inversion method is

$$
\begin{aligned}
T = Bt_r + Ft_p + & \qquad \text{(read and parse)} \\
R(1.2k \log k)t_c + I'(t_r + t_d) + & \qquad \text{(sort, compress, and write)} \\
\lceil \log R \rceil \left(2I'(t_r + t_d) + ft_c\right) + & \qquad \text{(merge)} \\
(I' + I)(t_r + t_d) & \qquad \text{(recompress)}
\end{aligned}
$$

seconds. Here, $k = (M - L)/10$ is the number of records that can be held in main memory after the space for the structure S is allowed for, $R = \lceil f/k \rceil$ is the number of runs, and I' is the size of the temporary file, including the extra cost of storing the unary-coded t-gaps and the compression leakage. Based upon the discussion above and the results in Table 3.8, a typical value is $I' \approx 1.35I$.

Evaluating this expression for the hypothetical inversion yields a time in the vicinity of 26 hours. The space requirement is twice 540 Mbytes because the sorting algorithm requires two copies of the data at any given time, which is 680 Mbytes more than the space needed for the final inverted file. The use of compression has reduced the disk space requirement by a factor of eight, yet the processing time has increased by only 25 percent. This is the first method discussed that is generally applicable to collections of any size. It would certainly be surprising if a machine being used to invert a 5 Gbyte collection to make a 400 Mbyte inverted file could not muster an additional 680 Mbytes of temporary disk space and 40 Mbytes of memory. Nevertheless, further improvement is possible.

Multiway merging

The merging process is now processor-intensive rather than disk-intensive, and a further reduction in time can be achieved by the use of a multiway merge, leading to the sort-based, multiway merge variant in Table 5.5. For example, suppose that a four-way merge is used. Then $\lceil \log_4 400 \rceil = 5$ passes are required for the hypothetical inversion, and the total inversion time is reduced by 6 hours to approximately 20 hours.

This approach can be taken further. Suppose that all of the R runs are written to the temporary file, following which a single R-way merge takes place. If there are 40 Mbytes of memory available, each strand of a 400-way merge can be allocated a buffer of 100 Kbytes. To read the 540 Mbyte temporary file as a sequence of 100 Kbyte blocks in random order requires 5,400 transfers and 5,400 seeks. These seeks add 54 seconds at the rate specified in Table 5.4, an inconsequential overhead. That is, once the temporary file has been written, the merge can be arranged so that each compressed pointer needs to be decoded and recoded only once—the only penalty being a minute or so of disk seek time.

To perform an R-way merge requires the use of a priority queue such as a heap (described on page 42) to allow the minimal element of a slowly changing set of candidates to be found efficiently. Each of the f triples that comprise the final inverted file will pass through this structure at a cost of $\lceil \log R \rceil$ record comparisons and swaps. Hence, the running time is reduced to

$$
\begin{aligned}
T = Bt_r + Ft_p + & \qquad \text{(read and parse)} \\
R(1.2k \log k)t_c + I'(t_r + t_d) + & \qquad \text{(sort, compress, and write)} \\
f \lceil \log R \rceil t_c + I'(t_s/b + t_r + t_d) + & \qquad \text{(merge)} \\
I(t_r + t_d) & \qquad \text{(recompress)}
\end{aligned}
$$

seconds, where $b \leq M/R$ is the size of the input buffer that is allocated to each of the runs, and k, R, and I' are as above. This results in a predicted inversion time for the collection of Table 5.4 of about 11 hours, under half the time required by the previous merge-based methods. Because all the merging is done as one operation, the space cost of this method is lower too—400 Mbytes for the final inverted file and 540 Mbytes for the temporary file containing the runs.

In-place multiway merging

During the R-way merge described above, one block of b bytes from each run is present in memory, feeding candidates into the heap. At the beginning of the merge, the first block from each run is read. Whenever the last triple from any particular block is taken into the heap, a replacement block is read. Suppose the last block in each run is padded so that it too is exactly b bytes long. The padding slightly increases the size of the temporary file but means that each compressed run occupies an integral number of blocks; as we will see shortly, this permits a considerable space saving elsewhere.

The merge proceeds by repeatedly taking the next smallest $\langle t, d, f_{d,t} \rangle$ candidate from the heap and adding it to an output block. The output blocks can also be constrained to be exactly b bytes long. So, provided that pages of the temporary file can be written in a random order, each output block can be written back into the temporary file at any vacant block position—almost as if the temporary file were being treated as a paged memory. All that is necessary to make sense of the output is a *block table*, showing the physical location of each logical block of the sorted output file. This takes just a few bytes per block and requires that a small amount of memory be reserved for this purpose.

At the commencement of the merge, there are R vacant blocks on disk that can be used for output since those blocks have already been copied into memory to provide the first candidates for the heap. This means that the first R output blocks can be written before the pool of vacant blocks can possibly become exhausted. But if R output blocks have been written, at least one of the runs must have already replaced its first input block, so there is now at least one more vacant block available. This process continues throughout the merge, until the last block of each run is processed, and the last block of output is written neatly into the last vacant block position. At any given moment that space is required for an output block, there must be at least one possible vacancy to hold it. Figure 5.5 shows the situation at an intermediate point of a merge of three sorted runs. Three blocks—one from each

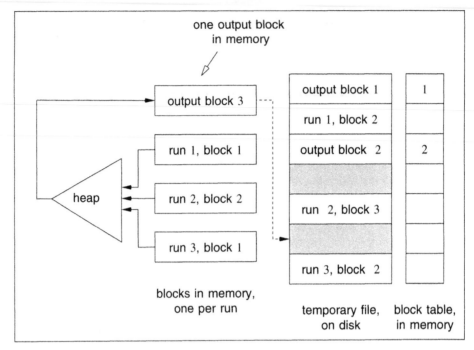

one output block
in memory

output block 3

run 1, block 1

heap

run 2, block 2

run 3, block 1

blocks in memory,
one per run

output block 1	1
run 1, block 2	
output block 2	2
run 2, block 3	
run 3, block 2	

temporary file,
on disk

block table,
in memory

Figure 5.5 In-place merging.

run—are in memory, two vacant blocks are on disk, and two output blocks have been written so far.

Employing a unary code for the t-gaps has the advantage of ensuring that there is no possibility of the compressed runs becoming longer and the output process getting ahead of the input process, and they can be safely recoded as γ-represented f_t values. The conversion during the merge of a sequence of t-gap codes to a single γ code indicating how many pairs are stored in the inverted list is safe because the "final" code can never be longer than the "initial" code. For example, a term that appears once has at least two bits used by the single t-gap and requires only one bit for a γ code; a term that appears twice has two t-gap codes totaling at least three bits, exactly the length of the γ code that replaces them; and so on. As the recoding takes place, the output process tends to lag behind the input process as the unary t-gap codes become shorter and as the padding at the end of each run is stripped away. A growing gap opens between the bit-reading process and the bit-writing process.

It is also desirable at this stage of the process to recode the d-gaps and $f_{d,t}$ values using whatever compression method is most appropriate for the final compressed inverted file. All of the parameters or explicit frequency distributions that might be required are now available since the entire text has been read once. However, if the inverted lists themselves are being recoded, there is some risk of temporary expansion—of having a block to write but nowhere to write it to because the corre-

To permute blocks so that page i holds block i, assuming that, initially, the ith page holds block *block_table*[i],

1. For $i \leftarrow 1$ to *nblocks*, if $i \neq$ *block_table*[i] then

   (a) Read page i into memory.

   (b) Set *holding* $\leftarrow$ *block_table*[i].

   (c) Set *vacant* $\leftarrow i$.

   (d) While *holding* $\neq$ *vacant* do

      i. Find j such that *block_table*[j] = *vacant*,

      ii. Copy page j to page *vacant*,

      iii. Set *block_table*[*vacant*] $\leftarrow$ *vacant*,

      iv. Set *vacant* $\leftarrow j$.

   (e) Write block in memory to page *vacant*.

   (f) Set *block_table*[*vacant*] $\leftarrow$ *holding*.

Figure 5.6 In-place permutation algorithm.

sponding input block has not yet been fully processed. This problem arises because there is no length guarantee when, for example, Elias δ-coded d-gaps are replaced by equivalent Golomb codes. Fortunately, the solution to the problem is simple. When necessary, the file is extended by exactly one more block, and the block currently in memory is written there.

At the end of the merge, the compressed inverted file is pseudosorted—each block is sorted and the block table allows recovery of the sorted file—but the blocks themselves are disordered. To permute the blocks so that the file is sorted, the block table is used to drive an in-place permutation so that each block is moved to its correct location. This can be done in linear time provided only that two b-byte buffers are available, with each block being read at most once and written at most once. The algorithm to do this is sketched in Figure 5.6. The step "Find j such that *block_table*[j] = *vacant*" is easily implemented as an array lookup. No decoding of compressed records is necessary, and the cost is relatively small. For example, if a file of 400 Mbytes is processed as blocks of $b = 50$ Kbytes, at most 16,000 seeks are required, and a maximum of 800 Mbytes of data are transferred. These cost 160 seconds and 400 seconds, respectively—about 9 minutes total.

Once this has been done, the inverted file can be truncated from its temporary size to the final size, releasing all of the now-unused space at the end. Figure 5.7 shows the complete process, assuming that no extra blocks need to be written.

The complete inversion algorithm is described in Figures 5.8 and 5.9. Values for $L = |S|$, k, and R are calculated and updated on the fly, and there is no need for any a priori estimates of any of these parameters. The only problem is that it is difficult

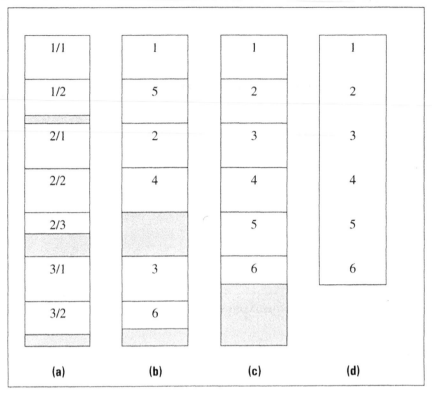

Figure 5.7 Adding slack and permuting blocks: (a) after the creation of runs; (b) after merging and recoding; (c) after permutation; (d) after truncation.

to choose a value for b, the block size. This can be solved by giving it an initial value that is a multiple of a large power of two, so that it can be halved as required while still ensuring that the runs already written remain an integral multiple of the new block size. This halving at step 2.c.v in Figure 5.8 is necessary to ensure that $R + 1$ blocks can be held in memory during the merging stage. Once this facility is included, the method is completely open-ended.

Let us estimate how much space is available for these block buffers. The only additional demand that has been placed upon memory is the need for a block table. This requires several words per block since the vacant blocks must be linked into a free list. Nevertheless, the total requirement is small. For the hypothetical text there will be $R = 400$ runs, so 401 block buffers must fit into memory. If each block is 50 Kbytes, then the buffers will occupy a little over 20 Mbytes, leaving plenty of space for the free list and block table. The blocks could be made larger, but that would increase the size of the temporary file because more space would be wasted by padding. With $R = 400$ runs and $b = 50$ Kbyte blocks, in total about 400×50 Kbytes $\times 1/2 = 10$ Mbytes of padding will be added, assuming an average wastage of half a block per run.

To produce an inverted index for a collection of documents,

1. /* Initialization */
   Create an empty dictionary structure S.
   Create an empty temporary file on disk.
   Set $L \leftarrow |S|$.
   Set $k \leftarrow (M - L)/w$, where w is the number of bytes required
       to store one $\langle t, d, f_{d,t} \rangle$ record.
   Set $b \leftarrow 50$ Kbytes.
   Set $R \leftarrow 0$.

2. /* Process text and write temporary file */
   For each document D_d in the collection, $1 \leq d \leq N$,

   (a) Read D_d, parsing it into index terms.

   (b) For each index term $t \in D_d$,

       i. Let $f_{d,t}$ be the frequency in D_d of term t.

       ii. Search S for t.

       iii. If t is not in S,
              insert it,
              set $L \leftarrow |S|$,
              set $k \leftarrow (M - L)/w$.

       iv. Add a record $\langle t, d, f_{d,t} \rangle$ to the array of triples.

   (c) If, at any stage, the array of triples contains k items,

       i. Sort the array of triples using Quicksort.

       ii. Write the array of triples, coding t-gaps in unary; d-gaps with δ;
            and $f_{d,t}$ values in unary.

       iii. Add padding to complete a block of b bytes.

       iv. Set $R \leftarrow R + 1$.

       v. /* Reduce the block size if memory looks threatened */
            If $b * (R + 1) > M$,
               set $b \leftarrow b/2$.

Figure 5.8   Improved sort-based inversion algorithm, part A.

In terms of the parameters in Table 5.4, the running time is

$$
\begin{array}{ll}
T = Bt_r + Ft_p + & \text{(read and parse)} \\
\quad R(1.2k \log k)t_c + I'(t_r + t_d) + & \text{(sort, compress, and write)} \\
\quad f \lceil \log R \rceil t_c + (I' + I)(t_s/b + t_r + t_d) + & \text{(merge and recode)} \\
\quad 2I'(t_s/b + t_r) & \text{(permute)}
\end{array}
$$

3. /* Merging */

    (a) Read the first block from each run,
add each block number to the free list.

    (b) Build heap with R candidates, one from each run.

    (c) While the heap is nonempty,

        i. Remove the root of the heap.

        ii. Add it to the output block, recoding the d-gap and $f_{d,t}$ values.

        iii. Replace it by the next candidate from the same run.

    (d) Each time the output block becomes full,

        i. Use the free list to find a vacant disk block. If there is no vacant disk block available, create one by appending an empty block to the file.

        ii. Write the output block.

        iii. Update the free list and the block table.

    (e) Each time an input block becomes empty,

        i. Read the next block from this run.

        ii. Update the free list.

4. /* In-place permutation */
Reorder the blocks so that the physical order corresponds to the logical order using the algorithm of Figure 5.6.

5. Truncate the index file to its final length.

Figure 5.9 Improved sort-based inversion algorithm, part B.

seconds, where $k = (M - L)/10$, $R = \lceil f/k \rceil$, $b < M/(R + 1)$, and I' is the peak size of the inverted file, assumed in these calculations to be $I' = 1.35I$. This works out to about 11 hours to invert the hypothetical collection, using 40 Mbytes of main memory and 150 Mbytes of disk space in excess of that required for the compressed inverted file. It corresponds to the sort-based multiway in-place method of Table 5.5.

Finally, we need to verify the claim that the search structure S can be implemented in about 30 bytes per word. In suggesting 30 bytes, generous allowance has been made for the characters of the word, with an average of 9 characters and an extra byte to store the length (10 bytes), a pointer to indicate the start of those characters (4 bytes), an "appeared last in document number x" field (4 bytes), a "frequency within current document" field (2 bytes), and a "next in chain" pointer (4 bytes), assuming a hash table implementation. There will also be a "head of chains" array of pointers; perhaps 2 bytes per word should be allowed for this. This comes to 26 bytes. Even allowing for memory fragmentation as the head of chains array is periodically resized, the total is less than 30 bytes per word. Applications in which the average term is longer than 10 bytes will, of course, require more memory. But this is a problem for all of the methods discussed and is not particular to the calculations made here.

5.4   Compressed in-memory inversion

We now leave sort-based inversion and return to the in-memory techniques that were introduced in Section 5.1. These can be combined with compression to produce feasible schemes that have different trade-offs from sort-based methods.

In this section, three further methods for inversion are described: the in-memory compressed method and the two lexicon-based methods of Table 5.5. The first, which is explored by Moffat (1992), falls into the same category as the simple sort-based inversion method—acceptable for collections of moderate size but impractical for large collections. It requires about 420 Mbytes of main memory to invert the hypothetical collection. This technique is then modified to allow for the situation where only restricted amounts of main memory are available, in much the same way as the sort-based methods led to a disk-restricted inversion algorithm. Two further methods emerge (Fox, Harman, et al. 1992; Fox and Lee 1991). Using the second of these, the hypothetical collection can be inverted in less than 16 hours using just 30 Mbytes of memory and about 50 Mbytes of disk more than the 400 Mbytes needed for the inverted file.

Large memory inversion

Suppose a machine is available that has a very large main memory. If for each term t the document frequency f_t is known when inversion begins, a large in-memory array could be allocated of exactly the right size to store the list of document numbers d and frequencies $f_{d,t}$. Compared to the in-memory technique discussed in Section 5.1, space is saved in two ways. First, there is no need for the "next" pointer field in each list node. Second, assuming that the number of documents N is known, $f_t \times \lceil \log N \rceil$ bits can be allocated to term t for the d components of the inverted list, rather than a "safe" value such as $32 \times f_t$ bits; if, for term t, the maximum within-document frequency m_t is known, the array of $f_{d,t}$ values for term t can be similarly coded in $f_t \times \lceil \log m_t \rceil$ bits. Together, these two economies reduce the memory space required to invert the hypothetical collection from 4 Gbytes to about 1.5 Gbytes. Of course, to find the values N, f_t, and m_t, a preliminary pass must be made over the entire collection—an appreciable, but perhaps acceptable, overhead.

Suppose that this approach is feasible. A single large array of the correct size is allocated to store the $\langle d, f_{d,t} \rangle$ pairs, with a lexicon entry for each term having an index pointer into the array indicating where the next document number for that word should be stored. The second pass of the inversion is illustrated in Figure 5.10. All terms have already been identified, so a minimal perfect hash function can be

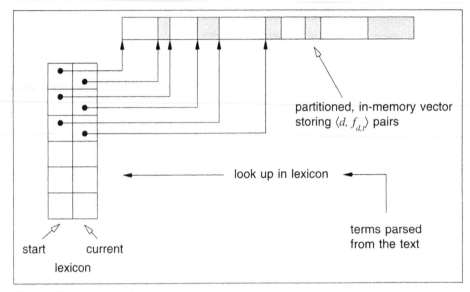

Figure 5.10   In-memory inversion.

designed for the set of terms, eliminating the need to store them. This allows the lexicon to be represented in about 10 bytes per term, or 10 Mbytes total for the sample collection of Table 5.4.

What is actually shown in Figure 5.10 is an inverted file being built up in main memory in random access fashion. The file uses a flat binary coding, without any compression. This raises the possibility of applying the compression methods described in Chapter 3 to provide a more efficient coding. The same first pass that accumulates the f_t and m_t values could also accumulate, for each term t, the total number of bits required to store the corresponding inverted list using any other fixed codes, such as δ for the d-gaps and unary or γ for the $f_{d,t}$ components. Using the compression figures of Table 3.8 (page 129) as a guide, it should be possible to reduce the memory requirement of 1.5 Gbytes to perhaps 420 Mbytes.

The time required to invert the hypothetical collection using this large-memory inversion approach is estimated as follows. First, 5 hours must be allowed for the initial statistics-gathering pass. Then, during the second pass, a further 5 hours is required for reading, parsing, and stemming. Moreover, the cost of three complete encodings and decodings of the inverted file must be allowed for—a random access encoding into memory as the inverted file is built up, a sequential decoding out of memory to obtain the inverted lists, and finally a further encoding as the inverted file is written to disk, assuming that the final representation on disk uses a different coding method from the in-memory form. These three coding passes will require about 40 minutes each, for a total inversion time of approximately 12 hours. Using the parameters given in Table 5.4, the inversion time is

$$T = Bt_r + Ft_p + \qquad \text{(first pass, read and parse)}$$
$$Bt_r + Ft_p + 2I't_d + I(t_d + t_r) \qquad \text{(second pass, invert)}$$

seconds. In this case, $I' \approx 1.05I$, since there is still a compression leakage of about 5 percent but no equivalent to the t-gaps required in the sort-based methods. This corresponds to the in-memory compressed method of Table 5.5.

Table 3.8 also shows several other compression methods that give better compression than δ, and if one of these encoding methods were used, the compression leakage might be reduced or even eliminated. Use of a global observed frequency code during inversion would, however, require *three* complete passes over the input collection—one to accumulate the frequencies and build a Huffman code, a second to count the number of bits needed for each inverted list, and a third to actually perform the inversion into the in-memory array. This might save several megabytes of memory but at the cost of 5 extra hours of processing time. In general, the same also applies for local compression methods—three passes are required and for only relatively small savings in space. However, if the local Bernoulli model described in Section 3.3 is used, the inversion can be performed in two passes because it is possible in just one preliminary pass to gather enough information to allocate memory to each compressed inverted list.

Consider again the Golomb code described in Section 3.3. The value $b_t^A \approx 0.69(N/f_t)$ minimizes the *average* number of output bits per symbol, but to perform in-memory inversion, a strict upper bound on the *worst* that can happen for any particular value of b is required since the space must be allocated in advance and cannot be extended easily if the compressed representation is larger than expected. Given values for N, f_t, and b, the maximum number of bits required by a Golomb code is

$$f_t(1 + \lceil \log b \rceil) + \frac{N - f_t(2^{\lceil \log b \rceil} - b + 1)}{b}.$$

The value of b that minimizes this "worst-case" (superscript W) number of bits is

$$b_t^W = 2^{\lfloor \log((N - f_t)/f_t) \rfloor}.$$

That is, to minimize the *maximum* number of bits that can be consumed, b should be taken to be the largest power of two less than or equal to $(N - f_t)/f_t$. (Golomb codes in which the parameter b is a power of two are also known as Rice codes, after Robert Rice of the Jet Propulsion Laboratory in Pasadena, California, and will be encountered again in Chapter 6.) For example, suppose an inverted list for which $N = 10,000$ and $f_t = 187$ is to be compressed. To code this inverted list so that, on average, the least amount of space is consumed, $b_t^A = 37$ should be used. With this value for b, on average 1,360 and at most 1,437 bits are required. On the other hand, using the b_t^W value of 32, the upper bound on the number of bits decreases slightly

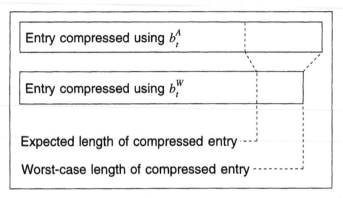

Figure 5.11 Using b_t^A and b_t^W to minimize average and worst-case lengths.

to 1,428, but the average number of bits consumed increases slightly to 1,363. This relationship between average and maximum coded lengths is shown in Figure 5.11.

For in-memory inversion, it is the upper bound on the number of bits that is of overriding importance, and to minimize memory usage during the second pass of the inversion, $b = b_t^W$ is used. Of course, if this maximum number of bits is allocated to each inverted list, each compressed representation will probably be a little short of filling the space allocated, so there will still be some leakage. This is tolerable provided that not too much space at the end of each compressed list has been wasted. What cannot be allowed is for any of the inverted lists to overflow since the space must be irrevocably allocated before any of the entries are filled in.

The "two-pass Golomb-coded in-memory" approach can now be described. The first pass counts, for each term t, its document frequency f_t and absolute frequency F_t and writes these to a lexicon file. To minimize the space required for data structures and maximize the space available in the second pass for inverted lists, the first phase calculates a minimal perfect hash function for the terms in the collection. One possible way to do this is described in Section 4.1.

The second pass reads the lexicon and calculates for each term t the value b_t^W, using that to determine the maximum number of bits that can be required by the Golomb code for the inverted list for this term. In addition, F_t bits are added to allow for unary-coded $f_{d,t}$ values. This information is used to allocate partitions that are guaranteed to be large enough for each compressed inverted list. Next, the text is processed again, building in random access fashion a compressed in-memory inverted file, using the worst-case local Golomb code and, for each term t, the corresponding value b_t^W to drive the code, with a unary-coded frequency value. Finally, at the end of the second pass over the text, the in-memory inverted file is sequentially decompressed and recompressed (perhaps using the Golomb code and b_t^A, with γ used for $f_{d,t}$ values) to form the final inverted file. This process is detailed in Figure 5.12.

To produce an inverted index for a collection of documents,

1. /* First pass—count term frequencies */
   Create an empty dictionary structure S.
   Process the text, counting, for each term t
   f_t, the number of documents containing t, and
   F_t, the total number of appearances of term t.
   Write these values to a lexicon file.

2. /* Second pass—encode into memory */
   Set $total \leftarrow 0$.
   Read the lexicon file.
   For $t \leftarrow 1$ to n do
   (a) Set $b_t = 2^{\lfloor \log((N - f_t)/f_t) \rfloor}$.
   (b) Set $B_t = f_t(1 + \lceil \log b_t \rceil) + (N - f_t(2^{\lceil \log b_t \rceil} - b_t + 1))/b_t$.
   (c) Set $start_t \leftarrow total$.
   (d) Set $current_t \leftarrow start_t$.
   (e) Set $total \leftarrow total + B_t + F_t$.

3. Allocate a single vector of $total$ bits.

4. /* Process the text */
   For each document D_d in the collection, $1 \leq d \leq N$:
   (a) Read D_d, parsing it into index terms.
   (b) For each index term $t \in D_d$,
   i. Let $f_{d,t}$ be the frequency in D_d of term t.
   ii. Append Golomb-coded d-gap using b_t and a unary-coded $f_{d,t}$ value at bit position $current_t$, updating $current_t$.

5. /* Decode, and recode to output */
   For $t \leftarrow 1$ to n do
   (a) Use b_t to decode the f_t pairs in inverted file entry for term t, starting at bit position $start_t$.
   (b) Recompress inverted file entry using output compression code.
   (c) Append this inverted file entry to the inverted file.

Figure 5.12 In-memory inversion algorithm.

On the *TREC* database, the worst-case memory allocations average about 6.1 bits per d-gap, which means that the leakage is about 5 percent and suggests that $I' \approx 1.05I$.

This still corresponds to a great deal of memory space—420 Mbytes for the hypothetical inversion of Table 5.4. Like the simple sort-based inversion, this "large memory" method is appropriate only for collections of moderate size. Clearly, some way of further reducing the amount of memory required is needed.

Lexicon-based partitioning

To attain this goal the inversion is subdivided into smaller tasks, each of which can be carried out using an in-memory vector within the available memory. One possible subdivision is to make multiple "second" passes over the text, each processing one *load*. For example, if the calculations based on the b_t^W values indicate that the memory required is three times the amount available, three "second" passes are made. The first load processes (roughly) the first third of the lexicon, discarding any words that fall outside this range, and writes the first third of the inverted file. Then a second "second" pass processes the text, extracting the next third of the words. Finally, the last third of the inverted file is produced by yet another "second" pass. The exact partitioning of the lexicon can be performed at the end of the (single) first pass when the f_t and F_t values are known. At this stage, the number of loads required can be determined and the *boundary words*—words that bound those terms that will be processed in each second pass—are determined. For obvious reasons, we will call this method of subdividing the work a *lexicon-based partition*; two such schemes will be discussed.

Suppose that the hypothetical collection is to be inverted in 40 Mbytes of memory and that the compact second-pass lexicon requires only 10 Mbytes. Since the inverted file occupies 420 Mbytes, allowing for 5 percent leakage, 14 loads must be inverted. These take 70 hours for parsing and stemming. Including another 5 hours for the first pass, and the time required by the three compression steps per pointer, this technique requires about 80 hours. Given such a long running time, it is wise to write the lexicon and the boundary words to disk, so that processing can be restarted at the beginning of the current load should a machine failure occur. For example, the first pass could generate, as its last action, an executable script that contains all the instructions for the second passes and then transfer control to that script.

In terms of the computational model established in Table 5.4, the time required is

$$T = Bt_r + Ft_p + \qquad\qquad \text{(read and parse)}$$
$$l(Bt_r + Ft_p) + 2I't_d + I(t_r + t_d) \quad \text{(process loads)}$$

seconds, where l is the number of loads and $I' = 1.05I$, as above. Assuming again that the static second-pass lexicon takes one-third the space of the dynamic first-pass lexicon, then $l = \lceil I'/(M - L/3) \rceil$. This corresponds to the first lexicon-based method of Table 5.5.

The time can be greatly reduced if extra disk space is available. In this case, the text need be parsed only twice since a set of temporary files can be written by the second pass, one for each load. The records in each temporary file contain a term number t, a document number d, and a frequency $f_{d,t}$, where all the t values are within the range of the boundary words for that particular load. Moreover, since the first pass has already determined the number of records that are written to each temporary file, they can be implemented as partitions within the same large file. This latter arrangement is necessary on systems with a limitation on the number of files that can be manipulated simultaneously.

Once the records have been distributed across the l temporary files, each load can be processed, drawing its data from the corresponding temporary file. This reduces the running time to

$$
\begin{aligned}
T = Bt_r + Ft_p + & \quad \text{(read and parse)} \\
Bt_r + Ft_p + 10f(t_s/b + t_r) + & \quad \text{(reread, write temporary files)} \\
10ft_r + 2I't_d + I(t_r + t_d) & \quad \text{(read and process loads)}
\end{aligned}
$$

where again it is assumed that each record $\langle t, d, f_{t,d} \rangle$ requires 10 bytes of storage and b is some convenient block size. This corresponds to the second lexicon-based method of Table 5.5. It allows the hypothetical inversion to take place in about 12 hours but assumes that 4 Gbytes of temporary disk space is available. The latter requirement makes the method unattractive. Moreover, compression of the temporary files is ineffective because they are written in order of document number d and so the t component is, for all intents and purposes, random.

Text-based partitioning

The space overhead of the lexicon-based partitioning method is small, assuming that no temporary disk file is used, but the time is much greater than for the in-place merging technique described in Section 5.3. However, the bulk of the time is now spent parsing and processing the data, 15 times in total for the hypothetical text.

As the basis for subdividing the work, suppose the text itself is partitioned rather than the lexicon: this corresponds to the text-based partition method of Table 5.5. First, an inverted file is produced for an initial "chunk" of documents, then for a second chunk, and so on, merging all the partial inverted files into a final inverted file. We have already seen one situation in which the merging can be performed in place, and here is a similar application where another in-place merging strategy can be used.

Imagine that the partitioned vector of Figure 5.10 is laid out on disk rather than in memory, as shown in Figure 5.13. After an in-memory inverted index has been constructed for a chunk, it is merged with the full inverted index that is being constructed on disk. To do this, the entire inverted index is read off disk, block by block, and written back with the new entries added. Since the space for each term's list is preallocated on the disk, the merged disk file can be written back to the same place from which it was read. The only extra requirement is that a *disk_current* bit pointer must be maintained for each term, to indicate where the next chunk's records should be appended. At the end of the text, after all the chunks have been inverted and merged, a final pass over the inverted file is performed, compacting

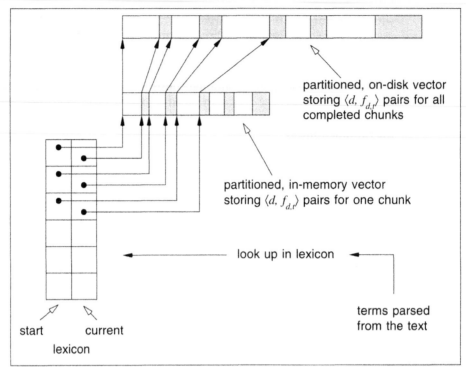

Figure 5.13 Inversion and merging of chunks.

out the unused bits at the end of each inverted list and perhaps recompressing using a different code. Once the compaction process is complete, the file can be truncated and any remaining free space at the end released.

The first pass is now responsible for deciding how many documents can be placed into each of the chunks. For every chunk it writes an information file that records the local within-chunk frequency of each term so that the chunk inversions can use accurate term frequencies to partition their regions of the inverted lists. This file will be a small overhead on the disk space. Term frequencies coded using γ take just a few bits each, so for the hypothetical text, the 14 chunks require a temporary chunk description file of less than 10 Mbytes. A second temporary disk file is required to maintain, for each term t, the value of the $disk\_current_t$ pointer, indicating how much of the space allocated to term t in the disk inverted file has been already consumed. Even stored as a file of 32-bit integers, this takes only 4 Mbytes. Both of these files are processed sequentially, so there is no need to keep them in memory.

Including these two files and the fact that the initial disk allocation for the d-gap component of the inverted file is in terms of b_t^W rather than b_t^A, the hypothetical inversion requires 435 Mbytes of disk storage to generate a 400 Mbyte inverted file an overhead of less than 10 percent and a further improvement on the 35 percent overhead of the in-place multiway merge of Section 5.3.

It remains to justify this *text-partitioning* technique in terms of running time. During the second pass the text is processed once, taking 5 hours. Each document number is now handled five times: random access compression into memory during the inversion of a chunk; sequential decompression out of memory and batched sequential compression into the partial inverted file at the end of that chunk; and, finally, sequential decompression and recompression during the compaction process. For this another 3 hours should be allowed. The partial inverted file is also read and rewritten sequentially once for each of the chunks and once again during the compaction process, accounting for $420 \times 15 \times 2$ Mbytes of data transfer. At 2 Mbytes per second, this takes 2 hours. The total processing time, including the first pass, is thus estimated to be 15 hours. More generally, the predicted running time for an inversion is

$$
\begin{aligned}
T = Bt_r + Ft_p + & & \text{(read and parse)} \\
Bt_r + Ft_p + 3I't_d + 2cI'(t_s/b + t_r) + & & \text{(invert in-place)} \\
(I' + I)(t_s/b + t_r + t_d) & & \text{(compact)}
\end{aligned}
$$

seconds, where $c = I'/(M - L/3)$ is the number of chunks the text is broken into, and, as before, $I' \approx 1.05I$ and b is a suitable block size.

This method can operate in less than the 40 Mbytes of memory allowed in all the previous calculations. If the memory for each chunk inverted file is reduced to 20 Mbytes, both passes require 30 Mbytes in total, and the memory requirements are balanced. Now, 21 chunks are generated, and the processing time increases by 1 hour to a total of 16 hours.

5.5   Comparison of inversion methods

Let us now stand back for a moment and put these algorithms into perspective. Using the final method, text partitioning with in-memory compression:

A 5 Gbyte collection can be inverted in just the memory space required by the lexicon for that collection, using less than 10 percent more disk space than the final compressed inverted file and at an overall rate of about 300 Mbytes of text per hour.

This is quite a remarkable improvement over the naive methods explored at the beginning of this chapter. Of all the possibilities:

The algorithms that cope best with a large collection are the sort-based, multiway merge, in-place method of Section 5.3, and the text-based partitioning technique described in Section 5.4.

The text-partitioning approach has the advantage of requiring less temporary disk space and can operate in less main memory if required to do so, but, according to the costs assumed in Table 5.4, requires slightly more running time.

The sort-based method has a major advantage in that it requires only one pass over the text. The model used to derive the results of Table 5.5 includes the cost of reading and parsing the text but excludes one other important cost—the time taken to decompress the raw text of the collection if it is stored compressed. Typical high-speed compression methods such as those based upon the Ziv-Lempel paradigm decompress at a rate of about 100 Mbytes per minute, so each pass during the hypothetical inversion requires another hour of CPU time for decompression. In this case, the time difference between the one-pass and two-pass methods will be greater than is recorded in Table 5.5. The balance may swing even further toward the one-pass method if there are other processing steps to be performed on the text. For example, if the text is large, it may be stored on drives mounted on other machines in the network, and in this case, network transmission costs may intrude. Certainly, the fewer passes made over the collection the better, so the sort-based method may well be preferable, even though the disk overhead is 35 percent rather than 10 percent.

Although these two methods are the only ones suited to large-scale inversion, the others have their uses. For one thing, not every inversion is 5 Gbytes. Many applications require the indexing of 100 Mbytes, and in this case, most of the preceding algorithms can be employed. In our own work, the in-memory compressed method was used successfully for quite some time until the needs of the *TREC* collection forced the development of an alternative.

The second reason we have described all these methods is, of course, for completeness. There is a great deal of folklore surrounding the true cost of index construction, and we hope to have cleared the air by giving a detailed account of all known methods.

5.6   Constructing signature files and bitmaps

The construction of a bitsliced signature file index (described in Section 3.5) is simpler than the convoluted processing required to build an inverted index but is not necessarily less time-consuming.

Suppose that enough main memory is available to hold the complete signatures of k documents and that N, the number of documents (or an overestimate of it), is known in advance. The value of k is easily calculated from the signature width W (in bits) and the amount of main memory M (in bytes) as $k = \lfloor 8M/W \rfloor$ since the signature of every document is the same length. That memory is then partitioned into partial bitslices, each k bits long. Once this is done, the text is processed in chunks of k documents. In this case, one pass over the input text is sufficient. For each document a signature is constructed by hashing each word that appears the requisite number of times and setting the bit corresponding to that document in each of the indicated bitslices. After k documents have been processed, all the partial bitslices are flushed to disk, writing each k-bit section into the correct place within the preallocated signature file. All the addresses and offsets involved are easily calculated, since each bitslice is exactly N bits long. The memory bitslice buffer is then reset, and the next chunk of k documents processed. At the completion of the input, the last set of partial bitslices is flushed and the process is complete—a mechanism with a strong resemblance to the text-based partitioning method for inverted file indexes.

Now consider the cost of this process for the 5 Gbyte example database. Suppose that queries may contain as few as one term, an average of one false match per query is sought, and a total of eight bitslices are to be retrieved to obtain this performance. This situation corresponds to the figures of Table 3.13 (page 136). Given these requirements, the signature width W must be 4,100 bits, and each term sets 8 bits. Recall that there is no need for a lexicon to be maintained because the hash functions are calculated directly from the term, so all of the 40 Mbytes of memory is available for partial slices. Thus, the text can be processed in chunks of $k = 78,000$ documents, and 65 chunks are necessary. The time required is 4 hours for reading and parsing the input text, saving 1 hour because of the absence of dictionary lookup; perhaps 2 hours to apply the hash functions 6.4 billion times and generate the partial bitslices; and 65 lots of 4,100 writes to the signature file, each writing a 10 Kbyte partial bitslice. Allowing 10 milliseconds for each seek (t_s in Table 5.4) and 5 milliseconds for data transfer, each of these 267,000 operations takes 15 milliseconds, for a total of 1 hour. Thus it should be possible to construct a signature file for the sample collection in about 7 hours.

In fact, the time-critical part of this process is not the input and output operations but the application of the hash function. The estimate supposes that each application will take a microsecond, the same time as was earlier allowed for an integer comparison and record swap. For most hash calculations this is, in fact, optimistic by an order of magnitude. For example, it is not unusual for hash function evaluation on a string argument to require several multiplications and at least one division, in which case an evaluation time of 10 microseconds is more likely. If this is the case, 18 hours are required by hash function evaluation and 23 hours by the indexing process in total. Evaluating the hash function is the dominant cost of building a signature file, and it is a CPU-intensive operation.

There is another aspect of signature file creation that also costs a nontrivial amount of time—the need to calculate the signature file parameters. The formulas presented in Section 3.5 require that the average document length and total number of index pointers be known prior to the index being created, and these can only be ascertained through a preliminary inspection of the collection. Creating a signature file is really a two-pass process if the index parameters are to be calculated rather than merely estimated.

Given that a bitmap can be thought of as a wide, sparse signature file, it is tempting to consider using the same technique for bitmap construction. However, the realities are somewhat different. The bitmap for the sample collection is one million "slices" wide, and so it would be necessary to use $k = 320$ and make 16,000 writing passes. Even if only 1 percent of the partial slices contain any 1 bits and so actually cause an output operation, the disk seeks alone will take 450 hours (18 days) of disk access time. This is clearly excessive. In fact, to build a bitmap, the best method is to build a compressed inverted file, then decompress it and store it with a unary code. More to the point, given the discussion in Chapter 3, and the fact that a bitmap for the hypothetical collection would require 580 Gbytes, it is difficult to see why you would ever want to construct it in the first place.

5.7   Dynamic collections

Throughout the previous description of indexing techniques, we have assumed that the database is static. However, it is rare for a database to be truly static. Even such collections as *The Complete Works of Shakespeare* undergo occasional expansion as new sonnets are discovered and authenticated, and dictionaries and encyclopedias are the subject of almost continual revision. The problem of dynamic collections cannot be ignored.

A collection can be dynamic in one of two ways. First, it might provide an "insert" operation that appends a new document to an existing collection but does not change any of the current documents. More radically, it might also be necessary to support an "edit" operation that allows current documents to be altered and perhaps even removed.

Expanding the text

Consider the operation of inserting a new document. First, the text of the collection must be expanded. Most file systems support an "append" operation on previously created files, so it is relatively straightforward to append the new document to the text of the collection. Care must be taken if the documents are being compressed, and the compression model must be able to cope with hitherto unseen symbols. If nothing else, the model should provide an "escape" flag that indicates that a document or part of a document is stored uncompressed. However, as the collection grows, the model will become less appropriate and the compression less effective. To limit the extent of this degradation, the retrieval system should periodically be completely rebuilt, creating a new compression model appropriate to the current text that is stored.

Several compression schemes designed specifically for the text of dynamic document collections are described by Moffat, Zobel, and Sharman (1997). For example, a word-based model might incorporate an escape flag to indicate that the next word is not in the lexicon and is coded as a sequence of eight-bit characters. Experiments with such a scheme show that the degradation in compression is relatively small. In one experiment, for example, a compression model was created by processing the first two-thirds of the *Comact* database and then used to compress the entire collection—this is equivalent to increasing the size of the database by 50 percent. Less than 5 percent extra space was required when *Comact* was compressed using the "two-thirds" model than when the same text was compressed using the full "three-thirds" model.

A more detailed solution to this problem is described in the section on dynamic collections in Chapter 9 (page 412), and the results show that two- and fourfold expansion of the text can be tolerated without significant degradation in compression rates using very simple expansion strategies; more complex expansion strategies allow 10- or 50-fold expansion. In a general database, adopting a conservative approach and rebuilding every time the collection has, say, trebled in size means that a total of 10 recompressions will see a collection grow from 10 Mbytes to 600 Gbytes. This latter quantity is sufficiently large that it seems safe to conclude that periodic recompression is an acceptable approach to the problem of maintaining a compression model in the face of document insertion and that just 10 rebuildings will be more than sufficient during the life expectancy of a database.

Expanding the index

More problematic is the effect that document insertion has on the index. The simplest way to handle this is to accumulate updates in a "stop-press" file that is checked for each query issued. When the stop-press grows too large, or when the opportunity arises, the entire collection is rebuilt. The drawback of this approach is that it takes ever longer to reindex the data, and this operation has to be performed relatively frequently. Recompression of the text need only be carried out when the collection has doubled or trebled, but to defer reindexing until two-thirds of the data is in the stop-press is unthinkable. A more continuous approach is required to keep the index up-to-date, and this has been investigated by Zobel, Moffat, and Sacks-Davis (1993b).

Consider first an inverted file. Since each newly inserted document contains many terms, there are many inverted lists that need to grow slightly longer. The inverted file must support *multipoint* expansion rather than a simple append mode of expansion. Since the inverted lists are already of widely varying lengths, we are faced with the problem of supporting a collection of dynamically changing variable-length records. This section describes one mechanism that provides the functionality required. First, a suitable file structure is described, then record extension is considered, and finally, record insertion is discussed.

Central to these operations is the disk file, which is organized into fixed-length blocks, each containing b bytes, for some suitable value of b such as 64 Kbytes. Each block contains a *block address table*, some *records*, and some *free space*. The block address table lists the number of records stored in the block, as well as, for each record stored, the record number and an address within the block for the record. The records themselves are packed at the other end of the block from the block table, and between the block table and the records there is some free space. This structure is shown in Figure 5.14.

In memory, a *record address table* is maintained that stores, for each record number, the block number currently containing that record. Also in memory is a *free list* that describes blocks that currently have an amount of free space greater than a given *tolerance*. Finally, the current *last block* of the file is kept in main memory rather than on disk.

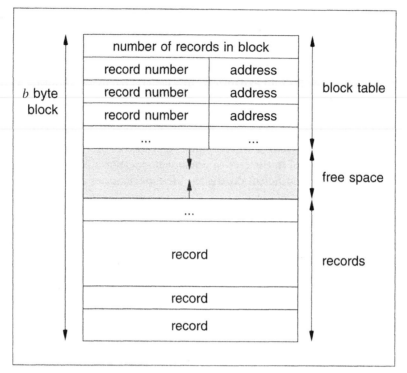

Figure 5.14 Block structure.

To access a record given its ordinal record number, the record address table is used to find the correct block number. The whole of that block is read into memory, and the block address table searched for the record number. This yields the address of the record within the block, so the record can then be located and its contents used.

Now, consider the problem of extending a particular record. First, the block that contains the record is retrieved. If the block contains sufficient free space that the extended record can still be accommodated, records are linearly shifted in the block to make the correct space, the extension added to the record, the block table updated, and the altered block written. This may also have some effect on the free list.

If, on the other hand, there is insufficient free space within that original block, the smallest record whose removal leaves enough space for the extended record is deleted from the block. If there is no such record, the record being extended is removed. Again, the block table and the free list should be updated, and the block written back to disk. In this case, however, still extant is a record that has no block—either a record that was removed to make space for the extension or the newly extended record itself. This record is treated as an insertion.

To insert a record, the free list is consulted to determine if there is any block in the file that has space for it. If there is, that block is retrieved from disk; the record is inserted; the block table, record address table, and free list are all updated; and the block is written back to disk. If there is not—if all the blocks on the free list are sufficiently full that they cannot absorb this record—attention is switched to the last block of the file, which is maintained in main memory. If the last block can take the record, it is inserted and the various tables are updated. If it cannot, the last block is written and perhaps added to the free list, and a new, completely empty, last block created in memory. Finally, the record can be inserted into this empty block.

In most cases, a record extension can be carried out with one block read and one block write. The worst that can be required is four disk operations: a block read to retrieve a block that does not have enough space; a block write, once a record has been removed from that block; a block read to retrieve a block that does have enough space; and a block write, as it is returned to disk. While constant, this requirement is sufficiently high that in this raw form the scheme is not likely to be useful. For example, it seems unlikely that 4×200 disk accesses totalling perhaps 30 seconds— four for each distinct term that appears in the document—is acceptable just to add one *TREC*-sized document to a collection. If it were, it would take 9 months to build a *TREC* index incrementally and close to 2 years to index the hypothetical 5 Gbyte collection.

To reduce the number of disk operations, an *update cache* is used to buffer requests and so allow multiple operations on each block once it is read into memory. A cache of 1 Mbyte and a block size of 64 Kbytes is sufficient to allow *TREC*-sized documents to be inserted in an average of one to two disk operations each.

The key to the success of the record management strategy described in this section is the relatively high cost of input and output operations compared with in-memory table lookup and shifting operations. For example, to extend a record with $b = 64$ Kbytes, on average 32 Kbytes must be copied sideways some small number of bits or bytes. On a typical computer, this copy takes a few milliseconds, much less than the 20 milliseconds that would be required by, say, two extra disk operations.

More space is used than would be required by a static inverted file for the same data, since each block contains some free space. Experiments have shown, however, that this loss is small (Zobel, Moffat, and Sacks-Davis 1993b). For example, a complete inverted file for the *TREC* collection, constructed by repeated insertion of documents, ended up with only about 5 percent unused space for a wide range of block sizes and cache sizes.

The indexing lexicon must also be designed to allow expansion, since new documents might contain completely novel query terms. The appropriate structure here is some kind of indexed file such as a B-tree. Certainly, in the face of expansion, minimal perfect hashing cannot be relied upon.

Having designed a system that is extensible, it is possible to create the inverted index in the first instance by repeated insertion in a single pass over the collection, in much the same way as was suggested for creating signature files. In this case, as much memory as possible should be employed for the update cache to minimize the number of disk operations required. Nevertheless, the time taken is likely to be more than that required by a tailored inversion process, and even for a dynamic collection it is probably better to use a special-purpose inversion method during database creation if the initial collection contains a large amount of data.

If editing of existing documents is allowed, the text of the collection must be stored using a dynamic file structure such as that described above. Moreover, if documents can be edited and perhaps deleted, inverted lists can change in the middle rather than just at the end. To meet this need, a parameterless code to compress inverted lists should be considered, so that the effect of document editing can be localized to small sections of inverted lists and the remaining codes simply copied rather than having to be decompressed and then recompressed.

Query processing with a dynamic collection is unchanged from the operations described in Chapter 4. Boolean queries are processed using no structures other than the lexicon and the inverted lists, and they pose no problems. On the other hand, ranked queries also require an array of document weights W_d. It is now possible to reveal one of the significant advantages of the variant of the cosine measure described by Equation 4.3 on page 187, namely, that the document-term weights $w_{d,t}$ and document weights W_d are independent of any parameters external to each document. In particular, by explicitly excluding the term weight w_t from the calculation of $w_{d,t}$, that cosine variant allows documents to be added to a collection without all of the other document weights W_d becoming invalid.

Finally, it is worth noting that the issues of dynamic collections are not in any way alleviated by the use of signature file indexing, contrary to popular belief. Having all of the bitslices of the same length does not make memory management in the face of insertion any easier since the lists must still be expanded as the collection grows. If anything, signature files are less efficient since having all of the slices exactly the same length means that fragmentation becomes a significant problem. There are no short slices to soak up the bits that would otherwise be wasted, and compared to an inverted file index, average space utilization will be very low. Insertion of records is also likely to be slower with a signature file index. As we have seen (in Tables 3.8 and 4.10), a document of t distinct terms causes approximately eight bits to be appended to each of t inverted lists if an inverted file index is being used. With a signature file index, however, around $8t$ slices must each have one bit set.

Editing documents with a signature file index is particularly difficult and involves processing every bitslice in which, for that document, the bit changes. For a deletion, all 1 bits must be zeroed, so as many as 1,500 or more bitslices must be edited.

Further reading

Inverted indexes. Experiments with a large inverted index have been described by Harman and Candela (1990), including the 13-day disk-based inversion. This material also appears in (Fox, Harman, et al. 1992). Lesk (1988) and Somogyi (1990) discuss the problem of inverting large collections. Recent papers describe the use of compression in conjunction with sort-based inversion and in-place merging as an aid to inversion (Moffat and Bell 1995), and the in-memory inversion technique of Section 5.4 (Moffat 1992). Fox and Lee have considered the problem of building an index within a limited amount of memory, and the two lexicon partitioning methods are due to them (Fox and Lee 1991; Fox, Harman, et al. 1992). The final text-partitioning approach is unpublished work of Alistair Moffat and Peter Thompson at the University of Melbourne. Moffat and Zobel (1994) give details of the work undertaken with the *TREC* collection and describe the use of the in-memory compressed bitvector method to build an index.

Dynamic collections. Several compression schemes designed specifically for the text of dynamic document collections are described by Moffat, Zobel, and Sharman (1997). The method for supporting dynamically changing files of variable-length records (Section 5.7) was described by Zobel, Moffat, and Sacks-Davis (1993b), and Figure 5.14 is taken from that paper. Similar structures have been described by many authors, including Lomet (1988), Carey et al. (1989), Cutting and Pedersen (1990), Biliris (1992a, 1992b), Faloutsos and Jagadish (1992), and Manolopoulos and Christodoulakis (1992).

Signature files. Zobel, Moffat, and Ramamohanarao (1998) examine the process of constructing a bitsliced signature file and give experimental results that show it to be slower than the time taken to construct a compressed inverted index.

Sorting and hashing. Bentley and McIlroy (1993) give an excellent derivation of the Quicksort internal sorting algorithm that has been assumed throughout this chapter. The cost of evaluating hash functions is considered by Ramakrishna and Zobel (1997).

Image Compression

The compression, indexing, and storing of text is only one side of the story. Much of the information we receive is communicated in the form of images. Of course, in ordinary language this generally means pictures, but in this book an even more important kind of image is one that contains text—text that is not immediately machine-readable. In fax transmission, for example, images that are predominantly textual are digitized, processed, and communicated by machine, but they are not machine-readable: they are handled and reproduced by the system as a matrix of digital picture elements, or *pixels*, not as text. Only people interpret fax images as text.

There are two advantages to having machines handle textual images as pictures rather than interpreting them as text. One is that the interpretation process—optical character recognition—is error-prone. Mistakes, once made, cannot be corrected except by human intervention. This contrasts with errors incurred by digitization, which can be controlled to within designed tolerances, and errors of transmission, which can be detected and corrected by suitable communication protocols. The second advantage is that documents that contain real pictures are accommodated naturally by a communication scheme that operates on images alone. If the images were converted to text first, special provisions would have to be made for pictures.

Set against these are two good reasons to attempt to recognize the content of the images before compressing and storing them. If textual images are interpreted as a stream of characters, much greater compression can be gained. Even more importantly, only by recognizing the text can we hope to be able to automatically index the information contained in the images in order to support content-based searches. Provided the document image itself can be reproduced correctly, some misrecognition is not normally a serious problem if it affects only what is contained in the index. It may make it harder to find the document, but once it is located it will be shown in its original form. Our job, then, is to find a way to achieve high compression of documents that have been "read" by optical character recognition, without incurring the problems of misrecognition and inability to cope with non-textual material. This can be done—and in the next two chapters, we will see how to obtain the best of both worlds. But we are getting ahead of ourselves.

In the last few years there has been a great deal of activity aimed at producing formal international standards for image compression. This has been prompted by the very rapid development of international computer networks since the 1960s, in particular by the incredible growth over the last decade of the Internet and, even more recently, the World Wide Web—in which digital pictures play a pervasive role. Two groups of standards in particular have been developed: JPEG, for compressing continuous-tone "photographic" images that are represented in grayscale or color, and JBIG, for compressing two-tone "bilevel" images that are (usually) black and white. The acronyms stand for Joint Photographic Experts Group and Joint Binary Image Group, respectively; the groups are "joint" in that they represent both the CCITT[1] telecommunications standards body and the ISO (International Standards Organization). Both groups have developed initial standards in their respective areas, and both are in the process of developing follow-on variants of the standards that address issues that were left unresolved, or inadequately resolved, in the initial effort. JPEG preceded JBIG historically, and its standardization process is a little more advanced—although it is a much larger committee, which tends to slow things down.

This chapter looks at the representation and compression of images. The techniques described here can be used directly to store scanned documents and will be extended in Chapter 7 to obtain better compression for documents containing predominantly text. We begin by reviewing in Section 6.1 the different types of digital images and the parameters that affect their digitized representation. The subsequent three sections describe compression methods for bilevel, or black-and-white, images. First, in Section 6.2 we introduce the CCITT international fax standard that governs how present-day fax machines encode the images they transmit. Section 6.3 then studies more effective methods of compression that are based on the techniques developed for compressing text surveyed in Chapter 2, and Section 6.4 looks at the JBIG standard for compressing bilevel images. (A more complex variant of JBIG is currently under development that uses techniques described in Chapter 7.) Following that, in Section 6.5 we turn to continuous-tone—that is, grayscale and color—images. We look at the standard lossless methods that are in widespread use today and also at some higher-performance methods to get a feel for the upper end of the spectrum. We conclude this look at lossless compression by describing (on page 296) the new JPEG lossless standard that is currently undergoing a standardization process. Section 6.6 turns to lossy compression and examines the continually evolving JPEG standard, which focuses primarily on lossy compression. JPEG has already had a significant impact on how lossy images are stored in practice, and later

---

1   Comité Consultatif International de Télégraphie et Téléphonie (International Telegraph and Telephone Consultative Committee), part of the International Telecommunications Union of the United Nations.

Table 6.1   An assortment of devices and their resolutions.

Device	Resolution (dpi)
Standard VDU (24-line, 80-character)	80×60
Low-end matrix printer	75×75
CCITT fax standard	204×98
high-resolution version	204×196
Apple Laserwriter (models I and II)	300×300
Many common scanners	300×300
Medium-quality Laserwriter	600×600
Low-cost phototypesetter	$1,200 \times 1,200$
High-resolution phototypesetter	$4,800 \times 4,800$

versions of the standard are emerging that incorporate state-of-the-art lossless compression methods too. Finally, Section 6.7 reviews ways of encoding images so that they can be displayed "progressively," with a rough version shown very quickly and refined as time goes by into successively more accurate renderings.

6.1   Types of images

When an image is digitized, its appearance depends on the resolution—that is, the number of pixels per linear unit—as well as on the number of bits that are used to represent each pixel. For example, ordinary fax has a resolution of around 200 dpi (dots per inch) in the horizontal direction and 100 dpi vertically. Faxes vary a great deal in quality because of deficiencies in the low-cost scanning mechanisms that are typically used. Another familiar example of image resolution is the ubiquitous Laserwriter, which (in its original version) prints 300 dpi in both directions. Table 6.1 shows the resolution of several different imaging devices.

The number of bits used to represent each pixel also helps to determine image quality. Most printing devices are bilevel: one bit is allocated to each pixel. When putting ink on paper, bilevel representation is natural—either a pixel is inked or it is not. However, display technology is more flexible, and many computer displays have several bits per pixel. Monochrome displays often show 16 levels of gray, while color displays range up to 24 or even 32 bits per pixel, perhaps encoded as 8 bits for each of the colors red, green, and blue, or perhaps in some more sophisticated form that separates the chromatic, or color, information from the achromatic, or brightness, information. Grayscale and color scanners are available for capturing images with more than 1 bit per pixel, although the lowest-cost scanners are bilevel ones.

More bits per pixel can compensate for a lack of linear resolution and vice versa. Research on human perception has shown that if a dot is small enough, its brightness and size are interchangeable—that is, a small bright dot cannot be distinguished from a larger, dimmer one. The critical size below which this phenomenon takes effect depends on the contrast between dots and their background. It corresponds roughly to a 500×500 pixel display at normal viewing levels and distances. One application of this phenomenon is that if text is generated on a display with grayscale capability, visual clarity can be improved by using shades of gray in letters. This is somewhat counterintuitive because it seems that sharper definition would always be obtained by using just black and white. However, using grayscales, distinctions can be made between different fonts that would not otherwise be possible, and text generated this way is usually easier to read and causes less eyestrain than bilevel text on a display of similar resolution. This technique is called *antialiasing*.

The converse situation occurs when grayscale pictures are reproduced on a bilevel device—for example, as print in a newspaper. This involves a technique known as *halftoning*. Using traditional analog technology, the picture is projected through a mesh of regularly spaced holes called a *halftone screen*. This process, a kind of optical sieving, creates a grid pattern of different-sized dots, large ones to represent darker shades and small ones for lighter. The grid can easily be seen in newspapers. The most widely used screens have from 65 to 150 lines per inch—newsprint occupies the lower half of the range. Digital methods are available that perform a similar job, but most of these use rather different techniques, achieving the same effect by creating blocks of pixels whose dot density approximates the desired grayscale value in each local neighborhood. Whichever method is used, it is clear that halftoning trades off the ability to represent shades of gray against spatial resolution.

An important question when storing or transmitting images is whether exact or approximate reproduction is required. While the former would nearly always be preferred by users, it can exact a heavy price in the volume of information involved for little payoff in perceived image quality—in some cases, none at all. When images are compressed using the techniques described in this chapter, the amount of information stored is greatly reduced. But, particularly with grayscale or color images, it may be that the lower-order few bits of each pixel are really just generated by noise in the digitization process and are therefore effectively random. This means that they have no appreciable effect on image quality and also that they are incompressible since it is impossible to compress random data. Consequently, you may find that a significant fraction of the bandwidth needed to store or transmit the image is dedicated to conveying information that is completely irrelevant! Of course, this makes an overwhelming case for approximate rather than exact representation.

Finally, there is the question of how the image is built up at the receiving end. Pictures on a conventional TV or printer are drawn in raster order—left to right, top to bottom, across the screen or paper. But when transmission is slow, there are advantages to creating the image in a different way. For example, 10 percent of the way through a raster transmission, only the top tenth of the picture can be seen, and this is not usually very informative. It would generally be better to be able to see the whole picture at a tenth of the final resolution. Figure 6.1 shows an example of

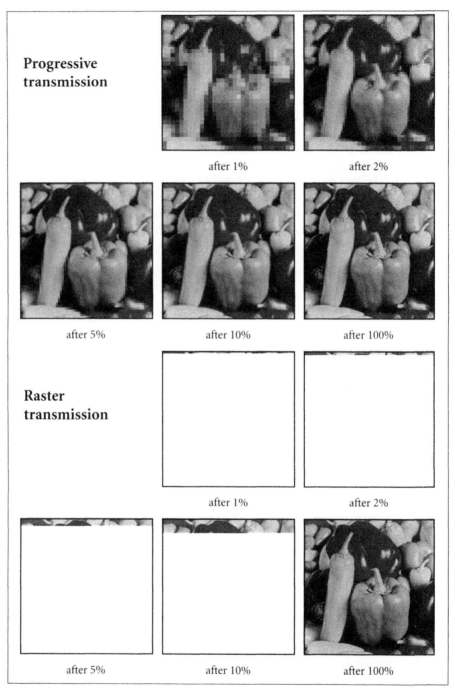

Figure 6.1 Progressive versus raster transmission. Reprinted by permission of the University of Southern California Image Processing Institute USC-IPI image database.

progressive transmission, which builds up gradually to the full resolution, contrasted with ordinary raster transmission. The full resolution in this case is rather greater than can be displayed by the halftoning process for this size of image, and the final picture is hardly distinguishable from the version created from only 10 percent of the information. Progressive transmission is also clearly advantageous in an interactive situation where you have an opportunity to stop transmission if the wrong picture appears or when browsing casually through many pictures. Even with no such opportunity to cancel transmission, it is much less frustrating to see an initial image that is progressively refined than it is to have it revealed, slowly and tantalizingly, line by line.

In this book we have chosen to concentrate primarily on exact reproduction of images that are predominantly textual, bilevel images, and grayscale pictures. However, you should be aware of other possibilities, such as color pictures, inexact (that is, lossy) reproduction, and progressive buildup, which are considered in Sections 6.5, 6.6, and 6.7, respectively.

6.2   The CCITT fax standard for bilevel images

Standards are very important in the communications business. We expect to be able to pick up the telephone and call people in other countries without encountering inconsistencies in voltage or signaling conventions. When you think about it—which we rarely do—this is quite amazing, especially given the differences in electricity supply voltage in different countries. When we buy a fax machine, we expect quite unthinkingly to be able to use it not just nationally but internationally, to distant countries, transcending barriers of language and culture—again a little surprising given differences in, for example, television encoding formats. Inconsistencies in the gauge of railways and the side of the road we drive on are inconvenient but tolerable in the transportation business, but such inconsistencies are unthinkable in communications. Indeed, the communications industry is driven by twin forces: technology and—even more importantly—standardization.

In the late 1970s, CCITT, the international communications standards body, recognized the potential of emerging technologies for fax transmission and sought a standard for fax. This was finalized in 1980 as the Group 3 standard and forms the basis of the fax machines that are in everyday use (Hunter and Robinson 1980). Because the standard incorporates simple data compression techniques, fax machines usually take up to a minute to transmit one page over a standard telephone circuit, depending on just what is being transmitted. This represents a worthwhile advance over the earlier Group 1 and 2 fax standards, which took about 6 and 3 minutes, respectively. In 1984 CCITT published the Group 4 standard, which is essentially the same as Group 3 but is intended for use on digital networks rather than conventional analog telephone circuits. The only real difference is that it dispenses with certain features that are designed to give robustness in the face of transmission errors, on the assumption that these are corrected by lower-level protocols. Because error correction and detection ability imply redundancy of representation, the omission of these gives rise to a more compact encoding and hence to faster transmission.

The CCITT standard begins by specifying details like paper size and scanning resolution. It is based on the international A4 paper-size standard rather than the U.S. norm of $8^{1}/_{2} \times 11$ inches. Resolution is specified as 1,728 pixels along a standard scanline length of 215 millimeters for an A4 page, which translates to 204 dpi horizontally. The standard vertical resolution is 3.85 lines per millimeter (98 dpi), but there is a high-resolution option that doubles the vertical resolution, giving 7.7 lines per millimeter. Thus, to a good approximation, the resolution is either 200×100 dpi (standard) or 200×200 dpi (high resolution). The Group 3 specification covers bilevel documents only, although Group 4 does include provision for optional grayscale and color images.

In summary, a one-page A4 document (about 210×300 millimeters) at standard resolution contains $1,728 \times 1,188$ black-and-white pixels, or 2.05 Mbits of information before compression. The transmission rate is normally 4,800 bits per second, which can be achieved comfortably over an ordinary telephone line. If no compression were used it would take 430 seconds, or about 7 minutes, to send the one-page document. This contrasts with an average time, for typical documents, of around 1 minute using the Group 3 standard.

The Group 3 standard specifies two coding methods: a one-dimensional scheme that treats each line independently and a two-dimensional one that exploits coherence between successive scanlines. Basically, the latter scheme identifies the positions along each line at which the image changes from black to white, or from white to black, and codes them relative to the corresponding positions on the previous line. To get things started, the one-dimensional scheme is used to transmit the first line.

Each scanline is regarded as a sequence of alternating black and white runs. Lines are assumed to begin with a white run so that the receiver can maintain black/white synchronization; ones that start with black are treated as though they begin with a zero-length white run. This is why codewords are needed (Figure 6.2) for runs of zero length. In the one-dimensional scheme, which is often called the *modified Huffman* method, a line is represented by coding the length of each run using a prespecified, nonadaptive Huffman code, as illustrated in Figure 6.2. Separate code tables are used for black and white runs because their statistical distribution is different—textual images are normally black on white, and black runs of a few pixels are much more common than white runs of the same length. Each code table can represent a run-length value up to 1,728 pixels, the maximum length of a scanline. To keep the table down to a reasonable size, codes are defined for run lengths from 0 to 63 and then for 64, 128, 192, . . . , 1,728; values of 64 or greater are coded with a two-part codeword in a manner similar to some of the encodings described in Section 3.3. The code tables were obtained by optimizing the codes for a particular set of test documents.

Coded lines are terminated by a special end-of-line codeword. This is a unique binary sequence that cannot occur in a valid line of coded data, and it has the effect of forcing codeword synchronization (see Section 2.7 for a discussion of how this can

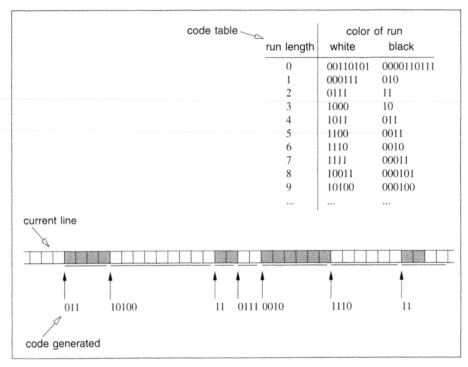

Figure 6.2 Example of one-dimensional coding.

be achieved). Even if transmission errors corrupt the scanline data, the end of the line will still be detected reliably. The worst that can happen is that the end-of-line codeword itself is corrupted, and in this case one whole scanline might be lost before synchronization is reestablished.

The two-dimensional code, sometimes called the READ (relative element address designate) code,[2] is a line-by-line scheme in which one row of pixels, the *current line*, is coded with respect to the previous, already-transmitted, row, the *reference line*. This first possibility is called *vertical mode*. The position of each color change (white to black or black to white) in the current line is coded with respect to a nearby change position (of the same color) on the reference line, if one exists. "Nearby" is taken to mean within three pixels, so the vertical-mode code can take on one of seven values: −3, −2, −1, 0, +1, +2, +3. If there is no nearby change position on the reference line, the second alternative is for the ordinary one-dimensional code—called *horizontal mode*—to be used. A third condition is when the reference line contains a run that has no counterpart in the current line, then a special *pass*

---

2   Strictly speaking, this is called the *modified READ* code. The original READ code was slightly different and more complex.

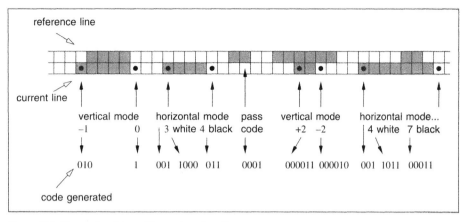

Figure 6.3 Example of two-dimensional coding.

code is sent to signal to the receiver that the next complete run of the opposite color in the reference line should be skipped.

Figure 6.3 shows an example of coding in which the second line of pixels—the current line—is transformed into the bitstream at the bottom. Black spots mark the changing pixels that are to be coded. Both end points of the first run of black pixels are coded in vertical mode because that run corresponds closely with one in the reference line above. In vertical mode, each offset is coded independently according to a predetermined scheme for the seven possible values. The beginning point of the second run of black pixels has no counterpart in the reference line, so it is coded in horizontal mode. Whereas vertical mode is used for coding individual change points, horizontal mode works with pairs of change points. Horizontal-mode codes have three parts: a flag indicating the mode, a value representing the length of the preceding white run, and another representing the length of the black run. These values are taken from the white-run and black-run code tables of the one-dimensional coding mode. The second run of black pixels in the reference line must be "passed" because it has no counterpart in the current line, so the pass code is emitted. Both end points of the next run are coded in vertical mode, and the final run is coded in horizontal mode. Note that because horizontal mode codes pairs of points, the final change point shown is coded in horizontal mode even though it is within the three-pixel range of vertical mode.

The two-dimensional coding scheme is more susceptible to errors than the one-dimensional method because any transmission error in a line will likely propagate all the way down the rest of the page. Consequently, some lines are transmitted using one-dimensional coding, and the two-dimensional code is used only for the remaining lines. The Group 3 standard provides for at least every kth line to be transmitted using the one-dimensional method, and k is set to 2 for the standard resolution. In this case, an error can destroy at most two consecutive lines. In high-resolution mode, k is set to 4, so that greater compression can be achieved. Errors

Table 6.2 Typical compression for the CCITT fax standard.

Resolution	Low (200 × 100 dpi)		High (200 × 200 dpi)	
Scheme	Group 3 1-D ($k = 1$)	Group 3 2-D ($k = 2$)	Group 3 2-D ($k = 4$)	Group 4 ($k = \infty$)
Compression	13%	11%	9%	7%
Bits per pixel	0.13	0.11	0.09	0.07
Seconds (4,800 bits per second)	57	47	74	61

can then destroy as many as four lines, but this corresponds to only two lines at standard resolution.

The one-dimensional scheme achieves a transmission time of around 57 seconds, averaged over a set of typical fax documents, at ordinary resolution over a 4,800 bits per second line. This corresponds to compression to about 13 percent of the original size. The two-dimensional scheme with $k = 2$ reduces the time to about 47 seconds for ordinary resolution (compression to 11 percent); in high-resolution mode with $k = 4$, it takes around 74 seconds (compression to around 9 percent of the original size, the original image being twice as large as it is in ordinary-resolution mode). These results are summarized in the first three columns of figures in Table 6.2.

The compression improvement of Group 3 two-dimensional coding is limited by the fact that every kth line is transmitted using one-dimensional coding, to localize the effect of transmission errors. In digital transmission systems where errors are detected and corrected at a lower level of protocol, this is unnecessary: the two-dimensional scheme can be used for every line on the page, assuming an all-white reference line at the beginning to get things off the ground. This is the Group 4 fax standard.[3] As shown in the final column of Table 6.2, it reduces transmission time to about 61 seconds per page in high-resolution mode (about the same as Group 3 with ordinary resolution), with a corresponding compression of about 7 percent.

Unfortunately, all these compression results are highly dependent on the particular test images used. Even different scanners operating at the same resolution and scanning the same documents can give images that admit significantly different amounts of compression. Indeed, widely differing results have been reported in the literature for what are ostensibly the same algorithms working on the same suite of test images (Pratt et al. 1980; Yasuda et al. 1985; Bodson et al. 1985). However, the results shown in Table 6.2 do capture the relative performances of the methods.

---

3 It is also called the *modified modified READ* coder, or MMR.

6.3 Context-based compression of bilevel images

Although the CCITT fax standard provides reasonable compression of many bilevel images, it is possible to do significantly better using a context-based prediction method coupled with arithmetic coding, in much the same way as was described in Chapter 2 for text compression. To provide a feeling for the amount of compression that might be attainable, consider first the results produced by six simple compression methods:

1. An ad hoc byte-based run-length coding scheme, which replaces multiple occurrences of the same byte-aligned eight-bit pattern within the raster image by an escape byte, a repeat-count byte, and one instance of the byte to be repeated. Although it performs poorly in comparison with most of the other methods, this ad hoc compression scheme is supplied by at least one manufacturer of image processing systems.

2. A bit-based run-length encoder with a static model, which is just a slightly modified version of the one-dimensional scheme described in the previous section that forms part of the Group 3 fax standard.

3. A bit-based run-length encoder with an adaptive model, which is similar to the previous method but uses adaptive arithmetic coding rather than fixed codes to transmit the run lengths.

4. A standard text compression tool, the PPMC program described on page 63 in Section 2.5, using raster order. Although designed for text rather than images, PPMC can be applied to any data stored as a string of bytes. Since binary images are usually stored in raster order, the application of PPMC to a file holding an image yields a compression regime in which between 24 and 31 pixels are used to predict the value of the next, if three bytes of prior context are used to predict the next byte (eight bits). The pixels used for predictions are taken only from the same scanline as the predicted pixel.

5. The PPMC program again but using column order, which is the same as the method above except that the image is processed as a two-dimensional array of eight-bit bytes in column order—that is, working with eight-bit-wide vertical stripes of the image.

6. A two-dimensional READ encoder implementing the Group 4 fax standard but adjusted to deal with images of arbitrary size. (Strictly speaking, this should be called a "modified modified modified" READ coder!)

In order to compare the six methods, their performance has been measured on a commonly used test suite of eight images created by the CCITT standards organization to provide a standard for the comparison of fax encoding schemes (see Hunter and Robinson 1980 for details of the images). Figure 6.4 shows the average compression obtained on these images. The compression factors are expressed as the ratio of the total of the original file sizes to the total size of the compressed files, so the larger the number, the better the compression. Values less than 1.0 indicate

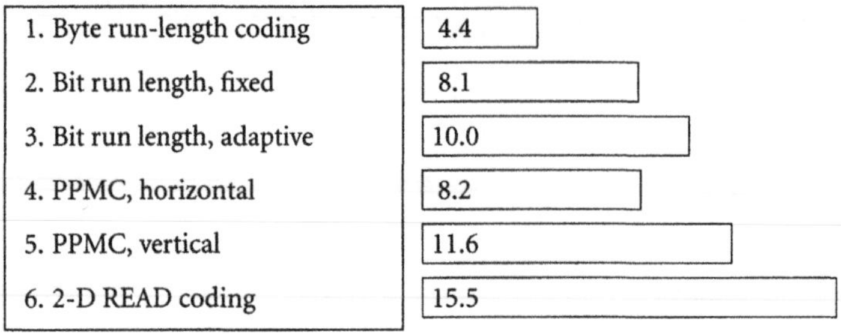

1. Byte run-length coding	4.4
2. Bit run length, fixed	8.1
3. Bit run length, adaptive	10.0
4. PPMC, horizontal	8.2
5. PPMC, vertical	11.6
6. 2-D READ coding	15.5

Figure 6.4 Compression factors on the CCITT test images.

expansion, not compression. The compression factors vary greatly over the images; for example, the 2-D READ coding method (method 6) ranges from a low of 7 on one image to a high of 48 on another.

It is worth noting that the amount of compression obtained depends strongly on the kind of images that are used. The images in the CCITT test suite contain fairly large areas of white (or, in one case, black), which means that excellent compression is achieved. They contain text, tables, and line drawings rather than halftone pictures. In order to provide a second, more demanding, test, another suite was assembled containing 79 bilevel images that were digitized from a range of drawings and photographs and chosen to be representative of what might appear, for example, in the nontextual parts of an electronic newspaper. Image sizes ranged from 323×252 to $1,152 \times 900$ pixels, and the images averaged about 400,000 pixels each. One of the more complex ones is the image of the cheetah shown in Figure 6.5.

The performance of the same six methods on these images is shown in Figure 6.6. The compression factors are substantially smaller than those of Figure 6.4, and an enlarged horizontal scale has been used for the bars. In fact, it can be seen that the two-dimensional READ coding, far from compressing, actually expands the images by a factor of two, on average. It is certainly not unknown for "compression" schemes to end up expanding instead of contracting; however, most actual implementations would automatically catch this behavior and switch compression off when it turns out to be ineffective. In this case, the poor performance is because the READ scheme is designed for textual rather than halftone images, and the Huffman codes that it uses are static and optimized for a particular type of image—underlining the advantages of adaptive over static compression that were mentioned in Section 2.2 in the context of text compression.

For each method there is again a wide variation in the individual compression factors attained on the test files. Typically, even the best methods gave a compression factor of only slightly over 1 for the very complex cheetah image, and compression factors ranged up to 30 or more for a test file—a picture of stars—that was almost entirely black. The factors shown in Figure 6.6 represent a realistic overall measure and generally capture the relative performance of the six methods on nontextual bilevel pictures.

Figure 6.5   One of the test images.

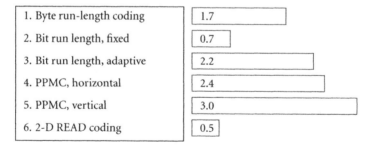

Figure 6.6   Compression factors on a test suite of pictures.

Context models

The two PPMC methods used in the experiments summarized in Figures 6.4 and 6.6 use context models to predict upcoming pixels. As explained in Chapter 2, context models of text condition the probability distribution of the upcoming character using the previous few characters. For each context that occurs, both encoder and decoder maintain a next-character probability distribution. The actual next character

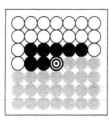

Figure 6.7 Seven-pixel context for image compression.

can be coded with respect to this distribution using arithmetic coding and recovered without error by the decoder since it has access to exactly the same distribution.

This works for bilevel pictures too. The probability distribution of a pixel being black or white is dependent on which of the preceding pixels are black and which are white. In text, which is essentially one-dimensional in nature, it is also clear that the best letters on which to condition the distribution are the directly preceding ones. On the other hand, for two-dimensional pictures we must decide whether to use the pixels above the current one or to the left of it—or, more likely, both.

One attractive plan is to use as context a template of pixels surrounding the current one but preceding it in raster transmission order. Experiments have shown that a good template is the seven-pixel one in Figure 6.7 (Langdon and Rissanen 1981). A black dot marks each pixel included in the template, and a bull's-eye marks the position of the pixel about to be coded. The gray pixels are ones whose values are not yet known by the decoder so they cannot be included in the context, and the open circles indicate pixels whose values are known but that are not included in the context.

The seven pixels in the template give, at most, 128 different contexts. The number of occurrences of a white pixel and a black pixel in each context are recorded—256 counts in all. Then, during coding, the pixels in the template are used as the context to determine which pair of counts to use, implemented by concatenating the seven bits together to form a context number and using the resultant number between 0 and 127 to index the list of occurrence counts. The counts are used to drive an arithmetic coder as described in Section 2.4. Note that this is one application in which arithmetic coding really is required—no Huffman or other prefix-free code can represent the symbols of a binary alphabet in fewer than one bit per symbol, and blocking to make runs and thereby enlarge the alphabet (as is done by the Golomb code of Section 3.3) is not effective because the probability of a 1 is almost certainly different in every context.

Sixteen bits is sufficient to store the counts since nothing is gained by making them more precise, and a pair of counts can be halved whenever one of the two threatens to exceed $2^{16} - 1$. On the other hand, eight bits may be insufficient, for much of the image is often white, and performance can be degraded quite noticeably if the maximum probability that can be represented is 255/256. The counts can be predetermined based on an analysis of representative images or computed individually for each image and transmitted to the decoder before coding begins. Alternatively, they can be accumulated adaptively and transmitted implicitly, as described in Section 2.2. Under the adaptive scheme, each pixel is coded according to the current set of counts and then used by both encoder and decoder to update the appropriate count. This raises the zero-frequency problem: how to code a pixel in a context in which it has never occurred before. The simplest solution is to start all counts at one instead of zero and to round up when halving.

Figure 6.8 shows the results achieved using adaptive coding with templates of different sizes on the same set of 79 test images as was used for the results of Figure 6.6. (Ignore the segments to the right of the lower bars for now.) For each size, the template shown is the shape that yields the best overall compression for the test suite. Using templates with seven or more pixels, this method outperforms all those shown in Figure 6.6.

Two-level context models

The trade-off between the compression accuracy attained and the "learning" cost of using a large model can be clearly seen in Figure 6.8. For models based on templates of fewer than about 12 pixels, the learning cost is small, so compression improves if the template is enlarged. With 12-pixel templates there are 8,192 counts—two for each possible template—and with an average of 400,000 pixels in each test image, there is a good chance that most different contexts will occur reasonably often—often enough to make a good model. On the other hand, when more pixels are used in the template, the model does not converge to a useful state within the number of pixels being encoded, so compression degrades as the template grows.

The learning cost of a large model can be quantified by determining the improvement in compression when the final values of the counts are used as a static model to compress the same image on a second pass. This measures the "self-entropy" of the image according to that template. It is not a physically possible compression method because it does not take into account the information needed to specify the set of counts, which is very large—16 Mbytes for 16-bit counts and a 22-bit template. Rather, it indicates the maximum compression that can be obtained when using that particular template. The incremental improvement is shown in the right-hand bars in Figure 6.8 for the templates with 12 or more bits. It is miniscule for the smaller templates.

The 18- and 22-bit templates offer a very detailed context in which the next bit can be predicted, but each of these large contexts needs to be initialized before it can be relied on, and this is why compression with these templates is actually worse than it is with the smaller 12- and 14-bit models. A two-level coding scheme enables the counts for a large template to be learned without paying a high learning cost (Moffat 1991). This is done by coding each pixel in the full context only if that context has already been observed a certain number of times before. If, because of insufficient prior occurrences, the full context is not regarded to be a reliable predictor, a subset is used to generate a smaller template. Figure 6.9 shows the compression that can be achieved with suitable two-level templates. The pixels used for the subordinate

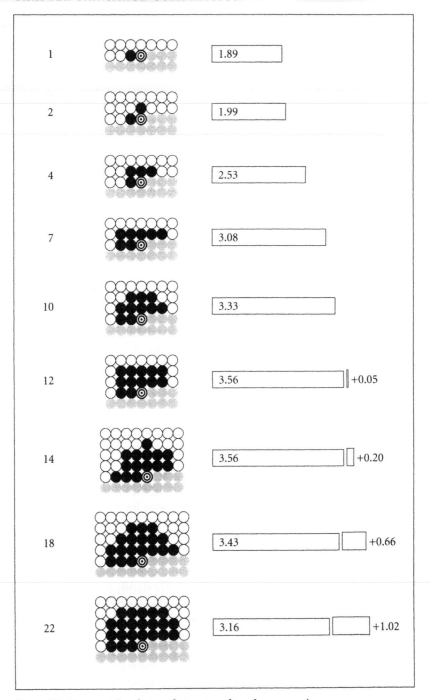

Figure 6.8 Compression factors for context-based compression.

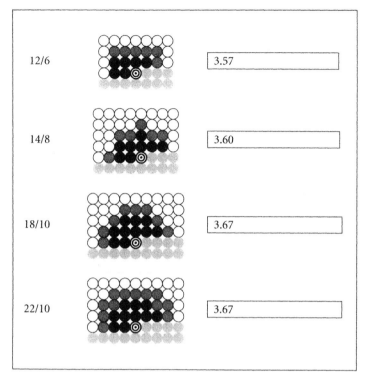

12/6   3.57

14/8   3.60

18/10   3.67

22/10   3.67

Figure 6.9 Compression factors for two-level compression.

context are black, and the extra pixels for the larger context are gray with dark borders. Again, the templates shown are those that give the best results out of a wide range of templates that were tested.

Small improvements were obtained by two-level coding for the 12- and 14-pixel templates, but the overall compression was still only a little better than that given by the corresponding one-level templates in Figure 6.8. More marked improvement was obtained with the 18- and 22-pixel templates. All of these "better" methods give virtually identical compression behavior on this test suite, and the large relative improvement achieved for the 18- and 22-pixel templates served only to make them as efficient as the model using smaller templates, for which smaller relative gains were achieved.

"Clairvoyant" compression

To gauge whether some other technique might improve on the context-based method, consider a hypothetical "absolute best" compression scheme. Imagine that contexts can include pixels from the "future" as well as from the "past." Such a scheme is impossible, but it does provide another way to estimate a bound on compressibility. We call these templates *clairvoyant*: by making use of more information than any real compression scheme can possibly have access to, they indicate

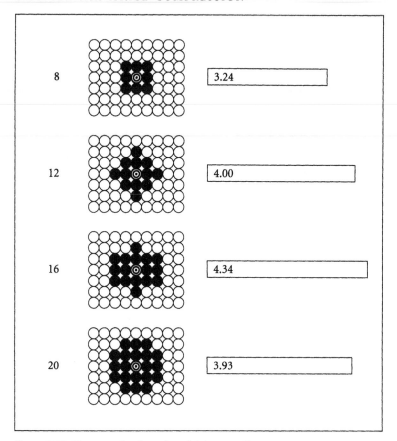

Figure 6.10 Compression based on "clairvoyant" contexts.

an upper bound on the compression that can be achieved by any actual algorithm. Figure 6.10 shows a number of clairvoyant templates and the corresponding compression results. For each template, the value given reflects the adaptive compression that would result if that template could be used, and it may be compared with the values in Figure 6.8.

The corresponding self-entropy figures are correspondingly larger: 4.97 and 5.27 for the 16- and 20-pixel templates, respectively. It is difficult to contemplate any legitimate compression scheme that has more information available to it than knowledge of all of the neighbors of each pixel that is to be coded together with the actual occurrence counts for each of those contexts. Consequently, these values can be viewed as a model-independent upper bound on the compression that might be obtained by any lossless image compression scheme.[4]

---

4 Implicit in this argument is the assumption that the image is statistically stationary. If the pixel statistics change over the image, then actual global occurrence counts may not perform as well as localized estimates.

For the test suite considered, the one-level templates with 12 or 14 bits (Figure 6.8), and the two-level templates with 12 or more bits (Figure 6.9), achieve within about 30 percent of this upper bound, which is certainly an impressive performance. Indeed, for this test suite of images it is questionable whether it is worthwhile in practice to go to the larger two-level templates at all because they only offer about 3 percent extra compression. However, on other test suites the situation is different. For example, on the CCITT test images, the larger two-level templates give nearly 10 percent more compression than the 12-bit one-level one. And the two-level models are robust: their performance does not degenerate as the template size grows beyond the optimum. Consequently, two-level modeling with the larger template sizes is the preferred method if the best compression performance is sought.

Before leaving the topic of clairvoyant compression, it is worth remarking that although the name sounds like a joke, the idea has proved to be strangely suggestive. We will meet it again in the next chapter: in Section 7.4 it is used in a powerful kind of template matching, and in Section 7.6 on page 342 it plays a key role in textual image compression.

6.4   JBIG: A standard for bilevel images

Context modeling forms the basis of the JBIG international standard for lossless compression of images (CCITT 1993). The standard is designed for bilevel images, although it can also be used for grayscale images with a small number of bits per pixel, by compressing each bitplane separately.[5] Once the resolution exceeds about six bits per pixel, however, more effective compression can be obtained using algorithms designed expressly for the task.

The compression method can be applied to the full image, or it can be used in a progressive mode, giving an approximate version first whose fidelity is improved over time. This is achieved by starting with a low-resolution image and then successively doubling the resolution. The starting image is called the *base layer*, and the others are called *differential layers*. The user can choose the base resolution and the number of differential layers that occur before the final layer is reached. It is anticipated that the coarsest base resolution used in practice will be either 12.5 or 25 dpi, which gives an image whose page layout is discernable but whose details are illegible. Setting the base resolution to be the same as the final one, and specifying that there are no differential layers, achieves an ordinary nonprogressive, or *sequential*, transmission.

One drawback of progressive compression is that it makes greater demands on the decoder's memory space than normal sequential transmission. The decoder

---

5 Better performance is achieved by encoding pixel values using so-called Gray codes before dividing the image into individual bitplanes. These codes, which are named after their inventor, F. Gray, have the property that consecutive numeric values are represented by codes that differ in just one bit position.

needs a buffer in which it can store the previous resolution level while it is decoding the next one. In order to reduce the amount of memory required, there is a provision in the standard to divide the image into stripes, each one being a horizontal bar with a user-definable height. Stripes are coded and transmitted separately, and the user can specify the order in which stripes, resolutions, and bitplanes are intermixed in the coded data.

The JBIG method is essentially a context-based encoder as described in the previous section, adapted to incorporate progressive transmission. At the lowest level, coding is based on a template model, and adaptive arithmetic coding is used to encode the predictions. Because only one-bit quantities (pixel values) are being encoded, the arithmetic coding process can be streamlined by using a reduced-precision implementation that does not involve multiplication. The JBIG2 standard includes a method specifically designed for textual images, which are the subject of the next chapter.

Resolution reduction

One of the most interesting features of the JBIG standard is the method that it suggests for computing lower-resolution images (Yoshida et al. 1992). The obvious way to halve the resolution of an image is to group the pixels into 2×2 blocks and average the four grayscale values in each block. Unfortunately, with bilevel pictures it is not clear what to do when two of the pixels are 1s and the other two are 0s. Consistently rounding up or down tends to wash out the image very quickly. Another possibility is to round the value in a random direction each time, but this adds considerable noise to the image, particularly at the lower resolutions.

Figure 6.11a illustrates the problem. The three images shown were obtained by reducing an original image (not shown) by successive factors of two, using random rounding. The original image was digitized at 150 dpi. Clearly, the overall tone of the image is quickly lost, and the third version, which is about 20 dpi, gives little information about the layout of the page.

A better image can be produced by using a more complex rule for aggregating pixels. Figure 6.12a shows a portion of the high- and low-resolution image, where for each square group of four pixels, the corresponding pixel at the next lower resolution is drawn as a circle. Figure 6.12b illustrates the pixels that participate in the resolution reduction. The value of the target pixel—marked by a bull's-eye—is calculated as a linear function of the pixels shown in black. Each of these is weighted in the sum by the weights shown in Figure 6.12c. The basic pattern of weights appears in the square pixels. Of the participating pixels, the central one is weighted most heavily at 4, the ones horizontally and vertically adjacent to it are weighted by 2, and the ones diagonally adjacent have weights of 1. The already-committed pixels at the lower resolution—the round ones—participate in the sum with negative weights that exactly offset the corresponding positive weights. This means that if the already-committed areas are each either uniformly white or uniformly black, they do not affect the assignment of the new pixel. If black and white are equally likely

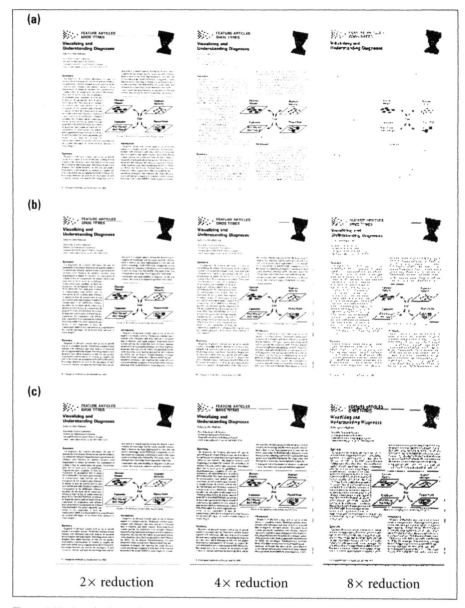

Figure 6.11 Resolution reduction using three different methods: (a) simple resolution reduction; (b) resolution reduction without exceptions; (c) full resolution reduction, including exceptions. Reprinted by permission of *Canadian Artificial Intelligence*.

and the pixels are statistically independent, the expected value of the bull's-eye pixel is 4.5. It is chosen to be black if the value is 5 or more and white if it is 4 or less.

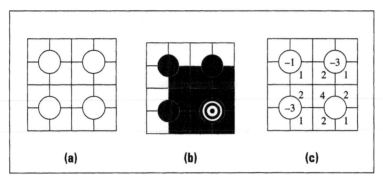

Figure 6.12 Pixels and pixel weights for resolution reduction: (a) two grid resolutions; (b) participating pixels; (c) pixel weights.

This method preserves the overall grayness of the image. It was used to produce the three images of Figure 6.11b, and it is clear that the overall tone is preserved much more faithfully than in Figure 6.11a. The layout of the page is still apparent even at the lowest resolution. However, problems occur with lines and edges because these deteriorate rapidly. For example, even in the first image of Figure 6.11b, the lines around the figure are beginning to disappear, and a line at the bottom of the page has disappeared completely. At the lowest resolution most lines have gone.

To address this problem, a number of exception patterns can be defined that, when they are encountered, reverse the polarity of the pixel that is obtained from thresholding the weighted sum as described above. The resolution reduction method in the JBIG standard defines four ancillary tables that specify the exception patterns, each in the form of a 12-bit number defining a particular configuration of the 12 participating pixels of Figure 6.12b. The edge preservation table has 132 such patterns, the line preservation table has 420, and the periodic pattern preservation and dither pattern preservation tables have 10 and 12 patterns, respectively. The last two are designed to preserve certain shading patterns and patterns arising from halftoning.

To convey the spirit of these exceptions, Figure 6.13 shows three sets of patterns. The first is aimed at preserving single-pixel horizontal lines. If the pixels marked 0 are white and those marked 1 are black, then the linear sum would assign white to the target pixel; however, because this pattern is stored as an exception, black is assigned to the target instead. The pattern applies regardless of the values of the three shaded pixels; thus, it covers eight cases. Moreover, the symmetric pattern obtained from reflection about the main diagonal is also defined as an exception, in this case aimed at preserving single-pixel vertical lines. Consequently, Figure 6.13a accounts for $8 \times 2 = 16$ of the 132 line preservation patterns. Finally, the pattern also applies when the pixels marked 0 are black and those marked 1 are white, in which case the exception causes the target pixel to be white.

The pattern in Figure 6.13b is aimed at preserving slightly thicker horizontal or near-horizontal lines. Again, it overrides the linear sum's assignment of 0 to the

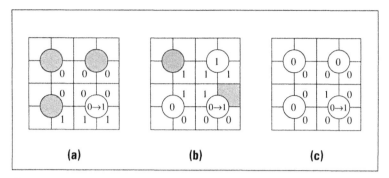

Figure 6.13 Some exception patterns for resolution reduction: (a) one-pixel lines; (b) two-pixel lines; (c) isolated pixel.

target pixel and assigns it 1 instead. For example, a two-pixel-wide black horizontal line will result in a line at the next lower resolution whose width alternates between one and two pixels. The upper row of black (1) pixels will all be preserved by the pattern in Figure 6.13a, and when processing the next scanline, the pattern in Figure 6.13b will cause pixels in the lower row to alternate, because it does not override the value of a pixel unless the previous pixel at the lower resolution (the bottom left circle in Figure 6.13b) is white (0). Again, the pattern applies to the symmetric configuration, with a vertical rather than a horizontal line. Thus it covers a further $4 \times 2 = 8$ of the 132 line preservation patterns.

Figure 6.13c is aimed at preserving isolated pixels of the kind that may be produced when a grayscale picture is converted to a black-white halftone one by the standard dithering process, which represents a gray region by a corresponding density of black pixels. It accounts for just 1 of the 12 dither preservation patterns and applies to an isolated black pixel on a white background and vice versa.

Figure 6.11c shows the effect of the exceptions. The rendition is considerably improved over Figure 6.11b, and in particular the lines—even the diagonal ones around the boxes in the figure—are preserved quite faithfully.

The complete JBIG resolution reduction algorithm is remarkably simple to implement. The result of the thresholded linear sum can be represented as a table of 4,096 bits, one for each possible configuration of the 12 dark pixels of Figure 6.12b. And of course, the exceptions can be readily incorporated into the same table simply by reversing the sense of the bits defined by the exception patterns. The result is a simple table lookup procedure that implements resolution reduction very effectively. The algorithm is identical for all resolution layers and all bitplanes. Use of this algorithm is not mandatory, however: the JBIG standard is constructed in such a way that alternative resolution reduction methods can be incorporated if desired.

When an image's resolution is reduced by a particular reduction algorithm, it sometimes happens that the receiver can determine a pixel's value unambiguously from pixels that have been received previously. When this occurs, the pixel is said to be "deterministically predictable." An algorithm can be designed that spots such

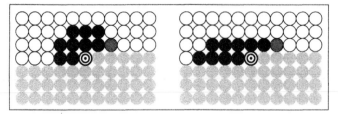

Figure 6.14 The base-layer templates in the JBIG standard.

pixels and assigns them their value without needing anything to be transmitted. This improves compression by around 7 percent.

Templates and adaptive templates

The JBIG standard defines two kinds of contexts: one for the base, or lowest, resolution layer and the other for the differential, or higher, resolution layers. Figure 6.14 shows the templates that can be used for coding the base layer, which, as noted at the beginning of this section, is often either 12.5 or 25 dpi in practical applications. There are two options depending on whether the context is to be taken from one or two preceding lines of pixels, and both involve 10 pixels. The encoder can specify which option is being used. Not surprisingly, one of them is the 10-bit template of Figure 6.8.

The single dark-gray pixel in each template of Figure 6.14 has a special status. Known as an *adaptive pixel*, it is allowed to change position during the course of processing an image. Figure 6.14 shows its default position, but at any time the encoder can specify that a different pixel is to be used instead. The intention of the adaptive pixel is to improve compression efficiency on images containing halftones, which have a regular grid structure that is usually much larger than the template size. By setting the adaptive pixel to the previous position in the halftone grid, significantly more effective contexts can be obtained for coding.

As well as pixels in the layer being coded, differential-layer templates contain pixels in corresponding positions in the lower-resolution layer. Progressive transmission works in the direction opposite to resolution reduction because lower-resolution layers are known when higher ones are being transmitted; with resolution reduction, higher layers are known, and lower ones are computed from them. Four templates are used for progressive transmission, depending on the phase of the pixel being coded, as shown in Figure 6.15. In each case, the template includes four pixels of the lower-resolution layer, marked by black circles, and six pixels of the current layer, five of which are marked by black squares and the sixth by a dark-gray square. In Figure 6.15, as in Figure 6.14, pixels whose values are not yet known are lightly shaded and have no outlines. There are 10 pixels in these templates and four phases; thus, $2^{12} = 4,096$ different contexts are maintained by the encoder and decoder.

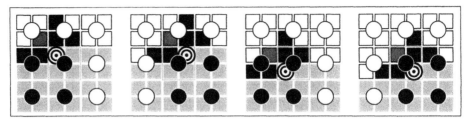

Figure 6.15 The differential-layer templates in the JBIG standard.

The dark-gray pixel in each part of Figure 6.15 is an "adaptive" pixel. Like the adaptive pixel in the base-layer templates, its position is allowed to change as the image is processed. Figure 6.15 shows its default position.

Coding and probability estimation

According to the earlier description of template models, for each of the 4,096 contexts, two associated counts should be stored—one for black target pixels and the other for white ones. However, JBIG does not represent the counts explicitly but buries them inside the arithmetic coding process itself, principally to make the implementation more efficient.

Recall from Section 2.4 that arithmetic coding works by maintaining an interval, defined by two numbers *low* and *high*, which represents the input that has been processed so far (modulo any bits of output that have been generated). Instead of upper and lower bounds to the probability interval, the JBIG arithmetic coder keeps a lower bound, called the *interval base*, and an *interval size*. The interval size is kept within an allowed range by renormalizing it, doubling it every time it falls below a particular value so that it remains the same size to within a factor of two. At each renormalization, the encoder generates one bit of compressed output.

In binary arithmetic coding, suppose one of the symbols has probability p and the other has probability $1 - p$. When the first symbol is coded, the interval size is reduced by a factor of p, and the interval base remains the same. When the second symbol is coded, the interval size is reduced by a factor of $1 - p$, and the interval base is increased so that the upper bound of the interval remains the same. JBIG keeps track of which is the *more probable symbol* (that is, the most probable pixel value, black or white), abbreviated MPS, and the *less probable symbol*, or LPS; p is the probability of the LPS and, if it were to exceed one-half, the MPS and LPS would be swapped.

Whichever symbol is coded, altering the interval size involves a multiplication. The JBIG coder avoids this by capitalizing on the fact that the interval size is maintained approximately constant. If the interval were to stay exactly constant, the multiplication would be unnecessary and could be avoided by suitable scaling. The JBIG coder omits the multiplication anyway and accepts the element of approximation that this introduces. It arranges scaling so that the interval size is between 0.75 and

1.5, keeping it centered around 1.0 so that the arithmetic approximation incurred by omitting the multiplication is reasonably good.

For each context, the coder uses one bit to keep track of which symbol (black or white) is the MPS and which is the LPS and seven bits to index a table of quantized LPS probabilities. Together with the interval base and size, these are the parameters used in the coding operation. No counts are stored.

The template models described on page 275 in Section 6.3 update the probability estimate—that is, the counts—as each symbol is encoded; in other words, for every bit of *input*. However, JBIG updates the LPS probability estimate only when renormalization occurs—that is, for every bit of *output*. The update is performed by using the quantized LPS probability to index into one of two tables, one for when the renormalization is triggered by the coding of the MPS and the other for when it is triggered by the LPS. On average, update occurs far less frequently than once every coding cycle, particularly when good compression is being achieved.

Pixel statistics often alter from one region of an image to another, and the design of the JBIG probability estimation mechanism ensures that changing probabilities can be tracked at an appropriate rate. This rate is controlled by the amount of precision in the LPS probability, which in turn governs the size of the tables. The lower the precision, the more quickly the estimator responds to a change of probability. Conversely, the greater the precision, the better the code performs if the statistics are stationary. Thus, there is a trade-off between response in nonstationary situations and coding efficiency in stationary ones.

The advantage of this coding and probability estimation technique is that it is very fast. No multiplication is involved in the arithmetic coding. The estimation is invoked only when renormalization is needed—that is, when a compressed bit is being generated—and even then, it is table driven and requires only an index and memory access. And, despite the approximations involved, little coding efficiency is lost. Full details of the methods of probability estimation and arithmetic coding in JBIG can be found in the descriptions given by Pennebaker et al. (1988) and Pennebaker and Mitchell (1988).

6.5   Lossless compression of continuous-tone images

Continuous-tone images are often compressed in a *lossy* manner, where the original image cannot be recovered exactly from the compressed version. Lossy techniques can be used to obtain remarkably compact representations—well under a bit for each eight-bit pixel. However, there are also many situations in which exact representation is considered to be essential and lossless compression must be used. These include image data that must be certified for medical or legal reasons and data such as remotely sensed images for which the final use is yet unknown and for which regenerating an approximation may be inadequate. In the case of satellite imagery there is also a matter of cost—it is far less expensive to store such images than to create them in the first place, and lossy compression might well be a false economy. Archival storage of images of historical documents may also require lossless compression: again, the needs of future scholars cannot be anticipated. For these reasons we examine five methods for the lossless compression of grayscale images in this section before proceeding to lossy compression in Section 6.6.

We consider first the standard lossless methods that are in widespread use today: the popular GIF format and the more recent PNG method that is gradually superseding it. Both are based on Ziv-Lempel coding of a sequence of pixel values. Techniques that take into account the two-dimensional context of the image give much better results, and the third method described is FELICS, developed specifically for lossless compression of grayscale pictures. Then we outline CALIC, a much more elaborate method that represents the current state of the art in lossless compression performance of continuous-tone images. The final mechanism described is the new JPEG standard for lossless compression, called "JPEG-Lossless." As noted earlier, lossy methods for continuous-tone images are discussed in Section 6.6.

The GIF and PNG lossless image formats

Probably the most widely used lossless image compression format prior to 1995 was GIF, the Graphics Interchange Format (pronounced "jiff"). This was adopted by CompuServe in 1987 in order to minimize the time required to download pictures over modem links; it was intended as an exchange medium for graphic images that could be displayed on a variety of graphics hardware platforms.

GIF applies to images in which each pixel is represented by eight bits or less. The code for a pixel is an index into a table that specifies a color map for the entire image. Thus with eight-bit pixel descriptors, there are 256 possible colors for every pixel in the image. However, the color map may itself contain colors chosen from a far larger palette. The GIF format allows the color map to be specified along with each image, or for a group of images to share the same color map, or for the color map to be omitted entirely. If it is included, it forms a prefix to the image file and may specify up to 256 color table entries each of 24 bits—8 bits for each of the three primary colors red, green, and blue. The color table is uncompressed.

The compression scheme used for the sequence of pixel values is not tailored for images at all: it is the LZW scheme that is designed for text compression. Recall from Section 2.6 that LZW is a variant of LZ78, the dictionary-based Ziv-Lempel compression method, that initializes the dictionary to contain the alphabet and then parses off successive phrases from the input string, each phrase being one that is found in the dictionary, at each stage adding to the dictionary the phrase augmented by one additional character.

Suppose we are working with eight-bit pixel descriptors. Then the GIF encoding scheme initializes the dictionary with the 256 possible pixel codes—though this is only notional; it is not necessary to actually load the dictionary with these values— and two extra codes, a "clear" code and an "end-of-information" code, and proceeds to LZW-encode the sequence of pixel values in raster scan order.

One additional feature is included to make it easy to skip quickly over a particular image in an image file—for one file may contain several images. The LZW-coded information is grouped into blocks of up to 255 bytes, each preceded by a byte count. This means that an image can be skipped over without actually being decompressed.

At the beginning of 1995 Unisys announced that royalties would be levied on programs implementing GIF because of a long-standing patent they held on the LZW compression scheme that lies at the core of the method. This caused widespread dismay because GIF was at that time the primary means of storing images on the World Wide Web, and it catalyzed the development of a new lossless image format, PNG, for Portable Network Graphics (pronounced "ping"), designed specifically for the public domain, which is steadily replacing GIF in practical applications.

Like GIF, PNG generates a sequence of pixel values and compresses the sequence using a general-purpose Ziv-Lempel compression scheme. It yields somewhat better compression because rather than LZW it uses the *gzip* compression scheme described on page 78 in Section 2.6; in practice the improvement in compression ranges from 10 to 30 percent.

The PNG standard incorporates an optional element of context-based compression by allowing the encoder to specify one of a small number of "filters" that are applied to the pixel values before compression. The default is to compress the pixels in raster scan order. However, alternative filters allow some context to be taken into account. For example, the *horizontal difference* filter subtracts the previous pixel value from the current one, so that it is pixel differences that are encoded.[6] Alternatively, the *vertical difference* filter subtracts the pixel value from the corresponding one above, the *average difference* filter subtracts it from the average of the one above and the one to the right, and a further filter performs a slightly more complex operation that involves a nonlinear function of the three neighboring pixel values. The PNG standard recommends that encoders optimize the filter for each scanline by trying all possibilities and using a heuristic criterion to select the best, choosing a different filter for each scanline.

PNG incorporates several other important practical improvements over GIF. Pixels are not restricted to 256 possible colors: they can include up to 16 bits of grayscale or up to 48 bits of full color information, as well as being drawn from a 256-color palette. Whereas GIF specifies one special pixel value to indicate transparency, so that an image can assume the background color underneath it, PNG allows 256 possible transparency values, again on a per-pixel basis, so that (for example) a picture can fade gradually into the background. Images can be stored in interlaced order, which gives a crude form of progressive display (see Section 6.7). PNG also incorporates a facility for correcting for differences in how computer monitors interpret color values via a "gamma correction" feature. It seems inevitable that PNG will gradually take over from GIF as the standard lossless image format for the World Wide Web.

---

6 In fact, the difference operation is applied to individual bytes rather than to pixel values. Each pixel may be represented by more than one byte, in which case the difference is taken between corresponding bytes. Bytewise operation applies to all the filtering operations.

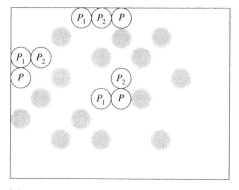

(a)

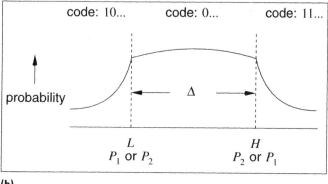

(b)

Figure 6.16 How a pixel's coding region depends on its two neighbors: (a) defining a pixel's neighbors; (b) the three coding regions.

FELICS: Fast, efficient, lossless image compression system

The third of the five lossless image compression methods we consider is FELICS, a simple and effective technique for grayscale images. The idea is to code each pixel based on two of its neighbors and use a specially tailored scheme to represent its value. FELICS substantially outperforms methods like GIF and PNG and on many images performs almost as well as the best-known methods for lossless image compression. However, it does not work well for highly compressible images and, in particular, can never compress to less than one bit per pixel, no matter how redundant the image. More recent lossless compression techniques incorporate a run-length coding mode so that images with long runs of the same grayscale value (for example, white) are coded effectively; this is particularly important for images containing text.

When a picture is transmitted in ordinary raster scan order, each pixel has two nearest neighbors whose values are known, as shown in Figure 6.16a. For interior pixels, these are the one above and the one to the left. For pixels on the top row, they are the two preceding ones. And for pixels on the left-hand side of the image, they are the first two pixels of the preceding line (an equally good alternative would be to use the first pixels of the two preceding lines instead). The only pixels not handled by these rules are the very first two in the image, and these can be encoded using the standard binary representation, with negligible impact on performance.

Suppose that pixel P, with neighbors P_1 and P_2, is being encoded. Overloading the notation slightly, we also use P, P_1, and P_2 to represent the grayscale values of these pixels. There are three cases: either the value P lies between the other two, or it lies above their maximum H, or it lies below their minimum L. These three situations are illustrated schematically in Figure 6.16b, in which $L = \min\{P_1, P_2\}$ and $H = \max\{P_1, P_2\}$ and the curve represents the estimated probability that P takes on various values relative to L and H. Actually plotting such a probability histogram for a real image is complicated by the need to normalize for all the different L and H values, particularly since for the vast majority of pixels L and H are very close together—if not the same. Normalization can be done, but the histograms that result are very noisy and tend to look quite different for different pictures. Figure 6.16b is thus very much an idealization and really serves only to motivate the coding method.

Typically, P lies in the central region about half the time, and this fact can be conveniently encoded in one bit. A special case occurs when the neighboring pixels P_1 and P_2 have grayscale values that are equal. Then the probability that P has the same value tends to be somewhat less than half because only one value is available, and it makes sense to widen the central region artificially to include, say, three gray levels rather than just one. When P lies outside the central region, the above/below situations are symmetrical and can be distinguished by a second bit. The codes for these three regions are shown in Figure 6.16b.

Figure 6.16b also shows the distribution of P relative to L and H. When P is within the central region, its values are distributed almost uniformly, so a standard binary encoding is appropriate. When P is outside the central region, its probability drops off sharply as the value moves further to the left of L or right of H, and the Golomb code described on page 119 in Section 3.3 is a good choice.

Define $\Delta = H - L$ to be the size of the central region, as marked in Figure 6.16b. To encode a pixel P between P_1 and P_2, the offset $P - L$ is coded within the range $[0, \Delta]$. If $\Delta+1$ is a power of two, a binary code with $\log(\Delta+1)$ bits is used. Otherwise, the code is adjusted by assigning $\lfloor\log(\Delta+1)\rfloor$ bits to some of the values and $\lceil\log(\Delta+1)\rceil$ to others. For example, if $\Delta = 10$, then 5 three-bit codes and 6 four-bit codes are used, a total of 11 codes in all. Table 6.3a shows a specific example of how the codewords might be assigned when $L = 20$ and $H = 30$. The middle column shows the 0 bit that indicates that P lies within the central region. It is advantageous to assign the shorter codes to the middle of the range since, as Figure 6.16b suggests, these values are marginally more likely. Consequently, the five three-bit codes are allocated in the center, with three of the four-bit codes at the beginning and the other three at the end.

It turns out that if we set $k = \lfloor\log(\Delta + 1)\rfloor$, then $a = 2^{k+1} - \Delta - 1$ of the values should be assigned k-bit codes ($a = 2^{3+1} - 10 - 1 = 5$ in Table 6.3a), and

Table 6.3 Example of coding when L = 20, H = 30, Δ = H − L = 10, and using m = 2: (a) within the central region; (b) above the central region.

(a)	Value P	Region bit	Code		(b)	Value P	Region bits	Code
	$L = 20$	0	0000			$H + 1 = 31$	11	000
	21	0	0010			32	11	001
	22	0	0100			33	11	010
	23	0	011			34	11	011
	24	0	100			35	11	1000
	25	0	101			36	11	1001
	26	0	110			37	11	1010
	27	0	111			38	11	1011
	28	0	0001			39	11	11000
	29	0	0011			40	11	11001
	$H = 30$	0	0101			...	...	...

$b = 2(\Delta + 1 - 2^k)$ should be assigned $k + 1$–bit codes ($b = 2(10 + 1 - 2^3) = 6$ in the table). The sum of a and b is $\Delta + 1$, as expected. Moreover, b is always even, so there is never any difficulty splitting the set of $k + 1$–bit codes into two equal halves, as illustrated in Table 6.3a.

Now consider the use of Golomb codes to represent values above and below the central region. In Section 3.3 (page 119) we described the Golomb code. It is controlled by a parameter b, and the number $x > 0$ is coded as $q + 1$ in unary, where $q = \lfloor (x - 1)/b \rfloor$, followed by $r = x - qb - 1$ coded in binary, requiring either $\lfloor \log b \rfloor$ or $\lceil \log b \rceil$ bits. Very little coding efficiency is lost by using the special case of Golomb coding in which b is restricted to a power of two, $b = 2^m$, which is also known as Rice coding. In a Rice code the binary part is the lower m bits of x, and the unary part is the number represented by the upper bits. The codes for the first few integers using each of these values are shown in Table 6.4.

Table 6.3b shows how the Rice code is used for the upper region in the same case as before, $L = 20$ and $H = 30$. The codes in the example are produced under the assumption that $m = 2$ and are the same as those in the $m = 2$ column of Table 6.4. The middle column shows the two bits that indicate that the values being coded lie above the central region. The value actually being coded is $P - H$, and the low-order two bits of the code give the low-order two bits of this value. The unary part of the code is given first, terminated by a 0 bit.

The Rice code works best when the value of m is chosen to suit the particular distribution that is being coded. It seems reasonable to employ Δ as a context to determine what value of m to use. In order to optimize m for each context, a record

Table 6.4 Example of Rice coding with different values of m.

Value	$m = 0$	$m = 1$	$m = 2$	$m = 3$
1	0	00	000	0000
2	10	01	001	0001
3	110	100	010	0010
4	1110	101	011	0011
5	11110	1100	1000	0100
6	111110	1101	1001	0101
7	1111110	11100	1010	0110
8	11111110	11101	1011	0111
9	111111110	111100	11000	10000
10	1111111110	111101	11001	10001
...	...	...	...	...

can be kept of how each value performed in the past. For an eight-bit grayscale image, there are only 255 possibilities for Δ and hence only a few values of m to be considered. Indeed, experience shows that it is seldom necessary to use anything other than $m = 0, 1, 2,$ and 3, which correspond to parameters of $b = 1, 2, 4,$ and 8 (Howard and Vitter 1993b).

It is a simple matter to maintain a table that records, for every value of Δ and m, the cumulative total code length that would have ensued if parameter m were used in the context Δ. The parameter with the smallest cumulative code length is selected to encode the next value encountered in that context. Of course, the decoder maintains the same table so that it can decode the Rice codes successfully. In this way, a suitable parameter value is used for each value of Δ, and very little overhead is needed to maintain the necessary information.

CALIC: Context-based adaptive lossless image codec

CALIC—the fourth of the five methods we consider—represents the state of the art in performance for lossless image compression algorithms; for example, it ranked top among the schemes that were evaluated by the JPEG committee prior to the development of the JPEG-Lossless standard. Although it is capable of efficient implementation, CALIC is conceptually rather an elaborate scheme, and only the main ideas will be sketched here; full details can be found in papers by Wu (1996) and Memon and Wu (1997). An important practical feature is that implementations only need sufficient storage space to hold three rows of the image, along with a small amount of memory, which is independent of image size.

CALIC encodes an image in conventional raster scan order and bases all its computation on a small local neighborhood of 12 pixels that precede the current one in transmission order. Like FELICS, it predicts the value of a pixel based on those pixels in its neighborhood and then transmits a correction that represents the discrepancy between the actual pixel value and its predicted value. However, both the prediction mechanism and the means of error transmission are considerably more involved than FELICS.

To predict a pixel value, four local estimates of the pixel gradient are obtained from the pixels in the local neighborhood, in the horizontal, vertical, and both diagonal directions. The gradient estimates are then used to detect the magnitude and orientation of edges in the input image so that adjustments can be made to the prediction. A total of eight different cases are distinguished, depending on whether sharp or not-so-sharp edges are detected in any of the four directions—for example, horizontal edge, sharp 135 degree diagonal edge, and so on—and the actual prediction formula is different for each case. Adjusting the prediction to take account of gradient is an explicit attempt to accommodate lines and edges in images.

Once this "gradient-adjusted" prediction is obtained, a correction is applied based on the particular pattern exhibited by the six closest neighboring pixels. This correction is necessary because gradients alone cannot adequately characterize some of the more complex relationships between the predicted pixel and its surroundings. Context modeling can exploit higher-order structures such as texture patterns in the image and is achieved by quantizing the six-pixel neighborhood into several hundred different conditioning classes and estimating the expected prediction error in each of these classes separately. Conditional expectations are estimated rather than conditional density functions to ensure that sample counts are sufficiently large to obtain good estimates and to reduce the time and space complexity. The conditional error expectation estimate is then used to correct the gradient-adjusted prediction. The net effect is a nonlinear, context-based predictor that corrects itself by adapting to errors made in the same context in the past.

Finally, the difference between the actual pixel value and the corrected prediction is entropy-encoded. In driving the entropy coder, the probability distribution of the prediction error is estimated within (only) eight different conditioning classes. Use of a range of conditioning classes allows the scheme to adapt to different spatial texture patterns. The appropriate conditioning class is determined by an estimate of the predictability of the signal at that point, measured by a linear function of the horizontal and vertical gradient and the prediction error at the preceding pixel. Optimal coefficients can be calculated using offline linear regression to yield a further improvement in coding efficiency. If this final correction stage is omitted, a lossy coding scheme results that is competitive with the JPEG lossy compression standard described in Section 6.6; in fact, it is claimed to yield significantly higher compression than JPEG for the same objective quality measure (Memon and Wu 1997).

Another important innovation in CALIC is that it distinguishes between binary and continuous-tone regions of pictures on a local, rather than a global, basis. It does this by examining the same neighborhood of six local preceding pixels as mentioned above; if they have no more than two different values (which need not necessarily be black and white), the upcoming pixel is coded in binary mode, otherwise it is coded using the predictive method described above. In binary mode, the six-pixel neighborhood is used to condition the distribution of the upcoming pixel values, as described in "Context models" (page 275). There is, of course, provision to "escape" to a pixel value that is different from the two that occur in the neighborhood.

JPEG-LS: A new standard for lossless image compression

The final scheme for lossless image compression that we consider has been under development since 1995 and has now nearly completed the lengthy standardization process. (When approved, it will be IS-14495.) Called JPEG-Lossless or JPEG-LS, it is a follow-on from the JPEG standard for continuous-tone images discussed in the next section. The original JPEG standard included a "lossless" mode, but its performance was inferior to other lossless methods, and it received little use. An intensive effort to produce a new and better standard has stimulated the development of a new generation of lossless image coders (of which CALIC, described in the previous subsection, is one example), and techniques from a variety of sources have been incorporated into the new standard, with the core of the standard being derived from the sc-i algorithm of Weinberger, Seroussi, and Sapiro (1996), using the MELCODE coder developed by F. Ono at Mitsubishi.

Like CALIC, JPEG-LS encodes in raster order and begins with estimates of the local pixel gradient at the current pixel position. However, these estimates are based on a context of only four pixels: the one directly preceding on the current scanline (which we will call W for west) and three in the preceding scanline, one directly above the current position (N for north) and both its neighbors (NW and NE). These four values are used to calculate three local gradients, two in the horizontal direction ($NE - N$ and $N - NW$) and one in the vertical ($NW - W$). If the three gradients are all zero, the encoder enters a "run" mode that encodes a run of identical pixels as a count of the number of pixels in the run. Otherwise, the encoder continues with context-based compression by quantizing each of the three local gradients into one of nine possible values, according to predetermined thresholds, giving a total of $9^3 = 729$ possible contexts (including one that corresponds to run mode). Symmetry is used to reduce this number to 365 contexts.

The next step is an edge-detecting predictor. It represents a significant advance: it is both simpler and more effective than previous predictors. Unlike CALIC's, it is not based on gradients—they come into play later. Instead, it attempts to detect horizontal and vertical edges by examining the three pixels N, W, and NW. The value of N is used as a prediction if a vertical edge is suspected, and the value of W is used if a horizontal edge is suspected. If neither kind of edge is detected, planar interpolation is used. This predictor is implemented by

$$
\text{prediction} = \begin{cases} \min(N, W), & \text{if } NW \geq \max(N, W) \\ \max(N, W), & \text{if } NW < \min(N, W) \\ N + W - NW, & \text{otherwise.} \end{cases}
$$

This predictor is sometimes called a "median" predictor, not because it takes the median of the three pixel values (it doesn't), but because if you consider three separate predictors that predict the values N, W, and $N + W - NW$, then the result is the median of the three predictions. Extensive evaluation by its developers has shown it to perform at least as well as linear and gradient-based predictors, despite its simplicity.

The prediction so far is based on the local gradient alone. However, this cannot characterize complex relationships between a pixel and its surroundings. Consequently, the predicted pixel value is corrected by adding to it an amount governed by the appropriate one of the 365 gradient contexts determined above (with a further adjustment to take symmetry into account). Called a "context-dependent bias cancellation" term, this is essentially the same as was discussed earlier for CALIC, although it involves a rather smaller number of contexts.

Now that a final prediction has been obtained for the new pixel value, the pixel error is calculated and transmitted. Despite the efforts made to obtain an accurate prediction, statistical redundancy still remains, and the variance of the prediction error is correlated strongly with the smoothness of the image around the predicted pixel. To model this, two further quantities are maintained for each of the 365 gradient contexts and used as parameters for the compression: the number of times that each context has occurred and the total absolute value of the prediction errors for this context. However, rather than implementing a time-consuming arithmetic coding step, these quantities are used to determine the parameter for a Golomblike code (see Section 3.3, page 119), which is finally used to encode the prediction error. Despite the simplicity of the Golomb coding procedure, the compression performance achieved is surprisingly close to that obtained by arithmetic coding (within 3%).

The overall result is a lossless compression method that comes very close to CALIC's compression performance but is considerably less demanding computationally. An implementation of JPEG-LS is available at *www.hpl.hp.com/loco/*.

6.6 JPEG: A standard for continuous-tone images

This section examines lossy compression of images. The JPEG method was designed to be general-purpose so that it can support a wide variety of image communication services and computer image applications such as photovideotext, desktop publishing, graphic arts, color fax, newspaper wirephoto transmission, and medical imaging. As a result of the care that went into its specification, it has now become the standard technique for compressing still images. Successively more detailed accounts of JPEG have been written by Wallace (1990, 1991); Pennebaker and Mitchell (1993) give a comprehensive description.

JPEG was motivated by the realization that state-of-the-art image coding techniques could yield an algorithm that compressed well enough to produce excellent image quality at around one bit per pixel and that was sufficiently low in complexity that economical implementations could keep pace with 64 Kbits per second communication channels. One bit per pixel—the starting point for fax—is impressive compression for grayscale or color images, which generally have anything from 8 to 32 bits per pixel when digitized. And of course a 64 Kbits per second channel has several times the capacity of the 4,800 bits per second channel normally used for fax. However, unlike fax, the JPEG standard is designed for interactive use. Compressed to one bit per pixel, a 720×576 pixel image would take 6.5 seconds to transmit over a 64 Kbits per second line, a tolerable wait for occasional image viewing.

Current schemes for lossless image compression cannot reduce typical continuous-tone pictures to one bit per pixel, and given the energy that has been invested in lossless image coding, it seems unlikely that they ever will. In order to go further, it is necessary to accept approximate rather than exact coding. Consequently, the JPEG method is a lossy one and does not reconstruct the original image exactly. The coding method was selected from among many possibilities based on an assessment of subjective picture quality. JPEG is divided into a baseline system that offers a limited set of capabilities and a set of optional extended system features. The baseline system gives a plain lossy, high-compression image coding/decoding capability and preserves image fidelity at compression rates competitive with or superior to other known techniques. However, it is not designed for very low bit rates, and at rates of around 0.25 bits per pixel or less, subband or wavelet compression techniques begin to outperform JPEG—particularly for images that exhibit sharp edges.

A delay of several seconds is frustratingly long for browsing, so the JPEG standard incorporates the possibility of progressive transmission, where the image is first transmitted approximately and then gradually refined to the final image quality. This is one of the extended system features. Progressive transmission usually ends when the image is the same as would have been transmitted in the normal (lossy) case, but JPEG also contains an option of progressive lossless coding, which continues until the final version is almost identical with the original—the only discrepancies being due to the finite-precision arithmetic employed in the encoder and decoder.

The original JPEG standard also incorporated a much simpler means of lossless image transmission that nevertheless yields reasonable bit rates for continuous-tone compression. Called the *independent lossless* scheme, it produces an image that is bit-for-bit identical to the original. However, it is being superseded by the new JPEG-LS standard described in the previous section, and so we will not cover it here.

Unlike the fax standards, which specify the exact page size and pixel resolution, JPEG is designed for pictures of arbitrary size and resolution. It operates on an image that has first been divided into 8×8 pixel blocks, in which each component sample is represented by eight bits. Higher-resolution options, with more bits per pixel, are among the extended system features. The algorithm encodes color image components independently and is suitable for use with any of the commonly used color spaces.

Figure 6.17 depicts the encoding and decoding processes. Each 8×8 block is subjected to a signal-processing technique known as the *discrete cosine transform*, which maps the 64 pixel values into 64 output coefficients. These 64 numbers characterize the input block exactly and can be used to faithfully reproduce the block if they are known to sufficient precision. They represent image components at different spatial frequencies and are more suitable than the pixel values themselves for lossy quantization. In 8×8 blocks in which sample values vary slowly from point to point—and this is the case for most parts of nearly all images, particularly ones of natural objects—the transformation concentrates most of the signal in the

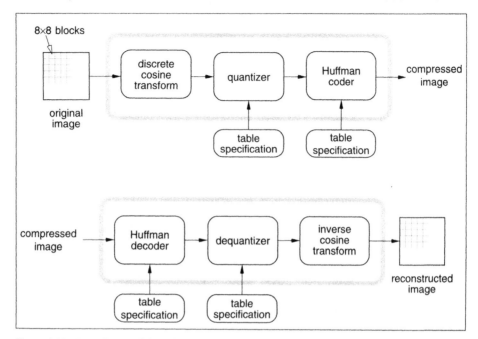

Figure 6.17   Encoding and decoding processes in baseline JPEG.

lower spatial frequencies. Of course, some pictures do have significant higher spatial frequencies—for example, ones that contain regular patterns such as brick walls or tiled roofs—but this rarely occurs for natural images because they tend to be irregular and fractal-like. For a typical 8 × 8 sample block from a typical source image, many of the higher spatial frequencies have zero or negligible amplitude and need not be encoded at all.

To show what the discrete cosine transform coefficients mean, Figure 6.18 presents an image after each successive coefficient has been received. The original 512 × 512 image has been divided into an 8 × 8 matrix of blocks, each block having 64 × 64 pixels. JPEG actually uses blocks of 8 × 8 pixels, but to demonstrate the effect, we use larger ones. The first version of the image is made from each block's zero-frequency, or DC,[7] coefficient; this represents the overall grayness of the block, so each block is a uniform shade of gray. After receipt of the second coefficient for each block, horizontal cross-sections through the blocks still have uniform shading, though vertical cross-sections do not. By the time the 32nd coefficient is received, the image is starting to look a lot like the final version. However, it would require 64 × 64 = 4,096 coefficients per block for full, error-free reconstruction of our example picture. (The corresponding figure for JPEG is 8 × 8 = 64 coefficients.)

_____

7   DC is an abbreviation for "direct current," using an electrical engineering analogy.

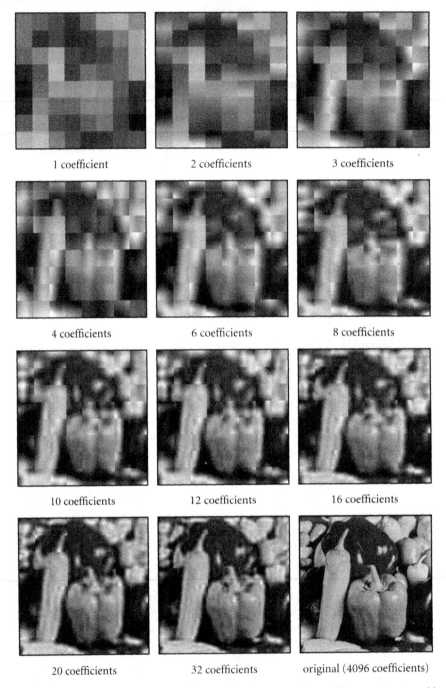

Figure 6.18 Transform-coded images reconstructed from a few coefficients. Reprinted by permission of the University of Southern California Image Processing Institute (USC-IPI) image database.

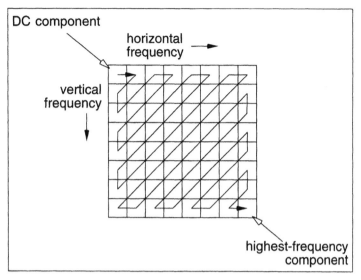

Figure 6.19   Zig-zag encoding sequence.

Following the discrete cosine transform, the nonzero coefficients are independently rounded to discrete values by a uniform quantizer—this is the lossy part. The quantizer step size—that is, the difference between successive levels—is different for each coefficient. The encoder may specify with each picture the quantization tables that are to be used for that picture—they could be derived for a particular picture and transmitted to accompany that image. Alternatively, it may specify that previously installed tables are to be used instead. The JPEG standard includes an example set of quantization tables that are particularly appropriate for natural scenery. The zero-frequency, or DC, coefficient is differentially encoded—that is, represented by the difference between it and the previous block's DC value—because it is highly correlated from block to block since it is basically the average intensity over the block. The other 63 coefficients are not differentially encoded. They are sorted from low to high frequency using the zig-zag sequence of Figure 6.19, in the order indicated by the arrowheads; then they are coded to reduce statistical redundancy. The baseline system uses Huffman coding for this purpose. First, since many of the coefficients are zero, the number of zero coefficients before the next nonzero one is specified—a kind of run-length encoding. Then the nonzero coefficients are Huffman coded. An example code table is provided in the JPEG specification, but the encoder can again determine codes appropriate to the particular picture and embed them in the compressed data stream.

Although the baseline system uses Huffman coding, the standard accommodates the option of using arithmetic coding instead, and this yields slightly greater compression at the expense of execution speed. The Huffman coding method is about twice as fast as the arithmetic coding method, but—at least in software implementations—throughput is dominated by other parts of the JPEG scheme, so

(a)   **(b)**   **(c)**

Figure 6.20 Images reconstructed from different numbers of bits: (a) 0.1 bit per pixel; (b) 0.2 bit per pixel; (c) 1.0 bit per pixel.

the overall difference is not so great in practice. The arithmetic coding option is exactly the same method of adaptive binary arithmetic coding that is employed by JBIG, reviewed above (page 287), along with the same scheme for probability estimation. The compression advantage of arithmetic over Huffman coding is about 10 percent for high-quality reconstructions of the relatively noisy test images used to develop JPEG. For lower bit rates and cleaner images, the advantage of arithmetic coding is even greater.

The difference between the baseline system and the progressive transmission mode begins once the coefficients produced by the discrete cosine transform have been quantized. Instead of transmitting all coefficients for each block in turn, many passes are made through the picture, and successively higher bands of coefficients are transmitted at each pass. Thus, in early passes, the low-frequency, rough-detail information is sent, leaving for later the high-frequency, fine-detail information. This is called the *spectral selection* method of progressive transmission. An alternative, called *successive approximation*, is also specified, in which the coefficients are first sent with reduced precision. Successive approximation yields much better visual quality at low bit rates, but the number of progressive stages is limited. Spectral selection allows more progressive stages and, since it is a simple extension of the sequential mode, is easier to implement. Successive approximation—particularly, it turns out, the Huffman coding version—is more difficult to implement.

The progressive lossless feature involves sending a spatial correction signal, which gives the per-sample difference between the final lossy image and the original one, as the last stage of encoded data. Again, there may be small discrepancies in reproduction because of the use of finite-precision arithmetic.

Figure 6.20 shows three stages of lossy transmission from a JPEG-like encoding scheme, at 0.1, 0.2, and 1.0 bit per pixel, respectively. The differences in resolution are just discernable—despite the low-quality halftone reproduction—if you look very closely, particularly around the straight edges in the pictures. The JPEG standard describes a postprocessing operation called *AC prediction*[8] that can be used to suppress blocking artifacts and improve quality at low bit rates; it is not used in these examples.

As a general guide to the results attainable with a lossy compression method:

For color images of moderately complex scenes, several levels of picture quality can be obtained at different compression factors:

- 0.25–0.5 bit per pixel: moderate to good quality, sufficient for some applications;
- 0.5–0.75 bit per pixel: good to very good quality, sufficient for many applications;
- 0.75–1.5 bits per pixel: excellent quality, sufficient for most applications;
- 1.5–2 bits per pixel: usually indistinguishable from the original, sufficient for the most demanding applications.

6.7 Progressive transmission of images

Progressive transmission was touched on in the sections on the JBIG and JPEG standards. The idea is to arrange for the quality of an image to increase gradually as data is received, which is an attractive way to communicate an image over a low-bandwidth channel. For example, when viewing an image on the World Wide Web, it is possible to get an early idea of what the image will be and stop it loading if it is not needed. In striking contrast to the raster format, the most "useful" information in the image is sent first, so that the viewer can begin to use the image before it is completely displayed and much sooner than if the image were painted in ordinary raster order.

There are three basically different ways to achieve progressive transmission, and they can be classified according to which feature of the image is improved with time. The first is to use *transform coding* to transmit spatial frequency information progressively, so that the image grows sharper as more data is received. This can be done either by transmitting low-frequency components first, followed by higher-frequency information (the technique used by the JPEG "spectral selection" progressive transmission mode) or by transmitting coefficients with reduced precision first (the JPEG "successive approximation" mode). The second is to use *vector quantization* to begin with a limited palette of colors or grayscales and gradually provide more, so that it is color detail that increases with time. The third, *pyramid coding*, is to begin at a low resolution and gradually increase the number of pixels used to represent the image, so that it is image resolution that increases with time.

---

8 AC stands for "alternating current," using the same electrical engineering analogy.

In our experience:

Transform coding, vector quantization, and pyramid coding are similar in terms of the subjective or objective quality of the images they produce after a given number of bits have been transmitted. However, they differ greatly in encoding and decoding speed.

Transform coding provides medium-speed encoding and slow decoding; vector quantization is very slow to encode but fast to decode; and pyramid coding is fast for both encoding and decoding. With pyramid coding, image quality can be enhanced significantly by smoothing the image during decoding, but this is very slow.

In all cases, bandwidth can be saved by allowing transmission to be lossy. An attractive feature of any progressive coding method is that lossy compression can be obtained simply by truncating the transmission before it is complete. The level of distortion depends on the amount of data sent, and the user can determine the trade-off between compression and quality.

The textual image compression technique described in the next chapter can be thought of as a specialized type of progressive transmission. As we will see, it allows a rough version of a textual document to be transmitted very quickly and then slowly refined to produce an exact copy. However, for documents that contain continuous-tone pictures, it will be necessary to adopt another technique to yield the benefit of progressive transmission for the image information. JPEG is one possible candidate; another is pyramid coding.

Pyramid coding

In pyramid coding, an image is approximated by aggregating adjacent pixels—usually pairs or quadruples—to produce a lower-resolution version. The process is repeated recursively, as shown in Figure 6.21, until the image resolution is just 1×1. Then this single pixel value is transmitted, followed by each higher-resolution image, down to the original one. Various stages of reception using pyramid coding are shown in Figure 6.1 on page 267. Note that when compressing a pyramid-coded image, the pixel value at one level provides an excellent prediction of those below it at the next level down, and it should be used as part of the context for coding those lower pixels if compression effectiveness is to be maximized.

Compression for pyramid coding

There are four compression methods that can be used in pyramid coding. The simplest is to average 2×2 blocks of child pixels to form the parent pixel. If compression techniques are not used, then pyramid coding will expand the image because there are 33 percent more pixels in the pyramid than in the original image.

A second technique, the *reduced-sum* method, is one way to bring the size back to near the original. If the average values are transmitted with their full precision (that is, the average of four pixels is represented using two more bits of precision

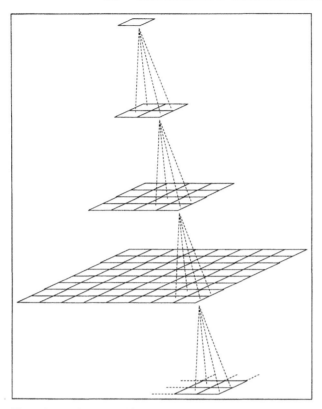

Figure 6.21 The pyramid tree.

than the original pixels have), then only three of the four child pixels need to be transmitted since the fourth can be calculated from the parent and sibling values. In this case, the number of nodes in the pyramid is the same as the number of pixels in the original image, although those at higher levels—a relatively small proportion—require greater precision.

The *difference pyramid* method—the third of the four techniques considered in this section—achieves a more compact representation by using the parent pixel to predict the values of its four children. Instead of transmitting the child values directly, we send the difference between each pixel value and the aggregate. These "error" values must be coded so that the most likely ones are represented by short codes. The best compression is obtained if the probability distribution of the error values is recorded and a Huffman or arithmetic coder is used to code the pixels.

The probability distribution, or model, can be constructed adaptively by starting with a bland probability distribution and increasing the probability of particular error values as they are encountered. As discussed in Section 2.2, a count is stored for each error value, initialized to one so that no error value has zero probability, and incremented after each error value is encoded. If the increment amount is greater than one, counts of nonoccurring values will become less significant more quickly. In practice, increments of about four give the best compression in pyramid coding applications, although performance is quite insensitive to the exact value.

Compression can be improved by predicting a pixel from its siblings as well as from its parent. In the final mechanism considered here, the *reduced-difference* method, only the differences between three pairs of siblings are stored. The fourth sibling's value can be reconstructed from these three differences, given the parent value. If the child pixel values that are averaged are c_{00}, c_{01}, c_{10}, and c_{10}, and we transmit the three differences

$$d_1 = c_{00} - c_{10}$$
$$d_2 = c_{10} - c_{11}$$
$$d_3 = c_{11} - c_{01},$$

then given the parent value $b = (c_{00} + c_{10} + c_{11} + c_{01})/4$, the child values can be reconstructed using

$$c_{00} = b + (3d_1 + 2d_2 + d_3)/4$$
$$c_{10} = c_{00} - d_1$$
$$c_{11} = c_{00} - d_1 - d_2$$
$$c_{01} = c_{00} - d_1 - d_2 - d_3.$$

In practice, the value of b, the mean of the four child pixels, will be truncated, but this can be accommodated in the calculations. When the difference values are coded using adaptive arithmetic coding, this gives an appreciable improvement over the difference method.

Median aggregation

There are other ways to aggregate a block of pixels into a single pixel of a lower-resolution image, apart from averaging them. Simply taking the maximum or minimum of the values decreases the quality of the image by gradually washing out the grayscale information. A more viable alternative is to use the median. This involves sorting the child values at each stage and selecting either the second or third child as the median. If one is chosen consistently throughout coding, then the image will be lightened or darkened on average, but this can easily be avoided by alternating between the two choices for each child that is transmitted.

The median is attractive because it helps with predictions and can improve image quality. It helps with prediction because in the tree, (at least) one of each node's children has the same value as the node itself, and this can be exploited in the coding. It can improve image quality because the median filter ignores single extreme values, and on high-quality displays, the median images tend to have a slightly higher contrast, although the median does tend to accentuate the stepped appearance of sloping edges. Set against this is the computational expense normally associated with median filtering, although in this application only four to five comparisons are required to sort four items, and the division operation required by the mean is avoided.

The child values can be coded by transmitting which of the four children is the median (this requires two bits), then using the difference method to transmit the other three. Compression can be improved by observing that once the median is known, it is also known how many of the other three values are greater and less than it. For example, if the median chosen was the child ranked second, and one child has been received whose value is smaller, then the other two children must have values greater than or equal to the median. This can be exploited for compression by maintaining three frequency tables: one for when the child is known to be less than the median, one for when it is known to be greater, and one for when its relation to the median is not known.

Error modeling

In general, it is very difficult to achieve worthwhile compression of continuous images if you insist on exact reproduction, whether or not progressive transmission is used. The problem is that each pixel value invariably contains some component of the noise that has arisen from the sampling or digitization process, and noise is inherently incompressible. Consequently, any hard-won improvement that compression yields tends to be swamped by the incompressible noise component.

Modern approaches to lossless compression of continuous-tone images, such as CALIC and JPEG-LS, attempt to separate the image structure from the noise and encode each using an appropriate model. The idea is to begin by identifying as much of the image structure as possible, ignoring the effect of noise. This is done by predicting a value for each pixel based on its neighbors. Then the discrepancy between the predicted value and the actual one is calculated and encoded as efficiently as possible, according to an appropriate probability distribution, or *error model*, that is known to characterize noise in images. The parameters of the distribution are estimated from the data itself, and the actual prediction errors are encoded with respect to the error model (Endoh and Yamakazi 1986; Howard and Vitter 1992b, 1992c).

The idea is applied to progressive transmission by encoding the picture in a series of levels, with increasing resolution. When we begin to encode any particular level, the pixels with known values lie on a square grid corresponding to the level above. Using the values of pixels on these grid points only, the value of the pixel at the midpoint of each grid square is predicted. This is done by taking either the 4 nearest pixels or the 16 nearest pixels and performing polynomial interpolation on their values. Then the error in this prediction is transmitted, to create a faithful representation of the level being encoded. Once all pixels in the level have been dealt with, the set of known pixels forms a checkerboard pattern at the midpoints of the previous grid squares. By rotating and scaling the coordinate system, a new square grid of pixels with known values is obtained, and the distance between adjacent pixels is only $1/\sqrt{2}$ as much as before. Figure 6.22 illustrates the pixels at two consecutive levels of the procedure.

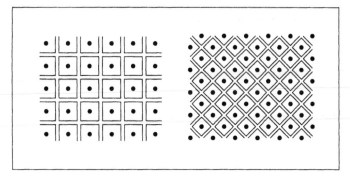

Figure 6.22 Pixels at consecutive levels in progressive encoding.

A suitable method for predicting the value of a pixel is to use a linear combination of the values of a group of nearby pixels at the level above. A 4 × 4 array of pixels works well in practice. The coefficients applied to this group are selected using a standard interpolation polynomial. In addition, the variance of the actual pixel values from the prediction is estimated over the whole level. This is simply transmitted to the receiver and used to encode all the errors at the present level. It creates very little overhead.

Prediction errors can be modeled quite accurately as a Laplace probability distribution with zero mean. This has the probability density function

$$f(x) = \frac{1}{\sqrt{2\sigma^2}} \exp\left(-\sqrt{\frac{2}{\sigma^2}} |x|\right),$$

where the variance is σ^2. An arithmetic coder is used to code each actual error value relative to the Laplace distribution with the appropriate variance.

This technique can encode certain images to one-half or even one-third of their original size in a way that is completely lossless, and it also has the advantage of progressive transmission.

6.8 Summary of image compression techniques

The capture, storage, retrieval, and manipulation of electronic images of pictures and documents offers capabilities that far surpass both traditional paper filing systems and film-based techniques like microfilm and microfiche. Unfortunately, pictures, when digitized, occupy a great deal of space. When an $8^{1}/_{2} \times 11$-inch document is scanned at a resolution of 200 dpi, an image file of 467,500 bytes—nearly half a megabyte—is produced. Higher spatial resolution, or the use of grayscale or color scanners, greatly amplifies the problem. As was noted in Section 1.1, in raw form, the figures in this book occupy about 40 times as much space as the text. Indeed, this book has about 175 figures and over 200,000 words, so there is roughly one figure for every thousand words. Whether they are "worth" the same is open to question, but certainly, on average, each figure occupies far more space than the words. Image compression is clearly important.

Different compression techniques are appropriate for bilevel and multilevel (grayscale and color) images. Bilevel techniques are normally lossless, and in this chapter we have examined the current fax standards, the general idea of context-based image compression, and the JBIG standard for bilevel images. JBIG is a fairly complex standard that offers the implementer numerous options, ranging from resolution reduction to adaptive pixels in templates, and that incorporates novel techniques such as those for probability estimation and efficient, approximate arithmetic coding. An even more complex variant of JBIG that is aimed at predominantly textual images has been under development since about 1996, and the techniques it uses are the subject of the next chapter, with Section 7.9 describing the emerging JBIG2 standard.

Turning now to grayscale and color images, they are sometimes encoded in a lossless manner and sometimes using lossy techniques. Widely used de facto standards for lossless image compression include GIF and PNG; higher-performance schemes include FELICS, which is very fast and obtains very good compression; CALIC, which is much slower but obtains excellent compression; and the new JPEG-LS method, which is designed to represent the ultimate compromise between compression performance and speed for today's implementation technology. For lossy image compression, the comprehensive and complex JPEG standard presents implementers with a vast array of options that allows them to explore, within the standard itself, the intricate interplay between reproduction fidelity, compression performance, execution speed, progressive transmission, and implementation complexity.

Intertwining compression and presentation is the question of progressive transmission. The ability to view an image at different resolutions is so useful that many current document imaging systems actually store two versions of each image, one at display resolution and the other at a higher resolution. A more elegant solution, which simultaneously increases display flexibility and storage economy, is to embed progressive transmission into the image coding scheme. Both JPEG and JBIG incorporate progressive transmission, the former in the transform domain through the spectral selection and successive approximation techniques, and the latter through an interesting and well-thought-out algorithm for resolution reduction of bilevel images. JBIG resolution reduction is a kind of pyramid coding, and the idea of pyramid coding has been successfully applied to grayscale images too. Finally, error modeling attempts to separate the image structure from the noise and encode each using an appropriate model.

We have been looking at techniques that are designed for general images. But many document images are pictures of text, and (as always) tailored compression techniques can be expected to yield better compression than general-purpose methods. The next chapter looks specifically at how such textual images can be represented efficiently.

Further reading

Fax compression. The CCITT fax standards are discussed by Hunter and Robinson (1980); their paper includes the eight test pictures that are widely used for evaluating fax transmission methods and were used for Figure 6.4. A number of authors have published results for compressing these images using the Group 4 fax method (Pratt et al. 1980; Yasuda et al. 1985; Bodson et al. 1985).

Context-based compression of bilevel images. Langdon and Rissanen (1981) undertook early, and seminal, work on context-based compression of bilevel pictures, and Moffat later explored the use of two-level context models (Moffat 1991).

The JBIG standard has completed the involved process of becoming an international standard, IS 11544 (ITU–T T.82) (CCITT 1993). The arithmetic coder and probability estimation method used in both JBIG and JPEG was developed by Bill Pennebaker and his colleagues at IBM (Pennebaker et al. 1988; Pennebaker and Mitchell 1988). Parts of JBIG are patented, including the resolution reduction method (Yoshida et al. 1992).

Lossless compression for continuous-tone images. The FELICS method for lossless encoding of grayscale images in Section 6.5 is due to Howard and Vitter (1993b) and Howard (1993), while CALIC is described by Wu (1996) and Memon and Wu (1997). The techniques incorporated into the JPEG-LS standard are from Weinberger, Seroussi, and Sapiro (1996); the MELCODE coder it uses is by F. Ono at Mitsubishi. The draft JPEG-LS standard itself is available from the International Standards Organization as ISO/IEC JTC 1/SC 29/WG 1. Standard IS-14495 is likely to have been approved by the time this book goes to print. A software implementation is available at *www.hpl.hp.com/loco/*. Rabbani and Jones (1991) give a good general tutorial on digital image compression techniques for continuous-tone images, and Ulichney has published an excellent book on the representation of continuous-tone images on bilevel devices (Ulichney 1987).

JPEG. Successively more detailed descriptions of the JPEG standard, IS 10918-1 (ITU-T T.81), have been written by Wallace (1990, 1991); Figure 6.17 is adapted from the second of these. The 1993 "JPEG Book" by Pennebaker and Mitchell (1993) contains a comprehensive description of JPEG and also includes information on JBIG. Work on JPEG continues, and the existing standard is just the first of a multipart set of standards for still-image compression.

Progressive transmission. The idea of combining compression with progressive transmission first appeared in the early 1980s (Anastassiou et al. 1983; Witten and Cleary 1983), and pyramid coding has been studied by Sharman (1992) and Sharman, Bell, and Witten (1992). The "error modeling" method outlined in Section 6.7 was first reported by Endoh and Yamakazi (1986) and further developed by Howard and Vitter (1992b, 1992c) and also in Paul Howard's 1993 Ph.D. thesis.

Textual Images

The more you know about whatever it is that is being compressed, the greater the amount of compression you can achieve. When text is to be compressed, it is assumed that the source is a string of characters that is read from left to right—that is why context-based methods like PPM work so well. If the text is known to be English, the compression scheme can be primed with samples of English text to improve performance; if we know that it is Hemingway, it can be primed with samples of Hemingway to improve performance further. When we compress an inverted file, our knowledge of the ordering and distribution of pointers is applied to devise coding schemes that are much more effective than if the file were just treated as a textual concordance. Similarly, more effective compression of an image can be achieved if it is known what sort of image it is.

Many images that are encountered in daily life—particularly in the office environment—are images of documents that contain mainly typed or typeset text. As discussed in Chapter 1, we call these *textual images*. It was pointed out at the beginning of Chapter 6, for example, that the digitized images used in fax transmission are generally business documents and hence predominantly textual. In fact, most office work deals with a mixture of machine-readable text and traditional paper documents, and huge problems arise from the fact that the documents are stored and transmitted in different physical forms. In archiving, documents are scanned and stored electronically for later retrieval. Though they sometimes contain line drawings or halftone pictures, more often they comprise text alone or text mixed with a small assortment of other image types. Consequently, it is well worth examining whether techniques of general image compression can be specialized to work with predominantly textual images. Documents that contain both textual and pictorial information are treated in the next chapter; in this chapter we consider images that are entirely textual.

One possibility for textual image compression is to perform optical character recognition on the text and represent the document as a sequence of character codes in some standard alphabet such as ASCII. Depending on the document's layout, and the application, it may be necessary to include the position of characters on the page as well as their sequential order.

However, there are some drawbacks to representing a document in this form. OCR is not completely reliable, particularly with poor-quality source documents. Imperfections in the original document, incorrect contrast settings when scanning, varying typefaces, and unusual characters all conspire to produce errors. Stylized fonts, foreign languages, and mathematical expressions can cause havoc.

An obvious difficulty in OCR is the need to deal with many different typefaces and sizes—and in some ways, the advent of computerized word processing has exacerbated the problem by vastly increasing the typographical repertoire of typical office documents. OCR systems need to be "trained" to learn a new font, and the document input procedure may have to be interrupted to deal with such problems. For a particularly badly printed word, recognition may be impossible because to decipher it requires background knowledge and careful examination of the context in which it appears.

Other ambiguities are caused by the nature of the letterforms themselves. For example, it can be difficult to distinguish between the letters *o, 0, O, Q,* and *D,* and often the context must be taken into account and linguistic knowledge used to make the distinction. Similarly, it may be hard to distinguish a punctuation character such as a dot or comma, or an accent or other diacritical mark, from a speck of noise or a staple hole. A different problem is that adjacent letters sometimes merge. For example, we have had to work with a scanned document in which the letters *r* and *n* were invariably run together and read as an *m,* causing particular amusement when words like *burn* occurred in the text. In cases like this, the operator may have to edit the document by hand or adjust parameters such as the contrast of the scan to improve the result.

When OCR is used, the final image will look much cleaner than the original because badly printed letters are corrected and small marks are removed from the page. Ironically, although the image may look better, it is actually noisier because it does not faithfully represent the original image. Smudged or badly printed characters are replaced by whatever symbols they are read as by the OCR system, instead of leaving human viewers to make their own interpretation. Dirt or ink stains, which in some archival applications have given valuable clues to a researcher, are at best lost and at worst interpreted incorrectly as text. The typeface may not be reproduced accurately, affecting the look of a document. For typed business letters, this sort of noise may be acceptable—even desirable—but for many legal, medical, and historical purposes, including archives where the interests of future readers are unknown, there is a strong motivation to record the document as faithfully as possible.

In this chapter we describe a compression method for textual images that has much in common with the OCR method but avoids these fidelity problems. The method has two levels. The base level is a lossy technique, for which the compression factor is high, but what is restored on decompression is only an approximation of the original digitized document. Built on top of the base level is a lossless second level, which enables the original document to be reproduced exactly from its compressed form. This is achieved by augmenting the information encoded by the lossy technique with enough further information to allow the original to be reproduced exactly. These two levels are achieved by separating the text and noise in the document image and compressing the two components separately using a method appropriate for each.

The two levels combine naturally into a two-stage procedure for progressive transmission: the lossy image is sent first, and then, if desired, extra information is transmitted to refine it into an exact copy of the original. This provides an advantage even when images are being stored rather than transmitted because the approximate image can be reconstructed much more quickly than can the additional information required to make it into an exact reproduction. Moreover, the information needed to regenerate the lossy image is far less voluminous than that required to refine it into an exact copy. In many applications, it is possible to store the information for the lossy image on a device that can be accessed relatively rapidly, relegating the latter information to some slower secondary storage medium. An approximate rendition of the document is often adequate for browsing purposes, particularly when several pages are displayed in miniature on a screen.

In practice, most images contain more than just printed text; they include logos, signatures, pictures, annotations, and so on. Though the textual image compression method is very effective when dealing with the purely textual part, it is often advantageous to separate out the graphical material and treat it separately. Methods for doing this are described in the next chapter. It is also important that the image is correctly oriented and any skew that occurred during digitization is corrected; this is also covered in Section 8.1. Thus, in this chapter we assume a perfectly oriented, wholly textual image.

After a brief overview of the idea of textual image compression in Section 7.1, we review how the idea developed (Section 7.2). The form of textual image compression described here is unique in that it includes a second step to make transmission lossless, a development that recent work in image compression (in particular the clairvoyant method described in Section 6.3, on page 279) has made possible. The following sections develop the idea of textual image compression in detail by examining how to locate marks on the page and extract them from it (Section 7.3), how to perform template matching so that marks can be matched to corresponding versions in a library (Section 7.4), and what information must be stored for each mark extracted from the page (Section 7.5). In Section 7.6 we examine how the individual components are coded, and in Section 7.7 we present some results on the amount of compression that can be expected, obtained from sample collections of images. In Section 7.8 we review the role of textual image compression in a document storage and retrieval system. Finally, in Section 7.9 we describe JBIG2, an embryonic international standard that will extend JBIG by incorporating a textual image compression mode.

7.1   The idea of textual image compression

Textual image compression works by building a library of shapes that occur in an image. These "shapes" usually correspond to characters. The shapes that occur in the image are then replaced with pointers into the library. In general, the process comprises the following steps, although there are many variants, and some schemes omit some of the steps:

1. Find, isolate, and extract all the *marks*—that is, connected groups of black pixels—in the image.

2. Construct a library containing the marks found in the image.

3. Identify the symbol in the library that corresponds the closest to each mark in the image, and measure the coordinate offsets between one mark and the next.

4. Compress and store the library, the symbol sequence, and the offsets.

From the information stored in step 4, an approximation to the original image, called the *reconstructed text*, can be created. To make the reconstruction lossless, a fifth step is included:

5. Store enough additional information to restore the original image from the reconstructed text.

Figure 7.1 shows an example image used to illustrate the procedure. It is part of a page from the 1872 printed catalog of the library at Trinity College, Dublin. The catalog has a rather old-fashioned look and contains a wide variety of symbols from many different typefaces, including italics and small capitals, and text in several different languages, such as Flemish, Latin, and Greek.

Step 1 of the textual image compression procedure identifies marks, which are generally characters. However, letters with disconnected parts like *i* and *j* are represented by pairs of library elements, one for the body and the other for the dot on top. This incurs a negligible penalty in storage size because of the adaptive compression that follows. Size thresholds may be applied to prevent very small specks, or very large marks, from being recognized.

As each mark is extracted, it is checked against the library symbols seen so far (step 2). If no sufficiently close matches are found, the mark may be added to the library as a new symbol, represented as a matrix of pixels. Figure 7.2 shows the library that is created from the example image. Symbols occur in order of their appearance in the document itself; thus they begin — , *R*, *e*, and so on. These are extracted as bitmaps from the image and placed in the library, and the fact that in Figure 7.2 they are (arbitrarily) aligned at the top emphasizes that they have not been recognized as characters but are simply being treated as bitmaps.

Table 7.1 shows the sequence of symbols in the order in which they are extracted from the document (step 3). The second column records the symbol number, and, using the library shown in Figure 7.2, the symbols can be identified and read off the

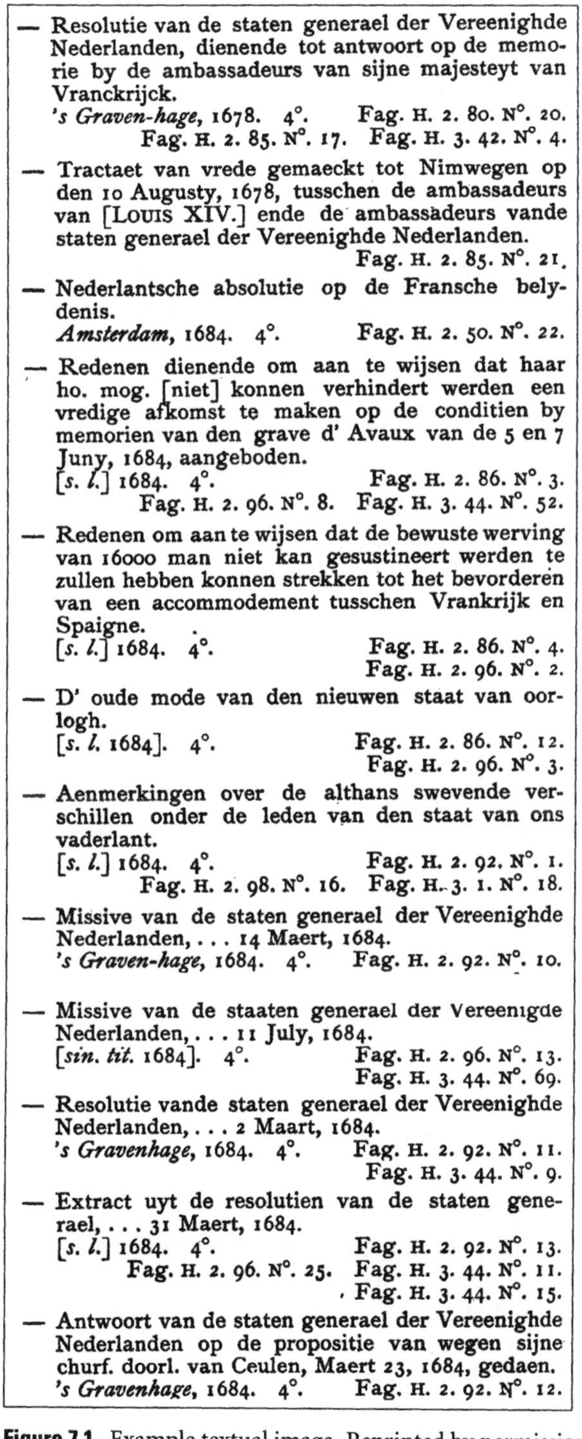

— Resolutie van de staten generael der Vereenighde Nederlanden, dienende tot antwoord op de memorie by de ambassadeurs van sijne majesteyt van Vranckrijck.
's Graven-hage, 1678.   4°.   Fag. H. 2. 80. N°. 20.
Fag. H. 2. 85. N°. 17.   Fag. H. 3. 42. N°. 4.

— Tractaet van vrede gemaeckt tot Nimwegen op den 10 Augusty, 1678, tusschen de ambassadeurs van [LOUIS XIV.] ende de ambassadeurs vande staten generael der Vereenighde Nederlanden.
Fag. H. 2. 85. N°. 21.

— Nederlantsche absolutie op de Fransche belydenis.
Amsterdam, 1684.   4°.   Fag. H. 2. 50. N°. 22.

— Redenen dienende om aan te wijsen dat haar ho. mog. [niet] konnen verhindert werden een vredige afkomst te maken op de conditien by memorien van den grave d' Avaux van de 5 en 7 Juny, 1684, aangeboden.
[*s. l.*] 1684.   4°.   Fag. H. 2. 86. N°. 3.
Fag. H. 2. 96. N°. 8.   Fag. H. 3. 44. N°. 52.

— Redenen om aan te wijsen dat de bewuste werving van 16000 man niet kan gesustineert werden te zullen hebben konnen strekken tot het bevorderen van een accommodement tusschen Vrankrijk en Spaigne.
[*s. l.*] 1684.   4°.   Fag. H. 2. 86. N°. 4.
Fag. H. 2. 96. N°. 2.

— D' oude mode van den nieuwen staat van oorlogh.
[*s. l.* 1684].   4°.   Fag. H. 2. 86. N°. 12.
Fag. H. 2. 96. N°. 3.

— Aenmerkingen over de althans swevende verschillen onder de leden van den staat van ons vaderlant.
[*s. l.*] 1684.   4°.   Fag. H. 2. 92. N°. 1.
Fag. H. 2. 98. N°. 16.   Fag. H. 3. 1. N°. 18.

— Missive van de staten generael der Vereenighde Nederlanden, . . . 14 Maert, 1684.
's Graven-hage, 1684.   4°.   Fag. H. 2. 92. N°. 10.

— Missive van de staaten generael der Vereenigde Nederlanden, . . . 11 July, 1684.
[*sin. tit.* 1684].   4°.   Fag. H. 2. 96. N°. 13.
Fag. H. 3. 44. N°. 69.

— Resolutie vande staten generael der Vereenighde Nederlanden, . . . 2 Maart, 1684.
's Gravenhage, 1684.   4°.   Fag. H. 2. 92. N°. 11.
Fag. H. 3. 44. N°. 9.

— Extract uyt de resolutien van de staten generael, . . . 31 Maert, 1684.
[*s. l.*] 1684.   4°.   Fag. H. 2. 92. N°. 13.
Fag. H. 2. 96. N°. 25.   Fag. H. 3. 44. N°. 11.
Fag. H. 3. 44. N°. 15.

— Antwoort van de staten generael der Vereenighde Nederlanden op de propositie van wegen sijne churf. doorl. van Ceulen, Maert 23, 1684, gedaen.
's Gravenhage, 1684.   4°.   Fag. H. 2. 92. N°. 12.

Figure 7.1   Example textual image. Reprinted by permission of the Board of Trinity College, Dublin.

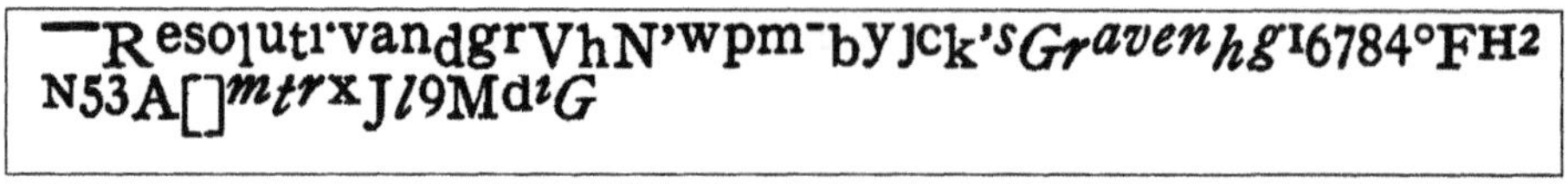

‾Resolutı·vandgrVhN'wpm‾byJck's*Graven*ₕ*g*'6784°FH2
N53A[]*mtrx*J*ℓ*9Md*ı*G

Figure 7.2 Library of symbols created from the example image.

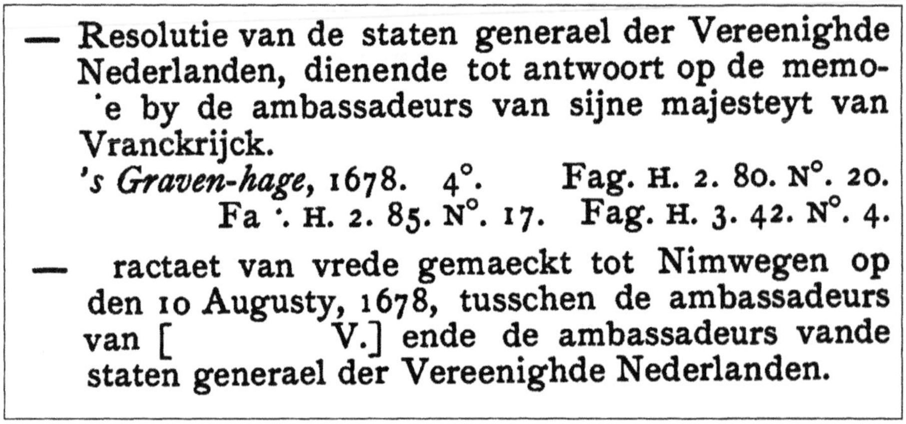

— Resolutie van de staten generael der Vereenighde
Nederlanden, dienende tot antwoort op de memo-
·e by de ambassadeurs van sijne majesteyt van
Vranckrijck.
's Graven-hage, 1678.   4°.   Fag. H. 2. 80. N°. 20.
         Fa ·. H. 2. 85. N°. 17.   Fag. H. 3. 42. N°. 4.
— ractaet van vrede gemaeckt tot Nimwegen op
den 10 Augusty, 1678, tusschen de ambassadeurs
van [V.] ende de ambassadeurs vande
staten generael der Vereenighde Nederlanden.

Figure 7.3 The "reconstructed text" image. Reprinted by permission of the Board of Trinity College, Dublin.

original picture. For easy reference, the first column shows a printed approximation to the corresponding library symbol. The intersymbol gaps of step 3 are recorded in the last two columns of Table 7.1, which shows the x and y offsets from the lower-right corner of one mark to the lower-left corner of the next. Occasionally, the x offset is small and negative (for example, following the body of an i when returning to the dot on top) or large and negative (when returning from the end of one line to the beginning of the next).

The outcome of the lossy encoding stage (step 4) is the reconstructed text, part of which is shown in Figure 7.3. It differs from the original image in three ways. First, small or very large groups of pixels may have been rejected by the segmentation process; these correspond to specks or nontextual marks in the image and do not appear in the reconstructed text. Second, because matching is approximate, characters that are merely similar in the original image will actually be identical in the reconstructed one. Third, marks that seldom occur may be pruned from the library, and if they are, they do not appear in the reconstructed text. When processing the example, marks that occurred only once on the page were pruned. Thus the letters *Louis XI* do not appear in the ninth line of Figure 7.3 because they are printed in a little-used typeface (small capitals) and occur only once each. If the system were tailored for the lossy mode of encoding, however, these symbols would not have been omitted, so that the reconstructed image would have been a very close approximation to the original.

Table 7.1 Symbols and x and y offsets created from the example image.

Symbol (approximate)	Symbol number	x offset	y offset
start-of-page	0	19	62
—	1	24	7
R	2	2	−1
e	3	3	0
s	4	4	0
o	5	2	−1
l	6	3	0
u	7	3	0
t	8	3	0
I	9	−8	−25
.	10	7	25
e	3	15	0
v	11	3	−1
a	12	3	0
n	13	17	0
d	14	4	0
e	3	25	0
s	4	3	−1
t	8	3	0
a	12	3	0
t	8	3	0
e	3	3	−1
n	13	23	10
g	15	2	−10
e	3	3	−1
n	13	4	0
e	3	3	−1
r	16	3	−1
a	12	3	0
e	3	2	0
l	6	18	0
d	14	3	0
e	3	3	0
r	16	18	0
V	17	3	−1
e	3	1	0
r	16	3	0
e	3	3	−1
e	3	3	0
n	13	4	−1
I	9	−8	−24
.	10	6	35
g	15	0	−11
h	18	3	1
d	14	3	−1
e	3	−1,012	53
N	19	4	0
e	3	2	0
d	14	4	0

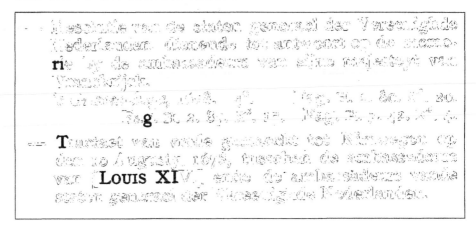

Figure 7.4 The "residue" image.

Step 5 produces enough information to generate the complete original image from the reconstructed image that approximates it. One way of doing this is to exclusive-OR the original image (Figure 7.1) with the reconstructed text (Figure 7.3) to form a *residue bitmap*, shown in Figure 7.4, which can then be coded using image compression techniques. In fact, however, this image is difficult to compress satisfactorily because it mainly contains random noise. As can be seen, much of the text can be made out from the residue in the form of *haloes* caused by small mismatches around the character edges. This indicates that the reconstructed text should be of considerable help in compression. In other words, it is profitable to use the reconstructed text as part of the context used to code the residue. The procedure used to do this is described in Section 7.6.

7.2 Lossy and lossless compression

The basic idea of textual image compression was first proposed in the mid-1970s (Ascher and Nagy 1974) and has been revived by several different groups of researchers since then—including the present authors (Witten et al. 1992; Witten, Bell, Emberson, et al. 1994). Although it has never found application on a large scale as a practical compression technique, with the advent of the JBIG2 standard, sketched in Section 7.9, that will no doubt change very quickly. Most implementations that have been described are lossy and are often built in a way that makes them suitable only for images that comprise text alone. Early systems stored the symbol sequence and offsets uncompressed, which meant that a considerable price was paid for having to represent the position of each symbol. Nevertheless, even the earliest systems reported an overall compression ratio of at least 16:1 over the raw bitmap representation.

In order to improve the technique so that it could deal with nontextual material as well as plain text, later systems incorporated the idea of encoding infrequently used marks, including nontextual material such as line drawings, using a different method. One way of doing this is to remove symbols from the image once they have been matched with a library element. This leaves the symbols that do not match as a residue that can then be compressed using a conventional image compression method.

This provides an image that is a good approximation to the original. However, it is still lossy because when a mark is matched with a library symbol, it is entirely removed from the image, even though the match may not have been a perfect one. In other words, the faint outlines, or haloes, that form around imperfectly matched symbols do not appear in the residue. Had they been left there, conventional image compression techniques would have performed disappointingly poorly on the residue.

The next development was to improve the coding of the offsets of the symbols extracted from the image, and in some experiments the patterns in the library were also compressed. Tests on the CCITT standard faxes (the same as those mentioned in Section 6.3) yielded an average compression ratio of around 25:1.

Compression can be improved by preloading common fonts into the library and discarding the residue. For example, experiments have been reported with a scheme that used a static library loaded with characters from three IBM Selectric typewriter fonts (Prestige Elite, Letter Gothic, and Courier), in both upper- and lowercase. It was also loaded with the 150 most common words in the English language, which account for around half the words in an average document; whenever any of these was encountered it was sent as a single symbol. Tests indicated that the system could achieve a compression ratio of about 145:1 provided the documents were English and were printed in one of the stored fonts. Again, compression was lossy because, although everything that failed to match was coded in the residue, haloes around characters were not coded.

Other improvements have been achieved by decomposing large figures into non-symbols so that matching techniques can be used to compress graphical information as well as text. Compression performance can also be enhanced by incorporating better pattern-matching methods that generate fewer library patterns. Speed of operation can be increased by positively identifying pattern matches, so that matching can stop as soon as the match is found instead of continuing through the entire library looking for the closest match.

Further improvements on lossy textual image compression schemes are possible. Generally, the bitmap from the first instance of each symbol is used in place of the marks that match that symbol. Performance can be improved slightly by averaging the bitmaps of all the marks that match a particular symbol and using this average as the template. The pattern-matching algorithms are not exact; if they were, the library would quickly fill up with subtly different copies of the same symbol. Inexact pattern matching can produce errors of substitution, when one character (say, a *c*) is matched to another's template (say, *o* or *e*). Errors of omission can occur when two patterns bleed into one during the printing or scanning process and are matched to a single character (for example, the digram "2." may be matched with "2"). Errors of commission can arise when the accidentally joined pattern occurs first and is placed into the library. Pattern matching is critical because mismatches lead to misrepresentations in the retrieved document, which can cause serious errors in interpretation.

To make compression lossless, step 5 encodes the entire residue, including specks and haloes, so that the original is reproduced completely, pixel-perfect. To code the residue effectively, so that it does not take up as much space as the original image would, requires novel techniques; these are described in Section 7.6.

This provides an opportunity to tailor the same scheme to work in either lossy or lossless mode. Omitting the residue encoding of step 5 gives a lossy encoding scheme that takes far fewer bits to encode a textual image. In fact, tests show that storing the residue image is responsible for perhaps three-quarters of the bits required to encode a typical textual image in lossless mode. Thus, there is a tremendous incentive to use lossy encoding in noncritical applications in which exact reproduction is not required. Unfortunately, as Figure 7.4 illustrates, the residue can contain a few important characters, so the lossy version of Figure 7.3 is deficient. However, these characters are only omitted from the library, and hence from the reconstructed text, because of the library management policy used, which in this case omits marks that occurred only once as well as marks smaller than a certain minimum size and larger than a certain maximum. Instead, all the marks larger than a minimum "speck" size could be included; this would produce an almost-perfect reconstructed image—one that was missing just the haloes in Figure 7.4—but would slightly reduce the compression that was obtained for lossless coding. The solution is clear: allow the scheme to be tailored either for lossy compression, in which case symbols are not omitted from the library, or for lossless compression, in which case a suitable library management policy is put in place to maximize the compression obtained. This gives the best of both worlds using the same basic mechanism in each case.

7.3   Extracting marks

The first step in textual image compression is to extract marks from the document. It is scanned from left to right, top to bottom, and the first nonwhite pixel is used as a "seed" to extract a mark. This means that the tallest leftmost mark is located first. Once a seed pixel is found, a boundary-tracing algorithm is applied that tracks the border of the mark. The purpose of identifying the border is to allow a bitmap of appropriate size to be set up to hold the mark itself. The next step is to actually extract the mark from the image. This is not quite so trivial a matter as it first seems because of the need to deal correctly with nesting, where one mark appears within a white region inside another mark. These do not occur in ordinary typefaces, although there are some nested marks in ideographic languages like Chinese. However, it is quite common for documents to contain paragraphs and figures surrounded by enclosing boxes, and in these cases it is important that the entire box and its contents are not extracted as a single mark. The same mark detection process will be used in the next chapter for examining whole pages of nontextual material, so we present here a general scheme that does indeed cope with arbitrarily nested marks.

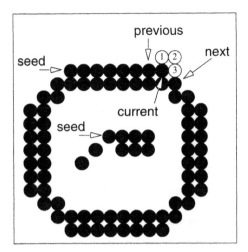

Figure 7.5   The boundary-tracing procedure.

Tracing the boundary of a mark

Boundary-tracing algorithms rely on the connectivity of the pixels in a group, and it is necessary to decide first what is meant by pixels being "connected." Each pixel has eight immediate neighbors, one in each of the eight principal compass directions, and all are considered to be connected to it. That means that a diagonal line of pixels is treated as a connected group, so that (for example) the symbol in the middle of the circle of Figure 7.5 is a single mark. This property is called *8-connectivity*. A different convention could have been used, that a pixel is only connected to its neighbors in the four primary compass directions (*4-connectivity*), but we adopt 8-connectivity as our standard.

Three pixels are used to explain the tracing process: *current*, the last pixel that has been located on the boundary so far; *previous*, the pixel processed just before the *current* one; and *next*, the pixel about to be located as the next member of the boundary. These are illustrated in Figure 7.5. The tracing procedure examines the neighbors of the current pixel in eight directions, starting two steps clockwise from the previous one (Johnsen, Segen, and Cash 1983). If a black pixel is encountered, it becomes the next member of the contour, and the operation proceeds. At the current point indicated in Figure 7.5, the first three pixels examined are marked 1, 2, 3, and once these have been scanned, the next black pixel in the contour is encountered. The boundary-tracing operation will continue clockwise all the way around the outside of the outer mark.

Progress continues along the contour until the seed pixel is met again, though this may not be the end of the operation. For example, the seed pixel of the interior mark in Figure 7.5 will be revisited before the left part of the mark has been examined, and tracing should continue past that point. The job is not complete until the seed is entered from a direction that makes the next pixel that would be encountered in the scan the one that originally followed the seed.

To trace the boundary of a mark,

1. Set *dir* ← right.

2. Repeat until back at starting pixel,

    (a) If pixel(turnright(*dir*)) is white then set *dir* ← turnright(*dir*),
        else if pixel(*dir*) is white then leave *dir* unchanged,
        else if pixel(turnleft(*dir*)) is white then set *dir* ← turnleft(*dir*),
        else set *dir* ← reverse(*dir*).

    (b) Go one step forward in direction *dir*.

    (c) Adjust bounding box parameters if necessary.

Figure 7.6 Fast procedure for boundary tracing.

During the operation, a record is kept of the minimum and maximum x and y values encountered, so that an array can be set up to hold the mark. During boundary tracing, pixels outside the border of the image are assumed to be white.

There is a substantially more efficient way to identify the boundary of a mark. It is a simple but (at first sight) strange fact that if a set of black pixels is 8-connected, the set of white pixels that surround it is 4-connected. For example, the white pixels marked 1, 2, and 3 in Figure 7.5 form part of the exterior boundary of the mark, and they are 4-connected—as are all the other pixels that lie just outside the boundary. It is quicker to identify a 4-connected boundary than an 8-connected one since fewer tests are involved. Consequently, a more efficient procedure is to begin at the pixel just above the seed and trace around the outside of the mark.

In order to explain this procedure, we use the notion of *current direction*, which may be right, left, up, or down. The direction is initially rightward, and the current pixel is the one just above the seed. The procedure checks the next pixel. If it is white, it can move ahead—but before doing so the pixel to the right is checked to see if it is white, and if so, it turns right instead of moving ahead. If the next pixel is black, however, the direction must be changed. (This situation will not arise in the first instance because the mark cannot contain any pixels above the seed pixel, but in general it can happen later on.) The procedure turns left if possible, to ensure that the perimeter is traced in the clockwise direction. However, if this is not possible—in other words, if the left pixel is black—we have found ourselves in a cul-de-sac. The appropriate thing to do is reverse direction.

The procedure is perhaps explained better in the pseudocode of Figure 7.6. Here, pixel(*dir*) checks the next pixel in the specified direction. Turnright(*dir*), turnleft(*dir*), and reverse(*dir*) are new directions obtained from the current one by turning right and left and reversing, respectively. The starting pixel is the one just above the seed pixel, and the process terminates when it returns to this starting pixel. In contrast to the previous boundary-following procedure, there is no need to check that the starting direction has been reached because the starting pixel is not the seed but the pixel above.

This 4-connected boundary-following method is more efficient than the previous 8-connected one. Our own tests on typical boundary shapes have shown that it requires an average of about two comparisons for each point on the boundary, while the other method uses about three comparisons. This advantage is very slightly offset by the fact that the white "outside" boundary traced by the 4-connected algorithm is longer than the black one that represents the 8-connected boundary of the mark. Generally, it is only a little longer—with a rectangle, for example, the difference is only four pixels—and the 4-connected boundary-following method is still 50 percent faster than the 8-connected one.

Removing the mark from the image

Once its boundary is identified, the mark is removed from the document. Care must be taken to cope correctly with nested marks. This can be done using a region-filling algorithm, except that in this case the black region containing the seed pixel is *emptied* from the image into the target array that has been set up to receive it.

The simplest region-filling procedure is known as the *flood-fill method*. The idea is to start with the seed pixel, copy it into the target array and remove it from the image, then recursively apply the flood-filling procedure to each of its eight neighbors. In general, the procedure, when applied to a particular pixel, first checks the color of that pixel. If it is white, the procedure exits immediately; otherwise, the pixel is copied to the target array and cleared in the source array, and the procedure is recursively invoked on each neighbor. The entire operation terminates when the original call of the flood-filling procedure—the one whose argument was the seed pixel—returns.

This simple method turns out to involve a large number of unnecessary recursive calls. An obvious modification is to check the color of each neighbor before recursively calling the procedure on that pixel; this does reduce the problem, but an excessive number of calls still remain. Any particular pixel will be processed up to eight times, as it has eight neighbors that will all check it as they are processed. The number of recursive calls will be up to eight times as many as necessary, creating a penalty in both execution time and stack space.

A better alternative is the *run-based region-fill algorithm*, which avoids making so many unnecessary recursive calls. Figure 7.7 illustrates this method on an *H*. First, the seed pixel is put onto a stack—items in the stack are gray. The procedure removes the next pixel from the stack and proceeds to empty the horizontal run of contiguous pixels to the right of it in the figure; it should check the pixel to the left as well, in case there is a run of pixels there. Clearly, this will not happen in the case of the seed pixel but may in the general case. As each pixel of the run is processed, the ones that are 8-connected to it in the lines above and below are checked. Any that begin a run of pixels in the figure are stacked. Thus, when the second pixel is emptied, the pixel below is stacked because it begins a run of pixels. In the version of *H* in Figure 7.7c, the first run of pixels has been emptied and there is one pixel on

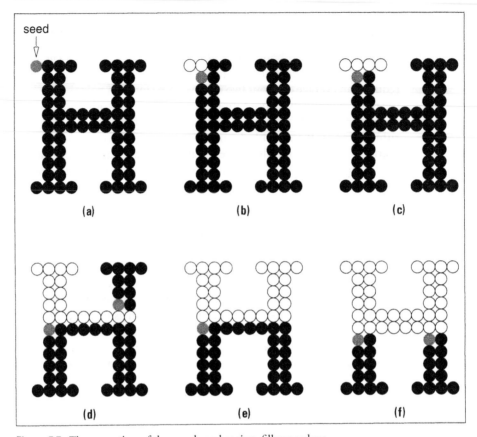

Figure 7.7 The operation of the run-based region-fill procedure.

the stack. The pixel beside the gray one is not stacked because it is only the leftmost pixel of a run—in other words, the one that begins it—that is placed on the stack. The algorithm removes the pixel from the stack and repeats.

By the time Figure 7.7d has been reached, the top left arm of the *H* has been emptied, as has the first row of the crossbar. Two pixels are now on the stack: the one beginning the second crossbar row and the one at the bottom of the top right arm. The latter is the first to be unstacked, and it results in the whole top right arm being extracted. When this is complete (Figure 7.7e), the former is unstacked and the second crossbar row is emptied. This causes two further pixels to be stacked (Figure 7.7f); these are subsequently unstacked and the legs are processed, beginning with the rightmost. The algorithm terminates when the stack is empty.

Recall that the purpose of identifying the border is to allow a bitmap of appropriate size to be set up to hold the mark itself. If there is no shortage of space, it is possible to omit the border identification step and instead allocate a scratch area for the mark whose size is the same as the original image. Then the process of determining the exact size of the map can be combined with the region-filling procedure, and no separate boundary-tracing operation is needed. It is a simple matter in the run-based region-fill algorithm to check each pixel that is unstacked, and each pixel that ends a run, against the bounds of the mark so far and enlarge the bounds if necessary. Once the mark has been transferred from the original image to the scratch area and its size is known, an appropriate space can be allocated for it in the library, and it is simply copied there. More details about region-filling algorithms can be found in computer graphics texts such as Foley and Van Dam (1982).

When the mark has been extracted from the image and the pixels that comprise it have been set to white, the left-to-right, top-to-bottom scan continues in order to locate a seed pixel for the next mark. This procedure deals correctly with nested marks because once an exterior mark has been removed, any interior ones will be encountered during future scanning. For example, after the outer mark in Figure 7.5 has been located and removed, the inner one will be found.

Sorting marks into natural reading order

It is not easy to find the lines of text in document images reliably for a variety of reasons, such as incorrect orientation of the document during scanning, multiple columns, and nontextual regions on the page. As noted previously, however, we are assuming that any skew has been corrected and regions containing textual material have been isolated, using methods described in Section 8.1. Consequently, a very straightforward method of detecting lines of text is quite satisfactory. It is sufficient simply to project the image onto its left-hand border and use this projection to determine where the lines of text are. The gaps between the lines will correspond to points where no values have been projected, and the lines themselves will be contiguous humps in the projection profile. These can easily be detected.

Once the lines have been identified, marks lying within each line's region are separated out and sorted by horizontal position, which puts them into the order in which they appeared on the page. In general, a symbol should be placed before any disconnected part that lies above it, and to do this, any ties in the sorting should be broken by vertical position, giving preference to marks lower on the page. For example, the body of an *i* will be encountered before its dot, the accent on an *é* will come after the letter itself, and both dots in the umlaut on *ü* will follow the *u*.

7.4 Template matching

As marks are extracted, they are matched against those already in the library. A set is kept of all marks that match each library member. If the current mark matches an existing one closely enough, it is added to the set of matches for that library symbol. Though it may be more reliable to match a mark with every library template to see which is the closest, it is much more efficient to terminate the operation as soon as a template is found that comes within a specified threshold. If no sufficiently close match is found, then the mark is added to the library.

Template matching is critical to the successful identification of marks. Matching procedures generally operate by examining an *error map*, which is the bitwise exclusive-OR between the new symbol and a library member. Before computing the error map, the two must be registered appropriately. The new symbol is superimposed upon each symbol in the library by aligning some fixed reference point. Aligning the lower-left corners is one possibility, but more reliable results are obtained by aligning the centroids—that is, the average position of the black pixels in each bitmap (this and other results in this section are from Inglis and Witten 1994). Several registrations may be tried to find the one that matches best. For example, nine matches might be performed, corresponding to the original registration plus constant (perhaps one-pixel) displacements in the eight principal compass directions. In each registration, the exclusive-OR between old and new symbols is calculated to yield the error map, and the tests described below are repeated (perhaps many times) until the template is accepted in one of the registrations. To save time, matching may be terminated when the first acceptable registration is found, or it may continue to the end so that the registration with the best fit can be used.

Many different matching methods have been described in the literature and are reviewed below. They can be divided into two categories, depending on whether they use global or local criteria. Global methods measure the overall mismatch between the new symbol and a library template, summing up contributions to the error map from the entire area occupied by the symbol. Local methods base their judgment on particular areas of mismatch that involve just a few adjacent pixels. A new approach to global template matching, which from the viewpoint of textual image compression is very natural, is to base it on the idea of image compression using the context models of Section 6.3. This provides an extremely effective template-matching technique that outperforms earlier methods. Many template-matching systems use a *screening* strategy, based on gross attributes such as overall size, to select just a few likely library marks to be presented to the matcher for a more detailed comparison with the unknown mark. This can substantially reduce both the amount of computation involved and the number of mismatches that occur. In fact, sometimes the screening strategies are so effective in reducing the number of comparisons made that they should really be considered part of the template-matching procedure itself.

Global template matching

The starting point for global template matching is to measure the difference between the two symbols by the total number of pixels that are set in the error map—that is, the number of positions in which pixels of the two symbols differ. However, it is best to weight the error pixels differently depending on the context in which the error occurs. Two identical characters—for example, two versions of *e*—may differ in several places around the boundary of the character. Two different characters—for example, *c* and *o*—may differ by a smaller number of pixels, but because the error pixels occur in a cluster (the gap between the arms of the *c*) they are more significant. Figure 7.8 illustrates the situation. The two *e*s at the top differ by 29 pixels, while

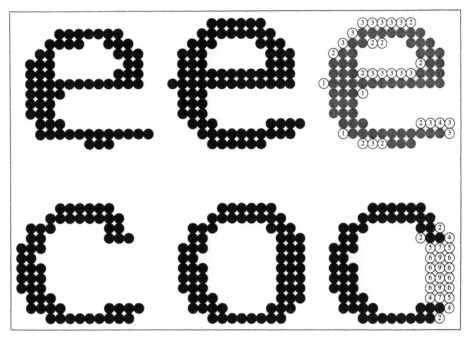

Figure 7.8 Template matching using the error map.

the *c* and *o* differ by only 23 pixels; however, the latter difference is clearly more significant. A solution is to weight error pixels more highly if they occur in a cluster (Pratt et al. 1980). This can be done by calculating the *weighted exclusive*-OR, in which each error pixel contributes an amount that equals the number of error pixels in its 3 × 3 neighborhood. These numbers are written in the small open circles in the figure. The total weight is 73 for the two *e*s but 131 for the *c* and *o*, indicating that these exhibit a far more significant difference.

Using this idea, a match is rejected if the weighted error exceeds a preset threshold. In order to make the scheme size-independent, the threshold should depend on the number of black pixels in the symbols and may be chosen to be a linear function of it. The best way to set the threshold is to train the system on the fonts being used. A more sophisticated approach, which has been found to work better in practice, is to make the threshold dependent on the symbols' perimeter length rather than on the black pixel count. The reasoning behind this is that when two similar symbol patterns are superimposed, the matching errors are randomly distributed along the inner and outer perimeters of the symbols, so this is an appropriate metric to use when normalizing the number of error pixels.

Another improvement is to look more carefully at the error map itself. Exclusive-ORing the two bitmaps amalgamates errors caused by an extra pixel in one bitmap with errors caused by an extra pixel in the other. According to the weighting mechanism, two neighboring error pixels increase each other's weights

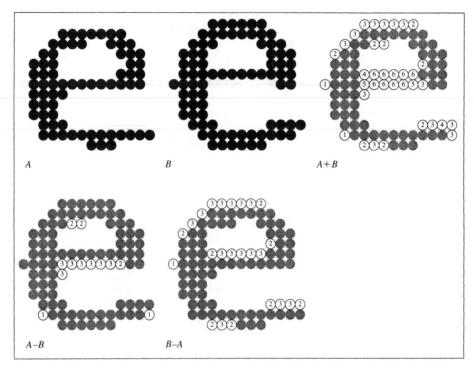

Figure 7.9 A problem with global template matching.

regardless of whether they are due to black pixels in the same pattern or to one black pixel in each pattern. The latter error is less serious since it corresponds to a single displaced pixel. Figure 7.9 illustrates the problem. The two *es* are very similar—just as similar as the ones in Figure 7.8—but the displaced horizontal line contributes highly weighted pixels to the error map, and in fact the total error weight between the *es* in Figure 7.9 is 129, almost the same as that between the *c* and *o* in Figure 7.8.

A solution is to differentiate two error maps, one (call it $A - B$) containing pixels that are set in the first image but not the second, and the other (call it $B - A$) containing pixels that are set in the second image but not the first (Holt and Xydeas 1986). These two maps are shown in the lower part of Figure 7.9. The weighting procedure gives each $A - B$ pixel a weight equal to the number of $A - B$ pixels in a 3×3 neighborhood centered on the element in question. Similarly, each $B - A$ error is weighted according to the number of neighboring $B - A$ errors. The weighted errors are then summed over the whole error map. The result is that, for example, a line that is displaced by a single pixel carries a lighter penalty than it would in the original weighting scheme. In Figure 7.9, the sum of the weights is reduced to 93. However, when a block of pixels is present in one bitmap but not the other—as with the *c* and *o* of Figure 7.8—the weighting is not affected because all the error pixels appear in just one of the two error maps.

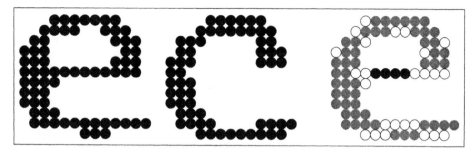

Figure 7.10 Detecting a one-pixel line using local template matching.

Local template matching

Local methods look at individual areas of the error map rather than summing all discrepancies across the whole map. A match is rejected if any black pixel in the error map is found to have more than a certain number of neighbors that are also black (Johnsen, Segen, and Cash 1983). We refer to this as Rule A and suppose that the threshold is four. This would cope correctly with the examples of Figure 7.8, since there is no place in which an error pixel for the two *e*s is surrounded by four black error pixels, and there are many places in which an error pixel for the *c* and *o* is surrounded by four or more black error pixels. Unfortunately, a threshold of four would erroneously reject the match between the two *e*s in Figure 7.9—it does not cope well with the displacement of a line in the bitmap.

Moreover, and more seriously, this Rule A alone will not be able to detect mismatches due to the presence of a thin stroke or gap in one image but not the other—like the fine line that differentiates the *c* from the *e* in Figure 7.10. To do this, a second, more complex, rule is needed. One that has been suggested is Rule B: reject a match if

- a black pixel in the error map has two or more black neighbors, at least two of which are not connected to each other, and
- the corresponding pixel in either one of the bitmaps is entirely surrounded by either white or black pixels.

As Figure 7.10 illustrates, this will detect a one-pixel-wide line that appears in one bitmap but not the other. The line causes an identical line in the error map, the center pixels of which, shown as solid black circles, have two disconnected black neighbors in the error map and are entirely surrounded by white in the *c* bitmap.

It turns out that Rule B often produces false matches on small characters. To combat this, tighter versions of Rules A and B can be defined. For Rule A, instead of rejecting a match if any black pixel in the error map has four or more black neighbors, any 2×2 neighborhood in the error map with all four pixels black can be taken as sufficient evidence for rejection. For Rule B, the last clause can be tightened by checking just four of the surrounding pixels rather than all of them: the ones above, below, and to either side.

Unfortunately, local methods are sensitive to the size of the symbols being considered, since they look for local patterns containing a certain number of pixels. This is illustrated by the erroneous rejection of the match between the two *es* in Figure 7.9 when the rejection threshold is set to four pixels. To achieve some degree of invariance, the size of the symbols can be checked to decide which version of the rules to apply. For example, if the width or height of either symbol is 12 pixels or less, the tighter version might be applied; if either exceeds this, then the original, weaker version could be used. This is called the *combined size-independent* strategy (Holt 1988).

Compression-based template matching

An entirely different approach to template matching, which fits well with the idea of textual image compression, is to quantify the information required to transmit a mark using each library symbol as a model and choose the symbol that enables transmission in the smallest number of bits (Inglis and Witten 1994). This approach works very well:

Compression-based template matching is probably the best choice for template matching unless speed is a major issue.

The basic idea is to calculate the entropy of the unknown mark with respect to each symbol in the library and choose the one with the lowest value. Recall from Section 6.3 that a context model can be used to expedite the transmission of a binary image. The *context* is a mask that singles out certain pixels surrounding the current one and uses their values as a context for prediction. Note that the word "template" was sometimes used in Chapter 6 in a different sense, denoting the mask used for context-based compression. Henceforth, we avoid this usage.

To use model-based compression for matching marks, instead of applying the mask to the image that has been transmitted so far to predict the next pixel of the same image, it is applied to the library mark that is being matched to predict the next pixel of the unknown mark. This means that the mask is not restricted to using prior pixels only and may include pixels from ahead of the current one; thus it is what we called "clairvoyant" in Section 6.3. Figure 7.11 shows two marks that are being matched. The first one, *H*, is from the library, while the second, *A*, is the unknown mark. Of course we do not expect a very good match between *H* and *A*; a much better score will result from using the library *A* for prediction.

In the figure, a symmetric 3×3 mask is shown in the same position over both letters and is used to predict a pixel in the unknown mark (the *A*). The two marks are aligned with each other by placing their centroids together, and then the mask is passed over them. The nine pixels in the library pattern are used to predict the mask's central pixel in the unknown pattern. Thus, in this position, the 3×3 configuration at the bottom is used to predict the pixel shown to the right, which in this case happens to be black. Prediction statistics are gleaned from typical pages, so that for this 3×3 context a black pixel count, say, c_b, and a white-pixel count, c_w, are

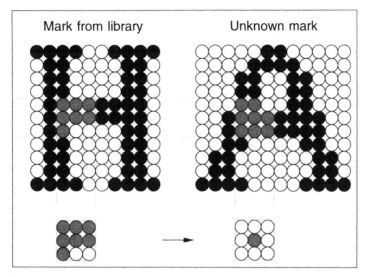

Figure 7.11 Using a mask to predict pixels of one mark based on another.

known. Coding this particular pixel would consume

$$-\log \frac{c_b}{c_b + c_w}$$

bits. For matching we are not actually interested in doing the coding, just in how many bits are required. Consequently, all that is calculated is the total of the bits required to code each pixel. This figure is the numeric value of the match between the two marks: small numbers mean better matches. It is essentially an entropy measure of one mark with respect to the other: we call it the *cross-entropy*.

In compression, it is normal to use an adaptive model, accumulating the counts as compression proceeds, because otherwise the model must somehow be communicated to the decoder. However, when obtaining an entropy figure, there is no need to communicate the model, so a static one can be used. Like the clairvoyant context, this provides a lower bound on the amount of compression that could possibly be achieved in practice. The template-matching procedure begins by building the model of one mark with respect to the other. It would be much faster to calculate a single model and use it for all matches. However, this degrades performance very seriously.

Suppose the two marks to be matched are designated by L and M. For any particular pixel $L_{i,j}$ in the first, there is a corresponding pixel $M_{i+\Delta x, j+\Delta y}$ in the second, where $(\Delta x, \Delta y)$ is the displacement due to registration. Figure 7.11 shows two different marks with the nine-pixel clairvoyant mask superimposed at the same position of each. The values of the nine pixels under the mask in the first mark, L, taken together, determine a particular context. The value of the central mask pixel in the other mark, M, gives a color, black or white, and the corresponding count for that context value is incremented. The process is repeated for every pixel to build a complete model. The marks are assumed to be surrounded by white space, and, once they have been registered, the maximum extent in both the horizontal and vertical directions is used as the area over which the entropy is calculated.

Once the model has been created, a second pass is taken over the marks, and the counts in the models are used to calculate the entropy of the second mark, M, with respect to the first one, L. The process is not symmetric, and both model and entropy will depend on whether the calculation is done for M with respect to L or for L with respect to M. Both are calculated and the maximum is taken as the final cross-entropy measure.

This method of matching is particularly attractive for textual image compression because from the numerical match value we can estimate the number of bits that are saved by using the library symbol and coding the differences from the unknown mark, versus simply leaving the mark in situ and coding it as part of the residue; we return to this in the subsection on "Library construction" (page 338). The method does have the drawback of being rather more computationally intensive than the other template-matching techniques. Taking the logarithms is not a problem: the log of the ratio can be obtained by subtraction, and the logs of all counts precalculated and stored in a table. However, passing the mask over the library symbol involves more bit shifting and pixel manipulation than the other methods.

Screening library templates

As marks are extracted, they are matched against the symbols already in the library. However, it is advantageous to screen the library symbols to reduce the number of matches that must be computed. There is no need to match templates that are obviously dissimilar to the input. For example, templates that differ greatly in width or height are obviously dissimilar: there is no point in comparing an M or W library template with a small punctuation character like a comma or a period (assuming, of course, that they are not of radically different font sizes). Screening reduces the number of template-matching operations that are undertaken, while simultaneously minimizing the number of matchable marks that are excluded.

Screening might be based on characteristics other than width and height. The features must be easy to compute and compare, and they must also be resistant to the noise that inevitably occurs during the digitization process. Two obvious possibilities are the mark's area and its perimeter, which are easy to obtain when extracting the mark. However, they do not seem to be particularly useful in practice, partly because they are correlated with width and height and also because they tend to be rather sensitive to noise and digitization parameters such as contrast. Other features that show more promise are the number of horizontal and the number of vertical white runs that are enclosed in the pattern. Thus, for example, a sans serif letter I would have none in either direction. A sans serif H would have none in the vertical direction but several in the horizontal direction corresponding to the number of white rows that run from one leg to the other. Sans serif E would have none in the horizontal direction but several in the vertical direction.

An even better basis for screening is to compare the overall spatial distribution of mass—that is, black pixels—in the two marks. This can be done by registering them according to their centroids, then dividing them into quadrants around the centroid. For each quadrant, a local centroid is calculated, and for each of the four local centroids the distance between its position in the two marks is determined. Finally, these four distances are averaged. The process could be continued recursively, defining a distance at level 0 based on the original centroids (that distance is 0 since centroid registration is used), a distance at level 1 as described above, and further higher-level distances. However, tests show that excellent screening results are obtained with the level-1 distance, and further elaboration is unnecessary.

Compression-based matching may lend itself to more rational—but also more expensive—forms of screening. For example, each symbol in the library can be stored at a reduced resolution, and a reduced-resolution version of the unknown mark can be calculated. Then the reduced versions are matched using model-based compression, and only the most promising matches are pursued to higher resolutions. The resolution reduction method of the JBIG standard (Section 6.4) is very suitable for this purpose. Reduced-resolution matching is much less time-consuming than the full matches and so is suitable for screening purposes.

Regardless of which screening method is chosen, it can also be used to sort the library templates that are to be matched, so that the most likely matches are tried first. This can be done on grounds of both feature similarity and probability of occurrence, where templates that have often been matched tend to be tried first. This reduces computation time because matching can cease as soon as a template is found that matches within a specified threshold. This threshold is generally chosen by trial and error.

It may also be worth considering a two-stage screening procedure, where the first screening attempts only to match library templates whose features are very similar to the unknown mark's features; in the few cases where no match is found, a much looser screening criterion is applied. This kind of technique has been reported to greatly reduce the average number of matches attempted per mark.

Evaluation of template-matching methods

In order to compare the performance of various template-matching procedures, a large collection of marks was obtained by extracting connected groups of pixels from several test images. The images included Figure 7.1, along with other pages from the same source. They had been scanned at 400 dpi with no noticeable skewing, and careful attention was paid to contrast settings so that there was little fragmentation of characters or bleeding of one into another.

The marks were labeled by hand, and ones that could not be identified easily were discarded. This left approximately 2,500 marks, each with a well-defined, unambiguous classification. Most were in roman font, but some were italicized and were labeled as such so that they were assigned to a different class from the corresponding roman letter. Six marks were *false ligatures* formed by two characters bleeding together—for example, *rt* occurred twice—and were labeled as such. There was some minor variation in type size—for example, letters in a small capitals face were assigned to the same class as regular capital letters. In total, 80 classifications were used with an average of just over 30 marks in each class. Twelve classes had just one member, while six contained more than a hundred members.

Several experiments were performed on this collection to test the processes of registration, template matching, and screening. Artificial noise models were used to investigate the effect of noise on classification accuracy. Six template-matching methods were tested. (The labels are those used in the template-matching literature.) Three of them are the global ones described above: XOR (exclusive-OR), which simply counts the number of pixels set in the error map; WXOR (weighted exclusive-OR), which weights the pixels according to the number of neighboring pixels that are set; and WAN (weighted AND-NOT), which does the same but treats black-to-white errors separately from white-to-black ones when calculating the weights. Two are the local methods described earlier: PMS (pattern matching and substitution), which rejects a match if any position in the error map is found to have four or more neighbors that are set, and CSIS (combined size-independent strategy), which augments this rule by two heuristics to detect thin strokes or gaps. The last, CTM, is compression-based template matching.

The result of any matching method depends critically on the registration, and in particular, for those that use the error map, it is clear that this map is extremely sensitive to the precise alignment of the images. Some systems align the upper-left corner of the bounding boxes, while others use the lower-left corner instead. A third possibility is to align the geometric center of the marks' bounding boxes; a fourth is to use the marks' centroids. Each of these was tested by registering pairs of marks and matching the two templates. The result in each case was a binary decision, match or no match. Repeating the operation over all pairs of marks with the same label gives an overall correctness figure for each registration choice. The resulting scores were highest for centroid alignment. In fact, for this test data the centroid turned out to be, on average, very close to the position of the geometric center. Registering based on the upper-left and lower-left corners gave classification accuracies that were measurably lower than when the centroid was used.

In order to test the six template-matching methods, each mark was compared with every other using that method. The result of every comparison was again a binary decision: match or no match. Only positive identifications are considered. If the true classification of the two marks according to the hand-assigned labels is the same, and the outcome is match, this is counted as a correct positive identification. If the true classification is different and the outcome is match, this is counted as an incorrect positive identification. The percentage of correct and incorrect positive identifications is used as a measure of the matching method's performance.

All the template-matching methods have parameters that need to be chosen. Each method was assessed under the most favorable possible conditions. Parameters were determined by searching the parameter space to maximize the number of correct minus the number of incorrect identifications. For example, for the XOR method, the range of the rejection threshold was varied to get the best result, which was in fact 81 percent correct and 6 percent incorrect identifications. In both the

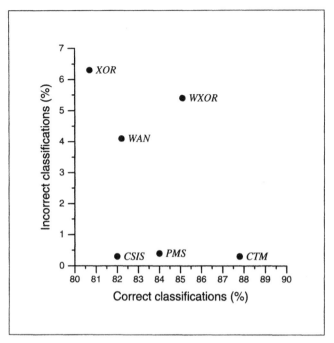

Figure 7.12 Results of different methods of template matching.

PMS and CSIS methods, each localized criterion for rejecting matches was treated as a parameter that was then subject to optimization. For example, the number of times an error pixel has more than a specified weight became a variable parameter. For the CTM method, a five-pixel symmetric clairvoyant template—four adjacent pixels and the central one—was used, and an experimentally determined two-part threshold, based on both the entropy per pixel and the absolute cross-entropy value, was used to decide whether a match should be accepted or rejected. It would be interesting to investigate whether experimentally determined thresholds could be avoided by setting an absolute threshold based on whether one mark could be coded more effectively with respect to the other, or whether it would be coded more effectively if the other were ignored.

Figure 7.12 shows the result of these experiments. CTM clearly outperforms the other methods, obtaining the best results in both classification dimensions. The percentage of correct classifications exceeds that of the closest competitor, WXOR, and the number of incorrect classifications is lower than the lowest of the other methods, PMS and CSIS.

Each method of template matching responds differently to different kinds of noise. Three types of noise were added to the marks to emulate such conditions. The first is salt-and-pepper noise, in which a certain percentage (10 percent) of pixels within a mark's bounding box are reversed. The second is the kind of edge noise caused by variations in paper quality or evenness of inking. This is modeled by

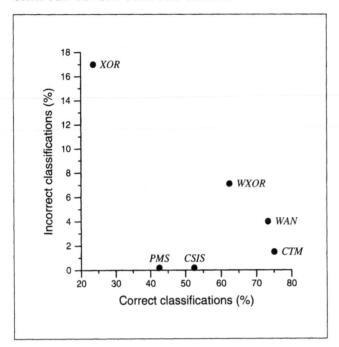

Figure 7.13 Results of template matching with added noise.

adding black pixels around the perimeter of the mark, with a certain probability (again 10 percent) that each white pixel around the perimeter is changed to black. The third type of noise is a more extreme kind of edge noise, intended to emulate the blurring that occurs when images are scanned at too high a contrast, and is obtained by repeating the previously described edge noise process several times.

The same testing process as above was undertaken for each noise model. Every mark was corrupted as described above, and the entire process of comparison was repeated using the same parameters as before. The results show that CTM continues to achieve the highest number of correct matches under all conditions. However, it no longer achieves the lowest number of incorrect matches: the PMS and CSIS methods are consistently better in this regard. Unfortunately, their performance with respect to correct matches is very much worse, reducing to only 25 percent for high edge noise. CTM is still the best choice overall.

Figure 7.13 shows the result of averaging the performance with different kinds of artifical noise. CTM continues to classify more marks correctly than the other methods, and while the rate of incorrect classification is slightly higher than both PMS and CSIS, the latter methods make major sacrifices in correct classifications. The method with the closest number of correct classifications is the WAN method, but this has almost twice as many incorrect results.

Finally, five methods of screening were investigated, based on the features discussed earlier. Each screening method can be used as a prefiltering step to any of the template matchers. The screening method determines the value of a numeric pa-

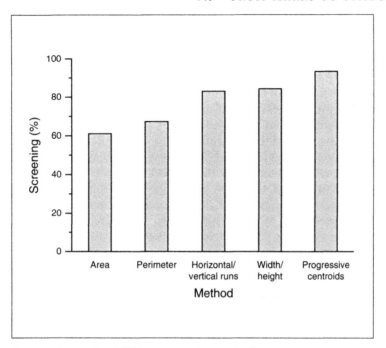

Figure 7.14 Results of different screening methods.

rameter. If the parameters for the two marks differ by more than a predetermined threshold, the match is rejected without further consideration; if it differs by less, a full template-matching operation is undertaken. For each method, an appropriate threshold was determined in a preliminary series of experiments. It was chosen to be as selective as it possibly could be without affecting the outcome of the classification process. For example, using area as a screening function, the best cutoff value for the threshold eliminated 61 percent of the matches from further consideration, without affecting any of the classifications.

Results for each of the methods is shown in Figure 7.14. Area was the least effective criterion, followed by perimeter. The simplest method—width and height of the mark—fared much better, as did the number of horizontal and vertical runs. The progressive centroid scheme gave the best performance, achieving 93 percent screening, with no impact on classification accuracy. A faster version using Hamming or "city block" distance instead of Euclidean distance performed only slightly worse.

7.5 From marks to symbols

Several issues arise when deciding which symbols should be stored in the library and how their positions on the page should be represented.

Library construction

In general, each library symbol is matched to several marks in the document image, and the set of corresponding marks is stored along with the library symbol. If the current mark matches an existing symbol, it is added to the set of matches for that library symbol; if not, it is added to the library as a new symbol.

The compression-based template-matching method described on page 330 is probably the best choice. However, in our original work on the Trinity College Library images we used the pattern-matching strategy developed in the "Local template matching" section on page 329. Because these images are scanned at 400 dpi, we found it necessary to modify the method slightly to enhance its size independence; the unmodified algorithm is probably more suitable for ordinary fax images. Of course, although in OCR mismatches are serious errors, when textual image compression is used in lossless mode, they merely cause a small penalty in compression efficiency. The reproduced image will still be a faithful copy of the original.

The result of template matching is a provisional library that stores the first-encountered variant of each symbol, along with the set of all marks that matched it. Each template in the library can be replaced by an averaged version in which a pixel is set if it appears in more than half the marks that matched. This removes the arbitrariness of storing the first-encountered variant. The averaged marks are the ones that will be used to make the image of the reconstructed text.

The final stage of library processing depends on whether performance is to be optimized for lossy or for lossless mode. If the system will normally be used in lossless mode, with step 5 included, it may be beneficial to prune the library by discarding *singletons*, or symbols that have occurred just once. If it will normally be used in lossy mode, marks should only be discarded if they comprise fewer than a fixed number of black pixels—say, half the number of black pixels in a period (.). Discarding singletons removes almost all the noise symbols. However, it also removes genuine characters that occur only once, which can create gaps in the reconstructed text (for example, the *Louis XI* of Figure 7.3). If the reconstructed text is to be used directly, singletons should remain in the library so that such gaps are avoided.

If compression-based template matching is used, pruning can be done on a more rational basis. Consider the fate of each mark in the image. There are three possibilities.

First, it may be matched to an existing library symbol. In this case, there is the cost of coding this occurrence in the symbol stream, the cost of transmitting the x and y offsets of the symbol, and the contribution that the difference between the mark and the library symbol makes to the residue. Second, a mark may be placed in the library as a new symbol. This incurs the cost of transmitting an extra symbol in the library, amortized over the number of other marks that match this symbol, as well as the cost of coding this occurrence in the symbol stream and transmitting its x and y offsets. It also incurs the cost of the mark's contribution to the residue. Third, the mark can simply be left in the residue and not matched to a library symbol at all.

As discussed earlier in this section, this is not a good option in lossy compression mode unless the mark is smaller than a certain minimum size.

Most of these costs can be estimated reasonably accurately, and it is not generally worthwhile to ascertain them exactly by performing the coding on a trial basis. The cost of coding a new member of the symbol stream obviously depends on how likely the new symbol is in the present context. However, an average figure can be used for estimation purposes. The same goes for the x and y offsets. When a mark is matched to an existing library symbol (the first case), its contribution to the residue is given by the matching distance, measured in bits. Again, this is only an approximation because different statistics and templates are used for coding the residue, as will be described in Section 7.6. When a mark is placed in the library as a new symbol (the second case), the cost of coding it as part of the library can be estimated as the average cost of transmitting library symbols. Its contribution to the residue is in principle zero, since the library symbol is the same as the mark; however, this is only an approximation because of the averaging process mentioned above. When a mark is left entirely in the residue (the third case), its cost can be estimated as the average cost of a library symbol since similar coding methods are used in each case (though with different templates).

Of course, careful pruning of the library does take time. However, it should be emphasized that, although it slows down encoding, it has no effect on decoding speed, which is often the critical parameter in practice.

Symbols and their offsets

The symbols in the final library are assigned unique identification numbers. For example, zero might be reserved to indicate start-of-page and the symbols numbered from one upward, in order of appearance. The sequence of marks that constitute the characters in the text will be represented as a list of symbol identifiers. This stream will be compressed using adaptive coding, so no penalty is paid for the fact that the identifiers do not correspond to a conventional character coding such as ASCII.

The x and y offsets from one symbol to the next are measured from the lower-right corner of one mark to the lower-left corner of the next. For proportionally spaced typefaces, this convention reduces variation in the mark-to-mark distances by factoring out the size of the marks involved. These offsets must be compressed and stored. The mark extraction process does not recognize white space as a symbol in its own right—any space following a mark will manifest itself merely as an unusually large x offset.

Experiments with ordinary text files show that the presence of white-space characters generally improves compression, even though these characters increase the number of items that have to be coded. For example, removing all the spaces (including newlines) from Hardy's *Far from the Madding Crowd* reduces its uncompressed size by 16 percent. However, when this spaceless version is compressed using the PPM method, the compressed file is 0.6 percent *larger* than the compressed form of the full book. It seems that space characters give important clues to the context-based compression system. Therefore, you might consider inserting a special code, known in advance to encoder and decoder, into the text between words and at the end of lines. The size of the x and y offsets associated with the preceding symbols is what distinguishes spaces from tabs (and newlines).

The points at which white space should be inserted can be located by seeking bimodality in the distribution of x offset values. If two peaks are separated by at least a certain amount, a cutoff point is placed halfway between them, and a space is inserted whenever the actual x offset exceeds this threshold (and also after large negative offsets). The average (mode) value of the offset associated with each symbol is then calculated, ignoring those occurrences where a space has been inserted. Then the x and y offsets associated with symbols that precede space are set at the modal values for that symbol, and the balance is assigned to the following white space. For all this effort, the white-space identification procedure generally improves overall performance by only a very small amount because the representation of the symbols is just a small component of the output. For this reason, it is probably not worth going to the trouble of identifying white space.

7.6 Coding the components of a textual image

Each component of the decomposed image is encoded into a single bitstream. Despite the variety of models used for the different components, they can all be used to drive a single arithmetic coder. Some components might be coded more simply using other methods, but the use of a uniform coding regime means that all components can be mixed into the same bitstream without any need to define a format for the information and without any penalty for starting and stopping the coding of each component. The arithmetic coder is driven by different probability distributions for each component of the image.

Library

The number of symbols in the library must be transmitted first. This can be done by employing a fixed, precomputed probability distribution. In fact, the number of symbols in the library costs only a few bits for the whole file no matter how it is coded, so the particular method adopted does not really make any practical difference. However, we will develop a code that will also serve other purposes.

Consider first a fixed code such as the γ code, described in Section 3.3. This has the advantage of allowing numbers of any size to be encoded, in a way that favors short numbers over long ones. If the γ code is to be adopted, we need to find a way to achieve its effect with arithmetic coding. The length of a γ-coded number $n \geq 1$ is $2\lfloor \log n \rfloor + 1$. Recall that a symbol of probability p, when coded arithmetically, contributes $-\log p$ bits to the output stream. Equating these yields the probability distribution that is implied by the γ code, and, as we saw in Section 3.3, this turns out to be $1/(2n^2)$. Therefore, using arithmetic coding with this probability distribution will yield the same code lengths as the γ code. However, coding is a little more efficient if the distribution is normalized. In fact, $\sum_{n=1}^{\infty} 1/n^2$ evaluates to $\pi^2/6$ (technically, this is the value of the Riemann zeta function $\zeta(s) = \sum_{n=1}^{\infty} 1/n^s$

when $s = 2$). Thus the appropriate coding distribution is

$$\Pr[n] = \frac{6/\pi^2}{n^2} \approx \frac{0.608}{n^2}.$$

The cumulative values of this distribution are easily calculated in advance and stored in a table.

After transmitting the number of library symbols, each one is sent separately. First its height and width are encoded. The same fixed probability distribution discussed above can be used, or the height and width of each library symbol can be coded using a simple model of the heights and widths seen so far, which gives slightly improved compression. Then the bitmap contents are encoded using the two-level method described in Section 6.3.

Symbol numbers

Next, the symbol numbers can be encoded using the PPM technique described in Chapter 2. The method has to be modified slightly to accommodate an alphabet with a variable number of symbols because normally it will be designed for a pre-determined alphabet (often of only 256 symbols). The performance of symbol sequence encoding will depend on the success of the template-matching process. If, for example, two variants of a certain character find their way into the library, up to one extra bit will be needed whenever the character occurs to distinguish between the two variants.

Symbol offsets

The x and y offsets can be compressed by conditioning them on the symbol with which they are associated and using adaptive coding. All offset values associated with each symbol so far are stored, along with the frequency of occurrence of each offset value. If the present value has followed the symbol before, it is coded (using arithmetic coding) according to this frequency distribution. If not, an escape code is sent and the offset encoder reverts to a second-level model. This model contains the frequency distribution of all values that have occurred so far, regardless of which symbol they followed. If that particular offset value has never occurred before, a further escape is sent and the encoder reverts to a third-level model that corresponds to the γ distribution encoder mentioned earlier.

Original image

The difference between the original image and the reconstructed text can be computed as the residue, the bitwise exclusive-OR of these two bitmap images. Because of the success of the symbol extraction process, far fewer bits are set in the residue than in the original image. For example, the image in Figure 7.1 contains 386,993 black pixels (out of a total of 4,368,000), while the reconstructed text, part of which appears in Figure 7.3, contains 382,606 of them. The residue of Figure 7.4 contains only 73,797 bits set to 1—that is, pixels at which there is a discrepancy between the original and reconstructed text images. This would seem to indicate that the residue can easily be coded much more efficiently than the original. However, this is not so. Even when a good compression method is applied, in practice there is little difference between the compressed sizes of the residue and the original.

For example, the two-level context modeling scheme described in Section 6.3 is a very efficient way of coding the original image. It reduces the image in Figure 7.1, which originally consumes 546,000 bytes, to only 34,176 bytes (using a 22/10-bit context). The same method reduces the 546,000-byte residue to 37,966 bytes. Remarkably, the residue is compressed into more bits than the original image—even though it has fewer than one-fifth the number of bits set.

This apparent paradox is actually quite easily explained. The original image is far more compressible than the residue precisely because most of the black pixels it contains form predictable parts of characters. When the marks are extracted, what is left is the noise—the irregularities around the edges that are caused by deficiencies in the printing and scanning processes—and noise is very difficult to compress. For example, when using the above method to compress the residue, nearly twice as many different contexts are encountered (20,000) as in the original image (11,000).

Fortunately, the residue can be coded more efficiently. There is considerable overlap in information content between it and the reconstructed text image since many of the characters can be discerned just from their haloes in the residue. To take advantage of this, the coding of the residue can use pixels in the reconstructed text image as a context to predict pixels in the residue, as well as pixels in the part of the residue that has been coded so far. This is particularly effective because the entire reconstructed text is known before any of the residue is coded. This means that the clairvoyant context method of Section 6.3 can be used.

Recall that these context templates are called clairvoyant because pixel values ahead of the current one will not be known by the decoder until after they have been decoded, rendering them useless for actual compression. As explained in Section 6.3, the idea was originally introduced only as a theoretical device for bounding compression performance. In this application, however, the reconstructed image is known by both encoder and decoder at the time the residue is processed. Consequently, we can use a clairvoyant template on the reconstructed text image. It is also beneficial to combine this with a regular (nonclairvoyant) template on the residue coded so far, to capture local correlations in the residue image.

For example, suppose the clairvoyant template in Figure 7.15a is used on the reconstructed image, where, as in Chapter 6, a black dot marks each pixel included in the template and a bull's-eye marks the position of the pixel about to be coded. This is a 13-bit template, not a 12-bit one, because the center pixel's value in the reconstructed image is known—as are all the other pixels. The template used on the residue might be the 4-bit template in Figure 7.15b. Here, the gray pixels (and the bull's-eye) are ones whose values are not yet known by the decoder and so cannot be included in the template—because, although the decoder knows the values of future pixels of the reconstructed text, it does not yet know the values of future pixels in the residue. When it comes to coding the residue pixel marked with the bull's-eye, the context will then contain a total of 17 bits, 13 from the reconstructed text image and 4 from the residue. To determine the probability estimate with which

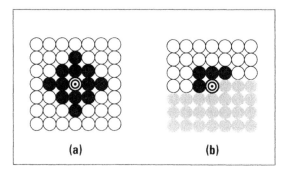

Figure 7.15 Two templates for compressing the original image: (a) clairvoyant template; and (b) regular template.

to encode the pixel, the 17-bit word that gives the value of the context is looked up in a table that stores counts of the number of times white and black pixels have already occurred in that context. The white count and black count are used in the standard way to encode the next pixel, just as in Section 6.3.

A final twist is to use this method not to encode the residue as described, but *to encode the original image.* This yields slightly better compression performance because the exclusive-OR operation used to construct the residue reverses the polarity of some pixels. It uses the reconstructed text as an aid to compressing the original image. The way this works is that while the clairvoyant template continues to act on the reconstructed image, the regular 4-bit one acts on the original image rather than on the residue. The pixel being predicted is one in the original image, and the 4-bit context refers to previous pixels of the original image. The residue does not need to be calculated at all.

The original image will replace the reconstructed one on the display screen. Rather than clearing the image and redrawing it from scratch, it is easy to arrange for the decoder to use the information to gradually enhance the reconstructed text on the screen. Thus, an approximate (though usually quite accurate) initial image can be displayed very quickly; it is slowly cleaned up as more data is decoded.

7.7 Performance: Lossy and lossless modes

In order to assess the performance of textual image compression, two collections of 20 textual images were digitized, scanned at 300 dpi. Each image in the first collection is a page of a different technical publication, and the typefaces, sizes, and column layout vary widely. This allows the performance of textual image compression to be assessed on a typical mix of textual images from different sources. The second collection comprises consecutive double-page spreads from a novel, where each page has the same simple layout and uses a consistent family of typefaces. This allows us to investigate the advantage of using a shared library of symbols to com-

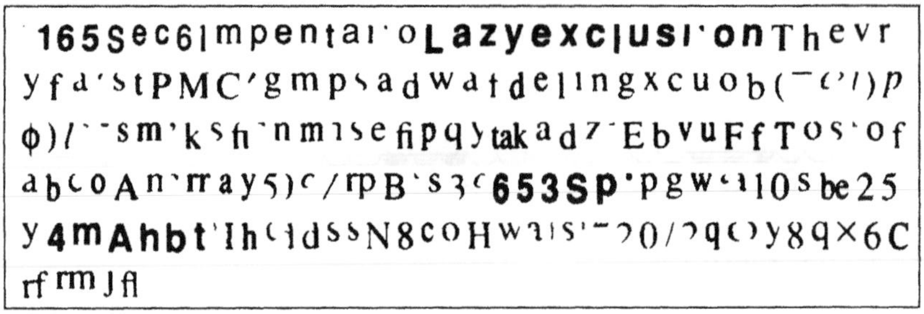

Figure 7.16 The library for an image of Collection 1.

press several different textual images at once. Due to the different typefaces and sizes that are used, a shared library has little to offer for the first collection.

Figures 7.16 and 7.17 show the libraries for a single sample image from the first and second collections, respectively. The bitmaps for the individual symbols have been collected into a single large bitmap for display, separated by a small amount of white space. For example, the first line of Figure 7.16 shows 37 separate library symbols, starting with a very small speck that is hardly visible and ending with an *r*. The first collection was scanned at a rather light contrast setting. This results in much fragmentation of symbols, and although most of the fragments are identifiable to the human eye as characters, the library contains several small pieces that could have originated from any of a number of different characters. The second collection was scanned at rather too high a contrast setting, and there is a large amount of bleeding together of strings of characters. For example, the last line of Figure 7.17 contains just four symbols in the library, corresponding to the strings *easin, gl, in,* and *terested*. The book from which this collection is taken was printed on paper of much lower quality than the journals and books used for the first collection, and many of the characters are not separated even on the printed page. The too-dark scanner setting exacerbates the problem.

Further information about the composition of these libraries appears in Table 7.2. The textual image compression procedure identifies a total of 193 symbols in the first document, which account for a total of 3,376 marks extracted from the page. A rough visual classification is shown in the table, breaking the symbols down into valid typographical symbols; duplicate copies of symbols; false ligatures, which are double or multiple characters formed by separate ones that have run together in the printing process; unidentifiable fragments where a printing imperfection has broken a symbol into parts and one of the parts cannot be identified as a character; and symbols that are classified as noise and should not have formed part of the typographical description of the image. The corresponding numbers when singleton marks are removed from the library appear in parentheses.

Partly because of the fragmentation, a large number of duplicate copies of symbols find their way into the library for the first image: on average, each valid typographical symbol has about one duplicate. Despite the light contrast used during scanning, the image contains six false ligatures, of which some are connected on the

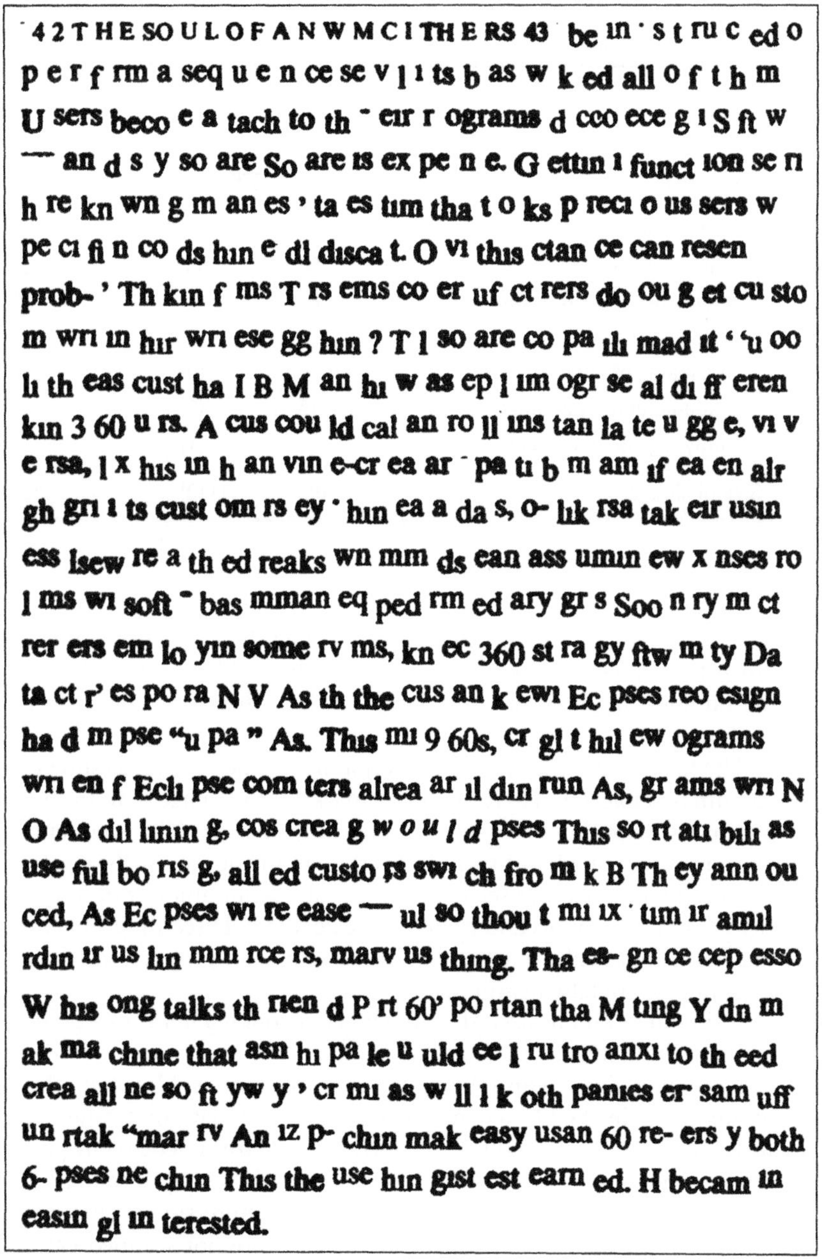

`42 THE SOUL OF AN W M CI THERS 43 be in · s t ru c ed o
p e r f rm a sequ e n ce se v l l ts b as w k ed all o f t h m
U sers beco e a tach to th ~ eir r ograms d cco ece g l S ft w
— an d s y so are So are is ex pe n e. G ettin l funct ion se n
h re kn wn g m an es ' ta es tim tha t o ks p reci o us sers w
pe ci fi n co ds hin e dl disca t. O vi this ctan ce can resen
prob- ' Th kin f ms T rs ems co er uf ct rers do ou g et cu sto
m wri in hir wri ese gg hin ? T l so are co pa ili mad it ' 'u oo
li th eas cust ha I B M an hi w as ep l im ogr se al di ff eren
kin 3 60 u rs. A cus cou ld cal an ro ll ins tan la te u gg e, vi v
e rsa, l x his in h an vin e-cr ea ar ¯ pa ti b m am if ea en alr
gh gri l ts cust om rs ey ' hin ea a da s, o- lik rsa tak eir usin
ess lsew re a th ed reaks wn mm ds ean ass umin ew x nses ro
l ms wi soft ~ bas mman eq ped rm ed ary gr s Soo n ry m ct
rer ers em lo yin some rv ms, kn ec 360 st ra gy ftw m ty Da
ta ct r' es po ra N V As th the cus an k ewi Ec pses reo esign
ha d m pse "u pa " As. This mi 9 60s, cr gl t hil ew ograms
wri en f Ech pse com ters alrea ar il din run As, gr ams wri N
O As dil linin g, cos crea g w o u l d pses This so rt ati bili as
use ful bo rs g, all ed custo rs swi ch fro m k B Th ey ann ou
ced, As Ec pses wi re ease — ul so thou t mi ix ' tim ir amil
rdin ir us hn mm rce rs, marv us thing. Tha es- gn ce cep esso
W his ong talks th rien d P rt 60' po rtan tha M ting Y dn m
ak ma chine that asn hi pa le u uld ee l ru tro anxi to th eed
crea all ne so ft yw y ' cr mi as w ll l k oth panies er sam uff
un rtak "mar rv An iz p- chin mak easy usan 60 re- ers y both
6- pses ne chin This the use hin gist est earn ed. H becam in
easin gi in terested.

Figure 7.17 The library for an image of Collection 2.

Table 7.2 Symbol identification and library construction for two images.

	Image from Collection 1		Image from Collection 2	
Marks extracted	3,376		2,834	
Library composition:				
valid typographical symbols	89	(53)	67	(48)
duplicates of valid symbols	81	(46)	80	(42)
false ligatures	6	(1)	272	(69)
duplicates of false ligatures	0	(0)	116	(25)
unidentifiable fragments	15	(9)	0	(0)
nontypographical noise	2	(1)	2	(1)
Size of library	193	(110)	537	(185)

paper original and others are artifacts created during the scanning process. Even discarding singletons does not really affect the incidence of duplicates, as shown by the numbers in parentheses in Table 7.2, though it does eliminate nearly all false ligatures.

The image from the second collection fares much worse, as shown in the second column of Table 7.2. There are fewer marks in the image than in the first example, but nearly three times as many symbols in the library. The fragmentation problem does not occur at all, but there is a very high incidence of false ligatures due to the excessively dark scanner setting. There is also a fair amount of duplication of valid typographical symbols and even of false ligatures. Discarding singletons reduces all the counts markedly, but there is still a significant proportion of duplicates and a large number of false ligatures.

It should be emphasized that much better-looking libraries would have been obtained on both image collections if the images had been scanned more carefully, with due attention given to optimizing the contrast settings. Moreover, the large number of duplicates in the library indicates that the template-matching procedure is not working as well as it might be. The combined size-independent pattern-matching strategy mentioned earlier was chosen because it is simple and fast, and it was not optimized at all for these images. Significant compression is obtained using textual image compression even though the images were not scanned carefully and even though the template matching is far from perfect—and these shortcomings do not affect the quality of the reconstructed image.

Singletons were not pruned from the library for any of the compression results given in Tables 7.3 and 7.4. This means that the result of lossy compression is a very close approximation to the original and differs from it in only two respects: very small specks are omitted because they are not coded as symbols, and the de-

Table 7.3 Results for lossy and lossless coding of two document collections.

	Collection 1	Collection 2	
	Separate images	Separate images	Combined images
Image size (pixels)	2,464 × 3,224	2,464 × 1,883	
Marks (per image)	3,353	2,640	2,640
Specks	573	38	38
Symbols in library	199	512	267
Compression, two-level coding	21.8	10.9	10.9
Compression, Group 4 coding	14.8	8.2	8.2
Library (bits per library symbol)	161.9	269.1	307.8
Symbol sequence (bits per mark)	4.9	7.7	10.7
x and y offsets (bits per offset)	4.3	5.2	4.7
Total bits per image, lossy	77,730	185,280	134,926
Lossy compression ratio	102.2	25.0	34.4
Coded original image	209,018	219,095	227,425
Total bits per image, lossless	286,748	404,375	362,351
Lossless compression ratio	27.7	11.5	12.8

tailed outlines of the marks are different because of the approximation inherent in the matching process. In other words, the residue image contains only specks and haloes. The image specks are taken to be connected groups of fewer than 16 pixels. Thus, a 4 × 4 block of pixels would not be discarded, which at 300 dpi corresponds to a mark just a third of a millimeter high. In the tests described below on images of different resolutions, the 16-pixel speck threshold is scaled accordingly.

Table 7.3 shows the compression obtained. The two broad columns of numbers refer to the first and second collections, respectively. The upper part of the table contains pertinent facts about the images: the average number of marks, specks, and symbols in the library and the average compression factor for both two-level context modeling and Group 4 fax coding. As in Chapter 6, compression factors are expressed as the ratio of the total of the original file size to the total size of the compressed file; the larger the number, the better the compression. Thus, context modeling comfortably outperforms Group 4 coding, as expected.

For the first collection, all results are averaged over the 20 images, compressed individually. For the second, results are given both for the average over the images treated separately and for the 20 images amalgamated into one. In the latter case, the total figures are divided by 20 to make the numbers directly comparable. For example, the average number of marks per image in the first collection is 3,353, and

Table 7.4 Results for coding the same images at different resolutions.

Resolution (dpi)	100	200	300	600
Image size (pixels)	608 × 894	1,216 × 1,786	2,464 × 3,224	3,632 × 5,332
Marks (per image)	2,513	2,572	2,486	2,552
Specks	173	287	417	60
Symbols in library	135	172	174	304
Compression, two-level coding	6.0	11.3	28.2	34.8
Compression, Group 4 coding	3.4	7.7	18.8	23.1
Library (bits per library symbol)	52.7	94.1	157.7	241.7
Symbol sequence (bits per mark)	5.8	5.5	5.2	6.2
x and y offsets (bits per offset)	3.5	3.9	4.4	5.7
Total bits per image, lossy	39,566	50,394	62,208	118,456
Lossy compression ratio	13.7	43.1	127.7	163.5
Coded original image	55,937	121,028	165,187	322,629
Total bits per image, lossless	95,503	171,422	227,395	441,085
Lossless compression ratio	5.7	12.7	34.9	43.9

the average number of symbols in the library is 199. For the second collection, the average number of marks per image is 2,640, and the number of library symbols averages 512. However, when the images are combined, the average library size is reduced from 512 to 267 symbols per image. This makes a total combined library of 5,340 symbols for all 20 images—a surprisingly large figure considering that the same typeface and size was used for all images. Examination of the individual images reveals that many marks bled together during the scanning process, as shown in Figure 7.17.

The sizes of the various components of textual image compression are given in the lower part of Table 7.3. The "original image" line shows the number of bits required to compress the original image given the reconstructed one—recall from the end of Section 7.6 that it is better to code the original image than the residue. The overall result for the first collection is a lossy compression ratio of 102.2 and a lossless compression ratio of 27.7. The latter figure comfortably exceeds the compression ratio obtained using two-level context modeling, namely, 21.8. For this collection, results are not given for the images combined; however, tests showed that the overall compression ratios deteriorate slightly in this situation because the economy in library transmission that results from sharing symbols between documents is outweighed by the fact that the symbol identifiers are larger. This is not unexpected since the images are taken from quite different sources.

The contribution of each component to the total number of bits can be calculated from the numbers in the table. For example, the library contributes an average of 161.9 bits per symbol, and there are an average of 199 library symbols, so transmission of the library accounts for 32,218 bits, or about 40 percent of the total amount required for lossy compression. Similarly, the symbol sequence accounts for 4.9 bits per mark over 3,353 marks, or about 20 percent; offsets—two per mark, making 8.6 bits per symbol—account for the remaining 40 percent.

For the second collection, compression is generally much worse than for the first, as shown by the lower compression ratios. This is principally because the image size was chosen to leave almost no white space around the border, so the images were packed with text, making for poorer compression. The compression achieved was a factor of 25.0 or 34.4 for lossy compression, depending on whether the images are amalgamated or not, and 11.5 or 12.8 for lossless compression. Again, the lossless compression outperforms two-level context modeling. In this case there is a significant improvement in the compression ratio when the libraries are combined because the images were taken from a single source with a single typeface and size. However, as noted above, due to character bleeding in the scanning process, the library was still much larger than might be expected. A still greater improvement in compression could have been obtained from the combined libraries if the images had been scanned more carefully; even so, we must expect such problems when dealing with scanned images.

To investigate the effect of coding documents at different resolutions, five members of Collection 1 were scanned at four different resolutions: 100, 200, 300, and 600 dpi. Table 7.4 shows the results of textual image compression in each case. Both lossy and lossless compression ratios increase markedly with resolution, which is only to be expected: the former from 13.7 to 163.5 and the latter from 5.7 to 43.9. At the lowest resolution, lossless textual image compression is not as good as two-level coding, but it significantly outperforms it at higher resolutions. More economy is achieved at higher resolutions by having a single library copy of a symbol shared by all occurrences because large areas of black need be coded only once per library symbol. Table 7.4 also shows that the number of bits required to encode the original image grows approximately linearly with resolution. This is because the action is taking place around the perimeter of the characters.

7.8 System considerations

Let us stand back and reflect on the role of textual image compression in a full retrieval system. We mentioned earlier the Trinity College Library catalog (and showed a page from it in Figure 7.1); it is instructive to consider the overall needs of such an application. A typical catalog will contain one thousand to one million images. Users will access it in different ways: browsing from page to page, giving a page number, or specifying other information such as a book title or author name (in which case all matching pages must be retrieved). Textual image compression makes sense only if all access is through bitmapped display screens because the image is reconstructed as a bitmap rather than as a succession of character codes.

For almost all queries, an approximate image is sufficient, and for this, textual image compression is particularly useful. To display a page in full, first the symbol library must be decoded, then the list of marks and (x, y) offsets, and finally the residue. The residue is many times larger than the other components, and, although necessary to obtain an absolutely faithful reproduction, it certainly is not needed for an overview of the page. Even in the reconstructed image of Figure 7.3 from which singletons are omitted, the original text can be read without difficulty, well enough for a casual browser to decide whether it is of interest, and in most cases sufficiently clearly for a user to find the shelf location of a book being sought. For the experiments of Section 7.7, singletons were not omitted from the library, so the lossy reconstructed text is extremely accurate. Only by express command, or on a request for a faithful printed copy, would the residual bitmap be retrieved and decompressed.

Although access will normally be to a single catalog page, compression can be improved by building the symbol library for several pages and coding the marks as a longer sequence. Decoding the residual image is the most intensive part of accessing the database, both in terms of bandwidth and processor time. Batching the remainder of the information into blocks of pages has little impact on retrieval performance, but yields a small compression saving and may improve the quality of the reconstructed text image by making library characters more representative. If the images are scanned carefully to reduce character fragmentation and bleeding, considerable economy will be realized by combining the images. In this case, if you are aiming at very high compression, it may be desirable to eliminate singletons from the library to reduce the impact of the occasional badly printed character on compression. Of course, if this is done, you must accept that the reconstructed image may be missing a few characters.

The separation between the information required to reconstruct the lossy image and that required to refine it into a lossless one allows different media to be used for the different components. The symbol library and symbol list might be retained on fast magnetic disk, while the residual image could be held on a bulk storage device such as an optical disk or even a robotic jukebox of optical disks. This two-level structure caters particularly well to casual browsers, who tend to flick rapidly from one page to the next after scanning them for just a few seconds. If the residual images are required only very occasionally, they could even be retained in low-cost, offline storage on high-capacity optical disks or magnetic cartridge tapes.

To provide keyword access, a standard full-text retrieval indexing mechanism can be employed as described in Chapters 3 and 4. The keywords would need to be entered manually at the time the images were scanned since the list of symbols corresponds only loosely to the characters of the text and cannot be used to generate index terms automatically. Alternatively, conventional OCR software might be employed to identify the terms appearing in the page so that an index could be created automatically.

This compression technique is applicable to more general tasks of document archiving. Despite the phenomenal capacity of "write once, read many" (WORM) optical disks, the space requirements of raw images make compression even more desirable than for textual databases. For example, a company might retain online copies of all signed contracts; most queries will require just the text of the contract—obtainable by decompressing the list of marks. Occasionally it will be necessary to produce a faithful reproduction in which the signature and any other hand annotations are also visible, when, for example, a document is to be submitted as legal evidence. Because of the dynamic nature of such a database and the variability of typeface, it may be inappropriate for the page blocking to span more than one document. However, within a document, the pages should again be blocked.

Compared to decompression, the compression phase is relatively time-consuming. For Trinity College's historical library catalog application, this is of little concern; the database is static and compression is performed only once. In a document-archiving environment, the cost of compression must also be considered. Compression could be carried out as a background process, with new documents spooled to some temporary holding area until they can be added to the permanent collection. Alternatively, the amount of compression could be traded off against speed by allowing the system to be "lazy" in places. For example, the template-matching process could be accelerated by allowing more approximate matches to be accepted, or the coding of the output could be accelerated by using a simpler method than arithmetic coding.

7.9   JBIG2: A standard for textual image compression

Textual image compression will likely form the basis of a new version of the JBIG standard for bilevel image compression called JBIG2. JBIG2 is in the process of going through the lengthy international standardization process—it is not expected to actually become an approved standard until approaching the year 2000—and so full details are not available as we write.

It seems likely that the new standard will embody many of the ideas developed in this chapter (Howard 1997). It will have provision for lossy as well as lossless coding, which will yield substantial compression gains over existing bilevel image compression methods even at imperceptible levels of image degradation. There will be a facility for multiple-page transmission, so that gains can be made by reusing marks transmitted for this page in subsequent pages.

There is a trend in data communications standardization circles toward having a standard specify how a decoder is to interpret a transmitted bitstream without placing restrictions on the ways in which encoders can generate it. For example, JPEG allows an encoder to come up with its own quantization tables; JBIG allows an encoder to decide on the location of the adaptive pixel itself. Inevitably, the more sophisticated the compression scheme, the more opportunities there are for clever encoding techniques, perhaps tailored to particular classes of images.

JBIG2 will push this trend still further. It is not necessary to specify the particular template-matching method to be used—that can be left up to the encoder because it does not affect decoder operation at all. There is no need to standardize screening techniques to reduce the number of template matches that must be computed— that has no effect except on encoder speed. There is no need to dictate how to decide what symbols should go in the library—that affects compression rate but not the mechanics of decoding. By defining a standard for *decoding* the result of textual image compression, JBIG2 will leave plenty of room—and incentive—for the development and refinement of innovative *encoding* procedures.

The new standard will include provision for the transmission of halftone images in the document page. It will be up to the encoder to segment the image into textual and halftone regions. Halftones may be transmitted by regular JBIG techniques using an "adaptive pixel" to indicate the location of the previous screen dot, or by using regular textual image transmission but with halftone dots as the library elements that are matched, or by "descreening" the image—that is, calculating a grayscale image at correspondingly lower resolution that approximates the halftone picture—and using a continuous-tone image standard such as JPEG. In accordance with the above philosophy, the question of how—or indeed whether—the encoder segments an image into textual and halftone areas is likely to be left open. We will return to the problem of segmentation in Section 8.2.

One interesting and worthwhile innovation is in the actual coding of any discrepancies between a mark and the library element used to represent it. In Section 7.6 (page 341) we discussed how to use the reconstructed text to transmit a "residue" image that contains the pixel-by-pixel difference between the reconstructed text and the original image, and we learned that instead of transmitting the residue it is slightly more effective to use the reconstructed text as a basis for reencoding the original image itself. A context template of pixels is formed, the major part of which is clairvoyant and looks at surrounding pixels on the reconstructed image (which can include pixels in the "future," that is, to the right and below), and the remainder, which is nonclairvoyant, looks at pixels in the part of the image that has so far been transmitted. The innovation that JBIG2 will likely use is "soft pattern matching," which refers to exactly the same technique, but at the level of individual marks rather than the entire page. A particular mark is communicated by first sending the identity of the best match and then transmitting sufficient information to encode the actual mark with respect to that best match. Doing this for each mark individually is likely to be better than doing it for the whole page because the surrounding context does not interfere with the processing of each mark.

Moreover, and perhaps more importantly, a new mark that has been communicated in this way, by identifying its corresponding library element and then transmitting the mark with respect to it, can be installed in the library and used for future matches. This provides an incremental means of transmitting the library that is likely to be more effective than the nonincremental scheme described earlier of sending it as individual bitmaps. Of course, it may be worthwhile imposing a template-matching threshold to prevent unlikely characters from matching. The JBIG2 standard will probably specify a variety of methods for transmitting library elements, from the regular JBIG method to this new scheme using soft pattern matching.

JBIG2 will have provision for lossy transmission but will probably not incorporate it into the standard itself. Instead, it is anticipated that encoders may, at their discretion, subject the image to a lossy preprocessing stage. Thus the standard is lossless with respect to the image that the encoder decides to transmit but not necessarily with respect to the original image. This preprocessing can be tailored closely to the encoding process to provide much more effective transmission with only a small degree of loss.

The idea of textual image compression has been with us for 25 years, but it has not found large-scale application as a practical compression technique. However, with JBIG2 that is about to change. This is a technology whose time has come at last.

Further reading

Textual image compression. The earliest published account of a textual image compression scheme appeared in 1974 (Ascher and Nagy 1974). Since then, several other lossy systems have been developed (Pratt et al. 1980; Wong, Casey, and Wahl 1982; Johnsen, Segen, and Cash 1983; Holt and Xydeas 1986). The first to research the idea of lossless schemes was Mohiuddin in his 1982 Ph.D. project, subsequently describing a system that embodied many of the ideas presented in this chapter in a seldom-cited conference paper (Mohiuddin, Rissanen, and Arps 1984). Our own work in this area developed independently, and precursors to the textual image compression scheme described here, based upon preliminary work by Hugh Emberson at the University of Canterbury, appeared in 1992 (Witten et al. 1992).

Template matching. The simple method of mark boundary tracing was described in one of the early papers on textual image compression (Johnsen, Segen, and Cash 1983), and the faster algorithm that traces the 4-connected outside boundary is well known in the graphics area. Standard region-filling algorithms, including the run-based one of Figure 7.7, are described in computer graphics texts (Foley and Van Dam 1982). Examples of global methods of template matching are the "combined symbol matching" (CSM) method (Pratt et al. 1980), from which Figure 7.8 is adapted, and the "weighted AND-NOT" (WAN) method (Holt and Xydeas 1986). Local methods include the "pattern matching and substitution" method (Johnsen, Segen, and Cash 1983) and the "combined size-independent strategy" (CSIS) (Holt 1988). Several methods of screening library marks to reduce the number of template matches that need to be performed have been described (Pratt et al. 1980; Johnsen, Segen, and Cash 1983; Holt and Xydeas 1986). A fuller account of compression-based template matching and its evaluation is available (Inglis and Witten 1994).

JBIG2. The proposed JBIG2 standard is described by Paul Howard (1997), who coined the term "soft pattern matching."

Mixed Text and Images

Textual image compression is more effective if the parts of the image that contain line art or halftone graphics are identified and treated differently from the text itself. It is also helpful if the orientation of the image has been analyzed and the image itself has been corrected for skew. This makes it easy to sort characters into their natural textual order, which makes coding of both the offsets and the sequence of marks more efficient—the former because offsets tend to be smaller and the latter because compressing the letters of text in natural order is more effective than compressing them in some arbitrary ordering.

Figure 8.1 shows an example of a scanned document with regions that contain different types of data: text, two graphics, and a halftone. In Figure 8.2, rectangles have been drawn (manually) around these regions. This particular layout is interesting because it contains a region—the large text block halfway down the left-hand column—that is clearly nonrectangular and one that is tilted. Subdividing the image into regions and identifying the region types are important preliminary steps for any further document processing. Of course, with the kind of textual image compression described in Chapter 7, it is not essential to perform these operations correctly—or even at all—because enough information is retained to allow the original image to be restored exactly from the reconstructed text. Correctly recognizing the textual regions merely enhances compression; it is not needed to ensure exact reproduction. However, for sophisticated processing of the document image—like OCR—it is important that different regions of the document be classified correctly.

This chapter examines the problem of how to separate the textual part of a document image from line drawings and halftones so that each component can be compressed effectively. There are three steps in the process. The first is to examine the orientation of the image and correct it for skew. The second is to segment the document into visually distinct regions, like blocks of text (columns, paragraphs,

FEATURE ARTICLES
GROS TITRES

Visualizing and Understanding Diagnoses

Suhayya Abu-Hakima

Knowledge Systems Laboratory
Institute for Information Technology
National Research Council, Ottawa, Canada
email: suhayya@ai.iit.nrc.ca tel: (613) 991-1231

Sommaire

Le diagnostic de systèmes physiques tels que les automobiles et les moteurs d'avion est une activité complexe. Les techniciens allient les manuels textuels (qui incluent des schémas) avec l'analyse des données mesurées pour diagnostiquer et réparer les moteurs. Les concepteurs de système à base de connaissance ont ajoutés l'heuristique, pour lier le texte avec les graphiques (hypermedia) pour simplifier la tâche des techniciens, tel qu'implanté dans le projet JETA (Halasz92). Des outils pour examiner la connaissance sont utilisés par les concepteurs de tels systèmes pour structurer et injecter la base de connaissance et sont aussi utilisés pour aider l'expert à visualiser la connaissance et les différentes relations possibles. De tels outils ont été conçus pour afficher et éditer la base de connaissance du projet JETA. Dans RATIONALE, un système de diagnostics qui raisonne en fournissant des explications, les explications sont utilisées pour comprendre le raisonnement du système |Abu-Hakima90]. Cet article argumente que même si ces approches à base de connaissances aident à la visualisation et à la compréhension des systèmes physiques, ils ont besoin d'être améliorés et mieux intégrés.

Summary

Diagnosis of physical systems such as car or aircraft engines is a complex activity. Technicians combine textual manuals with schematics and some analysis of measured data to diagnose and repair engines. Knowledge-based system designers have added heuristics to link text and graphic (hypermedia) representations of manuals to simplify the tasks of the technicians as implemented in JETA [Halasz92]. Knowledge browsers are used by the developers of such systems to structure and input the knowledge base and are

also used in a limited capacity to help the domain experts visualize the knowledge and the various possible relations. Such a browser has been implemented to view and edit JETA's knowledge. In RATIONALE, a diagnostic system that reasons by explaining, explanation is used to understand system reasoning [Abu-Hakima90]. This paper argues that although these knowledge-based approaches help in the visualization and understanding of diagnoses in physical systems, they need to be improved and better integrated.

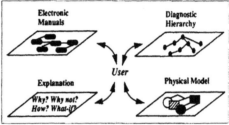

Figure 1: World of user in knowledge-based system

Introduction

Diagnosis of physical systems such as car or aircraft engines is a complex activity. Technicians combine paper manuals with schematics and some analysis of measured data to diagnose and repair engines. Knowledge-based systems provide the technicians with electronic manuals organized using hypermedia techniques as well as diagnostic hierarchies that represent the failure, test and repair actions of the diagnostic cycle. Such an approach has been followed for JETA, the Jet Engine Troubleshooting Assistant [Halasz92]. Other systems have followed modelling and simulation techniques that represent the actual physical system and attempt to diagnose it on the basis of the expected behaviour of the model [MBR91]. Some diagnostic systems

Figure 8.1 A document image containing different types of data. Reprinted from *Canadian Artificial Intelligence Magazine*.

or perhaps individual lines), headers and footers, and illustrations. The third is to classify the regions into text, line drawings, and halftones so that appropriate compression methods can be applied to each one. These three issues are examined in Sections 8.1, 8.2, and 8.3, respectively.

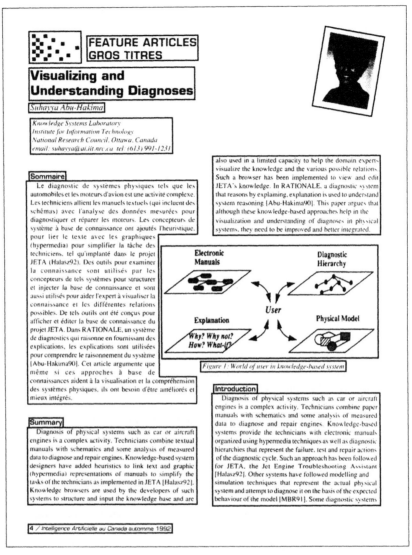

Figure 8.2   The document image segmented into different regions. Reprinted from *Canadian Artificial Intelligence Magazine*.

8.1   Orientation

The first problem is that the entire document image may be skewed, perhaps because it has been photocopied or fed through the digitizer at a slight angle. It is necessary to identify any skew before embarking on further processing.

Three approaches have been proposed for determinining the orientation, or skew angle, of a document image. The first is to examine the left margin of the text, which is usually clearly defined, straight, and vertical. The second is to look down the page for the gaps that occur between horizontal lines of text and determine the skew angle that makes the gaps look cleanest and sharpest. A correctly oriented page of text has clearly defined white space, called *leading*, between lines of text. The third approach is to look at the slopes of imaginary lines joining pairs of marks on the page and see which is the dominant direction of alignment; in a correctly oriented page this is invariably horizontal. This section discusses actual techniques based on these three approaches.

Once the document's orientation is known, the image can be corrected by rotating it appropriately. Some care must be taken to rotate it in such a way that connected regions do not become fragmented as a result of rotating a discrete grid. It turns out that the best way to rotate a digital image is not to take each pixel in the original image and transform it to its new position, but rather to take each pixel position in the new image, transform it to the old coordinate space, round the result to integer coordinates, and assign it the color of that point in the original image. Doing the transformation backward reduces the problem of fragmentation. However, it is frequently unnecessary to go to the trouble of performing a full rotation operation. The much faster shear transformation is as good as a rotation if the angle is not too large—even up to $8°$, the error is less than 1 percent. Alternatively, to save even the preprocessing time required for a shear, the image can be manipulated in ways that take its skewness into account. For example, to find lines of text in a correctly oriented image, we might scan a horizontal line down the page. In an image whose skew angle θ is known, we can scan down the page with a line that is itself rotated by the angle θ, which requires only a small amount of additional computation while the image is being processed.

A basic technique that is often useful when processing document images is the *Hough transform*, devised by P. V. C. Hough and patented in 1962 (Hough 1962). It assists in locating straight lines (or curves) in images. Essentially, the Hough transform maps straight lines in a two-dimensional image into points in another space called the *Hough domain*; conversely, it maps points in the image into sinusoids in the Hough domain. The next subsection is a slight digression that describes the transform and explains how it can be used to find straight lines; following that we return to our main topic of determining the orientation of document images. Although we refer to the use of the Hough transform in subsequent sections, it is not necessary to understand the details of how it works, and if you are not mathematically inclined, you can safely skip the following description.

Detecting straight lines using the Hough transform

The Hough transform is a line-to-point transformation that, when applied to a bilevel image, can be used to detect sets of pixels that lie along a straight line. It was originally described in a patent (since expired, so it may now be freely used) and has found numerous applications in pattern recognition. It can be extended to detect circles, quadratic curves, and indeed any parametrically representable curves—

though the computational cost of doing so increases with the number of parameters involved.

Imagine being given n points in a source image and being asked to decide which subsets of them lie on straight lines. One possible solution is to first find all lines determined by every pair of points and then find all subsets of points that are close to particular lines. Unfortunately, this is computationally very complex: there are $n(n - 1)/2 \approx n^2/2$ lines, and each of the n points must be compared with every line.

A different way to look at the problem is to consider all the lines that pass through a given point (x_0, y_0). The general equation of a straight line is $y = ax + b$, and this passes through the point (x_0, y_0) if and only if a and b are related by $y_0 = ax_0 + b$. An infinite number of straight lines pass through (x_0, y_0), and they are all obtained from different values of a and b that satisfy this relationship.

Consider the plane defined by varying the parameters a and b, which is called the *parameter space* for the line-finding problem. All lines passing through (x_0, y_0) have a and b values that satisfy the equation $b = -x_0a + y_0$. In fact, if a and b are quantized into k levels each, and a $k \times k$ matrix is set up, the set of lines passing through (x_0, y_0) can be characterized by writing a one in all the cells of the matrix that correspond to values of a and b satisfying the equation.

Now suppose we are given n points rather than just one, and we are interested in the lines that pass through them. For each original point (x_i, y_i), increment the matrix value for each of the (a, b) cells that satisfy $b = -x_ia + y_i$, after first initializing all of the k^2 matrix cells to zero. If a particular matrix cell has a final value of, say, 5, that means that five points lie on the line corresponding to those a and b values.

This procedure finds approximately colinear sets of points, to an accuracy that depends on the number of quantization levels k. Since a has k possible values, there are k matching b-values for each point (x_i, y_i). Thus, since there are n points in the source image, the operation takes time proportional to k^2 (for initialization) plus nk—that is, for a given accuracy k the time required is linear in the number of points being processed.

A problem with the procedure described so far is that vertical lines cannot be represented—they correspond to an infinite value of a. The solution is to use a different way of representing a parameterized line, say, $x \cos \theta + y \sin \theta = \rho$.

Here, θ is the slope of the line from the y-axis, varying from $0°$ to $180°$, and ρ is the closest distance that it passed to the origin. Figure 8.3a illustrates the meaning of the parameters. The origin is placed in the center of the source image and the x-axis extends across the page. Thus, $\theta = 90°$ corresponds to horizontal lines in the image. The bold line marked A has equation $x \cos 30° + y \sin 30° = 200$, where the dimensions of the original image are 512×512. In the Hough domain, shown in Figure 8.3b, θ ranges from $0°$ to $180°$, and the maximum value of ρ is the distance from the origin to a corner of the source image, namely, $256\sqrt{2} = 362$. The parameter ρ is positive for lines that pass above the origin and negative for lines that

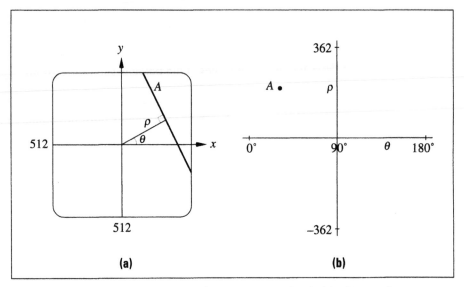

Figure 8.3 Meaning of the Hough transform parameters (ρ, θ): (a) a line on the page; (b) Hough transform domain.

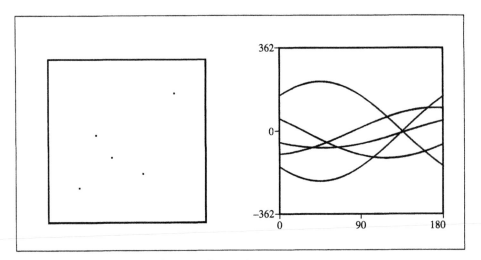

Figure 8.4 A simple image and its Hough transform.

pass below it. The bold line in the image domain (Figure 8.3a) corresponds to the point marked A in the Hough domain (Figure 8.3b).

A point in the original image corresponds to a straight line in the (a, b) parameter domain. However, in terms of the (ρ, θ) parameters, a point in the original image corresponds to a sinusoidal curve. Figure 8.4 shows a source image comprising five points, along with its Hough transform. The image points map into sinusoids, and the lines joining them correspond to the crossing points of the sinusoids in the Hough domain. The three-way intersection toward the right of the transform at around 145° corresponds to the three points stretched along the main bottom-left to top-right diagonal of the source image in Figure 8.4a. Note that the angle on the Hough transform is 90° different from the slope of the line in the original image, as shown in Figure 8.3a. The three-way near-intersection toward the left (at 45°) of the transform in Figure 8.4 corresponds to the near-colinearity of the three points in the original image close to the top-left to bottom-right diagonal.

In order to detect a straight line in the original image, we calculate the Hough transform and search for quantized points with large values in the Hough domain. The value of a cell in the Hough domain is the number of source image points that lie on the line represented by that Hough point. When implemented digitally, the Hough domain is actually a matrix of discrete cells, and the accuracy with which the Hough parameters are quantized reflects the accuracy with which the line is represented. When applying the transform to any particular problem, it is necessary to consider carefully what resolution is appropriate (Illingworth and Kittler 1988).

Left-margin search

Now let us return to our main problem: detecting the orientation, or skew angle, of a document image. The most straightforward way—the first of the three methods summarized at the beginning of this section—is simply to search for the left margin of the text (Dengel 1992). Most printed documents have an easily identifiable vertical left margin. It can be found by scanning rightward along each scanline until the first black pixel is encountered. Figure 8.5 illustrates the scan for a version of the test image that has been rotated by 2°. Each horizontal line of pixels is darkened until the first black pixel is encountered. Notice that in a couple of places the scan has sneaked through a miniscule gap in the box surrounding the diagram in the center of Figure 8.5, presumably caused by a printing or digitizing imperfection in the box. In general, the first black pixel is at the beginning of a text line. However, lines corresponding to paragraph indentations and interline spaces need to be discarded. One way to do this is to employ the Hough transform as a way of detecting the straight line that corresponds to the left margin.

Unfortunately, this method is not robust because sometimes the left margin is broken up by illustrations and also the text may not be left-justified. Consequently, the approach is not particularly reliable in practice.

The projection profile

The second of the three ways of determining the orientation of a document image is to first project the pixels onto the vertical axis by counting the number of black pixels on each line and then to examine the histogram that results (Srihari and Govindaraju 1989). If the document is oriented correctly, valleys will occur in the histogram between the lines of text, as illustrated in Figure 8.6a for the example document of Figure 8.1. The histogram will not necessarily reach zero in these

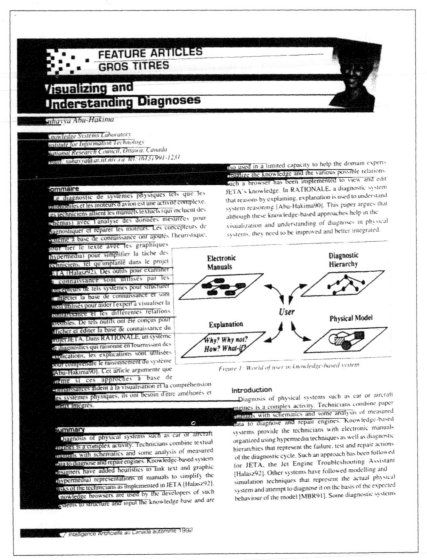

Figure 8.5 Searching for the left margin of the text. Reprinted from *Canadian Artificial Intelligence Magazine.*

valleys because occasionally, with narrow line spacing, an ascender on one line may intrude into the space reserved for descenders of the line above or—perhaps more likely—a nontextual mark such as a vertical line down the page may dilute the effect of the interline spacing. However, it is certain that pronounced valleys, if not actual zeroes, will occur.

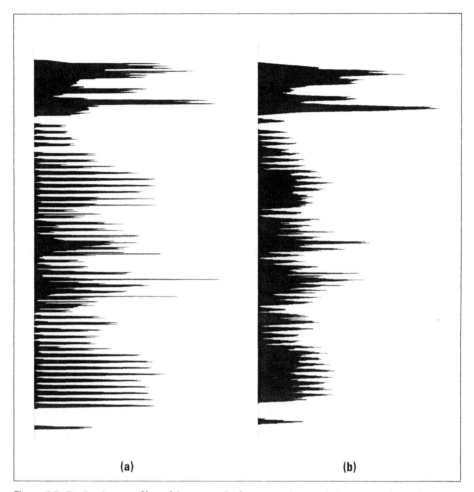

Figure 8.6 Projection profiles of the example document image: (a) correct orientation; (b) rotated by 2°.

Any skew in the document can be corrected by rotating the image gradually until its histogram, or *projection profile*, displays marked valleys. The angle at which the sharpest valleys are obtained almost certainly represents the skew of the document. An unskewed document will display the sharpest valleys when it is not rotated at all. Figure 8.6b shows the histogram of the example document after it has been rotated by an angle of 2°. While the valleys are still clearly distinguishable, they are not so well defined as in the nonrotated version of Figure 8.6a.

The sharpness of the valleys can be quantified by looking at the *autocorrelation function* of the histogram (Bones, Griffin, and Carey-Smith 1990). This is defined

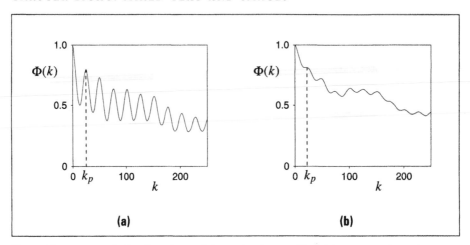

Figure 8.7 Autocorrelation functions of the projection profiles: (a) correct orientation; (b) rotated by $2°$.

as

$$\Phi(k) = \frac{\sum_n h(n)h(n+k)}{\sum_n h(n)^2},$$

where $h(n)$ represents the value of the histogram at vertical position n on the image and the sum is taken over all vertical positions. The autocorrelation function Φ can be computed for any value of the parameter k, which is commonly called the *lag*. The denominator is merely a normalizing factor to ensure that $\Phi(0) = 1$. The function oscillates, as shown in Figure 8.7, for the nonrotated and rotated histograms. When the orientation is correct, the autocorrelation function shows definite oscillations, with marked peaks and valleys. The autocorrelation function of the histogram of the skewed document, however, has peaks that are much less definite.

A measure of the sharpness of the original projection profile can be obtained by looking at the first oscillation of its autocorrelation function. Autocorrelation functions always peak at a lag of $k = 0$, and if the next peak occurs at lag $k = k_p$ (shown on the graphs), then the quantity

$$\frac{\Phi(0) + \Phi(k_p)}{2} - \Phi(k_p/2)$$

is a good indicator of the sharpness of the valleys in the projection profile. This represents the average height of the first two peaks above the first trough. One way to estimate the skew is to calculate the autocorrelation function for various rotation angles and to select the one with the largest value of this measure. For the auto-correlation functions of Figures 8.7a and 8.7b, its value is 0.4 and 0.04, respectively. The correctly oriented image is preferred because its measure is greater.

This method of determining the skew angle is computationally demanding, first because of the need to calculate the projection profile for different skew angles, and

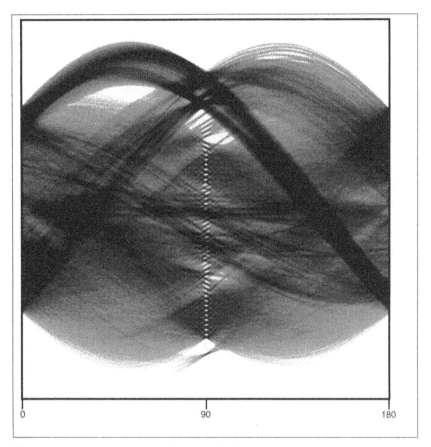

Figure 8.8 Hough transform of the example document image.

second because the autocorrelation function of each profile must be calculated and the position of its first peak determined. We address these two components in turn.

The projection profile of an image, calculated for every possible angle, forms a two-dimensional matrix that is in fact exactly the same as the Hough transform. Figure 8.8 shows the Hough transform of the example document page of Figure 8.1. The transform is a grayscale image in which low histogram values—that is, small projection counts—are represented by white and high ones by black. The histograms of Figure 8.6 correspond to vertical slices through Figure 8.8 at points $\theta = 90°$ and $\theta = 88°$, respectively. The latter corresponds to the projection of the original image onto a line at 88° instead of a vertical line, or—equivalently—the projection of the 2° rotated version of the image onto the vertical. The projection of the original image onto a *horizontal* line is represented by the vertical slice at $\theta = 0°$, while its projection onto the diagonal of the page—the longest projection profile—occurs at approximately $\theta = 60°$ and $\theta = 120°$.

The Hough transform maps points in the image into sinusoids in the Hough domain. For example, the wide swath that starts near the top left of Figure 8.8 and travels upward, turning over and descending to the lower right of the figure, is due to the photograph in the top right of Figure 8.1. The Hough transform can be obtained more rapidly than by explicitly projecting each black pixel of the image onto lines at every different angle. Nevertheless, the method still requires a number of operations that is approximately the square of the number of pixels in the image (more precisely, it is the number of black pixels times the total number of pixels), so it is very computation-intensive. There are no "fast" methods for calculating the Hough transform that are analogous to, say, the fast Fourier transform. However, the Hough transform is amenable to massively parallel implementation, so it can readily be obtained on special hardware.

The second part of the problem is calculating the autocorrelation function of each profile and determining the position of its first peak. The basic problem is to quantify the sharpness of the valleys in the projection profile so that profiles like Figure 8.6a can be chosen over those like Figure 8.6b. There are heuristic-based ways to do this that do not involve the autocorrelation function. The method that we describe here is to estimate the sharpness of a projection profile by finding the sum of the squares of the gradient at each point:

$$R = \ell(\theta) \sum_n [h(n+1) - h(n)]^2,$$

where $\ell(\theta)$ is the relative length of the projection profile at that angle:

$$\ell(\theta) = \begin{cases} 1/\cos(\theta), & \text{for } 0° \leq \theta < 45° \text{ and } 135° \leq \theta < 180°, \\ 1/\sin(\theta), & \text{for } 45° \leq \theta < 135°. \end{cases}$$

The scale factor $\ell(\theta)$ is intended to compensate for the fact that if θ is close to the diagonal positions of 45° or 135°, the contributing black pixels are distributed among more bins, so the peaks are lower, compared to profiles having θ close to the horizontal or vertical. For the two histograms of Figures 8.6a and 8.6b, the values of R are around 1,500,000 and 275,000, respectively. The correctly oriented image is preferred because its R value is greater.

It has also been suggested that the projection profile can be used to tell when the text is upside down. The argument is as follows. Consider a line of ordinary text. Most of the letters will be lowercase. Of these, five—g, j, p, q, and y—have tails that descend below the baseline of the text, and nine—b, d, f, h, i, j, k, l, and t—ascend into the region above the body of the letter. Ignore the regions of the profile above and below the bodies of the letters and consider the part that corresponds to the top of the body (say, the top of a letter x) and the bottom of the body (the bottom of the x). In the case of x, the contribution to the histogram will be about the same at the top and bottom. This is the case for most letters (b, c, d, e, and so on). For some, like f, h, m, n, r, t, v, w, and y, the contribution is larger at the top of the body than at the bottom. And for a few, certainly u and perhaps a, it will be smaller. All of these depend, of course, upon the typographical appearance of the font that is being

Figure 8.9 Magnified portion of the histogram of Figure 8.6a.

used. The histogram for a complete line of text is the sum of the contributions of the characters in it. Considering that in English the letter *e* occurs most frequently, followed by *t, a, o, i, n, s, h, r, d, l,* and *u* in approximately that order, it seems plausible to suppose that the overall histogram will tend to be larger at the top of the bodies of the letters than at the bottom of the bodies.

Unfortunately, examining detailed projection profiles does not support this analysis. For example, Figure 8.9 shows a magnified portion of Figure 8.6a corresponding to five lines of text near the bottom. Within the regions occupied by each line, subpeaks are readily apparent at the top and bottom of the letter bodies. The ascenders cause a shoulder above the uppermost subpeak of each pair, and the descenders cause one below the lower one. However, contrary to the prediction, in each case the *lower* peak of the pair is larger. This is due to the detailed structure of letterforms— in particular, the serifs. Figure 8.10 shows some more examples for text in different fonts. While there are a few exceptions, the general tendency is clearly for the lower peak to dominate the upper one. A more detailed examination of this phenomenon may lead to general rules for determining whether the text is upside down.

It may be thought that inverted text is fairly unusual in practice and that any method for detecting it is of academic interest only. However, it is likely to be reasonably common in daily operation because paper is often fed into a fax machine or scanner the wrong way round. It would certainly be nice if this could be detected reliably and corrected automatically.

From slope histogram to docstrum

The third and final way to detect the orientation of a document uses histogram-based techniques that reflect the pairwise relationship between marks in the image (Saheed 1993). Recall that a mark is a connected group of black pixels and usually corresponds to a character or a disconnected part of a character. Suppose the slope between every pair of marks is calculated, and the histogram of these slopes is displayed. To calculate the slope, a reference point is defined for each mark at the lower-left corner of its bounding box or perhaps at the centroid of the pixels in it. The histogram will almost certainly have a peak that corresponds to a dominant slope of $0°$—the baseline of the text. If the page is skewed so that all baselines are slanted, the peak will occur at the angle of skew.

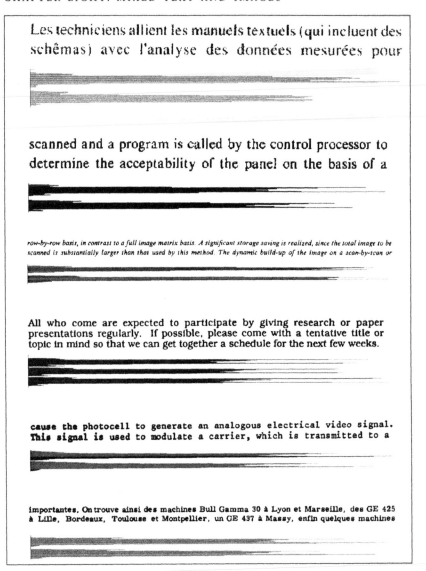

Figure 8.10 Magnified histograms of a few lines of various documents.

Figure 8.11 shows the histogram of slopes in the image of Figure 8.1. The dominant peak occurs at an angle of 0°, which indicates that the document is correctly oriented. If it had been skewed by 2°, the peak would have occurred at 2° as well. Of course, a huge number of other slopes are also present, corresponding to lines drawn between each mark and every other mark in the image. However, each individual line of text will contribute an overwhelming number of zero, or almost zero,

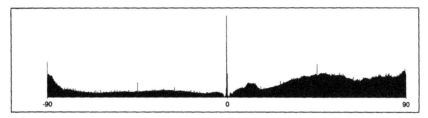

Figure 8.11 Histogram of mark-to-mark slopes in the example image.

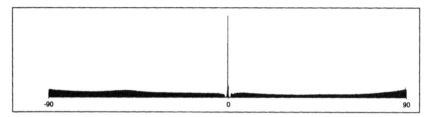

Figure 8.12 Histogram of the example image with the photograph removed.

slopes because all characters share the same baseline—at least, all characters that do not descend below the line, as *g*, *j*, *p*, *q*, and *y* do.

Although you might think that the histogram should be symmetric around 0°, this is not so. This particular histogram is strongly asymmetric because of the halftone picture at the top right of Figure 8.1. In fact, this small picture contributes a large proportion of the total marks in the document because the image has been digitized at a resolution that allows individual halftone dots to be separated. Consequently, there is a plethora of lines from other marks toward the top right of the image, and these all have slopes between 0° and 90°. Figure 8.12 shows a histogram of the same document but with the photograph removed. Most of the marks have gone!

The secondary peaks in Figure 8.11 at ±45° are also caused by the halftone picture. Halftone dots occur in a regular grid pattern, and this creates strong peaks at ±45°. Notice that even though the photo is tilted in Figure 8.1, the halftone screen is upright and the tilting does not distort the skew that is measured from the peak of the histogram.

If there are *n* marks on the page, then about $n^2/2$ slopes will have to be calculated and displayed on the histogram. For example, if the page contains 45 lines averaging 60 characters each, there will be nearly four million slopes between marks. Although this sounds like a lot of calculation, it is not necessarily worse than other methods of skew detection. For example, any method that uses pixels rather than marks must work with the total number of pixels in the image, which will probably be at least four million. To plot the histogram, very little calculation need be done for each pair of marks. Slopes need not be turned into angles since the histogram can plot slopes directly, and, once the peak value is detected, the corresponding angle can be found

Figure 8.13 Docstrum of the example document image.

by taking the inverse tan function. Finally, it is not necessary to use all the marks: a small random sample of a few percent will be perfectly adequate for line detection in practice, provided the image has a consistent, homogeneous, appearance.

An interesting transformation of the image that is related to the histogram of slopes is the *document spectrum*, or *docstrum* (Story et al. 1992). This is rather more sophisticated than the histogram and contains considerably more information. It is based on local rather than global information—just a few neighboring marks are used to create the histogram. A small constant k, usually four or six, is chosen first, and for each mark its k nearest neighbors are found. For example, with $k = 4$, a mark might pair with its left and right neighbors, another in the line above, and a fourth in the line below. Alternatively, depending on the width-to-height ratio of the adjacent marks, it might instead pair with its two left and two right neighbors. If the line spacing is large compared with the font size, it might pay to choose $k = 6$ instead to ensure that some information about line spacing is contained in the docstrum.

With the value $k = 4$, only 11,000 slopes need to be calculated for a 45-line, 60-character page. Rather than taking the lower-left corner of the bounding box as the reference point of a mark, the docstrum uses the centroid of the pixels it contains. Finally, instead of plotting a histogram of slopes, each pairing of marks—k pairs for every mark on the page—is plotted as a two-dimensional vector. The vector is translated to begin at the origin of the graph, the radial distance from the origin is the nearest-neighbor distance, and the angle from the horizontal is the nearest-neighbor angle.

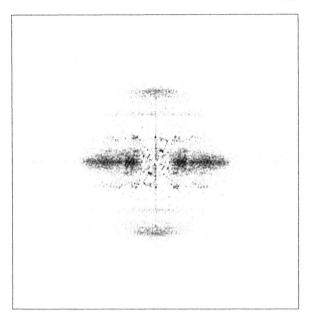

Figure 8.14 Docstrum of the example image with the photograph removed.

The docstrum is so named because of its similarity in appearance to the two-dimensional power spectrum of an image and because, like the power spectrum, it conveys a sense of the image's overall properties. (The power spectrum is explained in most image processing texts—for example, Gonzalez and Wintz 1987, Chapter 3.) The docstrum for the example page, calculated with $k = 6$, is shown in Figure 8.13. The darker streaks to the left and right of the origin are caused by the intercharacter and interword spacing in the horizontal direction; it is just possible to see where the intercharacter spacing ends and the interword spacing begins. The outer clusters are wider than the inner ones because interword spacing is more variable than intercharacter spacing. The image's orientation is given by the rotation angle of these dark streaks. The uppermost and lowermost horizontal bands above and below the central axis are due to the interline spacing; notice that the text of Figure 8.1 is quite generously spaced vertically—in fact, the line spacing is considerably greater than the average word spacing. The other horizontal bands are due to the different centroids of characters with descenders and ascenders and to accents and dots on i and j characters.

The curious central pattern of symmetric spots very close to the origin in Figure 8.13 is caused by the dot structure in the halftone photograph at the top right of Figure 8.1. This pattern is upright even though the photograph is tilted because of the orientation of the halftone screen used in printing. Figure 8.14 shows the docstrum of the same document with the photograph removed, and it is the same as Figure 8.13 without the central pattern.

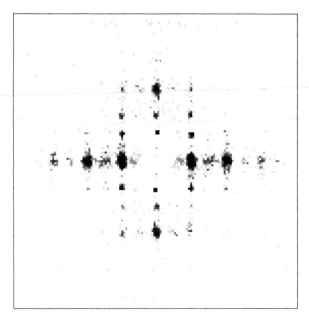

Figure 8.15 Docstrum of an image of typewritten text.

As might be expected, documents containing monospaced typewritten text exhibit a much simpler and more regular structure, as shown in Figure 8.15. The intercharacter spacing can be seen very clearly in the horizontal direction, with a separation of one character width (that is, adjacent characters) being most common, then a two-character separation (word spacing), then a three-character separation (which usually indicates sentence spacing). The vertical line spacing is also clearly seen, with some intermediate positions corresponding to, for example, the dots on *i*s and *j*s.

8.2 Segmentation

The aim of the segmentation process is to divide the document image into regions that contain either text, graphics, or a halftone picture. There are three critical issues to be considered. First, it is convenient to constrain the regions to be rectangular, though, as Figure 8.1 shows, this constraint is often violated in practice. Even an extension to accommodate arbitrary regions bounded by horizontal and vertical lines may not be general enough, for in some cases—as exemplified by Figure 8.16—there is an implied continuous boundary between text and illustration, and this would allow only piecewise approximations to it.

The second issue is that the scale of the attempted separation between text and graphics must be chosen carefully. For example, a fine-grained analysis may be able to separate textual annotation from graphical diagrams, even when the text occurs

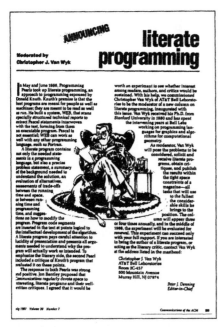

Figure 8.16 A page with a nonrectilinear region. Copyright © 1987 by Association for Computing Machinery, Inc. Reprinted by permission.

in small phrases that are not necessarily printed horizontally. Alternatively, it might be considered acceptable merely to isolate and identify the major text blocks and leave textual annotations as part of the graphic.

The third issue is whether to take account of any prior information that may be available concerning the layout style of the document, or even the individual fonts used. This can assist materially in making reliable, robust layout decisions—provided that the images really do satisfy the assumptions.

We will begin by considering the case where a document image is to be segmented into rectangular blocks that contain text, graphics, or halftone pictures. The segmentation is intended to be approximate in that small textual annotations are to be left in graphics blocks. No prior knowledge of the layout is assumed. There are two diametrically opposing philosophies for segmentation: top down and bottom up. The former views the entire image globally in terms of its horizontal and vertical projection profiles and uses these to cleave it into progressively smaller subdivisions. In the latter, individual marks or letters are merged together into progressively larger blocks based on their physical proximity. Frequently, top-down processing is performed on the result of bottom-up processing. This section also examines two other segmentation processes: extraction of short text strings and segmentation using a document grammar.

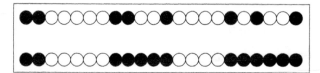

Figure 8.17 Example of run-length smoothing.

Bottom-up segmentation methods

The bottom-up method, called the *run-length smoothing algorithm*, starts by blurring, or more accurately, smearing, the binary image by filling in the pixels between any two black pixels that are less than a certain threshold distance t apart. For example, if the image were as shown at the top of Figure 8.17 and the threshold were $t = 3$, the smearing operation would result in the image beneath it.

This operation is applied separately in the horizontal and vertical directions, yielding two distinct bitmaps. Figures 8.18a and 8.18b show the result of the run-length smoothing algorithm on the example image of Figure 8.1. The thresholds in the x and y directions need not be the same. They are normally chosen to be quite large, spanning many characters and many lines, respectively, and for this example are chosen to be four centimeters (nearly half a column width) in each direction.

The two images are then combined together pixel by pixel, the result being black when the horizontally and vertically smeared images are both black. (This is an AND operation if black is represented by 1 and white by 0; it is an OR if the opposite convention is used.) The resulting image, which is black wherever text occurs, is shown in Figure 8.18c. The method produces reasonable results on simple layouts but is not very successful in this case because the column structure is disturbed by the diagram in the middle of Figure 8.1. Generally, the image can be made neater by taking the bounding box of each connected component. If the image is oriented correctly, each line of text will be represented by a black rectangle. If it is slightly skewed, the lines may be merged into paragraph-sized blocks.

A variant on the run-length method, which is intended to achieve much the same effect, is to perform smoothing in both directions simultaneously, determining the value of a pixel in the new, or *reduced*, image by examining the $k \times k$ neighborhood of the original image around that position. If the number of pixels in that neighborhood exceeds αk^2 for some constant α, then the pixel in the reduced image is made black. As an example, $k = 1.5$ millimeters and $\alpha = 0.1$ yields the reduced image in Figure 8.19a. To complete the operation, a second filter is passed over the reduced image, which sets a pixel to black if any of the pixels in a larger $n \times n$ neighborhood is black, giving (with $n = 4.5$ millimeters) the result shown in Figure 8.19b. This procedure is considerably more time-consuming than run-length smoothing, though it produces a more robust result.

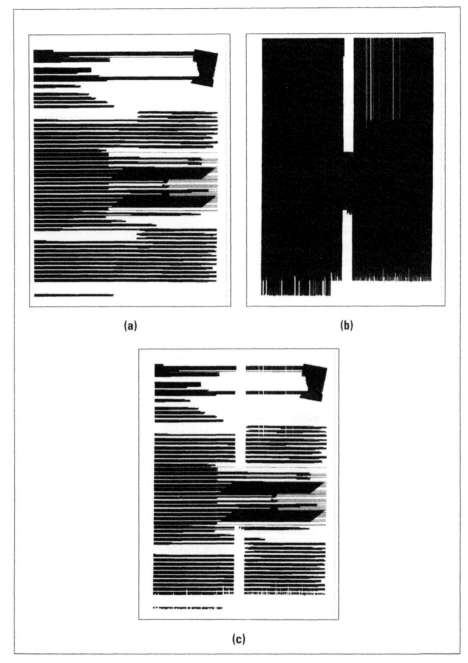

(a)

(b)

(c)

Figure 8.18 The result of the run-length smoothing algorithm: (a) horizontal smearing; (b) vertical smearing; (c) combined smearing.

Top-down and combined segmentation methods

Top-down segmentation decomposes an image recursively into a set of blocks in a technique known as the *recursive X-Y cut*. At every step, the projection profile is calculated in both horizontal and vertical directions. Then a cut is made at the most prominent valley in either profile, and the process is repeated recursively on each part. The procedure ends when no sufficiently deep and wide valleys are left. A test may be included to ensure that any block that results from cleaving has a minimum aspect ratio so that, for example, single lines of text do not end up as individual blocks.

Figure 8.20 shows the operation of the recursive X-Y cut algorithm on a simple example image. The effect is to represent the document in the form of a tree with nested rectangular blocks; this structure is often called an *X-Y tree*. The figure shows the cuts as horizontal and vertical lines, with thicker lines corresponding to earlier cuts. On this simple image, the procedure works perfectly, but on ones with a more complex structure, such as the example document of Figure 8.1, it does not, and its effect depends on just how the thresholds of valley depth and width are chosen.

Top-down and bottom-up segmentation can be combined by performing the recursive X-Y cut algorithm on the result of some kind of image-smoothing algorithm—for example, on Figure 8.18c or Figure 8.19b. This makes it somewhat more robust in that accidental cleavings are less likely to occur. In general, bottom-up procedures are preferred when it is desired to distinguish individual lines of text and top-down ones when the blocks are to be paragraph-sized or larger. Both procedures break down if the image is skewed.

Mark-based segmentation

If the marks in the document have already been identified, segmentation can be performed by working directly with marks instead of pixels. A simple bottom-up policy is to enlarge the marks' bounding boxes slightly to cover the intercharacter and interline gaps—possibly interword ones too—and then segment them into connected groups. Figure 8.21 shows pseudocode for this algorithm. It takes the list of marks in the document and creates a set of lists, each of which contains those marks belonging to a particular region. The algorithm is iterative: a new region is created for the next mark, and all remaining marks are tested against the one in that region to see if they overlap its extended boundary. The process repeats for all marks that are placed in the region until none of the marks left in the original mark list overlap any in the newly identified region. At that point a new region is begun and the process repeated. The result is that marks in the same line and the same paragraph are blocked together.

Figures 8.22 and 8.23 show an original image and the result of mark-based segmentation. The number of marks in each region is also given in Figure 8.23. In this case, the image has been segmented successfully, except for the merging of the heading "Forthcoming titles" with the first block of text and the merging of the page number with the lower-left block. This procedure can identify nested regions where one lies entirely within another. For example, the picture just underneath the

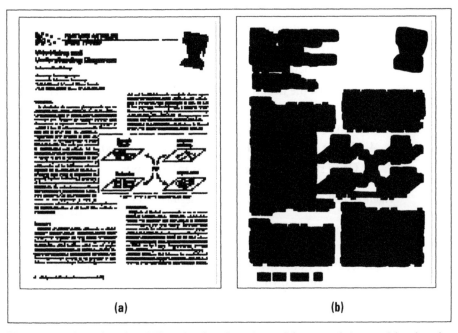

Figure 8.19 The reduced and filtered reduced versions of the example image: (a) reduced; (b) reduced and filtered.

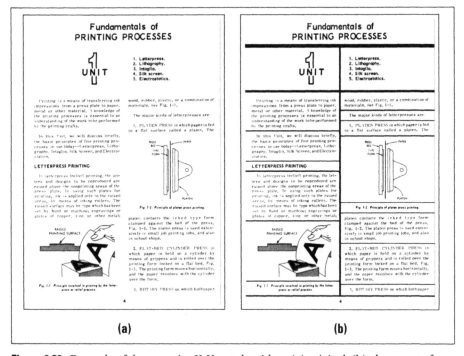

Figure 8.20 Example of the recursive X-Y cut algorithm: (a) original; (b) placement of cuts.

To segment a document into regions

1. Remove the next mark from the mark list ml.

2. Create a new region list r and place the mark in it.

3. Let m be the next mark on r. Create an enlarged boundary $e(m)$.
   For each member of the mark list ml, check whether its bounding box overlaps $e(m)$, and if so append it to r.

4. Repeat step 3 until the region list r is exhausted.

5. Go to step 1 until the mark list ml is empty.

Figure 8.21 Pseudocode for mark-based segmentation.

"Forthcoming titles" heading in Figure 8.22 has been identified as a nested region and is placed on its own as the second block in Figure 8.23. However, the procedure does rely on there being a certain minimum spacing between regions. It will not produce the grouping of Figure 8.2 on the image of Figure 8.1 unless the parameters are very carefully tweaked because the spacing between some regions is very small. One of the regions in Figure 8.2 is nonrectangular, and although the method can in fact deal with such regions, it behaves more robustly if the ability to identify nonrectangular regions is sacrificed and each region is bounded with a rectangle. This trade-off of representational power against robustness is typical of many image processing operations and of document image processing in particular.

Mark-based segmentation is more efficient than pixel-based methods, even when the overhead of mark extraction is included, because there are far fewer marks than pixels.

Segmenting short text strings

When extracting text from document images, a fine-grained approach is also possible (Fletcher and Kasturi 1988). Using a sufficiently careful and detailed analysis, it is possible to guarantee that virtually all text strings can be located in images containing mixed text and graphics, even short ones that may be printed at an angle. The conditions under which this feat can be achieved are reasonably modest:

- The image must include substantially more textual marks than graphics ones.

- The image must not exhibit an excessive range of font sizes (say, a ratio of less than 5:1 in point size).

- Each text string must contain type of similar size (a range of less than 2:1 in point size).

- The leading, or interline spacing between lines of text, must not be too small (it must be more than 25 percent of the average letter height).

Figure 8.22 Mark-based segmentation: original image.

- The interword gaps must not be too large (they must be less than 2.5 times the local average character height).

- Text strings can be identified only if they are printed along a straight line.

The first step is to identify the marks in the image. Next, marks that definitely do not correspond to characters or parts of characters are weeded out. Finally, straight lines of text are identified and removed from the image one by one.

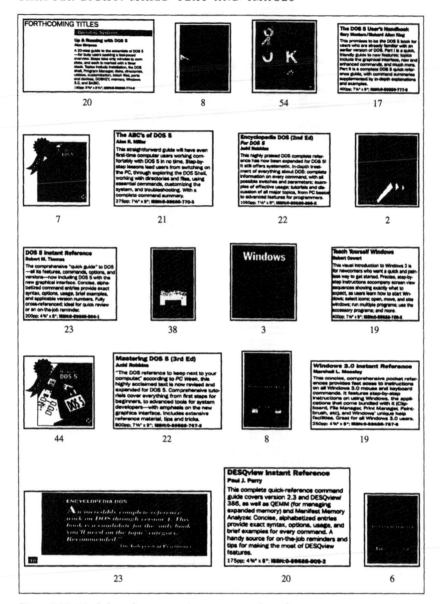

Figure 8.23 Mark-based segmentation: segmented result.

There are two heuristics for weeding out marks that are clearly not textual. The first is to eliminate any whose bounding boxes have extreme aspect ratios—say, greater than 20:1 or less than 1:20. The most extreme textual marks are the em dash (—), the vertical bar (|), and the exclamation mark (!); their aspect ratios normally lie between these bounds. The second heuristic for weeding out marks is to examine a histogram of the area of the marks' bounding boxes and determine an area threshold that broadly separates larger graphics from the text components. The threshold is determined by locating the most populated area of the histogram, using locally averaged histogram values so that neighboring areas are grouped together. Say this occurs at area value A_{mp}. It is assumed that this most popular area comprises chiefly textual marks; all marks whose area is greater than five times A_{mp} are rejected as graphical. To be more conservative, it may be worth calculating the average area A_{avg} of all the marks and only rejecting marks that are greater than five times the larger of A_{mp} and A_{avg}.

Now that most nontextual marks have been eliminated, all that remains is to identify lines of text. The Hough transform described in Section 8.1 (page 358) is an appropriate tool for this purpose. This transform is applied to the centroids of all remaining marks. The result is a two-dimensional matrix of integer counts in which the largest elements correspond to groups of marks that lie along a straight line. Recall that each point of the two-dimensional Hough matrix corresponds to a straight line in the image. The matrix value is a measure of the number of marks whose centroids lie on this line. Finally, the coordinates of that point define the actual line: they correspond to θ, the line's orientation in the image, and ρ, the closest distance it passes to the center of the image.

The vast majority of text strings in documents are parallel to the axes, and it is advantageous to remove these first. Consequently, the Hough transform is first performed for a restricted range of angles: $0° \leq \theta \leq 5°$, $85° \leq \theta \leq 95°$, and $175° \leq \theta < 180°$. From this, all lines containing three or more marks are extracted. Lines with more marks are removed first, and as each one is removed, the contributions of its marks are deleted from the Hough transform. Then, as a second step, the transform is recalculated for the full range of angles $0° \leq \theta < 180°$, and the extraction process is repeated. The procedure is summarized in Figure 8.24.

One of the difficulties in applying the Hough transform is deciding on an appropriate resolution for the distance parameter ρ, and this accounts for much of the complexity of the algorithm in Figure 8.24. An angular resolution in θ of 1° is appropriate for detecting lines of text. When choosing the resolution of the parameter ρ, it must be taken into account that the centroids of the marks along a line of text will not be exactly colinear. Too fine a resolution will result in marks belonging to the same text string contributing to different Hough matrix cells. Too coarse a resolution will cause marks from different lines of text to be grouped into a single line. The solution is rather complicated. The first step is to base the resolution on the average height of all marks currently under consideration as textual marks (step 1 of Figure 8.24). Even then, it may happen that some ascenders and descenders belonging to a line may contribute to the wrong Hough cell. Once a line is located, neighboring Hough cells are examined and temporarily amalgamated with the one corresponding to the line (step 5.a). The average height of all marks contributing to these cells is used to calculate a new clustering factor that determines how many Hough cells should be amalgamated in the final analysis (step 5.b).

Figure 8.24 leaves open the details of the string segmentation in step 5.c. The purpose of this step is to identify separate text strings that just happen to be colinear

To extract all text strings from an image,

1. Set H to the average height of the marks being considered.

2. Set the Hough domain resolution in θ to 1° and in R to 0.2 × H.

3. Apply the Hough transform to all marks, using θ in the ranges $0° \leq \theta \leq 5°$, $85° \leq \theta \leq 95°$, and $175° \leq \theta < 180°$.

4. Set the mark count threshold to $T = 20$.

5. For each cell (ρ, θ) of the Hough transform having a count greater than T (which corresponds to a line comprising T or more marks):

   (a) For the cluster of the 11 cells $(\rho - 5, \theta), (\rho - 4, \theta), (\rho - 3, \theta), \cdots,$ $(\rho + 5, \theta)$, calculate the average height H_{local} of marks that contribute to this cluster.

   (b) Compute a new clustering factor $f = H_{local}/R$ and re-cluster the cells $(\rho - f, \theta), (\rho - f + 1, \theta), \cdots, (\rho + f, \theta)$.

   (c) Perform string segmentation on the marks that contribute to this new cluster.

6. Update the Hough transform by deleting the contributions from all components discarded in step 5.c.

7. Decrement T by 1, and, if $T \geq 3$ go to step 5.

8. Compute the Hough transform for the entire range of θ, $0° \leq \theta < 180°$, and go to step 4.

Figure 8.24 Extracting strings of text from the Hough domain.

and to confirm that the strings really do comprise text. There are three stages to this step. First the marks are sorted along the line on which they lie to put them into natural reading order. The second stage is to scan the line to estimate the intercharacter spacing and interword spacings. This is where the constraint that interword gaps do not exceed 2.5 times the local average character height comes into play: gaps that do exceed this amount are assumed to be separate text strings. It is a good idea to extract long strings before short ones, and if the number of marks in a string falls below the current threshold (T in Figure 8.24), the string is not extracted at this stage but is left in the Hough transform to be dealt with later when the threshold has been decremented sufficiently.

The final stage of step 5.c is to check the strings to ensure that they really are text. The simplest kind of check merely rejects strings that comprise repeated small graphics (like lines of dots or dashes), all of whose marks are the same overall size and contain the same number of black pixels. More sophisticated tests are discussed in Section 8.3, which focuses on the classification issue.

- The title lines are set in Melior 36/38 point boldface, centered.

- There are one to four lines in the title: the second part of a long title is sometimes set in 24-point type.

- The byline is set in Melior 12/14-point boldface, centered; affiliations may either follow the authors' names set in the same typeface or are set on the same line.

- The title line precedes the byline, and the two are separated by at least 38-point leading.

- Every paragraph is indented except the first and the beginning of the conclusion section, which begin with a 40/40-point drop cap.

- The body type (main text) is TimesTen Roman 9/11.

- The page numbers and month-year (in body type) are set flush with the margin and alternate between left and right.

- Footnotes (rare) are set TimesTen Roman 7/8, separated by a hairline rule with a blank line before and after the rule.

Figure 8.25   Partial layout specifications for a journal. Reprinted from *IEEE Computer* (Nagy, Seth, and Viswanathan 1992) Copyright © Institute of Electrical and Electronics Engineers, Inc.

Segmentation using a document grammar

The final approach to segmentation is to invoke specific prior knowledge of the layout that is expected. For example, if the image is a page from a known journal, then information about exactly how pages of that journal are laid out can assist immensely with the segmentation process (Nagy, Seth, and Stoddard 1986; Nagy, Seth, and Viswanathan 1992). Figure 8.25 shows partial layout specifications for the journal *IEEE Computer* in 1991. It states that each article's title page starts with one to four lines of 36-point centered text (the title) separated by 2 points of spacing (the "36/38" gives the type size and the baseline-to-baseline spacing). This is followed by a space of at least 38 points; then the authors' names (the byline), centered, in 12-point text separated by 2 points of spacing (12/14); and so forth. These specifications can be interpreted at the pixel level as expectations for the vertical projection profile and at the mark level as expectations for the size and positioning of the marks that begin the first page.

The page layout specifications can be codified into a formal *document grammar* that governs the parsing of the image into regions. The grammar is a two-dimensional one that specifies how the page is divided recursively, sometimes by horizontal divisions—as with the title, byline, and page footer specifications of Figure 8.25—and sometimes by vertical ones, as when multiple text columns are specified. A full document grammar typically contains hundreds of productions for a single journal, and its creation is a time-consuming exercise. To make matters worse, the task is never-ending even for a single journal because styles change regularly.

- Lines of print are roughly horizontal.
- The baselines of characters are aligned.
- Each line of text is set in a single point size.
- Ascenders, descenders, and capitals have consistent heights. In roman fonts, serifs are aligned.
- Typefaces (including variants such as italic or bold) do not change within a word.
- Within a line of text, word and character spaces are uniform, and word spaces are larger than character spaces.
- Lines of text in a paragraph are spaced uniformly.
- Each paragraph is left-justified or right-justified (or both), with special provisions for the first and last line of a paragraph.
- Paragraphs are separated either by wider spaces than lines within a paragraph or by indentation (or both).
- Illustrations are confined to rectangular frames.
- In multicolumn formats, the columns are spaced uniformly.

Figure 8.26 Generic typesetting conventions. Reprinted from *IEEE Computer* (Nagy, Seth, and Viswanathan 1992) Copyright © Institute of Electrical and Electronics Engineers, Inc.

A document grammar gives prior, publication-specific information about the layout of a document image. In contrast, the segmentation methods discussed earlier rely implicitly on generic conventions of typesetting, some of which are summarized in Figure 8.26. It is clear that the much more specific rules in a document grammar will facilitate robust and accurate segmentation, at the expense of generality and flexibility. Moreover, such rules allow labels to be assigned to components of the document—title, authors, affiliation, abstract, page number, publication date, and so on—that will prove immensely valuable in many document display systems and in document retrieval. Most likely, the future will see a convergence between the two approaches. Document description languages such as SGML and XML already specify structure rather than presentation, and as a result the same document can be formatted in different ways simply by using different structural styles. Similarly, generic typesetting conventions will be codified and used by segmentation schemes in explicit form. They will be specialized in many ways to deal with different styles of documents. Meanwhile, document grammars will be generalized and mechanisms put in place to recognize variants of a page and even to infer grammar rules from sample images.

8.3   Classification

Once a document image has been segmented into regions, the final step in analyzing the layout is to classify the regions as text, line drawings, and halftone images. There are many clues that can be used for this, and a wide range of schemes is possible.

If the segmentation method aims to separate out individual lines of text, the overall size and shape of a region is an excellent indicator of its classification, for few graphics are as long and thin as lines of text are. Size and shape might be measured in terms of height, which is small for lines of text, and eccentricity or width/height ratio, which is large. If text lines are to be distinguished from solid ruled lines, this can be accomplished using parameters such as the overall blackness ratio and the mean black run length, which should both be small for text. A simple classifier will simply take all these parameters and compare them with prespecified thresholds to decide which class a particular region belongs to.

A more sophisticated approach is to perform some kind of texture analysis on the region. One method is to identify all the black-white horizontal runs and quantize the proportion of black to white into rough categories: say, less than 10 percent, between 10 and 20 percent, and so on. A matrix $p(i, j)$ is formed whose element i, j is the number of times that the image contains a horizontal run of length j whose black-white proportion is in category i. Then measures of short-run emphasis and long-run emphasis can be calculated from the matrix, for example, by

$$F_{short} = \frac{\sum_i \sum_j p(i, j)/j^2}{\sum_i \sum_j p(i, j)},$$

$$F_{long} = \frac{\sum_i \sum_j j^2 p(i, j)}{\sum_i \sum_j p(i, j)}.$$

F_{short} will be large for text regions, while F_{long} will be small (Galloway 1975). For regions containing line drawings, the reverse is likely to be true. If the image contains halftone pictures, F_{short} will be extremely large and F_{long} extremely small.

These features separate the different kinds of regions into different areas of the plane defined by the two parameters F_{short} and F_{long}. It then becomes a simple matter to carve up the plane so that each region can be classified from its parameter values. In order to provide even better discrimination, it may be advantageous to use additional basic features, such as the distribution of black-white-black runs as well as black-white ones. This method has been used successfully to classify regions into one of five categories—large-font text, medium-font text, small-font text, graphics, and halftones—by analyzing their textural characteristics.

As with many aspects of document image processing, it is often faster and more reliable to base region classification on marks rather than on pixels. For example, the number of marks in the region, and the mean and standard deviation width and height of the marks, are strong clues to the type of the region.

The histogram of mark-to-mark slopes, which was developed on page 367 of Section 8.1 for orienting the image, is a useful tool for classifying regions too. Each segmented region is examined, and the slopes within it are calculated. Regions containing text, line art, and halftones have different distributions of slopes. All of them generally exhibit a major peak at the horizontal. However, for text the distribution is otherwise fairly flat, except for a marked, but narrow, dip each side of the main peak. Halftones produce a very marked peak at $\pm 45°$ because of the regular layout of the halftone screen used to create them. Graphics have no particular distinguishing pattern except for a generally much lower density of marks.

Figure 8.27 shows typical histograms for regions of the three different types. It also exemplifies a practical problem that occurs when dealing with halftones. The scanning resolution for this particular image (300 dpi) was not nearly great enough to allow individual halftone dots to be resolved. Marks that are close together are smudged; indeed, whole dark areas run together. Despite the evident poor quality of the halftone, definite sharp peaks do occur at angles of $\pm 45°$, and it is still possible to use this clue to identify halftone images.

The docstrum (for example, in Figure 8.13 on page 370) provides additional clues for textual regions—namely, the characteristic pattern of four symmetric clusters due to the interline and intercharacter spacing, and the division of the left and right clusters into two subclusters due to the intercharacter and interword spacing.

The projection profile of individual lines of text provides an even more sensitive clue to the presence of text, even in very small quantities. Assuming that the Roman alphabet is being used, all lines of text in the region are superimposed, and their combined projection profile is checked to see if it conforms with expectations such as those discussed on page 367 of Section 8.1.

The projection profile method relies on the conventional shape of the letters and would be fooled by decorative or obscure type fonts. However, the mark-based approach to textual image compression provides an even better clue for detecting text: the frequency of reoccurrence of marks. In all natural languages, the number of different letters in a piece of text grows in a characteristic way with the total number of letters it contains. This is reflected in the growth of the mark dictionary for a region as a function of the number of marks in the region. Moreover, if the frequency of occurrence of the most popular letter is compared with the frequency of the next most popular letter, and so on, the distribution that results is a stable characteristic of natural language (see the discussion of Zipf's "law" on page 183 in Chapter 4), and this also can be used—on marks instead of letters—as a test for text. It should, however, be kept in mind that these methods involve statistical tests and so will not work for regions that contain just a few words.

We have discussed a number of possible features that can be used to discriminate regions of different types. In practice, most classification schemes are based on several features that are combined together using a linear discriminant function. For example, if there are n features with values $f_1, f_2, \ldots, f_n$ for a particular region and two classes, A and B, then a linear discriminant function involves n fixed numeric weights $w_1, w_2, \ldots, w_n$. The rule is to choose class A whenever

$$w_1 f_1 + w_2 f_2 + \cdots + w_n f_n \geq 0,$$

otherwise choose B. The weights are determined based on a training set of regions whose classifications are known, and there are standard procedures for coming up

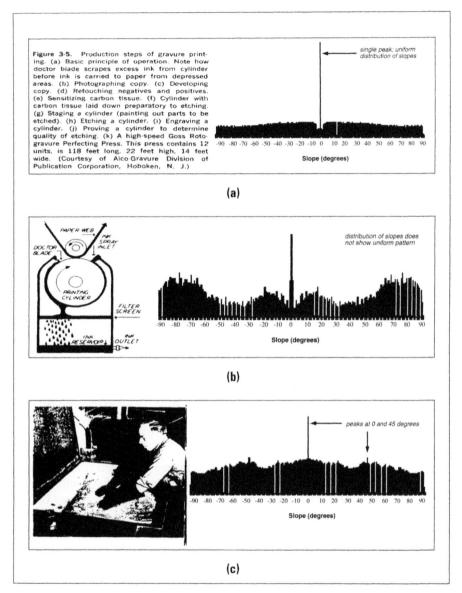

Figure 8.27 Slope histograms for three different types of region: (a) textual region; (b) graphics region; (c) halftone region.

with appropriate weight values (Fu 1982). For document image analysis there will normally be three classes—text regions, line drawings, and halftones. In this case, each pairwise discrimination can be treated separately (text versus line drawings, text versus halftones, halftones versus line drawings) and a different set of weights determined for each one.

Further reading

Image analysis. There is a collection of papers on document image analysis that provides excellent general descriptions of the problems involved (Baird, Bunke, and Yamamoto 1992); the chapters by Bayer, Franke, Kressel, et al. (1992) and Nagy (1992) are particularly relevant to the topics covered here. The "backwards" method for rotating discrete images is mentioned briefly by Russ (1992). The original description of the Hough transform is by Hough himself (1962). A tutorial introduction to the transform can be found in the image processing text by Gonzalez and Wintz (1987).

Skew detection. The method of skew detection by left-hand margin search is described by Dengel (1992). The use of the Hough transform for detecting skew in an image is due to Srihari and Govindaraju (1989), who also performed the detailed analysis of the projection profile in Section 8.1. The autocorrelation function approach to determining skew from the projection profile is presented by Bones, Griffin, and Carey-Smith (1990), who also detail a combined bottom-up and top-down blocking and cleaving algorithm for segmenting document images. The use of the slope histogram for orientation was developed by Saheed (1993), and the term *docstrum* was coined by Story et al. (1992).

Segmentation. A number of papers discuss the processes of segmentation and block classification (Wong, Casey, and Wahl 1982; Wang and Srihari 1989). The approach in Section 8.2 for identifying text strings in images containing mixed text and graphics is due to Fletcher and Kasturi (1988), and the algorithm of Figure 8.24 is adapted from that source.

The document grammar approach for segmentation is due to George Nagy and his coworkers (Nagy, Seth, and Stoddard 1986; Nagy, Seth, and Viswanathan 1992), and Figures 8.25 and 8.26 are reproduced from the latter paper. The measures F_{short} and F_{long} of short- and long-run emphasis are from Galloway (1975).

The distribution of letter frequencies, which was mentioned at the end of Section 8.3 as a means of detecting text, is discussed by Bell, Cleary, and Witten (1990). Appropriate procedures for selecting weights for linear discrimination functions are discussed by Fu (1982).

Implementation

The other chapters of this book have been rather general and have not endorsed particular methods. Nevertheless, we have implemented and tested many of the ideas presented and have an operational retrieval system that incorporates most of the components described in those earlier chapters. In order to arrive at an implementation, we had to choose between various alternative techniques, and this has provoked us into considering a wide range of detailed issues. The experience so gained is the subject of this chapter.

In the sections that follow, the various parts of a retrieval system for documents and images are described and justification given for the many choices that were made along the way. The system described—the mg retrieval system—is available free of charge via the Internet. It is "only" a research prototype, and to date its main use has been as a testbed for research into the techniques described in this book and as a basis for the derivation of empirical results concerning compression, access speed, and retrieval effectiveness. It has also been the main mechanism used by the Melbourne-based research group involved in the *TREC* project and the search engine for the New Zealand Digital Library described in Appendix B. As far as modern software goes, the system is relatively unpolished—for example, input and output is via a terminal interface rather than through a graphical user interface. Nor is there any provision for multiple users, for dynamic insertion of new documents, or for multiprocessing on parallel machines. Database creation is assumed to be a batch job, and, unless a recompilation is undertaken, there is only limited provision for customizing of the many options and parameters. Addition of these features is left to those who are interested in interface design and human factors experiments. Our interest has been in the algorithmics embedded at the heart of the system.

This chapter is about the design of the mg system. It is not in any way a user manual—that appears as Appendix A at the end of the book. Instead, the various decisions that led to the system in its current form are discussed and documented. For this reason, the material in this chapter is, by its nature, quite technical in places. Despite this, the discussion is relevant to nontechnical readers. In the sections that follow, we describe the document compression subsystem, the image compression subsystem, the index compression subsystem, the index construction methods, and the query processing techniques used in the mg system. We also give detailed performance figures derived from the implementation.

During the several years of mg-related development, a number of different computer systems have been used to carry out experiments. Almost all of the results given in the first edition made use of a SunSPARC 10 computer, which in 1993 was a reasonably powerful workstation. The inexorable advance of technology since then has meant that new experiments are inevitably carried out on faster machines. Now, in 1998, much of our experimental work is carried out on an Intel Pentium II 266 MHz platform, and many of the results in this chapter have been measured on that machine. In terms of raw processor speed, the latter machine is between five and six times faster than the SPARC (and was approximately one-quarter the price, not even counting inflation). Disk *capacity* has also decreased enormously in cost during these last four years, but in terms of disk *speed* the two machines are comparable, highlighting the need for compression—as CPUs become relatively faster, it becomes more and more attractive to decompress data on demand, saving on disk transfer costs.

9.1 Text compression

First, let us consider the process of compressing documents stored as ASCII text. Chapter 2 describes this area in detail; here, we discuss the specific application to large amounts of text stored as individual documents in a full-text retrieval system. In a typical small application there is likely to be 100 Mbytes of text and 100,000 documents. At the upper end we have been dealing with *TREC* at 2 Gbytes and 750,000 documents and have been considering hypothetical collections of 5 Gbytes and 5,000,000 documents. Moreover, the size of text collections is growing at an alarming rate.

There are three requirements for the text compression process. First, it should achieve good compression. Even when compressed, the text is the dominant consumer of disk space in a typical document retrieval system, and a small improvement in compression on a multigigabyte database returns a much greater saving than a small improvement in the efficiency of the index compression algorithm.

Second, and no less important, decoding should be fast. There are two usual scenarios for the use of a retrieval system, and both rely on fast access. In the first, an online system is accessed simultaneously by many users, all sharing the same central processing server and disk files and all paying real money for their connection time and other resources. In this case, the system must process queries efficiently if the required transaction rate is to be supported. Expensive hardware can sometimes achieve the same effect as elegance of design, but the latter will win out in the long run.

The second scenario is when all users have their own copy of the document collection. In this case, users buy the data and the software, rather than the service.

For example, they might buy a CD-ROM containing an encyclopedia and access the information on a home computer. Although there is no direct expense incurred by the user if access is slower than necessary—the owner of a personal computer pays no more for a million CPU cycles than for a hundred—users of such systems can be notoriously fickle in their choice of software, and if a particular piece of software is reputed to be slow, it is unlikely to prove a commercial success.

The third requirement is that individual documents must be decodable with a minimum of overhead. To do this, the compression regime must readily admit synchronization points. Without being able to access the text randomly, there can be no hope of accessing, decoding, and presenting individual documents within a reasonable time, and the system will not be viable unless the collection is small. We might, for example, consider a retrieval mechanism based on a pattern matcher such as the Unix grep command—in fact such systems can be quite useful (Manber and Wu 1994). Despite the fact that the entire text is scanned for each query, search times on collections of up to a few megabytes are reasonable, even if the documents must be decompressed. But response on a multigigabyte collection will be measured in tens of minutes, and that is unacceptable.

A final observation concerns the encoding subsystem. In both of the usage scenarios described above, decoding must be fast, but there is no such requirement for encoding. An important factor to take into account when designing the text compression regime is that, if necessary, encoding can be resource-intensive.

Choice of compression model

The requirement for synchronization points means that it is not possible to use a conventional adaptive model unless the model is reset frequently. However, more than one pass can be made over the original text, so a semi-static model is an appropriate choice.

Chapter 2 discusses several kinds of models that could be adapted to work in a semi-static manner. The best compression is obtained by finite-context models such as the *ppm*, *bzip2*, and *dmc* methods. However, two of these rely on arithmetic coding and, even worse, involve multiple coding steps per byte of text. The bit-by-bit *dmc* scheme requires that eight symbols be coded for each byte, and even the *ppm* method averages closer to two than to one because of the escape codes. In combination this means that fast decoding with these two methods can be achieved only on powerful hardware because the processes involved are intrinsically expensive. The *bzip2* transformation is faster to decode, especially so when coupled with a Huffman coder rather than an arithmetic coder, but compression is relatively poor unless large blocks of text can be processed.

The various Ziv-Lempel models are also candidates. If an LZ77-type model is used, a *priming text* should be chosen with which to initialize the window at the start of the encoding of each document. Priming the model is important because the documents will often be short. For example, the average verse in *Bible* is just 28 words long, so few copy pointers will be found if the window is initially empty. The priming text might be a representative section from the data itself or, more usefully, a pseudotext generated by considering some attributes of the collection as a whole.

For example, the most frequently appearing words might be identified and used to make up the initial window. Then the priming text assumed as the window prior to the compression of each *TREC* document would include

> *the of a in to and s is on The for that an as at be by it or DOC are was TEXT from said will with DOCNO.*

Moreover, there is no reason to make all of the interword gaps a single blank. Other sequences of characters should also be interposed to reap the maximum benefit from the priming text.

Another way to generate a priming text is to build a model of the text using a sophisticated technique such as the *ppm* scheme and then drive it backward by using that model and accumulated probabilities to "decode" a stream of random bits. This approach is not guaranteed to produce anything sensible, but if the model used to produce the text is good, the output will look remarkably similar to the original input. Indeed, running a decompressor backward is a very good way to gauge how good the model is—if the output looks like the input, the model is appropriate.[1]

The text in Figure 9.1 was generated by feeding random bits into a *ppm* model that was built for *Bible*. It bears a striking similarity of style to the real *Bible* text on page 107—although we know it is meaningless, the eye is lured into trying to read it.

Notice that the model exhibits a very good understanding of word and sentence structure, and even the verses have a typical length. However, as the decoder "decodes" more and more white noise, the randomized text degenerates because of the explicit feedback that takes place in an adaptive model. By way of contrast, the text in Figure 9.2 was generated randomly from a zero-order character model of *Bible*. About the only thing that can be said for it is that the eye is not deceived into trying to read it. The first example is without doubt the better priming text.

Once suitable text for the initial window has been selected, compression proceeds normally. The compressor is, of course, free to adapt within each document by sliding the window and phasing out the priming text. If this is done, then on long documents the compression efficiency will approach the rate that would have been achieved without breaking the collection into individual documents. Doing so may mean that execution rates are reduced because of the need for encoder and decoder to use dynamic data structures, but it is equally valid to not adapt the model and use the priming text as the window throughout the compression of each document.

If an LZ78-type model is used, a dictionary of strings must be chosen as the initial state of the model. One way to set up the dictionary is simply to note all of the words that appear in the text. That way every word is codable as a copy.

In reality, however, these suggestions are just an approximation of a word-based model. A model that is explicitly based on words has three advantages. First, it is natural for textual data (in English, at least); experiments such as those described in Section 2.8 have shown that it gives excellent compression on English text. Second,

---

1 Witten, Bell, Moffat, et al. (1994) take a whimsical look at the characteristics of randomly generated text.

```
acts
27
35
Sheft:  and men eius of man be fulfilled the Lord entered favour
way of the body is salloh;

jeremiah
52
233
Jibshan, which are escape the fulfilled indeed Peter came, the
wife?

romans
1
17
For he way of darken us to this gardeth a reproved him;

rber':  in the know not:

zechariot, and almug tree the truth.

jeremiah
52
12
Behold.
```

Figure 9.1   Random text generated by a fifth-order *ppm* model for *Bible*.

```
odeum
2y
.   oB
?eeeio,y
ueeem7ssK noo s,,?mm2wsmH
ee


s
euuv,oe?t?t emaet e
edyueve8oWesHne
oHos'tNneeoe,e wweGyLedeuuCCLGuN9HuwuHtG2Nw uGuRGLdT
GeNe Cow
G
dTwwu ew:Neww8
e.CeRHeTGewwCwfeCNf
```

Figure 9.2   Random text generated by a zero-order character model for *Bible*.

each symbol is several bytes long, so the average number of coding steps per byte is well under one. This means that decompression is fast. Third, an intrinsic part of the compression model for a word-based scheme is a list of all the words that appear in the text, and this list might have other uses in a full-text retrieval system.

For these three reasons:

The mg system uses a zero-order word-based semi-static model for ASCII text.

The encoder makes two passes over the text. In the first, a lexicon of *words* and *nonwords* is built up, and the frequency of each token is counted. In mg a word is defined to be a maximal-length contiguous sequence of up to 15 alphanumeric characters but containing not more than 4 numeric characters. The final clause of this definition was added to include short numeric strings such as 1994 and 100 as single words, but to force long numeric strings such as 1000000 to be split into multiple words. Since the empty string is permitted as both a word and a nonword, tokens that exceed these limits are simply broken into multiple parts. For example, the string "1000000" would be parsed as (word, "1000")+(nonword, "")+(word, "000"). The motivation for forcing these breaks after a relatively short number of numeric characters came from one of the test databases: *Comact* contains 261,829 documents, each of which is individually numbered. In the absence of a strict rule on numeric characters, this means that the compression model for *Comact* effectively contains 261,829 entries just for the page numbers, more than eight times the number of "real" words.

After the lexicon has been built, a second pass is made in which the text is compressed using the parameters accumulated in the first. At the beginning of each document, the address in the output file is noted and written to an index file. These addresses are stored to the nearest byte, rather than the nearest bit, in order to cope with large collections such as *TREC*, resulting in an average of 3.5 bits per record lost due to fragmentation. (The compressed form of *TREC* occupies about 605 Mbytes, which would require more than 32 bits to index to the granularity of a bit.) The issue of synchronization will be taken up again below.

Choice of coder

There are three main candidate coding methods that might be used with a word-based model. The first, and simplest, is a flat binary code in which word number $1 \leq w \leq n$ is coded as a $\lceil \log n \rceil$–bit binary integer. Binary coding ignores the actual probabilities accumulated by the model and assumes instead that all symbols are equally likely. For this reason, it is likely to introduce some compression "leakage." However, it has the advantage of being very fast during both encoding and decoding. All that is required is a simple loop that either takes an integer and then extracts and writes $\lceil \log n \rceil$ bits or, in the decoder, builds up a value by accumulating $\lceil \log n \rceil$ bits.

Second, and at the other end of the spectrum of coders, is arithmetic coding. The probability distribution implied by the observed symbol frequency counts is used exactly by the coder, and the resulting compression is only a small fraction more than the self-entropy. Arithmetic coding is, however, slow. In most implementations, several multiplicative operations are required per symbol, and a small number of shifting and masking operations are required per bit of output. If these costs can be accepted, then good compression will result.

The third candidate is Huffman coding. Here, the probability distribution is used to generate an optimal assignment of prefix-free codewords, which gives much better compression than a binary code if the distribution is nonuniform, but is inefficient compared to the arithmetic coder because all of the probabilities are, in effect, being approximated by negative powers of two. In Section 2.4 it was noted that the inefficiency of a Huffman code is bounded by $p_{max} + 0.086$ bits per symbol, where p_{max} is the probability of the most likely symbol. On the text *Bible*, for example, the most likely word is *the*, with probability $p_{max} = 0.075$; the most likely nonword is a single blank, with $p_{max} = 0.807$. Using the bound given above, the inefficiency for each word/nonword pair is bounded at 1.05 bits, a penalty of less than 10 percent overall, since the entropy of the word distribution is about 10 bits per word token, the entropy of the nonword distribution around 2 bits per symbol, and a word is always followed by a nonword. Furthermore, this is just an upper bound. On the text *Bible*, the actual loss through the use of Huffman coding compared to arithmetic coding is only 3.2 percent.

The need for synchronization further reduces the relative inefficiency. In a Huffman coder with bit-aligned addresses, synchronization costs nothing; in an arithmetic coder it adds about one bit at the end of a compressed document. An arithmetic coder must also reserve some small amount of bandwidth for an end-of-document symbol since codes are not bit-aligned and it is difficult otherwise for the decoder to know when it has exhausted the message. For example, on a message of 200 symbols and perhaps 1,000 bytes, the end-of-document symbol will typically have a probability of about 1/200, so in encoded form it adds about 8 bits to the compressed string. Each of the other symbols must have a correspondingly reduced code space, and in total the implicit appearance of "not end-of-document" 200 times costs another 1.5 bits. Together, these three effects add 10 to 12 bits to the arithmetic representation—an inefficiency of about 1 percent of the compressed size of a 1,000-byte document.

Thus, there is very little difference in compression between Huffman and arithmetic coding when used with a word-based model. Moreover, for semi-static decompression, during which there is no alteration to the set of codes, Huffman coding is much faster than arithmetic coding. For these reasons:

The mg system uses a Huffman coder for text compression.

The other coding method mentioned was binary. Surprisingly, when implemented for speed as was described in the subsection on canonical Huffman codes (page 36), Huffman decoding is just as fast as binary coding because both methods can be reduced to almost the same sequence of basic operations per decoded bit. Hence Huffman decoding is faster on probability distributions that are skew because the better compression of the Huffman coder means that fewer bits need to be processed through this operation sequence. In semi-static applications, there is no reason to prefer binary coding to Huffman coding, with the single exception that it is easier to write the programs.

Table 9.1 Example "bad" frequency distributions and corresponding Huffman codes.

	$n = 5$			$n = 6$			$n = 7$	
i	c_i	Code	i	c_i	Code	i	c_i	Code
1	1	0000	1	1	00000	1	1	000000
2	1	0001	2	1	00001	2	1	000001
3	1	001	3	1	0001	3	1	00001
4	3	01	4	3	001	4	3	0001
5	4	1	5	4	01	5	4	001
			6	7	1	6	7	01
						7	11	1

Limitations on Huffman codes

There is, however, one problem that might arise with the Huffman coding implementation described in Chapter 2. If codes longer than 32 bits are required, it is no longer possible to store them as a single integer, complicating the decoding process. As with arithmetic coding, this problem is completely eliminated by the use of a 64-bit machine; but also as with arithmetic coding, it can be avoided through the use of a modified technique. This is an interesting issue that we discuss extensively in this subsection and the next. However, we should warn you at the outset that the solution is not actually incorporated into the mg system (although to do so would not be difficult).

First, it is instructive to determine just how likely codeword overflow might be. An initial—and very tempting—approximation is to say that if a code is to be 33 bits long, the symbol represented must have a probability of approximately $1/2^{33}$. Since every symbol will have a frequency count of at least 1, this must mean that we need worry about codeword overflow only after about 2^{33} symbols have been processed. For a word-based model, where each symbol corresponds to an average of 5 or 6 bytes, this is equivalent to about 5×10^{10} bytes, or roughly 50 Gbytes. This is large even by the standards of the collections discussed in this book.

However, although $1/2^{33}$ is a reasonable first approximation, it is not correct. Consider the codes shown in Table 9.1. In the table, Huffman's algorithm is used to construct codes for each of three sets of symbol frequencies, and a quite disturbing trend is evident: despite the rule that "to minimize the length of the longest codewords, ties should be broken by giving precedence to single symbols ahead of packages of symbols," codewords of growing length are required. Nor is it difficult to create larger alphabets with even longer maximum code lengths. For example, if an eighth symbol is added to the seven-symbol list and given a frequency of 18, it is necessary for Huffman's algorithm to generate a seven-bit code. If a ninth symbol with frequency 29 is then added, the longest codeword will be eight bits long. For these frequency counts to arise and create an eight-bit codeword, as few as $75 = 29 + 18 + 11 + 7 + 4 + 3 + 1 + 1 + 1$ symbols are needed to appear in the input stream. This is substantially fewer than the 2^8 estimated by the simple logic sketched in the previous paragraph.

The set of frequencies that forces Huffman's algorithm to generate these long codes is related to the well-known Fibonacci numbers, which are defined in a standard way by the recurrence $F(1) = 1$, $F(2) = 1$, and $F(k + 2) = F(k + 1) + F(k)$. The Fibonacci sequence has many surprising properties (Graham, Knuth, and Patashnik 1989), not the least of which is that the cumulative sums of the sequence are closely related to the sequence itself:

$$\sum_{i=1}^{n} F(i) = F(n + 2) - 1 .$$

In the case of the modified Fibonacci sequence suggested by Table 9.1 and defined by $F'(1) = F'(2) = F'(3) = 1$, $F'(4) = 3$ with the same subsequent $F'(k + 2) = F'(k + 1) + F'(k)$ recurrence, a similar relationship holds when $n \geq 2$:

$$\sum_{i=1}^{n} F'(i) = F'(n + 2) - 1 .$$

Moreover, when $n \geq 4$,

$$F'(n) = F(n - 1) + F(n - 3) .$$

Hence the cumulative sum of the first $n + 1$ values, which is the total number of symbols necessary to force a code with a codeword of n bits, is given by

$$\sum_{i=1}^{n+1} F'(i) = F(n + 2) + F(n) - 1 .$$

In closed form the original Fibonacci sequence can be calculated from

$$F(n) = \frac{\phi^n + \hat{\phi}^n}{\sqrt{5}} = \left\lfloor \frac{\phi^n}{\sqrt{5}} + \frac{1}{2} \right\rfloor$$

where

$$\phi = \frac{1 + \sqrt{5}}{2} \approx 1.618$$

and

$$\hat{\phi} = \frac{1 - \sqrt{5}}{2} \approx -0.618.$$

Table 9.2 Values and cumulative sums for the modified Fibonacci function.

n	$F'(n)$	$\sum_{i=1}^{n+1} F'(i)$	2^n
1	1	2	2
2	1	3	4
3	1	6	8
4	3	10	16
5	4	17	32
6	7	28	64
7	11	46	128
8	18	75	256
9	29	122	512
10	47	198	1,024
33	3.01×10^6	1.28×10^7	8.59×10^9
65	1.47×10^{13}	6.21×10^{13}	3.69×10^{19}

The value ϕ is sometimes known as the golden ratio: ϕ and $\hat{\phi}$ are the roots of the equation $x^2 = x + 1$. Hence, since $F(n + 2) \approx \phi^2 F(n)$,

$$\sum_{i=1}^{n+1} F'(i) \approx (\phi^2 + 1)F(n) \approx (\phi^2 + 1)\frac{\phi^n}{\sqrt{5}} = \phi^{n+1}.$$

This last approximation illustrates one of the most remarkable things about equations involving ϕ—they can almost always be reduced by use of the fact that $\phi^2 = \phi + 1$ and other equivalent relationships. In this case, $(\phi^2 + 1)/\sqrt{5} = \phi$ is used.

From this final expression—or by simple addition—cumulative sums of the function F' can be calculated. The second column of Table 9.2 shows values of $F'(n)$, and in the third column the corresponding cumulative sum to $F'(n + 1)$ is listed, indicating the minimum number of symbols required to force a codeword of n bits. For example, to force a four-bit codeword, a message of just 10 symbols is sufficient, provided that the message contains 5 distinct symbols and the symbol frequencies are 1, 1, 1, 3, and 4—exactly the arrangement shown in the first part of Table 9.1. The fourth column of Table 9.2 shows the equivalent power of two. As can be seen, as few as 13 million symbols in a message can, in a pathological situation, force the assignment of a codeword 33 bits long, considerably fewer than the limit of 9 billion that was estimated at the commencement of this discussion.

These results do not, however, mean that Huffman coding is feasible only when the total number of symbols is less than a few million. There are several different ways to extend the range. Before describing them, however, it should first be recognized that these are extraordinarily contrived arrangements of symbol frequencies.

In any real application involving 13 million—or even 100 million—symbols, the alphabet will almost certainly include many thousands of symbols with small frequency counts, and the construction required to cause overflow works only if there are just a few such symbols. Rather than abort the code construction if more than 10 million symbols are encountered, it is much more useful to process as far as possible and terminate only if some code has definitely become longer than 32 bits.

We will describe four solutions to the problem—three in this subsection and the fourth, most satisfactory, one in the next. First, an implementation could make use of extended precision arithmetic. It is possible to arrange for pairs of 32-bit integers to be used as 64-bit words, and, in any case, 64-bit architectures are increasingly making their presence felt. This gives a great deal more power—to be precise, 62,113,250,390,417 symbols at least—which at 5 bytes per symbol corresponds to about 300 Tbytes of text. Even in the absence of a full 64-bit architecture, many machines already support extended precision operations. For example, on the Sun architecture used to develop mg, double-precision floating-point numbers have a 53-bit mantissa, so 53-bit integers can be manipulated as "doubles" without fear of rounding error. There are also software implementations of high-precision arithmetic, though they tend to be slow.

A second way to limit the maximum length of any codeword is to scale the frequency counts until they form a safe arrangement. For example, if no codeword is to exceed four bits, the total frequency count must be less than or equal to 16, since a total of 17 admits a five-bit maximum code length. More generally, an appropriate scaling rule is

$$\hat{c}_i = \left\lceil c_i \frac{\sum_{i=1}^{L+1} F'(i) - 1 - r}{(\sum_{i=1}^{r} c_i)/c_{\min}} \right\rceil,$$

where c_i is the actual frequency count for symbol i, $c_{\min}$ is the minimum frequency count, $\hat{c}_i$ is the scaled approximate count for symbol i, r is the number of symbols in the alphabet, and L is the maximum bit length permitted in the final code. Counts must, of course, be rounded up, so that no symbol is assigned a count of zero. To allow for the worst-case amount of rounding up of one per symbol, the target total frequency of $\sum_{i=1}^{L+1} F'(i) - 1$ is adjusted downward by r before the scaling ratio is calculated.

Table 9.3 shows the application of this one-shot scaling rule. The first two columns show the original symbol frequencies c_i for the pathological seven-symbol code and the codewords that result from the calculation of a canonical code. In the absence of scaling, the output for these frequencies is a code of maximum length 6 bits, and the overall cost of using the code to represent any source message that gives rise to this set of symbol frequencies is 66 bits. When scaled with $L = 4$ and the corresponding ratio $9/28 \approx 0.32$, the frequencies of the third column are obtained. These yield the codes of the fourth column: a total frequency of 13; a maximum length, as planned, of 4 bits; and a total output length of 68 bits for the coded data, just 2 bits longer than before. Note that in forming this code, ties have been broken by using the original frequencies c_i as a secondary key. Without this rule, symbol

Table 9.3 Codewords before and after application of one-shot count scaling.

c_i	Code	$\hat{c}_i$	Code
1	000000	1	0000
1	000001	1	0001
1	00001	1	001
3	0001	1	010
4	001	2	011
7	01	3	10
11	1	4	11

4 with $c_i = 3$ and $\hat{c}_i = 1$ might have been assigned a longer code than symbol 1 with $c_i = 1$ and $\hat{c}_i = 1$, and this is clearly undesirable. In the more highly stressed situation with $L = 3$ and $\hat{c}_i = 1$ for all symbols, the final code is still only 73 bits long. It is, of course, impossible to scale a distribution on seven symbols to yield a code of maximum length 2 bits.

Although it is simple to implement and requires just a linear amount of extra time, this one-shot count scaling process is a crude tool and has a number of drawbacks. For example, count scaling guarantees only that the longest codeword of the output code will be no more than L bits long. It might happen that the scaling is unnecessarily savage, and an output code with a maximum length $L - 1$ bits or less is the result. Worse, count scaling might actually fail in some perfectly valid situations. An example of this is when $r = 32$ symbols are to be coded in codewords with no more than $L = 5$ bits; this is clearly possible using a binary code. However, the worst-case assumption of maximum loss through rounding up yields a numerator in the scaling ratio of $28 - 1 - 32 = -5$ and negative frequency counts $\hat{c}_i$, which normally indicates that no code can be constructed.

A third solution, more time-consuming but not subject to these drawbacks, is a process that we call *iterative scaling*. The idea is very simple. First, a Huffman code is constructed using the frequencies as given. If the longest codeword is less than or equal to L bits long, the code is accepted and no more work need be done. If not, all the counts are reduced by some constant ratio (perhaps 2, or the golden ratio 1.618), rounding up to ensure that no counts reach zero, and a new Huffman code is constructed. This process is continued until a code of maximum codeword length L or less is generated. A number of codes might need to be generated before an acceptable one is found, but when the iterative scaling factor is two, each code is typically one bit shorter than the previous one, so the total effort cannot exceed approximately $n \log n + (H - L)n$ steps, where H is the longest codeword in the first unrestricted Huffman code. (If the symbol frequencies are sorted, a Huffman code can be calculated in time proportional to n, the number of symbols, rather than the usual $n \log n$ steps. In the case of iterative scaling, the $n \log n$ cost of sorting is incurred only once as an explicit stage, rather than appearing implicitly as part of the heap manipulations.) By the arguments above, $H \leq \lfloor \log_\phi \sum_{i=1}^{n} c_i \rfloor - 1$. On the distribution of frequencies in the example of Table 9.3, just one halving is necessary—resulting in frequencies $\hat{c}_i = 1, 1, 1, 2, 2, 4, 6$—to arrive at a safe situation that yields the same set of codewords as the cruder one-shot scaling method. In this case, $\sum_{i=1}^{n} \hat{c}_i = 17$. On the more extreme example described above, where $r = 32$, the iterative method will reduce the frequencies until all are sufficiently close to one another that Huffman's algorithm when applied generates a set of 32 codewords each of five bits. The "warm-up" algorithm of Milidiú and Laber (1997) implements a mechanism similar to the iterative scaling process we have described.

Length-limited coding

There is a fourth method for generating an approximate prefix code when codeword overflow would result from a direct application of Huffman's algorithm—*length-limited* coding (Hu and Tan 1972; Garey 1974; Van Voorhis 1974; Larmore and Hirschberg 1990), in which an a priori upper bound L is placed on the maximum length of any codeword and a special-purpose algorithm is used to devise an optimal code subject to this constraint. In effect, length-limited coding is a formal mechanism for achieving a code that is guaranteed to be minimal subject to the length constraint. As with the scaling techniques, the price paid is extra time spent constructing the codes and a certain amount of compression degradation. But the compression loss is usually small since it is the infrequent symbols that have their codewords adjusted, and there is no impact upon encoding and decoding speed since the resultant code is still just a prefix code, and the canonical coding mechanism of Section 2.3 can still be employed.

In order to build a minimum-cost L-limited code, we sort the symbols into increasing frequency order, so that $c_1 \leq c_2 \leq \cdots \leq c_n$. The procedure begins by assigning each of the n symbols a codeword length $l_i = 0$, giving a code that certainly satisfies the length limit but is infeasible since none of the codes have any bits. Then this code is adjusted repeatedly until it meets a feasibility constraint. In general, the feasibility of a prefix code can be determined from the Kraft sum $K = \sum_{i=1}^{n} 2^{-l_i}$; it is well-known that $K \leq 1$ is both necessary and sufficient for a prefix code to be constructed in which each codeword is l_i bits long (Kraft 1949; McMillan 1956; Karp 1961). In the example above, the Kraft sum adds up to n, so the code would only be feasible if $n = 1$. The value of K can only be reduced if one or more of the l_is are increased. We will see how to reduce it step by step in increments of 0.5, until it becomes equal to 1 and the code becomes feasible.

The first step is to increment l_1 to reduce the sum K by 0.5. Over all possible changes, this has the minimum impact upon the number of output bits since c_1 is the smallest frequency count. The second step is to increment l_2 to 1, which is guaranteed to achieve a further 0.5 reduction in K with minimal impact upon the number of output bits. (The alternative, one or more further increments in l_1, would not be sufficient to achieve a reduction of 0.5.) After these two steps, K is reduced to $n - 1$, and—unless $n = 2$—the code is still infeasible. If a message that matched the symbol frequencies were to be coded, it would have a total length of $\sum_{i=1}^{n} c_i l_i$, so the (currently infeasible) code implies a message length of $c_1 + c_2$.

The third step is not so obvious. There is now a choice—either the third least frequent symbol can be assigned $l_3 = 1$, or the same 0.5 reduction in K can be obtained by jointly incrementing the first two symbols, setting $l_1 = l_2 = 2$. In the first case, the increase in the length of the compressed message is by c_3, and in the second, the message grows by $c_1 + c_2$. To follow the path of minimal increase, the smaller of these two is chosen, and the l_is are incremented accordingly.

Continuing in this way for a total of $2n - 2$ "increments," each of which reduces K by 0.5, takes the code to a point at which it becomes prefix-free ($K = 1$). Provided that the set of symbols chosen in each increment generates a minimal increase in output bits and that no increment is allowed to boost any l_i value beyond the limiting value of L, then the final set of l_is describes a minimum-cost L-limited code.

The problem of determining which length to increment at each step becomes more complex after c_3. However, the *package-merge algorithm* of Larmore and Hirschberg (1990) stipulates a mechanism for enumerating packages of symbols that allows easy recognition of which $2n - 2$ increments should be performed to obtain $K = 1$, with minimal increase in message length. It uses a process of pairwise merging of lists, each of which contains packages of source symbols constructed to be of a uniform weight in terms of the quantity K mentioned above.

The full package-merge process is sketched in Figure 9.3. In Figure 9.3, Q is a list of lists, so that $Q[i]$ is the ith list. The algorithm generates, in a bottom-up manner, a list $Q[L]$ of *items*. A total of $L - 1$ other lists are formed on the way, and these are stored as lists $Q[1]$ through $Q[L - 1]$. Each item in list $Q[i]$ is a binary tree whose leaves describe which l_ks to increase to yield a $2^{-(L-i+1)}$ reduction in K. That is, each item describes some of the increments mentioned above and is either a singleton item—a leaf—or a *package* of items from the previous list $Q[i - 1]$. Each list is generated in ascending order of impact upon total compressed message length, and so the first $2n - 2$ items of $Q[L]$, each of which account for a 0.5 reduction in K, describe a minimum-cost L-limited code since they serve to reduce the Kraft sum K by $n - 1$ from its initial value of n down to the target value of 1.

The generation of $Q[L]$ is based upon the original list of probabilities $\langle c_i \rangle$ and the previous list of items $Q[L - 1]$, which represents increments each of which decrease K by 0.25. List $Q[L - 1]$ is, in turn, built out of an earlier list; provided that there are exactly L lists in total, no single l_i value can be incremented more than L times. The items in list $Q[1]$ are leaves with weight equal to their original frequency in $\langle c_i \rangle$; each increment on this list takes one codeword to $l_i = L$ bits long, reduces K by 2^{-L}, and adds c_i to the message cost. Once $Q[L]$ has been generated, it is simply a matter of choosing the first $2n - 2$ of its items and increasing the l_is corresponding to each leaf in the tree rooted at each item.

Table 9.4 shows an example of the package-merge algorithm when applied to the symbol frequencies $\langle 1, 1, 3, 5, 6, 11, 13 \rangle$ with $L = 4$. A minimum-cost code has codeword lengths of $\langle 5, 5, 4, 3, 2, 2, 2 \rangle$ and a message cost of 97 bits. Restricting codeword lengths to 4 bits results in the first two symbols having their codeword

To calculate an optimal L-limited prefix code for a set of n symbol frequencies
$$c_1 \le c_2 \le \cdots c_n,$$

1. If $L < \lceil \log_2 n \rceil$ return with failure, no prefix code is possible.
2. /* First list is a copy of the input frequencies */
   Set $Q[1] \leftarrow \langle c_i \rangle$.
3. /* Calculate $L - 1$ more lists */
   For $i \leftarrow 1$ to $L - 1$ do
   > Set $Q[i + 1] \leftarrow merge(\langle c_i \rangle, package(Q[i]))$.
4. Set $l_i \leftarrow 0$ for $1 \le i \le n$.
5. For $j \leftarrow 1$ to $2n - 2$ do
   - (a) Recursively expand the jth package of the final list $Q[L]$, tracing its composition through the pointers established by function *package*.
   - (b) For each symbol k that appears as a leaf in the tree described by the jth package of list $Q[L]$
     > Set $l_k \leftarrow l_k + 1$.
6. Return $\langle l_i \rangle$ as a set of optimal codeword lengths.

where to *package* a list $\langle q_i \rangle$ of n' elements,

1. Create an empty *output_list*.
2. For $j \leftarrow 1$ to n' div 2 do
   - (a) Make a new node.
   - (b) Link q_{2j-1} and q_{2j} as left and right subtrees, respectively, of the new node.
   - (c) Set the weight of the new node to the sum of the weights of q_{2j-1} and q_{2j}.
   - (d) Append the new node to *output_list*.
3. Return *output_list*.

and where *merge* is a standard list merge based upon item weights.

Figure 9.3 Package-merge algorithm.

Table 9.4 Application of the package-merge algorithm to the frequencies $\langle 1, 1, 3, 5, 6, 11, 13 \rangle$ with a length limit of $L = 4$. Boldface items are packages.

List	Item weights												
Q[1]	1	1	3	5	6	11	13						
Q[2]	1	1	**2**	3	5	6	**8**	11	13	**17**			
Q[3]	1	1	**2**	3	5	5	6	**11**	11	13	19	30	
Q[4]	1	1	**2**	3	5	5	6	**10**	11	13	**17**	24	49

lengths reduced and one or more other symbols having longer codewords to compensate. To calculate the code, the first 12 items from $Q[4]$ must be expanded, where $12 = 2n - 2$ is the number of 0.5 increments necessary to reduce K from 7 to 1. These items are shown to the left of the stepped boundary line, with the packages indicated by the use of a bold font. The set of 12 involves, not surprisingly, all of the seven l_i values, plus the expansion of five packages, which correspond in turn to the first 10 items of $Q[3]$. Inspection of the list $Q[3]$ shows that to obtain these 10 items, seven leaves must be traversed, causing increments so that $l_i = 2$ for all i, and three packages must be expanded. These three packages are drawn from the first six items in $Q[2]$; they in turn cause one packet—two items—to be expanded out of $Q[1]$. Accumulating all of the individual increments on symbols (all of the nonpackage items to the left of the boundary line), the final code is $\langle l_i \rangle = \langle 4, 4, 3, 3, 3, 2, 2 \rangle$ and results in a message cost of 98 bits. By taking the first 12 items from $Q[3]$, the same table can also be used to generate a 3-limited code; in this case the answer is $\langle l_i \rangle = \langle 3, 3, 3, 3, 3, 3, 2 \rangle$ and a message cost of 107 bits.

Let us now examine the resources required by the package-merge process. Implemented as described here, L lists are generated, $Q[1]$ to $Q[L]$, and each contains a mixture of n symbols and at most $n - 1$ packages, $(2n - 1)L$ items in total. Hence both the time and space costs of the method described in Figure 9.3 are proportional to nL. The cost of sorting the initial symbol weights should not be forgotten and adds a further $n \log n$ steps. But since $L \geq \log n$, the sorting cost does not dominate the running time.

The nL running time is quite acceptable. What is problematic is the nL space requirement—to generate a 30-bit limited code for the *TREC* word-based compression model, for example, would require as many as $2 \times 893{,}131 \times 30$ list nodes, each of at least 12 bytes, around 600 Mbytes in total. Fortunately, a number of techniques can be used to reduce the space consumption. For example, in Table 9.4 it was implicitly assumed that the items to the *left* of the boundary line must be calculated; but in fact it is equally valid to subtractively calculate the items to the *right* of the boundary, and there are far fewer of them (Turpin and Moffat 1995). It is also possible to calculate packages in an "on demand" manner and release the space they occupy when the period of need for that package has passed (Katajainen, Moffat, and Turpin 1995). Finally, the same run-length mechanism as was sketched on page 50 of Chapter 2 for the standard Huffman algorithm can also be employed (Moffat and Turpin 1998). In combination, these techniques allow implementation of the package-merge algorithm in surprisingly small amounts of space—even for an alphabet of $n = 1{,}000{,}000$ symbols, as little as a few kilobytes above and beyond the memory required to store the frequencies $\langle c_i \rangle$ is sufficient (Turpin and Moffat 1996; Turpin 1998).

Limiting the length of Huffman codes was not necessary for any of the four large test collections. A straightforward Huffman code can be used even for the 2 Gbyte *TREC* collection without the 32-bit limit being exceeded. In the *TREC* database, there are 354,775,451 word symbols, of which 893,131 are distinct. The longest word code assigned by a conventional Huffman code is 28 bits, and the shortest is 4 bits (for the word *the*). Similarly, there are 39,217 distinct nonwords; the longest

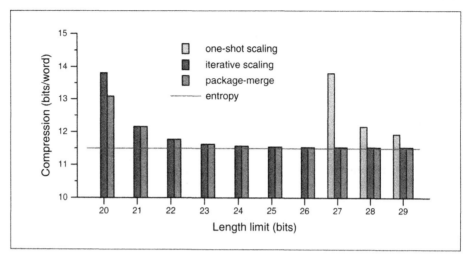

Figure 9.4 Compression loss through length-limited coding.

nonword code is 29 bits, and the shortest nonword code is 1 bit long (for a single blank character). Notice that the maximum code length is slightly greater for the smaller alphabet of the nonwords; that distribution is the more skewed.

Figure 9.4 shows the overall effect of using the three length-limiting techniques discussed here when applied to the *TREC* word distribution. The "one-shot scaling" method is quite inaccurate and predicts that no code is possible for values of L less than or equal to 27. It also results in poor codes when $L = 28$ and $L = 29$, unaware that no compression loss at all need take place for these two limits. As one example of its pessimism, for $L = 27$ the calculation suggests a scaling ratio of 1,382, which results in a 20-bit maximum codeword length. On the other hand, the iterative scaling (with a twofold increase in the scale factor at each iteration) performs extremely well in all but the most severely restricted case (when $L = 20$), giving compression performance indistinguishable from that of the package-merge algorithm. Compared to the package-merge algorithm, iterative scaling has the additional benefit of being somewhat simpler to implement, but the drawback of being more expensive to calculate in terms of memory space and computation time.

Figure 9.4 also shows the slight extent to which a length limit degrades overall compression. Even when $L = 22$ the compression loss is just a few percent compared to the self-entropy of the message stream. Based upon experiments with large document collections:

The practical limit of 32-bit Huffman coding is around 10–20 Gbytes if a word-based compression model and unrestricted-length coding is used, and if a length limit is applied, the upper bound on size is very large indeed.

The mg system currently does not incorporate a length-limiting method.

Table 9.5 Compression performance on sample texts (size of compressed file as a percentage of the uncompressed size).

Method	Compression, percent remaining				
	Bible	GNUbib	Comact	TREC	Average
pack	57.5	64.5	63.2	63.0	62.0
char	57.2	64.2	62.8	62.4	61.6
lzrw1	52.0	44.7	42.1	59.3	49.5
compress	34.2	31.6	32.3	40.4	34.6
gzip-f	35.8	26.6	25.3	39.9	31.9
huffword	27.1	26.6	26.2	29.4	27.3
gzip-b	28.8	22.3	19.2	33.3	25.9
dmc	22.1	17.6	16.6	27.1	20.9
bzip2	20.5	15.9	14.2	24.8	18.8
ppm	19.0	14.0	14.2	23.0	17.6

9.2 Text compression performance

The true measure of any compression scheme is the triple test of how well it compresses typical inputs, how quickly compression and decompression are achieved, and how much memory space is required for the method to operate. This section gives performance results for the scheme we have chosen.

Compression effectiveness

The method that has been suggested for compression in a full-text retrieval environment is the semi-static zero-order word-based compression regime of Section 9.1, referred to in Chapter 2 as the *huffword* method. Here we compare its compression performance with that of general-purpose compression methods. In Section 2.8, representative compression methods were evaluated on the Canterbury corpus. However, the majority of those files are under a megabyte in size, far smaller than the files likely to be used in a full-text retrieval system. Table 9.5 shows the result of using a range of compression methods on the four example document collections that were described in Table 3.1 (page 107). Here we have chosen to use percentage remaining as a measure of compression rather than the bits-per-character yardstick of Chapter 2. We chose percentage remaining because we are now interested in the text as just one component of a compressed retrieval system, which makes it less natural to express the size of the lexicon or index in terms of bits per character of original text.

None of the adaptive methods provide any synchronization, and so the only compression figures that are directly comparable to *huffword* are those listed for *pack*, the bytewise Huffman coder. Nevertheless, the adaptive mechanisms provide useful reference points for assessing compression effectiveness. Some experiments are described below that show how much the *ppm* compression deteriorates if synchronization must be provided to individual documents.

As can be seen from the compression ratios in Table 9.5, the best overall performers for these four texts are the *dmc*, *bzip2*, and *ppm* methods; all benefit from the large (as much as 16 Mbyte) memory that they are configured to use. The *ppm* implementation used for these experiments started each prediction with a fifth-order context.

The *gzip* implementation also gives excellent compression, within much less memory. At the other end of the table, the arithmetically coded *char* method again gives slightly better compression than the model-equivalent *pack*. This difference can be attributed almost entirely to the slight extra efficiency of arithmetic coding when no synchronization is required. However, both are comprehensively outperformed by the other methods. In defense of the *char* implementation (and the *cacm* program that preceded it in 1987), it should be noted that *char* was never intended as anything other than a framework in which different coders could be evaluated, and it was used purely as an adjunct to the discussion of arithmetic coding—a point which is reinforced by the use of arithmetic coding in the high-compression *ppm* and *dmc* methods. The *huffword* program performs reasonably well on these large textual collections—after all, this is exactly the sort of data for which it is intended. For these large files the cost of storing the lexicon is only a small fraction of the total output size. On the *TREC* collection, *huffword* is better than *gzip-b*, so its use in text retrieval systems is supported by its compression performance.

As further justification for the choice of *huffword* as the text compression subsystem in mg, experiments were carried out on *Comact* using an earlier version of the *ppm* method to determine how much compression degradation occurs if synchronization is provided. When a third-order *ppm* method is applied to *Comact* without any synchronization requirement, the compression achieved is 18.5%. If synchronization is added by simply restarting the context model from an empty initial state at the beginning of each document, the compression effectiveness is much worse, at 52.9 percent. That is, if *Comact* is compressed as 261,829 individual documents, they are sufficiently short that within each document there is little scope for the model to learn much more than zero-order statistics.

One simple technique to improve performance is to prime the compression of each document by preprocessing some data that is representative of the text to be compressed. In the *ppm* implementation used, this is easily achieved by compressing the priming text and, at the end of that training run, saving to disk the exact internal state of the model. In subsequent runs this memory image is retrieved and used as the initial state of the data structure during the compression of each document. The model is still allowed to grow and adapt while each document is processed, but it is reset back to the same initial state at the start of the next document.

In the document database application being considered here, the most direct place to obtain priming text is from the text collection itself. To obtain the data in Table 9.6, priming texts of different sizes were created by sampling the original 132 Mbytes of *Comact* at even intervals, taking 1 Kbyte of text at each sam-

Table 9.6 Synchronizing third-order *ppm* on *Comact* (size of compressed file as a percentage of the uncompressed size).

Volume of	Priming context			
priming text	0	1	2	3
10 Kbytes	49.8	40.6	35.0	33.3
100 Kbytes	49.8	39.9	31.3	26.9
1 Mbyte	49.9	41.8	31.3	—
10 Mbytes	50.1	42.0	32.9	—

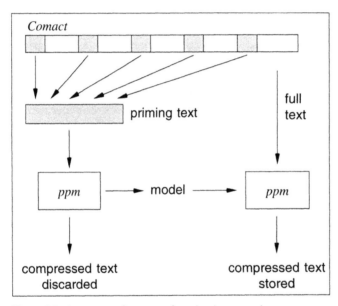

Figure 9.5   Structure of *ppm* synchronization experiments.

ple point, and concatenating the samples. This experimental structure is shown diagrammatically in Figure 9.5.

The amount of improvement in compression depends on two things. First, it is affected by the volume of priming text used. If the entire text is used for priming, the result is nothing more or less than a semi-static compression regime. There is, however, a problem with using all of the source text to establish a model—the amount of storage necessary to hold the memory image. The particular *ppm* implementation used places a limit of 65,536 on the number of nodes in the data structure used to represent the finite-context model, and when this limit is reached, it flushes the data structure and starts again from scratch. For *Comact*, this occurs about every 1 Mbyte of text if a third-order model is being used. Thus, there is no point considering priming texts of more than 1 Mbyte.

There is a way to extend this limit, and that is the second parameter in choosing a priming model. There is no reason why a second- or first-order model cannot be used to bootstrap a third-order model for the actual compression. The advantage of doing this is that more documents can be incorporated into the priming text, and this may outweigh the fact that the initial predictions are likely to be less accurate because fewer characters have been used to produce them.

Table 9.6 explores both of these parameters. It shows the compression that results when a third-order *ppm* is used on the individual documents of *Comact*, with priming texts of 10 Kbytes, 100 Kbytes, 1 Mbyte, and 10 Mbytes, and priming models constructed by passing this text through a *ppm* coder of order 0, 1, 2, and 3. Entries marked "—" represent situations that were infeasible because the priming model already exceeded the 900 Kbyte limit on the finite-context data structure imposed by this particular version of *ppm*.

The best performance is achieved with a third-order model based on 100 Kbytes of priming text. But even so, compression is no better than the semi-static *huffword* method, and it is nowhere near as efficient as the same third-order *ppm* method when applied sequentially to the text as a single stream.

Decompression speed

The speed of the different compression programs has already been presented in Figure 2.44 in Chapter 2 (page 98). The compression rates used to generate that graph were in fact the decoding rates the different methods attained on the *TREC* text. We focused on decoding speed because it is of more concern than encoding speed in a text retrieval environment. For further information on coder performance, Moffat et al. (1994) have measured the speed of a wide variety of coding methods under testbed conditions.

The observed performance justifies the use of the *huffword* scheme in a text database environment. Compression is only a little worse than that obtained by the very best of the adaptive methods, but decoding is very much faster. It is also worth repeating that none of the other "good" methods listed in Figure 2.44 support random document access since their use of adaptive models makes it impossible to insert synchronization points.

To some extent, the importance of decoding speed depends on what is happening to the decoded documents. If they are to be passed to another computer program for postprocessing, no speed is "fast enough." However, if they are to be browsed by a user, the main concern is the time taken to display some set of documents. In the *TREC* database, documents are about 3 Kbytes long on average. The *huffword* program decodes these documents at around 300 Mbytes per minute on the test machine (the 266 MHz Pentium II processor), which means that a document takes roughly half a millisecond to decode on average, an insignificant time to a user browsing documents out of a menu of titles, selecting with a mouse.

Table 9.7 Memory required by *huffword* during decoding, in kilobytes.

	Bible	GNUbib	Comact	TREC
Words	147	764	729	10,371
Nonwords	1	8	89	408
Total	148	772	818	10,779

Thus, *huffword* is eminently suitable for full-text retrieval since its use of canonical coding allows decompression rates that are fast enough for most applications, even on slow machines, while the word-based model achieves excellent compression.

Decompression memory

There is one more resource required by compression programs—memory space. Table 9.7 shows the amount of memory required during decoding using the word-based *huffword* model. This includes the cost of storing the tokens themselves, together with the cost of a four-byte string pointer to each. This latter component corresponds to the *symbol* array of Figure 2.10 on page 40. These sizes do not include any savings that could be made by front coding, the application of which is discussed below, and so correspond most closely to the method of lexicon storage illustrated in Figure 4.2.

Most of the adaptive methods listed in Table 9.5 are designed to work for arbitrary texts and so incorporate some a priori bound on the amount of decoding memory that may be used. For example, the *ppm* implementation used for the priming experiments (Table 9.6) uses at most 896 Kbytes of memory for data structures, and the *ppm*, *bzip2*, and *dmc* implementations used to derive the results in Table 9.5 use as much as 16 Mbytes. When this is exhausted, they discard their data structures and start afresh. The other adaptive methods operate within tighter limits, typically just a few hundred kilobytes. Less abrupt strategies for dealing with excessive model growth are to stop adapting and use the current model for the remainder of the text or to attempt to selectively reuse parts of the model by reclaiming nodes that have not been used recently.

By these standards, the decoding memory requirements shown in Table 9.7 for the *huffword* method on *Bible*, *GNUbib*, and *Comact* are not excessive. *TREC*, however, is another story: in raw form the decoding model takes over 10 Mbytes. Moreover, front compression and 1-in-4 indexing on the text model is not as effective as was described in Section 4.1 on page 159 because the use of a canonical code means that front coding can be applied only within the sorted list of tokens for each particular Huffman codeword length.

There is another method by which the model space for the word-based decompressor can be reduced, based upon the observation that if an *escape* mechanism is provided that allows words not in the lexicon to be "spelled out," then not every word need be included (Moffat, Zobel, and Sharman 1997). For example, a word that appears only once in the text of *TREC* has a 28-bit Huffman code and occupies perhaps 10–12 bytes of memory in the model. However, if an escape to a character-level coder is available, that memory can be reclaimed with only a slight compression loss. A 6-byte word coded according to a subsidiary character model would be represented in about 30 bits, plus perhaps 5–7 bits for an escape code to say "next word is not in the lexicon." On *TREC*, more than half the words appear only once, and even at a cost of 10 extra bits for each, the total compressed text size grows by just 0.5 Mbyte, less than 0.1 percent. This is a very small price to pay to save more than half of the required decode-time memory. Furthermore, eliminating low-frequency symbols from the lexicon is another effective way to reduce the maximum code length and avoid codeword overflow.

More generally, a target size for decoding memory can be decided in advance and then words selected for the lexicon to utilize that memory. Once this is done, the frequency of the characters in the remaining words, in conjunction with the word frequencies themselves, are used to compute a character-level model for the escaped words. Escape codes must also be inserted into the word and nonword distributions.

We outline three strategies for choosing words to fit some given amount of lexicon memory. The first and simplest is to take words in order of first appearance and to stop accepting them when the lexicon has reached the desired bound. This has the advantage of also bounding the memory required by the encoder. However, if the encoder is allowed to accumulate statistics about all possible tokens, there are obviously better strategies. The second, and most complex, is to actually calculate the cost of representing each word either as a word code or a sequence of character codes and weigh this against the cost of storing the word code in the lexicon. The intention is to arrive at an optimal lexicon—to be able to state categorically that no other selection of words generates a compressed output of fewer total bits. Such an optimal solution, while desirable, is difficult to compute for lexicons of practical size. The third approach, which is easily implemented, is to select words based on decreasing frequency of appearance, as was suggested earlier for *TREC*. This strategy gives good results in practice.

Figure 9.6 shows the effect of lexicon size on compression rate for *Comact*. Two techniques are shown: selection of tokens based on order of first appearance and selection based on frequency. The latter technique is clearly superior, and a lexicon of about 50 Kbytes is sufficient to allow a compression rate for *Comact* of better than 30 percent. Using the same technique on *TREC* is even more productive. Reducing the lexicon size by a factor of 10, from 10 Mbytes to 1 Mbyte, degrades the compression rate from 29.4 percent to just 30.0 percent. Table 9.8 shows the result of applying similar memory restrictions to the decode-time lexicon of the other test collections.

If memory space during text retrieval and decoding proves to be a problem in some application, the most effective way to economize is to make use of a selective compression model; 100–500 Kbytes are ample decoding memory space for the four test collections used here. Moreover, compared with the savings achieved by

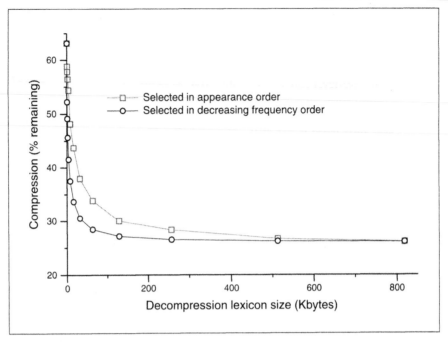

Figure 9.6   Effect on compression for *Comact* of reduced model size.

Table 9.8   Compression effectiveness based upon restricted lexicons (size of compressed file as a percentage of the uncompressed size).

Lexicon size	Bible	GNUbib	Comact	TREC
All	26.4	27.0	26.1	29.4
1 Mbyte	26.4	27.0	26.1	30.0
100 Kbytes	26.7	30.1	27.6	34.5
10 Kbytes	31.9	38.6	36.3	45.5

selective inclusion of tokens into the model, there seems little need to employ front coding. Front coding requires additional processing per token decoded, and speed of decoding is likely to be more important than the small amount of memory that is saved.

Dynamic collections

The discussion of the mg text compression subsystem has assumed that the collection is static and that it is feasible to make two passes over the input text. In practice, this is not necessarily the case, and we would like to be able to handle dynamic col-

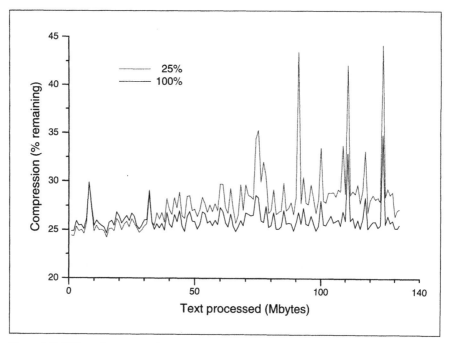

Figure 9.7 Effect of text growth on compression for *Comact*.

lections. This was discussed briefly in Section 5.7 on page 256, where it was claimed that periodic rebuilding was sufficient to maintain acceptable compression rates. Results presented by Moffat, Zobel, and Sharman (1997) to support this claim are reviewed here.

The previous subsection discussed the use of an escape code to indicate a non-lexicon symbol and the use of two subsidiary zero-order character models to code unknown symbols, one for words and the other for nonwords. These facilities are the key to handling dynamic collections. Provided that every possible character is allocated a code in the two zero-order character distributions, every text can be encoded. There is, however, one crucial difference when the text is dynamic. In the static case, probabilities for the character model and the escape code itself can be determined accurately because the entire text has been scanned. But in the dynamic case, both of these must be estimates since it cannot be known how many novel words will appear in the text yet to be inserted, nor can it be known what characters will be used to compose those tokens. Thus, in the dynamic situation, the compression model must estimate both of these. One solution is for the character distribution to be approximated by the characters of the words that have been seen and for the novel-word symbol to be given a probability based upon an understanding of the zero-frequency problem (Section 2.2).

Figure 9.7 shows the instantaneous compression rates obtained during the processing of *Comact* using two different models. To obtain the graph, the number of

Table 9.9 Compression effectiveness based upon partial models (size of compressed file as a percentage of the uncompressed size).

Expansion factor	Fraction processed	Bible	GNUbib	Comact	TREC
1	100.0%	26.5	27.1	26.1	29.5
2	50.0%	28.8	29.7	27.1	31.5
4	25.0%	31.2	32.4	27.9	34.1
8	12.5%	33.0	34.0	29.2	35.6

output bytes produced for each 1 Mbyte section of text was plotted, meaning that the overall compression efficiency is the integral of the curve. Two compression runs are shown. The first, with a dark line, is *Comact* processed assuming a lexicon based upon a complete first pass over the entire collection. This is the static mode of compression described in the previous sections. Notice the spikes—even with a complete statistics-gathering scan of the text, there is still enough local variability that some of the 1 Mbyte chunks are much less compressible than others.

The gray line shows the instantaneous compression rate obtained when a model based solely upon the first quarter of the text is used to compress the whole text. The "quarter model" gives slightly better compression throughout the first 25 percent of the text, which is to be expected, since in this region it is a more accurate model than the larger global model. But it also continues to give good compression through the remaining 75 percent of the text, and it gives an overall compression rate only slightly less than that achieved by a complete preprocessing. The reason is that any word that appears for the first time in the latter three-quarters of the text is almost certainly rare, and the inefficiency in coding that results from the use of an imprecise character model has almost no effect—exactly the same observation as was exploited in the previous section.

Table 9.9 shows the overall compression rates obtained for the four test collections based upon models created after various fractions of the collections have been processed. The "100 percent" compression is in some cases slightly different than those reported in Tables 9.5 and 9.8 because of the inclusion of the escape code, which forces some of the other codewords to be slightly longer, and the use of slightly different versions of the programs and data. These experiments were designed to mimic the situation where an initial database is created using a relatively small amount of the collection and then more and more documents are inserted into the retrieval system and compressed using the same set of model parameters.

The message of Table 9.9 is clear: dynamic databases can be handled quite successfully by providing an escape code and a subsidiary character-based model and simply allowing the collection to grow. There is some small degradation— "leakage"—in compression, but it is hardly significant even when the collection has more than doubled in size.

Moreover, this is the simplest of possible methods. Two more elegant techniques are possible that result in even less compression leakage. First, words that appear for the first time in inserted documents might be added to a "stop-press" section of the lexicon and allocated codes. The word-level escape code then indicates to the decoder that it should refer to the stop-press lexicon and decode, say, a flat binary code to indicate the word. To be decodable, each compressed document must be prefixed with an integer code to note the size of the stop-press at the time this document was compressed, but the code is a small overhead. The second technique is to make the stop-press lexicon self-adjusting, so that after a word has appeared once in an inserted document, it is allocated a shorter code. This results in even greater savings. Experiments with a 500 Mbyte database comprising two of the *TREC* sub-collections have shown that, in combination, these techniques allow expansion by factors in excess of 10 with negligible compression loss (Moffat, Zobel, and Sharman 1997).

9.3 Images and textual images

Mg contains some simple facilities for incorporating images and textual images into a full-text database. These are intended to demonstrate how such information can be included and to exemplify some of the state-of-the-art lossless compression methods described in Chapters 6 and 7. They are not intended to represent anything like a full-fledged document image management system. Considerable attention has been paid to honing the time and space efficiency for indexing and decompressing text, but our implementations of image compression methods remain relatively straightforward. They are slow—perhaps not fast enough for many practical applications—and much more could be done to speed them up, probably by substantial factors. We merely wanted to demonstrate how this kind of information can be incorporated and to show the power and flexibility of the idea of compressed full-text indexing in realms that are not entirely textual.

The three schemes that mg incorporates are the two-level context modeling technique of Section 6.3, the FELICS method for lossless compression of grayscale images described in Section 6.5, and an implementation of the lossy/lossless textual image compression developed in Chapter 7. These provide the capability of dealing with bilevel images, grayscale images, and textual images, respectively. It would certainly be useful to include implementations of the JPEG and JBIG methods, partly to allow lossy compression and color images and partly to accommodate international standards for image compression, and we encourage others to incorporate these into mg and make them available for general use (though there are patent issues that need to be considered). It would also be useful to include a scheme to incorporate compressed voice documents and multimedia documents—the MPEG (Moving Picture Experts Group) standard would be suitable for the latter (LeGall 1991). However, we have not done this. Rather than striving, inevitably in vain, to be comprehensive, we put forward the image compression methods that are incorporated as a kind of "proof of concept" of how nontextual information can be included in a document database. The problems presented by other image compression methods and by other media will not be radically different.

We have not included any facility for dealing efficiently with scanned documents that contain a mixture of text and images, as described in Chapter 8, because the methods of that chapter rely on heuristics that are sensitive to the exact details of the document image—not just its resolution but various aspects of the layout, too. Rather than include a scheme that deals satisfactorily with only certain styles of image, we prefer to omit this capability altogether until more robust methods become available. This is clearly an important area for future research.

One of the problems that plagues image compression is the large number of de facto standards that are used for representing images. Mg accommodates just two types of image format the PBM (portable bitmap) format, and the PGM (portable graymap) format. These are widely used on Unix computer systems as lowest-common-denominator graphics formats, and there are utilities for converting between them and most other image formats. Both kinds of files begin with a "magic number" that identifies the file type, then give the width and height of the image and, in the case of the PGM format, the maximum grayscale value, and finally the content of the bitmap or graymap. With PBM, the contents are expressed as a string of the appropriate number of pixel values, 1 being interpreted as black and 0 as white. There are two variants: one where pixel values are stored one per byte as the ASCII characters 0 and 1, and the other where they are packed eight per byte. With PGM, the gray values are expressed as a list of numbers between 0, which is interpreted as black, and the specified maximum value, which is interpreted as white. Again, there are two variants—one where the values are expressed as decimal numbers separated by spaces and the other where they are stored one per byte. In the latter case, the maximum grayscale value obviously must not exceed 256.

Compression of bilevel images

The method implemented for compressing bilevel images is the two-level context modeling technique of Section 6.3. To facilitate experimentation, and to allow compression to be optimized for different kinds of images, the particular size and shape of the two-level template can be specified at compression time. So that compressed images can be decoded without any additional information, the template is recorded at the beginning of the compressed image and picked up by the decoder whenever the file is decompressed.

Dealing with images on a pixel-by-pixel basis tends to be very slow because of the large number of pixels that most images contain. The basic operation of two-level modeling is to place the template over a particular pixel of the image and to massage the pattern of pixels under the template into a number that is used to index an array of counts. In order to expedite this operation, the mg implementation stores each line of the template separately and shifts a new bit into each line as the template is moved horizontally. In case there is insufficient main memory to hold the entire table of counts for each possible context value, a hashing scheme is implemented so that all contexts are hashed into a table of predeclared size. No account is taken of collisions; they will just cause the frequency values for the colliding contexts to be amalgamated, with some loss of compression but no impact on decodability.

There are three parameters upon which any implementation of two-level modeling must decide (Moffat 1991). The first parameter is the number of times a pixel has to be seen in the full context before that context is used in preference to the smaller one. Experiments have shown that it is worth going to the full context as soon as it has been observed at least twice, so this is the value that is used. The second parameter is the number to which the counts are initialized. Of course, they cannot be initialized to zero because that would introduce a zero coding frequency the first time they occurred, and arithmetic coding cannot accommodate zero frequencies. Best results are usually obtained when all counts are initialized to 0.5. To avoid having to deal with noninteger counts, the same effect is achieved by initializing counts to 1 and increasing them by 2 (instead of 1) whenever they are to be incremented. The third parameter is the maximum size that counts are allowed to reach before they are halved—this is necessary to prevent them from growing indefinitely. As noted in Section 6.3, eight bits may be insufficient for the counts because if much of the image is white, performance can be degraded quite noticeably by limiting probabilities to 255/256. Thus, 16-bit counts are used. However, it turns out that on typical image collections, it is better to impose a smaller maximum value than $2^{16} - 1$ on the count size because there are local adaptation effects that can improve the amount of compression achieved. The mg implementation uses a maximum value of 8,192. When, for a particular context, the black pixel count plus the white pixel count exceed this value, both are incremented by one and then halved—the increment being simply to avoid a result of zero.

Compression of grayscale images

Recall that the method implemented for compressing grayscale images is called FELICS (fast, efficient, lossless image coding system). It is implemented as described in Section 6.5. Once a pixel's two neighbors are determined, the pixel's value lies either between the two neighboring pixels' values or outside this range. In the former case, it is coded using an adjusted binary code. In the latter, a Golomb code is used with parameter b restricted to a power of two, that is, $b = 2^m$. The value of m is optimized by keeping a record of the compression that would have been achieved so far with each different possible value. For images with at most 256 gray levels, totals are kept for the eight different values $m = 0, 1, \ldots, 7$; if the image has more than this number of levels, totals are kept for $m = 0, 1, \ldots, 31$. Some speed can be gained—often at negligible expense in compression—by reducing the range of m, and, if desired, a smaller maximum value can be specified when compression is invoked.

Compression of textual images

The textual image component of mg is a straightforward implementation of textual image compression as described in Chapter 7. Compression can be either lossy or combined lossy/lossless. In the former case, much greater compression is normally achieved but at the expense of the final image being only an approximation to the original, with very small marks omitted and the outlines of marks reproduced inexactly. In the latter case, the final image is an exact replica of the original. Moreover, the compressed information is stored in such a way as to allow the lossy image to be reconstructed first and then to be elaborated into the final version as a separate, much more time-consuming step.

The normal mode of operation is to work on a collection of images and produce a common library for them. In some cases, particularly if the images are from different sources, it is more economical to compress them individually, and an option is provided for this. This facilitates experimentation on precisely when it is worthwhile to group images together so that they share a library.

Textual image compression works best if it is tailored to suit the actual resolution at which the images are digitized. Since this is not recorded in the PBM file format, it must be specified when compressing. This information is used for two purposes: to determine the size threshold that is applied to prevent very small specks from being processed as marks and to select a suitable size and shape for the clairvoyant and nonclairvoyant templates that are used to encode the original image with respect to the reconstructed one. Higher-resolution images benefit from somewhat larger templates. A table of default templates for several different resolutions is included in the implementation; these have been calculated by testing different templates on a sample set of images. The procedure finds the resolution that most closely matches the image's and selects the templates accordingly. However, it is possible to override this and specify the templates directly in just the same way as for two-level context modeling. The templates are recorded in the compressed file as before, along with the resolution, so that the decoder can reconstruct the original image without any additional information.

There are a number of internal switches that are designed mainly for testing purposes but that could prove useful for experimentation. When template-matching, registration can be switched between different methods: centroid alignment and upper- and lower-left corner alignment. Normally, once the library has been accumulated, symbols are refined by averaging the bitmaps of all the marks that match a particular symbol; this averaging can be turned off so that the first-encountered variant is used as the library template instead. Finally, pruning can be enabled so that the library is reduced by discarding "singletons," that is, symbols that have occurred just once. This may slightly improve compression but risks losing entire marks from the text reconstructed in lossy mode.

Although the experiments reported in Section 7.7 used the combined size-independent pattern-matching strategy developed in the "Local template matching" subsection on page 329, the mg implementation uses the compression-based template-matching method described on page 330. The two principal problems with template matching are fragmentation (a symbol is broken into two or more pieces on the printed page, and each piece is identified as a separate mark) and segmentation (two or more symbols on the printed page bleed together into one and must be separated). Some attempts are being made to ameliorate both of these problems, but they are likely to be resource-intensive, and it is not clear whether the improved compression will be worth the cost in processing time.

A solution to the fragmentation problem is to leave the mark being matched on the page, instead of extracting it. When a library template is matched against an unknown mark, the entire area of the page covered by the template participates in the match. This means that nearby fragments on the page will be taken into account in the match if they are close enough. Furthermore, when the unknown mark is registered with the library template, it is registered provisionally, and then any fragments that come within the ambit of the library template are taken into account to improve the registration further. If the match is successful and that library symbol is used to represent the mark, those fragments must be removed from the mark list. If the fragments have already been processed and identified as symbols, care must be taken to erase them from the symbol list.

Segmentation is a more difficult problem but must be tackled if excessive library growth such as that shown by Figure 7.17 is to be avoided. One solution is to take a great deal of care when scanning documents to optimize the contrast settings; however, this is probably unrealistic in practice. One way of separating false ligatures is to make it possible to identify symbols and peel them off from the end of the unknown mark. This can be accomplished when matching a mark with a library template by provisionally registering their left-hand boundaries. Registration can then be adjusted by excising that part of the mark that falls under the template and registering its centroid with that of the template. Compression-based matching is then used to determine the quality of the match; if it is sufficiently good, the part of the mark that falls under the template is peeled off, and the process is repeated with the truncated mark.

9.4 Index construction

Once the text and images of a retrieval system have been compressed, the next step is to index them. Ten algorithms for doing this were presented in Chapter 5 (they are summarized in Table 5.5 on page 227). Of these, only two are viable for large collections when memory and disk are limited, and operation in the face of such resource limitations has been one of the driving themes of our development. For this reason, the mg system makes use of the inversion method described in the "Text-based partitioning" subsection on page 251. There is no real reason to prefer this algorithm to the multiway in-place merge technique described on page 239; text-based partitioning is used only because it was developed earlier. Prior to its development the large memory inversion method was used (page 245). It proved perfectly adequate for the three smaller test collections, but about 200 Mbytes of memory was needed to invert *TREC*, and the biggest machine available at the time had just 48 Mbytes. Some initial experiments were carried out on a borrowed machine, but it is always difficult to avoid making an impact when fine-tuning a program that uses so much memory and time, and the improved algorithms described in Sections 5.3 and 5.4 were developed in response to a tangible need. Some of the problems associated with

Table 9.10 Inversion performance for *TREC* using Pentium II hardware.

Stage	Memory (Mbytes)	CPU time (hh:mm)
First pass	39.1	0:24
Calculate hash function	10.4	0:01
Second pass	39.2	0:36
Total	39.2	1:01

the sheer size of the *TREC* collection, and performance figures for the first round of experiments, are described by Moffat and Zobel (1994). In fact, we now have at our disposal relatively cheap hardware that could support in-memory inversion for current collection sizes.

Table 9.10 shows the cost of inverting the *TREC* collection using the text-partitioning method of Section 5.4. The results are for the Pentium II hardware. The second-pass memory limit was set so that the two passes would require the same memory. Use of minimal perfect hashing during the second pass meant that 32 Mbyte chunks could be processed, and five chunks were required. The program to construct the minimal perfect hash function required much less memory, and so in total, 40 Mbytes of main memory were sufficient to invert the 2 Gbyte *TREC* collection.

The text was indexed at an overall rate of about 30 Mbytes per minute, and similar rates were observed on the other three collections. The computational model used in Chapter 5 to estimate the relative cost of the various inversion methods suggested a *TREC* inversion time of 5.5 hours, rather more than the observed time of 1 hour. The discrepancy is partly the result of the hardware improvements that were mentioned at the commencement of this chapter and partly because the model also includes the time taken by input and ouput operations, which are not included in Table 9.10 but cost about 30 minutes. With the older SPARC hardware a *TREC* inversion required about 4.5 hours of CPU time.

The two passes of the text compression process are additional to this requirement, and so, in total, a retrieval system can be built on 1998 hardware at a combined rate of about 15 Mbytes per minute, or a little under 1 Gbyte per hour. Starting from scratch, it takes the Pentium a little over 2 CPU hours to build the *TREC* retrieval system and less than 30 seconds to compress and index *Bible*.

In some situations, there is a fixed cost of making each pass over the source text. For example, the raw data itself may be compressed, or it might be stored on several different disk drives on a network, in which case network latency can be expected. If main memory is plentiful, the first pass of the mg inversion process can be piggy-backed with the first pass of the text compression, and the two second passes similarly combined, with each joint pass requiring approximately 80 Mbytes. This

Table 9.11   Index compression on sample texts.

Method	Bible	GNUbib	Comact	TREC
Index size (Mbytes)	0.62	1.97	11.36	128.62
Percentage of input text	14.4%	14.0%	8.6%	6.3%
Auxiliary files (Mbytes)	0.47	1.62	3.15	19.80
Percentage of input text	10.9%	11.5%	2.4%	1.0%
Total retrieval system (Mbytes)	2.25	7.40	48.98	753.51
Percentage of input text	51.7%	52.6%	37.1%	36.7%

reduces overall building time by twice the cost of each preprocessing stage. Moreover, if a multiprocessor computer is available, the two first passes can be organized to run in parallel, piping the input text from one to the other. Similarly, the two second passes can be implemented to run in parallel, further saving on construction time. In this case, a retrieval system for *TREC* might be built in as little as an hour, a quite remarkable feat compared to the manual mechanisms that were described in Chapter 1. All of the times listed in this section are independent of any preprocessing to format or otherwise prepare the source text and assume only the use of a single processor. The mg system supports piggybacking but not parallel execution. The latter can easily be achieved at the operating system level.

9.5   Index compression

Chapter 3 describes several methods for compressing inverted files. Given that the compressed text occupies about 25 percent of the space of the original source data, and the index about 10 percent, there is little incentive to invest great energy into complex index compression techniques. The mg system uses a local Bernoulli model and the Golomb (or infinite Huffman) code to represent the document d-gaps. This provides fast decoding with quite acceptable compression (see Table 3.8 on page 129). The within-document frequencies $f_{d,t}$ are stored using the γ code, which again was chosen in preference to more complex methods that achieve better compression. Compression results for the within-document frequencies of the four test collections are shown in Table 4.10 on page 200. Each inverted list is prefixed by a γ-coded integer f_t to indicate the number of $\langle d, f_{d,t} \rangle$ pairs in that inverted list and to allow the calculation of the Golomb parameter b; this adds very slightly to the final size of the inverted file. Inverted lists are stored byte-aligned.

Table 9.11 shows the total index size for the four test collections, both as a raw amount in megabytes and as a percentage of the original text. For the small files, the augmented inverted file consumes less than 15 percent of the original text; for the two larger files, the augmented inverted file requires less than 10 percent.

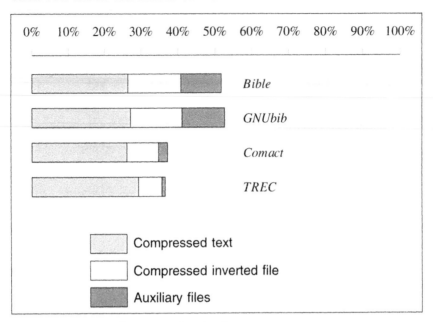

Figure 9.8 Total cost of compressed retrieval systems.

The second section of the table shows the total size of all auxiliary files required by the final retrieval system, again as a percentage of the initial uncompressed and unindexed text. Included in this are the files required by a disk-based lexicon for the index vocabulary, the file storing the compression model, files storing record addresses in both the compressed text and the compressed inverted file, and a file storing document weights used by the ranking process. The third section of the table includes the cost of the compressed text of each system and gives the overall amount of disk space required to effect Boolean and ranked queries using the methods described here. For the two small collections, the complete retrieval system occupies a little more than 50 percent of the space of the initial text. For the two large collections, less than 40 percent of the space needed by the unindexed text is used. Figure 9.8 shows the same percentage sizes graphically.

These results suggest that a CD-ROM—storing, in raw form, about 660 Mbytes—should comfortably hold a retrieval system for about 1.5 Gbytes of text. It is also interesting to consider the same retrieval systems but without the use of any compression. Clearly, the text itself will take 100 percent of its original size. Suppose that a four-byte integer is used for each document number in each inverted file posting, a two-byte integer for each within-document frequency $f_{d,t}$, and a four-byte integer for each f_t value stored in the inverted file. Based on the values listed in Table 3.1 on page 107, the inverted files for the four test collections occupy 93 percent, 92 percent, 57 percent, and 38 percent, respectively. The use of compression has effectively multiplied the amount of data that may be stored and indexed on a device such as

```
expanded, memory, equipment, suppose, computer, 640k, ram, runs,
finish, building, worksheet, solve, problem, install, board, lets,
work, data, fit, dos, limit, ideal, solution, boards, expensive,
intel, corp, 800, 538, 3373, oreg, 503, 629, 7369, 2, megabytes,
costs, 1, 445, configured, software, buy, 3, releases, 01, growing,
number, programs, release, os
```

Figure 9.9 Terms used for sample Boolean queries.

a CD-ROM by a factor of between three and four, a very satisfactory state of affairs. Let us now turn to the question of how the use of compression affects the speed of query processing.

9.6 Query processing

The usual cost when compression techniques are applied is increased access time. However, this need not always be the case. In this section, we discuss the cost of performing queries on the compressed retrieval system. Results are given that show compression of the inverted file to be a "win-win" situation: both storage space and retrieval time can be reduced, under quite a general set of computational assumptions. We first consider Boolean queries and then examine the cost of evaluating ranked queries using the cosine method. Details of the experiments carried out to measure the effectiveness of skipping on Boolean and ranked queries are given by Moffat and Zobel (1996), and the experimental work described in this section was originally undertaken for that paper.

Boolean queries

To measure the response time for Boolean queries, 25 pseudoqueries were generated by taking documents from *TREC* and extracting from each a collection of 50 terms, discarding stop words and words with identical stemmed forms. Although all of the stop words are indexed in mg, it was felt that to use them in queries would be atypical and might distort the results of the experiments because of their different frequency characteristics. Figure 9.9 shows one of the lists of words that was generated.

Then, to make a query of r terms, the first r words were taken from each of the lists. For example, the five-term query produced from the list shown in Figure 9.9 is

> *expanded* AND *memory* AND *equipment* AND *suppose* AND *computer*

This construction method guarantees that each query always has at least one answer, and it results in reasonably sensible-looking queries. Queries were run on a "paged" form of *TREC* in which the indexing granularity was taken to be 1,000 bytes—about one screenful of text. In effect, the location of words was recorded to within 1,000 bytes rather than to the nearest document, allowing more precise query formulation but with a larger index. This pagination resulted in a collection of 1,743,848 "documents," and an inverted file storing $F = 195,935,531$ pointers. On average,

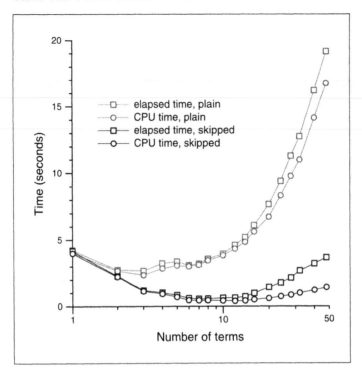

Figure 9.10 Time required by mg for Boolean queries.

each query term corresponded to an inverted list containing about 60,000 document numbers.

Figure 9.10 shows the time taken by mg to resolve a query as a function of the number of terms in it. Two sets of times are shown: for a "plain" compressed inverted file, without the inclusion of skipping information, and for a skipped inverted file (see the subsection "Random access and fast lookup" on page 176), built assuming that each inverted list must be resolved against $k = 100$ candidates. These experiments were run on a SPARC 10 Model 512, with all files on local disks and no other active user processes.[2] The difference between elapsed and CPU times shown in Figure 9.10 is a reasonably accurate reflection of the cost of any input and output operations. The times were measured from the moment that the query was issued until the moment that a final list of answer documents was ready but did not include any costs associated with retrieving and decoding any of those documents.

With the plain inverted file, typical queries of 5–10 terms are resolved in 3–4 seconds of CPU time, and in slightly more elapsed time. In the mg system, resolving a conjunctive query of r terms involves r seeks into the lexicon file (but the operating

2 Comparable query times for the 266 MHz Pentium II hardware are three to five times faster.

system has probably buffered most of this into memory by the end of the first query of the run), r seeks into the inverted file (which probably are not buffered because of its size), and decoding of approximately $60,000r$ compressed pointers, each occupying on average one byte in the inverted file. On the SPARC the speed of this latter operation was measured to be about 250,000 pointers per second, so a query with $r = 10$ can be expected to spend about 2.5 seconds decoding pointers and, with a seek time of 10 milliseconds and a transfer rate of 2 Mbytes per second (as assumed in Table 5.4), about 1 second actually fetching the data. This model accounts for the bulk of the measured times. There is a small amount of additional processing that is performed on a "per answer" basis, which is why the curves initially decrease from $r = 1$. On average, the single-term queries had 60,000 answers; after four terms each query had 60 answers; and by $r = 10$, there was on average only fractionally more than one answer per query.

When the index incorporates skipping, queries with $r = 10$ were processed by decoding about 13,000 pointers, together with about 9,000 skips. Thus, the total decoding effort was reduced to about 31,000 values (counting two values for each skip), or 5 percent of the previous cost. That is, the CPU cost of resolving the query decreases to about 0.1 second, plus about 0.5 second of fixed overhead. Added to this are the same disk transfer costs, which now constitute a sizable fraction of the retrieval time. Nevertheless, total query processing time is substantially decreased. The use of skipping allows queries of 5–10 terms to be answered between four and six times faster.

Furthermore, the overhead cost of inserting the skips is very small. The plain inverted file for this paged *TREC* occupied 184.36 Mbytes, and when skipped assuming $k = 100$, the size increased by less than 6 percent, to 194.74 Mbytes. For the time savings achieved, this small increase in disk space seems well worthwhile.

It was claimed above that the use of skipped compressed inverted files is a win-win situation. To justify this, consider the situation where no compression is employed. The CPU cost of resolving a query is negligible since a binary-searching process can be employed. However, at six bytes per pointer, each of the inverted lists is about six times larger. Because of this, the transfer time alone for a query of $r = 10$ terms involving 600,000 pointers and 3.6 Mbytes of data is about 2 seconds. This is the final proof of the technique: the use of a compressed inverted file not only saves space compared with an uncompressed inverted file, but also, if skipping is used, it provides faster query processing as well. It is, just occasionally, possible to have your cake and eat it too.

Ranked queries

Section 4.4 described a mechanism for ranking the document collection with respect to an informal query. The mg system includes support for ranked queries, where similarity is evaluated using the cosine measure. In the quest to make retrieval and decoding accessible to users of limited-power hardware, several of the memory reduction strategies described in Section 4.6 have been implemented. The first is the use of approximate document weights to guide the retrieval process (page 203).

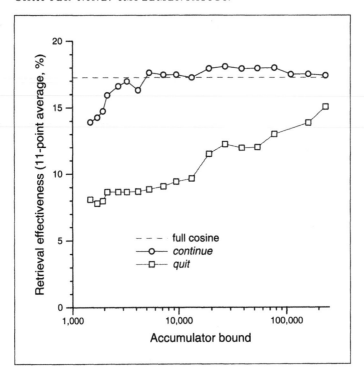

Figure 9.11 Ranking effectiveness: *quit* and *continue*.

Experiments on the *TREC* collection show that the use of approximate ranking using as few as six bits per document weight gives only slight degradation in retrieval effectiveness. Approximate weights can also be used as an aid to the calculation of exact cosine values. Again, experiments on *TREC* have shown that eight-bit approximate weights are sufficient to reduce the number of full document weights to only slightly greater than the number of retrieved answers. Both of these forms of ranking are supported in the mg system.

Also implemented is the facility to use a hash table as a set structure for maintaining accumulators, thereby saving space if the number of accumulators is kept small (page 206). Both the *quit* and *continue* strategies are available. They differ markedly in their computational requirements and also, unfortunately, in their retrieval performance. Figure 9.11 shows the 11-point retrieval effectiveness achieved by the two strategies on stopped and stemmed versions of 50 of the *TREC* queries, plotted as a function of the number of accumulators actually used by the query, with terms processed in increasing f_t order until the predetermined bound on the number of accumulators is reached. The database used was the paged variant of *TREC* described in the previous section. The dotted line shows retrieval effectiveness if every document is permitted an accumulator. Surprisingly, the *continue* strategy can achieve better retrieval performance than the full cosine method. It is clearly

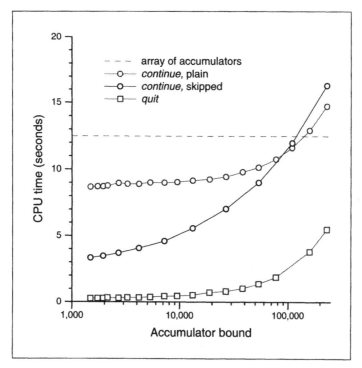

Figure 9.12 Time required by ranked queries.

advantageous to prohibit from consideration documents that contain only frequent terms. On the other hand, the poor performance of the *quit* strategy shows that all terms contribute to the ordering of the selected candidates and that discarding the cosine contributions of frequent terms greatly reduces retrieval effectiveness.

The results shown in Figure 9.11 support the claim that ranking can be carried out with a bounded number of accumulators and within a restricted amount of memory. For example, a bound of 10,000 accumulators easily gives retrieval performance as good as the full cosine method and requires only 140 Kbytes of storage. On average, 1,304,115 of the pages contained at least one of the query terms, and so, in the absence of any accumulator bound, an array would be the most economical data structure, requiring 7 Mbytes of memory.

Figure 9.12 shows the time taken to process these queries, again on the paged *TREC* collection and using the 1993-era SPARC 10 hardware. After stemming and stopping, the queries averaged 42.4 terms, involving an average of 3,131,050 inverted file pointers per query, or 74,000 per term. The dotted horizontal line shows the time taken by an array-based implementation of the cosine measure. These experiments again include all computation from the time of issue of the query until a ranked list of documents is produced, but exclude the cost of retrieving and decoding the answers. In all cases, the top $r = 200$ documents were identified.

The two gray lines show the time taken by the *continue* and *quit* strategies using a nonskipped inverted file. For small numbers of accumulators, the *quit* strategy is—not surprisingly—very fast. The *continue* strategy is also faster than the full array-based implementation when the number of accumulators is small because it both avoids the cost of initializing the large array and eliminates a large fraction of the floating-point calculations. Further time can be saved with the *continue* approach if a skipped inverted file is used. The black line in Figure 9.12 shows the time taken when the inverted file is built assuming that $k = 10,000$ candidates must be checked against each inverted list. Processing time is roughly halved when the accumulator bound is less than about 10,000. As Figure 9.11 shows, this is enough accumulators that retrieval effectiveness is as good as the full cosine measure. With the addition of skipping, the inverted file grows by more than is required to process purely Boolean queries because of the larger number of candidates anticipated (recall that $k = 100$ was used for the Boolean queries), and in this case the unskipped file is extended by 20 percent to 220.33 Mbytes.

In all cases except *quit*, the elapsed times are greater than the CPU times by the same constant amount of about 1 second because all of each inverted list must be read. The input time for the *quit* method varies with the number of terms processed and is akin to the difference between the CPU and elapsed times in Figure 9.10.

In summary, the use of a limited-accumulators policy and a skipped inverted file allows ranked queries of 40–50 terms to be executed within 3–5 seconds, only slightly slower than Boolean queries designed to access the same set of answers.

Further reading

Text compression and modeling. Moffat et al. (1994) have measured the speed of a wide variety of coding methods under testbed conditions. References to research on Huffman and canonical codes can be found in the "Further reading" section at the end of Chapter 2. Witten, Bell, Moffat, et al. (1994) take a whimsical look at the characteristics of randomly generated text. Bookstein and Klein (1993) examine the relative costs of Huffman versus arithmetic coding for short strings.

Length-limited Huffman coding. Extensive discussions of the Fibonacci and re-lated sequences are available (Graham, Knuth, and Patashnik 1989). Buro (1993) considers the maximum length of Huffman codes. Length-limited Huffman codes have been studied by several authors (Hu and Tan 1972; Garey 1974; Van Voorhis 1974). Larmore and Hirschberg (1990) described the package-merge algorithm, and the efficient implementation of that mechanism has been an interest of the second author since writing the first edition of this book sparked his curiosity in the prob-lem (Katajainen, Moffat, and Turpin 1995; Turpin and Moffat 1995, 1996; Moffat and Turpin 1998). Much of the thesis investigation of Andrew Turpin has also been in the area of length-limited coding (Turpin 1998). The "warm-up" algorithm of Milidiú and Laber (1997) implements a mechanism similar to the iterative scaling process described on page 400.

Unindexed retrieval. The GLIMPSE system is an example of a retrieval mechanism that makes use of fast exhaustive searching (Manber and Wu 1994), and it is especially powerful when coupled with an approximate pattern matcher (Wu and Manber 1992).

Experiments with *TREC*. Some of the problems associated with the sheer size of the *TREC* collection, and performance figures for the first round of experiments, are described by Moffat and Zobel (1994). Moffat, Zobel, and Sharman (1997) describe methods that allow static compression models to be extended to accommodate dynamic texts; Figures 9.6 and 9.7 are based upon that work. The same paper also considers mechanisms for limiting the decode-time memory required by the word-based model. Details of the experiments carried out to measure the effectiveness of skipping on Boolean and ranked queries are given by Moffat and Zobel (1996); Figures 9.10, 9.11, and 9.12 are based upon experimental work originally undertaken for that paper. Zobel and Moffat (1995) give further experiments that show that fetching and decoding a small number of documents from a compressed document collection is faster than fetching the same documents uncompressed.

The Information Explosion

00001
00010
00011
00100
00101
ten

People have been complaining about the information explosion for years, but in some ways it is only just beginning. It was estimated in 1975 that some 50 million books had been published up to that time[1] (Gore 1976). But the real problem is the rate of increase: it has also been estimated that the amount of information in the world doubles every 20 months (Piatetsky-Shapiro and Frawley 1991). These mind-boggling statistics may not be precisely accurate, but they do serve to underscore the problem that we all feel: information is getting out of control. To put the situation into perspective, it is instructive to look at how information has grown in the past and compare that with what is happening today. Next we will look at how people are coping with the information explosion. Full-text retrieval seems to be one very important and widely applicable lifeline that may help us keep our heads above the tide of information. We consider improvements that can be made to the methods that have been described in this book, and particularly to the mg system and systems like it. We also look at the increasingly important role that compression is playing in scientific thinking. Finally, we return to the vision, mentioned in Chapter 1 (page 6), of the personal prosthetic memory into which you can scan and store every document that passes your way in a lifetime.

10.1 Two millennia of information

In the beginning was the fabled library of Alexandria in Egypt. Created in 300 B.C., it grew at a phenomenal rate and, according to legend, contained some 200,000 vol-

---

1 On the assumption that half the people who ever lived are still alive, the total number of people who ever trod the planet up to 1975 is around 8 billion, which means that on average one person in every hundred or two writes a book. That sounds reasonable—although it all depends on what you mean by a "book."

umes within 10 years. Working in the acquisitions department in those days was pretty exciting. During a famine, the king refused to sell grain to the Athenians unless he received in pledge the original manuscripts of some leading authors. The manuscripts were diligently copied and the copies returned to the owners, while the originals went into the library. By far the largest single acquisition occurred when Mark Antony stole the rival library of Pergamum and gave it lock, stock, and barrel—200,000 volumes—to Cleopatra as a love token; she passed it over to Alexandria for safe keeping. By the time Julius Caesar fired the harbor of Alexandria in 47 B.C., the library had grown to 700,000 volumes. More than 2,000 years would pass before any other library would attain this size, notwithstanding technological innovations such as the printing press. Tragically, the Alexandrian library was destroyed. Much remained after Caesar's fire, but this was wilfully laid waste (according to the Moslems) by Christians in 391 A.D. or (according to the Christians) by Moslems in 641 A.D. In the Arab conquest, Amru, the captain of Caliph Omar's army, would apparently have been willing to spare the library, but the fanatical Omar is said to have disposed of the problem of information explosion with the immortal words, "If these writings of the Greeks agree with the Koran, they are useless and need not be preserved; if they disagree, they are pernicious and ought to be destroyed."

Moving ahead a thousand years, let us peek at what was happening in a major university library a century or two after Gutenberg's invention of the moveable-type printing press around 1450. Trinity College, Dublin, one of the oldest universities in Western Europe, was founded in 1592 by Queen Elizabeth I. In 1600 the library contained a meager collection of 30 books and 10 manuscripts. However, this grew rapidly, by several thousand, when two of the fellows mounted a shopping expedition to England, and by a further 10,000 when the library received the personal collection of Archbishop Ussher, a renowned Irish man of letters, on his death in 1661. Another great event in the development of the library occurred in 1801, when an act was passed by the British Parliament decreeing that a copy of every book printed in the British Isles was to be donated to the Trinity College Library.

There were no journals in Ussher's collection. The first scholarly journals appeared just after his death: the *Journal des Sçavans* began in January 1665 in France, and the *Philosophical Transactions* of the Royal Society began in March 1665 in England. These two have grown, hydralike, into some 50,000 scientific journals today.

In the 18th century, the technology of printing really took hold. For example, more than 30,000 titles were published in France during a 60-year period in the mid-1700s. The printing press that Gutenberg had developed in order to make the Bible more widely available became the vehicle for disseminating the European Enlightenment—an emancipation of human thinking from the weight of authority of the church—some 300 years later.

In the United States, President John Adams created a reference library for Congress when the seat of government was moved to the new capital city of Washington in 1800. He began by providing $5,000 "for the purchase of such books as may be necessary for the use of Congress—and for putting up a suitable apartment for containing them therein." The first books were ordered from England and shipped across the Atlantic in 11 hair trunks and a map case. The library was housed in the new Capitol until August 1814, when—in a miniature replay of Julius Caesar's exploits in Alexandria—British troops invaded Washington and burned the building. The small congressional library of some 3,000 volumes was lost in the fire. Another fire destroyed two thirds of the collection in 1851. Unlike Alexandria, however, the Library of Congress has regrown, to approximately 22 million volumes today.

The information explosion began to hit home in Ireland in the middle of the 19th century. Work started in 1835 on the production of a printed catalog for the Trinity College Library, but by 1851 only the first volume, covering letters *A* and *B*, had been completed. The catalog was finally finished in 1887, but only by restricting the books that appeared in it to those published up to the end of 1872. (Part of one of the pages of the catalog is reproduced in Figure 7.1 on page 315.) Other libraries, however, were beginning to be faced with much bigger volumes of information. By the turn of the century, the Trinity College library had around a quarter of a million books, while the Library of Congress had nearly three times that number. Both were dwarfed by the British Museum, which at the time had nearly 2 million books, and the French National Library in Paris with over 2.5 million.

10.2 The Internet: A global information resource

Nearly a hundred years later, computer networks began and the floodgates really opened. As has often been observed, the real impact of computers is not so much in computation as it is in information and communication. The appearance of the personal computer two decades ago was a minor revolution. But what we have experienced in the past five years, with the advent of the Internet, the World Wide Web, and the CD-ROM, is a major revolution in information and the communication of information. Large-scale information technology has finally found its way into popular culture.

The Internet is the world's largest computer network—a network of networks, really—and one of its most long-standing and popular services is the Usenet news service. This is a loose collection of newsgroups contributed by a huge user community, and it's free. To give an idea of the information explosion on computer networks, Figure 10.1 shows its initial growth in terms of both the daily number of news articles and the number of megabytes they represent. While we were writing the first edition of this book in 1993, the volume of news broke 100 Mbytes (roughly the equivalent of 400 printed books) *per day*, and we included the graph in Figure 10.1 to show how Internet news traffic doubled each year. Today, as we put together the second edition, there is 1 Gbyte of daily news, and the entire collection of news from before 1994—all the news in Figure 10.1—is just 3 hours' worth at the current rate! Moreover, the volume of news is no longer newsworthy: we cannot even locate annual figures to update our graph.

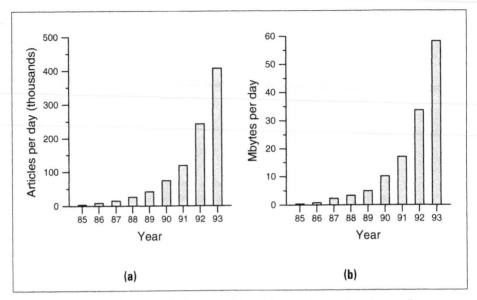

Figure 10.1 Growth of news on the Internet: (a) articles per day; (b) Mbytes per day.

Even more alarming, though, is the rate of growth: until very recently the number of articles, newsgroups, megabytes, users, and computers on the Internet had all been increasing exponentially since statistics began being collected in late 1984. Clearly, this cannot continue forever—there are some limiting factors. For example, at one time projections of the rate of growth of Internet users and the rate of growth of world population indicated that the former would overtake the latter in the year 2000![2] Inevitably things have slowed down somewhat: a 1997 projection put the number of electronic mail users at 110 million by 2000, and the growth of Internet hosts in the last three years appears to be "only" linear—but still massive, increasing from 26 million to 37 million between July 1997 and July 1998.

Today's Internet phenomenon is the World Wide Web. It has become so pervasive so quickly that we tend to forget how recently it developed. For example, it was so inconspicuous in 1993 that—amazingly—it was mentioned only in a passing reference in the first edition of this book. At present, there is estimated to be 4,000 Gbytes of data on the Web, and it continues to grow exponentially, doubling every 6 months. The average lifetime of a document is only 75 days, which accounts for the perceived unreliability of the medium as a serious information resource. To counter this, an organization called Internet Archive is aiming to archive the entire contents of the Web at regular intervals to preserve it for posterity (Kahle 1997).

---

2 To put this ludicrous projection into perspective, it is said that half the world's population does not live within 2 hours' walk of a telephone.

Much of the information on the Internet is ephemeral, trite, frivolous, and banal—and certainly does not compare with the information in the great libraries of the world. However, not all Internet activity can be written off in this way. Consider Project Gutenberg, whose goal is to encourage the creation and distribution of electronic text. Its aim is to have 10,000 electronic texts in distribution by the end of 2001. Conceived in 1971, the project's first achievement was an electronic version of the United States' Declaration of Independence, followed by the Bill of Rights and the Constitution. These were later followed by the Bible and Shakespeare—unfortunately, however, the latter was never released due to copyright restrictions. Like the Internet news, Project Gutenberg is a grassroots phenomenon—in fact, the Internet is full of grassroots phenomena. The amount of electronic text added to the Gutenberg collection doubles every year, with one book per month in 1991, two in 1992, four in 1993, and so on, so that the final goal should be reached in 2001; according to the latest available statistics the project was still on schedule through 1996. Text is input by volunteers, each of whom can enter a book a year or even just one book in a lifetime. The project does not direct the volunteers' choice of material; instead, people are encouraged to enter books they like and to enter them in the manner in which they are comfortable. Quality control is likely to be a problem.

In 1937, the renowned science fiction author H. G. Wells was promoting the concept of a "world brain" based on a permanent world encyclopedia (Wells 1938):

> ... our contemporary encyclopedias are still in the coach-and-horses phase of development, rather than in the phase of the automobile and the aeroplane. Encyclopedic enterprise has not kept pace with material progress ... the modern facilities of transport, radio, photographic reproduction and so forth are rendering practicable a much more fully succinct and accessible assembly of facts and ideas than was ever possible before.

It was supposed to give universal access to all human knowledge:

> This World Encyclopedia would be the mental background of every intelligent man in the world. It would be alive and growing and changing continually under revision, extension and replacement from the original thinkers in the world everywhere. Every university and research institution should be feeding it ... its contents would be the standard source of material for the instructional side of school and college work, for the verification of facts and the testing of statements—everywhere in the world. Even journalists would deign to use it.

It is hard to resist pointing to the Internet as the beginning of a phenomenon that might broadly resemble a world encyclopedia. With its 16 million computers (in 1997), each equipped with, say, 1 Gbyte of storage, it has been described as the world's largest library. If just 1 percent of this disk space were allocated for community use, the total space would amount to over 150 Tbytes (150,000,000 Mbytes). Even a tenth of this should be enough to accommodate a full-text database containing the text of the 50 million books estimated to have been published by 1975, compressed and indexed using the techniques we examined in earlier chapters—and the remaining nine-tenths might provide space to add all the books published since 1975![3]

There are two main problems with the Internet as a source of information. One was mentioned above: quality control. The mechanisms that have been put in place for protecting the integrity of the material that is published—the peer review mechanism for scholarly publishing and publishers' careful selection procedures—do not really exist on the net. The second is access, to which we will return in Section 10.4.

10.3   The paper problem

In 1978 a book was published entitled *Toward Paperless Information Systems* (Lancaster 1978). The title reflects the ethos of the time. While people still talk about "paperless offices," the "paperless society," and the all-electronic "library of the future," such phrases have become somewhat *outré*, and it is clear that paper documents are going to be with us for the forseeable future, at least. Although many indexes and abstracts are available electronically, they often have to be entered manually, possibly supported by OCR, which makes the cost of information services based on them much higher than it would be if the text were already available in digital form. Publishers are certainly in a position to establish centralized text databases as a by-product of computer typesetting, although it is not clear what the economic incentives are for them to make the information generally available. Even then, there is an opposing trend: it has become common for authors to supply their work in the form of "camera-ready copy" and for publishers to print it directly from paper, so that the electronic copy resides with the author. And because of the anarchic mixture of technologies to which people often resort when creating papers, that electronic copy may be a mess of incompatible files and formats.

The problems with paperless document distribution are graphically illustrated by the history of digital journals.[4] There have been quite a few experiments with digital journals, but surveys in the late 1980s indicated that none of these journals had by that time succeeded in establishing a viable publication (Gaines 1993). For example, in an experiment funded by the National Science Foundation, a psychological journal on mental workload was developed and operated on a computer conferencing system, but the results fell short of initial aspirations, and many of the participants found the system inconvenient or difficult to use. The experience inspired one researcher to write (in 1981) a paper entitled, "I Have Seen the Future and It Doesn't Work: The Electronic Journal Experiment" (Senders 1981). Another project in the

---

3 A well-known joke in the compression community observes that the Internet is so enormous that it can be used to compress any piece of text into just 13 bytes by the following strategem. Since any possible text must appear *somewhere* on the Internet, a 4-byte node address, plus a 5-byte disk address, plus a 4-byte character count, are enough to specify it fully.

4 "Graphically illustrated" is, of course, a double entendre that is really at the root of the problem!

early 1980s involving the electronic journal *Selected Papers from Social Sciences and Humanities* again resulted in criticism of the technology, in particular its inability to provide an environment conducive to convenient and efficient text reviewing. Some digital publications that seemed to offer a useful service during the 1980s have now been discontinued (Dixon 1988).

Many technical problems that plagued early digital journals, such as difficulty of network access, suitable terminals not being readily available in readers' offices, and lack of adequate graphics equipment and standards, are now well on the way to being solved. Many electronic journals now seem to be flourishing, and more are appearing continually, some adopting traditional scientific refereeing and acceptance processes and others pioneering more innovative mechanisms. It seems that digital journals are arriving at last. However, the problems that have been encountered by the academic community, which has a very strong motivation to develop new methods of information distribution and quality control in order to overcome traditional publication delays, will no doubt recur in far more serious forms and hamper the spread of paperless technology in other spheres.

Consequently, it would be naive to assume that in the future all important information will be available electronically and that the problem of handling paper images will simply go away if we ignore it long enough. Paper will probably always be with us, and the problem of integrating both machine-readable documents and optically scanned ones into a uniform electronic storage and retrieval system is going to grow ever more prominent.

There is already significant commercial interest and activity in electronic document image management systems (Thiel 1992). The need to manage an ever-increasing morass of paper is causing many organizations to convert all their paper documents into electronic image form for storage on optical disks. Firms often have to keep historical records of documents, like tax forms or company accounts, that are needed for legal reasons. Traditionally, document collections have been archived on microfiche, but after a couple of decades these begin to "bleed" and lose their clarity—in fact, restoring such documents is a popular current application of image processing techniques today. Properly managed, digital image storage does not suffer from problems of decay because a digital signal—unlike an analog one—can be read and rewritten afresh without any degradation. Of course, any given digital record will eventually become corrupted and illegible, but, provided it is copied in time, the new version will be exactly the same as the old, so the information can be passed down unaltered from digital generation to digital generation. Nevertheless, it is salutory to note that digital technology certainly does not have a good track record for information preservation. Although we can read the 400-year-old books printed on Gutenberg's press, it is often difficult to read a 15-year-old computer disk, and more often than not quite impossible to revisit a 3-month-old Web page.

Scanning and optical storage are solid and mature technologies, but OCR is not reliable enough for most organizations. Moreover, many documents contain handwritten parts, particularly signatures and handwritten entries on forms; it is essential to reproduce these faithfully. When documents are stored in image form, indexing becomes very cumbersome, and some organizations are resorting to bar-coding to automate the document-indexing step. Fortunately, OCR may well be adequate to extract text for indexing purposes, particularly when the cost of manual indexing is taken into consideration.

A rather more specialized demand for document images comes from scholars who need to have access to an exact facsimile of the original manuscript. For example, there are book preservation projects in which decaying books are scanned onto a digital storage medium to preserve them for posterity while there is still an opportunity to do so. In this way we may be able to avoid tragedies like the one in Alexandria, and future Antonys can treat their Cleopatras to a box of CD-ROMs.

10.4 Coping with the information explosion

Finding information has always been very difficult. Computer networks are certainly making it much easier, but along the way they are completely changing our expectations about what it is reasonable to try to find. For example, Internet users now expect to be able to discover anyone's electronic mail address given the name and perhaps some vague additional clues ("somewhere in the Midwest," "a Japanese philosopher"). They expect to be able to locate a file containing an interesting program given just the name of the program or to identify the latest papers on a particular specialized topic and immediately download them. Just a decade ago it would have seemed naive and unrealistic to predict that such incredible facilities for obtaining information would be in common use today.

Web search engines

In recent years, World Wide Web search engines have rapidly become a primary access point for electronically stored information. These systems seek, download, and index Web pages on a massive scale. Typically they permit a full-text search on the contents, or partial contents, of Web pages and some of the files that they point to—although most files are excluded unless they are expressed in the HTML language that is the basis for Web documents. In a phenomenon unique in the history of technology, companies—including major computer vendors—vie with each other to provide services that require vast computer resources, at no financial cost to the user. Search engines receive a large proportion of the total daily hits on the Internet, and their information-gathering software accounts for a substantial fraction of total traffic. Their primary purpose is usually to promote the wares of their hardware and software suppliers, although almost all are also supported by general advertising revenue. We are beginning to see whole product lines being built around searching technology.

It is interesting to trace the historical development of such systems. In the pre-Web era, a menu-based scheme called Gopher was set up for exploring Internet resources, and later a system called Veronica was built to index the resources that Gopher made available. Veronica claimed virtually complete coverage of the documents pointed to by the Gopher menu structure—although no attempt was made to index the document text. Early Web indexes such as Aliweb were based on specially formatted submissions from service providers. JumpStation provided three separate indexes to HTML pages: one for titles, a second for headings, and the third for the most frequent words in the text. The Lycos system, at least in its original version, restricted the text searched to the first few lines of each page and certain high-information-content keywords that appear later in the page. By 1995 Lycos had encountered several million pointers to Web pages, but 75 percent of these were unexplored; at that time new documents were being indexed at the rate of 15,000 per day.

Although these early Web indexes were academic efforts, present-day search engines are created by commercial firms to promote their services and products in the information retrieval area and are funded by advertising. Search engine operators have been unable to resist the temptation to generate revenue directly from the searching service they provide, and in some cases it has been possible for Web sites to pay to ensure that their pages figure prominently in the information retrieved by searches. The indexes are competitive in nature; consequently all claim to provide the best service, and it is very difficult to say with any accuracy how many pages they index—all tend to mention figures of around 50 million Web pages, which is generally accepted as about the size of today's World Wide Web (it doubles every 6 months, or at least did so until publication of the second edition of this book). Consequently the focus of advertising has shifted to extol the virtues of the quality of the indexing service offered, rather than boasting about the quantity of material covered.

Infoseek and WebCrawler are early commercial systems that resemble Lycos, although at least at the beginning they offered considerably less coverage. OpenText appeared later and offered ranked, Boolean, and proximity searches that could be confined to summaries, titles, first headings, links, and body text. AltaVista, a high-profile operation of Digital Equipment Corporation (Ray and Ray 1997), offers a basic ranked search facility in which you can additionally specify that certain terms are mandatory and others are prohibited. Terms can take the form of words, phrases, and partial words. An advanced search facility allows Boolean expressions of search terms as well, separating the query specification from the way in which the results are to be listed. Like other contemporary search engines, AltaVista is exceptionally well resourced to ensure that it provides impressive performance, and it is said that within a few months of operation it became so pervasive that it generated more brand-name recognition than its parent company. Finally, the Excite search engine site is eager to announce that its index is 50 percent bigger than its nearest competitor, that its indexing technology produces more relevant hits, and that its speed is unmatched by other search facilities.

And yet surprisingly little information is to be had about the search technology itself. User interfaces to current search engines are easy to toy with but require skill to use productively. Often the information necessary to interpret what the results mean is simply not there, and you must resort to experimentation and guesswork. The interface features that a search engine can provide depend to a crucial extent on the precise way in which indexing is done. Knowledge of full-text indexing techniques is rare even among computer professionals; moreover, the details of how indexing is done—details that are essential to interpreting the results—remain confidential. But commercial search engines are gaining a stranglehold: never in the history of information have so many depended on so few for so much—and been kept so utterly in the dark about what it is that they are actually getting (and, more to the point, not getting).

Agent-based information retrieval

The idea of an "agent" has emerged recently to assist with the task of finding information on the Internet. In a sense, the programs—sometimes called "crawlers"—that search engines use to explore the Web, gathering information and returning it to a central point for indexing, can be viewed as agents that operate autonomously on behalf of their owner, the Web index provider. But the use of agents for information retrieval has been proposed in contexts that are simultaneously far broader and far more personal than this. The notion of agents—better still, "intelligent" agents—has captured people's imagination and become widely talked about, and as the term has gained in popularity, it has become overhyped and defocused. The central idea is that an agent works semiautonomously, usually on behalf of an individual user. In this age of interactivity, background processing has been reinvented.

One kind of agent is an information retrieval tool, a robot librarian that mediates retrieval tasks for users. Programmed with data about different mechanisms for locating and retrieving information, it might take the form of a "software worm" that crawls from source to source looking for answers to your question. As it proceeds, it may discover and learn about new sources and check these too. Like a resourceful librarian, an agent may consult sources that the user knows nothing about. When it has exhausted all its sources, it returns with what it has found. The "worm" metaphor is a flight of fancy: it conjures up an image of the agent constantly relocating itself from computer to computer. Present-day agents don't do this, but—who knows?—one day they might.

Other kinds of agents are used for personal information filtering. An information-filtering agent will scan incoming information—papers submitted to a digital journal or digital library, news articles, Web pages, responses to a retrieval query, even email—looking for ones that match your interest profile. It may be adaptive: silently watching you read the matching articles, it notes which ones you spend most time on, or scroll all the way through, or print, or click links on—and uses that information to update its model of what interests you.

In contrast to personal information filtering, "collaborative" information filtering draws on a community of users to provide selection. This is nothing new—people have a long tradition of gaining information by networking in the right circles. Smart as they are, however, people have limited capacity to store and share information. But automated agents are beginning to be used for collaborative filtering. For example, a scheme called Firefly allows people to rate music recordings, so that you can find recommendations from audiophiles (or rock fans) with similar tastes and share your own recommendations—anonymously, of course—with others. This has now been extended to many information retrieval domains; it allows users to locate Web sites that they are likely to find of interest, to track down like-minded people, and to navigate through the Web in a personalized way. The recommendation scheme draws its data from other users' ratings. The idea is that as the system collects more ratings and learns more about your personal preferences, it is better able to match, so you receive better and more pertinent advice.

Another application for autonomous agents in information retrieval is the organization of information. Finding good ways of organizing information is extremely difficult, and finding them automatically is much harder! The real problem is enabling automatic agents to come to grips with—let's not use the overworked term "understand"—enough of the content of the information to do a useful job of organization. One way is by analyzing user behavior rather than information content: it has been proposed that Web servers should dynamically restructure their pages to optimize access for the observed patterns of user requests. Another is through human-assigned "metadata" that is attached to the information expressly to allow automatic algorithms to make some sense of it.

Data mining

There is another interesting development, this time not connected with the Internet, aimed at making sense of the information explosion. This is the idea of "data mining" (Piatetsky-Shapiro and Frawley 1991). If the amount of information in the world doubles every 20 months, the size and number of databases is probably increasing just as quickly. There is a huge amount of knowledge locked up in databases—knowledge that is potentially important but has not yet been discovered or articulated.

Data mining, or "knowledge discovery," is the extraction of implicit, previously unknown, and potentially useful information from data. The idea is to attempt to build computer programs that troll through databases automatically, fishing for such information. Techniques of machine learning and statistics are applied to look for "interesting," or at least unexpected, patterns. Of course, most real data is imperfect—some information is garbled, some missing. Anything that is discovered in such data will be inexact, and there will be exceptions to every rule and cases not covered by any rule. Algorithms need to be robust enough to cope with imperfect data and to find in it regularities that are inexact but useful.

This kind of search for valuable information in large volumes of data can be a cooperative effort between user and computer. Users define the problem and set goals; computers sift through the data, looking for patterns that match these goals. Strong patterns, if found, will likely generalize to make accurate predictions on future data. At present, data mining usually takes place on well-structured classical databases, not on the less formal, but perhaps more informative, media of text and pictures that we have been talking about in this book. The blockade to textual data mining is, of course, the problem of automatic understanding of the content of text, a long-standing challenge of artificial intelligence. But people are already talking about "text mining"—a classic example is the classification of a large collection of newswire stories—and, given the practical importance of the problem, activity in this area will only increase.

10.5 Digital libraries

Digital libraries will likely figure among the most important and influential institutions of the 21st century. Long a dream, the early prognostications of visionaries such as Bush, Nelson, and Licklider of large-scale, sustainable digital libraries are progressively becoming a reality with the initiation of major digital library projects at national levels (Lesk 1997). Future digital libraries will not only improve access to the world's knowledge dramatically but also act as "collaboratories" out of which new knowledge is crafted and refined by widely distributed teams and organizations—knowledge that right from conception is fully interconnected with previous work.

A digital library is an organized collection of digital information. Like the classical libraries with which this chapter began, they aim to provide uniform access to very large document collections. Like the Internet, they are global in scope and can transcend political and geographic boundaries. They combine the traditional library functions of collecting, classifying, and archiving information with the almost instant access and location independence that is the hallmark of modern computer networks. And since their raw material is digital in form, they support the kind of automated techniques for coping with the information explosion that we have seen in the previous section.

Digital libraries are libraries without walls. But they do need boundaries. The very notion of a collection implies a boundary: the fact that some things are in the collection implies that others must lie outside it. And they need a kind of presence, a conceptual integrity, that gives them cohesion and identity. Digital collections often present an appearance that is extremely opaque, a screen (typically a Web page) with no indication of what, or how much, lies beyond—whether a carefully selected collection or a morass of worthless ephemera, whether half a dozen documents or many millions. At least physical libraries occupy physical space, present a physical appearance, and exhibit tangible physical organization. When standing on the threshold of a large library, you gain a sense of presence and permanence that reflects the care taken in building and maintaining the collection inside. No one could confuse it with a collection of dated magazines in a doctor's waiting room. Yet in the digital world the difference is not so palpable.

Creating a publicly available digital library presents interesting challenges, particularly if the library is intended for serious professional work rather than casual browsing. First, the raw material: the collection must comprise text that can be placed in the public domain. Second, the selection of material: although a huge amount of public domain text is available on the Internet, its quality is extremely uneven and only a tiny fraction is appropriate for inclusion in a library. Third, the format of material: since most people prefer to do serious, sustained reading offline rather than online, it is helpful if the collection resembles the traditional form of typeset pages rather than raw electronic text so that it can be printed for subsequent reading. Fourth, cataloging: appropriate bibliographic information in a usable format may be difficult to find and onerous to provide manually. Fifth, information retrieval: a uniform, easy-to-use, publicly accessible interface is necessary.

A wide spectrum of experimental digital libraries have been created and are available on the World Wide Web. Some research projects focus on the underlying computer science technology and are particularly concerned with standards and interoperability of libraries that are distributed both in terms of the location of the information itself and in terms of the organizational responsibility for collecting and cataloging that information. Other projects focus on collections, the digitizing and preservation of information objects. In some cases the digital library is intended to showcase particular national resources—for example, historic, literary, or artistic treasures—while in others it is intended to support access to information that is more international in character and oriented toward particular business or academic functions. Some projects provide full professional cataloging of the information in the library; others rely on catalog information donated by the institutions or even individuals who supply the library material.

Cataloging tends to be a serious bottleneck in digital collections—as indeed it is in conventional library collections, as the Trinity College librarians discovered in the mid-19th century. The professional judgments of trained and experienced librarians are in short supply and cannot—in principle—cope with a world of exponentially growing information. This factor is somewhat mitigated by the sharing of catalog information that networked access makes possible; however, the responsibility for properly cataloged material rests with the individual library and is difficult to devolve.

More and more information today is becoming subsumed within the category of so-called gray literature, ranging from the enormous volume of material that emanates from large organizations like the United Nations down to the technical reports issued by individual university departments. The principal distinguishing feature of gray literature is that it lies outside the normal bookselling channels, which makes it more difficult to identify and acquire. Gray literature includes research reports, committee reports, conference papers, government reports, theses and dissertations, trade literature, and so on. It is particularly well suited to digital library technology because, not being produced for profit, it is often released in electronic form, which can be freely distributed on computer networks. However, the provision of formal cataloging information is a major obstacle to the creation of digital libraries for gray literature. And without a title, author, and subject database, it seems hard to offer the searching facilities that are expected in physical libraries.

This is where automated tools for coping with the information explosion come in. If full text is available electronically, the search techniques explained in this book can be used to approximate the facilities offered by a conventional library catalog. And full-text searching of content can provide ways of locating information that are far in advance of those available in a conventional library. No conventional back-of-the-book index can compare with a computerized text search—the brute power of the machine more than compensates for the human intelligence and effort that goes into a carefully prepared index.[5] Moreover, automatic agents can attempt to organize the information into clusters and categories. Methods of textual data mining can attempt to identify author and title information from the raw text and perhaps identify references to other documents so that automatic hyperlinks can be made to them. Appendix B describes just such a system, so that you can get a feeling for what it might be like to interact with a digital library and use it to retrieve a variety of different kinds of information.

10.6 Managing gigabytes better

No one can keep pace with the information explosion. And it's getting worse. The full-text indexing techniques that we have seen in this book provide a base level of accessibility without requiring anything other than the space that would have been needed to hold the text in the first place. There are no disadvantages aside from a modest processing requirement. No manual indexing is necessary: the index terms are drawn from the text itself. Nothing is missed: every word is indexed. No extra space is required: indeed, space is saved because the text and index compress into a smaller space than was originally required by the text alone. Full-text retrieval provides a fast, comprehensive, low-level access mechanism that can be obtained at essentially no cost.

Full-text retrieval systems that cope with text and images have a long way to go, and what we have seen in this book is just the beginning. There are some fairly obvious but nevertheless worthwhile developments that would benefit mg and systems like it. In Chapter 3 (page 104), the idea of representative terms was introduced; these are the terms by which a document is indexed. For text documents, we have assumed that the entire text itself constitutes the set of representative terms. In general, however, the text should be filtered first. For example, if it is the description of a document for a document preparation system, it will be expressed in a certain formatting language (such as HTML or LaTeX) and should be filtered by removing the formatting commands. If it is a source program, it should be filtered to leave just the user-defined names and comments, removing keywords, numbers, operators, and syntactic markers. Different filters will be needed for PostScript files, bibliography files, folders containing electronic mail, and so on. The possibilities are legion. Each new file type incorporated into the system would add the capability of dealing elegantly with information of that type.

Obtaining suitable representative terms for images is a much more difficult prospect. We have already suggested that OCR could be used to obtain terms from images comprising text. A challenging research problem is to develop ways of indexing other image types (Niblack and Fletcher 1993). It is relatively easy to index images on the basis of overall hue and intensity, so that queries like "retrieve

---

5 Nevertheless, this book includes a manually prepared index.

all images that are predominantly greenish-blue" can be answered. Texture is another indexable attribute, with components such as coarseness, which measures the texture's scale or grain size; directionality, which measures whether or not it has a favored direction; and contrast. Texture can be specified either linguistically, using words or numbers to represent feature values, or visually, by selecting from a menu something that matches the desired texture. Shape features, like area, circularity, eccentricity, and fractal dimension can be measured and used for indexing. It would be even more sophisticated to retrieve images by sketching some of the objects they contain, and this can be approached by calculating the major edges that appear in the images and using some sort of pattern-matching strategy.

It would be interesting to study how people remember images and see whether some cues that people use could be automated. Certainly, there is great scope for more sophisticated image retrieval in well-defined, or even loosely defined, subdomains where all the pictures are of similar things and differ only in certain respects. For example, structured drawings might be recognized and indexed on the basis of the number or pattern of boxes, lines, and so on, that they contain; weather maps might be indexed by the weather patterns they contain.

A much easier enterprise will be to extend the compression techniques that are incorporated into information management systems. It is fairly straightforward to include standard image compression methods like JPEG and JBIG into a system like mg and also to accommodate image files of different formats—TIFF, PNG, and so on. Compression methods for speech and other audio information could easily be provided too. The mechanism for indexing audio would be the same as for images, using a separate text file containing representative terms for each sound bite, possibly using voice recognition. Further extension to multimedia, perhaps using the MPEG standard, is also technically straightforward. Examples of more specialized kinds of documents that future retrieval systems might index include musical scores that can be searched for a given theme or harmonic sequence, engineering drawings that can be searched for a particular component or structure, and geographical information systems that can be searched for a specified combination of landscape features.

Another direction is to increase the flexibility with which different media are used. For example, the index might be stored on local disk and the text on CD-ROM. In response to a query, the system would tell you which CD to take off the shelf. Adding this sort of functionality is straightforward. We have explained in this book how to do the tricky jobs of compressing and indexing, and all that is necessary is to augment these modules with more flexible means of tracking files. Mg provides a lightweight, fast, and compact full-text retrieval engine that can be built into different systems to yield various different stylish, high-performance products.

10.7 Small is beautiful

We find ourselves in the midst of a practically important and intellectually fascinating convergence between the desire for more and better compression and the need to learn about what "structure" there is in data. The medieval philosopher William of Occam (or Ockham), who lived around 1300 A.D., enunciated the celebrated principle that has become known as Occam's razor: *entia non sunt multiplicanda praeter necessitatem*, literally "entities should not be multiplied without necessity." A more blunt and matter-of-fact rendition, much favored by programmers, is the KISS slogan: "keep it simple, stupid." Occam would probably have approved; he sounds like an earthy fellow, better known for his constant polemical warfare against the authority of the Pope than for his contribution to the philosophy of science. He led an interesting life, being born in Ockham in southern England and educated at Oxford and Paris. He was then imprisoned in Avignon by the Pope, escaped to Italy, was excommunicated, and ended his days in Munich.

The idea of Occam's razor is that the best scientific theory is the simplest one that explains all the facts. As Einstein is reputed to have said, "Everything should be made as simple as possible, but no simpler." It is sometimes hard to assess objectively whether a particular theory really does "explain" all the facts on which it is based. In order to make this notion more precise, we can insist that it must be possible to *regenerate* the facts upon which the theory is based from the theory itself. In other words, the best theory for a set of data is the most compact representation of that data. Science is compression.

Imagine an imperfect theory, for which a few exceptions are known. Not all the data can be explained by the theory, but most of it can. What we do is simply adjoin the exceptions to the theory, specifying them explicitly as exceptions. That makes the theory larger, and this is the price that must be paid for its inability to explain all the data. However, it may be that the simplicity—perhaps we should call it *elegance*—of the theory is sufficient to outweigh the fact that it does not quite explain everything, compared with a large, baroque theory that is in fact more comprehensive and accurate. If Kepler's three laws of planetary motion did not at the time account for the known data quite so well as Copernicus's latest refinement of the Ptolemaic theory of epicycles, they had the advantage of being far less complex, which would have justified any slight apparent inaccuracy (Koestler 1964). Kepler was well aware of the benefits of having a theory that was compact, despite the fact that his theory violated his own aesthetic sense because it depended on "ovals" rather than pure circular motion. He expressed this in a forceful metaphor: "I have cleared the Augean stables of astronomy of cycles and spirals, and left behind me only a single cartload of dung."

The best theory for a set of data is the one that minimizes the size of the theory plus the amount of data necessary to specify the data relative to the theory—the smallest cartload of dung. In statistical estimation theory, this is known as the *minimum description length principle*, and it has been applied successfully to various parameter-fitting and decision tree problems. In machine learning, it is known as *complexity-based induction*. Suppose a set of observations, or examples, is given and you need to infer a generalization of them. To use a metaphor of communication, the examples must be transmitted through a noiseless channel, and any similarity that is detected among them can be exploited by giving them a more compact coding. According to complexity-based induction, the best generalization is defined to be the one that minimizes the number of bits required to communicate the generalization, along with the examples from which it was made.

Thus, there is a strong connection between compression and the evaluation of "theories"—be they widely applicable scientific theories or more modest ones that in some sense account for regularities in a certain set of data. Compression is more than just a way to save space: it actually influences the way we think about science and explanation. While this connection certainly is not germane to the practical job of managing large collections of documents and images, it does serve to indicate that something rather fundamental is going on when we try to squeeze out the utmost in compression.

We have seen examples of compression being used for more than just making things smaller. In Section 7.4 we looked at the use of compression as a means of quantifying the information required to transmit a particular mark using another as a model, and we saw how this idea could be used as a means of template matching. This approach provides the basis for a clean and elegant template-based method for OCR. In Chapter 8 we saw how recognizing the components in a document image—text, graphics, and halftones—permits better compression; conversely, compression could be used as a metric for deciding between alternative ways to segment the image, the best segmentation being the one that yields the most compression.

Compression is important not just from a pragmatic viewpoint but from a scientific viewpoint also. The study of compression methods is likely to have spin-offs in methods for evaluating scientific theories. Small is beautiful.

10.8 Personal information support for life

In Chapter 1 (page 6), we dreamed of a personal prosthetic memory into which you could scan and store every document that passes your way in a lifetime and recall it using full-text retrieval. This is reminiscent of the "memex" vision of Vannevar Bush. It also brings to mind the idea of a "dynabook," conceived in the late 1960s by Alan Kay, then a leader in the development of the contemporary, visually based paradigm of human-computer interaction at Xerox Palo Alto Research Center (Davidson 1993) and now a Disney research fellow, as a personal dynamic medium the size of a notebook that could be owned by everyone and would have the power to handle virtually all of its owner's information-related needs (Kay and Goldberg 1977). Kay concentrated on the need for instant reactivity; quality output, both visual and audio; excellent, immediately accessible applications for creative writing, drawing, painting, filing, and music making; simulation and animation systems that were completely natural to use and required no special training; and so on. He thought that the dynabook should be as responsive as, say, a musical instrument like a flute, which is owned by its user and responds instantly and consistently to its owner's wishes.

The hardware to support these ideas seemed very futuristic in the 1970s. The dynabook was prototyped on a desk-sized computer system with a huge removable disk-pack unit and a workstation-style display. Today, though, with the advent of personal digital assistants such as U.S. Robotics' PalmPilot, along with portable CD-ROM drives—not to mention wireless connectivity—the hardware seems to present almost no problem, and we have seen a plethora of applications appear for personal computers like the IBM PC, which can provide a vast range of services to an immense user community. However, we are still far from the immediate responsivity and wide freedom of access that was envisaged for the dynabook, and it is not clear that much real progress is being made in the direction of naturalness of use.

The dynabook proposal did not dwell upon the information retrieval problem of how to find what you want in an ever-increasing morass of information. However, technology is now close to making it feasible to store every document that you encounter, scanning the ones that come on paper and storing directly those that arrive electronically. Full-text retrieval provides the only feasible access mechanism for the vast majority of these documents, for only rarely would it be worth spending time and energy on filing them properly so that they could be retrieved when desired. Users would of course want their personal prosthetic memories to connect into networks and allow access to the world's wider store of information. Again, full-text retrieval is the lowest-common-denominator access mechanism, though here with shared resources it may be possible to provide better organizational structures, at least for certain types of information.

A subtle change is occurring in the way we handle the information that we store on computers. Until fairly recently, disk space was a costly resource. It was used quite carefully. People took the time to organize things properly so that space wasn't wasted; they tidied up their file space regularly and made sure that their usage was kept under system quotas—or, on a personal computer, quotas imposed by their pocketbooks. Now the trade-offs are altering. Often it is not clear that it is worth tidying up one's disk space; it may be more cost-effective simply to buy another disk. Once you start down this road, it is very hard to stop since the time required to clean up the larger space when it finally becomes full would be even greater. We are moving from filing systems where the cost of storage is the dominant factor to ones where the cost of organization is dominant. Instead of worrying about the expense of including items, we worry about the expense of not including them should they turn out to be needed later.

In a filing system where items are inserted far more often than they are retrieved, and only a minority are ever retrieved, it is clearly necessary for insertion to be effortless and very quick, even if this does cause difficulty when it comes to retrieval. One of the problems is that it is often very hard to predict when a document will be desired. This is tricky enough to manage in a professional office situation but will be much worse on a personal scale—and there will be fewer resources available to solve the problem.

Like many dreams, the personal prosthetic memory may not turn out to be as wonderful as it sounds. Will it increase the gap between the informationally rich—the plugged-in and switched-on—and the informationally poor? The gulf is already large, and growing. A United Nations statement on universal access to basic communication and information services warns of "a new type of poverty—information poverty" (*UNDP and the Communications Revolution*, available at *www.undp.org/ comm/*), while closer to home all email users know how they divide their friends into the connected and the disconnected. Will it ever really be possible to find what we want in such an enormous database? We already have a hard enough time with the comparatively miniscule collections that we work with today. Will we become too dependent on outside information and lose the ability to think for ourselves? Doomsayers warned that electronic calculators would turn into mental crutches and cause our brains to atrophy, and to this way of thinking, cheap and flexible information storage and retrieval systems surely present a far grimmer prospect. Will such systems enrich our lives or make us slaves to other people's information? Many social commentators believe that we already spend far too much of our time as spectators rather than participants in the theater of life. Will better information technology really improve our lives? The jury is still out.

Further reading

Historical aspects of information dissemination. The estimate of the number of books published by 1975 is from an article by Gore (1976), who also recounts the fascinating history of the Alexandrian Library. The information on Trinity College, Dublin, was supplied by David Abrahamson; that on the Library of Congress was retrieved from the Internet itself, as were the Internet statistics. The Internet archiving project is described in a *Scientific American* article (Kahle 1997). Some of the other historical information, including much of the information on digital journals, is from an excellent and thought-provoking paper by Gaines that is well worth reading (Gaines 1993). H. G. Wells's "world brain" idea was published in 1938 and is still being pursued (Wells 1938; Goodman 1987). Lancaster wrote the *Paperless Information Systems* book in 1978, and it was John Senders who looked into the future and saw that it didn't work (Senders 1981). Problems of electronic journals are also discussed by Dixon (1988), who cites the case of *Clinical Notes On-Line*, an electronic journal that eventually ceased publication. The problems of document image management are discussed by Thiel (1992).

Digital libraries, Internet searching, and data mining. A fascinating book entitled *Practical Digital Libraries* (Lesk 1997) gives a comprehensive account of this exciting new field, with particular emphasis on economic issues. An interesting bibliography on Internet searching points to articles that rank, review, explain, or critique Web search engines (*www.dpi.state.wi.us/dpi/dlcl/pld/new_srch.html*). The *AltaVista Search Revolution* (Ray and Ray 1997) describes Digital Equipment Corporation's AltaVista search engine and the Web interface to it. The idea of database mining is described in a book on *Knowledge Discovery in Databases* (Piatetsky-Shapiro and Frawley 1991), which is the source of the estimate that information growth doubles every 20 months. Indexing pictures according to what they contain is the goal of IBM's query by image content (QBIC) project (Niblack and Fletcher 1993).

Other sources. Kepler's discovery of his economical three laws of planetary motion, and his doubts about them, are recounted by Koestler (1964). The "dynabook" was described in 1977 when the idea was nearly 10 years old (Kay and Goldberg 1977), and an interesting article about its creator, Alan Kay—the "man who made computers personal"—appeared in 1993 (Davidson 1993). The United Nations statement that speaks of information poverty is *UNDP and the Communications Revolution*, available at *www.undp.org/comm/*.

Guide to the mg System

The mg system is a public domain full-text retrieval system that runs under the Unix operating system. It demonstrates some of the key ideas described in this book. This appendix explains how to obtain, install, and use the system to index and query large collections of documents. A technical description of how mg works, and the rationale for design decisions, is given in Chapter 9. A more thorough description of the various programs that make up the mg system can be found here and in the manual pages that come with the system.

The mg system provides only a simple user interface, as it is really only intended to be a retrieval engine. Also, it works only on static document collections: an entire collection must be indexed and compressed before it can be used, and it is not currently possible to add new documents to the collection without reprocessing all of the documents. Nevertheless, mg provides a powerful tool for full-text retrieval of very large collections of documents, and it is a high-performance implementation of some of the main indexing and compression methods presented in this book. It is written in ANSI C and executes under Unix. Current systems for which mg is available include several versions of Solaris and SunOS (Sun hardware); Debian GNU/Linux (Pentium hardware); and DEC Alpha hardware.

A.1 Installing the mg system

At the time of writing, the mg system can be obtained by anonymous ftp from the Web site at *www.cs.mu.oz.au/mg/*. This is the mg home page, which contains current information about the status of the mg system, including which systems it can be used on, a description of the format of the mg distribution package, and a link to an errata file.

451

To obtain a copy of the mg system, you will need to copy and unpack one of the mg.tar.* files using the tools tar and one of uncompress, gunzip, or unzip. For example, on most systems the appropriate command line for unpacking the file mg.tar.gz is

```
gunzip < mg.tar.gz | tar xf -
```

This will create a new directory mg-nn, where nn is the version number of mg, and place in that directory a large number of files and subdirectories. At the time of writing (early 1999) the current version is mg-1.2.1.

The most important file that will be created is called README. Among other things, it lists any differences between the system as described in this tutorial and the system you have copied. Because it is easy to change software and difficult to change a printed book, you are urged to read that file before attempting to follow the rest of this tutorial.

You also need to create a directory for the indexed files to be stored in. The name of the directory should be stored in the environment variable MGDATA. For example, if the data directory is called mgdata and placed in your home directory, then the command to set the environment variable (assuming you are using the csh shell) is

```
setenv MGDATA ~/mgdata
```

This command should be placed in your login script so that it is executed automatically.

To use the sample document collections as described below, the location of the SampleData subdirectory should be stored in the environment variable MGSAMPLE. For example, if the directory is in the mg subdirectory of your home directory, the variable is set using

```
setenv MGSAMPLE ~/mg/SampleData
```

The next step is to compile and install all the programs. Detailed instructions on how to do this are in the files INSTALL.mg and INSTALL. The simplest sequence is to run the configuration script to establish what kind of hardware and operating system you are using (and so what options must be selected) and then make the entire suite of programs:

```
./configure --prefix=`pwd`
make
make check
make install
```

These four commands will compile and link all the programs necessary and place all of the executables and scripts in a directory called bin as a subdirectory of the main mg directory. It may take some time—as long as 10–15 minutes.

If this completes successfully, you are now ready to feed documents to mg. You should add the `bin` subdirectory of the mg system to your search path if you wish the mg programs to be invoked conveniently from other directories.

A.2   A sample storage and retrieval session

A public domain file containing Lewis Carroll's *Alice in Wonderland* is provided with the mg suite and is used here to demonstrate the system. To index this text, simply type

```
mgbuild alice
```

The program `mgbuild` is a script that invokes several other programs that construct the various files needed for full-text retrieval of the input file. It relies heavily on a program called `mg_get`, which reads the file of text and breaks it up into "documents." If there are any problems at this stage, they are probably because `mg_get` cannot find the file containing the text. The original file may be stored in a compressed format, so the `mg_get` script also needs to have access to the appropriate decompression program (for example, the Unix *gzip* program).

While `mgbuild` is running, many statistics are produced relating to disk, memory, and CPU usage. At the end of the build, the command `mgstat` is invoked. Figure A.1a shows the main statistics for the `alice` data distributed with mg, as reported by `mgstat`. According to these statistics, the uncompressed and unindexed `alice` file was 151,600 bytes. It has been broken up into 835 "documents," where a document is actually a paragraph of the book. Various other statistics are displayed, relating to the number of words in the collection and the effect of stemming. The second part of the `mgstat` output lists the sizes of the various files that are created. In the case of the `alice` collection, the text has been compressed to 26 percent of its original size, although by the time various dictionaries and indexes are added, the final size of the database is just under 80 percent of its original size. This figure is fairly high and is a consequence of the small size of the collection. The mg system is really intended for collections 10,000 times larger. Figure A.1b shows the equivalent output for the *TREC* collection and is the data that was shown diagrammatically in Figure 9.8. In this case, the final collection is only 37 percent of the size of the original collection.

To perform queries on the `alice` collection, type

```
mgquery alice
```

This runs an interactive query program, using the files that the indexing programs have placed in the subdirectory `alice` of the MGDATA directory. Try typing the query *flamingo* when the > prompt appears. This locates and displays every paragraph containing the word *flamingo*. The output is shown in Figure A.2, where five matching paragraphs are displayed, separated by lines of dashes. The number beside each line of dashes is the paragraph number within the text. You may notice

```
Input bytes                        :      151600,      0.14 Mbyte
Documents                          :         835
Words in collection [dict]         :       27618
Longest doc in collection [dict]   :        1260 characters
Maximum ratio                      :        6.22
Words in dict                      :        3035
Non-words in dict                  :         260
Total chars of distinct words      :       17929
Total chars of distinct non-words  :        1526
Words in collection [stem]         :       27504
Words in stem                      :        1891
Indexed fragments                  :         835
Total chars of stem words          :       11072
alice.text                         :       40090 bytes    26.445%
alice.invf                         :       19209 bytes    12.671%
alice.text.idx.wgt                 :        6692 bytes     4.414%
alice.weight.approx                :         649 bytes     0.428%
alice.invf.dict.blocked            :       33210 bytes    21.906%
alice.text.dict                    :       17462 bytes    11.518%
SUB TOTAL                          :      117312 bytes    77.383%
```

(a)

```
Input bytes                        : 2170856865,   2070.29 Mbyte
Documents                          :      741856
Words in collection [dict]         :   354775450
Longest doc in collection [dict]   :     2637276 characters
Maximum ratio                      :        4.85
Words in dict                      :      893131
Non-words in dict                  :       37376
Total chars of distinct words      :     7036282
Total chars of distinct non-words  :      245953
Words in collection [stem]         :   333338738
Words in stem                      :      535346
Indexed fragments                  :      741856
Total chars of stem words          :     4476809
trec12.text                        :      606.55 Mbyte    29.298%
trec12.invf                        :      127.61 Mbyte     6.260%
trec12.text.idx.wgt                :        5.66 Mbyte     0.273%
trec12.weight.approx               :        0.53 Mbyte     0.026%
trec12.invf.dict.blocked           :        9.37 Mbyte     0.453%
trec12.text.dict                   :        4.18 Mbyte     0.202%
SUB TOTAL                          :      753.91 Mbyte    36.416%
```

(b)

Figure A.1 Statistics for mg databases: (a) alice; (b) *TREC*.

```
mgquery alice
> flamingo
------------------------------- 482
The chief difficulty Alice found at first was in managing her
flamingo:  she succeeded in getting its body tucked away,
comfortably enough, under her arm, with its legs hanging down,
but generally, just as she had got its neck nicely straightened
out, and was going to give the hedgehog a blow with its head, it
WOULD twist itself round and look up in her face, with such a
puzzled expression that she could not help bursting out laughing:
and when she had got its head down, and was going to begin again,
it was very provoking to find that the hedgehog had unrolled
itself, and was in the act of crawling away:  besides all this,
there was generally a ridge or furrow in the way wherever she
wanted to send the hedgehog to, and, as the doubled-up soldiers
were always getting up and walking off to other parts of the
ground, Alice soon came to the conclusion that it was a very
difficult game indeed.
------------------------------- 487
Alice waited till the eyes appeared, and then nodded.  'It's no
use speaking to it,' she thought, 'till its ears have come, or at
least one of them.'  In another minute the whole head appeared,
and then Alice put down her flamingo, and began an account of the
game, feeling very glad she had someone to listen to her.  The
Cat seemed to think that there was enough of it now in sight, and
no more of it appeared.
------------------------------- 502
The hedgehog was engaged in a fight with another hedgehog,
which seemed to Alice an excellent opportunity for croqueting one
of them with the other:  the only difficulty was, that her
flamingo was gone across to the other side of the garden, where
Alice could see it trying in a helpless sort of way to fly up
into a tree.
------------------------------- 503
By the time she had caught the flamingo and brought it back,
the fight was over, and both the hedgehogs were out of sight:
'but it doesn't matter much,' thought Alice, 'as all the arches
are gone from the side of the ground.'  So she tucked it away
under her arm, that it might not escape again, and went back for
a little more conversation with her friend.
------------------------------- 526
'I dare say you're wondering why I don't put my arm round your
waist,' the Duchess said after a pause:  'the reason is, that I'm
doubtful about the temper of your flamingo.  Shall I try the
experiment?'
```

Figure A.2 Output from a search for the word *flamingo*.

```
mgquery alice
> .set mode heads
> flamingo | hedgehog
481 'Get to your places!' shouted the Queen in a voice
482 The chief difficulty Alice found at first was in m
483 The players all played at once without waiting for
487 Alice waited till the eyes appeared, and then nodd
488 'I don't think they play at all fairly,' Alice beg
501 Alice thought she might as well go back, and see h
502 The hedgehog was engaged in a fight with another h
503 By the time she had caught the flamingo and brough
526 'I dare say you're wondering why I don't put my ar
```

Figure A.3 Output of *flamingo* OR *hedgehog* with mode heads selected.

that mg refers to the paragraphs as *documents*. This is because a document can be defined to be any unit desired, and in the case of the alice collection, documents are defined to be lines of text separated by blank lines. This definition corresponds to a paragraph in the input file.

The default is for the query program to expect Boolean queries, specified using operators & for AND and | for OR. For example,

        flamingo & hedgehog

locates the three paragraphs that mention both animals, while

        flamingo | hedgehog

locates the nine paragraphs that mention either animal. The output from this latter query—with .set mode heads selected, which limits the output to the first few characters of each answer document—is shown in Figure A.3.

Parentheses can be used to form more complex expressions. For example, paragraphs located by the following query will all contain the word *croquet* and either *flamingo* or *hedgehog* (or both).

        croquet & (flamingo | hedgehog)

A NOT operator, "!", is also available. The query

        croquet & !queen

finds the two paragraphs that mention croquet, but not the Queen.

Other types of queries are possible apart from the Boolean ones described above. For example, ranked queries simply take a list of terms and produce documents that are likely to be relevant (Section 4.4). To switch to ranked queries, type

        .set query ranked

```
mgquery alice
> .set query ranked
> .set maxdocs 4
> eat food drink chew swallow
-------------------------------- 404 3.170445
'What did they live on?' said Alice, who always took a great
interest in questions of eating and drinking.
-------------------------------- 189 2.994334
'Is that all?' said Alice, swallowing down her anger as well as
she could.
-------------------------------- 350 1.931998
'Not the same thing a bit!' said the Hatter.  'You might just
as well say that "I see what I eat" is the same thing as "I eat
what I see"!'
-------------------------------- 223 1.610610
She was a good deal frightened by this very sudden change, but
she felt that there was no time to be lost, as she was shrinking
rapidly; so she set to work at once to eat some of the other bit.
Her chin was pressed so closely against her foot, that there was
hardly room to open her mouth; but she did it at last, and
managed to swallow a morsel of the lefthand bit.
```

Figure A.4 Output from a ranked search for paragraphs relating to eating and drinking, top four paragraphs.

The initial period (.) is important; it is what distinguishes an mg command from a query. A similar .set mode command was used in Figure A.3, and we will encounter several more .set commands below. Once this change is made, the query

        eat food drink chew swallow

searches for paragraphs related to eating and drinking. Not all of the terms need to be present for a paragraph to match, but the paragraphs that produce the closest matches are displayed first. Figure A.4 shows the four paragraphs that are the closest matches. Now a second number is displayed beside each line of dashes; this is the *similarity score*—a measure of how closely the next document matches the query. These are calculated using the cosine rule, with a computation similar to that illustrated in Table 4.8 on page 188. The values are greater than one because the system does not factor in the query length W_q.

By default, the query system displays the full text of documents that match the query. Other information can be displayed instead. The mode heads just shows the first few characters of each answer document and has already been illustrated in Figure A.3; the mode count causes only the number of matches to be displayed. For example, the output from counting the paragraphs that contain the word *alice* is simply "355 documents match."

```
mgquery trec12
> .set query ranked
> .set timestats on
> .set maxdocs 100
> .set mode silent
> to be or not to be that is the question
100 documents match.
-=-=-=-=-=-=-=-=-=-=-=-=-=-=-=-=-=-=-=-=-=-=-=-=-=-=-=-=-=-=-
Time:   invf  00:00:03.94 cpu, 00:00:08 elapsed.
        text  00:00:00.05 cpu, 00:00:01 elapsed.
        total 00:00:03.99 cpu, 00:00:09 elapsed.

-=-=-=-=-=-=-=-=-=-=-=-=-=-=-=-=-=-=-=-=-=-=-=-=-=-=-=-=-=-=-
```

Figure A.5 Output with `timestats` (timing statistics) switched on.

Because mg is primarily intended for experimental purposes, it has extensive facilities for providing performance information. The command

> .set timestats on

causes timing statistics to be displayed for each query. The `invf` statistics give the time spent reading, decoding, and merging inverted file entries, and `text` gives the time spent reading, decompressing, and writing the answer text. Figure A.5 shows the speed of the mg system when executing on a 266 MHz Pentium II platform. Now the database is the *TREC* collection summarized in Figure A.1b. Mode `silent` fetches and decodes the answer documents but then discards them rather than displaying them; `maxdocs` indicates that the top 100 answer documents should be fetched. It takes just 9 seconds to perform a ranked query on the terms *to be or not to be that is the question*, during which time more than 2.5 Mbytes of compressed inverted lists are decoded and added to accumulators (comprising 3.5 million index pointers) and more than 90 Kbytes of text is decoded.[1]

Statistics for memory usage (`memstats`), disk usage (`diskstats`), and other quantities involved in the processing of a query (`sizestats`) can also be enabled. More information about these is given in the online manual for mgquery.

To leave the query system, type either `.quit` or control-D.

---

1 Sadly, for this query none of the top 10 documents refer to Shakespeare or his play *Hamlet*—the eight query terms are just too common. However, an extended query that included the additional terms *whether tis nobler to suffer* returned in the top 10 matches several transcriptions of speeches—including one by Prince Charles—parodying the famous soliloquy.

A.3   Database creation

Document collections are compressed and indexed by the mgbuild command. Raw documents are provided to mgbuild by the mg_get command, which is usually implemented or adapted by the user for the particular collection to be processed. This single command provides a clean means of input to mg because you are usually dealing with very large files, or collections of files, that could be stored in a variety of formats on a number of different media.

In general, an indexed collection is constructed by the command mgbuild name, where *name* is the name of a collection that mg_get understands. The mg_get script is stored in the bin directory of the mg suite so that it is on the search path and can be run by mgbuild.

The mg_get command is a program or shell script that takes the name of the collection to be processed as an argument (such as alice for the collection described in the previous section) and outputs all of the documents to be stored, with each document terminated by a control-B character (ASCII code 002, sometimes written as ^B). The documents can be any size and could be a sentence, verse, paragraph, page, chapter, paper, or even a whole book.[2] Queries that involve a combination of terms identify all documents containing the combination, so the granularity chosen will depend on the kind of retrieval required.

The mg_get command must read all the documents and insert control-B terminators after each one. The documents might be stored in files in a directory, in which case mg_get must read each file in the directory. In other cases the documents may be stored in a single large file, in which case mg_get must read the file, detect the end of each document, and put the terminators in the output as appropriate. Similarly, if the text file is compressed, mg_get must decompress it before outputting it. The collection of documents may even have to be obtained from a remote site or a removable medium such as a CD-ROM.

The mg_get command will be invoked several times during the indexing and compressing process, and it is important that it returns identical output each time. This can cause difficulties if a dynamic collection of files is to be indexed. If the data is being taken from tape, provision must be made to rewind the tape each time mg_get is used. The mg_get command supplied with mg provides several examples of ways to process a collection of documents. In the example in the previous section, the script for the mg_get command detects the name alice and decompresses (if necessary) and formats the appropriate file.

The building programs assume that a reasonably large amount of memory is available. If the program is running on a smaller machine, it is possible to specify a smaller memory usage (at the expense of processing time) by changing the -m parameter for the program mg_passes in the mgbuild script. This parameter

---

2 The mg system can optionally subdivide "documents" into "paragraphs," which are separated by control-C characters. Documents are then indexed at the paragraph level, but queries are answered at the document level.

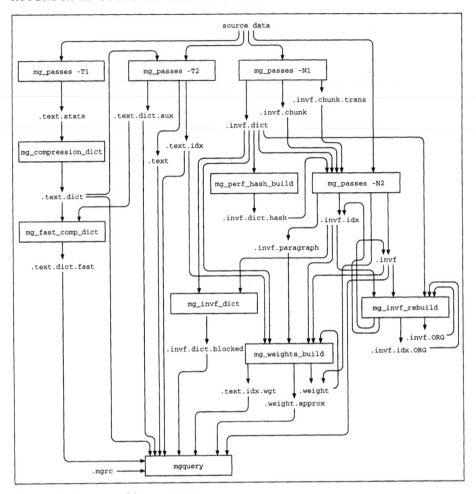

Figure A.6 Structure of the mg system.

specifies the number of megabytes that the program can use. Specifying a smaller amount of memory will allow the program to run on a smaller machine, and it should still run reasonably quickly if small files are being indexed.

Table A.1 shows the main steps carried out by mgbuild. Most of the work is done by the mg_passes program, which is called several times with different parameters to build a dictionary, compress the text, and create an inverted index. Ultimately the files generated are used by mgquery. Not all the files are necessary, but they reflect different storage methods that may be appropriate for different situations. Figure A.6 shows the various programs in the mg suite and the files that they use.

Table A.2 describes the files created by the building process. These files are stored in a subdirectory of the MGDATA directory. The sizes of some of these files for the

Table A.1 The steps of mgbuild.

Program	Purpose	Input	Output
mg_passes -T1	Create the statistics file for the text compression	text from mg_get	text.stats
mg_compression.dict	Create the compression dictionary	text.stats	text.dict
mg_passes -T2	Compress the source text	text from mg_get, text.dict	text.dict.aux, text, text.idx
mg_passes -N1	Create the stemmed dictionary for the inversion	text from mg_get	invf.dict, invf.chunk, invf.chunk.trans
mg_perf_hash_build	Create a perfect hash function for the stemmed dictionary	invf.dict	invf.dict.hash
mg_passes -N2	Invert the source text	text from mg_get, invf.dict, invf.chunk, invf.chunk.trans, invf.dict.hash	invf.paragraph, invf.idx, weight, invf
mg_fast_comp_dict	Build a version of the compression dictionary that is fast to load	text.dict, text.dict.aux	text.dict.fast
mg_invf_dict	Build a fast-access disk-based version of the stemmed dictionary	invf.dict, invf.idx	invf.dict.blocked
mg_weights_build	Build the document weights file	text.idx, invf.dict, invf.paragraph, invf.idx, invf, weight	text.idx.wgt, weight.approx, weight
mg_invf_rebuild	Rebuild the inverted file to contain skips	invf.idx, invf, invf.dict, invf.ORG, invf.idx.ORG	invf.idx, invf, invf.ORG, invf.idx.ORG
mgquery	Query mg databases	.mgrc, text.dict, text, invf.dict.blocked, text.idx.wgt, weight.approx, invf	

Table A.2 Files used by mg (nonessential files are marked with an asterisk).

File suffix	Description
text	The compressed text
text.stats*	Stores statistics about the text, such as the number of distinct terms
text.dict	A compressed list of all terms in the text
text.dict.fast*	A processed version of text.dict and text.dict.aux that is faster to load
text.dict.aux*	Novel words found during the second pass of the text compression
text.idx*	The compressed text index file, that is, a file of pointers to the start of compressed documents
text.idx.wgt	The text index and exact weights file merged together
invf	The inverted index
invf.dict*	The compressed stemmed dictionary
invf.dict.hash*	A perfect hash function for the terms in the stemmed dictionary
invf.dict.blocked	A version of the stemmed dictionary that resides on disk, a kind of B-tree
invf.chunk.trans*	Maps stemmed terms from occurrence order to lexical order
invf.chunk*	Describes where the source text is broken up into chunks for the inversion pass
invf.paragraph*	A file describing how documents are broken up into paragraphs (only generated when a paragraph-level inversion is performed)
invf.idx*	The index into the inverted index
invf.ORG*	The original inverted index (saved when a new format has been used)
invf.idx.ORG*	The original index into the original inverted index
weight.approx	The approximate weights file (used in ranking)
weight*	The exact weights file
.mgrc*	The mg start-up file

TREC collection are shown in Figure A.1b. Those listed are the files that are required under normal circumstances for the retrieval engine to operate and so represent the "final" size of a compressed database—what would be stored on a CD-ROM, for example. The file containing the compressed text (the one with the suffix .text) is usually the largest, with most of the remaining space being used for the inverted index file (.invf). The building process creates several files that are unnecessary— the ones marked with an asterisk in Table A.2—and these can be deleted to save disk space, although doing this may have an adverse effect on retrieval performance or on the start-up time for mgquery.

More details about mgbuild and the commands it uses can be found in the online manual pages that come with the mg suite.

A.4 Querying an indexed document collection

All queries to documents indexed by the mg system are through the program mgquery. This program has an interactive command-line interface. When the program is run, the document collection can be specified by giving its name. It is also possible to specify (with the -d flag) the directory in which the collection is stored, although usually this will be taken automatically from the MGDATA environment variable.

When mgquery is invoked, it reads various tables into memory and is then ready to reply to queries. Several types of queries are supported. By default, queries are Boolean and are constructed using a collection of terms linked by the Boolean &, |, and ! operators. Note that there are some limitations on the use of the NOT operator because it is implemented as a set difference operator rather than a true set complement. For example, it cannot be used with the only term in a command: the query !the does not work.

All terms used in queries are stemmed—that is, they are reduced to a root word so that they are more likely to match with words in relevant documents. The searching is also case independent and ignores punctuation. The indexing phase will already have stemmed the words in the documents. Stemming and case folding can both be disabled in the mgbuild script if required.

There are several other types of query that can be used, and these are summarized in Table A.3. To change the type of query, the internal query variable must be set to the type required using the .set command, as was shown in Figure A.4. For example, the document shown in Figure 3.4 on page 110 was retrieved from the *TREC* collection with the ranked query

```
managing gigabytes \
compressing and indexing documents and images
```

The backslash character (\) is used at the end of the line to continue a command on to a second line. Note that searching is case insensitive. Compared to ranked queries, the approx-ranked method is slightly faster, but less accurate, because it uses approximate weights to reduce the number of disk accesses. The use of approximate weights was discussed in Section 4.6.

Each document is numbered sequentially, and the last type of query—the docnums query—does no searching but merely fetches and displays the documents whose numbers are specified. Documents are numbered from 1, so the query

```
100 101 102
```

retrieves three consecutive documents starting at the 100th.

When mgquery is run, it checks for a file called .mgrc in the current directory or, if none is found there, in the user's home directory. If the file exists, it is executed as if its contents had been typed into the mgquery command-line interface prior to the first prompt. This can be used to customize the environment by setting variables

Table A.3 Query modes available in mg.

Query mode	Action
boolean	Boolean combinations of terms using &, |, and !
ranked	A list of terms to be processed using the cosine measure
approx-ranked	As for cosine, but the measure used is only approximate
docnums	Queries are simply a list of the sequence numbers of the documents to be retrieved—no terms or indexing are used

Table A.4 Some of the variables that can be set in mgquery. Default values are shown in italics.

Variable	Values	Description
mode	*text*, docnums, silent, count, heads, hilite	Determines how the retrieved documents should be displayed
query	*boolean*, ranked, approx-ranked, docnums	See Table A.3
maxdocs	*all*	The maximum number of documents to be displayed in response to a query
pager	*more*	The program used to display documents
qfreq	*true*, false	Determines if ranked queries take into account the number of times a term is specified in the query
verbatim	on, *off*	Specifies if program should do regular-expression matching on the retrieved text
mgdir		Specifies directory where indexed files can be found; normally this is taken from the MGDATA environment variable
mgname		Specifies the document collection to be used; normally this is specified on the command line when mgquery is run
briefstats	on, *off*	Switches on display of brief statistics after each query
diskstats	on, *off*	Switches on display of disk usage after each query
sizestats	on, *off*	Switches on display of size statistics after each query
timestats	on, *off*	Switches on display of timing statistics after each query
memstats	on, *off*	Switches on display of memory statistics after each query
expert	yes, *no*	Switches off display of information relating to operation of the program

such as the query mode and the output mode. This file may contain only commands and not queries.

Table A.4 summarizes the main variables that can be set to control the environment of mgquery. There are many other variables that control things such as the length of the string shown in mode heads, the format of the string that separates documents, and so on. The current settings of variables in mgquery can be obtained by typing the command .display. The system can be tailored to suit the user's purpose by changing any of the settings, giving considerable control over how queries can be specified and how the output is processed. This makes it possible to interface mgquery to other programs, such as a graphical user interface, or display utilities more suited to the data. A full description of the commands, queries, and variable settings available in mgquery can be obtained from the manual pages that are supplied with the mg software.

A.5 Nontextual files

Nontextual files, such as images, can be integrated with an mg database by using the mg_get script to explicitly store the data and getting mgquery to retrieve it. This approach is a little primitive but very flexible. Typically, the nontextual data will be compressed and stored in the same directory as the processed document collection during the initialization call to mg_get. A document is then created that contains the name of the compressed file, the method for decompressing it, and any related text that is available. This document will be indexed by mgbuild. If it is retrieved later, the method for obtaining the associated data file will be displayed, or the output from mgquery can be redirected to another program that automatically detects the display information and presents the data appropriately.

To demonstrate this idea, the sample data provided with mg includes a very small collection of documents and images by Leonardo da Vinci. To index and query the collection, type

```
mgbuild davinci
mgquery davinci
```

Typing the query *mona lisa* produces a small collection of documents relating to the famous painting. One of the documents returned is the painting itself—or rather, what is returned is a command that can be used to obtain the image from a compressed file. This command could be executed using mgquery's ability to redirect the output of queries to another program (using the .output command), which could execute the appropriate decompression program and direct its output to an appropriate viewing program.

Most of the work of integrating the images with the text is done using the mg_get command. For the davinci collection, mg_get works with a mixture of image and text files in a single directory. The images are all processed the first time mg_get is called. This processing involves compressing the images and creating temporary text files containing information about them that can be indexed by mg. The mg_build command makes it easy for mg_get to do some pre- or postprocessing by calling it with the flags -i (initialize) and -c (cleanup) at the very beginning and end of the building process. During these special calls, no output is expected from mg_get. To obtain the text, mg_get is called without any arguments or with the -t (text) argument.

The suffix of a file identifies how it should be processed. For example, a file ending with .txt contains ASCII text and is treated as a single document. Files ending with .pbm and .pgm are portable bitmap and portable graymap images, respectively, and are compressed with an appropriate program. Files that are closely associated with each other have the same *prefix*. For example, monalisa.pgm is a grayscale image of the Mona Lisa, while monalisa.txt is a brief textual description of the image. The text file provides terms that can be used to locate the image using a query. If an image has no associated text file, then a temporary one is created containing the name of the image file. For example, the file canal_excavation.pbm has no associated text describing it, yet a query on terms such as *canal* or *excavate* will retrieve the image. In principle, a descriptive text file could be created from the image itself by performing OCR on the image. Any terms that were successfully recognized could be used for queries, yet the original scanned image would also be retrieved, so a faithful reproduction of the original document would be provided. For scanned documents containing a mixture of images and text, the page segmentation techniques described in Chapter 8 could be used to extract the images and associated text.

The idea of using mg_get to associate different types of files is very flexible and could even be used to integrate audio and video files into an mg database. A recording of speech might be indexed using speech recognition in the same way as OCR could be used for textual images. Appropriate compression techniques should be applied to the data files—for audio and video data it is usually appropriate to use lossy compression.

A.6   Image compression programs

Three image compression programs are provided with the mg suite, and all of them are used to compress files in the davinci collection. The programs mgfelics and mgbilevel are for compressing grayscale and bilevel images, respectively. The third image compression program provided is mgtic, a textual image compression system that is suitable for scanned images of documents containing typed or typeset text. The algorithms embodied in these programs were described in Chapters 6 and 7, and implementation details can be found in Section 9.3.

The programs mgfelics and mgbilevel can take their input from a single specified file that is to be compressed or decompressed, and they can also read and write to standard input and output. The mgtic program can process multiple files at once, with each file typically being a separate, but related, scanned page. An additional argument is also required, which is the name of a library of symbols that will be used to code the document. The library is constructed using mgticbuild, which processes a collection of files and constructs a library based on marks found in the files. All three of the image compression programs have a command-line flag, which is used to specify whether the input should be encoded (-e) or decoded (-d). Uncompressed files must be in the portable graymap (PGM) format (for mgfelics) or the portable bitmap (PBM) format (for mgbilevel and mgtic). The programs write files to standard output, which should be redirected to the location where the file is to be stored. For example, the command to compress the file monalisa.pgm with mgfelics is

```
mgfelics -e monalisa.pgm > \
    $MGDATA/davinci/monalisa.flx
```

which creates the compressed file monalisa.flx in the directory where the other davinci files will be stored. The file is decompressed using the command

```
mgfelics -d $MGDATA/davinci/monalisa.flx > \
    monalisa.pgm
```

In this example, the decompressed output is stored to where the original file was, but in practice it is likely to be redirected to a viewing program or a printer.

Other options for these programs are described in the online documentation that accompanies them. An example of using these programs with the full-text retrieval system is given in the davinci section of the mg_get script.

Guide to the NZDL

T he New Zealand Digital Library (NZDL) is a repository of public information, freely available on the World Wide Web, that uses mg as its kernel. It gives full-text access to several substantial collections of information. This provides a large-scale application of some of the key ideas described in this book and also demonstrates the utility and flexibility of the mg software for information retrieval. This appendix explains the facilities that are provided and the mechanisms that are necessary to provide them.

Operated as a research project in the Computer Science Department at Waikato University in New Zealand since 1995, the system can be found at *www.nzdl.org*. It is still evolving, so—in the great tradition of the World Wide Web—what you get when you access it may not be precisely what you see described here. The project's goal is to develop schemes that impose structure on fundamentally anarchic, uncataloged, distributed repositories of information, thereby providing users with effective tools to locate the information they need and to peruse it conveniently and comfortably. The aim is not to run a new library but to develop the underlying technology and make it available so that others can use it to create their own collections.

B.1 What's in the NZDL?

Several different collections of public domain text are offered on an experimental basis. These collections are intended as independent individual demonstrations of the potential of full-text retrieval for information access, rather than as a unified library in their own right.

Computer Science Technical Reports

The flagship collection is a library of computer science technical reports, which currently (early 1999) provides a full-text index to 46,000 reports—well over a million pages, containing half a billion words—collected from hundreds of sites around the world. It indexes 2.7 Gbytes of text extracted automatically from 34 Gbytes of source information in PostScript format.

The interface allows documents to be located by either Boolean or ranked searches, the latter according to the cosine rule described in Chapter 4. In either case queries are answered quickly, and the plain text of each matching document is made available for browsing almost instantly.

The *Computer Science Technical Reports* collection is the most mature, and organizationally the most complex, collection offered by the NZDL. Intended as a serious research resource, it is used by computer scientists worldwide. Figure B.1a shows the query page, and Figure B.1b a typical response page. The searching options, which are entered on the query page, include

- choice of ranked or Boolean queries;
- the ability to stem terms and/or make them case insensitive, both on a whole-query basis and a term-by-term basis;
- phrase searching;
- choice of searching at the document or the page level; and
- searching first pages only.

In order to bound the resources consumed by each query, a maximum of 50 documents are returned. The "query results" shown in Figure B.1b contains information about 10 of them, including the first few words of the document and four or five icons that serve as buttons. From these the user can quickly retrieve

- the network location of the original document, with its size, creation date, and download date;
- the original document itself, downloaded from that location;
- a facsimile image of the first page or two of the original document;
- the text extracted from the original document, crudely formatted; and
- the figures extracted from it (if they are in encapsulated PostScript).

A typical use of this collection might be a case-sensitive, unstemmed query on a name such as *Moffat* to retrieve all documents that contain that name—perhaps as an author, perhaps in a reference.

Other collections

In order to demonstrate that digital libraries can benefit diverse groups of users, other collections of publicly available information have been constructed. They are organized in a similar manner to the *Computer Science Technical Reports*, although since they are not usually extracted from PostScript, they are somewhat simpler: the text is the original document, and there is no need to provide access to it separately nor to facsimile images of the first pages.

Figure B.1 (a) The *Computer Science Technical Reports* query page and (b) a typical response.

- *The Computists' Communique.* An online research news magazine in the field of artificial intelligence, operating since 1991, this includes grant and funding opportunities, industry news, Internet and Web news, online resources, research discussion lists, news and software offers, software development resources, and career or entrepreneurial tips. A typical query on this collection might be the word *wearable* (case insensitive, no stemming) to find news items on wearable computers.

- *FAQ Archive.* "Frequently Asked Questions" are an Internet phenomenon that arose as a way of helping newcomers get answers to their questions and also as a means of reducing repetitive traffic in discussion groups. They have developed into an extensive corpus of questions and answers on a huge variety of topics. This collection can be searched for terms appearing within the same Frequently Asked Questions list, under the same subject heading, or within the same paragraph. A user might issue the query *cappuccino foam* to find out how to make a nice coffee.

- *The HCI Bibliography.* This is an online bibliographic database on human-computer interaction, created in a project whose goal is to put an appropriate electronic bibliography on the screens of all researchers, developers, educators, and students in the field. With this collection, either reference entries alone, or reference entries and abstracts, can be searched. You might query on *synthetic speech* to find articles on speech synthesis.

- *The Humanity Development Library.* Put together by the Global Help Project, this collection aims to provide ideas, experiences, and solutions to workers in developing countries and is the fruit of a massive humanitarian and development information transfer project. Forty organizations are collating useful publications and resources to help reduce poverty, increase human potential, and provide education to all. The goal is to give any person in a developing country with access to the Internet, or to a personal computer with CD-ROM drive, direct low-cost access to a complete library of 3,000 books containing humanitarian aid information. You might like to learn about, for example, *snail farming.*

- *Indigenous Peoples.* This collection contains information on indigenous people found around the world. The material emanates from the Fourth World Documentation Project, which was started in 1992 to collect and distribute information of importance for indigenous people. The documents include essays, position papers, resolutions, organizational information, treaties, UN documents, speeches, and declarations on social, political, strategic, economic, and human rights issues. This project has become a primary information resource for universities, state and federal agencies, and Native American and tribal councillors. You might enjoy reading a satirical article on how Native Americans have been systematically denied their human rights; you will stumble across it if you search for information about *buffalo hunting.*

- *Oxford Text Archive.* The public domain texts in the Oxford Text Archive comprise 53 literary works ranging from *Wuthering Heights* to *The Red Badge of Courage.* This archive is provided by Oxford University Computing Services, which aims to serve the interests of the academic community by providing archival and dissemination facilities for electronic texts at low cost. Checking up on sexist writing by issuing a query for *her him he she* and examining the word frequencies returned, you will learn that *her* occurs significantly more often than *him*, whereas *he* occurs nearly three times as often as *she*. Interpreting the results of this search are beyond the scope of this book.

- *Project Gutenberg Collection.* This collection, which was mentioned in Section 10.2, currently contains around 1,000 public domain books: *The King James Bible*; classic literary works such as *Moby Dick, Alice in Wonderland*, and *Paradise Lost*; and reference books like *Webster's Dictionary*, the periodic table, and *The Hacker's Dictionary.* The quality of transcription, unfortunately, is uneven. You might be intrigued to learn that *God* appears more prominently in Daniel Defoe's *Robinson Crusoe* than it does in the Bible.

- *TidBITS.* This is a weekly electronic publication that covers news and views relating to the Macintosh computer, with a focus on Internet-related topics. News items are independent of each other, and it is possible to search individual items, individual paragraphs, or titles of news items. Search for *handwriting* to find information on the Newton handwriting recognizer. Use a Boolean search to get the documents retrieved in document order—for this collection, in time order, most recent first—rather than the similarity order that is implied by ranked searching.

The major difference between these collections is the source and format of information, the updating policy, the granularity with which searching can be done (document, page, paragraph, and so on), the different kinds of index that are provided (titles, references, abstracts), and the structure and format in which the output is displayed.

For example, Figure B.2a shows the query results page for the query *Perlman* made to the *HCI Bibliography* collection. Complete references are provided, and where more information is available—as in all but the third entry—a link is created to a fuller record. Figure B.2b shows two sample records, which contain abstracts along with the reference themselves. The *detach* button at the top is used to detach the page so that it is retained while a second document is shown.

As another example, Figure B.3a shows the result of a query for *marriage* in the *Humanity Development Library* (the repetitions in the list are caused by repeated sections in the original document collection), and Figure B.3b is the fourth document, *Closing the Gap Between Supply and Demand: Fertility Decline in Egypt.* Because this collection is structured as a hierarchical system of documents emanating from many different sources, it is rather hard to orient yourself in the collection. Consequently a navigational aid is presented at the top of the document returned (Figure B.3b) showing the section it resides in, along with the sibling subsections,

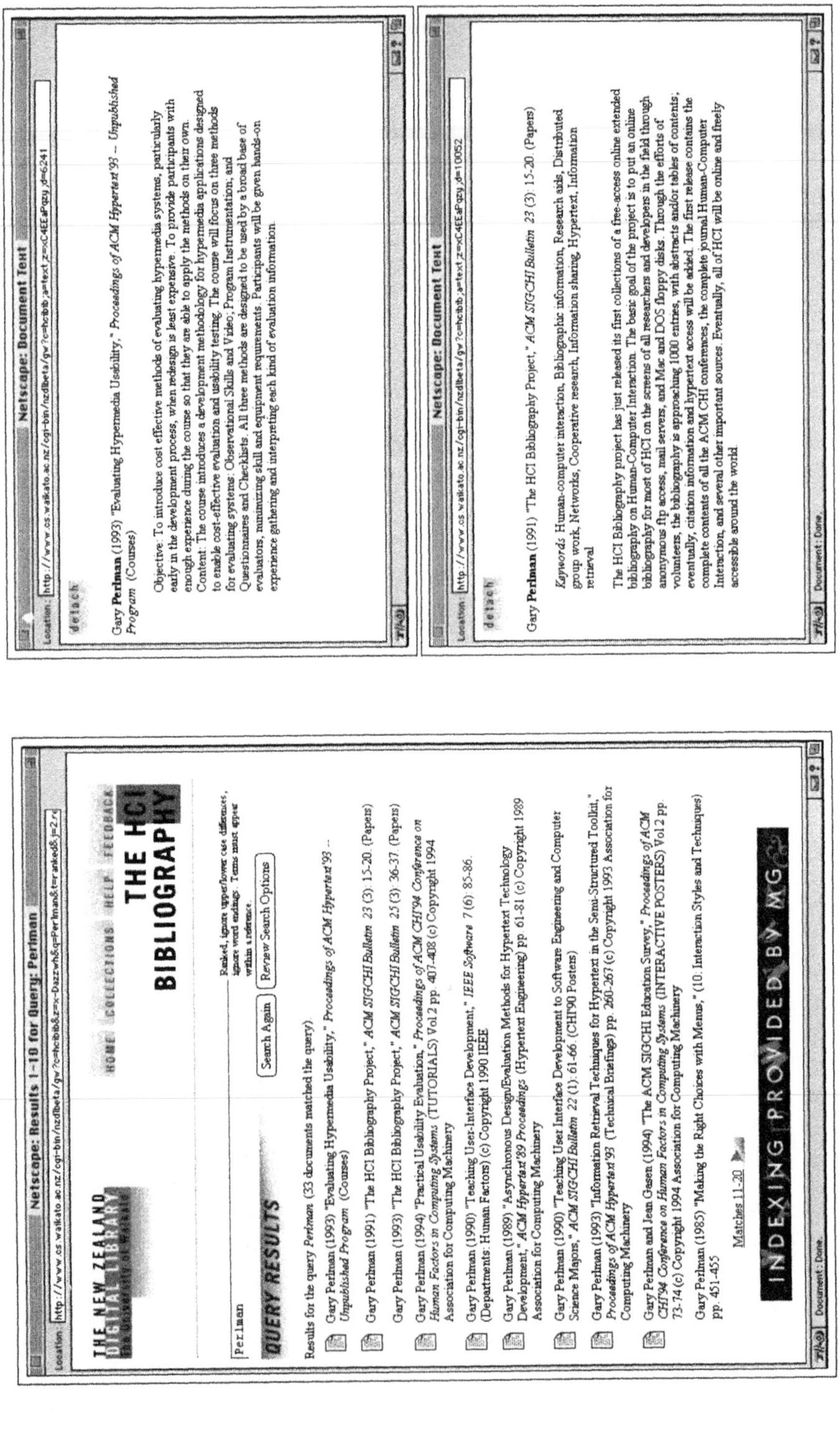

(a)

(b)

Figure B.2 (a) Query results page and (b) two sample records.

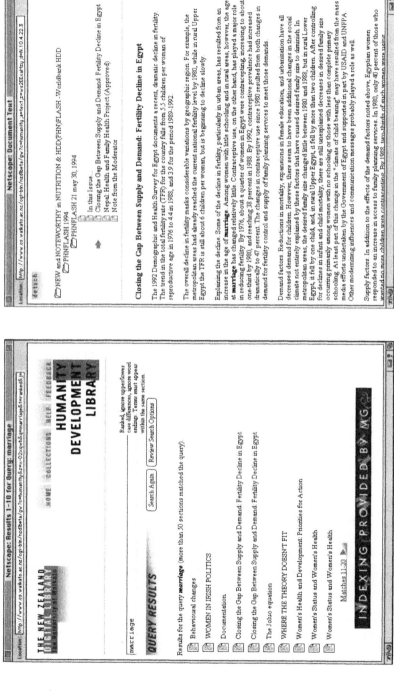

(a)

(b)

Figure B.3   (a) Query results page and (b) the fourth document returned.

preceded by the titles of hierarchically enclosing sections. This is generated automatically from the document structure, and by clicking on the folder and document icons the user can browse the collection very conveniently.

These are typical examples of how the structure of the information displayed needs to be tailored specifically for that kind of collection. Another example, which occurs in some of the other collections, is the provision of a summary of the contents of the collection—for example, a clickable list of titles.

Collection development

Work is under way on a number of other collections that to date have only been made available on a private basis. Of particular interest are those collections that create novel problems for full-text retrieval and that introduce new issues that have not yet been addressed in the project. Here are three that are being constructed.

- *City Council Minutes.* In an effort to increase public awareness and participation in local government, a local city council is planning to make available on the World Wide Web records of council meetings, along with related discussion papers. Having these in searchable form will greatly increase their accessibility and usefulness. For example, you can search just motions, or paragraphs, or whole sets of minutes, to find information relevant to particular decisions, people, or places.

- *Library Catalog.* A large library catalog containing about 10 million records has been converted into a fully indexed collection. While conventional search based upon named fields such as "Author" is appropriate when seeking an item that you know is there and have a good deal of information about, full-text search of library catalog entries is probably more convenient for nonprofessional users, in situations where you are not sure what you are looking for, and for casual browsing. We are adding author, title, and keyword fields, so that if necessary the user can disambiguate query terms by restricting them to one of those fields. Human factor experiments are planned to determine the relative efficiencies of field-based and full-text searching for various kinds of information retrieval tasks.

- *The Karlsruhe Bibliographies.* This is a large collection of bibliographies in the field of computer science, totaling about 700,000 bibliography entries. Requirements are similar to the *HCI Bibliography* collection, except that users may be offered a choice of reference format so that they can cut and paste references into documents they are working on.

Audio collections

The collections above are composed of conventional textual material. However, audio collections also present opportunities for using conventional search engines like mg as the basic searching mechanism. Here are two examples.

- *Oral History Collections.* Oral history is becoming available in both tape and transcript form from a number of sources. A timed transcript can provide precise full-text access to audio material, along with suitable methods of navigating around the recordings.

- *Visually Impaired Readers.* The World Wide Web offers interesting distribution possibilities for the visually impaired. Currently, many organizations for the blind produce audiotapes and large-print versions of books for distribution to such readers. Many potential readers have access to voice synthesis technology that enables them to read books that are available in electronic form. Such equipment can also give access to the Web, provided that information—and particularly choices—are presented textually rather than graphically. The construction of information retrieval services designed expressly for partially sighted readers is an attractive and worthwhile possibility.

Of course, the audio domain, by its very nature, suggests the development of search technology that is not text-based. In order to indicate the possibilities, we will stray slightly off topic and look at a collection that does not use mg but relies on an entirely different searching mechanism. It uses a special search engine that is capable of applying musical knowledge to match sequences of notes.

Melody Index

The *Melody Index* service retrieves music on the basis of a few notes that are sung, hummed, or otherwise entered (McNab et al. 1996). Music librarians are often asked to find a piece of music based on a few sung or hummed notes. The magnitude of this task may be judged by the fact that the Library of Congress holds over six million pieces of sheet music (not including tens of thousands of operatic scores and other major works), and the National Library of France has 300,000 hours of sound recordings, almost all music. Techniques such as optical music recognition technology will ultimately enable such collections to be placed online.

With the *Melody Index*, users can literally sing a few bars and have all melodies containing that sequence of notes retrieved and displayed—a facility that is attractive to casual and professional users alike. Such systems will form an important component of the music library of the future. With them, researchers will analyze the music of given composers to find recurring themes or duplicated musical phrases, and musicians and casual users alike will retrieve compositions based on remembered (perhaps imperfectly remembered) musical passages.

The *Melody Index* system transcribes melodies automatically from microphone input. It then searches a database for tunes containing melodic sequences similar to the sung pattern and ranks the tunes that are retrieved according to the closeness of the match. Experimental studies on how people remember tunes indicate that users need a choice of several matching procedures and should be able to explore the results interactively in their search for a particular melody. Thus different search criteria have been implemented involving melodic contour, musical intervals, and rhythm; both exact and approximate matching are available to users.

Figure B.4 shows two screen displays from the melody retrieval system. In each case the input sung was the first eight notes of "Auld Lang Syne." For the query in Figure B.4a, the "simple" query mode was used. The transcribed input is shown at the top, and titles of tunes returned by the database search appear below. Tunes are ranked according to how closely they match the sung pattern. Any of the returned tunes may be selected for display, and the user can listen to the displayed tune. Figure B.4b shows the "advanced" query mode, which allows the user to control the tightness of the matching by specifying pertinent parameters.

It is necessary to have a database of tunes stored in the form of music notation, and the database is a collection of international folk tunes from various countries formed by amalgamating a collection of nearly 2,000 tunes, most of North American origin, from the Digital Tradition folksong database, with the nearly 8,000 in the Essen database of European and Chinese melodies (Schaffrath 1992). There are just over half a million notes in the database, and the average length of a melody is around 50 notes. The database is segmented into the following parts:

- North American (and British) folksongs (1,700 tunes),
- German ballads and folksongs (5,500 tunes),
- Chinese ethnic and provincial songs (2,100 tunes), and
- Irish folksongs (50 tunes).

The greatest limiting factor for melody indexes is that few score collections are available in machine-readable form. As digital libraries develop, however, scores will be placed online through the use of optical music recognition technology (Bainbridge 1996; Bainbridge and Bell 1996). On an experimental basis, the NZDL offers a prototype *Optical Music Recognition* service that accepts images of music and returns an audio or MIDI file containing a performance of the music, or a file suitable for input to a music editing package. Eventually, music submitted for processing will automatically be added to the database of tunes that can be searched using the melody index.

B.2   How the NZDL works

Let us take a look at how collections are organized in the NZDL. The main issues in any noncommercial information collection are where the raw material comes from and what facilities are provided for users to access it. We examine these in turn.

The raw material

Source documents can be in any format from which ASCII text can be extracted. For example, the *Oxford Text Archives* are stored in SGML, which is related to the HTML language in which Web pages are written. The *Gutenberg* collection is stored in unadorned ASCII text. The *Humanity Development Library* is extracted from Microsoft Word documents. The *HCI Bibliography* is in a reference format called REFER, an

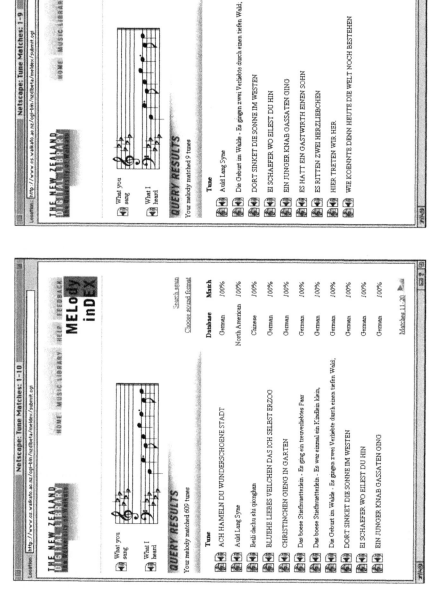

Figure B.4   (a) Results for a simple query and (b) results for the same query with tighter matching options.

example of which was shown in Figure 3.2 on page 108; the *Karlsruhe Bibliographies* are in BIBTEX. Scanned TIFF images of the textual documents that comprise the *City Council Minutes* collection are subjected to optical character recognition prior to indexing: the inevitable recognition errors reduce the quality of the index, but this is ameliorated by using ranked queries containing redundant terms.

In the world of electronic information, the PostScript format (along with its close relative PDF, a more recent derivative) provides the closest analog to paper as a document storage medium. PostScript is a page description language that is widely used on the Internet for storing technical reports and other more "serious" information. Unlike the HTML format used throughout the World Wide Web, PostScript cannot be read by ordinary Internet search programs and is therefore invisible to them. PostScript (and PDF) files are almost universal in computer science technical report archives, and for this reason the *Computer Science Technical Reports* collection includes only documents in these formats.

For this collection, archives of technical reports are located through lists maintained on the Internet. Each archive is automatically scanned for (possibly compressed) PostScript or PDF files. Each file is downloaded, along with its size and date, and the appropriate information is extracted. In order to build the index, it is necessary to extract plain, unformatted text automatically from the documents. While the words of a technical report usually appear as plain text within a PostScript file, they are thoroughly intermixed with PostScript language commands and internal data. Extracting plain text from such documents presents an interesting technological challenge (Nevill-Manning, Reed, and Witten 1997).

With any Internet-based information collection, a crucial question is how much information to store centrally. For the *Computer Science Technical Reports*, it was decided that the index and search engine would operate locally but the documents themselves would remain in their original repositories. In addition to the index, a facsimile image of each document's first page or two is retained at the NZDL site so that users can read the title and abstract and sample the look and feel of the original. The plain, unformatted text must be extracted from the documents to build the index, and it proves expedient to retain a full copy of this text locally as well. This is useful in its own right for browsing: users can examine the text without going to the trouble of downloading and printing the original document.

One source of growth for the collection is when new documents in known repositories are located during a routine examination of currently indexed sites, which is undertaken periodically to ensure that the documents indexed continue to exist. New sites are detected by various means: monitoring standard Internet lists for new additions, manually scanning the newsgroups that announce them, and encouraging users to email suggestions to a central coordinator.

Searching and indexing

The material in the NZDL collections has no cataloging information associated with it; consequently some of the services that are available in formally cataloged collections can only be approximated. This situation is at least partially by choice. If collections were limited only to those where cataloging were available or might be supplied, the scope would be greatly restricted. If it was necessary to find the means to catalog collections manually, new collections would be severely limited by human resources. Therefore, although most of the material is gathered from publicly available repositories of text, the system has been set up not to require any effort or action on the part of participating repositories. No special software, archive organizations, or file formats are required of the providers. The only information used for cataloging is derived from the documents themselves.

These considerations lead inexorably to the use of a full-text index instead of a library catalog as the principal retrieval mechanism. The NZDL indexes make the entire text of all documents available for searching, rather than some much more restricted list of keywords, as is the case in many computer-based text retrieval systems. From the point of view of building the system, this approach has the advantage that nothing more is needed to construct the index than the plain text of the documents in the library: there is no requirement that traditional bibliographic database information such as author, title, publisher, and so on, be entered. From the point of view of the user, full-text retrieval is a powerful tool for searching for information.

Consider the extent to which it can approximate the more traditional forms of library access—by author, title, date, subject, and so on—in the *Computer Science Technical Reports* collection.

- *Author/title.* In the vast majority of reports, the first page gives bibliographic information such as title and author. By limiting term matching to this page, a user who is familiar with the structure of the collection can approximate a search based on such information. For example, an initial page search for documents authored by *Knuth* will not retrieve documents that merely cite his work, since most reports begin with a title page.

- *Publication date.* Most reports also include the publication date on the front page, and the same technique serves for publication date searches. Alternatively, this facility could be simulated by permitting the user to search on the date in which a technical report was entered into its repository, although such a strategy is likely to produce uneven results because many reports are placed in repositories long after they were originally produced.

- *Page searching.* The full text of technical reports is stored, and searching over the complete document text is supported. This is very useful in performing very general searches with high recall. Of course, irrelevant documents can be expected as well. To achieve higher precision, a limited kind of proximity searching is supported by requiring the query terms to appear on the same physical page of the document. Phrase searching is implemented within mg by postprocessing query results: a string search for phrases can be performed on documents returned by any query.

- *Case folding/truncation/exact match.* A choice is offered of how query terms should be matched in the document returned. The user can specify whether terms can be folded to lowercase or whether a stemming algorithm is to be used to reduce them to root form. This allows you to search for names or for grammatical variants of a root word.

To support these kinds of search, a number of separate indexes to the collection are constructed that make it possible to search on a first-page, same-page, and same-document basis and to specify whether search terms should be stemmed and case-folded or not. As far as the user is concerned, however, all that is required is to specify the level of the search and whether stemming and case folding should be in force.

For a high-recall topic search, the user specifies a document-level search. This will match to search terms appearing in any portion of the document text (including the references section), and the terms can be widely scattered. For a more focused query, the user specifies a page-level search; the search terms must then appear on the same page of the documents, although they still need not be adjacent. With both page- and document-level searching, the user can either choose exact term matching or apply case folding and stemming to the query terms. The ability to turn case folding off is particularly useful when searching computing documents because names of software systems are often acronyms that are also common English words (for example, the SMART retrieval system).

To search by author, title, or date, the user typically specifies that only the first page of documents should be searched, with no stemming or case folding. This type of query is not as precise as a search over specified fields, of course, but in practice is an effective workaround for a collection that is not formally cataloged but is characterized by certain conventions in the structure of the items it contains. To find cited authors or papers, the user specifies a full document search with no stemming or case folding. This locates authors or titles within the body of a document, which generally includes references. Again, the search will be relatively imprecise. Nevertheless, anecdotal evidence from users suggests that this type of query is useful, particularly since commercial citation indexes such as SciCite provide relatively weak support for computer science.

B.3 Implications

Full-text retrieval technology has enormous practical implications for the dissemination of material, particularly noncommercial "gray literature." One of the original motivations for the NZDL project was efficient use of the expensive trans-Pacific Internet link. Computer scientists could search for and preview technical reports locally before downloading the full PostScript document file, thus encouraging exploration without concern for network charges.

But other collections have different aims. The *Indigenous Peoples* index gives people ranging from scholars and politicians through activists access to material that they would otherwise be quite unable to find. The *Humanity Development Library* is intended for deployment in developing countries to dispense practical advice and wisdom. The various newsletters reach specialized professional communities. The

City Council Minutes give ordinary people access to local information that they otherwise would never be able to find. Libraries for visually impaired users will empower whole new segments of society. Digital libraries will be a major force for social development and democratization throughout the coming millennium.

Further reading

The PostScript-to-text converter that is used to extract index terms for the *Computer Science Technical Reports* is freely available from the NZDL home page; it is described by Nevill-Manning, Reed, and Witten (1997). The *Melody Index* is described by McNab et al. (1996). An article by D. Greenhaus describing the North American folksong database, *About the Digital Tradition*, can be found at *www.deltablues.com/DigiTrad-blurb.html*, and an account of the Essen database of European and Chinese melodies is also available (Schaffrath 1992). The optical music recognition technology used in the NZDL was developed by David Bainbridge in his Ph.D. project (Bainbridge 1996; Bainbridge and Bell 1996).

References

Åberg, J., Y. M. Shtarkov, and B. J. M. Smeets. 1997. Towards understanding and improving escape probabilities in PPM. In Storer and Cohn (1997), pages 22–31. **63, 101.**

Adams, D. 1979. *The Hitchhiker's Guide to the Galaxy.* London: Pan Books. **20.**

Anastassiou, D., M. K. Brown, H. C. Jones, J. L. Mitchell, W. B. Pennebaker, and K. S. Pennington. 1983. Series/1-based videoconferencing system. *IBM Systems Journal* 22(1/2):97–110. **310.**

Anh, V. N., and A. Moffat. 1998. Compressed inverted files with reduced decoding overheads. In Croft et al. (1998), pages 290–297. **207, 222.**

Arnold, R., and T. Bell. 1997. A corpus for the evaluation of lossless compression algorithms. In Storer and Cohn (1997), pages 201–210. **102.**

Ascher, R. N., and G. Nagy. 1974. A means for achieving a high degree of compaction on scan-digitized printed text. *IEEE Transactions on Computers* C–23(11):1174–1179, November. **318, 353.**

Baeza-Yates, R. 1992. String searching algorithms. In Frakes and Baeza-Yates (1992), Chapter 10, pages 219–240. **170, 221.**

Baeza-Yates, R., and G. H. Gonnet. 1992. A new approach to text searching. *Communications of the ACM* 35(10):74–82, October. **221.**

Bainbridge, D. 1996. *Extensible optical music recognition* (Ph.D. thesis). University of Canterbury, New Zealand. **478, 483.**

Bainbridge, D., and T. C. Bell. 1996. An extensible optical music recognition system. In Ramamohanarao, K., editor, *Australian Computer Science Conference*, pages 308–317, Melbourne, Australia, February. **478, 483.**

Baird, H. S., H. Bunke, and K. Yamamoto, editors. 1992. *Structured Document Image Analysis.* Berlin: Springer-Verlag. **388.**

Barlow, H., and S. Morgenstern. 1949. *A Dictionary of Musical Themes.* London: Williams and Norgate Ltd. **12, 20.**

Barrett, P. H., D. J. Weinshank, and T. T. Gottleber. 1981. *A Concordance to Darwin's "Origin of Species."* New York: Cornwell University Press. **3.**

Bayer, T., J. Franke, U. Kressel, E. Mandler, M. Oberländer, and J. Schürmann. 1992. Towards the understanding of printed documents. In Baird, Bunke, and Yamamoto (1992), pages 3–25. **388.**

Belkin, N. J., P. Ingwersen, and A. M. Pejtersen, editors. 1992. *Proc. 15th Annual International ACM SIGIR Conference on Research and Development in Information Retrieval,* Copenhagen, June. New York: ACM Press.

Belkin, N. J., A. D. Narasimhalu, and P. Willett, editors. 1997. *Proc. 20th Annual International ACM SIGIR Conference on Research and Development in Information Retrieval,* Philadelphia, PA, July. **221.**

Bell, T. C. 1986a. Better OPM/L text compression. *IEEE Transactions on Communications* COM-34:1176–1182, December. **101.**

Bell, T. C. 1986b. *A Unifying Theory and Improvements for Existing Approaches to Text Compression* (Ph.D. thesis). Christchurch, New Zealand: University of Canterbury. **101.**

Bell, T. C., J. G. Cleary, and I. H. Witten. 1990. *Text Compression.* Englewood Cliffs, NJ: Prentice Hall. **xxv, 99, 102, 388.**

Bell, T. C., and D. Kulp. 1993. Longest-match string searching for Ziv-Lempel compression. *Software—Practice and Experience* 23(7):757–772, July. **101.**

Bell, T. C., and A. Moffat. 1989. A note on the DMC data compression scheme. *The Computer Journal* 32(1):16–20, February. **71, 101.**

Bell, T. C., A. Moffat, C. G. Nevill-Manning, I. H. Witten, and J. Zobel. 1993. Data compression in full-text retrieval systems. *Journal of the American Society for Information Science* 44(9):508–531, October. **150.**

Bell, T. C., I. H. Witten, and J. G. Cleary. 1989. Modeling for text compression. *Computing Surveys* 21(4):557–592, December. **99.**

Bell, T. C., I. H. Witten, and M. Fellows. 1998. Computer science unplugged: Offline activities and games for all ages. Available from *unplugged.canterbury.ac.nz.* **10, 20.**

Bender, T. K., and D. L. Higdon. 1988. *A Concordance to Henry James's "The Spoils of Poynton."* New York: Garland. Garland Reference Library of the Humanities, Vol. 648. **3, 4, 20.**

Bentley, J., and M. D. McIlroy. 1993. Engineering a sorting function. *Software—Practice and Experience* 23(11):1249–1265, November. **261.**

Bentley, J., D. Sleator, R. Tarjan, and V. Wei. 1986. A locally adaptive data compression scheme. *Communications of the ACM* 29(4):320–330, April. **101.**

Bentley, J., and A. C.-C. Yao. 1976. An almost optimal algorithm for unbounded searching. *Information Processing Letters* 5(3):82–87, August. **116, 150**.

Biliris, A. 1992a. An efficient data storage structure for large dynamic objects. In *Proc. IEEE International Conference on Data Engineering*, pages 301–308, February. Phoenix, AZ, February. **261**.

Biliris, A. 1992b. The performance of three database storage structures for managing large objects. In *Proc. ACM-SIGMOD Conference on Management of Data*, pages 276–285. **261**.

Bodson, D., S. J. Urban, A. R. Deutermann, and C. E. Clarke. 1985. Measurement of data compression in advanced group 4 facsimile systems. *Proc. IEEE* 73(4):731–739, April. **272, 310**.

Bones, P. J., T. C. Griffin, and C. M. Carey-Smith. 1990. Segmentation of document images. In *Proc. SPIE/SPSE Symposium on Electronic Imaging Science and Technology*, pages 78–88, February. California, February. **363, 388**.

Bookstein, A. 1981. Comparison of two systems of weighted Boolean retrieval. *Journal of the American Society for Information Science* 32(4):257–259. **222**.

Bookstein, A. 1983. Information retrieval: A sequential learning process. *Journal of the American Society for Information Science* 34(5):331–342. **222**.

Bookstein, A., and S. T. Klein. 1991a. Compression of correlated bit-vectors. *Information Systems* 16(4):387–400. **150**.

Bookstein, A., and S. T. Klein. 1991b. Flexible compression for bitmap sets. In Storer and Reif (1991), pages 402–410. **150**.

Bookstein, A., and S. T. Klein. 1993. Is Huffman coding dead? *Computing* 50(4):279–296. **87, 101, 428**.

Bookstein, A., S. T. Klein, and T. Raita. 1992. Model based concordance compression. In Storer and Cohn (1992), pages 82–91. **116, 150**.

Bookstein, A., S. T. Klein, and T. Raita. 1994. Markov models for clusters in concordance compression. In Storer and Cohn (1994), pages 116–125. **150**.

Bookstein, A., and D. R. Swanson. 1974. Probabilistic models for automatic indexing. *Journal of the American Society for Information Science* 25(5):312–318, September. **216, 222**.

Bookstein, A., and D. R. Swanson. 1975. A decision-theoretic foundation for indexing. *Journal of the American Society for Information Science* 26(1):45–50, January. **216, 222**.

Borwein, J. M., and P. B. Borwein. 1990. *A Dictionary of Real Numbers*. Pacific Grove, CA: Brooks/Cole. **20, 109**.

Bratley, P., and Y. Choueka. 1982. Processing truncated terms in document retrieval systems. *Information Processing & Management* 18(5):257–266. **172, 222**.

Buckley, C., and A. F. Lewit. 1985. Optimization of inverted vector searches. In *Proc. 8th Annual International ACM SIGIR Conference on Research and Development in Information Retrieval*, pages 97–110, Montreal, Canada, June. New York: ACM Press. **151, 206, 222.**

Buckley, C., G. Salton, and J. Allan. 1992. Automatic retrieval with locality information using SMART. In Harman (1992d), pages 59–72. **151.**

Bunton, S. 1995. The structure of DMC. In Storer and Cohn (1995), pages 72–81. **101.**

Bunton, S. 1997a. An executable taxonomy of on-line modeling algorithms. In Storer and Cohn (1997), pages 42–51. **100.**

Bunton, S. 1997b. *On-Line Stochastic Processes in Data Compression* (Ph.D. thesis). University of Washington, March. **63, 65.**

Bunton, S. 1997c. A percolating state selector for suffix-tree context models. In Storer and Cohn (1997), pages 32–41. **100.**

Buro, M. 1993. On the maximum length of Huffman codes. *Information Processing Letters* 45(5):219–223, April. **428.**

Burrows, M., and D. J. Wheeler. 1994. *A block-sorting lossless data compression algorithm*. Technical report 124. Digital Equipment Corporation, Palo Alto, CA, May. **65, 101.**

Bush, V. 1945. As we may think. *The Atlantic Monthly* 176(1):101–108, July. **6.**

Buyanovsky, G. 1994. Associative coding. *Monitor* (8):10–19, August. In Russian. **101.**

Cahoon, B., and K. S. McKinley. 1996. Performance evaluation of a distributed architecture for information retrieval. In Frei et al. (1996), pages 110–118. **218, 222.**

Cameron, R. D. 1988. Source encoding using syntactic information source models. *IEEE Transactions on Information Theory* IT-34(4):843–850, July. **101.**

Capocelli, R. M., and A. De Santis. 1991. New bounds on the redundancy of Huffman codes. *IEEE Transactions on Information Theory* IT-37(4):1095–1104, July. **100.**

Capocelli, R. M., R. Giancarlo, and I. J. Taneja. 1986. Bounds on the redundancy of Huffman codes. *IEEE Transactions on Information Theory* IT-32(6):854–857, July. **100.**

Carey, M. J., D. J. DeWitt, J. E. Richardson, and E. J. Shekita. 1989. Storage management for objects in EXODUS. In Kim, W., and F. H. Lochovsky, editors, *Object-Oriented Concepts, Databases, and Applications*, Chapter 14, pages 341–369. Reading, MA: Addison-Wesley. **261.**

CCITT. 1993. Draft recommendation T.82 & ISO DIS 11544: Coded representation of picture and audio information—progressive bi-level image compression, February. **281, 310.**

Chevion, D., E. D. Karnin, and E. Walach. 1991. High efficiency, multiplication free approximation of arithmetic coding. In Storer and Reif (1991), pages 43–52. **59**.

Choueka, Y., A. S. Fraenkel, S. T. Klein, and E. Segal. 1986. Improved hierarchical bit-vector compression in document retrieval systems. In *Proc. 9th Annual International ACM SIGIR Conference on Research and Development in Information Retrieval*, pages 88–97, Pisa, Italy, September. New York: ACM Press. **151**.

Choueka, Y., S. T. Klein, and Y. Perl. 1985. Efficient variants of Huffman codes in high level languages. In *Proc. 8th Annual International ACM SIGIR Conference on Research and Development in Information Retrieval*, pages 122–130, Montreal, Canada, June. New York: ACM Press. **100**.

Clarke, M. V. 1875. *The Complete Concordance to Shakespeare.* London: W. Kent and Co. **2, 19**.

Cleary, J. G., W. J. Teahan, and I. H. Witten. 1995. Unbounded length contexts for PPM. In Storer and Cohn (1995), pages 52–61. **65, 100, 101**.

Cleary, J. G., and I. H. Witten. 1984a. A comparison of enumerative and adaptive codes. *IEEE Transactions on Information Theory* IT-30(2):306–315, March. **100**.

Cleary, J. G., and I. H. Witten. 1984b. Data compression using adaptive coding and partial string matching. *IEEE Transactions on Communications* COM-32(4):396–402, April. **61, 100, 102**.

Collison, R. 1962. *Indexing Books: A Manual of Basic Principles.* London: Ernest Benn Limited. **223**.

Cooper, L. 1911. *Concordance to the Poems of William Wordsworth.* New York: Russell and Russell. **1, 19**.

Cormack, G. V., and R. N. Horspool. 1984. Algorithms for adaptive Huffman codes. *Information Processing Letters* 18(3):159–165, March. **32, 100**.

Cormack, G. V., and R. N. Horspool. 1987. Data compression using dynamic Markov modeling. *The Computer Journal* 30(6):541–550, December. **69, 101, 102**.

Cormack, G. V., C. R. Palmer, and C. L. Clarke. 1998. Efficient construction of large test collections. In Croft et al. (1998), pages 282–289. **221**.

Cormen, T. H., C. E. Leiserson, and R. L. Rivest. 1990. *Introduction to Algorithms.* Cambridge, MA: MIT Press. **100, 170, 210, 221, 222**.

Cover, T. M., and R. C. King. 1978. A convergent gambling estimate of the entropy of English. *IEEE Transactions on Information Theory* IT-24(4):413–421, July. **94, 102**.

Croft, W. B., A. Moffat, C. J. van Rijsbergen, R. Wilkinson, and J. Zobel, editors. 1998. *Proc. 21st Annual International ACM SIGIR Conference on Research and Development in Information Retrieval*, Melbourne, Australia, August. New York: ACM Press. **221.**

Cruden, A., C. J. Orwom, A. D. Adams, and S. A. Waters. 1941. *Cruden's Complete Concordance to the Old and New Testaments.* London: Lutterworth Press. **13, 19.**

Cutting, D., and J. Pedersen. 1990. Optimisations for dynamic inverted index maintenance. In *Proc. 13th Annual International ACM SIGIR Conference on Research and Development in Information Retrieval*, pages 405–411, Brussels, Belgium. New York: ACM Press. **261.**

Czech, Z. J., G. Havas, and B. S. Majewski. 1992. An optimal algorithm for generating minimal perfect hash functions. *Information Processing Letters* 43(5):257–264, October. **168, 221.**

Davidson, C. 1993. The man who made computers personal. *New Scientist* 1878:32–35, June. **447, 450.**

de Kretser, O., A. Moffat, T. Shimmin, and J. Zobel. 1998. Methodologies for distributed information retrieval. In Papazoglou, M., M. Takizawa, B. Krämer, and S. Chanson, editors, *Proc. 18th International Conference on Distributed Computing Systems*, pages 66–73, May, Amsterdam. Los Alamitos, CA: IEEE. **218, 222.**

Deets, P. 1989. A guide to litigation support for the small firm. *Legal Assistant Today* 6(4):40–46, Mar/Apr. **20.**

Dengel, A. 1992. ANASTASIL: A system for low-level and high-level geometric analysis of printed documents. In Baird, H. S., H. Bunke, and K. Yamamoto, editors, *Structured Document Image Analysis*, pages 70–98. Berlin: Springer-Verlag. **361, 388.**

Dixon, B. 1988. Science and the information society. *Scholarly Publishing* 20(1):3–12. **437, 449.**

Elias, P. 1975. Universal codeword sets and representations of the integers. *IEEE Transactions on Information Theory* IT-21(2):194–203, March. **116, 150.**

Endoh, T., and Y. Yamakazi. 1986. Progressive coding scheme for multilevel images. In *Proc. of the Picture Coding Symposium*, pages 21–22. Tokyo: SPIE. **307, 310.**

Faloutsos, C. 1985. Signature files: Design and performance comparison of some signature extraction methods. In *Proc. 8th Annual International ACM SIGIR Conference on Research and Development in Information Retrieval*, pages 63–82, Montreal, Canada, June. New York: ACM. **151.**

Faloutsos, C. 1992. Signature files. In Frakes and Baeza-Yates (1992), Chapter 4, pages 44–65. **151, 222.**

Faloutsos, C., and S. Christodoulakis. 1984. Signature files: An access method for documents and its analytical performance evaluation. *ACM Transactions on Office Information Systems* 2(4):267–288, October. **151.**

Faloutsos, C., and H. V. Jagadish. 1992. On B-tree indices for skewed distributions. In Yuan, L.-Y., editor, *Proc. 18th International Conference on Very Large Databases*, pages 363–374, Vancouver, Canada. **261.**

Fenwick, P. 1994. A new data structure for cumulative probability tables. *Software—Practice and Experience* 24(3):327–336, March. Errata published in 24(7):677, July 1994. **60, 100.**

Fenwick, P. 1996a. Block sorting text compression. In Ramamohanarao, K., editor, *Proc. 19th Australasian Computer Science Conference*, pages 193–202, Melbourne, January. **101.**

Fenwick, P. 1996b. The Burrows-Wheeler transform for block sorting text compression: Principles and improvements. *The Computer Journal* 39(9):731–740, September. **101.**

Fergusson, T., and J. Rabinowitz. 1984. Self-synchronizing Huffman codes. *IEEE Transactions on Information Theory* 30(4):687–693, July. **101.**

Feygin, G., P. G. Gulak, and P. Chow. 1994. Minimizing excess code length and VLSI complexity in the multiplication free approximation of arithmetic coding. *Information Processing & Management* 30(6):805–816, November. **59.**

Fiala, E. R., and D. H. Greene. 1989. Data compression with finite windows. *Communications of the ACM* 32(4):490–505, April. **101.**

Fletcher, L. A., and R. Kasturi. 1988. A robust algorithm for text string separation from mixed text/graphics images. *IEEE Transactions on Pattern Analysis and Machine Intelligence* 10(6):910–917, November. **378, 388.**

Foley, J. D., and A. Van Dam. 1982. *Fundamentals of Interactive Computer Graphics.* Reading, MA: Addison-Wesley. **325, 353.**

Fox, E. A., Q. F. Chen, A. Daoud, and L. Heath. 1991. Order preserving minimal perfect hash functions and information retrieval. *ACM Transactions on Information Systems* 9(3):281–308, July. **164, 221.**

Fox, E. A., D. K. Harman, R. Baeza-Yates, and W. C. Lee. 1992. Inverted files. In Frakes and Baeza-Yates (1992), Chapter 3, pages 28–43. **151, 245, 260, 261.**

Fox, E. A., L. Heath, Q. F. Chen, and A. Daoud. 1992. Practical minimal perfect hash functions for large databases. *Communications of the ACM* 35(1):105–121. **164, 221.**

Fox, E. A., P. Ingwersen, and R. Fidel, editors. 1995. *Proc. 18th Annual International ACM SIGIR Conference on Research and Development in Information Retrieval*, Seattle, WA, July. New York: ACM.

Fox, E. A., and W. C. Lee. 1991. *FAST-INV: A fast algorithm for building large inverted files.* Technical report TR 91–10. Blacksburg, VA: Virginia Polytechnic Institute and State University. **245, 261.**

Fraenkel, A. S., and S. T. Klein. 1985. Novel compression of sparse bit-strings— Preliminary report. In Apostolico, A., and Z. Galil, editors, *Combinatorial*

Algorithms on Words, Volume 12, NATO ASI Series F, pages 169–183. Berlin: Springer-Verlag. **150**.

Frakes, W. B. 1992. Stemming algorithms. In Frakes and Baeza-Yates (1992), Chapter 8, pages 131–160. **151**.

Frakes, W. B., and R. Baeza-Yates, editors. 1992. *Information Retrieval: Data Structures and Algorithms*. Englewood Cliffs, NJ: Prentice Hall. **129, 151, 221**.

Frei, H.-P., D. Harman, P. Schäuble, and R. Wilkinson, editors. 1996. *Proc. 19th Annual International ACM SIGIR Conference on Research and Development in Information Retrieval*, Zurich, Switzerland, August. New York: ACM. **221**.

Fu, K. S., editor. 1982. *Applications of Pattern Recognition*. Chapter 1, pages 1–13. Boca Raton, FL: CRC Press. **387, 388**.

Furness, M. H. H. 1875. *A Concordance to Shakespeare's Poems: An Index to Every Word Therein Contained*. Philadelphia: J. B. Lippingcott and Co. **3, 14, 19**.

Gailly, J. L. 1993. Gzip program and documentation. Source code available from *ftp://prep.ai.mit.edu/pub/gnu/gzip-*.tar*. **78, 102**.

Gaines, B. R. 1993. An agenda for digital journals: The socio-technical infrastructure of knowledge dissemination. *Journal of Organizational Computing* 3(2):135–193. **436, 449**.

Gallager, R. G. 1978. Variations on a theme by Huffman. *IEEE Transactions on Information Theory* IT-24(6):668–674, November. **32, 52, 100**.

Gallager, R. G., and D. C. Van Voorhis. 1975. Optimal source codes for geometrically distributed integer alphabets. *IEEE Transactions on Information Theory* IT–21(2):228–230, March. **116, 120, 150**.

Galloway, M. M. 1975. Texture analysis using gray level run lengths. *Computer Graphics and Image Processing* 4:172–179. **385, 388**.

Garey, M. R. 1974. Optimal binary search trees with restricted maximal depth. *SIAM Journal on Computing* 3(2):101–110, June. **401, 428**.

Gilbert, E. N., and E. F. Moore. 1959. Variable-length binary encodings. *Bell Systems Technical Journal*, pages 933–967, July. **87, 88, 101**.

Golomb, S. W. 1966. Run-length encodings. *IEEE Transactions on Information Theory* IT–12(3):399–401, July. **116, 119, 150**.

Gonnet, G., and R. Baeza-Yates. 1991. *Handbook of Data Structures and Algorithms*, second edition. Reading, MA: Addison-Wesley. **170, 221**.

Gonzalez, R. C., and P. Wintz. 1987. *Digital Image Processing*, second edition. Reading, MA: Addison-Wesley. **371, 388**.

Goodman, H. J. A. 1987. The "world brain/world encyclopaedia" concept: Its historical roots and the contributions of H. J. A. Goodman to the ongoing evolution and implementation of the concept. In *Proc. 50th Annual Meeting of the American Society for Information Science*, pages 91–98, Medford, NJ. **449**.

Gore, D. 1976. Farewell to Alexandria: The theory of the no-growth, high-performance library. In Gore, D., editor, *Farewell to Alexandria*, pages 164–180. Westport, CT: Greenwood Press. **431, 449.**

Gräf, U. 1997. Dense coding—A fast alternative to arithmetic coding. In *Proc. Compression and Complexity of Sequences*, Positano, Italy, July. Los Alamitos, CA: IEEE Computer Society Press. **100.**

Graham, R. L., D. E. Knuth, and O. Patashnik. 1989. *Concrete Mathematics: A Foundation for Computer Science*. Reading, MA: Addison-Wesley. **397, 428.**

Gravano, L., and J. H. Garcia-Molina. 1995. Generalising GlOSS to vector-space databases and broker hierarchies. In Dayal, U., P. M. D. Gray, and S. Nishio, editors, *Proc. International Conference on Very Large Databases*, pages 78–89, Zurich, Switzerland, September. **220, 222.**

Harman, D. K. 1992a. Overview of the first text retrieval conference. In *Proc. TREC Text Retrieval Conference*, Harman (1992d), pages 1–20. **150.**

Harman, D. K. 1992b. Relevance feedback revisited. In Belkin, Ingwersen, and Pejtersen (1992), pages 1–10. **214, 215, 222.**

Harman, D. K. 1992c. Relevance feedback and other query modification techniques. In Frakes and Baeza-Yates (1992), Chapter 11, pages 241–263. **214, 215, 222.**

Harman, D. K., editor. 1992d. *Proc. TREC Text Retrieval Conference*, November. Washington: National Institute of Standards Special Publication 500-207.

Harman, D. K. 1995. Overview of the second text retrieval conference (TREC-2). *Information Processing & Management* 31(3):271–289, May. **150, 192, 221.**

Harman, D. K., and G. Candela. 1990. Retrieving records from a gigabyte of text on a minicomputer using statistical ranking. *Journal of the American Society for Information Science* 41(8):581–589, August. **151, 206, 222, 230, 260.**

Havas, G., B. S. Majewski, N. C. Wormald, and Z. J. Czech. 1993. Graphs, hypergraphs and hashing. In *Proc. 19th International Workshop on Graph-Theoretic Concepts in Computer Science (WG'93)*, pages 153–165. Berlin: Springer-Verlag, LNCS 790. **168, 221.**

Hirschberg, D. S., and D. A. Lelewer. 1990. Efficient decoding of prefix codes. *Communications of the ACM* 33(4):449–459, April. **34, 100.**

Holt, M. J. 1988. A fast binary template matching algorithm for document image data compression. In Kittler, J., editor, *Proc. 4th International Conference on Pattern Recognition*, pages 230–239. Cambridge, England: Springer-Verlag. **330, 353.**

Holt, M. J. J., and C. S. Xydeas. 1986. Recent developments in image data compression for digital facsimile. *ICL Technical Journal*, pages 123–146, May. **328, 353.**

Horspool, R. N. 1995. The effect of non-greedy parsing in Ziv-Lempel compression methods. In Storer and Cohn (1995), pages 302–311. **101.**

Horspool, R. N., and G. V. Cormack. 1992. Constructing word-based text compression algorithms. In Storer and Cohn (1992), pages 62–71. **101**.

Hough, P. V. C. 1962. Method and means for recognizing complex patterns, December. U.S. Patent 3,069,654. **358, 388**.

Howard, P. G. 1993. *The Design and Analysis of Efficient Lossless Data Compression Systems* (Ph.D. thesis). Providence, RI: Brown University. Available as Technical Report CS-93-28. **63, 310**.

Howard, P. G. 1997. Text image compression using soft pattern matching. *The Computer Journal* 40(2/3):146–156. **351, 353**.

Howard, P. G., and J. S. Vitter. 1992a. Analysis of arithmetic coding for data compression. *Information Processing & Management* 28(6):749–763. **100**.

Howard, P. G., and J. S. Vitter. 1992b. Error modeling for hierarchical lossless image compression. In Storer and Cohn (1992), pages 269–278. **307, 310**.

Howard, P. G., and J. S. Vitter. 1992c. New methods for lossless image compression using arithmetic coding. *Information Processing & Management* 28(6):765–779. **307, 310**.

Howard, P. G., and J. S. Vitter. 1993a. Design and analysis of fast text compression based on quasi-arithmetic coding. In Storer and Cohn (1993), pages 98–107. **59, 62, 100**.

Howard, P. G., and J. S. Vitter. 1993b. Fast and efficient lossless image compression. In Storer and Cohn (1993), pages 351–360. **294, 310**.

Howard, P. G., and J. S. Vitter. 1994. Arithmetic coding for data compression. *Proc. IEEE* 82(6):857–865, June. **100**.

Hu, T. C., and K. C. Tan. 1972. Path length of binary search trees. *SIAM Journal of Applied Mathematics* 22(2):225–234, March. **401, 428**.

Huffman, D. A. 1952. A method for the construction of minimum-redundancy codes. *Proc. Inst. Radio Engineers* 40(9):1098–1101, September. **30, 100**.

Hunter, R., and A. H. Robinson. 1980. International digital facsimile coding standards. *Proc. IEEE* 68(7):854–867, July. **268, 273, 310**.

Ide, E. 1971. New experiments in relevance feedback. In Salton (1971), pages 337–354. **222**.

Illingworth, J., and J. Kittler. 1988. A survey of the Hough transform. *CVGIP: Computer Vision, Graphics and Image Processing* 44:87–116. **361**.

Inglis, S., and I. Witten. 1994. Compression-based template matching. In Storer and Cohn (1994), pages 106–115. **326, 330, 353**.

Jansen, B. P., A. Spink, J. Bateman, and T. Saracevic. 1998. Real life information retrieval: A study of user queries on the Web. *ACM SIGIR Forum* 32(1):5–17, Spring. **222**.

Jayant, N., editor. 1997. *Signal Compression: Coding of Speech, Audio, Text, Images and Video*. Singapore: World Scientific. **99**.

Johnsen, O., J. Segen, and G. L. Cash. 1983. Coding of two-level pictures by pattern matching and substitution. *Bell Systems Technical Journal* 62(8):2513–2545, October. **321, 329, 353**.

Kahle, B. 1997. Preserving the Internet. *Scientific American* 276(3):82–83, March. **434, 449**.

Karp, R. M. 1961. Minimum-redundancy coding for the discrete noiseless channel. *IEEE Transactions on Information Theory* IT-7(1):27–38, January. **401**.

Katajainen, J., and A. Moffat. 1998. In-place calculation of minimum-redundancy codes. Submitted. Preliminary version in *Proc. 1995 Workshop on Algorithms and Data Structures*, Kingston, Ontario, August 1995, pages 393–402. Source code available from *www.cs.mu.oz.au/~alistair/inplace.c*. **100**.

Katajainen, J., A. Moffat, and A. Turpin. 1995. A fast and space-economical algorithm for length-limited coding. In Staples, J., P. Eades, N. Katoh, and A. Moffat, editors, *Proc. International Symposium on Algorithms and Computation*, pages 12–21, Cairns, Australia, December. Berlin: Springer-Verlag, LNCS 1004. **404, 428**.

Katajainen, J., M. Penttonen, and J. Teuhola. 1986. Syntax-directed compression of program files. *Software—Practice and Experience* 16(3):269–276, March. **101**.

Kay, A. C., and A. Goldberg. 1977. Personal dynamic media. *IEEE Computer* 10(3):31–41, March. **447, 450**.

Kent, A. J., R. Sacks-Davis, and K. Ramamohanarao. 1990. A signature file scheme based on multiple organisations for indexing very large text databases. *Journal of the American Society for Information Science* 41(7):508–534, July. **138, 151**.

Klein, S. T., A. Bookstein, and S. Deerwester. 1989. Storing text retrieval systems on CD-ROM: Compression and encryption considerations. *ACM Transactions on Information Systems* 7(3):230–245, July. **149, 151**.

Knuth, D. E. 1985. Dynamic Huffman coding. *Journal of Algorithms* 6(2):163–180, June. **32, 100**.

Koestler, A. 1964. *The Act of Creation*. London: Hutchinson. **446, 450**.

Korfhage, R. R. 1997. *Information Storage and Retrieval*. New York: Wiley. **221**.

Kraft, L. G. 1949. *A device for quantizing, grouping, and coding amplitude modulated pulses* (Master's thesis). MIT, Cambridge, MA. **401**.

Lancaster, E. W. 1978. *Toward Paperless Information Systems*. New York: Academic Press. **436, 449**.

Langdon, G. G. 1983. A note on the Ziv-Lempel model for compressing individual sequences. *IEEE Transactions on Information Theory* IT-29(2):284–287, March. **101**.

Langdon, G. G., and J. Rissanen. 1981. Compression of black-white images with arithmetic coding. *IEEE Transactions on Communications* COM–29(6):858–867, June. **276, 310**.

Larmore, L. L., and D. S. Hirschberg. 1990. A fast algorithm for optimal length-limited Huffman codes. *Journal of the ACM* 37(3):464–473, April. **401, 402, 428**.

LeGall, D. 1991. MPEG: A video compression standard for multimedia applications. *Communications of the ACM* 34(4):464–473, April. **415**.

Lelewer, D. A., and D. S. Hirschberg. 1987. Data compression. *Computing Surveys* 19(3):261–296, September. **99, 100**.

Lelewer, D. A., and D. S. Hirschberg. 1991. Streamlining context models for data compression. In Storer and Reif (1991), pages 313–322. **62, 100**.

Lennon, M. D., D. Pierce, B. Tarry, and P. Willett. 1981. An evaluation of some conflation algorithms for information retrieval. *Journal of Information Science* 3:177–183. **151**.

Lesk, M. 1988. Grab—inverted indexes with low storage overhead. *Computing Systems* 1(3):207–220, Summer. **151, 260**.

Lesk, M. 1997. *Practical Digital Libraries: Books, Bytes, and Bucks*. San Francisco: Morgan Kaufmann. **221, 442, 449**.

Lomet, D. B. 1988. A simple bounded disorder file organisation with good performance. *ACM Transactions on Database Systems* 12(4):525–551, December. **261**.

Lovins, J. B. 1968. Development of a stemming algorithm. *Mechanical Translation and Computation* 11(1-2):22–31. **151**.

Lucarella, D. 1988. A document retrieval system based upon nearest neighbour searching. *Journal of Information Science* 14:25–33. **151, 206, 222**.

Macleod, I. A., T. P. Martin, B. Nordin, and J. R. Phillips. 1987. Strategies for building distributed information retrieval systems. *Information Processing & Management* 23(6):511–528, November. **218, 222**.

Majewski, B. S., N. C. Wormald, G. Havas, and Z. J. Czech. 1996. A family of perfect hashing methods. *The Computer Journal* 39(6):547–554. **168, 221**.

Manber, U. 1997. A text compression scheme that allows fast searching directly in the compressed file. *ACM Transactions on Information Systems* 15(2):124–136, April. **89, 101**.

Manber, U., and S. Wu. 1994. GLIMPSE: A tool to search through entire file systems. In *Proc. of the USENIX Winter 1994 Technical Conference*, pages 23–32, San Francisco, CA, January. **391, 429**.

Manolopoulos, Y., and S. Christodoulakis. 1992. File organizations with shared overflow blocks for variable length objects. *Information Systems* 17(6):491–510. **261**.

Maron, M. E., and J. L. Kuhns. 1960. On relevance, probabilistic indexing, and information retrieval. *Journal of the ACM* 7(3):216–244, July. **214, 222.**

McDonell, K. J. 1977. An inverted index implementation. *The Computer Journal* 20(1):116–123. **151.**

McIlroy, M. D. 1982. Development of a spelling list. *IEEE Transactions on Communications* COM–30(1):91–99, January. **150, 151.**

McKenzie, B. J., R. Harries, and T. C. Bell. 1990. Selecting a hashing algorithm. *Software—Practice and Experience* 20(2):209–224, February. **151.**

McMillan, B. 1956. Two inequalities implied by unique decipherability. *Institute of Radio Engineers Transactions on Information Theory* IT-2:115–116. **401.**

McNab, R. J., L. A. Smith, I. H. Witten, C. L. Henderson, and S. J. Cunningham. 1996. Toward the digital music library: tune retrieval from acoustic input. In Fox, E. A., and G. Marchionini, editors, *Proc. Digital Libraries '96*, pages 11–18. New York: ACM Press. **477, 483.**

Memon, N., and X. Wu. 1997. Recent developments in context-based predictive techniques for lossless image compression. *The Computer Journal* 40(2/3):127–136. **294, 295, 310.**

Milidiú, R. L., and E. S. Laber. Submitted 1997. The WARM-UP algorithm: A Lagrangean construction of length restricted Huffman codes. **401, 428.**

Moffat, A. 1989. Word based text compression. *Software—Practice and Experience* 19(2):185–198, February. **101.**

Moffat, A. 1990a. Implementing the PPM data compression scheme. *IEEE Transactions on Communications* 38(11):1917–1921, November. **63, 100, 102.**

Moffat, A. 1990b. Linear time adaptive arithmetic coding. *IEEE Transactions on Information Theory* 36(2):401–406, March. **61, 100.**

Moffat, A. 1991. Two-level context based compression of binary images. In Storer and Reif (1991), pages 382–391. **277, 310, 417.**

Moffat, A. 1992. Economical inversion of large text files. *Computing Systems* 5(2):125–139, Spring. **245, 260.**

Moffat, A., and T. A. H. Bell. 1995. In-situ generation of compressed inverted files. *Journal of the American Society for Information Science* 46(7):537–550, August. **235, 260.**

Moffat, A., R. M. Neal, and I. H. Witten. 1998. Arithmetic coding revisited. *ACM Transactions on Information Systems* (16):256–294. Source software available from *ftp://munnari.oz.au/pub/arith_coder*. **59, 100–102.**

Moffat, A., N. Sharman, I. H. Witten, and T. C. Bell. 1994. An empirical evaluation of coding methods for multi-symbol alphabets. *Information Processing & Management* 30(6):791–804, November. **100, 409, 428.**

Moffat, A., and L. Stuiver. 1996. Exploiting clustering in inverted file compression. In Storer and Cohn (1996), pages 82–91. **116, 126, 127, 150.**

Moffat, A., and A. Turpin. 1997. On the implementation of minimum-redundancy prefix codes. *IEEE Transactions on Communications* 45(10):1200–1207, October. **100, 102.**

Moffat, A., and A. Turpin. 1998. Efficient construction of minimum-redundancy codes for large alphabets. *IEEE Transactions on Information Theory* 44(4):1650–1657, July. **51, 100, 404, 428.**

Moffat, A., and J. Zobel. 1992. Parameterised compression for sparse bitmaps. In Belkin, Ingwersen, and Pejtersen (1992), pages 274–285. **116, 125, 150.**

Moffat, A., and J. Zobel. 1994. Compression and fast indexing for multi-gigabyte text databases. *Australian Computer Journal* 26(1):1–9, February. **151, 221, 261, 420, 429.**

Moffat, A., and J. Zobel. 1996. Self-indexing inverted files for fast text retrieval. *ACM Transactions on Information Systems* 14(4):349–379, October. **178, 207, 222, 423, 429.**

Moffat, A., J. Zobel, and S. T. Klein. 1995. Improved inverted file processing for large text databases. In Sacks-Davis, R., and J. Zobel, editors, *Proc. 6th Australasian Database Conference*, pages 162–171, Adelaide, January. **178, 222.**

Moffat, A., J. Zobel, and R. Sacks-Davis. 1994. Memory efficient ranking. *Information Processing & Management* 30(6):733–744, November. **203, 222.**

Moffat, A., J. Zobel, and N. Sharman. 1997. Text compression for dynamic document databases. *IEEE Transactions on Knowledge and Data Engineering* 9(2):302–313, March. **101, 256, 261, 411, 413, 415, 429.**

Mohiuddin, K. M. 1982. *Pattern Matching with Application to Binary Image Compression* (Ph.D. thesis). Palo Alto, CA: Stanford University, December. **353.**

Mohiuddin, K. M., J. Rissanen, and R. Arps. 1984. Lossless binary image compression based on pattern matching. In *Proc. International Conference on Computers, Systems and Signal Processing*, pages 447–451, Bangalore, India, December. **353.**

Moulton, W. F., and A. S. Geden. 1897. *A Concordance to the Greek Testament*, first edition. Edinburgh: T. & T. Clark. **1, 19.**

Moulton, W. F., and A. S. Geden. 1977. *A Concordance to the Greek Testament*, fifth edition. Edinburgh: T. & T. Clark. Revised by H. K. Moulton. **2, 19.**

Nagy, G. 1992. Towards a structured document utility. In Baird, Bunke, and Yamamoto (1992), pages 54–69. **388.**

Nagy, G., S. C. Seth, and S. D. Stoddard. 1986. Document analysis with an expert system. In Gelsema, E. S., and L. N. Kanal, editors, *Pattern Recognition in Practice II*, pages 149–159. Amsterdam: Elsevier Science Publishers B. V. (North-Holland). **383, 388.**

Nagy, G., S. Seth, and M. Viswanathan. 1992. A prototype document image analysis system for technical journals. *IEEE Computer* 25(7):10–22, July. **383, 384, 388.**

Nelson, M. R. 1996. Data compression with the Burrows Wheeler transform. *Dr. Dobb's Journal of Software Tools* 21(9):46–50, September. **101.**

Nelson, M., and J. L. Gailly. 1995. *The Data Compression Book: Featuring Fast, Efficient Data Compression Techniques in C*, second edition. Redwood City, CA: IDG Books Worldwide. **99.**

Nevill-Manning, C. G., T. Reed, and I. H. Witten. 1997. Extracting text from PostScript. *Software—Practice and Experience* 28(5):481–491. **480, 483.**

Newstrack. 1993a. "Media trials." *Communications of the ACM* 36(2):13, February. **20.**

Newstrack. 1993b. "Want ads." *Communications of the ACM* 36(2):13, February. **20.**

Niblack, W., and M. Fletcher. 1993. Find me the pictures that look like this: IBM's image query project. *Advanced Imaging*, April. **444, 449.**

Owolabi, O. 1993. Efficient pattern searching over large lexicons. *Information Processing Letters* 47(1):17–22, August. **221.**

Parrish, S. M., editor. 1959. *A Concordance to the Poems of Matthew Arnold*. Ithaca, NY: Cornell University Press. **3.**

Pennebaker, W. B., and J. L. Mitchell. 1988. Probability estimation for the Q-coder. *IBM Journal of Research and Development* 32(6):737–752, November. **288, 310.**

Pennebaker, W. B., and J. L. Mitchell. 1993. *JPEG: Still Image Data Compression Standard*. New York: Van Nostrand Reinhold. **297, 310.**

Pennebaker, W. B., J. L. Mitchell, G. G. Langdon, and R. B. Arps. 1988. An overview of the basic principles of the Q-coder adaptive binary arithmetic coder. *IBM Journal of Research and Development* 32(6):717–726, November. **288, 310.**

Persin, M. 1994. Document filtering for fast ranking. In Croft, W. B., and C. J. van Rijsbergen, editors, *Proc. 17th Annual International ACM SIGIR Conference on Research and Development in Information Retrieval*, pages 339–348, Dublin, Ireland, July. **208–210, 222.**

Persin, M., J. Zobel, and R. Sacks-Davis. 1996. Filtered document retrieval with frequency-sorted indexes. *Journal of the American Society for Information Science* 47(10):749–764, October. **208–210, 222.**

Piatetsky-Shapiro, G., and W. J. Frawley, editors. 1991. *Knowledge Discovery in Databases*. Cambridge, MA: MIT Press. **431, 441, 449.**

Porter, M. F. 1980. An algorithm for suffix stripping. *Program* 13(3):130–137, July. **151.**

Pratt, W. K., P. J. Capitant, W. H. Chen, E. R. Hamilton, and R. H. Wallis. 1980. Combining symbol matching facsimile data compression system. *Proc. IEEE* 68(7):786–796, July. **272, 310, 327, 353.**

Rabbani, M., and P. W. Jones. 1991. *Digital Image Compression Techniques.* Bellingham, WA: SPIE Optical Engineering Press. **310.**

Ramabadran, T. V., and D. L. Cohn. 1989. An adaptive algorithm for the compression of computer data. *IEEE Transactions on Communications* 37(4):317–324, April. **101.**

Ramakrishna, M. V., and J. Zobel. 1997. Performance in practice of string hashing functions. In Topor and Tanaka (1997). **151, 261.**

Ray, E., and D. Ray. 1997. *The AltaVista Search Revolution*, second edition. New York: Osborne McGraw-Hill. **439, 449.**

Rissanen, J., and G. G. Langdon. 1979. Arithmetic coding. *IBM Journal of Research and Development* 23(2):149–162, March. **100.**

Rissanen, J., and G. G. Langdon. 1981. Universal modeling and coding. *IEEE Transactions on Information Theory* IT-27(1):12–23, January. **100.**

Rissanen, J., and K. M. Mohiuddin. 1989. A multiplication-free multialphabet arithmetic code. *IEEE Transactions on Communications* 37(2):93–98, February. **59.**

Robertson, S. E., and K. Sparck Jones. 1976. Relevance weighting of search terms. *Journal of the American Society for Information Science* 27(3):129–146. **222.**

Rocchio, J. J. 1971. Relevance feedback in information retrieval. In Salton (1971), pages 313–323. **222.**

Rubin, F. 1979. Arithmetic stream coding using fixed precision registers. *IEEE Transactions on Information Theory* IT-25(6):672–675, November. **100.**

Russ, J. C. 1992. *The Image Processing Handbook.* Boca Raton, FL: CRC Press. **388.**

Sacks-Davis, R., A. J. Kent, and K. Ramamohanarao. 1987. Multikey access methods based on superimposed coding techniques. *ACM Transactions on Database Systems* 12(4):655–696, December. **137, 151.**

Saheed, A. 1993. *Processing textual images: Recognising the layout of digitised printed documents* (Master's thesis). Department of Computer Science, University of Waikato, New Zealand. **367, 388.**

Salomon, D. 1998. *Data Compression: The Complete Reference.* New York: Springer-Verlag. **99.**

Salton, G., editor. 1971. *The SMART Retrieval System: Experiments in Automatic Document Processing.* Englewood Cliffs, NJ: Prentice Hall.

Salton, G. 1989. *Automatic Text Processing: The Transformation, Analysis, and Retrieval of Information by Computer.* Reading, MA: Addison-Wesley. **221.**

Salton, G., and C. Buckley. 1990. Improving retrieval performance by relevance feedback. *Journal of the American Society for Information Science* 41(4):288–297, April. **214, 222.**

Salton, G., and M. J. McGill. 1983. *Introduction to Modern Information Retrieval.* New York: McGraw-Hill. **221.**

Schaffrath, H. 1992. The ESAC databases and MAPPET software. In Hewlett, W., and E. Selfridge-Field, editors, *Computing in Musicology*, volume 8. Menlo Park, CA: Center for Computer Assisted Research in the Humanities. **478, 483.**

Schindler, M. 1998. A fast renormalisation for arithmetic coding. In Storer and Cohn (1998), page 572. **100.**

Schuegraf, E. J. 1976. Compression of large inverted files with hyperbolic term distribution. *Information Processing & Management* 12:377–384. **116, 150.**

Sedgewick, R. 1990. *Algorithms in C.* Reading, MA: Addison-Wesley. **210, 222.**

Senders, J. W. 1981. I have seen the future and it doesn't work: The electronic journal experiment. In *Proc. Society for Scholarly Publishing 2nd Annual Meeting.* Washington. **436, 449.**

Shannon, C. E. 1948. A mathematical theory of communication. *Bell Systems Technical Journal* 27:379–423, 623–656. **25, 51, 99.**

Shannon, C. E. 1951. Prediction and entropy of printed English. *Bell Systems Technical Journal* 30:55. **94, 102.**

Shannon, C. E., and W. Weaver. 1949. *The Mathematical Theory of Communication.* Urbana, Illinios: The University of Illinois Press. **99.**

Sharman, N. B. 1992. *An empirical comparison of progressive image compression techniques* (Master's thesis). University of Canterbury, Christchurch, New Zealand. **310.**

Sharman, N. B., T. C. Bell, and I. H. Witten. 1992. Compression of pyramid coded images for progressive transmission. In *Proc. 7th New Zealand Image Processing Workshop*, pages 171–176. University of Canterbury, Christchurch, New Zealand. **310.**

Siemiński, A. 1988. Fast decoding of the Huffman codes. *Information Processing Letters* 26(5):237–241, May. **100.**

Sloane, N. J. A., and S. Plouffe. 1995. *The Encyclopedia of Integer Sequences.* New York: Academic Press. **20.**

Somogyi, Z. 1990. *The Melbourne University Bibliography System.* Technical report 90/3. Department of Computer Science, The University of Melbourne, Parkville, Victoria 3052, Australia, March. **150, 151, 260.**

Srihari, S. N., and V. Govindaraju. 1989. Analysis of textual images using the Hough transform. *Machine Vision and Applications* 2:141–153, summer. **361, 388.**

Storer, J. A. 1988. *Data Compression: Methods and theory*. Rockville, MD: Computer Science Press. **99.**

Storer, J. A., editor. 1992. *Image and Text Compression*. Norwell, MA: Kluwer Academic. **99.**

Storer, J. A., and M. Cohn, editors. 1992. *Proc. 1992 IEEE Data Compression Conference*, March. Los Alamitos, CA: IEEE Computer Society Press.

Storer, J. A., and M. Cohn, editors. 1993. *Proc. 1993 IEEE Data Compression Conference*, March. Los Alamitos, CA: IEEE Computer Society Press.

Storer, J. A., and M. Cohn, editors. 1994. *Proc. 1994 IEEE Data Compression Conference*, March. Los Alamitos, CA: IEEE Computer Society Press.

Storer, J. A., and M. Cohn, editors. 1995. *Proc. 1995 IEEE Data Compression Conference*, March. Los Alamitos, CA: IEEE Computer Society Press.

Storer, J. A., and M. Cohn, editors. 1996. *Proc. 1996 IEEE Data Compression Conference*, April. Los Alamitos, CA: IEEE Computer Society Press.

Storer, J. A., and M. Cohn, editors. 1997. *Proc. 1997 IEEE Data Compression Conference*, March. Los Alamitos, CA: IEEE Computer Society Press. **99.**

Storer, J. A., and M. Cohn, editors. 1998. *Proc. 1998 IEEE Data Compression Conference*, March. Los Alamitos, CA: IEEE Computer Society Press. **99.**

Storer, J. A., and J. H. Reif, editors. 1991. *Proc. 1991 IEEE Data Compression Conference*, April. Los Alamitos, CA: IEEE Computer Society Press.

Story, G. A., L. O'Gorman, D. Fox, L. L. Shaper, and H. V. Jagadish. 1992. The RightPages image-based electronic library for alerting and browsing. *IEEE Computer* 25(9):17–26, September. **370, 388.**

Strong, J. 1894. *Strong's Exhaustive Concordance of the Bible: Showing Every Word of the Text of the Common English Version of the Canonical Books, and Every Occurrence of Each Word in Regular Order; Together with a Comparative Concordance of the Authorized and Revised Versions Including the American Variations; also Brief Dictionaries of the Hebrew and Greek Words of the Original with References to the English Words*. Nashville, TN: Abingdon Press. **20.**

Stuiver, L., and A. Moffat. 1998. Piecewise integer mapping for arithmetic coding. In Storer and Cohn (1998), pages 1–10. **59.**

Teahan, W. J. 1998. *Modelling English Text* (Ph.D. thesis). University of Waikato, New Zealand. **102.**

Teuhola, J. 1978. A compression method for clustered bit-vectors. *Information Processing Letters* 7(6):308–311, October. **116, 150.**

Thiel, T. J. 1992. Automated indexing of document image management systems. *Document Image Automation* 12(2):43–49, Summer. **437, 449.**

Tomasic, A., and H. Garcia-Molina. 1993. Performance of inverted indices in shared-nothing distributed text document information retrieval systems. In

Carey, M. J., and P. Valduriez, editors, *Proc. 2nd International Conference on Parallel and Distributed Information Systems*, pages 8–17, San Diego, January. Los Alamitos, CA: IEEE Computer Society Press. **218, 222.**

Topor, R., and K. Tanaka, editors. 1997. *Proc. Database Systems for Advanced Applications*, April. Singapore: World Scientific.

Turpin, A. 1998. *Efficient Prefix Coding* (Ph.D. thesis). University of Melbourne, Australia. **100, 404, 428.**

Turpin, A., and A. Moffat. 1995. Practical length-limited coding for large alphabets. *The Computer Journal* 38(5):339–347. **404, 428.**

Turpin, A., and A. Moffat. 1996. Efficient implementation of the package-merge paradigm for generating length-limited codes. In Eades, P., and M. E. Houle, editors, *Proc. CATS'96 (Computing: The Australasian Theory Symposium)*, pages 187–195, January. University of Melbourne. **404, 428.**

Turpin, A., and A. Moffat. 1997. Efficient approximate adaptive coding. In Storer and Cohn (1997), pages 357–366. **100.**

Turpin, A., and A. Moffat. 1998. Housekeeping for prefix coding. *IEEE Transactions on Communications.* **100.**

Ulichney, R. 1987. *Digital Halftoning.* Cambridge, MA: MIT Press. **310.**

van Rijsbergen, C. J. 1979. *Information Retrieval*, second edition. London: Butterworths. **221.**

Van Voorhis, D. C. 1974. Constructing codes with bounded codeword lengths. *IEEE Transactions on Information Theory* IT-20(2):288–290, March. **401, 428.**

Viles, C. L., and J. C. French. 1995. Dissemination of collection wide information in a distributed information retrieval system. In Fox, Ingwersen, and Fidel (1995), pages 12–20. **218, 222.**

Vitter, J. S. 1989. Algorithm 673: Dynamic Huffman coding. *ACM Transactions on Mathematical Software* 15(2):158–167, June. **32, 100.**

Voorhees, E. M., N. K. Gupta, and B. Johnson-Laird. 1995. Learning collection fusion strategies. In Fox, Ingwersen, and Fidel (1995), pages 172–179. **218, 222.**

Wallace, G. K. 1990. Overview of the JPEG (ISO/CCITT) still image compression standard. In *SPIE/SPSE Symposium on Electronic Imaging Science and Technology*, Santa Clara, CA, February. **297, 310.**

Wallace, G. K. 1991. The JPEG still picture compression standard. *Communications of the ACM* 34(4):30–44, April. **297, 310.**

Wang, D., and S. N. Srihari. 1989. Classification of newspaper image blocks using texture analysis. *Computer Vision, Graphics and Image Processing* 47:327–352. **388.**

Weinberger, M. J., G. Seroussi, and G. Sapiro. 1996. LOCO-I: A low complexity, context-based, lossless image compression algorithm. In Storer and Cohn (1996), pages 140–149. **296, 310.**

Welch, T. A. 1984. A technique for high performance data compression. *IEEE Computer* 17(6):8–20, June. **81, 101, 102.**

Wells, H. G. 1938. *World Brain.* New York: Doubleday. **435, 449.**

Willems, F. M. J., T. Shtarkov, and T. Tjalkens. 1995. Context tree weighting method: Basic properties. *IEEE Transactions on Information Theory* 32(4):526–532, July. **63, 101.**

Willems, F. M. J., T. Shtarkov, and T. Tjalkens. 1996. Context weighting for general finite context sources. *IEEE Transactions on Information Theory* 33(5):1514–1520, September. **63, 101.**

Williams, R. N. 1991a. *Adaptive Data Compression.* Norwell, MA: Kluwer Academic. **65, 99–101.**

Williams, R. N. 1991b. An extremely fast Ziv-Lempel data compression algorithm. In Storer and Reif (1991), pages 362–371. **79, 102.**

Witten, I. H., and T. C. Bell. 1991. The zero frequency problem: Estimating the probabilities of novel events in adaptive text compression. *IEEE Transactions on Information Theory* 37(4):1085–1094, July. **29, 63, 100, 101.**

Witten, I. H., T. C. Bell, H. Emberson, S. Inglis, and A. Moffat. 1994. Textual image compression: Two-stage lossy/lossless encoding of textual images. *Proc. IEEE* 82(6):878–888, June. **318.**

Witten, I. H., T. C. Bell, M. E. Harrison, M. L. James, and A. Moffat. 1992. Textual image compression. In Storer and Cohn (1992), pages 42–51. **318, 353.**

Witten, I. H., T. C. Bell, A. Moffat, C. G. Nevill-Manning, T. C. Smith, and H. Thimbleby. 1994. Semantic and generative models for lossy text compression. *The Computer Journal* 37(2):83–87, April. **392, 428.**

Witten, I. H., T. C. Bell, and C. G. Nevill. 1992. Indexing and compressing full-text databases for CD-ROM. *Journal of Information Science* 17:265–271. **116, 150.**

Witten, I. H., and J. G. Cleary. 1983. Picture coding and transmission using adaptive modeling of quad trees. In *Proc. Int. Electrical, Electronics Conf.*, pages 222–225. Toronto, Canada. **310.**

Witten, I. H., R. M. Neal, and J. G. Cleary. 1987. Arithmetic coding for data compression. *Communications of the ACM* 30(6):520–541, June. **56, 59, 100.**

Wong, K. Y., R. G. Casey, and F. M. Wahl. 1982. Document analysis system. *IBM Journal of Research and Development* 26(6):647–656, November. **353, 388.**

Wong, W. Y. P., and D. K. Lee. 1993. Implementations of partial document ranking using inverted files. *Information Processing & Management* 29(5):647–669, September. **207, 222.**

Wright, E. V. 1939. *Gadsby*. Los Angeles: Wetzel; reprinted by Kassel Books, Los Angeles. **27, 102**.

Wu, S., and U. Manber. 1992. Fast text searching allowing errors. *Communications of the ACM* 35(10):83–91, October. **221, 429**.

Wu, X. 1996. An algorithmic study on lossless image compression. In Storer and Cohn (1996), pages 150–159. **294, 310**.

Yasuda, Y., Y. Yamazake, T. Kamae, and K. Kobayashi. 1985. Advances in FAX. *Proc. IEEE* 73(4):706–730, April. **272, 310**.

Yoshida, T., T. Endoh, N. Kawamura, and H. Kato. 1992. Image reduction system, October. U.S. Patent 5,159,468. **282, 310**.

Young, R. 1939. *Young's Concordance: Analytical Concordance to the Holy Bible*, eighth edition. London: United Society for Christian Literature, Lutterworth Press. **20**.

Young, I. D., editor. 1965. *A Concordance to the Poetry of Bunyon*. Austin, TX: Best. 4 vols. **2**.

Yuwono, B., and D. L. Lee. 1997. Server ranking for distributed text retrieval systems on the Internet. In Topor and Tanaka (1997). **218, 222**.

Zipf, G. K. 1949. *Human Behaviour and the Principle of Least Effort*. Reading, MA: Addison-Wesley. **183**.

Ziv, J., and A. Lempel. 1977. A universal algorithm for sequential data compression. *IEEE Transactions on Information Theory* IT-23(3):337–343, May. **75, 101**.

Ziv, J., and A. Lempel. 1978. Compression of individual sequences via variable rate coding. *IEEE Transactions on Information Theory* IT-24(5):530–536, September. **75, 79, 101**.

Zobel, J. 1997. Collection selection via lexicon inspection. In Bruza, P., editor, *Proc. Australian Document Computing Symposium*, pages 74–80, Melbourne, Australia, April. **220, 222**.

Zobel, J. 1998. How reliable are the results of large-scale information retrieval experiments? In Croft et al. (1998), pages 307–314. **221**.

Zobel, J., and A. Moffat. 1995. Adding compression to a full-text retrieval system. *Software—Practice and Experience* 25(8):891–903, August. **102, 429**.

Zobel, J., and A. Moffat. 1998. Exploring the similarity space. *ACM SIGIR Forum* 32(1):18–34, Spring. **185, 222**.

Zobel, J., A. Moffat, and K. Ramamohanarao. 1996. Guidelines for presentation and comparison of indexing techniques. *ACM SIGMOD Record* 25(3):10–15, October. **151**.

Zobel, J., A. Moffat, and K. Ramamohanarao. 1998. Inverted files versus signature files for text indexing. *ACM Transactions on Database Systems*, December. **151, 261**.

Zobel, J., A. Moffat, and R. Sacks-Davis. 1993a. Searching large lexicons for partially specified terms using compressed inverted files. In Agrawal, R., S. Baker, and D. Bell, editors, *Proc. 19th International Conference on Very Large Databases*, pages 290–301, Dublin, August. **172, 173, 221.**

Zobel, J., A. Moffat, and R. Sacks-Davis. 1993b. Storage management for files of dynamic records. In Orlowska, M. E., and M. Papazoglou, editors, *Proc. 4th Australian Database Conference*, pages 26–38, Brisbane, February. Singapore: World Scientific. **257, 259, 261.**

Zobel, J., A. Moffat, R. Wilkinson, and R. Sacks-Davis. 1995. Efficient retrieval of partial documents. *Information Processing & Management* 31(3):361–377, May. **221.**

Index

About the Authors

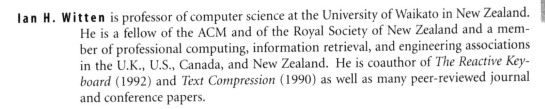

Ian H. Witten is professor of computer science at the University of Waikato in New Zealand. He is a fellow of the ACM and of the Royal Society of New Zealand and a member of professional computing, information retrieval, and engineering associations in the U.K., U.S., Canada, and New Zealand. He is coauthor of *The Reactive Keyboard* (1992) and *Text Compression* (1990) as well as many peer-reviewed journal and conference papers.

Alistair Moffat is associate professor of computer science at the University of Melbourne. He is the author of numerous peer-reviewed journal and conference papers, which have explored such areas as algorithms and data structures for text and image compression, self-adjusting data structures for dictionaries and priority queues, and algorithms for adaptive searching and sorting.

Timothy C. Bell is head of the Computer Science Department at the University of Canterbury. He is coauthor of *Text Compression* (1990) and the author of a number of peer-reviewed journal and conference papers covering text and image compression, computers and music, and computer education.

The authors regularly serve on the program committees of the IEEE Data Compression Conference and the ACM Information Retrieval and Digital Libraries Conferences.

Printed and bound by CPI Group (UK) Ltd, Croydon, CR0 4YY

03/10/2024

01040339-0009